BLAMING MOTHERS

FAMILIES, LAW, AND SOCIETY SERIES
General Editor: Nancy E. Dowd

Justice for Kids: Keeping Kids Out of the Juvenile Justice System
Edited by Nancy E. Dowd

Masculinities and the Law: A Multidimensional Approach
Edited by Frank Rudy Cooper and Ann C. McGinley

The New Kinship: Constructing Donor-Conceived Families
Naomi Cahn

What Is Parenthood? Contemporary Debates about the Family
Edited by Linda C. McClain and Daniel Cere

In Our Hands: The Struggle for U.S. Child Care Policy
Elizabeth Palley and Corey S. Shdaimah

The Marriage Buyout: The Troubled Trajectory of U.S. Alimony Law
Cynthia Lee Starnes

Children, Sexuality, and the Law
Edited by Sacha Coupet and Ellen Marrus

A New Juvenile Justice System: Total Reform for a Broken System
Edited by Nancy E. Dowd

Divorced from Reality: Rethinking Family Dispute Resolution
Jane C. Murphy and Jana B. Singer

The Poverty Industry: The Exploitation of America's Most Vulnerable Citizens
Daniel L. Hatcher

Ending Zero Tolerance: Students' Right to Rational Discipline
Derek W. Black

Blaming Mothers: American Law and the Risks to Children's Health
Linda C. Fentiman

Blaming Mothers

*American Law and the Risks
to Children's Health*

Linda C. Fentiman

NEW YORK UNIVERSITY PRESS
New York

NEW YORK UNIVERSITY PRESS
New York
www.nyupress.org

First published in paperback in 2019

© 2017 by New York University
All rights reserved

References to Internet websites (URLs) were accurate at the time of writing. Neither the author nor New York University Press is responsible for URLs that may have expired or changed since the manuscript was prepared.

Library of Congress Cataloging-in-Publication Data
Names: Fentiman, Linda C., 1949– author.
Title: Blaming mothers : American law and the risks to children's health / Linda C. Fentiman.
Other titles: Families, law, and society series.
Description: New York : New York University Press, [2016] | Series: Families, law, and society series | Also available as an ebook. | Includes bibliographical references and index.
Identifiers: LCCN 2016041759| ISBN 9780814724828 (cl : alk. paper) | ISBN 0814724825 (cl : alk. paper) | ISBN 978-1-4798-6718-9 (pb : alk. paper) |
Subjects: LCSH: Child abuse—Law and legislation—United States. | Mother and child—United States. | Mothers—Legal status, laws, etc.—United States. | Pregnant women—Legal status, laws, etc.—United States. | Children—Health and hygiene—United States. | Health risk assessment—United States.
Classification: LCC KF9323 .F46 2016 | DDC 362.1083/0973—dc23
LC record available at https://lccn.loc.gov/2016041759

New York University Press books are printed on acid-free paper, and their binding materials are chosen for strength and durability. We strive to use environmentally responsible suppliers and materials to the greatest extent possible in publishing our books.

Manufactured in the United States of America

10 9 8 7 6 5 4 3 2 1
Also available as an ebook

This book is dedicated to those
who showed me what it means to be a parent
and why it matters

My mother and father,
Janet Ralph Fentiman Crandell and Donald Sidney Fentiman

My husband,
Arthur Elliott Levine

and

My daughters,
Jamie Sloan Fentiman Levine and Rachel Elizabeth Fentiman Levine

CONTENTS

Acknowledgments   ix

PART I. INTRODUCTION TO RISK AND CHILDREN'S HEALTH

1. Are Mothers Hazardous to Their Children's Health?   3
2. The Social, Psychological, and Legal Construction of Risk   24
3. How Healthy Are America's Children? Myths and Realities   56

PART II. MOTHERS AS VECTORS OF RISK

4. Conceptions of Risk: Legal and Medical Interventions against Pregnant Women   71
5. Drug Use by Pregnant Women: Context and Consequences   109
6. Caught in the Crossfire: Breastfeeding (or Not) as Dangerous Behavior   155
7. The "Good Mother" and Crimes of Omission   178

PART III. ENVIRONMENTAL HAZARDS TO CHILDREN: TOXIC SUBSTANCES AND CONTAGIOUS DISEASES

8. Childhood Lead Poisoning and Other People's Children   207
9. The Vaccination Paradox   243

PART IV. A NEW FRAMEWORK FOR RISK ASSESSMENT AND RISK REDUCTION

10. Moving beyond Blame: Real Solutions for Children's Health   279

Appendix: Criminal Prosecutions of Parents Based on a Failure to Act   297

Notes   301

Index   403

About the Author   423

ACKNOWLEDGMENTS

This book would not have been possible without the generosity of time and spirit of many talented individuals. To my editors, Deborah Gershenowitz and Clara Platter, I owe great thanks—to Debby for helping me conceptualize the project and to Clara for helping bring it to fruition. Many colleagues—Bridget Crawford, Nancy Dowd, Debby Denno, Fran Miller, Wendy Parmet, and Liz Rapaport—gave generously of their time, reading many drafts of my proposal and book chapters along the way. Others shared their expertise and insights in the specialized fields of medicine, psychology, and law in which they teach and practice, often reading multiple drafts of chapters and articles and offering invaluable counsel that made this a much better book. This very long list includes Carol Anderson, Noa Ben Asher, Susan Bandes, Adele Bernhard, Anne Bloom, Kathleen Boozang, Melissa Breger, Bennett Capers, Martha Chamallas, Georganne Chapin, Elena Cohen, Karl Coplan, Bernard Dickens, Joshua Dressler, Dorothy Ehrlich, Joseph Espo, Gretchen Flint, Leslie Garfield, Lissa Griffin, Jill Gross, Elaine Heffner, Diana Hortsch, Peter Jacobson, Desiree Kennedy, Ellis Levine, Tom McDonnell, Michelle Oberman, Kathleen O'Connell, Lynn Paltrow, Patti Peppin, Phillipe Pierre, Ann Powers, Dorit Rubinstein Reiss, Marc Rodwin, Sanda Rodgers, Audrey Rogers, Susan Rozelle, Carol Sanger, Renata Schiavo, Janet Severson, Ross Silverman, Jill Sowards, Scott Smith, Deborah Spitalnik, Julia Spring, Audrey Stone, Stephanie Toti, Emily Gold Waldman, Jessica Waters, and Kelly Weisberg.

Pace Law School Deans Michelle Simon and David Yassky and Associate Deans for Research Bridget Crawford and Andrew Lund were incredibly supportive of my research. Associate Deans Horace Anderson and Jeff Miller made it possible for me to carry out my teaching responsibilities and find the needed time to write. My faculty assistants, Jennifer Chin and Kathleen Lambert, have been simply amazing, always going above and beyond the call of duty, helping with all manner of editing, formatting, and researching tasks. The law librarians at Pace Law School, under the extraordinary leadership of Marie Newman, were always knowledgeable and helpful; I give special thanks to Alyson Carney, Vicky Gannon, Jack McNeil, Margaret Moreland, and Cynthia Pittson.

I also want to thank Nancy Northrup and the Center for Reproductive Rights, who gave me a place to think and write during a sabbatical, and to the many friends at conferences who shared their latest research and insights with me. Special thanks go to the participants at the Pace faculty 10/10 research sessions, Fordham University students in Debby Denno's Advanced Criminal Law Seminar, and faculty participants at colloquia sponsored by Albany Law School and the Touro Law Center.

Portions of this book are derived from my previously published articles: *The New "Fetal Protection": The Wrong Answer to the Crisis of Inadequate Health Care for Women and Children*, 84 Denver University Law Review 537 (2006); *Pursuing the Perfect Mother: Why America's Criminalization of Maternal Substance Abuse Is Not the Answer*, 15 Michigan Journal of Gender & Law 389 (2009); *In the Name of Fetal Protection: Why American Prosecutors Pursue Pregnant Drug Users (and Other Countries Don't)*, 18 Columbia Journal of Gender and Law 647 (2009); *Marketing Mothers' Milk: The Commodification of Breastfeeding and the New Markets for Human Milk and Infant Formula*, 10 Nevada Law Journal 29 (2009); *Rethinking Addiction: Drugs, Deterrence, and the Neuroscience Revolution*, 14 University of Pennsylvania Journal of Law and Social Change 233 (2011); *Are Mothers Hazardous to Their Children's Health: Law, Culture, and the Framing of Risk*, 21 Virginia Journal of Social Policy and the Law 295 (2014); and *Sex, Science, and the Age of Anxiety*, 92 Nebraska Law Review 455 (2014). I am grateful to the editors of these journals for their questions, suggestions, and zealous Bluebooking.

I further want to acknowledge the important influence of countless scholars, in law and other disciplines, whose feminist insights have shaped my thinking over many years. This work would not have been possible without their trailblazing work, and I owe them a profound debt of gratitude.

Over the years I have been blessed with extraordinary research assistants who assisted with the research on multiple issues addressed in this book. They include Verona Benjamin, Cassandra Castellano, Malisa Chokshi, Kimberly Pierce Cortes, Heather Deichler, Lynn Donohue,

Amanda Evanson, Briana Fedele, Maria Finnochio, Nidhi Garg, Nicole Giordano, Carly Grant, James Healy, Deborah Heller, Timothy Henesy, Heather Ingle, Jennifer Kim, Rebecca King, Gillian Kirsch, Sabrina Lavail, Christine Love, Jennifer McAdam, Lauren Maier, Vito Marzano, Corinne Ortega, Jennifer Ramme, William Rapp, Nicole Sasaki, Jonina Sauer, Jake Sher, Devon Towner, Jennifer Turchetta, Meredith Van Horn, and Sara Wordsworth.

Most important to me has been the encouragement, patience, and support of my family, including my mother, Janet Crandell; my sister, Sandra Fentiman; and my daughters, Jamie and Rachel Levine. Above all, it would have been impossible to bring this book into being without my partner in love and life, Arthur Levine, whose creativity, insightful feedback, sense of humor, and staunch support made all the difference in the world.

    Linda C. Fentiman
    New York, New York
    March 2016

PART I

Introduction to Risk and Children's Health

1

Are Mothers Hazardous to Their Children's Health?

In 2007 Bridget Kevane, a mother in Bozeman, Montana, was charged with criminal child neglect after she dropped off her twelve-year-old daughter and a friend at the local mall, along with the two girls' younger siblings, ages eight, seven, and three. After the two twelve-year-olds momentarily left the younger children alone while they were trying on clothes at Macy's, the police were called. The police officers exercised their discretion to decide that the children were the victims of child neglect, and a prosecutor agreed that the mother had violated her duty of care.[1] Kevane, a university professor, wanted to fight the charges but ultimately agreed to a plea deal after the results of a mock jury trial convinced her that if she actually went to trial she would be convicted.

Nearly every day brings a news story—in a major newspaper or on the Internet—suggesting that mothers have fallen short in their obligation to protect their children's health and well-being. In 2011, in an article headlined "Teenage Obesity Linked to Poor Mother–Child Bond," the *New York Times* reported on a study published in the prestigious journal *Pediatrics* which purported to show that children who had poor relationships with their mothers as toddlers were more likely to be obese as teenagers.[2] Other studies have claimed that the more time mothers spend working outside the home, the more likely their children are to be overweight.[3] During the past three decades there has been a growing emphasis—by doctors, the media, government officials, and prosecutors—on the "risks" that mothers pose to their children's health. Mothers—and pregnant women—are increasingly seen as exclusively responsible for all aspects of their children's health and well-being.[4] At the same time, the enormous impact of poverty, genetics, environmental toxins, fathers, government, and private institutions on children's health is largely ignored.

Pregnant women have borne the brunt of criminal prosecutions and civil interventions. In 2004 Utah prosecutors brought murder charges against Melissa Rowland, a mentally disabled young woman, after she declined to have a caesarean section and subsequently delivered a stillborn child.[5] In 2009 a pregnant woman in New York, Jennifer Jorgensen, was charged with three counts of manslaughter after she was involved in an accident with another car. The prosecution claimed that she had been driving under the influence of alcohol and prescription drugs and that Ms. Jorgensen was reckless in driving without a seatbelt. Two of the victims were occupants of the other car; the third was Ms. Jorgensen's daughter, who was delivered prematurely and lived only six days. Astonishingly, while the jury acquitted Ms. Jorgensen of manslaughter in the case of the two adult victims, it found her guilty of manslaughter for causing her daughter's death. The trial judge sentenced Ms. Jorgensen to prison for three to nine years, and his ruling was upheld by a midlevel appellate court. Ultimately, Ms. Jorgensen's conviction was reversed by the New York Court of Appeals. The Court ruled that women could not be subject to criminal liability for manslaughter based on their conduct while pregnant, holding explicitly that a child who was injured *in utero* could not be a "person" under New York homicide law.[6]

Pregnant women have faced criminal charges for other accidents. In 2010 Christine Taylor, a pregnant Iowa woman, was arrested and held on suspicion of attempted feticide after she fell down a flight of stairs. The arrest was based on Ms. Taylor's statement to emergency room workers that she was not sure she wanted to have the baby because her husband had just abandoned her and her two young children. Eventually the case was dropped because Ms. Taylor's pregnancy was not sufficiently advanced to permit prosecution.[7]

Pregnant women have also been subject to other deprivations of liberty. In 2013 a Wisconsin judge ordered Alicia Beltran, a pregnant Wisconsin woman, to be civilly committed—involuntarily detained in a "treatment" facility—for seventy-nine days based on her *prior* dependence on opioids, despite negative drug tests, because of the risk that she might harm her fetus. In 2014 Marlise Muñoz, a pregnant paramedic who was brain-dead, was kept on life support for nearly four months at the insistence of the Texas hospital where she had been taken after suffering a stroke; the hospital's lawyer asserted that this was required by a Texas law that declared that life-sustaining treatment may not be withdrawn or withheld from pregnant women. And in 2010 a Florida judge ordered Samantha Burton, a pregnant woman, to be hospitalized for bed rest and treated over her objection, because Ms. Burton had declined to follow her doctor's recommendations. The judge declared that *because* she had disagreed with her doctor's advice her pregnancy was therefore "high risk" and posed a "substantial and unacceptable'" risk of harm to the fetus.[8] Many of these criminal and civil actions reflect an underlying view of pregnant women as mere vessels for developing fetuses. While this perspective is not new, it has been gaining prominence since the beginning of the twenty-first century, along with the rise of the "personhood movement" and increased efforts to limit women's access to abortion.

Moving beyond pregnancy, over the past decade a rising chorus of medical professionals and government officials has embraced the message that mothers who do not breastfeed are actively risking their children's health. From 2004 to 2006 the U.S. Department of Health and Human Services sponsored a series of public service announcements to promote breastfeeding. These included ads that equated the "risks" of not breastfeeding with the dangers of riding a mechanical bucking bronco while eight months' pregnant.[9] Since 2012 in an effort to get more mothers to breastfeed, some New York City hospitals have treated infant formula like a drug, which must be held under lock and key and is not available to new mothers without an approved "medical reason."[10]

Mothers have been criminally prosecuted for child abuse, manslaughter, and murder for failing to act to protect their children from sexual abuse or violent assault by a husband or boyfriend. Yet fathers are rarely prosecuted when they fail to protect their children from similar abuse by a wife or girlfriend. In nearly half of the cases, the mothers who are prosecuted are themselves the victims of intimate partner violence by the same man who has abused or injured their children.

This book proceeds in four parts. Part I, "Introduction to Risk and Children's Health" explores the multiple ways in which mothers are blamed for risking—or actually harming—their children's health. Chapter 1, "Are Mothers Hazardous to Their Children's Health?," documents the ever-expanding and insistent narrative that mothers are "risky" to their children. This chapter demonstrates the myriad ways in which mothers are portrayed as dangerous to their children's health—and often held legally responsible for it. Chapter 2, "The Social, Psychological, and Legal Construction of Risk," explores the psychosocial processes of risk construction, demonstrating how they interact with substantive legal principles to make a singular focus on mothers both possible and likely. The chapter first explains the processes of risk perception, risk communication, and risk management, which are highly value-laden, neither neutral nor objective. These psychosocial processes are both unconscious and very powerful, affecting the way we perceive and talk about risk and how we act on these perceptions. Subliminal biases and stereotypes, reflecting individual worldviews as well as enduring cultural scripts,[11] play out in the legal system in two distinct ways. First, American law expressly incorporates socially constructed legal norms. These include "the reasonable person," which defines the standard of behavior called "negligence," and the requirements of causation known as "actual cause" and "proximate cause." Second, deciding whether an individual's acts meet legal criteria involves the exercise of discretion, which is often affected by unconscious cognitive shortcuts and biases.

Discretionary decisionmaking pervades both the civil and criminal law arenas. On the civil side, discretion is exercised when investigators choose whether to pursue a case, lawyers consider whether to sue, juries decide whether a defendant was negligent (and thus liable for damages), and judges determine that a person's past behavior threatens future harm, justifying involuntary civil commitment for treatment. In the criminal setting, discretionary decisions are made when police officers choose to arrest or warn someone who has broken a law, prosecutors initiate or drop criminal charges, juries convict or acquit, and judges affirm or overturn a conviction. Each occasion for individual choice is also an opportunity for unacknowledged prejudices and cultural norms (including those based on gender, marital status, class, and race) to affect not only how key legal requirements are framed but also judgments about whether those requirements are met in a particular case; frequently these biases and unarticulated norms are outcome determinative.[12] Health care professionals—doctors, nurses, and others—wield tremendous power, deciding when—and when not—to disclose confidential patient information to law enforcement if they believe that a patient has engaged in "risky" behavior.

Chapter 3, "How Healthy Are America's Children? Myths and Realities," situates the health of America's children in historical and comparative context. Today the reality is that American children are quite healthy, compared with children in prior eras.[13] Life expectancy rates for American children are at historic highs. A baby born in 2013 can expect to live 78.8 years, the longest life expectancy for American children ever projected.[14] In contrast, in the early 1900s newborn American infants faced significant odds of an early death. One-fifth of children died before age five, and many did not reach their first birthdays. Infant deaths were so common that babies were often buried in unmarked graves.[15]

Even in the middle of the twentieth century the risk of a child's dying from an infectious disease, such as polio or pertussis (whooping cough), was alarmingly real. Before these afflictions were brought under control, more than a million Americans were infected each year with serious contagious diseases, with thousands dying each year. In the year 1950 alone there were 120,000 cases of pertussis, with 1,118 deaths; 33,000 cases of polio, with 1,904 deaths; and 319,000 cases of measles, with 468 deaths.[16] Today, all of these diseases are preventable through childhood vaccination. In the United States, childhood death is rare, because of achievements in sanitation,[17] child labor laws,[18] the discovery of antibiotics, breakthroughs against childhood cancer, and the development of vaccines.[19] For most diseases now preventable by vaccination, death rates have fallen by more than 90 percent from their twentieth-century peak.[20]

Yet compared with other economically developed countries, the United States falls far short, especially in measures of infant mortality, preterm birth, and childhood injury and death.[21] These differences can be attributed largely to significant racial and economic disparities in health care access in the United States,[22] as well as to the profound impact of economic and social disadvantages in all aspects of life. The Affordable Care Act ("Obamacare") has the potential to reduce these disparities, but class- and race-based differences in health care access and outcomes are likely to persist for some time.[23] There is also a strong correlation between childhood stressors (including physical and sexual abuse, domestic violence, and parental alcoholism and mental illness) and poor health as adults, resulting in a markedly shorter lifespan for some Americans. Many of these stressors are closely correlated with poverty and social and geographic isolation, whether in rural areas or the inner city. Mounting evidence shows that exposure to stress at a young age results in permanent damage to the brain and other organs.[24]

Chapter 3 also examines the impact of fathers and other men, the government, and environmental and social factors on children's health. Most obviously, fathers shape children's health through their genetic contributions. In addition, fathers contribute to the child's fetal and post-birth environment when they use tobacco, alcohol, or other drugs at home or are exposed to toxins at work. Men transmit HIV to children by having sex with the child's mother and by sharing contaminated needles with other drug users. Most notably, male sexual and physical abuse of children, particularly girls, not only causes immediate harm but also contributes to children's subsequent physical and mental illnesses and substance abuse.

The American legal system has largely taken a hands-off approach to domestic violence, which encompasses intimate partner violence and child abuse. In part, this reflects the value Americans place on protecting individual liberty and family privacy, although one can also see it as the legacy of a patriarchal system that accepted male "discipline" of wives and children as long as the harm was not too great. Tolerance of domestic violence by judges and the police, though much less prevalent today, continues. Since the 1980s the Supreme Court has twice rebuffed lawsuits seeking to hold the government accountable for failing to protect children whom they knew to be at risk of harm from abusive fathers. It remains an open question whether media coverage of the 2014 scandal exposing domestic violence in the National Football League will change the tenor of public discourse and lead to stepped-up enforcement of existing civil and criminal sanctions.

Government has also been dilatory in protecting children from environmental hazards. After a burst of environmental activity in the late 1960s and early '70s, there has been little government action to protect public health from pollution and toxic harms. Media discussions of children's health risks often omit environmental perils, particularly those that operate at a physical or temporal distance. Environmental harms include not only obvious dangers, such as exposure to toxic chemicals through indoor and outdoor air pollution, drinking water contaminated with lead or arsenic, and even toys and household products, but also the hidden risks lurking in substandard housing and impoverished neighborhoods. Exposure to lead from chipping and peeling paint leads to the identification of more than a half million children each year as suffering from irreversible lead poisoning. Infants and children have been exposed to lead in drinking water in several American cities, including Flint, Michigan, and Washington, D.C. Children who live in poor neighborhoods lack safe play spaces and access to affordable and healthful food; they are also exposed to physical dangers and psychological stress.[25] These children are more likely to be exposed to localized environmental risks, such as coal-burning power plants or locally caught fish, which frequently expose children to high levels of mercury and other toxins.[26]

Part II of the book, "Mothers as Vectors of Risk," examines four specific settings in which maternal behavior is singled out for special attention by the media, health care professionals, government, and the law.[27] The four chapters in this part demonstrate how the psychosocial processes of risk construction intersect with the social and biological aspects of pregnancy and motherhood to create an intense focus on mothers, which stands in stark contrast to the lack of scrutiny placed on fathers and others. Because pregnant women and mothers are literally "proximate" to the fetus or newborn child, it is understandable but inaccurate to view mothers as responsible for all of their children's health problems. Part II demonstrates how real biological differences between men and women are exaggerated and seized upon to justify differential treatment of fathers and mothers regarding their moral and legal responsibilities for children's health. Unconscious cognitive processes, gender biases, and popular cultural stereotypes shape the legal actions that are brought against mothers.

The first two chapters in this part examine pregnancy and explore the myriad ways in which media, health care professionals, and government have exaggerated the risks that prospective mothers can pose to their offspring. Chapter 4, "Conceptions of Risk: Legal and Medical Interventions against Pregnant Women," documents a wide range of legal and medical interventions against women claimed to improve the health of soon-to-be-born children, as well as criminal prosecutions of pregnant women for causing or risking harm. For more than fifty years judges have ordered pregnant women to receive medical treatment, despite their religious or other objections. These compulsory treatments include blood transfusions, caesarean sections, bed rest, and civil commitment for alcohol and other drug abuse. Not only do these judicial actions fail to guarantee the birth of healthy children,[28] but they also contravene the basic principles of informed consent, which are supposed to govern the doctor–patient relationship. Although judges have sometimes been reversed on appeal, these rulings usually come too late to prevent women from being harmed by physically invasive treatments and substantial deprivations of liberty and privacy. And, as noted in the case of Melissa Rowland, some women's choices not to follow medical advice have led to criminal prosecution.

This chapter first documents the historical shift in physicians' attitudes toward pregnancy that has taken place over the past fifty years. Many doctors today appear to believe that the fetus, not the mother, is the primary patient,[29] acting in part out of fear of becoming a defendant in a medical malpractice suit.[30] As a result, caesarean sections (C-sections) have become the default medical procedure whenever the there is an actual, or perceived, risk of harm to the fetus, even though such a procedure also increases the chances of maternal and fetal injury and death. Today nearly a third of all American babies are delivered via C-section.[31] This chapter also addresses the special concerns about women who are HIV-positive, who are especially likely to be subject to medical and legal interventions because of the risk that they might transmit the HIV virus to a fetus or infant during pregnancy, delivery, or breastfeeding.

Chapter 4 explores other ways in which the law treats pregnant women differently from other patients. Two-thirds of the states have laws that prevent the enforcement of living wills or advance medical directives when women are pregnant. As noted, in 2014 a Texas law prohibiting the removal of a pregnant woman from life support was challenged by Erik Muñoz, whose pregnant wife had collapsed and been deprived of oxygen for more than an hour before she was discovered and taken to a hospital. Despite doctors' determination that Mrs. Muñoz was brain-dead, the hospital would not allow her to be removed from a ventilator, insisting that Texas law required that she be kept "alive" until the fetus was viable. Ultimately, a judge ordered the "treatment" of Mrs. Muñoz halted, because she was in fact dead, so the law did not apply.[32] This chapter also considers recent criminal prosecutions of pregnant women, including murder cases growing out of stillbirths or other pregnancy losses.

Pregnant women's drug use is the focus of intense media, medical, and government scrutiny. Chapter 5, "Drug Use by Pregnant Women: Context and Consequences," examines the debate about whether women should be subject to enhanced medical and legal supervision of their behavior while pregnant, under the guise of promoting fetal and childhood health. While the abuse of illegal drugs garners the most attention, two legal drugs—alcohol and nicotine—threaten the greatest harm, both to pregnant women and the fetuses they carry. Alcohol is the most widely used drug in America and is associated with 85,000 deaths annually, including deaths due to cirrhosis of the liver, cancer, domestic violence, and automobile accidents. A small number of children are born each year with the symptoms of fetal alcohol syndrome, a combination of cognitive deficits and physiological impairments that can cause lifelong harm.[33]

About 10 percent of American women drink at least occasionally while pregnant. While pregnant women in previous generations drank (and smoked), during the past twenty-five years government has endeavored to curtail pregnant women's alcohol use through a variety of means, including social pressure, the use of "warning" and "labeling" laws, involuntary civil commitment, and criminal prosecution. Most scientists agree that significant alcohol consumption while one is pregnant is linked to fetal alcohol syndrome, but there is much less evidence that moderate or occasional alcohol consumption by pregnant women harms children.[34] More than thirty states make the use of alcohol or illegal drugs while pregnant grounds for involuntary civil commitment.[35] Women have also been criminally prosecuted for drinking alcohol while pregnant, although their convictions have universally been overturned.

Many states require health care professionals to report pregnant women who admit to, or are suspected of, using alcohol or other drugs. As noted, Alicia Beltran, a twenty-eight-year-old Wisconsin woman, made national headlines in 2013 after she was civilly committed "as habitually lack[ing] self-control" because of drug use. During a prenatal care visit Ms. Beltran had revealed her prior dependence on Percocet, an opioid drug, but stated that she had successfully weaned herself off it. Despite a drug test that confirmed her drug-free status, the physician's assistant in whom she had confided reported Ms. Beltran to law enforcement. She was arrested, handcuffed and shackled, and then brought before a family court judge, who committed her for involuntary "treatment." Alicia Beltran was confined for nearly three months before being released. And it was not until she challenged her confinement by suing in federal court that the Wisconsin prosecutor dismissed the case against her.[36]

Tobacco use is the largest single cause of death in the United States, contributing to at least 435,000 deaths a year; tobacco products are used by more than a quarter of Americans.[37] More than 15 percent of pregnant women smoke. *In utero* nicotine exposure is linked to preterm birth and childhood asthma.[38] In some cases courts have made child custody decisions in divorce cases on the grounds that one parent's smoking endangered the child's health.[39]

Many women who use alcohol, tobacco, and other drugs are highly motivated to decrease their use of drugs while pregnant. Unfortunately, there simply are not enough treatment programs available. Historically, programs for drug treatment often excluded pregnant women because they were seen as "high risk," while many obstetricians and their staffs were unsympathetic to pregnant women who acknowledged a drug problem, as evidenced by the *Beltran* case. As a result, women frequently concealed their substance abuse in order to get the obstetric care they needed.

Pregnant women's use of caffeine and prescription drugs has also become the subject of media and medical scrutiny. Some doctors' concerns about pregnant women's use of prescription drugs actually put their health at risk. Women who rely on antidepressant medication to maintain their mental health, take drugs to control asthma, or receive chemotherapy for cancer should generally not stop treatment based on a myopic concern with fetal development.[40] Women who stop treatment with anti-depressants prior to or during pregnancy have increased odds of becoming seriously depressed after their children's births, creating a real risk that they will injure or neglect their newborns. Similarly, women whose lack of medication during pregnancy results in serious illness or death will not be able to care for their children.[41]

Concerns about pregnant women's use of drugs are amplified when the focus switches to illegal drugs. About 5 percent of pregnant women use illegal drugs. This is not surprising, because one's twenties are the peak years for both drug use and childbearing. Over the past three decades, prosecutors in more than thirty states have indicted scores of

American women who used alcohol and other drugs while pregnant, invoking theories of "fetal protection" or "child endangerment."[42] In South Carolina alone, more than seventy women were charged with crimes based on drug use while pregnant between 1989 and 2003.[43] Since 1999 more than a dozen women in six states have been prosecuted for homicide, based on allegations that their drug use caused a child to be stillborn or to die shortly after birth. Those women who have been convicted have received sentences of as long as twenty years in prison.[44] Although almost all the convictions of pregnant drug users have been invalidated or overturned, in Alabama and South Carolina these prosecutions continue. Indeed, prosecutions have expanded after the two states' highest courts affirmed their propriety. Since 2006 more than sixty women in Alabama have been prosecuted for using drugs while pregnant under the state's "chemical endangerment" law.[45] Legislators in other states have enacted criminal laws to punish a broad spectrum of undesirable or "reckless" conduct by pregnant women, including drug use. In 2014 Tennessee became the first state to make it a distinct crime to use drugs while pregnant, despite objections that there were not enough facilities to provide treatment for all the women who needed it.[46] Elsewhere, prosecutors continue to charge pregnant women who use drugs with child endangerment,[47] even though most state court judges have ruled that such laws cannot be applied to pregnant women.[48] The case of Jennifer Jorgensen, who was convicted of manslaughter in her daughter's death due to a premature delivery, resulting from Ms. Jorgensen's alleged reckless driving and drug use, is a cautionary tale, demonstrating prosecutors' propensity to charge pregnant women for "reckless" conduct, even in politically liberal states like New York.

While legislators and prosecutors justify their actions as necessary to deter pregnant women from using drugs and risking their fetuses' lives and health, there is considerable debate over whether the prosecutions are achieving their avowed purpose. Many physicians and women's advocates contend that these prosecutions are counterproductive because they drive pregnant drug users underground, away from prenatal care and drug treatment, and may encourage some women to abort their pregnancies to avoid prosecution.[49]

Chapter 5 also reviews the empirical evidence on addiction and deterrence. It shows that drug addiction is a multifaceted illness, shaped by genetic predispositions, biology, and complex social forces, including poverty, domestic violence, lack of education, and insufficient social support. The chapter concludes by asserting that if governments really want to reduce the use of drugs by pregnant women, they must implement policies and programs that take the multiple causes of women's addiction into account and use carrots, rather than sticks, to encourage women to change their behavior.

The next two chapters examine the emphasis on mothers' actions after their children have been born as a means of improving children's health, exploring two very different contexts—infant nutrition and child abuse. During the past two decades, medical and governmental authorities have identified breastfeeding as the solution to a problem that few knew existed: the "risk" that not breastfeeding one's child will lead to a plethora of childhood ills, including upper respiratory infections, diarrhea, obesity, and impaired cognition or emotional development. Chapter 6, "Caught in the Crossfire: Breastfeeding (or Not) as Dangerous Behavior," explores the current debate over breastfeeding and demonstrates how easy it is for weak medical and scientific evidence to be manipulated and misused. At the beginning of the 1900s, babies who were not breastfed did indeed have high death rates, primarily because they drank unpasteurized or contaminated cow's milk.[50] One hundred years later, the evidence that American children are at risk of serious childhood illness as a result of a lack of breastfeeding is extremely weak, if it exists at all.[51] Nonetheless, many physicians and the federal government have enthusiastically endorsed breastfeeding as scientifically based and normatively preferred behavior for new mothers. The National Breastfeeding Awareness Campaign, launched during the presidency of George W. Bush, was explicitly designed to elicit a fear of disaster in parents of non-breastfed infants. The campaign targeted African-American women (asserted to breastfeed at lower rates than white women), using sensational, fear-based advertising, rather than considering how economic constraints and the cultural preferences of many low-income women and women of color might make nursing less feasible or desirable than formula feeding. The Obama administration has also advocated strongly for breastfeeding, with equally excessive claims about its benefits, accompanied by insufficient efforts to make it a realistic possibility for women who would like to breastfeed to do so.[52]

Women often face insurmountable obstacles to breastfeeding. Some cannot breastfeed for medical reasons. Others find it difficult to nurse while balancing work, school, and other child-care responsibilities, especially if they are single parents or otherwise lack a strong domestic support system. Workplace hurdles are daunting. Neither the Americans with Disabilities Act nor the Family and Medical Leave Act gives nursing mothers the legal right to compel employers to let them breastfeed or to pump their milk at work. There is a clear class divide in the workplace, with women who hold professional jobs finding it much easier than lower-salaried women to have both a private space and sufficient flexibility in their work day to be able to pump at work. Not until the Affordable Care Act (ACA) was enacted in 2010 were large employers required to provide their employees who are nursing mothers with the opportunity to take unpaid breaks in order to pump their milk, as well as a refrigerator in which to store it. The ACA also requires health insurers to provide nursing mothers with a free breast pump.[53] While wealthy women can afford lactation consultants to assist them in breastfeeding, the government does not provide routine breastfeeding support to lower- and middle-income women. The United States ranks last among thirty-six developed nations in its support of breastfeeding.[54] The gap between rhetoric and practice in regard to the "risks" of not breastfeeding illustrates the persistent tendency of American society—and American law—to exhort individual women to do everything possible to promote children's health while ignoring the systemic barriers to achieving that goal.

Chapter 7, "The 'Good Mother' and Crimes of Omission," addresses the complex circumstances under which mothers are criminally prosecuted for failing to protect their children from the physical violence or sexual abuse of another. Child abuse is a serious problem in the United States. In 2014 some 702,000 American children were estimated to be victims of abuse and neglect.[55] Girls, especially older girls, are more likely to experience sexual abuse,[56] but boys, especially young boys, are more likely to be the victims of physical abuse.[57] Each type of abuse—and of course many children are victims of both—threatens children with severe, long-lasting harm.

Physical and sexual abuse often results in serious injury or death; it can also have devastating psychological consequences. Abused children frequently have long-term cognitive impairments and emotional and behavioral problems. Victims of childhood abuse are much more likely than non-abused children to misuse drugs and to develop mental illnesses, particularly depression and posttraumatic stress disorder, in response to that abuse.[58] Abused children are more likely to engage in risky sexual behavior, increasing the odds that they will contract HIV or another sexually transmitted disease, or unexpectedly become a parent.[59] Abused children are also more likely than non-abused children to replicate the violence of their childhood—to enter the juvenile justice or prison system, or to become an abuser or a victim as an adult.[60] Many pregnant women who misuse legal and illegal drugs were sexually abused as children. As adults they often live with violent men. In many cases this increases the women's drug use, either because their boyfriends encourage it or because the women use drugs as a means of temporarily escaping from the harsh reality of domestic violence.[61]

Every year American mothers are prosecuted for homicide or child abuse when their children are killed or injured by the woman's male partner, either a husband or boyfriend. This chapter explores why the converse is much less likely to be true.[62] It does not argue that mothers are always blameless. Some mothers do terrible things to their children, and, sadly, mothers and fathers kill their children at roughly equal rates.[63]

Rather, this chapter asserts that mothers are more likely than fathers to find themselves facing criminal charges when an abusive partner harms the parent's child. This stems from a confluence of factors, including changing family structures, poverty, and a criminal and child protective system in which discretion plays an enormous role. Over the past fifty years the American family has undergone profound changes. In 1960 85 percent of American children lived with two parents. Today that number has declined to 64 percent.[64] Nearly one-quarter of American children under the age of eighteen live in a one parent home headed by a single mother.[65] More than three-quarters of children ages eight and younger who live in households headed by single mothers are poor or low-income,[66] which, in turn, is highly correlated with their being the victim of child abuse or neglect.[67] An astonishing 53 percent of children born to women under age thirty are born to single mothers.[68]

With this demographic reality as background, ostensibly "neutral" criminal law principles are often deployed to treat mothers differently from fathers. These principles include, first, the ever-expanding conception of parental duty, which is shaped by gendered conceptions of good parenting; second, the socially and legally constructed nature of "the reasonable person" and "the reasonable parent"; and, third, elastic criminal law causation principles. When decisionmakers with discretionary authority—police, investigators, prosecutors, juries, and judges—apply these "neutral" legal principles, it is highly likely that unconscious cognitive shortcuts, cultural norms, biases, and stereotypes will shape their application of these criminal law principles to increase the odds that a mother will be blamed for failing to act to protect her child.

Chapter 7 examines fifty years of criminal prosecution of parents for failing to protect their children from a partner's violence or abuse. In 108 appellate cases published since 1960, mothers have faced disproportionate prosecution. In eighty-seven of the cases the mother was the parent who was prosecuted based on an alleged failure to act. In eleven cases it was the father, and in the remaining ten cases the person prosecuted was a girlfriend or stepmother, or boyfriend or stepfather. Mothers' convictions were affirmed (in whole or in part) more often (in 72 percent of the cases) than convictions of fathers (63 percent). In 41 percent of the published cases in which mothers faced criminal charges, the mothers were themselves victims of violence by the men who brutalized their children. Frequently, although certainly not always, mothers tried to protect their children while endeavoring to placate their spouse or boyfriend. Yet the fact that the women stayed with their partners, out of economic or emotional dependence, was often used against them. Prosecutors and judges frequently invoked the rhetoric of "choice," asserting that these mothers *chose* to stay with violent or abusive partners, thereby deliberately putting their children's health at risk.[69]

The chapter concludes that unless and until the American legal system treats domestic violence against adults and children much more seriously and develops more effective interventions, which respond to the root causes of domestic violence as well as individual bad actors, children will continue to suffer significant physical and psychological trauma. These harms will accompany them into adulthood, increasing the odds that the cycle of violence and abuse will continue.

Part III, "Environmental Hazards to Children: Toxic Substances and Contagious Diseases," explores two external threats to children's health. Both lead, an environmental hazard found frequently in American homes, and infectious diseases pose substantial risks to children's health. Yet public perceptions and the legal system's response to these two disparate sources of harm are very different. At first glance, an observer might speculate that mothers play a minor role in protecting their children from these external health threats. But just as in the case of pregnant women, mothers of newborns, and mothers who live with abusive partners, the psychosocial construction of risk connects with basic principles of the American legal system to highlight the role of mothers in regard to these two distinct hazards. Here again, conceptions of the reasonable parent that embody unconscious stereotypes of gender, race, and class intersect with a legal system whose rules of causation favor *near*, rather than *distant*, sources of harm. As a result, in cases involving children poisoned by lead, their mothers are likely to be held solely responsible for their children's intellectual, physical, and emotional development, despite lead's well-known status as a neurotoxin, while landlords and lead product manufacturers are not held accountable. In contrast, in cases involving vaccination against contagious diseases, mothers who refuse to have their children vaccinated have *not* been held legally responsible for harm caused by their failure to vaccinate, harms that are suffered not only by their own children but also by other children in the community. Chapters 8 and 9 explore the reasons for these paradoxical differences in treatment.

Chapter 8, "Childhood Lead Poisoning and Other People's Children," examines lead, a ubiquitous environmental toxin. Lead is extremely hazardous to children, causing severe and irreversible cognitive and nervous system impairment, as well as behavioral problems. Even after a child is discovered to be the victim of lead poisoning, remedial treatment is expensive, painful, and insufficient to undo the permanent harm caused by lead. Every year more than 500,000 American children under age six have blood lead levels indicating toxic levels of exposure.[70] Historically, children were exposed to lead from multiple sources, including airborne lead from gasoline, lead from peeling paint, and lead in toys. This chapter explores the different approaches that have been used to reduce children's exposure to lead, strategies that have had varying success. Government has tended to act aggressively when *all* of the nation's children are at risk from lead exposure but has been much slower to act when the health of poor, inner-city children of color is at stake. This chapter illustrates how the American legal system supports this bifurcated approach to protecting children's health.

All of America's children benefited from the 1973 decision by the Environmental Protection Agency (EPA) to prohibit lead as a gasoline additive. The EPA relied on the Clean Air Act, which authorized it to limit pollutants that "will endanger" the public health. The EPA mandated a phased reduction of lead in gasoline; children's blood lead levels plummeted nationwide, precisely in sync with the reduction of lead in gasoline.[71] Less dramatically, Congress acted swiftly in the early twenty-first century in response to public concern about toys containing lead, especially toys imported from China, and enacted protective legislation.[72] At least one judge ordered medical monitoring of children who had potentially been exposed to lead from toys.[73] For these children, it appears that the precautionary principle was again successfully invoked.

In contrast, a core group of children remains at high risk of lead poisoning. These are the "Freddie Grays" of America, concentrated in the Northeast and Midwest. They live in old, deteriorating housing stock and are exposed to lead from chipped and peeling paint, lead dust created when windows are raised and lowered, and lead in public drinking water. These children are overwhelmingly poor and urban and predominantly African-American or Latino. Poor children, particularly boys, are especially vulnerable to lead's toxic effects. Lead exposure, even at low levels, results in intellectual impairments, physical motor problems, and aggressive behavior.[74] Indeed, lead poisoning has such severe impacts on cognition and behavior that it has been suggested as a potential defense to criminal responsibility by criminal law scholar Deborah Denno.[75] Yet American paint manufacturers aggressively marketed lead paint throughout the twentieth century, despite the widespread scientific recognition, as long ago as the mid-1800s, that lead paint was hazardous to children. Congress did not ban the use of lead-based paint in residential dwellings until 1978. The contaminated public water supply in Flint, Michigan, is a stark reminder of the impact of governmental indifference on children's health.

The American legal and political systems have failed to protect all children from the risk of lead poisoning, reflecting hostility to precautionary regulation and aggressive environmental enforcement, as well as difficulty in establishing causation under traditional tort law rules. Almost all states, as well as the federal government, limit the legal remedies available to children injured by lead exposure. In many states property owners' economic interests appear to receive greater protection than children's health.[76] It was not until 2014 that a landmark lawsuit succeeded in holding lead paint and pigment manufacturers accountable, using the tort of public nuisance. Under the trial judge's decision, the manufacturers have been ordered to clean up the lead paint that contaminates apartments and homes in major California cities.[77]

Some courts have held landlords responsible for harming children who were injured by exposure to lead paint and lead dust in the rundown homes where they live.[78] Yet, despite clear evidence of lead's toxicity, even when children's blood tests show alarmingly high levels of lead and the children display other symptoms of lead poisoning, in many cases landlords have denied responsibility, asserting a lack of causation.[79] Their defense, essentially, is that it is the mothers' fault. While landlords may concede that lead-based paint can cause the *type* of injuries asserted, they argue that in an individual child's case, the child's cognitive deficits and behavioral problems are attributable to his or her mother's genes (passed along to her child), poor parenting skills, poor housekeeping, or other factors for which the landlord is not responsible. These landlords seek to alter the narrative about who should be blamed for lead poisoning, shifting it away from the landlord's legal obligation—to maintain his property in habitable condition—to the mother. Some landlords have persuaded trial judges to order plaintiff children's mothers or siblings to provide their own school records and to submit to IQ tests. If the child has intellectual difficulties, the landlords argue, the mother is to blame, not the landlord. The potential for judges and juries to make decisions based on pervasive stereotypes of inner-city children of color and their mothers is at once obvious and dangerous.[80] Once again, mothers are deemed responsible for their children's well-being, which means that the substantial contributions to children's health of other, distant but powerful, sources of harm, including landlords, manufacturing corporations, and government are ignored. Because the American legal system has historically preferred to find one simple cause of harm, which then precludes holding others legally responsible, many children injured by lead exposure do not receive adequate treatment or compensation for the harm they have suffered.

Chapter 9, "The Vaccination Paradox," examines the role of mandatory vaccination laws in protecting the public's health, as well as the backlash against these laws. Vaccination has long been seen as a "public good," a cost-effective means of addressing a shared problem that benefits everyone in the community. Vaccination is regarded as a public good because it confers the benefit of "herd immunity" on those who cannot be vaccinated for medical reasons, including children with compromised immune systems, some pregnant women, and the elderly. When the vast majority of a population is vaccinated, widespread illness is prevented and society avoids the need to spend large sums of public and private money in the event of a disease outbreak.[81] Children whose parents choose not to vaccinate them are "free riders," protected by the herd immunity of the communities in which they live.[82] It is estimated that giving the standard set of childhood vaccines to American children prevents more than 42,000 deaths and 20 million cases of disease for each birth cohort, saving nearly $14 billion in direct health care costs and $69 billion in broader costs to society.[83]

Yet vaccines are the victim of their own success.[84] Today, childhood immunization rates are falling nationwide.[85] When immunization rates are low, especially in localities where vaccine "exemptors" may cluster, disease outbreaks are more likely.[86] For example, the year 2014 witnessed the most measles cases since 1994, with major outbreaks among Amish children in Ohio and across the United States as a result of exposure to an unvaccinated child at Disneyland in December 2014. Increasing numbers of parents have embraced "alternative vaccination schedules," which permit them to "individualize" the standard childhood immunization schedule recommended by the American Academy of Pediatrics and the Centers for Disease Control and Prevention (CDC).[87]

This chapter illuminates the psychosocial nature of risk perception and risk construction by exploring the clashing views about the risks of contagious diseases and vaccines by vaccine advocates and vaccine opponents. At a time when most parents, and many health care providers, have never seen a child afflicted with polio, pertussis, or measles,[88] growing numbers of parents are focused not on the risk that their children might contract a disease preventable by vaccination but on the fear that vaccination itself could cause autism or another childhood affliction whose cause is unclear.[89] Opponents of vaccination have publicized a variety of theories asserting that vaccines are dangerous to children. These theories have been uniformly tested and rejected; they lack scientific merit.[90] Nonetheless, some parents are still fearful that vaccines are not safe, and many are simply unsure.[91]

The controversy over childhood vaccination provides a striking counternarrative to earlier chapters. Exploring the construction of risk in the context of the debate over immunization mandates and parental opt-outs reveals the singular role that American law gives to parental choice in this one area of children's health. Only in the case of vaccine refusals are parents not held legally accountable *either* for risking their own children's health *or* for inflicting harm on other people's children because of a failure to vaccinate. No parent has been sued or criminally prosecuted for failing to immunize her child.

In contrast, over the past fifty years many parents have faced criminal charges for forgoing lifesaving medical treatment for their children. Christian Science parents, as well as others with strongly held religious beliefs, have been convicted of manslaughter and other crimes after they failed to seek medical treatment for a sick child who they thought was suffering from the flu or other minor illness.[92] In other cases physicians and hospital authorities have sought, and received, court orders compelling children to receive medical treatment over their parents' objections, whether the objections are religiously motivated or simply reflect parental beliefs that they know what is best for their children.[93] And, as noted earlier, many pregnant women have been ordered to undergo medical treatment as a means of protecting fetal health. Other women have been criminally prosecuted for using drugs while pregnant as well as for other allegedly dangerous behaviors. Finally, mothers who failed to intervene to protect their children from the violence or abuse of a partner have also faced serious criminal charges; many have been convicted. The chapter concludes by exploring why parents who oppose vaccination for their children have thus far not faced legal consequences for their omission to act.

Part IV, "A New Framework for Risk Assessment and Risk Reduction," responds to the concerns raised by the previous chapters. Chapter 10, "Moving Beyond Blame: Real Solutions for Children's Health," considers the risks to children's health comprehensively, reviewing the sources of health risks to children and exploring the connections among them. The risks to children's health and safety are multiple, complex, and synergistic. These threats cannot be reduced by resorting to simplistic solutions and the scapegoating of mothers. In order to promote healthy fetal development, as well as the health of infants, older children, and adolescents, it is necessary to respond to the systemic factors that put children's health at risk, including poverty and ethnic and racial discrimination.[94] The children most at risk for health problems are those who live in poor neighborhoods,[95] in substandard, toxic housing, who lack access to nutritious food and quality health care, who do not have safe places to learn and to play, and who are more likely to be sexually abused and physically assaulted. Without addressing the broader risks to childhood health, the cycle of childhood poverty, illness, injury, and violence will repeat endlessly.

Fundamentally, our goal must be to improve the health of all of America's children, not just those we know but children in all neighborhoods. We must finally acknowledge that America's children and families are all part of one community, with much greater interdependence than most of us care to acknowledge. It really does "take a village" to nurture the next generation.[96] To put it differently, despite our tendency to form close knit groups with like minded people, every parent's actions can affect the lives and health of children who live only two ZIP codes away.[97]

2

The Social, Psychological, and Legal Construction of Risk

Introduction

Risk is neither a fixed nor a neutral phenomenon. Rather, our understanding of risk—and response to it—is, at bottom, social and psychological, rather than scientific or quantitative. This chapter first examines how unconscious psychological and social processes affect the way we perceive risk, talk about risk, and make decisions about risk. The chapter then explores how these psychosocial risk construction processes intersect with the American legal system, both directly and indirectly. Some concepts of risk are incorporated directly into fundamental legal concepts. For example, the law defines "negligence" as acting unreasonably—that is, either not perceiving a risk that a reasonable person would have perceived or not acting to avoid or reduce that risk, even though one has perceived it.[1] The legal rules that govern causation and the principles that underlie the precautionary principle also reflect ideas about risk, even those ideas of which we are unaware. Risk construction is also indirect, as it unconsciously informs the decisions and actions of participants in the legal process. These include health care professionals, social service investigators, police, prosecutors, jurors, judges, and government policymakers. Subliminal mental processes, as well as conscious and unconscious biases and stereotypes, subtly but powerfully affect the impressions, judgments, and behavior of all of us, including these legal players. Unstated cultural values and assumptions, of which we are frequently unaware, also affect our views on risk and the ways that we apply them in legal settings.

I. Risk Perception

Like beauty, risk is in the eye of the beholder. For scientists and lawyers who work at the intersection of science and health, and perhaps for some members of the public, it can be tempting to believe that risk can be assessed objectively. We long to believe that a single number—like three in a million—represents the "true" risk of injury or death from a particular type of danger. We imagine that this number can be easily determined by calculating the potential magnitude of a particular harm and the probability that it will occur and then multiplying the two together.[2] To be sure, scientific and mathematical principles do provide quantitative approaches that can be useful in assessing and managing risk; they also carry an aura of objectivity. For example, in considering the potential injury from human exposure to a particular toxic chemical, such as lead, a quantitative risk assessment will take into account the means and duration of the exposure; the range of individual variation in response to that chemical; the mechanism of the chemical's toxicity, carcinogenicity, and so on; the dose–response relationship for these effects; and the uncertainty that accompanies each of these variables.[3] Yet even this already complex equation is incomplete without considering subjective factors—how large a margin of safety is necessary to protect more vulnerable populations (e.g., children and the elderly), what data points should be selected for analysis, and how useful are animal models for determining the risks to human health. Of course, in real life people are never exposed to just one chemical, thus complicating risk assessment further.[4] Each variable added, and each step taken to develop a theoretically more accurate analytical model, inevitably involves subjective value judgments that have important implications for the ultimate "answer"—the magnitude of the risk found.[5] In practice, the "safe exposure level" may change over time, as scientists learn more about each variable. For example, the Centers for Disease Control have reduced the "safe" level of exposure to lead several times in recent decades, as new research documents the harmful effects of lead even at very small "doses."[6]

Many "hard" scientists and social scientists have observed that risk—or the perception of it—is not a quantifiable, empirically discoverable fact.[7] As Paul Slovic, a leading researcher on the psychosocial construction of risk, says, "Risk does not exist 'out there,' . . . waiting to be discovered."[8] Rather, for scientists as well as for lay people, the identification and construction of risk is a highly subjective process, strongly influenced by one's gender, race, social class, individual values, and unconscious cognitive processes.⁹ Slovic further observes, "Whoever controls the definition of risk controls the . . . solution to the problem at hand." The very way in which a question about risk is framed influences the answer.¹⁰ "Defining risk is thus an exercise in power."¹¹ For example, when people were asked whether seat belt use should be mandated by law, they were more likely to support such laws when the risk of death or serious injury from an automobile accident was expressed as odds over a lifetime of driving rather than a single car ride.¹² Similar research on current public attitudes on health issues such as gun control, wearing motorcycle helmets, and global warming shows that how a question is phrased dramatically influences the answers given.¹³

A. Heuristics

There are many unconscious psychological influences on how people perceive risk or respond to it. Social science research has identified a variety of "'mental shortcuts'"—or "heuristics"—that people use in framing risk.¹⁴ For example, we tend to view a risk as more serious, or more likely, if we have experienced it personally or have heard about it from the media. This is often called "the availability heuristic."¹⁵ Thus a simple story of a terrible event can be much more emotionally powerful than a detailed and well documented statistical risk analysis, even if—or precisely because—the simple story lacks nuance and specificity.¹⁶ In practice, this means that many people are more concerned about newly discovered risks, such as BPA (bisphenol A), an industrial chemical used in plastic baby bottles and other consumer products,¹⁷ than longstanding risks that have faded into the background, such as lead poisoning as a result of exposure to lead from peeling or chipping paint.¹⁸ Similarly, people are much more likely to see drowning as a risk of summer recreation, as opposed to dying from skin cancer, even though skin cancer deaths are twice as likely as drowning.¹⁹

Rare events capture our imagination, but our ability to assess the odds of a rare event's occurring is actually quite poor.²⁰ This plays out in a variety of settings. For example, some parents are so concerned about the extremely small likelihood that their children will be seriously injured by vaccination that they choose not to vaccinate them, exposing their own children, as well as others, to the much more serious risk of contracting a harmful and potentially fatal disease.[21] People tend to overestimate the risk of events they dread, such as being diagnosed with cancer, at the same time that they underestimate familiar risks, such as being injured in a car accident.[22] Yet people are often overly optimistic about their own chances of *not* being affected by illness, which may reflect unconscious beliefs of personal moral superiority and being able to control their destiny.[23] Some parents who choose not to vaccinate their children against contagious diseases believe that their children are not at risk of becoming ill with a contagious disease because they are breastfed, eat healthful foods, and have a "natural" lifestyle.[24]

This self-referential view of risk also plays out in another unconscious psychological mechanism, "the fundamental attribution error," which affects daily decisionmaking as well as legal determinations. Most people have an underlying belief in a just world, in which "good things happen to 'good' people and bad things happen to 'bad' people." This provides reassurance that "the world is an orderly, predictable place," so that bad things will not happen to them.[25] As part of this self-reassurance, people engage in "defensive attribution." "The fundamental attribution error" is the unconscious tendency to "'explain' adversity . . . by assigning fault or blame," ascribing it to the character or choices of the victim, rather than to the victim's situation. This is easier, and more emotionally satisfying, than admitting that bad things do happen to good people and that we cannot control them.[26]

Another unconscious bias that affects risk perception is the "omission bias," the belief that action is riskier than inaction. For example, some parents decide that action—vaccinating one's child against contagious diseases—is riskier than choosing not to vaccinate, despite the data demonstrating that the risk of illness and injury is lower when children are vaccinated.[27] Another way of conceptualizing this bias is the idea that people often fail to act because they don't want to "tempt fate."

People also alter their perception of risk depending on what they know about other risks that they deem relevant, which is called the "anchoring and adjustment" heuristic.[28] Simply put, "anchoring" provides a point of reference—"compared to what"—which then unconsciously influences people to perceive another risk as closer to that anchor.[29] Trial lawyers can exploit the anchoring phenomenon by presenting jurors with verbal and visual cues—anchors—such as the amount of money damages sought, to help jurors assess the harm that a plaintiff or victim suffered.[30] Additional anchors are provided by our unconscious cultural biases, including racial, gender, and class stereotypes, and biased prototypes, which can affect how jurors and other legal players decide a case.[31] "Priming," the automatic activation of stereotyped responses, is another type of anchor. Studies have shown, for example, that the mere act of listening to rap (as opposed to pop) music makes listeners more likely to believe that black men are dangerous, hostile, and less intelligent.[32]

B. Racial Bias

Volumes have been written about the impact of unconscious racism, especially in the criminal justice system. The criminal justice system provides myriad opportunities for the exercise of discretion. Police officers decide whether or not to arrest;[33] prosecutors decide whether or not to indict, to seek the death penalty or a life sentence, or to offer an attractive plea bargain;[34] jurors decide whether or not to convict and whether or not to impose the death penalty;[35] and judges make decisions about setting bail, admitting evidence at trial, and, if a defendant is convicted, what sentence to impose.[36] No American who was an adolescent or older in the first two decades of the twenty-first century could fail to recognize the possibility that unconscious racism was at work in the multiple killings of unarmed African-Americans at the hands of police officers who exercised their discretion to shoot first and ask questions later.[37]

Even in more mundane interactions between citizens and government officials, unconscious racial biases can have a powerful effect. Harvard researchers examining potential bias in the voter registration process found, in a survey of more than 7,000 election officials in forty-eight states, that local election clerks responded differently to inquiries by prospective voters who appeared to be Latino compared with those posed by non-Latinos, by either failing to respond at all or responding less fully to e-mail requests from the putative Latino inquirers. This study illustrates the powerful impact of racial bias on the exercise of discretionary authority by such "street-level bureaucrats,"[38] demonstrating again how potent our unconscious biases can be.

C. The Impact of Worldviews

Cutting across all these unconscious mental shortcuts is a different set of psychocultural factors that profoundly affect how we perceive—and respond to—risk. A growing body of research shows that how people assess risk depends on their unarticulated worldviews: their visions of a good society.[39] Many researchers have documented "the white male effect." This is the persistent finding in studies of individual attitudes about risk that about 30 percent of white men perceive very little risk in a broad array of potential hazards, ranging from vaccination to lead paint to nuclear power plants to handguns.[40] In contrast, white women and African-Americans of both genders perceive much greater risk in the same lists of potential hazards.[41] The white male effect cannot easily be explained as the result of a person's education, income, status as a caregiver, or scientific literacy.[42] In fact, the extent of a person's actual knowledge about a particular hazard does not account for gender differences in risk perception, although it has been shown that, in general, women are more comfortable than men in expressing anxiety about particular risks.[43] Together with the white male effect, this might explain why mothers appear to be more likely than fathers to oppose vaccinating their children.[44]

Numerous studies have shown that people's perceptions of risk vary significantly depending on whether their outlook is "hierarchical" (as opposed to "egalitarian") and/or "individualist" (as opposed to "communitarian").[45] This may be most easily seen as a grid, as shown in figure 2.1.

According to Dan Kahan, Paul Slovic, and other social science researchers, responding to risk in accordance with one's worldview serves as a psychological defense mechanism against a type of "cultural identity threat." These researchers theorize that people with an "individualist" worldview tend to dismiss claims of environmental and technological risks, because recognizing them would threaten their preference for a market based, privately ordered society.[46] Similarly, those who hold a "hierarchical" worldview are less likely to perceive risk, because "assertions of environmental catastrophe" implicitly threaten the "competence of social and governmental elites."[47] In contrast, people with "egalitarian" and "communitarian" worldviews are more likely to perceive risk,

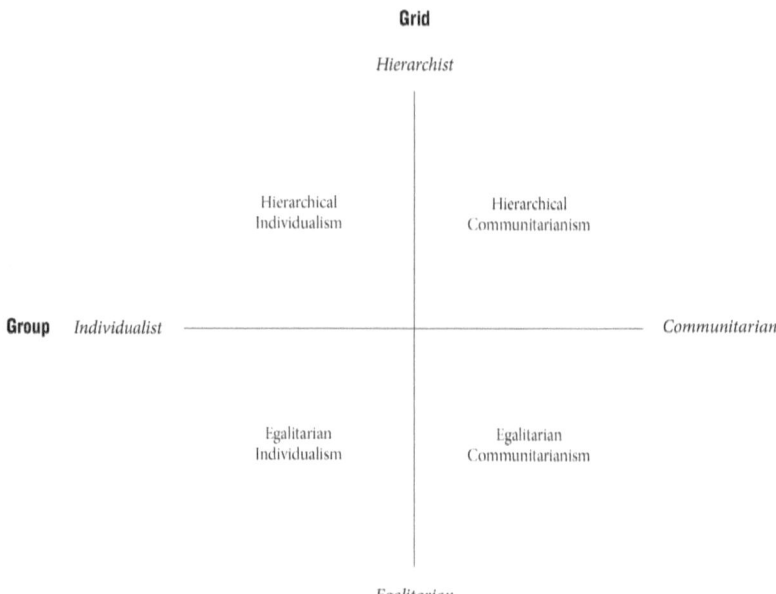

Figure 2.1. "Group-grid" worldview typology. Figure from Dan M. Kahan et al., *Culture and Identity-Protective Cognition: Explaining the White Male Effect in Risk Perception*, 4 J. Empirical Legal Studies 465, 468 (2007). This chart was originally created by Mary Douglas, *Natural Symbols: Explorations in Cosmology* (London: Barrie & Rockliff, Cresset Press 1970).

especially in the environmental and technological arenas. People with egalitarian worldviews, who reject preconceived roles based on status (such as age, gender, and family connections), are more likely than those with a hierarchical orientation to perceive technology as risky. Similarly, those whose worldview is communitarian, who understand life as requiring frequent interactions with others, and who want people to be able to depend on one another, are more likely than individualists to be concerned about environmental and technological risks. They "readily credit claims of environmental risk; they find it congenial to believe that commerce and industry, activities they associate [with] inequity and selfishness, cause societal harm."[48]

The strength of these cognitive biases, together with other unconscious psychosocial risk construction processes,[49] helps explain not only America's intense "culture wars" over the past four decades but also why scientists and other experts often find it so difficult to convince people to consider a new point of view simply by offering them new information. In recent years, this battle of worldviews has played out in the debate about climate change, exemplified by the fierce battle of money and media over the Keystone XL pipeline, which would carry oil extracted from the tar sands of western Canada to the Gulf Coast.[50] Similarly, in the debate about mandatory vaccination, one of the arguments raised by opponents is that vaccines are produced by a global medical-industrial complex, which is said to be greedy and untrustworthy.[51]

Finally, unconscious cultural understandings of risk have a powerful influence on how we perceive, talk about, and "manage" risk. Professor Deborah Lupton has observed that "risk" is itself a value-laden concept. *Risk* was once a neutral term, used as a substitute for *probability*, a simple way of conveying the odds of a particular event's occurring, which could be either positive or negative. Today, to say that something or someone is "risky" has a pejorative tone. "Risk has come to mean danger," and health risks appear to be everywhere.[52]

In the context of public health, *risk* is used in two distinct settings, with different consequences. First, risk applies to environmental hazards. They are "external" and difficult for individuals to control, leading them to experience anxiety, frustration, and fear. Second, *risk* refers to "'lifestyle' choices made by individuals," which are seen as being within their control.[53] In this context, *risky* often appears to be synonymous with *sinful*, a concept that is now seen as old-fashioned. A focus on individual "lifestyle" choices reinforces a belief that individuals are to blame for their situations, including poor health, resonating with the "ancient . . . 'desire to explain sickness and death in terms of volition—of acts done or left undone.'"[54] Here we can see the fundamental attribution error at play. These two views of risk are popularized by media accounts of diseases. For example, the threat of developing HIV/AIDS can be seen either as an "external" risk, imposed on a person with hemophilia who needed a blood transfusion, or an "internal" risk, assumed as part of a lifestyle "choice" by a person who used intravenous drugs or a man who had sex with another man. Health care professionals are not immune from unconscious risk judgments. One public health commentator observed, "'Many within the profession now think that anyone who has a [heart attack] must have lived the life of gluttony and sloth. . . . We seem to view raising a cheeseburger to one's lips as the moral equivalent of holding a gun to one's head."[55] Ensuing chapters will explore how health care professionals' unarticulated views about risk can influence their discretionary decisions, including a decision to divulge confidential medical information to law enforcement officials, a violation of patient privacy that occurs with distressing frequency, especially regarding pregnant women.

II. Risk Communication

The psychological and social-cultural factors that shape risk perception also figure prominently in the ways in which we communicate about risk. In everyday conversation, media discourse, and formal settings ranging from jury trials to legislative sessions, how a message is framed affects the way it is understood.[56] The availability heuristic, coupled with the average person's desire for straightforward explanations of complicated phenomena, can make it easy for the public—and others—to be persuaded by simple but incomplete risk stories. This makes it difficult for complex scientific explanations to compete with vivid anecdotes, even though we know, on an intellectual level, that the plural of anecdote is not data.

Deeply held worldviews may complicate efforts to "educate" people about "the real risks" of a particular technology or scientific phenomenon. A recent study of public attitudes toward the HPV vaccine illuminates the problem. The study was designed to test the hypothesis that people are more likely to accept the views about risk of those who share their underlying worldview. The researchers created fictional "experts" to present pro and con arguments about the HPV vaccine, which protects against the human papillomavirus, the cause of many types of cancer, as well as genital warts, in men and women. The "experts" were given profiles, including phony publications and photographs with distinctive attire and facial hair—think bearded, denim clad professor versus clean shaven, suit attired businessman or government official. Each pseudo-expert presented a coherent and clearly identifiable "cultural perspective." When the anti-vaccine expert fit a "hierarchical individualist" profile, people who "shared those values and who were already predisposed to see the vaccine as risky became even more intensely opposed to it." Similarly, when the putative expert appeared to hold "egalitarian and communitarian values and defended the vaccine as safe," those who held similar worldviews became even more vociferous in supporting vaccination. However, when researchers switched the expert personae, so that the hierarchical expert supported mandatory vaccination and the egalitarian expert opposed it, the experimental subjects responded in the opposite manner. People who held hierarchical worldviews now agreed with the hierarchical expert, and vice versa.[57]

This experiment about the impact of "expert" authority also illustrates the importance of trust, both in understanding and discussing risk. If the listener does not trust the person who is assessing or managing the risk, the communication will not be persuasive. Risk and trust are interactive. When government agencies charged with assessing and managing risk offer "highly confident statements about [a] . . . problem they can build public confidence [in the agency's competency but at the same time] lead citizens to question their honesty. [Conversely, f]ull and open expressions of uncertainty can make the agent appear more honest, but (alas) less competent."[58] This happened in the late 1990s, when an expert panel convened to study vaccine safety decided that the preservative thimerosal should be removed from childhood vaccines out of an abundance of caution. Not only did this action fail to reassure some vaccine skeptics, but it also led them to believe more strongly than ever that vaccines containing thimerosal *were* dangerous.[59] This is a telling example of the skill of "media and special interest groups" "in bringing trust-destroying news to public attention."[60]

The study of risk attitudes and HPV also provides important insights for communicating about public health and environmental risk. Information must be communicated in a manner that is compatible with people's core values in order for them to be open to a new understanding of risk. "*It is not enough that the information be true*; it must be framed in a manner that bears an acceptable social meaning."[61] One cannot persuade a skeptical public simply by presenting more facts.[62] Instead, the most effective way to communicate about risk may be to offer multiple sources of authority, with different cultural perspectives and worldviews, to reach and persuade the widest possible audience.[63] This is the approach now being encouraged by public health officials concerned about outbreaks of contagious diseases, such as measles and pertussis, which are the result, in part, of declining childhood vaccination rates. Today few parents of young children have seen firsthand the deadly consequences of a disease that is preventable by vaccination, while many have observed the adverse effects of vaccines, even if they are mild, like a low-grade fever or a sore arm.[64] This makes it easy for parents to focus on the potential risks, rather than the benefits, of vaccination, despite overwhelming evidence that vaccination does not cause autism or other serious illnesses.[65] As a result, many public health authorities are encouraging individual pediatricians, whom most parents trust, to talk directly with parents about the risks and benefits of vaccination. These doctors are likely to be better communicators about health risks for children than experts from the Institute of Medicine and the Centers for Disease Control, who, as representatives of the government, might be expected to take a pro-vaccination stance.[66]

Understanding the difference between absolute and relative risk is an essential step to improving discussions about risk. Virtually everyone, at all levels of education and expertise, has difficulty understanding—and applying—this key distinction. *Relative risk* describes the extent to which a particular behavior, treatment, or action increases or decreases the odds of a particular event's occurring. *Absolute risk* refers to the absolute numerical change in the odds.[67] Journalists tend to report relative risks, because they make for attention-getting headlines, but they are also frequently misleading. A classic example occurred in the mid-1990s. The British media reported that a new type of oral contraceptive increased by 100 percent the chances of one's developing a life-threatening blood clot in the lungs or legs. As a result, many women became alarmed. What the women failed to understand—because the media did not report it—was that the *absolute risk* of developing blood clots was still extremely low. The new type of contraceptive increased the absolute risk of a woman's developing a blood clot as a result of contraceptive use from 1 in 7,000 to 2 in 7,000. While this was indeed a doubling of the *relative risk*, or a 100 percent increase, the *absolute risk* of their developing a blood clot posed by the new contraceptive had changed very little and was still quite low. The absolute risk was also *lower* than the risk of women developing blood clots as a result of pregnancy, whether the pregnancy was carried to term or ended by an abortion. But because the media failed to distinguish between absolute and relative risk, many women stopped taking contraceptive pills. As a consequence, there was an increase in pregnancies and, in turn, more births and abortions. In sum, as a result of this misunderstanding of relative versus absolute risk, women stopped taking oral contraceptives and exposed themselves to a greater risk—and actual harm—from developing blood clots than if they had continued contraceptive use.[68]

Similarly, today American women are being bombarded with risk information, without guidance on how to use it. In pregnancy, for example, women are warned about drinking too much caffeine (because doing so might trigger a miscarriage or premature delivery) and eating unpasteurized cheese or deli meats (which can carry the Listeria bacterium, which could result in a miscarriage or cause meningitis or neurological problems in infants). While these are very small risks, in both absolute and relative terms, women who hear about the slight possibility of an adverse event may respond by choosing to avoid these substances altogether, following the "omission bias" by deciding to "err on the side of safety," even though that could have other unwanted consequences.[69]

In contrast with the widespread attention paid to small absolute risks, there is little candid discussion, in the media or between doctors and their patients, about the substantial risks of poverty and intimate partner violence (domestic violence) to fetal health and development. Poverty increases the risk of adverse health outcomes. Poor women, especially poor African-American women, have higher rates of stillbirth, and their children suffer higher rates of premature birth, infant mortality, and cognitive impairment. Estimates of the incidence of domestic violence among pregnant women range from 2 to 23 percent.[70] Homicide is the second leading cause of death for pregnant women, and most such homicides are committed by the women's violent partners.[71] Women who are abused while pregnant are more likely to use cigarettes, alcohol, and illegal drugs[72] and to suffer concurrent physical and psychiatric problems.[73] Their children are more likely to be born prematurely and at low birthweight; both conditions increase their chances of cognitive and physical impairments as children.[74] These health issues will be discussed at greater length in chapters 3, 4, and 5.[75]

III. Managing Risk

The same psychocultural forces that underlie risk perception and risk communication are also at work in "risk management." In practice, *risk management* means deciding how to minimize risk, while simultaneously acknowledging that in a democratic, pluralistic society there are often significant competing goals and values. The unconscious processes of risk construction have important implications for questions about how risk—economic, environmental, health, and technological—should be managed by public policymakers. Risk management also occurs in criminal and civil trials. Verdicts about who is responsible for a bad outcome necessarily involve assessments of risk and decisions about how that risk—which has now been realized—should be managed.

Trust is as essential to risk management as it is to risk communication. Paul Slovic argues that the unique style of American democracy, and its implementation in the American regulatory system, exacerbates inherent difficulties in risk communication and makes risk management—deciding what to do about a particular risk—more challenging. He asserts that ". . . in the US, risk-management tends to rely heavily upon an adversarial legal system that pits expert against expert, contradicting each other's risk assessments and further destroying the public trust."[76] Thus, the practice of administrative law, which relies on input from competing scientific and economic experts and demands procedural due process and open deliberation about risk, may make government agency decisionmaking more difficult, as well as confusing and unattractive to the public. When disagreements among scientists *are* made public, as they are in current debates about hydraulic fracturing and climate change,[77] citizens can easily become cynical and disaffected. Or, as noted earlier, members of the public may unconsciously adjust their assessment of a particular risk to match their worldview.[78] Contentious debates in Congress and the media may also reduce the public's trust in science and the concept of expertise. Some debate participants suggest that scientists and other experts are constantly changing their minds (as opposed to updating their theories based on new data) and thus that information (and sources) which purports to be scientific can be discounted.[79]

Similar processes take place in contested trials, which also rely on dueling experts. For example, when children injured by lead poisoning seek to hold lead-based paint and pigment manufacturers legally responsible, the experts presented by the plaintiff and the defense offer strikingly different testimony about the extent of harm due to lead exposure and the contributions of genetics and parenting to a child's intelligence and cognitive abilities. As we shall see in chapter 8, how credible those experts are to the jury may depend heavily on how good a match there is between the experts' apparent worldviews and those of individual jurors.

In addition, in order to make rational health decisions, both individuals and government policymakers need to pursue comparative risk analysis, to compare the risks created by different behaviors and exposures, to maximize overall health benefits.[80] Media portrayals of risk often fail to put risks in a broader context (recall drowning versus skin cancer from summer recreation). They also frequently omit consideration of confounding variables, factors that appear to be causally related to a particular outcome but in fact simply "overlap" with the real causal factor. Confounding variables make it more difficult to understand the causal relationships between particular behaviors and observed outcomes. For example, a report of a study which showed that coffee consumption was associated with an increased risk of heart attacks would be misleading if it failed to disclose that coffee consumption is also closely associated with smoking, and that it is smoking, not drinking coffee, that is the cause of the cardiovascular damage that makes some people more likely to suffer heart attacks.[81] Similar confounding variables appear to be at work in many studies about the health benefits of breastfeeding for children.[82]

Media accounts often overlook relative risk and confounding variables. Only recently have several long-term studies of children born during the "crack" cocaine epidemic of the 1980s and '90s provided hard data to debunk myths about so-called "crack babies," which were widely reported in the news. During this epidemic, media accounts insistently reported that children born to cocaine-using mothers were irreparably harmed, doomed to a lifetime of failure. The reality disclosed by these studies is far different. They found that the children of poor African-American mothers who used crack cocaine while pregnant displayed no significant differences when compared with children born at the same hospitals to similar poor African-American mothers who did *not* use drugs. Instead, the researchers found that poverty, not drug use, was the most significant contributor to the children's intellectual ability and academic achievements. Children born to *both groups* of mothers fell well below the national average in intellectual functioning and achievement.[83] Other studies have found that being born into poverty or living in substandard housing is the biggest predictor of long-term adverse health outcomes, creating risks of acute and chronic health problems that are much higher than for middle-class and suburban children.[84] As a result, pediatric experts in the United States and Canada are now focusing on poverty itself as a health risk to children, one that must be confronted directly because its impact on children's health is more profound than many of the after-the-fact medical and public health interventions that physicians can offer.[85]

Yet for decades, myths about crack babies and stereotypes about their mothers, as well as the failure to understand relative versus absolute risk, have animated media and public policy discussions about children's health. These myths and misunderstandings about risk have led legislators to enact, and prosecutors to enforce, punitive laws against pregnant women. These issues will be explained at greater length in chapters 4 and 5. For now we will turn to the questions of "why" and "how." Through what mechanisms do our innate, unconscious processes of risk construction find their way into the law and legal decisions?

IV. How the Law Reflects and Supports the Social-Psychological Construction of Risk

Why does it matter that the way people perceive, talk about, and manage risk depends, in important and unexpected ways, on their race, gender, social status, and personal worldview? It matters, of course, because law is also socially constructed. Law is not simply positive commandments and prohibitions—the criminal code and regulatory requirements—or a set of "blackletter" rules derived from prior court decisions. Instead, the law *also* embodies a worldview, built on underlying assumptions and cultural values, with the implicit aim of shaping human behavior. Both criminal law and tort law seek to change behavior through deterrence, the idea that the fear of being found criminally responsible or having to pay tort damages will motivate people to behave in "appropriate" ways, avoiding risky or dangerous actions.[86] Criminal law is also based on retribution, the belief that people must be convicted and punished when they commit a crime, to ensure that a convicted defendant suffers commensurately with the harm he has caused and to make a public statement about the wrongfulness of that harm.[87] Similarly, tort law's recognition of individuals' moral obligations to one another is reflected in the concept of "corrective justice."[88] Other bodies of law, including the tax code and environmental regulations, also seek to shape people's behavior through a structure of incentives and penalties.

American law is pervaded by the same psychosocial processes that underlie risk construction. These processes play out in multiple settings and in two dimensions, which the law categorizes as "substantive" or "procedural." Substantive law is the body of legal rules that govern our society. Historically, most of these rules were the product of the common law tradition, in which judges announced new legal rules by relying on the decisions of judges in prior cases.[89] Today the common law is supplemented by legislative, executive, or administrative agency actions, which are embodied in statutes, executive orders, and regulations, respectively. Procedural law is what its name implies, the procedures for making legal decisions. These include the rules for practicing civil litigation (the rules of civil procedure), conducting jury trials (the rules of evidence), and the rules for implementing legislative action by administrative agencies, such as the notice-and-comment rulemaking mandated by federal and state law.[90]

Substantive and procedural law frequently overlap. For example, the law governing duress, which is a defense to certain crimes, includes statements about the circumstances that constitute duress (substantive law) and the types of evidence (expert or lay testimony) which can be admitted to establish that those circumstances existed at the time of the crime (procedural law). Of course, substantive and procedural law are both created by individual human actors, who bring to their decisions the same psychosocial processes that animate risk construction and risk management generally. The next section examines three major venues in which the psychosocial modes of risk construction affect the law. First, when jurors are asked to apply abstract legal concepts like "negligence" or "the reasonable person" to the factual circumstances of an individual case, they are literally constructing the law. Second, when other participants in the legal system—social service investigators, police, prosecutors, and judges—exercise their discretion in a particular case, they are making law indirectly, as they advocate for—or reject—further legal action and establish precedents for future decisions. Individuals' discretionary judgments are affected by the same psychosocial processes of risk construction we have already discussed. Their unconscious biases, preconceptions, worldviews, and "cultural scripts" are channeled into their interpretation and enforcement of the law. Third, the psychosocial processes of risk construction affect lawmakers at all levels, including the legislators and administrative agency policymakers who make decisions about managing risk.

A brief tour of each of these settings demonstrates how the unconscious psychosocial aspects of risk construction interact with the American legal system, creating the potential for bias and distortion in legal decisions. These psychosocial forces are manifestly at work in decisions about risk and blame that emphasize mothers as the source of harm to their children, while often excluding others whose actions profoundly affect children's health.

A. How Juries Decide Cases

The psychosocial processes that undergird jury decisionmaking are similar to those involved in risk construction. In her book *Inside Jurors' Minds: The Hierarchy of Juror Decision-Making*, law professor and former prosecutor Carol Anderson explores the many unconscious as well as cognitive processes that shape jurors' experiences at trial and their ultimate deliberations.[91] These encompass mental shortcuts like the "availability heuristic," the processes of "anchoring and adjustment," and "accommodation and assimilation." They also include self-protective psychological mechanisms like cognitive dissonance, all of which color jurors' understanding of events, including the "facts" of a case at trial.[92]

We have already seen that the availability heuristic leads people to overestimate the likelihood of events occurring that are similar to those they can readily recall, including events that have been made "available" through extensive media coverage.[93] Thus, although jurors are instructed to render a verdict solely on the basis of evidence presented during trial, their decisions are inevitably influenced by what they already believe to be true, based on stories gleaned from the news media or casual conversations.

In addition, jurors (like the rest of us) come to understand new information through the psychological processes known as accommodation and assimilation. When we encounter new ideas or knowledge we try to place it within our existing cognitive frameworks or "schemata," the "mental file folders" that help us categorize information, beliefs, people, and events. If the framework we have chosen is actually a good fit, all is fine. If not, we have two choices. The first is to construct a new framework, a process called accommodation. Sometimes, however, it is easier psychologically to place the new information into an old framework that does not fit well, a process called assimilation. To do this, we distort or alter the new information to harmonize with the framework, as in cramming a square peg into a round hole. As a result of this distortion or alteration, our response to the new information is often inaccurate or inappropriate.[94]

One type of assimilation involves "biased prototypes." A prototype is a type of cognitive shortcut that permits people to place new situations in an appropriate category by searching for "a family resemblance between the new case and the prototypical case."[95] As explained by Professor Martha Chamallas, prototypes can shape jurors' decisions. Problems arise through jurors' unconscious reliance on a *biased* prototype, which does not represent the typical or average case, as a lens for viewing the actions of a particular defendant, victim, or other participant in court proceedings. In these cases the biased prototype imperceptibly reframes the legal issue that the jury is asked to decide. Jurors ask themselves not whether the case being tried meets the legal requirements for a particular crime (as explained in jury instructions) but whether the case fits the prototype. Rape law provides a vivid example. Rape requires that a defendant accomplish sexual intercourse by force or threat of force, without the consent of the victim.[96] For many jurors the prototypical rape is stranger rape, a sexual attack on the victim by a violent stranger. Nonconsensual intercourse that is not between strangers, whether it is between husband and wife or casual acquaintances, does not fit this prototype. As a result, some jurors can find it hard to believe that spousal rape or date rape is "real rape" because they are considering rape as defined by the prototype, not the law.[97] In consequence, some defendants whose conduct meets the legal requirements of rape will be acquitted.[98]

Jurors also employ the same cognitive strategies that we all use to come to terms with events, particularly unpleasant or tragic ones, in ways that are comforting and nonthreatening. These coping strategies may sharply skew their assessment of risk and responsibility. The "fundamental attribution error" prompts us to understand an adverse event by unconsciously assigning blame to internal factors—the character or choices of the victim or defendant, rather than external factors—the circumstances surrounding the event.[99] Another way in which people protect their unconscious view that they live in a just world is to attribute idealized character traits to themselves. Carol Anderson refers to this phenomenon as the "better-than-average effect";[100] devotees of the *Prairie Home Companion* might call it "the Lake Wobegon effect." As a result of this self-serving bias, when jurors compare their conduct with that of the parties at trial, they tend to employ a distorted standard of judgment, evaluating the parties' behavior using a standard derived from the jurors' ideal, not actual, selves.[101]

Like the rest of us, jurors act with the benefit of hindsight. In practice, this hindsight bias leads people to "believe that a certain outcome is inevitable" because they already know what the outcome is.[102] In a jury trial, in which both sides offer an opening statement—a narrative of the facts—jurors can be readily persuaded by a skilled trial lawyer that the events in the case were "inevitable, obvious, and predictable from the start. This makes it easier for them to blame one or both of the parties for failing to anticipate and avoid the harm that now seems so eminently foreseeable."[103] Further, because jurors want to believe in a just (and safe) world, they also tend to engage in "counterfactual" thinking, "imagining alternative scenarios to reality and [mentally] playing out the consequences." Professor Anderson provides a typical example of these so-called "if only" scenarios, positing a basketball player who misses the last shot as the buzzer sounds. In the public's reconstruction of the game, the player's final missed shot looms much larger than his overall high scoring throughout the game. In the legal context, jurors also engage in "if only" thinking. They are likely to blame a defendant if he or she is the last actor who, in the counterfactual construction of events, had the last chance to avoid harm.[104] In the case of harm to children, the last person is likely to be the child's mother or mother-to-be.

The recent Connecticut case of *State v. Scruggs* offers a striking example of the potency of counterfactual thinking. Judith Scruggs was the single mother of a seventeen-year-old daughter and a twelve-year-old son, Daniel. Ms. Scruggs worked sixty hours a week, full-time at Daniel's school and part-time at a local Walmart. Daniel was the victim of extreme bullying at school, and the State Department of Children and Families was working with his mother and school officials to arrange for Daniel to attend a different school. Because of the bullying, Daniel was frequently absent from school. Daniel suffered from very poor hygiene; he was also emotionally fragile, spending much time in his closet. Six days after the Department closed its case file on Daniel, he hanged himself. When investigators came to the Scruggses' apartment, they found it extremely cluttered and malodorous.[105]

As a result of the investigation into Daniel's death, Ms. Scruggs was charged with four counts of "risk of injury to a child" (child endangerment) and a jury convicted her on one count. When Ms. Scruggs asserted that the evidence did not support her criminal conviction, the trial judge ruled that while the conditions in the apartment did not place Daniel in physical danger, "the jury reasonably could have found that the conditions in the defendant's apartment were likely to cause injury to a child's mental health." The trial judge repeatedly referred to the jury's "knowledge of human experience" and "common sense," asserting that "[a]ny layperson with common sense could conclude that the squalor and home living environment here created a risk to Daniel's emotional health. . . ."[106] The Connecticut Supreme Court overturned Ms. Scruggs' conviction. It found that that the evidence did not show that it was foreseeable that living in a cluttered and smelly home could cause Daniel to suffer emotional harm, leading him to commit suicide. It further expressed its deep concern about the use of hindsight to find that this harm was foreseeable simply because it had occurred, implicitly recognizing the power of the hindsight bias and counterfactual thinking.[107]

In sum, jurists, legal scholars, and researchers on risk perception concur that jurors' construction of "the facts" of a case can never be totally objective. Instead, it is inevitably value-laden, a result of the psychological mechanisms that underlie risk construction and the ways in which all people respond to tragic and emotionally disturbing situations. Let us now turn to the substantive law contexts in which jurors and others make decisions about the actions, and inactions, of mothers.

B. Substantive Legal Principles and Discretionary Decisionmaking

Three core American legal principles both permit and reinforce the current emphasis on mothers as the source of harm to their children, interacting with the psychosocial processes we have just discussed. The first is the essential role that "the reasonable person" plays in imposing liability in tort and in criminal law. The second is the elastic set of legal rules that govern a finding of causation, an essential step in establishing both civil liability and criminal responsibility. The third is American law's emphasis on realized, rather than threatened, harm, evinced by profound skepticism about precautionary regulation.[108] Each of these three features of American law is significant in its own right. They are also linked by the common concept of foreseeability, a construct that is highly malleable, connected as it is to the hindsight bias. These core legal principles are present in multiple settings, in which American law not only reflects but also reinforces prevailing cultural norms regarding risk and the role of women in protecting their children's health.

1. "THE REASONABLE PERSON": A CONSTRUCTION OF THE JURY WITH AN ASSIST FROM JUDGES

All first-year law students learn about "the reasonable person" as a core legal construct. An individual who falls below the standard of behavior expected of the reasonable person—because she or he is too careless, too clumsy, or too clueless—and causes harm to another will be liable in tort[109] for negligence.[110] To put it another way, a person is negligent when he or she acts, or fails to act, when a reasonable person would have acted to avoid a foreseeable risk. Foreseeability is thus a central component of negligence.[111] In certain cases the negligent individual may be criminally responsible. For example, in *People v. Williams*, two Native American parents were found guilty of manslaughter based on their failure to seek medical attention for their seventeen-month-old son because they did not "understand the significance or seriousness of the baby's symptoms" (gangrene due to an abscessed tooth) whereas "reasonable" parents would have.[112] The negligence required for a criminal conviction must meet a higher standard, generally referred to as "gross negligence" or "criminal negligence."[113]

The construction of the "reasonable person" is not a neutral process. Professor Steven Hetcher has criticized many tort scholars for arguing about substantive tort law principles without considering the crucial role the jury plays in articulating that law.[114] Hetcher asserts, and jury researchers agree, that when juries decide cases, they bring their own moral intuitions and preconceived notions of appropriate behavior to their deliberations. This is precisely what research on the unconscious processes of risk construction and jury deliberations tells us. When jurors are told to apply "the reasonable person" standard in a negligence case, their mental shortcuts and conscious and unconscious biases have a major impact on how they construct "the reasonable person;" in reality, it can be outcome determinative.[115] Indeed, this is the point of the jury system—to bring to bear the views and values of the community in evaluating the conduct of fellow citizens, rather than leaving the decision solely to a judge, who is usually a person of a more privileged background.[116] Hetcher explains, "Thus, there is a de facto standard that results from the jury's application of the formal standard through the lens of its normative vision. The natural consequence of these de facto standards is that different jurors with different sets of norms can be expected to produce different outcomes.... *A neutral, objective application of the standard to the facts simply does not exist.*"[117] Thus, in practice, juries go far beyond their ostensible role of objective "fact finding" and actually make law.[118] While the jury's application of community norms has been applauded as anti-elitist and pro-democratic,[119] it necessarily brings individual jurors' preconceived notions about appropriate behavior into their decisionmaking.

Whether or not a particular action—or failure to act—is "risky" lies in the eye of the beholder. In deciding that a particular defendant was negligent, a jury is implicitly finding that a risk existed—that the defendant had a duty to protect against it,[120] failed to do so, and caused harm.[121] Making this complex risk determination depends on the context in which harm has occurred, about which jurors may hold preconceived notions of appropriate behavior, and on jurors' worldviews and other unconscious biases, including their attitudes toward women in general and mothers in particular. Judges similarly labor under conscious and unconscious biases, stereotypes, and value preferences based on their worldviews. These unconscious preferences often inform judicial actions, including discretionary decisions about whether to admit evidence, how to frame jury instructions, and whether particular defenses are available. Historically, the socially constructed reasonable person has been skewed toward the traditional views held by those in power. These tend to reflect a male viewpoint, simply because men were in control of the apparatus of the law for so long. As we will explore in more detail in chapter 7, some judges may not believe female witnesses, especially victims of domestic violence, because they cannot conceive of themselves in that situation.[122]

Professor Mayo Moran has studied "the reasonable person" in diverse areas of the law and has shown how unconscious gender biases can permeate judicial decisions. Moran observes, "Conceptions of what is ordinary or customary . . . [are key to determining] fault in negligence." Moran's research led her to conclude that "different kinds of shortcomings" are treated differently depending on whether judges see them as "ordinary" or "normal." Moran reviewed a series of tort cases involving injuries to children, including those in which the harm was caused by other boys or girls. Moran found that judges frequently determined that boys were not negligent, simply because "'boys will be boys'"—that is, more aggressive and less careful. In contrast, judges expected girls (and women) to be more cautious and to always act to keep within the margins of safety.[123] In an important nineteenth-century case, *Michigan Central Railroad Co. v. Hasseneyer*,[124] the Michigan Supreme Court found that a thirteen-year-old girl was herself negligent when she was struck by a train that was backing up, and thus precluded her recovery from the defendant railroad under the then prevailing theory of contributory negligence. Moran quotes the ruling by Judge Thomas Cooley, who declared: "If we judge of ordinary care by the standard of what is commonly looked for and expected, we should probably agree that a woman would be likely to be more prudent, careful and particular in many positions and in the performance of many duties than a man would. She *would, for example, be more vigilant and indefatigable in her care of a helpless child*; she would be more cautious to avoid unknown dangers; *she would be more particular to keep within the limits of abso-*

lute safety."[125] While *Hasseneyer* is an old case, the pattern of its reasoning carries forward to this day. Disparate views of the behavior to be expected of "reasonable" males and females continue to affect the decisions of judges and juries regarding the obligations of mothers and fathers to their children.

a. The Reasonable Pregnant Woman

A compelling example of the intersection of the psychosocial processes of risk construction, jury deliberations, and substantive law can be found in the emerging legal issue of whether mothers should be found liable, either in tort or in criminal law, based on their conduct during pregnancy because of potential risks to the developing fetus. This will be discussed in greater detail in chapters 4 and 5. Here, I will briefly sketch the way these issues have arisen in tort law.

Since 1980, six state appellate courts have considered the question of whether children can seek money damages from their mothers based on the mothers' actions while pregnant.[126] In the four decisions involving motor vehicle accidents, the lawsuits asserted that the pregnant woman was negligent in the way she drove or crossed the street.[127] The two other cases involved the mother's use of drugs while pregnant. In one, a legal drug, Tetracycline, resulted in the child's having discolored teeth.[128] The other case involved the pregnant woman's use of alcohol and cocaine, allegedly causing cognitive and physical harm to her child.[129]

The courts were split in their rulings. Three state courts found that pregnant women *do* have a legal duty to take care to avoid harm to their developing fetuses.[130] Implicit in these decisions was the view that no distinction can or should be drawn between a pregnant woman and a mother in her duty to avoid taking risks that might injure a child.[131]

Three other courts declined to find that pregnant women had a legal, as opposed to a moral, duty to behave in a risk-reducing manner. These courts recognized the difficulty of articulating a clear, objective standard of negligence for juries to follow. In the leading case, *Stallman v. Youngquist*,[132] the Illinois Supreme Court declared that the relationship between a pregnant woman and her fetus was "unlike the relationship between any other plaintiff and defendant." Acknowledging that a pregnant woman's "every waking and sleeping moment . . . shapes the prenatal environment,"[133] the court observed that it would be difficult to define or limit the scope of that duty, because so many actions taken in a woman's life, even prior to conception, could affect fetal development. Further, it would be impossible to articulate a truly objective standard to be applied to women of diverse socioeconomic backgrounds, whose situation in regard to access to health care and even knowledge of their pregnancy might be very different.[134]

b. "The Reasonable Parent" and "the "Reasonable Mother" in Criminal Law

The criminal law also relies on the concept of "the reasonable person," who, in specific cases, will be operationalized as "the reasonable parent" and "the reasonable mother." Every year American women are prosecuted for murder, manslaughter, child abuse, and other crimes when their children are killed or injured by the woman's male partner, either a husband or boyfriend.[135] The converse is much less likely to be true, as will be shown in chapter 7. This disparity is due in part to the demographic reality that the children of single mothers are disproportionately likely to be the victims of child abuse. It also reflects the intersection of unconscious risk construction with substantive legal principles, including "the reasonable person," elastic conceptions of parental duty,[136] and the legal rules of causation, to be explored in more detail shortly. Foreseeability also plays a big part in defining legal obligations in the context of non-abusive parents. Under established principles of criminal law and negligence law, a person has no duty to prevent harm unless that harm is foreseeable.[137] However, it is easy to say that for a mother, harm to her children is *always* foreseeable if her husband or boyfriend has any history of violent or dangerous behavior, thus creating a criminal law duty to act to prevent that harm. Finding such a duty also has major implications for the legal rules that govern causation.

2. CAUSATION AND ITS FOCUS ON FORESEEABILITY AND INDIVIDUAL ACTION

American law's historical bias in favor of finding a single, rather than a multifaceted, cause of harm makes it easy for American prosecutors, judges, and juries to focus on mothers as *the cause* of harm to their children. This emphasis on a unitary, rather than a multifactorial, approach to causation is, in part, a carryover from our pre-industrial legal system, which reflected moral and religious notions of personal responsibility and largely ignored the possibility of multiple contributors to harm. Today American society is still highly individualistic, emphasizing and preferring individual, rather than collective, responsibility.[138] The emphasis on individual actions and actors in the context of causation is evident in tort and criminal law, which both require "actual cause" (usually stated using the "but-for" test) and "proximate cause."[139] These principles were transported from English common law and formalized in the late nineteenth and early twentieth centuries. At that time scholars asserted that law was a science,[140] with "correct legal principles . . . [including the method for determining *the* proximate cause, being deducible] through logical and objective inquiry."[141] Proximate cause requires foreseeability.[142] Only if defendants could or should have foreseen the potential harmful consequences of their actions can they be found liable. As we saw in *Scruggs*, in light of the hindsight bias, proximate cause is often easy to establish; because a certain harm *did* occur, it is tempting to say that it was foreseeable.[143] Criminal law also relies on foreseeability in determining causation, although judges often take pains to point out that the criteria for proximate cause should be narrower in criminal law than in tort law, because the stakes (incarceration or a death sentence) are more serious than the standard tort remedy of paying money damages.[144]

Modern tort scholars have acknowledged some of the problems with causation theory, recognizing that making a determination of actual and proximate cause is inevitably value-laden. Prevailing theories of causation reflect cultural attitudes about individual and corporate responsibility and implicate specific legal policy goals.[145] Tort scholars Martha Chamallas and Jennifer Wriggins, in their book *Measure of Injury: Race, Gender, and Tort Law*, suggest that neither legal theorists nor jurors are able to separate "scientific" fact-finding from conscious and unconscious policy judgments.[146]

Similarly, criminal law scholars like Joshua Dressler recognize that "courts and juries don't *discover* the proximate cause of harm—they *select* it."[147] Indeed, the entire concept of foreseeability, or "objective probability," as it is sometimes called, has been challenged by criminal law scholars as incoherent, because there is no "non-arbitrary way of deciding what a reasonable person knows about [particular dangers]."[148]

Inevitably, jurors and judges are influenced by the hindsight bias, the fundamental attribution error, and other heuristics and biases. Other scholarly research finds that the way in which jurors and others draw "conclusions about cause and effect is not [a matter of science, that is,] . . . of passive discovery of objective fact." Rather, making decisions about causation is "an active process of social construction" that varies according to people's "'time, place, culture and interest.'"[149]

The natural tendency of jurors, as well as legal scholars, to think of causation primarily in terms of individual actors plays out in two distinct "maternal" contexts in the criminal law. The first involves pregnant women who use legal and illegal drugs and suffer an adverse birth outcome, which will be discussed in detail in chapter 5. In these cases, the primary causation issue is the lack of reliable evidence to establish beyond a reasonable doubt that the pregnant woman's ingestion of alcohol, cocaine, or methamphetamine caused a stillbirth, preterm birth, or other injury to her child. When physicians called by the prosecution testify that the pregnant woman's drug use was *the cause* of an adverse birth event, it may be difficult for defense lawyers to persuade a jury that other relevant contributors to the harm—poverty, poor nutrition, domestic violence, or maternal illness—should raise a reasonable doubt about causation and, thus, the woman's guilt. When the prosecution presents evidence that the pregnant woman behaved in an undesirable, if not illegal, manner by using drugs (thereby failing to live up to the standard of "the reasonable pregnant woman"), and the pregnant woman is literally "proximate" to the developing fetus, convincing the jury to consider more distant factors, external to the pregnant woman, will often be an uphill battle. In an emotionally charged criminal trial, unconscious cognitive shortcuts like the fundamental attribution error and the hindsight bias can profoundly affect jurors' thinking.

We will also examine the psychosocial construction of causation in chapter 7, considering the cases of parents whose children are injured by the abusive acts of their spouses or romantic partners. As noted, mothers are disproportionately prosecuted for failing to act to protect their children from abusive partners. In many of these cases, juries, armed with the socially constructed standard of "the reasonable mother" and acting with the benefit of hindsight, have found that a mother's failure to act to prevent foreseeable and harmful actions of her partner has "caused" that harm, and thus she should be held criminally responsible. In cases in which the mother was present when the child was injured by her partner, it appears that nothing less than proof that the mother herself was beaten so severely that she was physically unable to intervene will save her from prosecution. Frequently even this evidence will be insufficient to prevent a guilty verdict, either because the judge refuses to allow evidence to be introduced to prove that the woman was a victim of intimate partner violence, or because the prosecutor argues that this evidence demonstrates that the woman "chose to stay" despite the abuse, thereby "causing" the child's injuries.[150] In cases in which the mother did not witness the abuse, a prosecutor is likely to argue that she should not have left the child in the man's care, even if the abuser was the child's father or the reason for the mother's absence was that she was working to support her family.[151] If there is *any* evidence that the mother was aware of the possibility that the man would harm the child, the prosecution will argue first that the harm was foreseeable and that the mother therefore had a duty to act, and second that her failure to intervene was both the actual and proximate cause of that harm, thereby justifying a guilty verdict.[152] Here again, jurors are likely to be influenced by culturally constructed norms of what a "good mother" would do, as well as conscious and unconscious racial and class biases.[153]

C. Skepticism about the Precautionary Principle as a Basis for Government Action

We have seen the emphasis placed on the foreseeability of harm by civil plaintiffs and prosecutors seeking to hold mothers legally responsible for their children's health, and the impact of the hindsight bias on finding mothers civilly and criminally responsible. In contrast, foreseeability is invoked much less frequently, and with less success, in cases of environmental harm, both potential and realized. Particularly when the risk of harm has not yet materialized, many citizens—and government officials—are not willing to act to prevent harm, because such regulatory action has a cost, both in constraining economic development and in spending of taxpayer dollars. Thus, manufacturers of lead products and other environmental toxins, along with other distant contributors to the poor health of America's children, often escape legal accountability. Simply put, Americans are highly skeptical about the precautionary principle. This skepticism is, in part, a legacy of *laissez-faire* capitalism. It also flows from the unconscious processes of risk construction, which focus attention on risks that are readily "available" because they are highly publicized. Further, the hostility to precautionary regulation reflects Americans' collective worldview, which tends to favor individual, rather than community, responsibility. We will observe the impact of worldviews on the operation of law in discussions of legal responsibility for childhood lead poisoning (chapter 8) and parental obligations to have their children immunized against contagious diseases (chapter 9).

However, in the late 1960s and early 1970s a brief burst of activism put risk at center stage, as environmentalists successfully challenged the conventional wisdom about the proper role of government in safeguarding the public's health. Environmental law expanded rapidly beyond its common law roots during this decade. The common law torts of nuisance, trespass, and negligence are based on completed harm. They generally require that an injured party establish causation, as well as unreasonable behavior if negligence is alleged. Private nuisance law provided an imperfect tool to remedy many instances of environmental harm, because it authorized a court to balance the competing interests of the polluter and its injured neighbors. In many cases courts would not enjoin a polluter's activities because those activities were asserted to have economic benefits; as a result, the injured party would be only partly compensated for the harm suffered.[154] In contrast, public nuisance law permits government to sue for injunctive relief in the case of harm to the public, compelling the creator of a nuisance to abate (clean up) a hazardous situation.[155]

The genius of American environmental lawyers, as well as sympathetic legislators, was to acknowledge the limits of common law remedies and to push for the enactment of statutes based on the precautionary principle, to prevent, rather than simply ameliorate, health related harms.[156] In the heady days of the 1960s and early '70s Congress enacted, and President Richard Nixon signed into law, more than thirty statutes designed to protect the health of the population at large.[157]

Many of these statutes invoked the precautionary principle, permitting regulators to act before harm occurs.[158] In response, there was significant debate about how much risk must be demonstrated before an administrative agency, like the Environmental Protection Agency (EPA) or the Occupational Safety and Health Administration (OSHA), can act to prevent harm. In many cases, the people resolving this question were federal judges. Like other legal decisionmakers, these judges brought their personal biases, social identities, political philosophies, and worldviews to their work—the process of perceiving, assessing, and managing risk.

In the 1970s some federal judges did defer to an agency's interpretation of its statutory mandate, authorizing regulatory action despite a lack of definitive proof of a causal link between a specific type of pollution and harm to the public. The zenith of this judicial deference was Judge J. Skelly Wright's expansive interpretation of a key provision of the Clean Air Act, which permitted the EPA to act if it determined that a particular pollutant "will endanger . . . the public health or welfare." In *Ethyl Corp. v. Environmental Protection Agency*,[159] Judge Wright upheld the EPA's determination that atmospheric lead posed substantial risks to human health and development, finding that the agency's decision to phase out lead in gasoline was justified.[160] Essentially Judge Wright determined that the EPA could act without waiting for dead bodies.[161] "[E]ndanger," he said, "means something less than actual harm. When one is endangered, harm is *threatened*; no actual injury need ever occur."[162] *Ethyl Corp.* held that even though the EPA could not demonstrate *actual harm*—either that a significant portion of the population had very high lead levels, or that lead from gasoline was the cause of those high levels (which would be necessary for a successful tort suit)—the EPA had established a significant *risk of harm*. The court considered the facts that demonstrated risk: that high blood lead levels were known to be toxic, that 90 percent of atmospheric lead came from leaded gas, and that people living in urban areas, especially children, were likely to face greater lead exposure than those in less populated areas.[163] In Judge Wright's view, this significant *risk* of harm was sufficient to justify precautionary regulation under the Clean Air Act.[164]

In the 1970s American corporations and other conservative forces pushed back against the environmental movement, with important consequences in the federal courts and Congress. In 1971, Lewis Powell, the former president of the American Bar Association, and soon-to-be associate justice of the United States Supreme Court, wrote a memo for the United States Chamber of Commerce in which he denounced the leftist threat to the American free enterprise system, including civil rights, consumer advocacy, and environmental activism.[165] In 1980, the federal judiciary's embrace of the precautionary principle was halted, in significant part, by Justice John Paul Stevens' opinion in *Industrial Union Dept., AFL-CIO v. American Petroleum Institute*,[166] also known as "the Benzene case." Professor Robert Percival suggests that this decision may have been a throwback to traditional tort reasoning, reflecting Justice Stevens' apparent desire that the existence of a causal relationship be demonstrated by methods more consistent with common law tort requirements for *realized* harm rather than the mandate of a precautionary statute.[167] Justice Stevens interpreted the Occupational Safety and Health Act[168] to mean that before OSHA could establish a lower permissible exposure level for workers exposed to benzene, a known potent carcinogen, it had to demonstrate that current exposure levels represented a "significant risk of harm" that could be remedied only by lowering exposure to another specified level.[169]

Since the Benzene case, federal regulatory agencies have generally chosen to rely on heavily quantitative risk analyses, even though this approach inevitably relies on subjective policy choices about which quantitative approach or "conservative assumptions" to adopt.[170] With the federal courts' shift to the right, accomplished by Presidents Ronald Reagan, George H.W. Bush, and George W. Bush, judges have often demanded that agencies demonstrate risk in quantitative terms, rather than simply point to a foreseeable risk of harm.[171] Simultaneously, Congress and many state legislatures have backed away from their earlier enthusiasm for the precautionary principle, and governors and other state officials have often been slow to act, despite mounting evidence that a wide range of chemicals—heavy metals like lead and mercury, as well as endocrine disruptors like BPA and phthalates—may cause harm during prenatal development and childhood. The lead crisis in Flint, Michigan, is but the latest example of the failure of governments to act aggressively to protect children's health.[172]

Conclusion

Unconscious psychological processes and cultural assumptions have a powerful impact on the way we perceive, talk about, and manage risk. In turn, these constructions of risk both shape the meaning of core legal principles and affect the ways in which human actors exercise their discretion in the arenas of civil and criminal law. The following chapters will show how these unconscious risk construction processes frame our determinations of moral, legal, and social responsibility for the health of America's children.

3

How Healthy Are America's Children?

Myths and Realities

Introduction

In many ways, the health of America's children is at an all time high. When compared with their nineteenth- and twentieth-century forebears, our children live longer and healthier lives, largely free from the scourge of contagious diseases, agricultural and industrial accidents, many forms of cancer, and numerous illnesses and injuries that routinely afflicted children in the past. At the same time, American children born in the twenty-first century are more likely than their forebears to suffer from chronic health conditions, including asthma, autism, diabetes, mental illness, and obesity. Further, there are enormous racial and class disparities in children's health status. These reflect not only differing degrees of access to health care but also the insidious and long-term effects of poverty, which include physical and emotional stress and the negative impacts of substandard housing and poor nutrition. Health disparities among American children have widened in recent years, providing a partial explanation of why they are less healthy, on average, than their peers in other industrialized democracies, even though the United States spends more per capita on health care than any other nation.[1] This chapter explores the current status of children's health in the United States. It examines medical, social, economic, and environmental contributors to children's health and well-being and surveys important health indicators, including death, disease, and injury rates as well as other markers of childhood health. It considers the health of the "average" child as well as the health of more vulnerable children, and it puts the health of America's children in both historical and comparative perspective.

I. At the Beginning

To assess children's health one must begin before birth, even prior to conception. Many factors that affect a child's health are situated in the circumstances of the child's parents when they were children themselves. These preconception factors affect birth outcomes and infant and child health, as well as adolescent and adult health. Children's health prospects can vary dramatically depending on whether their parents were reared in poverty, middle-class comfort, or wealth; whether the parents had limited or ready access to health care; and whether they became parents as teenagers or older adults. The essential critique of the current fixation on mothers as *the* source of risk to children's health is that it focuses too narrowly on the mother's behavior while pregnant and parenting, ignoring the multiple structural and epigenetic determinants of both maternal and child health. Today, the evidence is overwhelming that children and adolescents who grow up in poverty, without adequate nutrition or access to health care, and who are exposed to stress, toxic chemicals, heavy metals, and other environmental hazards are very likely to have poorer health and to die earlier than their wealthier peers. Their children, in turn, are likely to become parents of children who also begin life facing health challenges.[2] Indeed, in writing this book I have been frequently reminded of James Carville's admonition to the Clinton campaign during the 1992 presidential election: "It's the economy, stupid!" More than any other circumstance, poverty is the greatest risk factor for poor health in children.[3]

Mothers and fathers each contribute to a child's health status, not only through their obvious donations of genetic material but also by exposing their child to a variety of substances and forces *in utero*. Although maternal drug use, both legal and illegal, has garnered the lion's share of media and medical attention, paternal drug use also can have a significant impact on children's health. Studies have found that children born to fathers and mothers who smoke are likely to weigh less at birth than the children of nonsmoking parents and are more likely to have birth defects and genetic diseases. Recent research suggests that paternal smoking *prior* to conception can alter a father's DNA, causing permanent mutations in his sperm that are transmitted to the child via conception and make the child more likely to develop cancer.[4] Fathers (and other men) can transmit HIV to children through sexual intercourse with the child's mother or by sharing contaminated needles with a drug-using woman who later gives birth to an HIV-positive child.[5] Older fathers are more likely to have genetic mutations in sperm that affect brain development in their offspring, leading to autism and schizophrenia.[6] Both fathers and mothers can be exposed to a variety of toxic substances and dangerous instrumentalities at work—pesticides, lead, mercury, organic compounds, and ionizing radiation—which can damage the parents' gametes and harm the developing fetus, resulting in miscarriages, stillbirths, and damage to developing organ systems. Sometimes parents bring these toxic chemicals home on their skin or work clothes. They may be spread throughout the home (and indirectly to the fetus) when parents hug their children or launder work clothes with the rest of the family wash.[7] Finally, parents' genetic contributions to their children may be shaped by the phenomenon of epigenetics. "A deleterious gene in one's DNA may not be harmful in the absence of certain triggers that 'turn on' gene expression and cause cancers [or other health problems] to develop. These modifications in gene expression . . . can be inherited and affect the health of offspring."[8] For example, many studies have documented what appears to be inherited stress in the children of survivors of the Holocaust and other genocides.[9]

II. Birth

The average American child born in 2013 can expect to live longer than ever before, nearly seventy-nine years.[10] This is greater than the sixty-nine years that was the average life expectancy of Baby Boomers, born between 1945 and 1961, and of the Boomers' parents or grandparents, born in the first third of the twentieth century or earlier, whose life expectancy was about fifty-nine years.[11] However, American children's life expectancy lags behind that of children in other developed nations, a gap that has been widening since 1980.[12] Many children born today face significant obstacles to a healthy childhood, either because they were born prematurely and/or at low or very low birthweight, suffer from birth injuries or genetic diseases, or are affected by childhood poverty and other environmental hazards.

About 12 percent of American children are born preterm (before thirty-seven weeks), placing the United States in the global company of Honduras, Kenya, Thailand, and Turkey. In contrast, in Canada, Australia, and most European nations preterm birth rates range from 7 to 9 percent.[13] Being born prematurely makes it much more likely that a child will die in infancy; those children who do survive are more likely to have persistent health problems and disabilities.[14] The American preterm birth rate has risen 30 percent since 1981. This is due in part to increased use of fertility treatment and other assisted reproductive technology, as well as the lack of prenatal care and other factors that are more difficult to pinpoint. It turns out, for example, that the longer an immigrant lives in the United States, the more likely she is to give birth prematurely.[15]

Being a teenage mother also increases the risk of a woman's delivering a premature or small baby.[16] American teen pregnancy rates have been cut nearly in half since their 1991 high, but they are still significantly higher than those in other developed countries.[17] Within the United States rates vary widely between adolescents of diverse races and locales: in 2010 the teen pregnancy rate was 15 per thousand in New Hampshire and 55 per thousand in Mississippi.[18] In turn, these variations reflect different cultural values, educational opportunities, and access to health care, including contraception and abortion.[19]

III. Childhood

A. Childhood Deaths

Today, it is extraordinarily rare for Americans to die in childhood, a phenomenon due largely to the implementation of basic sanitation and other public health interventions, the development of vaccines against most major infectious diseases, and substantial medical progress against many forms of childhood cancer.[20] The mortality rate for infants (under one year) has either remained the same or decreased significantly every year since 1958. Yet economic and racial disparities persist. Despite the continuing decline in infant mortality, in 2009 the death rate for black American infants was more than double that of white and Hispanic infants (12.71 per thousand infants versus 5.27 and 5.44, respectively).[21] An infant born to a mother without a high school diploma is twice as likely to die as one born to a college-educated woman.[22] These racial and socioeconomic disparities are a major reason that the United States ranks *fifty-first* in the world in infant mortality, well behind other developed nations.[23] The two leading causes of death for American infants are birth defects, which are either genetic or a result of abnormal fetal development or delivery, and illnesses related to preterm birth and low birthweight. The third leading cause of death is sudden infant death syndrome (SIDS), the diagnostic label that is given to infant deaths whose cause cannot be explained. SIDS has declined since 1988, attributable both to a change in pediatricians' recommendations for infant sleeping positions and narrowed diagnostic criteria. A number of factors are *associated* with SIDS, including parental smoking, poverty, maternal alcohol abuse, and preterm birth.[24] The other leading causes of infant death are a variety of birth-related complications, accidents, and circulatory diseases.[25] Fewer than 200 American infants are born each year with HIV, but almost all are able to be treated successfully with antiretroviral drugs.[26] Other infants die from vaccine-preventable diseases, either because they were too young to be vaccinated against a particular disease, they had a compromised immune system and could not be vaccinated, they received a vaccination that did not "take," or their parents chose not to vaccinate them.[27]

Among American children ages one to four, the leading cause of death is accidents, from motor vehicles and other sources, followed by birth defects, homicide, cancer, and heart disease. For children ages five to fourteen, accidents are again the leading cause of death, followed by cancer, birth defects, homicide, and suicide. Among adolescents ages fifteen to nineteen, the leading cause of death is accidents, followed by homicide, suicide, cancer, and heart disease. Indeed, motor vehicle accidents are the leading cause of death for children ages five to nineteen, as well as young adults.[28] Older children are the most likely to die because of a motor vehicle accident, reflecting the increased likelihood that teenagers will be the driver or passenger in a car involved in a fatal accident.[29] American children are more likely to die in accidents than their peers in other developed nations, a difference that is largely explained by America's higher motor vehicle fatality rates and the much greater use of firearms in the United States.[30]

B. Childhood Illness and Injury

The reality for most American children today is that they will suffer occasional acute illnesses and injuries (a cold, an ear infection, diarrhea, or a broken arm) but will be mostly "healthy," viewed from both historical and comparative perspectives. As noted, they are no longer likely to become ill, or die, from infectious diseases, thanks to the successful development and deployment of vaccines.[31] Today's children are, however, rather likely to live with a chronic illness or condition, including asthma, allergies, diabetes, developmental disorders, learning disabilities, and mental illnesses.[32] Environmental pollutants contribute to many of these conditions. Lead exposure causes significant neurological problems and learning disabilities, while motor vehicle exhaust and power plant emissions cause about 30 percent of childhood asthma cases. Mercury emissions from power plants also cause neurological harm to developing fetuses and children.[33] Increasingly, American children, as well as others living in the developed world, are seen to suffer from "a group of chronic conditions of multifactorial origin that have been termed the 'new pediatric morbidity.'"[34]

Over the past three decades, the number of children diagnosed with anxiety, depression, attention deficit disorder, or other mental illness, as well as autism or other developmental disorders, has grown rapidly. Indeed, autism spectrum disorders are now diagnosed in one of every sixty-eight children.[35] About one in a hundred children experience physical abuse and neglect. More than a fifth of America's children live in poverty; the likelihood that a child will live in a family with an income below the federal poverty level was higher during the past nine years than in 1975.[36] There is mounting evidence that childhood poverty is not merely statistically associated with poor childhood health but actively contributes to it. Some children are especially likely to have health problems as a result of genetic susceptibilities and birth injuries. Virtually all American children are exposed to an array of toxic chemicals in the environment. Children are more likely than adults to be harmed by such exposure because of their faster metabolism; the larger relative surface area of their bodies, which permits greater exposure; different rates of absorption of toxic substances; and the inherent "biologic sensitivity" of children because they are still developing.[37] Children can also be exposed to environmental toxins depending on what they eat and where they live. For example, the average child consumes more apples than an adult does. As a result, exposure to a dangerous pesticide used on apples could cause substantial harm to a child's developing systems.[38] Poor urban children of color are disproportionately exposed to lead from deteriorating paint in substandard housing. The extent of the harm caused by environmental exposure to toxic chemicals depends not only on the "dose" the child receives but also on the potentially protective effects of a supportive home, school, and community environment. Finally, because of widening economic and social disparities in the country as a whole, including poverty and a lack of family support, a large group of vulnerable children, particularly adolescents, are more likely to be in poor health,[39] a condition that they may "transmit" to future children.

C. Chronic Conditions

Asthma affects more American children than any other disease, requiring frequent visits to a pediatrician's office or a hospital emergency room for both acute asthma attacks and long-term disease management.[40] Children whose asthma is not well controlled are likely to miss school, contributing to lower educational achievement. Poor, inner-city, and African-American children are disproportionately likely to develop asthma, as they are exposed to more air pollution than suburban and rural children and frequently live in substandard housing, where mold, cockroach dust, and other asthma triggers are present. For example, after Hurricane Katrina up to a quarter of African-American children in New Orleans suffered from asthma, reflecting the confluence of environmental exposure to mold and other allergens in dilapidated housing and the lack of access to health care.[41] Parental smoking, before and after birth, is also associated with asthma and other respiratory diseases.[42] The United States has one of the highest asthma rates of all developed nations.[43]

The proportion of American children who are overweight and obese has tripled in the past thirty years, although recent data show that obesity's incidence has peaked and is beginning to decline.[44] Thirty-five percent of American children ages five to nineteen are overweight; 17 percent of American children are considered obese.[45] The United States has led the developed world in this regard for decades.[46] The debate over the factors that contribute to obesity is contentious. Some debaters focus on the individual food choices and nutritional practices of parents and children, while others point to an increase in children's "screen time," greater reliance on automobiles for transportation, increased corporatization of food production, and targeted marketing of unhealthy foods to children.[47] Regardless of the reasons why so many American children are overweight and obese, these conditions make them much more likely to develop diabetes, as well as cardiovascular, kidney, liver, and respiratory diseases that put them at risk of premature death.[48] Obese and overweight children are also disproportionately poor and members of ethnic and racial minorities; many live in rural areas.[49]

D. Abuse and Neglect: Physical and Psychological Impacts

Child abuse and neglect have been recognized as a problem in America since the late 1800s. Today an average of one in a hundred children is physically or sexually abused. An estimated 700,000 children a year are the victims of abuse (out of more than 3 million reports of child abuse); more than 1,600 deaths annually result from child abuse.[50] Since the early 1960s, when the term *battered child syndrome* was coined, child abuse has been the focus of intense medical, media, and political attention. Many experts agree that child abuse and neglect are both under- and over-diagnosed and that a broad array of government interventions has only partially succeeded in protecting children at risk for abuse and neglect.[51] As a result of violent assaults and sexual abuse, children suffer an array of physical injuries, including some that result in death. This abuse also predisposes these children to develop physical and mental illness and substance abuse.[52] Many children suffer from stress and mental illness as a result of living in poverty and unsafe environments. More than one-quarter of poor urban children have witnessed a murder. More than three-quarters of all urban youth have witnessed violence in some form—in their homes, at schools, or in their communities.[53]

E. Environmental Hazards

Increasingly, children are exposed to a vast array of toxic substances—at home, school, and in the larger environment—that can cause neurological harm, cancer, and other serious diseases. Nationwide, the incidence of lead poisoning has declined since the 1970s, after lead was banned as a gasoline additive and as an ingredient in interior house paint, but children who are African-American, poor, and living in dilapidated housing continue to suffer serious injuries from lead exposure.[54] The devastating impact of lead on children's health will be explored in depth in chapter 8. For now, it is enough to note that more than half a million American children under the age of six—*one in every thirty-eight children*—become the victims of lead poisoning each year.[55] Research has demonstrated that children are harmed by lead exposure at very low levels, with long-term, irreversible consequences for their intellectual and emotional development, as well as cardiovascular, immunological, and endocrine effects. Academic and behavioral problems are a common result of lead poisoning, especially among boys.[56]

Mercury, another heavy metal, causes substantial neurological and other harms to children and adults. Today, the major sources of mercury toxicity in the United States are elemental mercury, released into the atmosphere from coal-burning power plants, and methyl-mercury, which is created when this elemental mercury is acted upon by bacteria, eaten by fish, and ultimately consumed by humans.[57] Fish, which are good to eat because they are high in protein and omega-3 fatty acids, are the major source of mercury for most Americans. Although elemental mercury and methyl-mercury cause toxic brain injuries to all humans (for example, many European hat makers suffered the neurotoxic effects of occupational exposure to mercury in the nineteenth century, leading to the expression "mad as a hatter"), it has especially pernicious effects on the developing fetal brain.[58] Until 2011 the EPA had not regulated mercury emissions from older coal-burning power plants under the Clean Air Act, and industry opposition continues to make it difficult for the EPA to effectively and immediately regulate mercury emissions.[59] Nearly all American children and pregnant women still receive unsafe doses of mercury, because they eat fish or breathe air that is contaminated with mercury from power plant emissions.[60] Children who eat a lot of fish, particularly Native American children and children whose parents practice subsistence fishing, are exposed to much higher levels of mercury.[61]

In addition to heavy metals and known carcinogens, there is growing evidence that chemical compounds known as endocrine disruptors pose health risks to adults and children. Many studies have found an association, although not a causal relationship, between exposure to Bisphenol A (BPA), a potent neurotoxin widely used in the manufacture of baby bottles, children's products, and food containers, and some chronic conditions of childhood, especially obesity. The FDA has banned the use of BPA in baby bottles and children's toys, amid concerns that BPA poses epigenetic risks.[62]

F. Adolescents' Health

American adolescents are generally healthy. However, their health risks and health care needs are often different from, and harder to meet than, those of younger children, because the care they need is frequently preventative but they are less likely to see a doctor on a regular basis.[63] During adolescence children seek greater freedom from parental oversight and control, at the same time that they often lack the necessary maturity and life experience for appropriate independent decision-making. As a result, adolescents are more likely to engage in behaviors that are risky to life and health. These include driving while texting or drinking, having unprotected sex (exposing them to unwanted pregnancy and sexually transmitted diseases), and using alcohol, nicotine, and other drugs, which threaten immediate and long-term harms.[64] Despite significant public health efforts aimed at reducing childhood smoking, today about one-fifth of all high school students smoke,[65] a rate that has not changed since the beginning of the twenty-first century. In part this reflects the tendency of adolescents to believe that they will not personally suffer the known dangers of tobacco use,[66] and in part it is explained by expanding youth-focused marketing of candy- and fruit-flavored cigars, which are not as tightly regulated as cigarettes.[67] E-cigarettes, whose long-term health impacts are not yet known, are especially popular with adolescents.[68]

Adolescents are more likely than younger children to die in accidents, whether from motor vehicles, firearms, or other sources. About 20 percent of adolescents suffer from a chronic condition, such as asthma, or a mental illness, including depression, anxiety, and eating disorders. Adolescents are more likely than younger children to attempt and commit suicide and develop substance abuse problems.[69]

Recent national surveys show that more than 40 percent of teens ages fifteen to nineteen, both male and female, have had intercourse at least once, a decline from a high of 51 percent in 1988. In contrast to their peers in other developed nations, American teenage girls are much more likely to become pregnant and to have abortions. In 2007 the average number of births per thousand for American teenage mothers was forty-three; the average for Canadians was thirteen and for the Netherlands five. Other developed countries also have much lower abortion rates, because they make it easier for adolescents to use effective contraception.[70]

Several groups of adolescents are especially vulnerable and thus more likely to develop chronic physical and mental health problems. The first group includes victims of sexual and physical abuse, who are more likely than their nonvictimized peers to develop mental illness, abuse drugs, and attempt suicide.[71] Even children who have not been abused themselves but have witnessed family violence often display mental health or substance abuse problems.[72] Other vulnerable adolescents are those who are transgender, runaways, or homeless, who lack parental supervision and support, and those who are poor and members of racial or ethnic minorities. All of these groups are often less healthy than white or more affluent children, because of a lack of health insurance, infrequent visits to a primary care physician, exposure to environmental hazards, and the stress of living in a dangerous environment.[73]

Adolescents are less likely to be insured than younger children. For the past three decades, at least 12 percent of adolescents have lacked any insurance coverage, either public or private.[74] While most children of parents who receive health insurance through employment are covered until age twenty-one or older, many children who are covered by the two major public insurance programs—Medicaid and the State Child Health Insurance Program (SCHIP or CHIP)—are eligible for insurance only until they reach the age of nineteen. Historically, Medicaid covered children older than six only if their parents were extremely poor. With the introduction of CHIP in 1997, children from slightly more affluent families (up to 200 percent of the federal poverty level) became eligible for health insurance, but CHIP was criticized for offering a less robust set of benefits than Medicaid.[75] Children enrolled in Medicaid and CHIP often have a hard time finding a doctor willing to provide medical services, because of extremely low reimbursement rates, and thus many children cannot obtain the care mandated by law.[76] Other children are not enrolled because it is harder for their parents to navigate the complex Medicaid and CHIP enrollment process. This is sometimes made more difficult by the parents' poor English language skills and low educational levels, as well as lack of knowledge that public insurance is even available.[77] The Affordable Care Act was enacted to increase access to health care for poor children and adolescents, as well as adults. However, the United States Supreme Court ruled in *National Federation of Independent Businesses v. Sebelius*[78] that the ACA's expansion of Medicaid was optional with individual states. Today, nearly twenty states have elected not to participate in the Medicaid expansion, with the result that many fewer children are guaranteed access to health care coverage.[79]

Going Forward

The children's health concerns raised here will be explored in subsequent chapters, which focus on the risks to children's health at particular developmental and life stages. Chapter 10 responds to these concerns, by addressing the need to create and implement innovative strategies to intervene at multiple stages of children's development, to intercept the troubling cycle in which poverty, child abuse, environmental hazards, and lack of access to comprehensive health care reinforce existing health disparities, thus setting up a new generation at risk for poor health.

PART II

Mothers as Vectors of Risk

4

Conceptions of Risk

Legal and Medical Interventions against Pregnant Women

Introduction

Today, many American women find themselves the subject of intense surveillance during pregnancy. Even as pregnant women happily anticipate the birth of a healthy child, families, friends, health care providers, and government officials often scrutinize their actions for behavior that could potentially risk the health of the developing fetus. Increasingly, widely held beliefs about how the "good" pregnant woman should behave have resulted in legal interventions. Physicians, nurses, and other health care providers have often "referred" their patients to law enforcement, resulting in legal interventions that include court-ordered medical treatment, involuntary civil commitment, tort liability, and even criminal prosecution. This chapter examines the rising trend of legal intervention predicated on women's actions—or inaction—while pregnant, reflecting the convergence of psychological and cultural forces that shape our perceptions of risk. Put simply, mothers and mothers-to-be have become vectors of risk.[1]

At the outset, this chapter explores the dynamic connections among medical, media, political, and social attitudes toward pregnancy and the perceived obligation of pregnant women to promote fetal life at all costs. These changing attitudes are the product of new medical knowledge and the psychosocial processes of risk construction. This discussion also previews the significant shifts in legal doctrine governing the fetus that have taken place during the past century. Over the past four decades, coinciding roughly with the legalization of abortion accomplished by *Roe v. Wade*,[2] lawmakers, criminal prosecutors, and private litigators have increasingly endeavored to hold pregnant women legally responsible for threatening or causing harm to the fetuses contained within their bodies.

This chapter considers the diverse contexts in which ostensibly neutral principles of American law have been deployed to treat pregnant women as virtual guarantors of fetal and child health. The chapter first documents how the well-established legal principles of informed consent to medical treatment have been ignored in the context of pregnancy. By virtue of becoming pregnant, women are deemed to have given up significant legal rights—to exercise autonomy and control over their own bodies, make health care decisions, and to seek and retain employment. In the name of reducing perceived risks to the fetus, courts have ordered pregnant women to submit to unwanted medical treatment, including blood transfusions and caesarean sections, bed rest and hospitalization, psychiatric care, and insulin therapy.[3] The law also authorizes retrospective risk assessments, as pregnant women's behavior is increasingly scrutinized after the fact, through tort litigation and criminal prosecutions. Since the 1980s some children who suffered prenatal injuries have sued their mothers, seeking to hold them liable for alleged negligence—in driving, walking, or taking drugs (legal and illegal) while pregnant. An alarming number of pregnant women have been criminally prosecuted for allegedly risking or causing harm to the fetus, based on conduct such as choosing not to deliver by caesarean section, having accidents, or attempting suicide. Both tort and criminal cases show how core legal concepts—including causation, informed consent, and negligence—have been refashioned when they are applied to pregnant women.

The chapter then examines recently enacted statutes explicitly aimed at protecting fetal life. Frequently, these laws have the thinly disguised goal of making abortions harder to obtain, both legally and practically. These new statutes avoid difficult legal questions about when a fetus is, or should be treated as, the legal equivalent of a child. Instead, these laws target pregnant women directly and explicitly, authorizing either criminal prosecutions or civil interventions based solely on the women's pregnant status. The former include a broad array of fetal endangerment and fetal homicide laws that criminalize the conduct of pregnant women as well as the actions of third parties. The latter include laws that override a pregnant woman's advance medical directive, effectively requiring her to receive medical treatment over her objection in order that her life may be prolonged long enough to deliver a viable fetus. Additional laws, which will be addressed in chapter 5, target pregnant women who use legal and illegal drugs, authorizing both criminal prosecution and involuntary civil commitment.

The Evolving Media, Medical, and Political Landscape

How did we get to this point? Today's heightened emphasis on the risks of pregnancy—and the obligation of pregnant women to avoid these risks at all costs—is a product of converging medical, media, and political forces that have laid the foundation for changes in American cultural norms and law. Three phenomena stand out. First, over the past half-century the fetus has become much more visible, both literally and figuratively. In 1965, Swedish photographer Lennart Nilsson published *A Child Is Born*, a book that displayed spellbinding images of a fetus as a human being completely separate from its mother. While the book also addressed pregnancy's impact on the woman and her family, these two narratives—the changes in the body and life of the pregnant woman and the development of the fetus—were often divorced from one another. This disconnect was apparent in the April 30, 1965, issue of *Life* magazine, whose cover displayed one of Nilsson's colorized photographs of a fetus isolated within its mother's womb. This photograph lacked any indication that the womb was bounded by the pregnant woman's body. In effect, the woman was erased from the public portrayal of the fetus,[4] as was her essential role in its nurture and development.

Recently visual imagery of the fetus as a separate human being has become ubiquitous, presented not only in dramatic photographs of fetal surgery, showing a tiny hand reaching outside the mother's body, but also in images of routine fetal ultrasounds, mounted on family refrigerators and passed around to friends at baby showers.[5] Commercial ultrasound studios offer "3D" and "4D" imagery to expectant parents, who can post the images on Facebook or enter their fetuses into online beauty pageants.[6] These ultrasonic images have contributed to the social *construction* of fetal personhood, as the fetus now becomes "real" months before its birth.[7] The political implications of this have not been lost on anti-abortion activists. As the *New York Times* reported months before the 2016 presidential election, many Republican candidates emphasized the impact of seeing ultrasounds of their children and grandchildren, which brought home to them that these fetuses *were* children.[8] The ongoing debate about whether pregnant women should be required to view sonograms of their fetuses and listen to their heartbeats before they can obtain an abortion is merely the latest round in the legal and political struggle over whether women should have any right to an abortion at all.[9]

The heightened visibility of the fetus as a separate human entity has occurred in tandem with the second factor—the increased emphasis in medical research and media discourse on the factors that affect fetal and child health. From the Middle Ages until the mid–twentieth century physicians and midwives treated the fetus as part of the pregnant woman's body, a sort of appendage that was inseparable from it until the moment of birth. English common law followed medical understandings of fetal development. Pregnancy was essentially viewed as a black box, into which were poured the magic ingredients of sperm and egg. Nothing was known about the outcome until the fetus "quickened," and even then the exact result was not revealed until the baby's birth nine months later. Under the common law "born-alive rule," one could not be subject to criminal or civil liability based on actions that affected a fetus, unless it was born alive. Birth thus established a sharp "bright line" that precluded legal liability for harm that occurred prior to a child's birth.[10] The fetus was seen as a "'passenger' in a woman's body, [literally] propelled into existence through the birth 'passage.'"[11]

American legal doctrine tracked this understanding. For example, the 1894 case of *Dietrich v. Inhabitants of Northampton* concerned a pregnant woman who had slipped on a public sidewalk and delivered prematurely; her four- or five-month-old fetus survived for only a short time. When the woman sued the town of Northampton, Massachusetts, seeking damages for her loss, Oliver Wendell Holmes, Jr., sitting on Massachusetts' highest court, rejected the idea that the woman had grounds for a lawsuit. Justice Holmes observed that no American court had recognized a cause of action for prenatal harm, because "the unborn child was a part of the mother at the time of the injury";[12] thus only physical harm suffered by the mother herself was legally compensable. This was the prevailing view in the United States until 1946, when, in a medical malpractice case, *Bonbrest v. Kotz*, a Washington, D.C., court ruled that a child born alive could sue third parties for injuries allegedly suffered when it was a viable fetus.[13] Courts around the country rapidly accepted this view.[14]

Yet even at this time the medical community continued to regard the fetus as part of the mother. Mid-twentieth-century obstetrical practice, as well as textbooks, focused on the mother, not the fetus, as the patient. This reflected the prevailing medical wisdom that promoting the health of the pregnant woman was the best way to ensure the delivery of a healthy baby.[15] Today, the emphasis has shifted, in both medical research and clinical practice. Much more attention is paid to avoiding risks to fetal health as an independent goal of medical practice. Obstetricians now see themselves as taking care of two patients: the mother and the child-to-be-born. This view began to emerge in the late 1950s. At that time, researchers were trying to identify fetuses at risk for oxygen deprivation, with accompanying brain damage; they developed electronic fetal monitoring in a quest to identify appropriate occasions for intervening during labor.[16] Unfortunately, electronic fetal monitoring (EFM) has proved to be quite imprecise in identifying fetuses actually likely to be deprived of oxygen; EFM has an extremely high false-positive rate—50 percent. It has, however, led to an enormous increase in the incidence of caesarean sections.[17] The concern that a baby is too large to be delivered vaginally has similarly contributed to the rise in C-sections, even though most of the predictions of big babies turn out to be erroneous.[18] The rate of C-sections rose from less than 3 percent in the 1930s to just fewer than 5 percent in the mid-1960s and has climbed steadily since. Today almost one-third of American babies are delivered via C-section. Worldwide rates are lower, but still much higher than in previous decades.[19] Pediatricians, who are now heavily involved with fetal surgery and other pre-birth interventions, are even more likely than obstetricians to favor medical and legal interventions that they believe will promote the health of the child-to-be-born.[20]

I. Risks during Pregnancy: An Objective Appraisal

The past half-century has witnessed a significant increase in medical research focused on fetal development and on medical interventions during pregnancy and childbirth that might enhance fetal well-being.

However, some of the research on fetal risks is either inconclusive or inconsistent, with medical authorities in different countries offering differing recommendations.[21] Very little research on pregnant women and birth outcomes meets "the gold standard" of a randomized clinical trial, in which participants are randomly assigned to the "treatment" and "control" arms of a double-blinded research protocol.[22] This is because the United States stringently regulates research on human subjects, and pregnant women are rarely permitted to be part of randomized clinical trials. Indeed, not until 2014 did the National Institutes of Health require that research they fund be balanced in terms of male and female subjects. Historically, women were excluded from much medical and scientific research, despite mounting evidence that many physiological processes work differently in men and women.[23] As a result of the exclusion of pregnant women from randomized clinical trials, much of the research on "risk factors" for miscarriages, stillbirths, premature births, and connections between substance abuse and adverse birth outcomes shows only an association, rather than causation. This type of retrospective, observational research cannot show clear cause-and-effect relationships between pregnant women's actions and birth outcomes because it cannot control for the many confounding variables that can contribute to an observed outcome.[24] A significant proportion of adverse pregnancy events—stillbirths, miscarriages, and preterm births—cannot be attributed to a clear cause. However, the public is not well educated about the real chances of suffering a pregnancy loss, which occurs in more than 15 percent of pregnancies.[25] Physicians draw a somewhat arbitrary line between miscarriages and stillbirths. A miscarriage is a fetal loss that occurs before twenty weeks of pregnancy; a stillbirth is a fetal loss occurring at twenty weeks or later.[26] In 2008, 17 percent of pregnancies ended with a fetal loss, either a miscarriage or a stillbirth.[27] Miscarriages occur in one or two of every ten pregnancies.[28] Preterm birth occurs in about 12 percent of all American births,[29] and stillbirths "occur in about 1 in 160 pregnancies."[30] Rather than point out these facts, or the relative and absolute risks of pregnancy losses, the media appear to oscillate between publishing rosy stories of happy birth outcomes ("medical miracles")[31] and stories that emphasize the riskiness of many normal behaviors during pregnancy. These include consuming caffeinated beverages; eating (or not eating) fish, which are high in omega-3 fatty acids but may also contain mercury; or gaining excessive weight. As a result, the public may find it difficult to accurately identify significant pregnancy risks or to understand that many negative birth outcomes occur simply by chance.[32] The instantaneous availability of information on the Internet makes it difficult for prospective parents to objectively evaluate the reliability and value of particular information. It is even harder to challenge what is presented as authoritative medical judgment, even when it is not accurate.[33] As will be discussed shortly, some adverse events, like stillbirth, occur disproportionately among African-American women, regardless of their economic circumstances. Prosecutors and judges, like other members of the public, appear woefully uneducated about the objective odds of adverse events.

A. Domestic Violence

At the same time, the media and health care professionals often fail to consider other major risks to pregnant women and their future children. Among these is the risk of domestic violence. Every year an estimated 4 to 8 percent of pregnant women are battered by their partners, putting several hundred thousand women, and their offspring, at risk of serious harm.[34] Homicide is the second-highest cause of death for pregnant women, accounting for nearly a third of injury-related deaths among pregnant women (after automobile accidents), and batterers commit most of these killings. Younger pregnant women and those who are African-American are disproportionately likely to be victims of homicide.[35] Women who are battered are at risk not only for direct injury to themselves and their fetuses but also indirect harms, including stress, placenta previa, gestational diabetes, or high blood pressure, all of which jeopardize a healthy and timely birth.[36] Pregnant victims of domestic violence are also more likely than nonvictims to have anemia, first- and second-trimester bleeding, infections, and inadequate weight gain. They are more likely to suffer from mental illness and substance abuse, which also place pregnancies at risk. Women who are battered while pregnant have a 40 percent greater chance of having a low-birthweight baby. Only recently has there been a push to screen pregnant women for domestic violence.[37]

B. Poverty

What is also frequently overlooked in discussions of how to promote the birth of healthy children is the central role that poverty plays. Fifty years after President Lyndon Johnson declared a War on Poverty, nearly one-quarter of American children live below the federal poverty level; African-American and Latino children are disproportionately represented in this group.[38] Poor pregnant women are more likely to be young, single, and less well educated than their wealthier peers; they also lack access to health care. Women living in poverty are more likely than wealthier women to suffer from poor health *before* they become pregnant. They are less likely to have access to health care in general and prenatal care in particular.[39] Poor pregnant women are also more likely to suffer from stress and to be undernourished and/or overweight or obese. Each of these conditions predisposes them to medical problems during pregnancy and poorer birth outcomes.[40] Although Medicaid, the federal–state partnership that finances health care for low-income women, children, and disabled adults,[41] pays for nearly half of all births in the United States,[42] women frequently do not gain access to prenatal care until late in their pregnancies. African-American and Latina women are more likely than white Americans to lack access to early prenatal care.[43] Yet early access to prenatal care is critical to maximizing the potential for a healthy pregnancy and a favorable birth outcome. While the Affordable Care Act guarantees a full spectrum of reproductive health care for women and girls, many women still do not have routine access to appropriate care, as a result of the 2012 Supreme Court decision invalidating the mandatory expansion of Medicaid in *National Federation of Independent Businesses v. Sebelius*.[44] The most important time to promote fetal health is prior to conception and in pregnancy's early stages, when the developing embryo or fetus is most susceptible to environmental exposures, including heavy metals, pesticides, endocrine disruptors, contagious diseases, and legal and illegal drugs.[45] Nearly half of American pregnancies are unplanned.[46] More than 40 percent of all births are to unmarried women;[47] the rate exceeds 50 percent for children born to women who are age thirty years or younger.[48] In addition to struggling to receive adequate health care, many poor women lack a strong economic or social support system.

They are more likely than wealthier women to have suffered physical or sexual abuse as children and are more likely to be currently living with a physically abusive partner.[49]

C. The Real Risks of Stillbirths, Preterm Deliveries, and Other Adverse Birth Outcomes

Poor women suffer higher rates of stillbirths, deliver more preterm and low-birthweight infants, and have more children die in the first year of life than wealthier women.[50] Indeed, although infant mortality rates have declined among all socioeconomic groups since 1969, disparities between these groups have been growing since 1985. African-American infants and infants whose mothers dropped out of high school were more than twice as likely to die as white infants or those born to mothers who were college graduates.[51] Preterm births have increased by 30 percent since 1981; they now constitute nearly 12 percent of all births.[52] Preterm birth is the leading cause of death, injury, and illness among infants.[53] Preterm infants are born disproportionately to poor women, although preterm birth is also common among children conceived through assisted reproductive technology, who are overwhelmingly born to middle- and upper-class parents.[54] Preterm infants and those with low birthweight (less than 2.5 kilograms) are much more likely than their more mature and heftier peers to die.[55] If they survive, they are more likely to suffer long-term problems with their health and cognitive development.[56]

D. How Physicians and Lay Persons Perceive Risk

To appreciate how this information about pregnancy and risk is received and evaluated by pregnant women, the media, medical authorities, and legal decisionmakers, we must return to the social and psychological processes of risk assessment. As we learned in chapter 2, a purely objective, neutral assessment of risk does not exist. Deciding whether a particular activity is "risky" depends on multiple factors. Our initial assessment of risk depends on how it is framed—for example, as a relative or an absolute risk. Usually a risk is seen as much greater when couched in relative terms.[57] Our worldviews, which are closely tied to our social identities, also affect our perceptions of risk. Finally, risk perceptions are shaped by a complex array of psychological mechanisms that help us navigate an uncertain and often threatening world. For example, in perceiving risk we often revert to the availability heuristic, drawing conclusions about "riskiness" based on what we have previously heard about it, which then becomes "available" for assessing risk.[58] Other cognitive biases like the fundamental attribution error make it more likely that we will blame others—specifically their "bad" character traits—for adverse events that they encounter. Conversely, when unfortunate things happen to us, we tend to blame situational factors beyond our control. Causal attribution, the psychological means by which we identify and name a causal relationship between event A and event B, involves much more—or less—than determining how the laws of physics apply to a particular circumstance. More than 150 years ago, John Stuart Mill noted the prevailing "'assumption . . . that a phenomenon cannot have more than one cause.'" Most people prefer monocausal explanations of events. These simple explanations are often influenced by intuitive and unconscious assessments of moral blameworthiness.[59] Similarly, we often make decisions—in everyday life and as jurors—based on unconscious and biased prototypes that, because they *are* unconscious, can powerfully shape the conclusions we reach in assigning blame or determining responsibility. Further, the extent to which a specific behavior—or medical or legal intervention—is emotionally important to us can affect how we perceive it. Many researchers have found an "affect heuristic," in which individuals' overall emotional response to a particular phenomenon can affect their perception of both its risks and benefits, which usually are inversely related.[60]

A concrete example of this occurs with physicians' attitudes toward medical malpractice lawsuits. Physicians are frequently no better than lay people in understanding risk numbers.[61] They are, however, highly attuned to the risk of being sued for medical malpractice. Fear of being a malpractice defendant creates an emotional response to the risk of an unlikely but devastating outcome. As a result, physicians often practice medicine in ways they hope will reduce this risk.[62] In addition, physicians in general tend to be risk averse, reflecting a professional inclination to "err on the side of safety."[63] Practicing defensive medicine is especially common among obstetricians, who pay higher malpractice premiums than many other medical specialists. Increasingly, they serve patients who are older and more likely to have fewer babies than previous generations,[64] who often expect "perfect" babies.[65] These factors, as well as the nature of medical training, which instills in doctors the obligation to look for pathology, even if they ultimately rule it out,[66] encourage an interventionist approach toward pregnancy.

Finally, a tendency toward medical parentalism—that "doctor knows best"—is sometimes apparent in physician–patient interactions, particularly when those exchanges cross racial, gender, and class lines.[67] While the official ethical guidelines of the American College of Obstetricians and Gynecologists declare that the pregnant woman should be in control of all medical treatment decisions, in practice some physicians behave as if they are entitled to overrule the pregnant woman's judgment if they believe her decisions put her fetus at risk.[68] This is particularly likely in view of the increased attention that has been paid to fetal wellbeing in research and clinical practice in recent years. The result is much more aggressive medical oversight, and sometimes heavy-handed control, over pregnancy. Despite a brief burst of enthusiasm about "natural" childbirth during the 1960s and '70s, today American pregnancy, labor, and delivery are highly medicalized. Just over 1 percent of American babies are born outside a hospital, and women's decisions to give birth at home continue to be controversial.[69] Almost all hospital deliveries occur under a physician's supervision.[70]

While many women choose to defer to their obstetricians during pregnancy,[71] for others this deference is enforced by their doctors, who sometimes seek governmental intervention. Women are often tested for drug use or other medical problems without their consent, frequently based on the racial and class biases of doctors, nurses, and other health care professionals. In *Ferguson v. City of Charleston, S.C.*, the Supreme Court ruled that the nonconsensual drug testing of women who were "public" patients at Charleston City Hospital's maternity unit was a violation of the patients' Fourth Amendment right to be free from unlawful searches and seizures. The patients were overwhelmingly African-American. The largely white "private" maternity patients were not tested similarly.[72] Physicians also routinely withhold prescription medications for pregnant women that they would otherwise prescribe[73] and sometimes make stringent efforts to manage pregnant women's diet and exercise.[74]

E. Caesarean Sections—Emergency and Planned

Rates of caesarean sections in the United States have risen dramatically over the past fifty years, from about 5 percent in 1965 to nearly 33 percent today. This rise has been propelled by the widespread use of electronic fetal monitoring and physicians' (and sometimes patients') concern about the need to deliver a fetus who might be at risk of oxygen deprivation or in an awkward birth position, or whose delivery is taking longer than clinical norms.[75] Many obstetricians prefer to perform C-sections on women who have previously delivered by that method, despite guidelines from the American College of Obstetricians and Gynecologists (ACOG) indicating that VBACs (vaginal births after caesareans) are quite safe.[76] Increasingly, obstetricians try to persuade pregnant women to have their labor induced if they do not deliver within expected time frames.[77] However, new research questions the appropriateness of these norms for women who receive epidurals for pain relief, because those women tend to labor longer than their peers who have not received epidurals.[78] Similarly, rates of C-sections are higher for women who are told that their babies are likely to be very large, even though this prediction is frequently incorrect.[79]

In recent decades a small, but not insignificant, number of judges have given greater weight to physicians' risk aversion than to the legal right of pregnant women to choose how to manage their labor and have ordered pregnant women to undergo caesarean sections. At the same time, physicians and other health care providers now venture into the realm of legal interpretation, exercising their discretion to report their patients to law enforcement authorities for either civil commitment or criminal prosecution.[80] Here again, there are significant racial disparities in the rates of prenatal drug testing and reporting, with one study finding that black women were ten times as likely as white women to have their physicians report them for drug use, despite roughly equal rates of positive toxicology reports.[81] Fetal surgery, which of course takes place by invading the pregnant woman's body, placing both her and the fetus at significant risk, is becoming more common as well, although to date no woman has been forced to undergo such a procedure.[82] The legitimacy of all of these interventions must be evaluated under the doctrine of informed consent.

II. Legal Actions against Pregnant Women

A. Violations of Informed Consent and Deprivations of Constitutionally Protected Liberty

Compelling pregnant women to accept medical treatment in the name of promoting fetal health is contrary to the fundamental legal principles of informed consent, which form the ground rules for physician–patient interactions. At its heart, informed consent doctrine provides that is patients, not physicians, who have the ultimate authority to decide what medical treatment is best for them. The role of the physician is to provide sufficient information about a proposed treatment's pros and cons to permit patients to make a rational choice about what is best for them, in light of their medical condition, values, and beliefs. The requirement of informed consent has ancient roots, in the English tort of battery, defined as "an unconsented touching." One hundred years ago, in 1914, Judge Benjamin Cardozo declared, "Every human being of adult years and sound mind has a right to determine what shall be done with his own body."[83] Informed consent is the law of the land. Every state has adopted the doctrine of informed consent, by judicial opinion or statute, and federal law requires every hospital to advise patients of their rights under state law.[84] Initiating medical treatment without a patient's informed consent is a tort. Patients who have been harmed by a failure to secure their consent to treatment are entitled to sue for compensatory damages.[85] Court-ordered medical procedures may also violate patients' constitutional rights. The Supreme Court has recognized that competent adults have a liberty interest, protected by the Fourteenth Amendment, in deciding whether to accept or decline medical treatment. Compelled treatment can also infringe on patients' religious beliefs, which are protected by the First Amendment.[86]

B. Compulsory Medical Treatment: Blood Transfusions and Caesarean Sections

For more than fifty years, physicians and hospitals have repeatedly sought court orders to compel pregnant women to receive medical treatment over their religious and other objections. Most of the cases have involved blood transfusions and caesarean sections, although doctors have also sought to compel women to submit to other medical interventions. Many of the earlier cases reflect classic medical and judicial paternalism—a belief in physician infallibility, coupled with hostility to nonmainstream religious beliefs and condescension toward female patients and patients of color. A review of the cases makes it clear that while judges sometimes recognize that pregnant women are fully competent adults, with constitutional and legal rights to make independent medical treatment decisions, more frequently judges treat pregnant women as second class citizens, issuing orders compelling women to undergo unwanted and potentially dangerous medical treatment in the name of "fetal protection." Further, for every case in which treatment was initiated through court order, there are many more in which the patient was pressured into acquiescence.[87]

In the 1960s courts across the United States began to order pregnant women to receive blood transfusions, despite their religious objections to the treatment. A 1964 New Jersey Supreme Court decision, *Raleigh Fitkin–Paul Morgan Hospital v. Anderson*, was typical. The hospital requested a court order to compel a pregnant woman to accept blood transfusions if they became medically necessary. Although the woman left the hospital before a transfusion could take place, the court nonetheless found that court-ordered transfusions were justified if the attending physician believed that they were necessary to save the lives of the mother and the fetus.[88] In a similar 1985 decision, a New York trial judge declared that the state's interest in protecting the life of a not-yet-viable fetus outweighed a pregnant woman's First Amendment interest in exercising her religious beliefs (she was a Jehovah's Witness, who rejected blood transfusions as contrary to the Bible). The court compounded the insult by appointing the physician who had sought the court order as a "special guardian of the unborn child."[89]

Fortunately, within a few years the judicial tide shifted. Over the past three decades most courts have found court-ordered blood transfusions to be unconstitutional, whether the transfusions are sought to save the life of the fetus or the mother, and whether or not the child was born. Most recent decisions have recognized the right of competent adults, including pregnant women, to refuse all medical treatment under the principles of informed consent. These courts have refused to engage in a balancing of fetal and maternal interests.[90] Courts have also recognized that blood transfusions are not minimal, risk-free invasions of women's bodily integrity. Instead they have acknowledged patients' concerns about the risk of transmission of HIV and the hepatitis virus via transfusion.[91] Several courts have also rejected the argument that a legal guardian should be appointed to protect the medical interests of a fetus.[92]

Today, despite the progress made in the area of compelled blood transfusions, the struggle over the right of pregnant women to give informed consent plays out in the battle over whether courts should order pregnant women to deliver their babies via caesarean section if a physician testifies that failure to undergo a caesarean would endanger the life of the woman *or* her fetus. For decades, courts have ordered this surgery when requested by a health care provider, using language that resonates with earlier decisions authorizing transfusions over a pregnant woman's objections. *Jefferson v. Griffin County Hospital Authority* was decided in 1981. In *Jefferson* the Georgia Supreme Court affirmed a trial judge's order that a pregnant woman, Mrs. Jessie Mae Jefferson, should undergo a caesarean section and receive blood transfusions as necessary, based on a physician's declaration that she was likely to go into labor soon and that the fetus was in a placenta previa position, with the placenta blocking access to the birth canal. The trial court treated the physician's opinion as infallible, accepting his statement that there was "a 99 to 100% certainty that the baby [would] die" if Mrs. Jefferson attempted a vaginal delivery.[93] Mrs. Jefferson rejected the physician's recommendation based on her religious beliefs. In response, the trial court gave social service authorities temporary custody of the fetus (which of course was contained within Mrs. Jefferson's body) and ordered Mrs. Jefferson to submit to a sonogram. If that sonogram showed that the fetus was still placenta previa, Mrs. Jefferson would be required to undergo a caesarean section. Strikingly, by the time that she was ready to deliver, the fetus had changed its position and Mrs. Jefferson delivered her child vaginally at another hospital. In its decision upholding the trial judge's order, the Georgia Supreme Court explicitly balanced the mother's and "unborn child's" interests, ignoring the legal rules for informed consent that give patients the final say about their medical treatment. The court declared, "[When] the right of the mother to practice her religion and to refuse surgery on herself . . . [is weighed] against her unborn child's right to live . . . . [we must find] in favor of her child's right to live."[94] A concurring judge went further, invoking *Roe v. Wade* in a constitutional analogy. This judge concluded that the question of whether a state had a sufficiently compelling interest to override a pregnant woman's decision to have an abortion was controlling on the very different question of whether the state could override a pregnant woman's right to determine the manner of delivery. The judge further found that Georgia's compelling interest in preserving the life of the fetus outweighed the mother's religious liberty.[95] Bioethicists, feminists, and legal commentators have challenged this reasoning. First, they assert that the constitutional questions regarding abortion and caesarean section are distinct. Second, they point out that many of the women subjected to court-ordered caesareans were members of racial, as well as religious, minorities and suggest that unconscious bias may have played a role in court decisions.[96]

Simply stated, overriding a woman's right to decide the course of her medical treatment during pregnancy is contrary to the high value that American society places on autonomy in decisionmaking and the right to protect one's bodily integrity, both traditional hallmarks of American law. Court-ordered medical and surgical interventions against pregnant women are also inconsistent with a long line of cases declaring that people may not be compelled to use their bodies to promote another's health, even if the proposed medical intervention is likely to be successful. For example, in *McFall v. Shimp*, a Pennsylvania trial court held that a man could not be ordered to donate his kidney to a cousin in order to save the cousin's life.[97] Similarly, in *Curran v. Bosze*, the Illinois Supreme Court declined to order two minor twins to donate their bone marrow to a half-sibling, despite the fact that the procedure posed little risk to their health and that, without it, their half-sibling was likely to die.[98]

It was not until the decision of *In re A.C.*, a heart wrenching case involving a young woman who had survived cancer as a teenager only to have it recur when she became pregnant, that some courts began to reconsider their approach. In *A.C.*, a District of Columbia trial court ordered Ms. C.'s twenty-six-week-old fetus to be delivered via caesarean section, apparently concluding that although Ms. C.'s wishes could not be ascertained because she was being sedated to receive chemotherapy, it would order a caesarean section in an effort to prolong the fetus' life. Unfortunately, the baby died a few hours after the caesarean delivery and the mother died two days later.[99] The District of Columbia Court of

Appeals reversed the trial court. While it obviously could not undo the results of the prior decision,[100] the Court of Appeals declared that "in virtually all cases the question of what is to be done is to be decided by the patient—the pregnant woman—on behalf of herself and the fetus." If the patient is mentally incompetent or unable to give informed consent as a result of her underlying illness or its treatment, the trial court should undertake a "substituted judgment,"[101] a judicial procedure that seeks to decide what the patient would have chosen if she *were* competent, rather than what the court thinks is in the patient's (or others') best interests.

As a result of the appellate court's decision in *A.C.*, some physicians and judges have changed their approach in cases in which pregnant women and their doctors disagree about the appropriate course of treatment. Today all relevant national medical bodies—the American College of Obstetricians and Gynecologists, the American Medical Association, and the American Academy of Pediatrics—emphasize that the decision about a proposed medical intervention is to be made solely by the pregnant woman, with the benefit of neutrally presented information from physicians and other health care professionals.[102] As the ACOG ethics opinion states, "Although a parental decision may, in certain circumstances, be overridden for a child after birth, *even the strongest evidence for fetal benefit would not be sufficient ethically to ever override a pregnant woman's decision to forgo fetal treatment.*"[103]

Nonetheless, the actual attitudes—and behavior—of physicians in practice are often at odds with the "ethical best practices" advocated by their national membership bodies.[104] Despite the widely heralded decision in *A.C.*, as well as the policy statements of national medical groups, many pregnant women still find that their autonomy in decisionmaking is being challenged by physicians and, far too frequently, overridden by court order. Several cases decided during the past two decades make it clear that some judges are all too willing to overrule medical treatment decisions made by pregnant women. In 2004, Amber Marlowe, a woman who was pregnant with her seventh child, was told by physicians at a Wilkes-Barre, Pennsylvania, hospital that because her fetus was larger than the norm, she needed to deliver by caesarean section. When she disagreed, because she had successfully delivered six other large babies vaginally, the hospital obtained a court order compelling Ms. Marlowe to have a C-section. However, by that time, Ms. Marlowe had already had a successful vaginal delivery at another hospital.[105]

In two different Florida cases, judges deferred to the judgment of physicians and overruled a pregnant woman's choice of medical treatment. In 1999, Tallahassee mother Laura Pemberton planned to deliver her second child through a VBAC procedure (vaginal birth after caesarean), assisted by a midwife at home. When Mrs. Pemberton went to a hospital seeking intravenous fluids prior to delivery, the hospital requested a court order compelling her to undergo a caesarean section, asserting that there was a high risk of maternal and fetal death if she attempted a vaginal delivery. After the hospital's attorney contacted the local prosecutor, the prosecutor "deputized" him to represent the asserted state interests in the case. A state judge convened an *ex parte* hearing (without the presence of Mrs. Pemberton and her husband), ordering her to be transported to the hospital. Once Mrs. Pemberton arrived at the hospital, the judge took her testimony even as she was being prepared for surgery, signaling his eventual decision.[106] In accordance with the judge's order, Mrs. Pemberton had to undergo a caesarean section.[107] Strikingly, she later delivered three other children using the VBAC procedure,[108] calling into question the attending physician's absolute medical certainty and the judge's reliance on it. The *Pemberton* decision may have reflected larger concerns about the merits of the VBAC procedure, obstetricians' fear of malpractice liability, and the ongoing turf battle between obstetricians and nurse midwives. However, as far as Mrs. Pemberton was concerned, the bottom line of the court's decision was that because she was pregnant, she was not treated as a competent adult, entitled under the principles of informed consent law to exercise independent judgment to choose the type of medical treatment she wished.

Mrs. Pemberton later challenged the state judge's actions in federal court, asserting that her civil rights had been violated. The federal judge rejected her claim using the same balancing approach taken by the Georgia Supreme Court in *Jefferson*. The judge ruled that Florida's interest "in preserving the life of the unborn child" outweighed Mrs. Pemberton's constitutional rights to autonomy and self-determination.[109] The judge also cited the Supreme Court's decision in *Roe v. Wade*, declaring that because, under *Roe*, a state could preclude a woman from having a third-trimester abortion, it could also limit her ability to choose the method by which she would deliver her baby.[110]

Many critics have challenged this interpretation of *Roe*. They assert that the Supreme Court's decision in that case was limited to the question of when the government can limit women's access to abortion, and that *Roe* was not intended to be an open-ended disquisition on fetal life.[111] However, the Supreme Court's more recent decision in *Gonzales v. Carhart*, upholding a federal ban on so-called partial-birth abortions,[112] arguably makes it more likely that language from abortion cases will be applied in the very different context of pregnant woman who have chosen to carry their pregnancies to term. Many commentators have raised concerns about *Gonzales*' novel reasoning. Justice Anthony Kennedy's opinion for the Court justified the congressional ban on a specific abortion procedure, by citing, among other reasons, the risk that a woman who had this type of abortion might one day feel remorse about her decision.[113] This, of course, is exactly the kind of paternalistic argument that many other courts, like the court in *In re A.C.*, have resoundingly rejected. Today, some writers fear that future courts might rely on *Gonzales* to decide that a pregnant woman who wants to deliver her child in a particular way, for example vaginally rather than via caesarean section, can be deprived of her right to give informed consent to medical treatment, because of the possibility that she might later come to regret her choice if the delivery went badly.[114]

Ten years after *Pemberton*, Samantha Burton, a Florida mother of two, was hospitalized against her will and forced to stay in bed, accept intravenous medication, and undergo a caesarean section. Acting at the behest of a Tallahassee hospital, a trial judge accepted the testimony of Ms. Burton's physician and found that that there was "a 'substantial and unacceptable' risk of severe injury or death to the unborn child if [Ms. Burton] . . . continued to fail to follow the recommended course of treatment." The trial judge treated the fetus as the legal equivalent of a child and then applied principles of child welfare law. Citing the principle "that 'as between parent and child, the ultimate welfare of the child is the controlling factor,'" the court overrode Ms. Burton's constitutionally protected interests in autonomous decisionmaking and bodily integrity.[115] Several days later, Ms. Burton delivered a twenty-five-week-old stillborn fetus. When Ms. Burton appealed the decision, the Florida

Court of Appeals ruled that the trial judge had improperly employed a legal standard that applied only to born children. The court emphasized that pregnant women are not deprived of their constitutional right to independent medical decisionmaking. The court ruled that this right is not absolute and can, in certain circumstances, be overridden by a compelling state interest. However, to make such a determination a court must first find that the state interest is indeed compelling. Then, the court must narrowly tailor the remedy to limit the intrusion on the rights of the competent patient, whether or not she is pregnant.[116]

In 2006, a married, college-educated New Jersey woman, referred to in court proceedings as V. M., went into labor and sought to deliver at a nearby hospital,[117] where the rate of caesarean delivery was nearly 50 percent.[118] When the doctors tried to convince Ms. V. M. to undergo a caesarean, she objected, becoming boisterous and uncooperative and struggling with hospital personnel. In response, hospital staff requested a psychiatric evaluation. After the first psychiatrist found that Ms. V. M. was indeed competent to make treatment decisions, a second psychiatrist was consulted. Before he could render a decision, a healthy baby was delivered vaginally. However, the second psychiatrist referred the case for social services investigation. Eventually, a judge declared that the new baby was a neglected child, based in part on Ms. V. M.'s behavior during delivery. An attorney for child protective services assailed Ms. V. M., accusing her of taking "it upon herself to have her needs addressed first before having the needs of the child addressed." The judge found that "with the mother's life and baby's life in balance, I think it was negligent . . . [for Ms. V. M.] not to accede to what the doctors requested."[119]

Judges have also compelled pregnant women to submit to other types of medical treatment, again declaring that the goal of promoting fetal health must prevail over a woman's wishes. In 2000, Rebecca Corneau, a pregnant Massachusetts woman, was suspected of being a member of a religious sect whose members rejected Western medicine and were believed to have neglected their children. A prosecutor brought a proceeding in juvenile court, asserting jurisdiction on the ground that Ms. Corneau's fetus was a "child." A Massachusetts judge first compelled Ms. Corneau to be subjected to a medical examination and treatment over her objection, and then involuntarily committed her to a prison hospital, where she remained until her child was born. Thereafter, the court terminated Ms. Corneau's rights as a parent.[120] Pregnant women in other states have also had civil or criminal proceedings initiated against them based on a lack of prenatal care or the fact that they suffered from gestational diabetes or mental illness.[121] As in the case of Ms. V.M., a woman's very refusal to accede to a physician's treatment recommendations is sometimes considered as evidence of mental illness. Physicians often request a psychiatric evaluation in an effort to bolster their assertion that a woman is not competent to refuse a recommended medical intervention.[122]

C. HIV: Mandatory Testing and Treatment

The tensions between pregnant women's right to give informed consent to medical treatment and the interests of the state in promoting fetal health are highlighted in the debate about mandatory testing and treatment of pregnant women for HIV. Being diagnosed as HIV-positive is no longer a death sentence. Rather, HIV/AIDS is a chronic disease, managed like diabetes, heart disease, and many types of cancer—through monitoring, medication, and treatment as necessary. Yet because there is about a 25 percent risk that an HIV-positive pregnant woman may transmit the HIV virus to her infant, while it is *in utero*, during the birth process, or through breastfeeding, many physicians and public health advocates recommend mandatory HIV testing for all pregnant women, so that those who test positive for HIV can begin treatment with AZT and other drugs. The recommended protocol for pregnant women can reduce the risk of "vertical" transmission from a pregnant woman to her newborn from 25 percent to 1 percent.[123] Some advocates for women argue against mandatory testing and treatment, asserting, first, that some women may not want to know their HIV status. Revelation of one's HIV status can be emotionally overwhelming and stigmatizing; it can also put the woman in danger from an abusive partner. Second, even though most pregnant women would do anything to advance the health of their potential children, treatment to reduce the levels of HIV in one's system is neither pain- nor risk-free. Women can suffer many adverse side effects, including nausea, diarrhea, vomiting, bone marrow suppression, and neuropathy, as well as permanent damage to the heart, kidneys, liver, and the reproductive system.[124]

To date, only one published case has arisen that raises the issues of mandatory testing and treatment of pregnant women. In *Doe v. Div. of Youth and Family Services*, plaintiff Doe, a New Jersey woman, alleged that she was tested for HIV without her consent; after she was informed that she was HIV-positive she began treatment but stopped it because of adverse side effects. When Ms. Doe went into labor she again refused AZT. Thereafter, two different physicians discussed her HIV status in front of her family, who had been unaware of her illness. After Ms. Doe declined to take AZT during labor or to consent to treat her newborn daughter with AZT as a precautionary measure, her daughter was taken into protective custody by New Jersey social services officials. When Ms. Doe eventually regained custody of her daughter, she consented to have her treated with AZT but then revoked her consent when the treatment made her daughter sick. Subsequent testing revealed that Ms. Doe's daughter did not have HIV. This is a common occurrence, because blood tests of newborns at birth in fact reflect the mother's HIV status, not the child's.[125]

The *Doe* case illuminates multiple problems with the mandatory testing and treatment of pregnant women for HIV. Mandatory testing is contested because it can be emotionally devastating and stigmatizing, and it may place the woman in physical danger if the test result suggests, for example, that the woman's partner is not the child's father. As noted, HIV testing is also often erroneous. In many states, including Connecticut, Illinois, and New York, mandatory testing does not occur during pregnancy but only after the child is born.[126] This is too late to make a difference for a potentially afflicted child. It denies the pregnant woman the opportunity to choose to be treated with AZT while pregnant and to be advised about the risks of breastfeeding, while it still delivers devastating news that can put the woman at physical risk.[127] On the other hand, if mandatory testing occurs during pregnancy, women who do not consent to treatment might be subject to court-ordered treatment, which would mean a loss of liberty and possible enforced treatment for months, a prospect far more intrusive than a caesarean section. The onus of being HIV-positive is similar to the stigma of being a drug user, addressed in detail in chapter 5. Pregnant women may respond to the possibility of testing for HIV or illegal drugs as they might to the possibility of being forced to undergo a C-section. In each case they may decide not to seek prenatal treatment or not to be candid with health care professionals, out of fear that they will lose their ability to make independent medical decisions, and that their character and their conduct will be judged and denigrated. The unintended result of mandatory HIV testing is thus to drive women underground, away from medical care that might promote their health and that of their children.

The best way to reduce the incidence of HIV among newborns is to develop a contextual approach, which takes account of the circumstances in which their mothers contract HIV. In the United States, women who are HIV-positive are overwhelmingly African-American or Latina.[128] Historically they have had great difficulty in accessing medical care and they often deeply distrust the health care system. In addition, 80 percent of HIV-positive women were infected through sex with their male partners.[129] The most effective way to reduce infant HIV infection is to expand health care access to male and female adolescents and adults; encourage counseling and voluntary testing and treatment for sexually transmitted diseases, including HIV; and expand efforts to make condom use routine. Frequently women feel unable to ask their partners to use condoms, because of cultural norms as well as the women's economic dependence on, or fear of physical violence from, their partners.[130] Summing up, we see that fears of malpractice liability and general risk aversion, coupled with a high degree of medical paternalism, have prompted physicians and other health care professionals to seek legal intervention if they believe that a pregnant woman who disagrees with their treatment recommendations is jeopardizing the health or life of the developing fetus. In turn, many judges are highly deferential to medical authority, particularly when the doctors and judges share normative beliefs about appropriate behavior for pregnant women. The idea that "the good pregnant woman," like "the good mother" more generally, should always act to protect the fetus, also plays out in the context of tort suits and criminal prosecutions brought against pregnant women.

III. Lawsuits against Pregnant Women

In a half dozen cases litigated during the past three decades, children who suffered prenatal injuries have sued their mothers, alleging that they were harmed by her alleged negligence while pregnant.[131] All six cases addressed a foundational legal question—does a pregnant woman have a *legal* duty to protect her fetus? The cases illuminate the nature of risk construction and demonstrate the profound impact of unconscious psychological processes on legal decisions. Thus, they have ramifications far beyond tort law.

The six courts split evenly. Three courts held that children *could* sue their mothers for prenatal harm; the other three courts ruled that authorizing tort suits against pregnant women was bad law and unwise social policy. The apparent goal of the lawsuits was to provide economic compensation to the injured children, since in each case the mother was sued by the child's father or guardian. Four cases involved motor vehicle accidents, in which the pregnant woman was alleged to have been a negligent driver or negligent pedestrian.[132] Two involved the mother's alleged negligent drug use while pregnant. One pregnant woman took a prescription drug, Tetracycline, which allegedly caused her child to have discolored teeth.[133] The other mother used alcohol and cocaine while pregnant, allegedly causing cognitive and physical injuries to her child.[134]

The three judges who found that pregnant women do have an enforceable legal duty toward a developing fetus saw no reason to distinguish between suits brought against mothers for post-birth behavior, which are generally permitted, and suits brought based on their actions while pregnant.[135] These courts seemed untroubled by—or even unaware of—the implications of their decisions for future pregnant women. They reasoned that there was no ground for distinguishing between third parties and pregnant women who caused prenatal harm, apparently concluding that because the goal of the lawsuit was to compensate the child for prenatal injuries, it was immaterial who caused them.[136] Each appellate court sent the case back for trial, leaving it up to a jury to determine the question of the mother's negligence—that is, whether she fell below the standard of the reasonable person in driving her car, crossing the street, or taking Tetracycline while she was pregnant.[137]

In contrast, judges who determined that courts should not impose a legal duty of care on pregnant women cited the substantial negative consequences of permitting children to sue their mothers for prenatal harm. They recognized the risk of opening the floodgates of liability against pregnant women based on an infinite variety of prenatal acts or omissions. These courts were concerned that jurors might impose liability after the fact, based on their individual religious and cultural values about how a "good pregnant woman" should behave, without considering the real life medical, economic, and social circumstances of the particular pregnant woman. They also were concerned that the fear of being sued might lead some women to be less candid with physicians and others who could offer help and support during pregnancy.[138]

At the outset, these courts recognized the practical and policy problems that they would create by imposing on pregnant women a legal, as opposed to a moral, duty to exercise due care. These problems are inherent in the concept of negligence, which is based in part on foreseeability. Obviously, during pregnancy, and even prior to conception, everything a woman does has the potential to affect her future child.[139] As a result, courts and juries might be unable to place any limits on this duty, a problem known in the law as a "slippery slope." "Since anything which a pregnant woman does or does not do may have an impact, either positive or negative, on her developing fetus, any act or omission on her part could render her liable to her subsequently born child."[140] Everything a prospective mother inhaled or ingested could potentially put a developing fetus at risk; so too could exercising (or not exercising) and accepting (or refusing) medical treatment.[141] As a result, juries would be placed in the untenable position of trying to apply an ostensibly neutral negligence standard—"the reasonable pregnant woman"—to the facts of the particular case before it, which of course involves a child who did suffer harm *in utero*.

Three distinct problems arise. First, negligence is, by definition, situational. The classic test for negligence, articulated by Judge Learned Hand, requires jurors to assess the likelihood that harm will occur, its severity if it does occur, and the burden of taking adequate precautions against it.[142] That burden necessarily differs depending on the actor's circumstances.[143] Every woman is unique, in her wealth or poverty, age, educational attainment, religious beliefs, access to health care, and knowledge that she is pregnant or likely to become pregnant.[144] Inevitably there will be difficulty in attempting to determine, and apply, a uniform standard of "reasonableness," because the reasonableness of people's behavior depends in large part on the situation in which they find themselves.

Assessing risk through the prism of hindsight poses significant dangers. Hindsight influences not only the determination of whether the pregnant woman behaved "reasonably" but also the independent issue of causation.[145] As Baruch Fischhoff has found, the hindsight bias has incredible power to shape our understanding of past events. Knowing that an event *has* occurred has a huge impact on our belief that it was foreseeable that it *would* occur. He says, "'It is much easier after the event to sort the relevant from the irrelevant signals. After the event, of course, a signal is always crystal clear.'"[146] Therefore, we should not be surprised that jurors who are asked to evaluate a pregnant woman's conduct with the benefit of hindsight—including the fact that her child was in fact injured—might readily find that she fell below the standard of care expected of the hypothetical "reasonable pregnant woman." Similarly, because foreseeability is at the heart of causation analysis, serving as the litmus test for finding proximate cause, the fact that an adverse event occurred makes it easy for jurors (and judges) to say that a reasonable pregnant woman would have foreseen and avoided that risk, and that this woman's failure to take appropriate precautions was the cause of that harm, thus finding her liable.

Other unconscious cognitive distortions can have a similar impact on jury decisions, including the "fundamental attribution error" and the "better than average" bias. We also know that one's worldview significantly affects both the perception of risk and the determination of an appropriate response to that risk. Jurors, like the rest of us, are influenced by a host of other unconscious biases, reflecting our moral and religious beliefs and race-, class-, and gender-based stereotypes. Nobel laureate Daniel Kahneman has identified the deep problem that most of our conclusions and impressions are formed almost instantaneously, without conscious thought, yet we are usually unwilling to consider the possibility that these impressions and conclusions might be wrong, or that they might be reached impulsively rather than rationally.[147] Taken together, these factors make it virtually impossible for jurors to render the even-handed and neutral assessment of a particular woman's conduct contemplated by "the reasonable pregnant woman" standard. The inevitable result will be arbitrary, inconsistent, and unpredictable jury verdicts in different cases.[148]

The second objection to imposing a legal duty of care on pregnant women grows out of these inherent difficulties in jury fact-finding. Charging pregnant women with such a legal duty renders them the absolute guarantors of their developing fetus' physical and mental health. In part, this is consistent with the biological reality of pregnancy, in which the mother and fetus are uniquely, and completely, intertwined. That "the mother's every waking and sleeping moment . . . shapes the prenatal world of the developing fetus . . . is not a pregnant woman's fault: it is a fact of life."[149] Yet to recognize a legal, as opposed to moral, duty of care on pregnant women threatens significant undesirable consequences. These include a massive deprivation of women's constitutional and common law rights to liberty, autonomy, and bodily integrity, as well as potentially undesired health outcomes, as we have seen in the cases of court-ordered caesarean sections and other compelled medical treatment. The chilling impact of subjecting pregnant women to a legal duty of care is manifest. Pregnant or potentially pregnant women will inevitably fear that their actions, which might well be considered legitimate and noncontroversial if they were not pregnant, will be scrutinized, twisted, and judged negatively when viewed through the lens of "the reasonable pregnant woman."[150] The final undesirable result is that "mother and child . . . [become] legal adversaries from the moment of conception until birth."[151]

Third, those courts that declined to impose a duty of care on pregnant women recognized other unintended negative consequences of imposing a new tort duty. Women would be deterred from speaking candidly with their health care providers and discouraged from seeking prenatal care or substance abuse treatment. Chapter 5, which examines the involuntary civil commitment and criminal prosecution of pregnant women who have used alcohol and other drugs, demonstrates that this fear is well founded. Other women might choose to have an abortion rather than face legal liability.[152] Many medical and public health groups agree with the Illinois Supreme Court's statement in *Stallman v. Youngquist* that the best "way to effectuate the birth of healthy babies is not . . . after-the-fact civil liability in tort for individual mothers, but rather through before-the-fact education of all women and families about prenatal development."[153]

Significantly, the highest court in Canada has reached the same conclusion as these American courts. In 1999 the Supreme Court of Canada decided *Dobson v. Dobson*,[154] a lawsuit in which a husband sued his wife on behalf of their child, alleging that her negligent driving while pregnant caused a car accident in which the fetus was injured. The Court relied explicitly on the reasoning in *Stallman v. Youngquist*. The Court emphasized the unique relationship between the pregnant woman and the fetus, the privacy and autonomy rights of the pregnant woman, and the impossibility of devising an objective standard of pre-maternal conduct. The Court focused particularly on the inevitable slippery slope upon which courts, litigants, and juries would be launched in trying to determine the boundaries of appropriate behavior in a particular pregnant woman's case and ruled that women should not be liable to their children in tort for their behavior before the child was born.[155]

IV. Criminal Prosecutions of Pregnant Women

Five recent criminal prosecutions demonstrate the strength of the psychological processes of risk construction in affecting the decisions of health care workers, prosecutors, judges, and juries. That these cases were brought in the so-called "blue" states of Iowa, Massachusetts, and New York; the "red" state of Utah; and the "purple" state of Indiana demonstrates that unconscious biases and mental shortcuts affect everyone. In each case, prosecutors or other law enforcement officials seized on the tragic circumstances of vulnerable women to initiate criminal proceedings, arguing that these pregnant woman had breached an absolute duty to protect their fetuses. The cases arose in circumstances in which any pregnant woman could find herself, including falling down the stairs, refusing a caesarean section, being involved in an auto accident, unexpectedly going into labor at home, and becoming distraught after being abandoned by the father of one's future child.

The first of these outrageous criminal prosecutions occurred in 2004. As mentioned earlier, Melissa Rowland, a woman with a history of mental disability and drug use, was charged with murder after she declined to have a caesarean section. Ms. Rowland was unmarried and homeless; when she found herself pregnant with twins she decided to give them up for adoption. At the suggestion of an adoption agency she consulted, she moved to Utah because of its lenient adoption laws and low cost of living. As she neared her delivery date Ms. Rowland sought medical attention; although the nursing staff at a hospital recommended that she undergo a C-section, Ms. Rowland declined. The hospital did not seek legal intervention. Ms. Rowland subsequently went into labor and one of the twins was stillborn.

Ms. Rowland was charged with murder and faced the death penalty if convicted. Prosecutors explicitly based their case on a theory of maternal selfishness, asserting that Ms. Rowland's decision to decline a C-section was due to her vanity in not wanting an abdominal scar. Prosecutors also claimed that Ms. Rowland's failure to agree to a C-section was a criminal omission because she had a legal duty to act to protect her fetus. They further charged that her selfishness was sufficient to establish the culpable *mens rea* of "depraved indifference to human life" necessary to support a murder charge. Only after a massive public outcry, and perhaps recognizing the weakness in their case, did prosecutors offer Ms. Rowland a plea deal. After spending more than three months in jail, Ms. Rowland pleaded guilty to two counts of felony child endangerment and left the state.[156]

In 2007, Alissa Pugh, a twenty-eight-year-old single mother in Massachusetts, was charged with manslaughter after she unexpectedly gave birth at home and the child either was stillborn or died shortly after birth. Although Ms. Pugh had known she was pregnant, she had told no one else. After feeling ill at work, Ms. Pugh went home to rest. In the course of a few minutes her water broke and she began active labor. Ms. Pugh thought she was suffering a miscarriage, but after she reached inside herself she felt a tiny foot; she then realized that she was having a "breech" delivery. The baby was blue when it emerged, and Ms. Pugh was unable to revive it. After that, Ms. Pugh panicked; she did not report the birth to anyone and put the baby's body in the trash. Ms. Pugh was charged with involuntary manslaughter, an unintentional but "reckless" killing under Massachusetts law. The prosecution presented two theories of criminal responsibility: either that Ms. Pugh had acted recklessly in using excessive force in trying to deliver the baby, or that she had acted recklessly in failing to summon help mid-delivery, thus breaching her duty to act to protect the emerging child. A judge, sitting without a jury, found her guilty.[157]

The Massachusetts Supreme Judicial Court reversed the conviction. It first found that the prosecution failed to prove beyond a reasonable doubt that Ms. Pugh's act of pulling during delivery had caused the infant to suffer fatal injuries or, indeed, that the infant had been born alive.[158] The court then addressed a broader question—what is the legal duty of a pregnant woman who gives birth without medical assistance? The court was deeply concerned about standardless discretion. It declared, "What constitutes reasonable conduct during labor and childbirth defies ready articulation. Women give birth alone or with others in attendance, with or without complications . . . , each labor and childbirth posing its own challenges." Necessarily, there is no "'one size fits all' rule," an objective and uniform standard of behavior, which is essential to guide a jury in making its decision.[159]

The court expressly rejected the prosecutor's assertion that women in childbirth have a duty to summon medical assistance. The court noted that home birth is legal in Massachusetts and cited the fundamental principle that competent adults have the right to make their own medical treatment choices, including the decision to forgo medical treatment. The court relied on its decision in *Remy v. MacDonald*, which held that pregnant women could not be sued in tort for causing prenatal harm.[160] As in *Remy*, in *Pugh* the court was concerned that imposing a legal duty on pregnant women could lead to unwanted medical interventions such as C-sections. It could also result in arbitrary and selective prosecution, with decisions about "what is lawful and what is criminal conduct on the part of pregnant women and women in labor . . . left to individual law enforcement officials and judges."[161]

Just such selective law enforcement appears to have taken place in the case of Christine Taylor, a twenty-two-year-old woman living in Iowa who was arrested for attempted feticide in 2010. After Ms. Taylor fell down a flight of stairs, she sought treatment at a hospital emergency room. During her physical examination she confided to hospital staff that she felt ambivalent about being pregnant, because her husband had recently abandoned her and their two other children, leaving her alone in Iowa, without family or friends. Although the fall did not appear to have harmed her fetus, hospital workers summoned the police, violating their duty to preserve patient confidentiality. Ms. Taylor was questioned and then arrested, spending two days in jail while her young children were left alone.¹⁶² Prosecutors initially considered charging Ms. Taylor with attempted feticide, defined as an intentional effort to terminate pregnancy after the end of the second trimester, but backed off when they discovered that Ms. Taylor was within her second trimester of pregnancy, thus taking her case outside the feticide statute.¹⁶³ This case illustrates the growing tendency of health care providers to take it upon themselves to interpret the law, deciding, first, that they have a duty to report to law enforcement officials, and, second, that a pregnant woman's conduct violates a legal duty.¹⁶⁴

In 2010, Bei Bei Shuai, a thirty-two-year-old Chinese immigrant living in Indiana, became pregnant by her married boyfriend. When she was about thirty-three weeks pregnant her boyfriend broke off the relationship. Ms. Shuai was devastated and attempted to commit suicide by ingesting rat poison. Distraught, she wrote to her boyfriend that she was going to kill herself and was "taking this baby, the one you named Crystal, with me." After Ms. Shuai told a friend what she had done, she was hospitalized and treated to stabilize her mental and physical health, as well as that of her fetus. After a week of treatment the fetus exhibited an abnormal heart rate and Ms. Shuai agreed to a caesarean section. A daughter was born, approximately seven weeks premature. However, the baby's blood did not clot and the baby was found to have a severe brain hemorrhage. Ms. Shuai eventually agreed to remove her daughter from life support and the child died. Ms. Shuai remained in the hospital's psychiatric unit for another month because of doctors' concern that she might attempt suicide again. A month after being released from the hospital, Ms. Shuai was stunned when prosecutors charged her with murder and attempted feticide in her daughter's death. Ms. Shuai spent the next year in jail while her lawyer challenged the legal basis for the prosecution, as well as the refusal to grant bail while she awaited trial.¹⁶⁵

Ultimately, the Indiana Court of Appeals determined that although Ms. Shuai should have been released on bail because the prosecution's case was weak, the evidence was still strong enough to permit the prosecution to go forward. In a stinging dissent, Judge Patricia Riley criticized what she viewed as a distortion of Indiana statutes and case precedent to justify bringing charges of murder and attempted feticide. Judge Riley asserted that if Ms. Shuai were convicted and this prosecution upheld, Indiana feticide statutes "could have an unlimited scope and create an indefinite number of new 'crimes,'" based on pregnant women's use of "over-the-counter cold remedies and sleep aids," as well as legal drugs like tobacco and alcohol. In Judge Riley's view, the prosecutor's "interpretation might lead to a slippery slope whereby the feticide statute could be construed as covering a full range of a pregnant woman's behavior." She condemned this interpretation as both unreasonable and a usurpation of the legislature's role in defining criminal conduct, a violation of the constitutional principle of separation of powers. As a result of the Court of Appeals' decision the case was set for trial. At the last minute, shortly before trial was to begin, Ms. Shuai agreed to plead guilty to reckless endangerment, a misdemeanor. As part of the plea bargain she was sentenced to 189 days in jail, the precise length of time she had already served.[166]

Most recently, Jennifer Jorgensen was prosecuted for manslaughter in New York after she was involved in a fatal accident. The prosecution alleged that she was driving under the influence of alcohol and an antianxiety drug, although the evidence of drug use was sharply contested. The prosecutor argued that Ms. Jorgensen had been reckless by speeding and failing to brake, driving while talking on a cell phone, and driving without a seat belt. Ms. Jorgensen, who was eight months' pregnant, was also injured. After she was taken to the hospital she consented to a caesarean section. She delivered a daughter, who lived only six days. Ms. Jorgensen was charged with three counts of manslaughter for the three victims of the car crash—an elderly couple whose car she struck, and her daughter—as well as other drug- and driving-related charges. The case was tried twice. The first trial ended in a mistrial after the jury was unable to reach a verdict. At the second trial the jury acquitted Ms. Jorgensen of the manslaughter charges against the elderly couple, reckless driving, and driving under the influence of alcohol or other drugs. However, the jury found her guilty of manslaughter in her daughter's death. This was not surprising, perhaps, in light of the prosecution's efforts to portray Ms. Jorgensen as a selfish, bad mother. The prosecutor argued that her failure to wear a seat belt was analogous to a parent's failure to securely fasten an infant in a car seat. Further, he claimed that her attention at the scene of the accident to her own injuries—facial lacerations and a broken arm with bones protruding—demonstrated improper self-concern, arguing that her first concern should have been the safety of her unborn child. The trial judge sentenced Ms. Jorgensen to three to nine years in prison; a mid-level appellate court affirmed that decision in 2014. In 2015 New York's highest court, the Court of Appeals, overturned the conviction, ruling that a child injured *in utero* could not be a "person" under New York homicide law.[167]

Taken together, these five criminal cases raise ominous warning signs for pregnant women. They suggest that local prosecutors and law enforcement officials, who lack medical expertise, may respond to tragic situations involving preterm births, stillbirths, and complicated deliveries by proceeding against vulnerable pregnant women. Three of the five women were single mothers; most were also poor, socially isolated, and, in two cases, suffering from a mental illness or mental disability. Further, they demonstrate the power of retrospective risk construction. The hindsight bias makes it easy to find that a defendant—like Ms. Rowland, Ms. Shuai, or Ms. Taylor—intended or foresaw harm in light of the harm that actually occurred. Under the fundamental attribution error, the natural human tendency is to assume that when bad things happen to others—Ms. Jorgensen and Ms. Pugh—they are the result of their bad choices and character flaws, while when they happen to us they are the result of external circumstances beyond our control. These heuristics influence police, prosecutors, judges, and juries, along with conscious and unconscious racial, gender, and class biases. As a result, women who could have been offered social and economic support services instead faced criminal charges and public opprobrium.

Connecting the Abortion Debate and Civil and Criminal Actions against Pregnant Women

Anti-abortion sentiment appears to be the driving force in many of the civil and criminal actions against pregnant women, as well as in the enactment of new laws explicitly directed at women's conduct while pregnant. In *Roe v. Wade* the Supreme Court ruled that women had a constitutionally protected liberty interest in choosing to have an abortion, at least during the first trimester of pregnancy. Justice Harry Blackmun articulated an analytical framework based on then-current medical understanding, dividing pregnancy into three trimesters. The Court held that during the first trimester women's liberty and privacy interest outweighed the state's interest in potential life, and a pregnant woman is free to choose abortion. During the second trimester the state may regulate the abortion procedure in order to protect the woman's health. After the fetus becomes viable, the state may prohibit abortion, "except when it is necessary to preserve the life or health of the mother."[168] A key part of the Court's decision in *Roe* was its finding that a fetus was not a person within the meaning of the Fourteenth Amendment and thus did not have rights that were superior to those of a pregnant woman.[169] *Roe* made possible a revolution in reproductive health care, empowering women to control their biological, social, and economic destinies. At the same time, *Roe* unleashed an enormous political backlash that continues to this day, with religious and political conservatives fighting to overturn the decision and to limit access to contraception as well as abortion.[170]

In 1992, in *Planned Parenthood of Southeastern Pennsylvania v. Casey*, the Supreme Court maintained *Roe*'s essential holding that that women have a right to terminate their pregnancies prior to viability but moved beyond its trimester-based approach, which analyzed the competing interests of the woman and the state differently depending on the trimester of pregnancy.[171] In *Casey* the Court held that a woman's right to choose to have an abortion should be analyzed under an "undue burden" test, which declared unconstitutional any state regulation that "plac[es] . . . a substantial obstacle in the path of a woman seeking an abortion of a nonviable fetus." Written by Justice Sandra Day O'Connor, the plurality opinion in *Casey* emphasized that prior to viability the ultimate decision about whether to continue a pregnancy must be made by the woman, who will inevitably bear the physical and psychological burdens of that condition. Her opinion rejected the argument that because women have "so nobly born that burden" over centuries, giving their infants "a bond of love," "the state . . . [was justified in insisting] . . . upon its own vision of the woman's role, however dominant that vision has been in the course of our history and our culture."[172]

However, in 2007, in *Gonzales v. Carhart*, the Supreme Court invoked that maternal "bond of love" as the basis of a compelling state interest (grounded in the woman's psychological health) that justified limiting abortions, citing the possibility that women might later regret their decision to have an abortion, especially one carried out in a particular manner.[173] Justice Anthony Kennedy wrote the opinion in *Gonzales*, which upheld Congress' ban on partial-birth abortion, focusing on the type of medical procedure employed, rather than fetal viability. *Gonzales* is significant for its explicit reliance on cultural norms of how a good pregnant woman *should* feel, which the Court determined should trump the actual feelings and concerns of the real woman seeking abortion.[174]

In the forty-three years since *Roe* was decided, a vast array of legislation has been enacted that aims to undercut, if not overturn, *Roe* or seeks, outside the abortion context, to redefine the fetus as a "person" who can claim constitutional protection and other legal rights.[175] The clearest example of this is fetal homicide laws. Thirty-eight states, as well as the federal government, have enacted laws that make the killing of a fetus a homicide, a crime that is distinct from injuring or killing the pregnant woman. While anti-abortion activists praise these laws as supporting and protecting fetal life, others have criticized them. They assert that when laws declare a fetus to be a child in one context, they create a slippery slope that makes it more likely that pregnant women themselves will be held liable, civilly or criminally, for harming or risking harm to their fetuses.[176] This concern appears well founded, in light of the criminal prosecutions just discussed and the laws in twenty-three states that authorize the criminal prosecution for feticide of those who cause the "death" of a potential human being at the very earliest stages of development, beginning at fertilization and continuing to birth, regardless of viability.[177] Other opponents of fetal homicide laws charge that they place the concern for fetal wellbeing above the physical and emotional suffering of the pregnant woman who was the primary victim of an assault that also caused the death of the fetus, erasing the woman as an injured party and devaluing her own suffering due to her pregnancy loss.[178]

V. Overriding Pregnant Women's Advance Medical Directives

Many states have also exalted fetal interests over those of the pregnant woman through legislation that invalidates and overrides the advance medical directives of pregnant women. Every state authorizes and encourages competent adults to use "advance directives," "living wills," or "health care proxies," which enable them to express in writing their wishes for future medical care in the event that they become unable to voice those wishes themselves.[179] These laws were a response to judicial decisions in the 1980s and '90s, when courts were asked to make end-of-life decisions for formerly competent adults who had not documented their wishes in writing.[180] They stem from American law's emphasis on individual autonomy and self-determination, which is reflected in the doctrine of informed consent. Advance medical directives provide welcome and explicit guidance to family members and physicians about the kind of care that the person would choose if he or she were able to do so.

However, more than half of the states have enacted laws that invalidate advance directives if the woman is pregnant, once again privileging fetal health over women's health and autonomy. In twelve states a woman's advance directive is unenforceable *throughout* her pregnancy, simply because of that biological status. Texas is one of these states; its advance directive law provides that life-sustaining treatment may not be withdrawn or withheld from a pregnant patient.[181] In fourteen additional states the woman may have her treatment wishes overridden if it is probable that her pregnancy will progress to a live birth, and four more states suspend the implementation of an advance directive if the fetus is currently viable or likely to become viable. Another fourteen states' statutes are silent on the impact of pregnancy. In these states a pregnant woman's family cannot determine the enforceability of an advance directives without time-consuming and emotionally exhausting litigation. Only five states' laws provide that the choices made by a woman in her advance directive will always be honored and explicitly offer her the opportunity to express her wishes about treatment while pregnant.[182]

The legality of statutes prohibiting the enforcement of pregnant women's advance directives has rarely been litigated. In January 2014, a Texas man, Erick Muñoz, challenged the application of the Texas advance directive law to his wife, Marlise Muñoz, who had collapsed from a stroke when she was fourteen weeks' pregnant with the couple's second child. Mrs. Muñoz's collapse was not discovered for an hour or more; during that time she stopped breathing. After she was brought to the county hospital, doctors were unable to restore her to consciousness. Doctors determined that she was brain-dead and they were concerned that her fetus had also suffered irreversible damage to the brain and other organs, because of the length of time the fetus was deprived of oxygen.

However, the hospital decided not to "pronounce" Mrs. Muñoz dead because of its concerns about the pregnancy exclusion in the Texas advance directive law. The hospital interpreted the Texas law's mandate that life-sustaining treatment may not be withdrawn or withheld from a pregnant patient as requiring the hospital to maintain Mrs. Muñoz on life support even though she was brain-dead. Mrs. Muñoz had been a paramedic, along with her husband; both her husband and her parents asserted that she would not have wanted to be maintained on a ventilator if there was no chance that she could be restored to consciousness. Only after the case gained national attention and Mr. Muñoz sued the hospital did a Texas trial judge order that Mrs. Muñoz be removed from the ventilator, because she was in fact dead. The judge declined to rule on the Texas law's legality or constitutionality, declaring only that the law was inapplicable because Mrs. Muñoz was dead and the law applied only to living patients.[183]

The judge's opinion itself became a hot-button issue in the Texas primary election race that occurred shortly thereafter. Every Republican candidate for lieutenant governor criticized the decision, seeking, as one reporter declared, to "burnish[ ] their pro-life credentials." The comments of state senator Dan Patrick, who was later elected lieutenant governor, were typical. He declared, "Life is so precious and there's nothing more precious than the life of a baby in the womb."[184] Indeed, the basic tenet of abortion foes appears to be that the fetus' interest in potential life should always prevail over a woman's right to health and to make autonomous medical decisions.[185]

Thirty years earlier, another dead woman's body was mechanically sustained in order to promote fetal life. In 1986, a pregnant Georgia woman, Donna Piazzi, was declared brain-dead after an apparent suicide attempt, but the hospital refused to accede to her husband's request to remove her from life support, after her paramour (and apparent biological father of the fetus) objected. The hospital petitioned a court to continue treatment and the court agreed, determining that even if Mrs. Piazzi had executed an advance directive, it would not be enforceable under Georgia law. The court ordered Mrs. Piazzi to remain on life support until she could gestate and deliver a living child.[186] When the fetus' condition deteriorated at about twenty-five weeks of pregnancy it was delivered by caesarean section; it lived for less than forty-eight hours.[187]

Thereafter Mrs. Piazzi was removed from life support and allowed to die.[188]

Yet when women have asked judges to invalidate state laws making their advance directives inoperative during pregnancy they have been unsuccessful. In two cases, brought in North Dakota and Washington, the courts rejected lawsuits challenging these state laws. In both cases the courts found that because the women were currently healthy, mentally competent, and not pregnant there was no actual "case and controversy."[189] Laws that authorize a "pregnancy exclusion" to women's advance medical directives are objectionable because they impose other people's views about the risks that pregnant women should be willing to accept in order to avoid any risk of fetal harm, totally disempowering women who seek to control their medical treatment.[190] These laws enshrine a paternalistic view of women, directly overruling any other choice the woman has made. In essence, laws invalidating the advance medical directives of pregnant women assert that any reasonable woman would choose to receive medical treatment, no matter how invasive, painful, or futile, in order to give her fetus a chance at life. They are eerily reminiscent of the tragedy of Angela Carder, the young woman at the center of *In re A.C.*,[191] whose cancer returned mid-pregnancy, and the many other women who have been compelled to undergo a caesarean section rather than choose the method of delivery that reflects their medical preferences and personal values.

5

Drug Use by Pregnant Women

Context and Consequences

Introduction

Americans have long had a love affair with drugs, and pregnant women are no exception. Drugs include both legal substances—alcohol, tobacco, and prescription medications—and illegal, "controlled" substances. While pregnant women's use of illegal drugs captures the bulk of the headlines, in fact it is two legal drugs—alcohol and tobacco—that cause the most harm to the greatest number of children.[1] In the colonial era, Americans of all ages drank wine, beer, and hard spirits regularly, at home and in public.[2] Tobacco products were consumed regularly by Americans of all social strata,[3] following the successful introduction of tobacco at the English colony at Jamestown, Virginia.[4] Caffeine was also freely consumed, in coffee, tea, and cocoa.[5] Pregnant women use drugs for the same reason that everyone else does: it makes them feel good. It is hardly surprising that drug use and pregnancy frequently occur together, because the twenties are the peak years for both drug abuse and childbearing. Pregnant drug users come from all races and social classes. Their rates of drug use are similar across ethnic and income groups, although the drug of choice may vary.[6]

This chapter reviews more than a quarter-century of criminal prosecutions and involuntary "civil" commitments of pregnant women based on their use of legal and illegal drugs. Criminal prosecutions are the ultimate occasion for risk construction. They examine past acts and events and seek to determine, with the benefit of hindsight, whether a particular person's actions created an objectively foreseeable risk of harm, whether that harm was realized, and whether the person acted with a blameworthy state of mind or *mens rea*. Many individuals play key roles in criminal prosecutions, by rendering decisions to initiate criminal proceedings, bring a case to trial, convict or acquit, and impose a sentence. These players include health care workers, social services investigators, police officers, prosecutors, judges, and jurors; each makes decisions with a great degree of unconstrained discretion. Inevitably, their decisions are shaped by a host of unconscious biases and prejudices, stereotypes, and cognitive shortcuts that affect their perceptions of risk and assessments of responsibility for creating risk and causing harm. Similar psychological factors are at play with involuntary commitment, where the risk assessment is prospective. Here decisionmakers ask whether a pregnant woman who has admitted to past drug use will continue to use drugs and consider whether the potential risk to her fetus is so severe that she needs to be locked up to prevent future harm. Involuntary commitment for drug use raises many of the concerns we saw in chapter 4 concerning court-ordered caesarean sections and other compelled medical treatments.

A brief history of criminal prosecutions brought against pregnant women based on their drug use is revealing. Over the past forty years, prosecutors, often working in tandem with physicians, have taken increasingly punitive actions. In 1977 California prosecutors became the first to indict a pregnant woman for using drugs. Margaret Reyes was charged with felony child endangerment based on her use of heroin while pregnant. However, the California Court of Appeals halted the prosecution, concluding that the legislature did not intend the term *child* to encompass harm to fetuses.[7]

After *Reyes* there was a brief lull in prosecutions. Then, in the late 1980s and early 1990s, Presidents Ronald Reagan and George H.W. Bush declared a "War on Drugs." The media devoted extensive coverage to an "epidemic" of crack cocaine use. The War on Drugs was roundly criticized by many medical and public health experts. They charged that its battle cry, "Just Say No," ignored the complex genetic, biological, and social factors that contribute to drug abuse and addiction. Others saw the War on Drugs as a cynical political ploy, designed to appeal to the racial prejudices and economic insecurities of low-income whites, particularly in southern states.[8] Although the War on Drugs was popular with law enforcement and some members of the public, by the mid-1990s criminal prosecutions of drug-using pregnant women for child abuse or endangerment had been declared unconstitutional by courts everywhere they were brought, except for Alabama and South Carolina.

In 1999, the criminal landscape changed dramatically. That year Regina McKnight, a young South Carolina woman, became the first woman to be charged with *murder* based on her drug use while pregnant, after she delivered a stillborn child at thirty-four to thirty-seven weeks.[9] Ms. McKnight was a homeless African-American woman with an IQ of 72;[10] she was also addicted to crack cocaine, which she began using after her mother died.[11] After the stillbirth, cocaine metabolites were found in the bodies of Ms. McKnight and her child; she was charged with homicide by child abuse, a form of murder under South Carolina law.[12] A jury convicted Ms. McKnight of murder,[13] the judge sentenced her to twenty years in prison, and the South Carolina Supreme Court affirmed her conviction.[14]

In 2006 Mississippi prosecutors charged sixteen-year-old Rennie Gibbs with first-degree murder after she too delivered a stillborn child. Although an obvious and apparent reason for the stillbirth was the umbilical cord wrapped around the child's neck, Ms. Gibbs was nonetheless prosecuted after an autopsy found small amounts of cocaine metabolites in the child's body. The case was in legal limbo until 2014, when a Mississippi trial judge dismissed the indictment, although he gave the prosecutor leave to recharge.[15] In 2007 an Oklahoma trial judge sentenced Theresa Hernandez to fifteen years in prison based on her delivery of a stillborn child and her admitted use of methamphetamine while pregnant. Ms. Hernandez was charged with first-degree murder and pleaded guilty to second-degree murder. In fact, prosecutors had a weak case, because there is little reliable evidence that methamphetamine causes stillbirths.[16] Nonetheless, prosecutors were able to exert considerable pressure on Ms. Hernandez to plead guilty, because she had already spent more than three years in the county jail awaiting trial, unable to see her children.[17]

Meanwhile, Alabama prosecutors continued to charge drug-using pregnant women with the crime of "chemical endangerment of a child"; many indigent young women pled guilty in exchange for the prosecutor's promise that if they went to jail for a year they would not lose custody of their children.[18] In 2013, the Alabama Supreme Court upheld the convictions of Hope Ankrom and Amanda Kimbrough for this crime, ruling explicitly that the statutory term *child* encompasses a fetus *in utero*.[19] Ms. Ankrom's son was born with cocaine metabolites in his system, without apparent ill effects; she received a suspended sentence with one year's probation, on condition that she enter and complete a drug treatment program. Ms. Kimbrough's son was born extremely prematurely, at twenty-five weeks, and lived only nineteen minutes. Ms. Kimbrough admitted to using methamphetamine. After she pleaded guilty she was sentenced to ten years in prison.[20]

During the six-year period from 1999 to 2005 alone, more than 100 American women were arrested and subjected to criminal prosecution or other court-ordered intervention for using alcohol or other drugs while pregnant. The trend toward prosecution and other punitive sanctions appears to have accelerated over the past decade, with more than 300 pregnant women facing either criminal charges or involuntary civil commitment.[21] Women have been charged with crimes ranging from child abuse to first-degree murder and have received prison sentences of up to twenty years.[22]

In addition to facing criminal charges, scores of women have been civilly committed to inpatient drug treatment programs after they admitted to use of alcohol or other drugs. The most recent *cause célèbre* involved the involuntary civil commitment of Alicia Beltran, a twenty-eight-year-old pregnant Wisconsin woman who had become addicted to prescription painkillers but had weaned herself off them. In 2013, after acknowledging her prior drug use at a prenatal visit, she was arrested, handcuffed, and involuntarily committed for drug treatment, despite the fact that she was then drug-free. She spent seventy-eight days in involuntary confinement before being released.[23] Her case will be discussed in more detail in section V of this chapter.

As the twenty-first century unfolds, it appears more attractive than ever for politicians, prosecutors, and the media to denounce pregnant women who use drugs as monsters of maternal selfishness, who have "chosen" a dangerous "lifestyle" that risks the delivery of an infant who is stillborn, preterm or low birthweight, or suffering from fetal exposure to alcohol, cocaine, or methamphetamine. In Alabama, prosecutor Mitch Floyd has made it his mission to prosecute drug-using pregnant women, who, he avows, have violated a God-given duty to protect their children from all harm. In 2012 he campaigned for, and won, a local judgeship by touting his chemical endangerment prosecutions.[24] In the wake of the Alabama Supreme Court's decision in *Ankrom*, prosecutors in that state have become even more zealous in pursuing a criminal, rather than public health, solution to the complex problem of pregnant women's drug use.[25]

Discussions of the best way to respond to pregnant women's drug use frequently fail to acknowledge the complex biological, economic, and social circumstances which contribute to that behavior and, in turn, threaten harm to children not yet born. These circumstances include domestic violence, homelessness, poverty, and poor diet, as well as the lack of affordable and accessible health care. Each of these factors enhances the odds that women will use drugs at the same time that it contributes independently to adverse birth outcomes. Medical and public health authorities view drug abuse and addiction as illnesses, best responded to by offering treatment. In contrast, most law enforcement authorities assert that illegal drug use is simply a crime, undesirable behavior that should be addressed by the classic criminal law armament of retribution and deterrence. In either case, an exclusive focus on pregnant women overlooks the significant role that fathers play in promoting, or impairing, the health of a developing fetus. Fathers can cause both direct and indirect harm to fetuses and children. Thus, men who abuse their female partners can not only directly injure the fetuses the women are carrying through their physical violence but also push the women into drug use as a form of escape. When fathers buy or use drugs, they often encourage their pregnant partners to indulge as well, sometimes under a threat of violence. When fathers smoke cigarettes, the second-hand smoke reaches the fetus via the mother, contributing to premature births, lower birthweight, and poor lung development.

This chapter will first survey the wide range of drugs, legal and illegal, used by many Americans, including pregnant women. It will identify important differences between men and women in the way that their bodies respond to drugs, particularly the rapidity with which women can become addicted. The chapter also considers why some pregnant women continue to use drugs even after learning that they are pregnant, including the difficulty they can face in obtaining drug treatment. The chapter will also critically examine the strength of the evidence concerning the links between drug use and fetal development and childhood health.

The chapter reviews the history of four decades of criminal prosecutions of pregnant women who use drugs. It documents a stark trend of ever more draconian prosecutions, as district attorneys have upped the ante from bringing child abuse or child endangerment charges to obtaining indictments for murder and attempted murder. It also addresses state legislative efforts to respond to drug use by pregnant women and the creation of new crimes that explicitly target their behavior. In 2014 Tennessee became the first state to make it a separate crime for a woman to use drugs while pregnant, on top of the sanctions provided by existing drug laws. In 2016, the legislature ended the law, concluding that it had not achieved its purpose.

The chapter will next analyze *why* criminal prosecutions against pregnant women are increasing and *why* they are likely to succeed, if, of course, *success* is defined as putting women in prison. It identifies four unique aspects of the American legal system that make it possible for prosecutors to charge, and judges and juries to convict, pregnant women of crimes that risk harm to fetuses and infants. These facets of the American justice system are both procedural and substantive. They are: (1) the unbridled authority of American prosecutors, who exercise virtually limitless discretion in deciding whether or not to bring criminal charges, (2) the tendency, in rhetoric and in law, to conflate a fetus with a child, (3) the highly subjective and potentially biased criteria for evaluating "the reasonable pregnant woman," and (4) extremely malleable legal principles of causation. After considering these four factors in light of what we know about risk perception and the unconscious processes of making judgments and reaching conclusions, it will not be surprising that so many pregnant women have been prosecuted for and convicted of serious crimes after having suffered adverse birth outcomes. Almost all of these defendants are poor and/or racial or ethnic minorities. The tactics of American prosecutors will be compared briefly to those of their peers in Canada and France. While these prosecutors confront similar drug use by pregnant women, none have employed the punitive approach taken by American law enforcement.

The chapter also considers the desirability of involuntary civil commitment for drug use. Many medical and public health authorities have criticized both civil commitment and criminal prosecution as ineffective and counterproductive responses to drug use by pregnant women.

Neither approach is likely to help women quit. Instead, it appears that both approaches succeed only in deterring women from seeking medical help, exacerbating the already substantial barriers facing substance abusing women who seek treatment. The chapter will conclude with a discussion of alternative interventions that focus on harm reduction rather than on absolute cessation of drug use, in order to promote the birth of healthy babies.

I. Drugs: Their Use and Effects
A. *The History and Epidemiology of Drug Use*

The United States has a long history of drug use, both legal and illegal. Alcohol is the most widely used drug in America. Just over half of all Americans over age twelve drink on a fairly regular basis, at least once a month; nearly one-quarter engage in "binge drinking" at least once a month.[26] More than 8 percent of pregnant women drink on a fairly regular basis, and nearly 3 percent admit to binge drinking. In contrast, among nonpregnant women of childbearing age, 55 percent drink regularly and 24 percent admit to binge drinking.[27]

In the 1960s, 42 percent of all Americans smoked, with more than half of men and about a third of women being smokers. After 1964, when the Surgeon General issued a landmark report warning that smoking was dangerous to health, tobacco use gradually declined.[28] Today, just over 20 percent of all adults, but nearly 40 percent of young adults (ages eighteen to twenty-five), use some tobacco product. Overall, more than a third of men and about a quarter of women use tobacco.[29] One in six pregnant women smokes, compared with nearly one in four nonpregnant women.[30]

Americans are also big consumers of caffeine. Coffee is the caffeinated beverage of choice for most adults, followed by tea, soft drinks, and energy drinks. Coffee also provides more caffeine than any other beverage, except for concentrated energy drinks. Children, adolescents, and younger adults are most likely to get their caffeine through soft drinks, tea, and energy drinks. Women of childbearing age generally consume less caffeine than older women.[31] Perhaps it takes older women longer to get going in the morning.

Nearly 10 percent of Americans over age twelve use illegal drugs—either "street drugs" or prescription drugs put to an unauthorized use. Those most likely to use illegal drugs are young adults, who are at a stage of asserting independence from parental controls and are more likely than adolescents to have the money to buy drugs. Among these young adults, 21 percent used at least one illegal drug, followed by just under 10 percent of those ages twelve to seventeen, and 7 percent of those twenty-six or older. Slightly more than 7 percent of Americans over age twelve use marijuana, while much smaller percentages use other illegal drugs, including, in declining order, illicit prescription drugs, cocaine, hallucinogens, inhalants (glue, etc.), heroin, and methamphetamine.[32] In recent years methamphetamine use has declined, while the use of heroin, which is cheaper and more readily available than prescription painkillers, has increased sharply.[33] Slightly less than 6 percent of pregnant women use illegal drugs, compared with nearly 11 percent of non-pregnant women of childbearing age.[34]

B. Why People Use Drugs

People use drugs because drugs make them feel better. All drugs affect the brain, acting on brain cells called neurons and influencing the work of neurotransmitters, which send messages between brain cells.[35] Different drugs act through different mechanisms and at different brain locales, but, speaking generally, the brain responds to drugs by increasing or decreasing the availability of dopamine, a key neurotransmitter.[36] Dopamine plays an essential role in creating the sensations of pleasure humans normally feel—when eating, falling in love, and having sex—although the quantity of dopamine produced by drug use far surpasses the amounts released in these naturally pleasurable moments.[37] Addiction researchers are engaged in an ongoing debate about whether the transition from drug use to addiction is purely biochemical or whether addiction is similar to other kinds of learned behavior, which evolve in response to classical conditioning.[38] Everyone agrees that drug use is strongly reinforcing; that reducing, or eliminating, one's drug use is incredibly challenging; and that relapse is both frequent and predictable.[39]

Individuals' genetic makeup can increase their vulnerability to drug addiction, at the same time that the environment is a major contributor. "It is estimated that 40% to 60% of the vulnerability to addiction is attributable to genetic factors."[40] Of course, this must mean that 40 percent to 60 percent of the vulnerability to addiction is attributable to environmental factors. Scientists have long recognized that alcoholism and substance abuse[41] seem to run in families.[42] The genetic contribution to addiction is highly complex, acting through an individual's biology and his personality. For example, a person's genes may increase or decrease the risk that she will try drugs, use them frequently, become tolerant of their effects and use more, and relapse.[43] Certain genes may predispose people to risk-taking, making them more likely to experiment with drugs and to live "on the edge."[44] Environmental factors play a significant role in determining whether people who experiment with alcohol and other drugs will go on to become addicts. Neighborhood poverty, physical and sexual abuse, lack of parental support, lower socioeconomic status, stress, and the ready availability of drugs make drug abuse and addiction more probable. These are the same factors that promote mental and physical illnesses.[45]

C. How Gender Makes a Difference in Drug Use and Abuse

Gender matters in addiction. It affects the biological and environmental factors promoting drug use and dependency,[46] the way that drugs work in the brain and other organs, the factors that trigger or impede relapse, and treatment efficacy. Over the past two decades neuroscientists have discovered significant differences between men and women in terms of brain structure, biochemistry, and brain functioning that have major implications for understanding addiction. As one noted neuroscientist has observed, "[I]nvestigators have documented an outstanding array of structural, chemical and functional variations in the brains of males and females. These inequities are not just interesting idiosyncrasies that might explain why more men than women enjoy the Three Stooges . . . [but] raise the possibility that we might need to develop sex-specific treatments for a host of [mental] conditions. . . ."[47]

A striking example is found in the different ways that women and men metabolize alcohol. Women who drink alcohol have a higher blood alcohol level than men consuming the same "dose" per unit of body weight. This reflects two biological realties; on average, women have a higher percentage of their body weight in fat (which does not absorb alcohol) instead of water, and women have a much smaller amount of alcohol dehydrogenase, the key gastric enzyme necessary to metabolize alcohol.[48] Both of these lead women to have higher percentages of alcohol in their bloodstream, which transports it to the brain, liver, and heart. Women suffering from alcoholism have very little alcohol dehydrogenase; as a result, almost all the alcohol they consume is absorbed into the bloodstream. Women risk becoming alcoholic by consuming as few as eight drinks a week, compared with a threshold of twenty-one or more drinks a week for men.[49] Women can progress from nondrinker to alcoholic much more quickly than men, a process known as "telescoping."[50]

Women also respond differently to illegal drugs from men. Some drugs have longer half-lives in women than in men; thus they are likely to have a longer biological impact.[51] In addition, female hormones such as estrogen and progesterone interact with dopamine and other neurotransmitters to enhance drugs' addictive effects and make it easier for women to become addicted after even a short period of drug use.[52] As with alcohol, women who start using cocaine and other drugs are more likely than men to become dependent quickly.[53]

Cultural expectations also contribute to gender differences in alcohol and drug abuse. Historically, societal norms that only "bad" women used alcohol and other drugs meant that women were less likely to abuse and become addicted to drugs. During the American colonial period, women who were drunk in public were often condemned as promiscuous and neglectful of their children; they were frequently punished severely, with lengthy jail sentences, public shaming, and forcible sterilization.[54] In the twenty-first century these taboos have lessened for alcohol, but they are still strong for other drug use. As a result, women who abuse illegal drugs are more likely to experience shame and stigma than their male peers.[55] This censure leads some women to increase drug use as a coping mechanism; it also makes it harder for them to admit they have a problem and seek treatment for it.[56] Today women still use and abuse alcohol and other drugs at lower rates than men, but this gender gap appears to be closing.[57]

Drug-abusing and -dependent women are much more likely than men to have a coexisting mental illness, especially depression, anxiety, or posttraumatic stress disorder (PTSD).[58] Rates of PTSD among female substance abusers have been estimated to range from 30 to 59 percent. Substance abusing women are very likely to have experienced multiple traumas, including physical and sexual abuse, particularly when they were under age eighteen and had fewer internal and external coping mechanisms.[59] This abuse is especially disturbing because it arises in a close relationship. It often has long term negative effects, fostering both an inability to trust and a sense of lack of control over one's body and the larger world.[60] One study found that women and girls were five times more likely than males of similar ages to develop PTSD in response to trauma or violence;[61] other studies have found that PTSD is particularly likely to accompany opioid and cocaine dependence.[62] In general, women are more likely than men to suffer from depression, in part because of fluctuations in the hormones estrogen and progesterone.[63] Some writers assert that women's mental illnesses frequently precipitate alcohol and drug abuse as an attempt at self-medication, although this theory is not universally accepted.[64]

D. Pregnant Drug Users

Pregnancy compounds the problems of substance abuse, but pregnant drug users differ little from the larger group of women who use drugs, which includes women of all races and social classes, who use drugs at similar rates. About 90 percent of female drug abusers are of reproductive age.[65] Pregnant drug users are simply a subset of the large group of female drug users, who find it difficult to stop their drug use once they discover they are pregnant.[66] Despite media and politicians' stereotypical denunciation of pregnant women who use drugs as selfish and hedonistic, who have deliberately chosen to ignore the health risks for the developing fetus in their pursuit of pleasure, the situation of pregnant women who use drugs is much more nuanced and complex.

Many drug-using women have unintended pregnancies.[67] This is not surprising given that half of all American pregnancies are unplanned. Rates of unplanned pregnancy are much higher among women who are younger, poorer, less well educated, and African-American or Latina.[68] Addicted women frequently recognize quite late that they *are* pregnant. They stop having menstrual periods because of drug use, and their morning sickness is similar to the nausea that can accompany drug withdrawal. For many women, by the time they realize that they are pregnant their pregnancy is too far advanced to obtain a legal abortion.[69] This is especially true for poor women and those living in rural areas, because of state laws that ban the use of Medicaid funds to pay for abortions, as well as expanding state restrictions on abortion, all of which have led to an extreme scarcity in many parts of the country of physicians who perform abortions.[70]

Many pregnant drug users have had life experiences that have led them to feel choiceless, at the mercy of "fate" or other people, instead of believing that they can control their fertility or make other decisions involving their bodies.[71] It may be difficult for the well-educated, self-actualized readers of this book to place themselves in the shoes of pregnant drug abusers, but understanding this overwhelming sense of lack of agency[72] is essential to developing effective and realistic strategies to help pregnant substance abusers reduce their drug use and deliver healthy babies. Many pregnant drug users come from poor, unstable, and abusive family situations. Often they were raised by single parents, other relatives, or foster parents.[73] Frequently they were sexually and physically abused as girls, often at a young age, by a parent, step-parent, or other male relative.[74]

Many pregnant drug users were exposed to drugs as young girls, because there was easy access to drugs in their home or community or because drugs were a tool in their sexual abuse.[75] For girls for whom drugs were readily available, their use was not only normal but also an attractive way to escape, at least temporarily, from a chaotic and unhappy home situation or the stress of growing up in a violent urban neighborhood.[76] Many pregnant drug users, like addicted women in general,[77] are poorly educated and find it difficult to be economically self-sufficient.[78] They are often socially and physically isolated and lack close friends and family members. Frequently they are homeless.[79]

As adults, pregnant drug users often find themselves in dependent and physically abusive relationships that mirror those of their childhood.[80] After a woman becomes pregnant, her partner may become even more abusive or controlling, replicating a childhood pattern of coercive drug use and prompting women to try to escape the abuse by even greater drug usage.[81] Other partners may use violence to attempt to force the pregnant woman either to continue the pregnancy or have an abortion, at the partner's whim.[82]

Yet despite their difficult lives, many pregnant drug users try to minimize the harm their drug use may have on their developing fetuses.[83] Depending on the specific drug they are taking, it may be too dangerous for the women to stop using drugs altogether because of the effects of withdrawal on the fetus. Women addicted to heroin and other opiates must be weaned to methadone or other drugs and continue on that regimen throughout pregnancy and beyond.[84] Reducing their drug usage can minimize the drugs' potential harmful effects, particularly if this reduction occurs early in the pregnancy. Many addicts are successful in cutting back on drugs, especially if they are able to enter a treatment program that emphasizes harm reduction and provides the necessary social supports and incentives to encourage women to decrease their drug intake.[85] Alternatively, some women switch on their own to drugs that they perceive to be less dangerous (marijuana instead of cocaine, for example) or attempt to provide a healthier environment for fetal development by taking prenatal vitamins, eating better, and getting more rest.[86] Some women seek prenatal care and others try to find drug treatment, often with the goal of ensuring that they can keep the baby they are carrying or regain older children who were removed from their custody because of the mother's prior drug use.[87]

However, women have often found health care professionals to be unsympathetic and judgmental,[88] which may deter them from being candid about drug use in the future.[89] Many pregnant women delay seeking prenatal care, or skip appointments, to avoid being screened for drugs, out of fear of being reported to child protective services or law enforcement.[90] That this fear is realistic is confirmed by the numerous cases of criminal prosecution and involuntary civil commitment of pregnant drug users that begin with a call from a health care provider after a woman has admitted past or current drug use.

E. Harm from Drug Use

The harm posed by pregnant women's drug use is real. But it must be considered in light of overall drug use in America, as well as the larger context of other threats to childhood health and safety, including paternal behavior and the risks to the developing fetus posed by the social and physical environment. Today, legal and illegal drugs are the cause of thousands of deaths and hundreds of thousands of injuries and illnesses. Legal drugs cause far more harm than illegal ones. Tobacco use alone accounts for more than 435,000 deaths annually, or 18 percent of the total, contributing significantly to cancer, cardiovascular disease, emphysema, and other pulmonary diseases.[91] Alcohol is estimated to be the primary cause of more than 85,000 deaths annually (between 3 to 4 percent of all deaths), contributing to heart and liver disease, cancer, motor vehicle deaths, and homicides growing out of domestic violence and other assaults.[92] Men's alcohol use is a significant factor in domestic violence, child abuse, and motor vehicle accidents.[93] In contrast, illegal drugs account for less than 1 percent of all deaths, or about 17,000 people annually.[94]

While most researchers agree that drug use by pregnant women is potentially harmful to the fetus, they disagree profoundly about the severity and the permanence of the harm. Alcohol, a legal drug that is cheap and widely available, poses the clearest danger, but there is no consensus on the amount of prenatal alcohol exposure necessary to cause permanent damage. Most experts agree that when women drink both heavily and regularly, their children *may* be born with fetal alcohol syndrome (FAS) and suffer serious long-term physical and cognitive effects. Fetal alcohol syndrome was not recognized as a clinical entity until 1973, and there is still extensive debate about both the definition and the incidence of FAS. Estimates of its incidence in the United States range from 0.2 to 2.0 cases per 1,000 live births. Other researchers estimate that three times that number of children are born with fetal alcohol spectrum disorders, a much more broadly defined clinical entity.[95] Estimates of the prevalence of FAS in Europe are much lower, despite the much higher levels of drinking among pregnant women there.[96] This suggests either that different diagnostic criteria are used in Europe or that FAS is a more complex clinical phenomenon that is affected by a multitude of clinical and environmental factors, as detailed below.[97] Binge drinking, with its potential for the fetus to be exposed to high levels of alcohol for a longer period of time, appears to be the most harmful.[98] Alcohol exposure during the early stages of pregnancy, when the brain, central nervous system, and other organs are forming, poses a significant risk of harm; yet many women do not know that they are pregnant during these early weeks, given the large percentage of unplanned pregnancies.[99]

The timing and extent of maternal drinking are not the only predictors of fetal harm; poverty and other maternal health factors have a significant impact. Even among the children of alcoholic women, who by definition are heavy and regular drinkers, only about 5 percent are born with fetal alcohol syndrome.[100] Strikingly, the likelihood that a child born to a mother who drinks heavily will be diagnosed with FAS varies enormously by class.[101] A study of pregnant women who had at least three drinks a day found an FAS incidence of 71 percent among the children of low-income women but only 4.5 percent among women who were middle-class or wealthier. In addition to poverty, the incidence of fetal alcohol syndrome is strongly correlated with smoking, malnutrition, high parity (the number of births and stillbirths), small size, and advanced maternal age, each of which is an independent predictor of adverse birth outcomes. Several studies have found that mothers who lack access to basic nutrients, ranging from calcium, riboflavin, and omega-3 fatty acids to trace nutrients like zinc and copper, are more likely to deliver children suffering from FAS than other mothers who live in the same communities and have similar drinking patterns but are better nourished.[102]

Across all demographic groups, there is much less evidence that minimal or moderate alcohol consumption by pregnant women is dangerous. Yet, or perhaps because, so much is still unknown about the causal relationship between drinking during pregnancy and birth outcomes, American public health officials have taken the stance that no amount of alcohol is safe to consume; they recommend total abstinence during pregnancy. In 2016 the Centers for Disease Control recommended that any woman even contemplating pregnancy should abstain from drinking; the CDC recommended that women who wanted to continue to drink use birth control.[103] In contrast, many European nations have taken a less absolutist approach, emphasizing that there is no clear evidence that low or moderate levels of alcohol consumption pose a risk and recommending that women be discouraged from excessive drinking rather than being told that they must abstain from drinking throughout pregnancy or risk irreparable harm to their fetuses.[104] Studies recently conducted in Denmark have confirmed earlier findings that low to moderate drinking (as opposed to binge drinking) in early pregnancy has not been associated with measurable adverse effects on children up to age five.[105]

In sharp contrast to alcohol, tobacco use by pregnant women and their partners is much more clearly linked to preconception and prenatal harm as well as infant mortality and childhood illness. Prior to conception, paternal smoking can cause mutations in the germ cells that are passed along to children via the father's sperm, making children more likely to develop cancer.[106] Children exposed to tobacco *in utero*, either from the mother's smoking or exposure to second-hand smoke from another household member, are more likely to be born prematurely and to develop asthma and other respiratory problems as children. Scientists have found that nicotine may cause many of the harms that are popularly associated with cocaine use.[107] Sudden infant death syndrome (SIDS) is more common among children if one parent smokes.[108] Thus, reducing maternal and paternal smoking may have important health benefits for children. Several recent studies of the impact of public and workplace smoking bans have found striking reductions in adverse health outcomes for children, showing a 10 percent decrease in preterm births and the incidence of asthma attacks and a 5 percent reduction in children who were born small for gestational age.[109]

Even caffeine is sometimes portrayed as risky by physicians and the media. In January 2008 a report suggesting a link between caffeine intake and miscarriages received wide public attention, despite the statements of some scientists that the link might not be causal.[110] Pregnancy advice books and individual physicians vary in the extent to which they warn against "excessive" caffeine consumption,[111] but so far, no woman has been prosecuted for drinking too much coffee while pregnant.

In contrast to the well-documented harms of alcohol and tobacco use on fetal development, the evidence on the impact of illegal drug use is much more equivocal. While some researchers have concluded that maternal cocaine use may lead to subtle, long-lasting neurological deficits in their children, including "the ability to habituate or self-regulate" and small deficits in IQ and language ability,[112] others have found that most infants exposed *in utero* to cocaine "catch up to their peers in physical size and health status by age 2."[113] A 2001 meta-analysis reviewing many studies found that cocaine exposure *in utero* is much *less* harmful than exposure to alcohol and tobacco; fetal cocaine exposure has not been shown to result in any "major developmental consequences in early childhood."[114] More recent longitudinal studies have confirmed that prenatal cocaine exposure does not result in long-term physical or neurological deficits in children. Instead, poverty is the biggest contributor to cognitive and physical deficits.[115]

Pregnant women who use drugs have been charged with homicide and other serious felonies after suffering a miscarriage, stillbirth, or premature labor and delivery. Yet in many cases the medical evidence that the mother's drug use caused the adverse event is thin, if it exists at all. Strictly speaking, a miscarriage is a fetal loss that occurs before twenty weeks of pregnancy, while stillbirth is a fetal loss that occurs at twenty weeks or later. While each type of fetal loss is associated with multiple factors, there is still much that is unknown about their underlying causes. Thus, it is difficult to conclusively establish causation in an individual case. Approximately 26,000 infants are stillborn each year, or a little more than six for every thousand births. African-Americans are more than twice as likely as whites to suffer stillbirths, regardless of their educational level or social class. Half of all stillbirths are the result of unknown causes. Chromosomal, genetic, and placental abnormalities cause some stillbirths; other maternal risk factors are obesity, hypertension, diabetes, and infectious diseases, as well as poverty, single motherhood, and advanced age (e.g., over 35).[116] Similarly, preterm births, which increase the chances of early infant death and other physical and developmental problems, occur much more frequently in women who are poor, victims of domestic violence, African-American, malnourished, or unmarried, suggesting that both biological and social factors contribute to adverse birth outcomes.[117]

Despite the multiplicity of factors that lead to fetal loss and the great difficulty of proving a cause-and-effect relationship between maternal behavior and a particular adverse outcome, many prosecutors have been quick to seize upon a pregnant woman's drug use as the *sole* cause of a stillbirth or infant death and to initiate criminal proceedings whenever a pregnant woman has used drugs. We saw earlier, in the cases of Rennie Gibbs and Theresa Hernandez, that prosecutors may face obstacles to obtaining a conviction because their case on causation is weak. This could occur either because the use of a particular drug has not been connected with stillbirth (as in *Hernandez*, where there was no evidence that methamphetamine caused stillbirths) or because the evidence on causation in a particular case was problematic (as in *Gibbs*, when the stillborn child had its umbilical cord wrapped around its neck, undercutting the prosecution's argument that drug use caused the stillbirth). Nonetheless, the flexible rules of causation in American law often permit prosecutors to persuade a jury that a pregnant woman's drug use was *the* cause of her child's stillbirth or death, despite the rule in criminal cases that conviction requires proof beyond a reasonable doubt of every element of the crime.[118]

II. A Short History of Criminal Prosecutions of Pregnant Women for Drug Use

A. *The First Wave of "Fetal Protection" Prosecutions*

In 1977 Margaret Reyes was charged with child endangerment, becoming the first American woman charged with risking fetal harm based on her drug use during pregnancy. However, the California Court of Appeals ruled that the prosecution could not proceed, finding that the legislature did not intend to criminalize harm to fetuses through its use of the term *child*.[119] In *Reyes*, the court invoked the common law "born-alive rule," which declared that a person could not be held criminally liable for causing harm to one who was not yet born. The court's decision also reflected respect for two important constitutional law principles: separation of powers and due process. Under the federal and state constitutions, the principle of separation of powers means that only the legislature can authorize and define crimes, by enacting statutes. Due process, a central tenet of American democracy, requires that laws be written in a way that gives notice and fair warning of what conduct is prohibited. In the criminal law context this is called "the principle of legality."[120]

For a brief period after *Reyes*, prosecutions of pregnant drug users for child abuse or endangerment were rare. But after the War on Drugs was launched, many local prosecutors began to charge pregnant women with offenses such as child abuse and endangerment or delivering drugs to a minor (under the theory that the drug was "delivered" via the placenta or umbilical cord). An all too typical case occurred in 1990. Diane Pfannenstiel was a twenty-nine-year-old Wyoming woman who went to the police to report that her husband had beaten her. While news stories do not report what happened to her husband, we do know that after the police took her to the local hospital for treatment, she was arrested because her lab workup disclosed a blood alcohol level slightly above the limit for drunk driving. Because she was also four months' pregnant, Mrs. Pfannenstiel was charged with felony child abuse. A judge subsequently dismissed the charges, finding no evidence that the fetus had been harmed. Five months later, Mrs. Pfannenstiel delivered a healthy baby.[121]

Police and prosecutors often worked closely with health care personnel, as occurred in Diane Pfannenstiel's case. Charleston, South Carolina, provided a notable example of such a partnership. In the late 1980s, prosecutors outside of Charleston began to charge drug-using pregnant women with the crime of child abuse. When a nurse at Charleston City Hospital learned about these prosecutions, she contacted local law enforcement officials. Together they devised a policy to covertly test the urine of many women who delivered at the hospital. Under this policy, all positive drug tests were turned over to the police and local prosecutors. The criteria for deciding whom to test were aimed, consciously or not, at indigent African-American patients. Women who had received late, "incomplete," or no prenatal care, as is common among poor women, were automatically drug-tested. So were women whose labor and delivery were accompanied by complications such as placental abruption or unexplained premature labor, which were viewed as evidence of possible drug use. Initially all women with a positive drug test were automatically arrested. Some women who had just delivered babies were taken to jail in shackles, still bleeding. Subsequently Charleston City Hospital adopted a deferred prosecution policy, giving women the "option" of entering treatment or being jailed.[122] Virtually all of the women who were arrested were poor and African-American; the only white woman charged was noted by a nurse to have an African-American boyfriend.[123] It was not until 2001 that the United States Supreme Court ordered a halt to the hospital's covert testing program, finding that it constituted an unconstitutional search and seizure.[124]

Similarly, by the mid-1990s criminal prosecutions of drug-using pregnant women for child abuse or endangerment had been halted, declared unconstitutional by the courts in all states where they had been brought, except for Alabama and South Carolina. Courts that ruled against the prosecutors reasoned that criminal proceedings in these cases violated the constitutional requirement of separation of powers or the due process principle of legality. For example, in *Johnson v. State*, the Florida Supreme Court held that a law prohibiting delivery of a controlled substance to a minor did not make it a crime for cocaine to pass through the umbilical cord from a mother to a fetus. Many judges also questioned the underlying policy of these prosecutions, reasoning that pregnant women would be deterred from seeking prenatal health care or would even opt for abortion out of fear of prosecution.[125]

B. The Second Wave of "Fetal Protection" Prosecutions

Yet despite nearly universal judicial rejection of "child abuse" prosecutions against pregnant women, by the late 1990s some prosecutors had adopted an even more aggressive stance. For the first time, prosecutors charged pregnant women with homicide, including murder, manslaughter, and attempted intentional homicide. Prosecutors also indicted pregnant women for child endangerment and drug delivery, even though such prosecutions had previously been found legally unsound in almost every jurisdiction. In these new cases many prosecutors, as well as some judges, specifically invoked the rhetoric of the anti-abortion movement in support of their positions, emphasizing the "innocence" of the "unborn child."

The first case in the new round of prosecutions involved the legal drug alcohol. In 1996 Wisconsin prosecutors charged Deborah Zimmerman, a thirty-five-year-old pregnant woman who had a long history of alcohol abuse, with attempted first-degree intentional homicide and reckless injury.[126] The prosecution relied on confidential statements Ms. Zimmerman had made to emergency room nurses who sought to convince her to undergo a caesarean section. After she went into labor while drinking at a bar, her mother brought her to the hospital. While there, a highly intoxicated Ms. Zimmerman declared, "'[I]f you don't keep me here, I'm just going to go home and keep drinking and drink myself to death and I'm going to kill this thing because I don't want it anyways.'" As Professor Elizabeth Armstrong observed in recounting the story, some health care professionals might have viewed this as a suicide threat and sought psychiatric intervention.[127] These hospital workers did not and instead contacted law enforcement officials. In charging Ms.

Zimmerman, the prosecutor focused on her alleged intent to harm her fetus.[128] Ms. Zimmerman moved to dismiss the indictment, arguing that the crimes charged could be committed only against "human beings," which, under Wisconsin law, referred only to persons who were born at the time of injury.

Ms. Zimmerman spent three years in county jail while her case was on appeal to the Wisconsin Court of Appeals. Ultimately, that court agreed with her. Relying on the principle of legality, the court held that under the Wisconsin statute, a fetus was not a human being, thus precluding prosecution for attempted homicide.[129] In addition, the court identified several troubling aspects of the criminal prosecution of pregnant drug users. Questioning whether the problem of substance abuse was better addressed through punishment or treatment, it voiced concern that threatening prosecution could deter women from seeking prenatal care or treatment for substance abuse.[130] In addition, the court recognized that the prosecution of pregnant women created a "slippery slope." It observed that given the broad continuum of maternal behavior that could potentially harm a fetus, it would be difficult to draw a line on that continuum to clearly separate criminal from noncriminal behavior. To permit the prosecution to go forward would mean that "a woman could risk criminal charges for any perceived self-destructive behavior during her pregnancy that may result in injuries to her unborn child [, including] smoking or abusing legal medications . . . [or] 'the failure to secure adequate prenatal medical care and overzealous behavior, such as excessive exercising or dieting.'"[131]

Meanwhile, South Carolina prosecutors continued to rely on the criminal law to address the health care problems of indigent pregnant women. In 1997, the South Carolina Supreme Court upheld a conviction for "child endangerment" based on a woman's use of drugs while pregnant. In *Whitner v. State* the court declared that a viable fetus was a "child" within the meaning of the South Carolina child endangerment statute, rejecting the argument, accepted by virtually all other state courts, that such a conviction violated the principle of legality.[132]

Two years later, after suffering a stillbirth, another South Carolina woman, Regina McKnight, was indicted for murder based on her use of cocaine while pregnant.[133] As noted earlier, Ms. McKnight was African-American, young, and homeless, with an IQ indicating that she was borderline mentally retarded.[134] After the stillbirth, drug testing of Ms. McKnight and her stillborn child revealed cocaine metabolites; the prosecution contended that Ms. McKnight's cocaine use had caused the stillbirth.[135] While Ms. McKnight's first trial ended in a mistrial,[136] during the second trial prosecutors were much better prepared on the causation issue. Inexplicably, Ms. McKnight's lawyer failed to present much of the evidence contesting causation that she had offered at the first trial. After deliberating for thirty minutes, the jury convicted Ms. McKnight of murder.[137] The judge sentenced her to twenty years in prison.[138]

The South Carolina Supreme Court upheld Ms. McKnight's conviction, rejecting her argument that a homicide conviction based on prenatal "child abuse" violated the principle of legality and deprived her of due process of law. The court ruled that in light of its previous decisions, no woman in South Carolina could lack notice that the "homicide by child abuse" statute could apply to a woman whose fetus is stillborn. The court found first that its decision in *Whitner* provided public notice that using cocaine while pregnant was potentially dangerous to a fetus and, second, that the law was clear that such behavior constituted child neglect. The court thus deemed it entirely appropriate to leave it to the jury to decide whether Ms. McKnight had acted with the "extreme indifference to human life" necessary for a murder conviction. The court defined "extreme indifference to human life" as "'a mental state akin to intent characterized by a deliberate act culminating in death.'"[139] This meant, in effect, that as long as a defendant had acted intentionally in taking a drug, she could be found guilty of murder if that act resulted in death. There was no requirement that the defendant be consciously aware that her conduct created a risk of fetal loss. In light of what we know about how jurors deliberate and their reliance on heuristics such as the "better than average" effect, as well as other unconscious biases and stereotypes, the jury's conclusion that by using cocaine, Ms. McKnight demonstrated "extreme indifference to the value of human life" is not surprising. It is, indeed, what prosecutors count on in bringing these homicide prosecutions. The *McKnight* case signaled a new era of criminal prosecution of pregnant women based on illegal drug use. Although hers was not the first criminal case, it was the first to threaten a lifetime sentence for the use of drugs while pregnant. As it was, Ms. McKnight was imprisoned for eight years before her conviction was overturned on the grounds that she had been denied the effective assistance of counsel by her lawyer's failure to adequately challenge the prosecution's case on causation.[140]

Ms. McKnight's conviction appeared to embolden other prosecutors. Prosecutors in Hawaii, Maryland, Missouri, Oklahoma, and South Carolina also charged drug-using pregnant women with homicide when their infants were stillborn or died shortly after birth.[141] In 2003 a Hawaii prosecutor indicted Tayshea Aiwohi for manslaughter based on her methamphetamine use while pregnant, which allegedly caused the death of her two-day-old infant. Amazingly, the indictment was not brought for two years, despite the fact that by then Ms. Aiwohi had successfully completed a drug treatment program. The prosecutor and the trial judge asserted that a criminal prosecution was necessary, to hold Ms. Aiwohi accountable and to send a message to other women that they should not use drugs while pregnant.[142] Using reasoning that paralleled the South Carolina Supreme Court's decision in *McKnight*, the trial judge asserted, "[D]rug usage, including the use of crystal methamphetamine[,] is a matter of choice and not an illness. Certainly it is a conscious choice to obtain and use the drug initially and[,] worse yet, while pregnant." This use of the rhetoric of "choice" is typical of prosecutors and judges in prosecutions based on women's conduct during pregnancy. Those who seek to impose criminal liability on pregnant women focus solely on the actions of the individual woman, ignoring the multiple biological, genetic, and social determinants of addiction and drug use. After Ms. Aiwohi was convicted, the judge sentenced her to twenty years in prison, although he suspended the sentence on condition that she satisfy the terms of a ten-year probation.[143] On appeal, the Hawaii Supreme Court overturned the conviction, holding that a fetus was not a person within the meaning of the manslaughter statute.[144]

Although almost all state appellate courts have overturned the convictions of drug-using pregnant women on legal or constitutional grounds, the indictments have continued. Indeed, over the past two decades both the rhetoric of prosecutors and the severity of the charges they have brought have escalated. Prosecutors have moved from charging pregnant women with relatively low level felonies like child abuse or child endangerment to bringing murder charges, seeking lengthy prison sentences for women whose children were stillborn or who died shortly after birth. Despite the lack of compelling medical evidence that would enable them to meet their burden of proof on the essential element of causation, particularly in the case of stillbirths, prosecutors seem willing to gamble that a jury will convict a woman whose drug use makes her an unsympathetic defendant. In other cases in which defendants have faced homicide charges based on their drug use while pregnant, the defendants, who are frequently indigent and lack strong social support systems, have pled guilty to lesser crimes out of fear that if they challenge the prosecution and go to trial, they will lose custody of their children, particularly if they are being held in jail awaiting trial.[145] We now consider *why* prosecutors are so zealous in this area, exploring the unique aspects of American law that both encourage prosecution and make conviction possible. As noted earlier, these include (1) unconstrained prosecutorial discretion, (2) the tendency to conflate a fetus with a child, (3) the malleable concept of the reasonable person, and (4) highly elastic principles of causation.

III. Why Prosecutors Are Likely to Bring—and Win—Criminal Prosecutions against Pregnant Drug Users

At the outset it must be observed that America's criminal law "solution" to the problem of drug use by pregnant women reflects the American emphasis on individual, rather than collective, responsibility, explored in more detail in chapter 2. As Elizabeth Armstrong observes, American society tends "to locate explanations for . . . [adverse health outcomes] at the individual . . . level rather than to see . . . [the outcome] as the consequence of social conditions." She continues, "Biologizing problems also individualizes them—taking them out of the realm of society and embedding them in the bodies of individual women, children, and men. . . . It reinforces the belief that individual, not social, change is called for."[146] Similarly, American criminal law reflects a "belief in freedom of the human will and a consequent ability and duty of the normal individual to choose between good and evil."[147] Conservative politicians and media of all ideological stripes frequently emphasize that these crimes are *chosen* by individual defendants, rejecting the possibility that both their behavior and adverse events may be a response to challenging social and economic circumstances.[148] Yet the reality is, as we have seen in discussing the risk factors for stillbirth, preterm birth, and fetal alcohol syndrome, that poverty is the single biggest contributor to the adverse birth outcomes that have given rise to so many criminal prosecutions. That poverty is so highly correlated with these adverse outcomes reflects the complex synergy between a lack of adequate housing, nutrition, and health care and the physical dangers and stress that accompany economic insecurity, domestic violence, and living in a run-down and violent neighborhood.

A. Unrestrained Prosecutorial Discretion

The uniquely American institution of the prosecutor shapes both the criminal law landscape and the political debate over pregnant women's drug use. The United States stands alone among industrialized democracies in taking a punitive, rather than public health, approach to address concerns about prenatal drug exposure. To understand why this is so, we must examine the incentives for prosecutors to bring criminal cases, as well as the institutional structures that enhance their odds of winning convictions, even if the convictions are eventually overturned on appeal. Stated bluntly, American prosecutors are likely to prosecute because of three institutional factors: they are locally elected politicians, prosecutions of pregnant women advance their political ambitions, and their actions are unrestrained either by a hierarchical system of prosecutorial control or the judiciary. Let us examine each factor in turn.

First, on the state level, virtually all American prosecutors are locally selected. This practice began in the colonial era, when great geographic distances between British royal governors and local communities necessitated the appointment of local prosecutors who became, in practice, the sole authorities entitled to initiate criminal prosecutions. After the American Revolution, the system of appointed local prosecutors spread throughout the former colonies. Prosecutors were initially an arm of the judiciary, but after the Jacksonian period and the push for democratic, decentralized authority, they became independent officials, answerable only to the electorate. Over time, local prosecutors came to wield significant power. By the beginning of the twentieth century, concern was widespread about the concentration of prosecutorial authority and the possibility of corruption.[149]

American prosecutors apply state and local laws, rather than a single, national body of law. In contrast to Canada and France, for example, whose prosecutors apply a national penal code, written by the national legislature and interpreted by the nation's highest court, in the United States prosecutors apply law that differs in each jurisdiction. There are more than fifty distinct bodies of criminal law that govern prosecutions brought in the states, the District of Columbia, and Puerto Rico. There is also a federal penal code, enforced by the Department of Justice and individual United States Attorneys, but so far it does not include any crimes directed at the actions of pregnant women. Further, while the Supreme Court has a major role in developing constitutional law and criminal procedure (the law governing the criminal trial process), it exerts very little control over the substantive criminal law of the states, only rarely invalidating a criminal statute.[150]

Second, being a prosecutor in the United States is often a stepping stone to higher political office.[151] Prosecuting pregnant women for drug use or other acts of "fetal endangerment" can help local prosecutors further their political ambitions. Among the former prosecutors now serving in the United States Senate are Ted Cruz of Texas, Patrick Leahy of Vermont, and Claire McCaskill of Missouri. Former prosecutors who became governors include Earl Warren of California and Chris Christie of New Jersey. Charles Condon, the Charleston district attorney who prosecuted many pregnant women, has repeatedly sought higher office.[152] Mitch Floyd, the outspoken Alabama prosecutor who brought chemical endangerment cases against pregnant women, was elected a judge in 2012.[153]

Today, many prosecutors appear frustrated by the widespread and complex problem of drug abuse and addiction, which has resisted easy solutions. It may be tempting to seek harsh punishment as a "wake-up call" to individual women and a signal to the wider community. Indeed, the National District Attorneys Association has publicly favored expanding the definition of "child abuse" to include pregnant women's drug use and to authorize testing of all pregnant women and their newborns.[154] Even without new legislation, prosecutors can enhance their standing with a conservative electorate simply by "taking a stand" against drugs and declaring their desire to protect "innocent children" or "the unborn." Further, prosecutors who lose individual cases can still view their prosecutions as successful if they raise public awareness about pregnant women's drug use. As one Wyoming prosecutor observed, "We stuck our toe in the water on this thing.... People need to understand there's a big hole in the law that needs to be filled."[155] It is not surprising that the states where some of the most zealous criminal prosecutions of drug-using women have occurred are those in which religious and political conservatives are politically powerful, and where access to abortion, particularly for minors and for poor women, is increasingly tenuous and fragile. Examples include Alabama, Missouri, Mississippi, Oklahoma, South Carolina, Texas, and Wisconsin.

Third, American prosecutors have virtually unlimited discretion in deciding whether to bring criminal charges, unconstrained either by a higher prosecutorial authority or the judicial system. This discretionary power compounds the broader problem of a lack of transparency about charging decisions, including the criteria for indicting for particular crimes, overcharging (charging multiple crimes based on the same incident), and determining when a plea bargain is appropriate.[156] There is mounting evidence of racial disparities in prosecutors' charging decisions, particularly in the plea bargains they offer, which lead to disproportionately more severe sentences for African-American and Latina defendants.[157] Together these concerns raise the likelihood that prosecutors will bring weak cases, which they might be unable to win at trial, in the hope of inducing defendants to plead guilty to avoid a lengthy prison term.[158]

Unlike their peers in other Western democracies, American prosecutors are not overseen by any higher prosecutorial authority. In contrast, in Canada there is centralized review of cases that are brought at both the federal and provincial levels.[159] In France, a prosecutor's decision to bring serious criminal charges is overseen initially by an independent magistrate, the *juge d'instruction*, and then by the prosecutor's superiors in the Ministère Publique, as well as circulars that set forth general guidelines for prosecution. In the United States, even in the rare states in which the state attorney general provides some oversight of local prosecutors, there are virtually no limits on a prosecutor's exercise of discretion.

The lack of hierarchical constraints on American prosecutors is compounded by what many see as the judiciary's abdication of its role as enforcer of the constitutional requirement of separation of powers. More than thirty years ago, Yale Law School Professor Abraham Goldstein decried the tendency of judges to take a hands-off approach to prosecutorial actions. Goldstein declared that the lack of oversight was so profound that it should be called "judicial withdrawal" rather than "judicial restraint."[160] Observing the failure of judges to meaningfully review prosecutors' charging decisions and plea bargain offers, he concluded that judges appeared "to have forgotten principles of legality which they have enforced energetically elsewhere in the criminal law—principles that make the legislature the primary source of law and the judiciary its authoritative interpreter." Goldstein found that legislatures frequently failed to articulate a "clear cut legal rule" when enacting statutes and that courts have failed to meaningfully review prosecutors' expansive interpretations of those statutes, essentially granting prosecutors a license to fill in the blanks. This, Goldstein said, demonstrated a complete "misunderstanding of the relationship between the concept of discretion itself and the separation of powers."[161]

Nowhere is the lack of effective judicial oversight clearer than in the criminal prosecution of pregnant women. When trial judges fail to rein in prosecutors' decisions to treat fetal drug exposure as the equivalent of criminal "child abuse" without explicit statutory authorization, or when they decline to dismiss indictments brought without sufficient evidence that the alleged harm has been caused by the defendant, they are abdicating their judicial duty, leaving poor, uneducated women unprotected from ambitious and overreaching prosecutors. As dissenting Judge Riley asserted in the case of *Bei Bei Shuai v. State*, judges must insist that prosecutors respect the principle of separation of powers, in which only the legislature is authorized to create crimes, or pregnant women will be prosecuted without any guidance—or limit—on the conduct that can put them in prison.[162]

B. The Conflation of a Fetus with a Child

The American criminal justice system mirrors the nonlegal world in its view that fetuses and children are equivalent, making it highly likely that women will be prosecuted for "risking" fetal harm. In chapter 4 we observed that the media, medical personnel, and the public often conflate a fetus with a child. The increased ability to visualize the fetus prior to birth has led many people to consider a fetus as an entity entirely separate from the pregnant woman, even though a developing fetus cannot exist outside the woman's body until very late in pregnancy. Many doctors consider that they are treating two patients, rather than one pregnant woman carrying a potential life. Obstetricians have abandoned their earlier belief that the best way to ensure the birth of a healthy child was to promote the health of the pregnant mother-to-be, a belief that shaped the way they provided care. Today many physicians feel conflicted about their treatment obligations to the pregnant woman and the fetus; they tend, perhaps out of fear of malpractice suits, to emphasize the well-being of the fetus over that of the woman in whose body it is contained.

The crusade for "personhood," which posits that life begins at conception and that a fertilized egg is as fully human as a born child, has a significant impact on the criminal prosecution of pregnant women. The activism of the personhood and anti-abortion movements contributes to a political and legal environment in which it is no longer a huge step to treat a single cell organism as the moral equivalent of a child. Increasingly, this belief is being enacted into law. This has occurred legislatively, with thirty-eight states enacting fetal homicide statutes (which, in more than half of these states, declare that life begins at conception);[163] through judicial decisions that interpret the statutory term *child* to mean any human entity from the moment of conception on;[164] and by criminal indictments in which prosecutors allege that the mother's behavior during pregnancy has caused her "child" to be put at risk.

Prosecutors and judges frequently use language that collapses the distinction previously made between a fetus developing *in utero* and a born child, which the common law encompassed in "the born-alive rule." For example, Mitch Floyd, explaining why he prosecutes women who have used drugs while pregnant, declared, "A child is helpless, and God has put one person on this planet to be the last-line defense, to be the fiercest protector of that child, and that is its mother. . . . When that child's ultimate protector is the one causing the harm, what do you do [except prosecute her]?"[165] Charles Condon, the legal architect of the covert drug-testing program challenged successfully in *Ferguson v. City of Charleston*, exulted after Regina McKnight's conviction. He proclaimed,

"Today, South Carolina's unborn children have a much better chance at a long, happy life than they did yesterday [before she was convicted]."[166] Anti-abortion advocates have enthusiastically embraced the criminal prosecution of pregnant women. Troy Newman, the president of Operation Rescue, says that laws like Alabama's chemical endangerment statute can help the anti-abortion movement succeed. "'Look,' he says, 'we win every time we establish the precedent that the unborn child in the womb is a unique human individual.'"[167]

Similarly, judges who have upheld criminal convictions of pregnant women under statutes criminalizing child abuse or child endangerment have expressly equated a fetus with a child. In 2014 the Alabama Supreme Court decided *Ex parte Hicks*, another case in which a woman was charged with chemical endangerment, this time based on her use of cocaine while pregnant. Her child was born without apparent ill effects.[168] In *Hicks*, Justice Thomas Parker was apparently not content simply to rely on the court's decision in *Ex parte Ankrom*, which a year earlier had ruled that the term *child* in Alabama's chemical endangerment statute included a child *in utero* exposed to drugs by its mother's drug use.[169] Instead, Judge Parker launched a direct attack on the Supreme Court's abortion jurisprudence, declaring that *Roe v. Wade* and *Planned Parenthood of Southeastern Pennsylvania v. Casey* were improperly decided and that a child exists from the moment of conception.[170] His reasoning parallels the decisions of judges who have upheld court-ordered caesarean sections. These judges have also explicitly treated a fetus as the legal equivalent of a child when they "balance" the fetus' interest against that of the pregnant woman.

C. The Social Construction of "the Reasonable Mother" and "the Reasonable Pregnant Woman" Makes It Likely That Drug-Using Pregnant Women Will Be Found Criminally Liable

If, as prosecutors argue, a fetus is a child, then jurors in a criminal case are likely to evaluate the conduct of a pregnant woman through the lens of "the reasonable mother," an elastic and socially constructed standard. There are three problems with the use of this standard. First, as we observed in chapter 4, because the fetus is not yet born it is inappropriate to impose on a pregnant woman the same duties that the law imposes on parents of children who have already been born. Pregnant women should certainly be supported and encouraged to engage in behaviors that promote their own health, as well as the well-being of their developing fetuses, but they should not be held criminally responsible under the same legal standard that is applied to parents of born children.

That this makes sense becomes apparent by using what Professor Cynthia Lee calls a "gender-switching" exercise, a counterfactual analysis in which a jury is asked to consider how it would decide a particular case if the defendant were of the opposite gender, and then apply the insights gained from this process to the actual case at hand.[171] Applying this gender-switching approach, it is hard to imagine that an expectant father would be held criminally liable for child abuse because he smoked while his wife was pregnant, despite compelling evidence that second-hand smoke enters the developing fetus' environment and can cause a variety of adverse birth outcomes. Similarly, it is unlikely that an expectant father would be charged with, or convicted of, failing to seek substance abuse treatment even if that might make him less likely to assault his pregnant wife, which could also harm the fetus. Yet prosecutors have repeatedly justified bringing charges against women who used drugs while pregnant as necessary to protect "children," arguing that a pregnant woman should be treated like the parent of an already born child. The essence of Alabama prosecutor Mitch Floyd's argument was, "The mother is supposed to be the child's fiercest protector; a mother—or pregnant woman—who fails to fulfill this duty should be criminally convicted." Rebecca King, chief prosecutor for Amarillo County, Texas, declared, "All fetuses are legally individuals at all times during pregnancy." As a result, she charged pregnant women who used drugs with "delivering drugs to a minor." She also informed local physicians that they had a legal duty to report all pregnant patients who used drugs, effectively seeking to make an end run around physicians' ethical and legal obligations to maintain patient confidentiality.[172]

When pregnant women are charged with violating the same duties that parents owe to a born child it is almost inevitable they will be found liable, because, on an emotional level, we expect so much of mothers. Even if the jury is instructed to apply the standard of "the reasonable pregnant woman," the conflation of a fetus with a child means that the jury will actually be evaluating the defendant's conduct in light of "the reasonable mother" standard. By definition, a "reasonable mother" does not neglect her children to pursue her own selfish pleasures. In a society in which drug use is seen as a chosen and hedonistic act rather than an illness, it is highly likely that a pregnant woman charged with acting negligently will be found guilty.

Second, even instructions that use the concept of "the reasonable pregnant woman" are problematic. This standard is inherently elastic, shaped by unconscious biases and cultural norms. Legal scholars have long debated the appropriate contours of "the reasonable person." In the 1960s, when the traditional "reasonable man" standard was first challenged by feminists, American law revised the standard to become ostensibly gender-neutral. Thus, the "reasonable man" became the "reasonable person."[173] Yet questions remain about the extent to which the "reasonable person" should resemble the defendant, including age, race, sexual orientation, and physical and mental traits. Generally speaking, courts and scholars have chosen a hybrid persona for the "reasonable man/woman," striking a middle ground that takes into account those characteristics of the defendant that are seen to legitimately bear on his or her culpability. These are typically age, gender, physical strength or vulnerability, and sometimes race and sexual orientation. However, the prevailing view is that "the reasonable person" should not embody every characteristic of the defendant, because that would defeat the essential purpose of "the reasonable person" standard, which is to provide a neutral normative standard by which an individual's conduct may be judged.[174]

Even assuming that a "reasonable pregnant woman" standard could be properly articulated, there are still two major problems. First, as the Illinois Supreme Court held in *Stallman v. Youngquist*, it is impossible to develop a truly objective and neutral standard by which to evaluate a pregnant woman's conduct.[175] Such a standard would inevitably fail to take into account the unique situation of a *particular* pregnant woman, who may or may not be struggling with alcohol and other substance abuse, have access to good health care, be the victim of domestic violence, have economic and other social supports, or even be aware that she is pregnant. By definition, negligence is *contextual*—a person is negligent, in tort and criminal law, if she or he falls below the standard of the reasonable person *in that situation*.[176]

Further, to permit a jury to find a defendant guilty based on a "reasonable pregnant woman" standard tilts the balance impermissibly against drug-using pregnant women who lack the personal, economic, and social resources of a middle-class woman with a well-ordered life, even if she too uses drugs. As the court explained in *Stallman*, it would be impossible to keep "prejudicial and stereotypical beliefs about the reproductive abilities of women . . . [from the jury, which would affect its] determination of whether a particular woman was negligent at any point during her pregnancy."[177] Drug use by pregnant women transcends class and racial lines: women who are white and middle- or upper-class are just as likely to use drugs as women of color and women who are poor. Yet women in the latter group are much more likely to be brought to the attention of law enforcement and are therefore more likely to be prosecuted and convicted. In *Ferguson v. City of Charleston*, all but one of the forty-two patients at Charleston City Hospital referred to law enforcement were African-American, and most were poor. Indeed, the criteria used to decide which pregnant women would be tested included having late or no prenatal care, effectively targeting poor women, who were much less likely to have access to regular health care.[178] A landmark 1990 study showed that pregnant African-American and white women were equally likely to use illicit drugs, but that African-American women were *ten times* more likely than white women to be reported to public health or law enforcement authorities.[179] A more recent study found that about 15 percent of women in communities across the United States continued to use alcohol and/or illicit drugs after learning that they were pregnant. Indeed, the wealthiest community surveyed had the highest rate of substance use, driven by their significant wine drinking. This study also found that about one-fifth of the women smoked during pregnancy, which is a major contributor to preterm birth and low birthweight.[180] Yet jurors who are not informed about how widespread drug use during pregnancy really is are likely to impose their idealized views of how a "reasonable pregnant woman" should behave and convict a drug-using defendant, particularly if she is poor, a racial minority, or socially marginalized.

The possibility that a criminal trial will simply confirm the unconscious selection biases of health care providers and prosecutors is enhanced by the psychosocial dynamics of judge and jury decisionmaking. At every stage of a potential legal proceeding discretion is exercised by multiple actors, including health care professionals, social services investigators, police, prosecutors, judges, and jurors. All will inevitably bring a host of psychological shortcuts (heuristics) and other processes to the decisions they reach about liability and criminal responsibility. Daniel Kahneman and other social scientists have found that people are usually very good at reaching almost instantaneous judgments about a wide variety of social situations. However, while we are frequently right, we also have a hard time recognizing when we are wrong, or even likely to be wrong, and we cling to the belief in our own infallibility.[181] Like the rest of us, jurors are heavily influenced by unconscious and biased prototypes and tend to reach conclusions based on the extent to which a particular defendant does or does not fit such a prototype.[182] News media frequently frame the problem of drug use by pregnant women along racial and class lines, making those images highly "available" to jurors deciding a criminal case. Where the defendant is a poor, single mother struggling with substance abuse, particularly if she is African-American or Latina, jurors are likely to unconsciously summon mental images of appropriate mothering that can have a disproportionate impact on their decisions. Stereotypes of "good" and "bad" mothering are also deeply embedded in Western culture and have the potential for outsize influence on the decisions of jurors and judges.[183] Finally, as Professor Carol Anderson has noted, jurors are prone to the fundamental attribution error—that is, the tendency to see others' difficulties as problems of their own making while attributing the problems that befall us (the jurors) to external forces, beyond our control. For a jury considering the case of a defendant who used drugs while pregnant, this translates into a strong likelihood that the jury will overlook the specific circumstances of the woman's life (disregarding the rule of negligence law that those circumstances are *supposed* to be considered in deciding whether *this* woman fell below the standard of the reasonable pregnant woman) and will evaluate the defendant based on an idealized pregnant woman who would strive to do virtually anything to promote the health of her developing fetus. In this situation, application of the ostensibly neutral standard of "the reasonable pregnant woman" is likely to result in a criminal conviction.

D. The Rules of Causation Make Prosecution and Conviction of Pregnant Women More Likely

Two aspects of American law on causation make the criminal prosecution of drug-using pregnant women easier and more likely to succeed. First, the historical preference of American law for a unitary, rather than multifactorial, model of causation makes it easy for American lawyers, prosecutors, and juries to focus on the behavior of pregnant women, including drug use, as *the cause* of harm to their not-yet-born children, ignoring other environmental and human factors that may have contributed to the adverse birth outcome. Second, the highly elastic nature of legal causation, particularly the use of "foreseeability" in constructing proximate cause, makes the criminal prosecution and conviction of drug-using pregnant women likely.

As noted in chapter 2, this emphasis on the central role of individuals in causation has deep historic roots. It reflects not only the political views of the Enlightenment that all men were free agents, who, by acting together, could form a legitimate government but also deep-seated religious and moral notions of personal accountability before God. Other, more distant causes of harm were simply incomprehensible. In the Middle Ages, while one common response to misfortune was to view it as an act of God, another response, as in the case of periodic epidemics of plague, was to blame disfavored or deviant individuals, such as Jews or female healers, with the former being killed "en masse" and the latter being burned at the stake as witches.[184] Today, this emphasis on individual actions, rather than larger external forces, is a central theme in American culture. It is a significant and often unquestioned part of the narrative of American history, as well as a frequently offered explanation of current economic and social disparities.[185]

The focus on individual human action is also apparent in the law's two requirements for establishing causation: "actual cause" and "proximate cause." Discussions of actual cause, which usually rely on the "but for" test, proceed as if actual cause could be determined by applying the principles of physics and drawing an invisible straight line from the actions of the defendant to the prohibited result. Yet in reality, deciding whether one person's actions caused a result involves a complex process of causal attribution, in which the psychological framing of actions is critical.[186] Proximate cause is a limitation on legal responsibility that is predicated on foreseeability. Only if the defendant could have foreseen the potential harmful consequences of her actions can she be found guilty.[187] However, because hindsight is 20/20, proximate cause is pretty easy to establish.[188]

Today most legal scholars recognize that determining actual and proximate cause is inevitably value laden. Decisions about causation—either articulating general principles or applying those principles to the "facts" of a particular litigated case—reflect prevailing cultural norms about individual, corporate, and societal responsibility. As we saw in examining the psychosocial construction of risk, research on how we resolve questions about causation demonstrates that the way in which jurors and others draw "conclusions about cause and effect is not [a matter of science—that is,] . . . of passive discovery of objective fact."[189]

The malleability of the key concepts of foreseeability and causation, as well as the law's preference for single causes, helps to explain why prosecutors have been so successful in indicting—and convicting—drug-using pregnant women. Some of the crimes charged—child abuse or child endangerment—do not require *any* showing of causation, because the crime is complete when the woman acted, for example, by taking a drink or using cocaine. However, many of the serious criminal charges brought in recent years—homicide by child abuse (*McKnight*) and murder (*Aiwohi, Gibbs*, and *Hernandez*)—require the prosecution to establish causation. The prosecution must prove a causal relationship between the woman's behavior, the *actus reus*, and a prohibited result, death. The prosecution must prove that "but for" the woman's ingesting drugs, the fetus would not have been stillborn or born prematurely and died thereafter (establishing "actual cause") *and* that it was reasonably foreseeable that this drug use could cause the harm that occurred, so that it is "just" to hold the woman criminally responsible (establishing "proximate cause"). Further, the prosecutor must demonstrate causation by proof beyond a reasonable doubt. Although it might seem that prosecutors would find it difficult to meet this heavy burden of proof, this has not turned out to be the case. Let us consider why.

The prosecutor's first hurdle is to establish actual cause. We know that adverse birth outcomes—stillbirths, preterm delivery, and low birthweight—are frequently the result of multiple causes (including maternal disease and poor nutrition), that in many cases it is impossible to pinpoint any one cause, and that as a statistical matter these adverse birth outcomes occur disproportionately among poor women and African-American women. Thus, at first glance it might appear that prosecutors would often face an uphill battle proving actual cause—that but for the mother's taking drugs this adverse event would not have occurred—beyond a reasonable doubt. Yet in practice this has not happened. For example, in the *Hernandez* case there was little evidence that methamphetamine use is causally related to *any* stillbirths, let alone the death of Ms. Hernandez's child. The prosecutor avoided the evidentiary gap in his case by charging Ms. Hernandez with first-degree murder and pressuring her to plead guilty with the promise of a more lenient sentence. After Ms. Hernandez had spent three years in jail awaiting trial, the plea deal was surely a tempting offer, and she chose not to test the strength of the prosecution's case.[190] In the *Gibbs* case, when an African-American teenager suffered a stillbirth at thirty-six weeks, Mississippi prosecutors insisted on filing criminal charges based on an autopsy that found traces of cocaine in the stillborn infant, despite the fact that the infant was delivered with its umbilical cord wrapped around its neck. It took six years for a trial judge to dismiss the indictment on other grounds.

The case of Regina McKnight illustrates how hard it may be for defense counsel to counter a jury's inclination to find causation based solely on the presence of drugs or an admission of drug use by the pregnant woman. In *McKnight*, the prosecution presented testimony at the first and second trials that Ms. McKnight's cocaine use was the sole cause of the stillbirth, rejecting alternative explanations. At the first trial, the defense challenged the prosecution's expert witnesses by offering its own expert witness, who testified that the stillbirth was caused not by cocaine but by several maternal infections.[191] This expert also testified that recent medical research had shown that cocaine use during pregnancy could not be conclusively linked to stillbirth and pointed out flaws in the earlier research on cocaine and stillbirths. After lengthy jury deliberation, the first trial ended in a mistrial. However, at Ms. McKnight's second trial her lawyer, the county public defender, failed to call the same expert witnesses. Instead she called only one expert, whose testimony largely tracked that of the prosecution's two expert witnesses. The jury deliberated for just thirty minutes before finding Ms. McKnight guilty of homicide by child abuse. After Ms. McKnight had spent eight years in prison, the South Carolina Supreme Court found that the failure of her defense lawyer to offer testimony to rebut the prosecution's evidence on causation constituted ineffective assistance of counsel. Although in *McKnight* it was defense counsel, rather than the prosecutor, who did an inadequate job of presenting evidence about causation, the case stands as a cautionary tale about how easy it can be to establish causation to the satisfaction of a jury in these types of cases. Doctors' testimony that "to a reasonable medical certainty" a pregnant woman's drug use was the sole cause of a stillbirth, rejecting other plausible explanations, can be incredibly powerful. Jurors can readily envision cocaine metabolites crossing the placenta (thus making harm from cocaine use literally foreseeable) and may be tempted to disregard evidence that suggests other causes of stillbirth, or even that no cause has been established beyond a reasonable doubt, since the cause of stillbirth is unknown in nearly half of all cases.

In contrast, as Lynn Paltrow, Executive Director of the nonprofit organization National Advocates for Pregnant Women, points out, "If a pregnant, drug-using woman were a corporation, her case wouldn't even get to trial because the rules of evidence require that there be science to prove causation."[192] Prosecutions of drug-using pregnant women can indeed be usefully compared to criminal cases brought against deep-pocketed corporations, who rely on skilled lawyers and highly paid expert witnesses to challenge the prosecution's case on causation. In *People v. Warner-Lambert Co.*,[193] a case read by several generations of law students, a prosecutor indicted a major manufacturing corporation and four high-level employees after an explosion caused a devastating fire in its factory, killing six workers. The explosion had been predicted by the corporation's insurance carrier, who expressed concern that the factory contained high levels of magnesium stearate dust, which was potentially explosive. After a grand jury indicted Warner-Lambert, the trial judge ruled that there was not legally sufficient evidence of causation and dismissed the indictment. The New York Courts of Appeals agreed. The court ruled that because the actual cause of the spark that ignited the explosion could not be pinpointed, the prosecution was legally unable to establish that the actual cause was foreseeable and thus could not prove causation beyond a reasonable doubt. Yet here the risk of explosion that existed in the defendant's factory was not only foreseeable but was actually foreseen by the defendants. The Court of Appeals' decision prevented the case from going to trial out of concern that the jury would speculate about causation and improperly convict the manufacturer.[194] Similar concern over the possibility that juries will speculate about the causal connection between a pregnant woman's use of drugs and an adverse birth outcome has been largely absent from judicial decisions imposing and upholding lengthy prison sentences for pregnant women.

IV. New Statutes Criminalizing Pregnancy

In addition to prosecutors' expansive use of existing criminal laws to prosecute pregnant women who use drugs, state legislatures have recently enacted new laws that explicitly criminalize the use of illegal drugs while pregnant as well as other behavior that could be risky to fetal development. In 2010 the Utah legislature enacted a statute that made it a homicide, ranging from vehicular homicide to aggravated murder,[195] to intentionally, knowingly, recklessly, or negligently "cause the death of . . . an unborn child at any stage of its development." The precise crime that can be charged under this statute varies with the defendant's mental state, so that a convicted defendant can be sentenced to death if she acted intentionally or knowingly. The law was apparently enacted in reaction to a tragic case in which a pregnant Utah teenager responded to her boyfriend's threat to dump her if she did not "get rid of" her pregnancy by hiring a stranger to beat her in order to induce a miscarriage.[196] Although the law provides exemptions for legal abortions and refusal of medical treatment, it does not preclude prosecution for intentional or knowing acts that result in fetal death.[197] As a result, today women in Utah are vulnerable to prosecution for homicide based on drug use, with all the problems inherent in such prosecutions.

In 2014, the Tennessee legislature made it a crime to use illegal narcotics while pregnant. Supporters of the Tennessee law claimed that it would serve as a "velvet hammer" to force mothers to enter drug treatment, because the law provided an "affirmative defense" to women who began drug treatment while pregnant and continued drug treatment until after their babies were born. Opponents claimed that the law's real goal was to punish a targeted group of drug-using pregnant women, rather than to promote fetal health. Opponents pointed out that there were already not enough treatment programs available, particularly in rural counties. Medical and public health groups further asserted, to no avail, that the law would do nothing to assist women in getting off drugs and would instead only drive women away from treatment.[198] Two years later, the opponents prevailed. In 2016 the legislature decided not to reauthorize the law. In effect, the law identified a subset of drug-using pregnant women—those who abuse illegal, rather than legal, substances, and cannot afford or gain access to drug treatment—and singled them out for punishment. Further, because the law deemed it irrelevant whether the newborn was actually harmed by the mother's drug use, the law was both under- and over-inclusive. This leads inevitably to the question of whether compulsory substance abuse treatment of pregnant women who use drugs is ever appropriate or desirable.

V. Civil Commitment

Currently more than thirty states authorize the involuntary civil commitment—that is, compelled confinement—of pregnant women based on their use of drugs. In most states such commitment is permitted under broadly worded laws that authorize the confinement of adults who are mentally ill and dangerous to others;[199] in these states *others* is interpreted to include embryos and fetuses. Five states—Minnesota, Oklahoma, North Dakota, South Dakota, and Wisconsin—explicitly sanction the civil commitment of pregnant women who are using alcohol or controlled substances.[200] Minnesota was the first state to enact such a statute.[201] The Minnesota law requires physicians to test all pregnant women who they suspect may be using drugs, without their knowledge. This, of course, is precisely the sort of nonconsensual search and seizure that the Supreme Court declared unconstitutional in *Ferguson v. City of Charleston*.[202] If the drug test is positive, the physician is required to report the woman to child protective services, which may then initiate civil commitment proceedings. However, the law contains a giant loophole. Physicians are not obligated to report women who are using alcohol or marijuana *if* they are providing them with health care services. In effect this gives preferential treatment to women who have an ongoing physician–patient relationship and who are using drugs that are viewed by the legislature as less dangerous.[203] In 1998 the Wisconsin legislature passed a similar civil commitment law, apparently in reaction to the Wisconsin Supreme Court's decision in the *Angela M.W.* case that a fetus was not a "child" within the meaning of the child protection statute and that pregnant women could not be compelled to undergo treatment.[204] Oklahoma, North Dakota, and South Dakota enacted their laws more recently.[205]

The exact number of women involuntarily confined under these laws is unknown, but anecdotal evidence suggests that the laws are used frequently. Many women who are subjected to these laws are indigent and unable to afford a lawyer to represent them, so they cannot effectively fight their involuntary commitment. However, the recent case of Alicia Beltran garnered national headlines. In 2013 Ms. Beltran, a twenty-eight-year-old Wisconsin woman who was twelve weeks' pregnant and seeking prenatal care, confided her prior drug use to a physician's assistant during an intake interview. Ms. Beltran acknowledged her previous dependence on Percocet, a prescription painkiller, but stated that she had weaned herself off it by using another drug, Suboxone. The physician's assistant recommended that Ms. Beltran continue the use of Suboxone, but she declined to do so because she was already drug free. Two weeks later Ms. Beltran was arrested, handcuffed, and held in jail before receiving a hearing in front of a family court commissioner. Ms. Beltran was denied a lawyer to represent her, despite the fact that the district attorney's office was representing the local child protective services agency and a separate guardian had been appointed to represent the fetus. The family court commissioner ordered Ms. Beltran to be confined against her will in an inpatient drug treatment facility two hours from her home. She remained there for seventy-eight days; during that time she was offered counseling but no medical treatment *or* prenatal care, and she lost her job. Ms. Beltran brought suit in federal court in Wisconsin, challenging her confinement as a violation of her constitutional rights to privacy and autonomy, due process, and equal protection of the laws, as well as her right to be free from cruel and unusual punishment. The federal court dismissed her suit as moot because she was no longer pregnant or in custody and the state proceedings had been dismissed.[206]

Many legal and medical commentators have criticized civil commitment as a poorly designed response to concerns about pregnant women's drug use. They assert that involuntary treatment will not lead to a decrease in pregnant women's drug use but will, instead, simply drive it underground, since women will be afraid to be candid with health care providers and may even avoid prenatal care, ultimately leading to poorer outcomes for fetal and child health. A study of low-income women who delivered their babies at an inner-city hospital in Detroit bears this out. The study participants told researchers that if Michigan adopted a law mandating that women whose babies tested positive for drugs be sent to jail, substance-abusing women would be less likely to seek prenatal care, drug testing, or drug treatment. When the study's authors then sought to interview women in a state with a law that currently threatened incarceration, all known drug users refused to participate in the study out of fear of self-incrimination.[207] In contrast, if women are encouraged to enter substance abuse treatment voluntarily, are assisted in locating a treatment program, and can obtain comprehensive treatment responsive to the needs of pregnant women, they are more likely to be able to reduce, if not completely eliminate, their drug use.

This noncoercive approach was endorsed by the Supreme Court of Canada in *Winnipeg Child & Family Services v. G.D.F.*,[208] a tragic case involving a young aboriginal woman, referred to in court papers as Ms. G.D.F. She was addicted to sniffing glue ("solvents") and already had three children, two of whom had been injured by exposure to solvents *in utero*. When Ms. G.D.F. became pregnant again she oscillated between seeking and rejecting treatment, behavior that is typical of many women who use drugs. Treatment was unavailable when Ms. G.D.F first sought it. When a treatment slot later opened up, social workers came to Ms. G.D.F.'s home to take her to a treatment center. Because she was intoxicated at the time, she refused to go. The local social services agency sought a court order compelling her to enter treatment, and a trial judge granted it.

On appeal, the Supreme Court of Canada reversed the trial judge. The Court declared as a principle of tort law and civil commitment law that pregnant women could not be treated as the guarantors of fetal health. The Court first articulated a concern about a slippery slope. It reasoned that if it recognized *some* behavior by pregnant women as justifying either government intervention or tort suits brought on behalf of their children, there would be no principled way to draw a line defining permissible and impermissible acts. "[Women could] be held liable for any behavior during pregnancy having potentially adverse effects on her fetus, including failure to eat properly, [the use of legal or illegal drugs] . . . , exposing herself to infectious disease or to workplace hazards, engaging in immoderate exercise or sexual intercourse . . . [or other acts]," leaving them unable to control their bodies or make independent decisions. Significantly, the Court rejected the notion that pregnant women were "choosing" to use drugs and thereby put their fetuses at risk. It declared, "[L]ifestyle 'choices' like alcohol consumption, drug abuse, and poor nutrition may be the products of circumstance and illness rather than free choice capable of effective deterrence by . . . legal sanction."[209]

VI. In an Ideal World, What Treatment Works Best?
A. Gender Matters

Despite the insistence of many American prosecutors, legislators, and judges that criminal prosecution and civil commitment are necessary "to send a message" and "protect the unborn," recent research has identified many paths to successful voluntary treatment. Treatment works when it is tailored to the needs of pregnant women and recognizes that many women suffer from both substance abuse and mental illness, "co-occurring disorders." The biological, psychological, and social differences between men and women who use drugs necessitate differences in treatment, simply because their processes of addiction and relapse are different. Women face significant obstacles in gaining access to appropriate care for substance abuse and co-occurring mental illness.[210] First, the stigma surrounding the use of alcohol and other drugs makes it hard for women to seek treatment, particularly in cultural and ethnic groups where such use is taboo. Frequently, the families of addicted women are either in denial that the woman has a drug problem or are part of that problem.[211] Substance-abusing women are more likely than men to be poor, homeless, young, not well educated, unemployed, and/or members of racial minorities.[212] In practice, this means not only that they are less likely to be able to afford treatment, given the small number of publicly funded treatment slots,[213] but also that success in treatment will be harder to achieve, as a result of practical economic and structural barriers such as the lack of drug-free housing and affordable and efficient transportation to treatment centers.[214] Even when women are able to obtain substance abuse treatment, it is frequently not available in an optimal setting.[215] Women are more likely than men to have child care and other family obligations that make inpatient care and other intensive treatment impracticable, yet for many women this type of treatment offers the best chance of getting off drugs.[216]

B. Special Concerns in Treating Pregnant Women

As is the case with other women who abuse drugs, pregnant drug users face many barriers in obtaining high quality integrated health care services that address pregnancy, mental illness, and addiction. Many poor women are likely to avoid the public health care system (the only one they can access) if doing so means that their drug use will be detected and reported to authorities, as has been the case in Charleston, Amarillo, and elsewhere.[217] Pregnant women need immediate treatment in order to reduce their drug use and thus limit fetal drug exposure, but frequently it is difficult to obtain a place in any treatment program, let alone one designed to meet the special needs of pregnant and parenting women. Historically many drug treatment programs declined to provide care either out of a fear of legal liability if the woman or fetus should be injured or because many women lacked public or private health insurance.[218] In the 1980s, many substance abuse treatment programs would not accept pregnant women. While the situation has improved somewhat, it still is often difficult for women to find a treatment slot.[219]

Many pregnant drug users find that health care providers fail to understand their difficulties in reducing or abstaining from drug use, while substance abuse treatment programs often ignore the physical and psychological realities of pregnancy.[220] Federal law requires that pregnant women receive priority in obtaining drug treatment and that treatment be provided within forty-eight hours of a woman's requesting it. However, this mandate has not been met. Today less than 5 percent of pregnant drug users are able to access substance abuse treatment, and less than 13 percent of all substance abuse treatment programs in the United

States had programs for pregnant or postpartum women.[221] In addition, while only a small number of programs focus on pregnant women, even fewer programs offer services to new mothers.[222] Caring for a newborn is a daunting prospect under the best of circumstances. As a result, many new mothers relapse and increase their drug use under the stress of parenting.[223]

C. Innovative Treatment That Works

Neither draconian criminal justice strategies nor involuntary civil commitment will stop pregnant women with substance abuse problems from using drugs. Yet one "harm reduction" strategy that has been successful in reducing or ending drug use is treatment that uses "carrots," rather than "sticks," to encourage people dependent on drugs to voluntarily reduce their drug use. "Carrots"—the incentives of positive rewards—can be a powerful tool in helping them reduce or eliminate their drug use. Psychologist Gene Heyman and others have found that incentives can jump-start desirable behavior, setting the stage for a more permanent recovery from addiction. Many researchers have demonstrated that addicts can be motivated to become abstinent or to substantially reduce their drug use by contingent financial incentives, offered in conjunction with counseling and other supportive services.[224] Although so far most contingent management programs have treated pregnant women in regard to their tobacco addiction,[225] there is no reason that the programs could not be expanded to include pregnant drug addicts who use alcohol and illegal drugs.

Conclusion

If pregnant drug users are to succeed in ending or reducing their drug use, legislators, prosecutors, and proponents of involuntary treatment must give up the punitive, counterproductive strategy they have pursued in recent decades, trying to threaten or scare pregnant women into giving up drugs. While such a strategy may have superficial public appeal and carry short term political benefits for legislators and prosecutors, it does little to stop pregnant women's drug use. Instead, what pregnant drug users and addicts need, and what works best, is comprehensive, integrated health care that addresses their physical and mental health needs, provides substance abuse treatment, and offers individualized support in accessing services such as housing, transportation, and child care.[226] Contingent management programs that provide concrete financial incentives to initiate and sustain drug abstinence should be an important part of the overall treatment strategy.[227] Treatment and social service interventions must acknowledge the difficult economic and social realities that many pregnant drug users confront. They must also recognize the underlying causes of women's addiction, including the frequent co-occurrence of depression and PTSD, and their connection with childhood physical and sexual abuse and intimate partner violence in adulthood.[228] Until government and health care interventions make it possible for addicted women to live safely, away from drug-using and physically abusive partners, future generations of children will remain at risk.

6

Caught in the Crossfire

Breastfeeding (or Not) as Dangerous Behavior

Do you want to bring everyone back to his first duties? Begin with mothers. . . . The whole moral order degenerates; naturalness is extinguished in all hearts [when wet nurses, and not their mothers, nourish infants]. . . . Let women once again become mothers, men will soon become husbands and fathers again.
—Jean-Jacques Rousseau, *Emile*[1]

You wouldn't take risks before your baby's born. [On-screen text as a very pregnant African-American woman rides a gyrating mechanical bull. After the woman is thrown off the bull] Why start after? Breastfeed exclusively for 6 months.
—The National Breastfeeding Awareness Campaign, 2004[2]

No matter what, she was the mother. . . . She was failed, but she should have been strong enough to do more.
—Juror explaining why she voted to convict Tabitha Walrond of negligent homicide for breastfeeding her son despite evidence that he was losing weight, even though Walrond was not told that her breast-reduction surgery could make breastfeeding unsuccessful and bureaucratic obstacles prevented her from getting health insurance for her son[3]

Introduction

This chapter examines the medical, legal, and psychosocial construction of risk in the context of breastfeeding. Once again, the mother stands at center stage in public and private discussion of risk and children's health. Should the decision to breastfeed—or to refrain from breastfeeding—be a matter of personal choice for women and their families or is it instead a medical, moral, or legal imperative, essential for the promotion and protection of children's health?[4] Over the past three decades some physicians, government officials, and "lactivists" have framed breastfeeding as the key to assuring individual and public health, claiming that breastfeeding confers enormous benefits on children and mothers and asserting that mothers who elect not to breastfeed are "risking" their children's health and intellectual development. Others push back, contending that opting to breastfeed—or not—is a minor event in a lifetime of parenting, one of many childrearing decisions that women and their partners should be free to make in the context of their personal preferences, values, and resources. So far only a handful of cases have arisen in which a mother's decision to breastfeed has led to legal action. However, this is beginning to change in the wake of the Affordable Care Act, which requires large employers to accommodate nursing mothers.

Regardless of one's beliefs about the extent of breastfeeding's benefits, one may well ask why the focus should be on individual mothers, rather than on government and corporate policies, especially those governing health care access and the availability of paid maternity and paternity leave. The lack of health care and parenting leave makes it difficult for many mothers who would otherwise choose to breastfeed to do so. While government and medical authorities emphasize the "risks" of not breastfeeding, the United States is the only developed nation that does not mandate paid maternity leave,[5] which would, of course, make it much easier for new mothers to have the time and other resources to nurse their infants. We previously encountered this individualistic, mother-centric approach in pregnancy. There, we noted that some physicians, and many politicians and prosecutors, treated maternal substance abuse solely as a medical or criminal problem, located within the mother's body, while ignoring the multiple external and societal factors that contribute to both substance abuse and potential adverse outcomes for infants exposed to drugs *in utero*.[6]

This chapter considers the pivotal role of the medical profession in shaping mothers' views about breastfeeding, as well as the attitudes of society at large. It documents a history of remarkable shifts in "expert" professional opinion over time concerning the desirability of nursing, as opposed to bottle-feeding, newborn children and infants. The chapter will scrutinize the strengths and weaknesses of the medical and scientific case for breastfeeding, emphasizing the crucial distinction between association and causation and paying particular attention to the difference between absolute and relative risk. The chapter examines the current debate over breastfeeding in order to explore how the law both reflects and reinforces prevailing cultural norms. In breastfeeding, like other areas of childrearing, risk is socially and legally constructed in a way that makes mothers the virtual guarantors of their children's health, ignoring the many other factors that contribute to healthy child development. Over the past forty years, government policy and law have influenced American mothers' choices about breastfeeding. Unlike the context of pregnancy, in which civil and criminal actions against individual mothers-to-be provide the frame for questions of risk, the debate about breastfeeding focuses primarily on law as an instrument of social and health policy.

I. A History of Breastfeeding in America

For millennia, there was not much to discuss about breastfeeding. Nursing at a woman's breast was essential to the health of individual children and the survival of the species. When a woman could not breastfeed or the mother died in childbirth, other mothers who were already nursing their own infants stepped up to feed her child, because women's milk production expands to meet the demand. In societies ranging from the ancient Greeks to French and English aristocracies, the position of wet nurse evolved to assist elite women who preferred not to breastfeed.[7] In colonial America, Puritan ministers preached that women had a religious duty to breastfeed. Cotton Mather delivered a sermon in which he declared, "You will *Suckle Your Infant your Self* if you can; Be Not Such an *Ostrich* as to Decline it, meerly [sic] because you would be one of the *Careless Women living at Ease*."[8]

After the Civil War, patterns of infant feeding began to change, following Swiss chemist Henri Nestlé's invention of infant formula in 1867 and the advent of commercial formulas in the United States.[9] By the close of the nineteenth century, more than three-quarters of "'well-to-do'" children were "'fed at some font other than the maternal breast,'"[10] reflecting their mothers' desire to be free of the discomfort and other constraints of breastfeeding. Frequently poor women also did not breastfeed, finding that nursing was too labor intensive because they were working full time, inside and outside the home.[11] In urban areas bottle-fed infants died at rates as high as fifteen times the death rate for breastfed babies, because cow's milk, the available substitute, was often unpasteurized or was adulterated with chalk or other substances. Many infants died from dehydration, diarrhea, and other illnesses contracted from tainted cow's milk.[12]

During the last quarter of the nineteenth century and the beginning of the twentieth century, pediatricians, members of a newly emerging medical specialty searching for a *raison d'être*, responded to the high infant mortality rate in multiple ways. Some pediatricians continued to encourage breastfeeding, believing it was the healthiest choice. In urban areas, squads of public health nurses were deployed to make personal contact with mothers and assist them in breastfeeding. Other pediatricians sought to introduce greater hygiene and pasteurization to the production of cow's milk, making it safe to drink for infants and children living in the cities. Still others sought a solution in the development of "scientific" infant formulas to replace human milk.[13] As a result, by the early twentieth century, many American women did not breastfeed, although the majority of infants were breastfed through the 1920s.[14]

Ironically, pediatricians' quest for a technological fix accelerated the decline in breastfeeding. By the 1930s, a new generation of pediatricians had not experienced the crisis in infant deaths of the early twentieth century. These pediatricians tended to believe that formula was just as good as human milk and frequently counseled new mothers against breastfeeding.[15] As a result, formula use began to rise.[16] Middle- and upper-class women were again the most likely to bottle-feed their infants.[17]

By the mid–twentieth century, breastfeeding rates had fallen sharply. Although the American Academy of Pediatrics' official policy was that breastfeeding was preferred,[18] individual pediatricians often took a different position. Many were not knowledgeable about breastfeeding, and their views were influenced significantly by the visits of infant formula "detail men." These were representatives of formula manufacturers, who extolled the advantages of their particular brand of formula in office visits and by offering physicians paid vacations,[19] employing a practice known, apparently without irony, as "ethical marketing."[20] Pediatricians *and* formula companies promoted formula as a "scientific" product whose chemical content was known and whose intake could be measured.[21] "Modern" women who left the paid workforce after World War II and wanted to continue to enjoy the freedom they had enjoyed as working women also chose formula-feeding.[22] Breastfeeding rates plummeted, falling by 50 percent from 1946 to 1956, the era when most Baby Boomers were born.[23] This trend continued through the 1960s. By 1971 only 21 percent of American infants were breastfed at the time of hospital discharge; only 6 percent were still nursing five to six months later.[24]

In the 1970s, pediatricians and other childrearing experts promoted a new paradigm of the mother–child relationship that helped build demand for breastfeeding. Specifically, pediatricians and childrearing experts propounded the theory of "bonding," a connection between mother and infant in the post-birth period that was touted as both a mystical union and the human analogue to the joining of two pieces of wood by Super Glue.[25] Advocates declared that bonding was essential in order to avoid child abuse; they urged mothers to breastfeed to build the requisite physical closeness between mother and infant. When the "bonding" hypothesis was developed, an emphasis on maternal–infant closeness made sense as a counterweight to the heavily medicalized notions of childbirth prominent in the mid–twentieth century, which did indeed separate mothers from their newborns for many hours after birth. But the ever-lengthening time frame of "bonding" proponents, which expanded the importance of mother–infant closeness from the period right after birth to the entire first year of a child's life, was not scientifically supported. Instead, it reflected a distorted view of parental caregiving, heavily skewed by gender bias.[26] Indeed, as professor and psychologist Diane Eyer has observed, despite the fact that the scientific justification for the theory of bonding was extraordinarily weak, it readily became accepted wisdom, catching on precisely because it offered a simplistic solution to complex medical and social problems. Bonding also affirmed the authority of physicians at the very moment that the need for pediatricians' expertise was being eroded by the conquering of major childhood illnesses and the hegemony of obstetricians in the birth process was being challenged by feminist critics.[27]

In response to pro-bonding arguments as well as other trends in labor and delivery, breastfeeding rates grew in the late 1970s and early 1980s.

Middle- and upper-class women led the new trend toward increased breastfeeding.[28] After a sharp decline from 1984 to 1989, breastfeeding rates increased until the end of the twentieth century, when they plateaued for several years.[29] Recently, breastfeeding rates have risen again, slowly and gradually. Among infants born in 2011, 79 percent were breastfed at least once and 26 percent were still breastfeeding at one year. However, rates of exclusive breastfeeding (no other food or formula) drop dramatically between three months (40 percent) and six months (less than 19 percent), reflecting the reality that relatively few women can breastfeed 24/7 once they return to work.[30] Of course, these numbers are averages, concealing significant geographical, educational, racial, class, and age differences in breastfeeding practices among women. The women most likely to breastfeed are older, wealthier, white, and well-educated, who have good health insurance, live in western states, and do not work full time outside the home.[31] Immigrant women are more likely to breastfeed than their non-immigrant peers. Strikingly, the likelihood of breastfeeding decreases about 4 percent a year for each additional year an immigrant woman lives in the United States.[32]

II. Is It "Risky" Not to Breastfeed?

A. The American Academy of Pediatrics: How a "Recommendation" Became a Mandate

Over the past twenty years the American Academy of Pediatrics (AAP) has pushed to make breastfeeding the norm for all infants and their mothers, increasingly emphasizing breastfeeding as an obligation, not an option. In 1997, the Academy's Committee on Breastfeeding released a policy statement supporting breastfeeding for all infants.[33] It recommended that women breastfeed exclusively for the first six months after birth and continue breastfeeding throughout the infant's first year, even while providing solid food after six months.[34] However, the Academy declared that "[t]he ultimate decision on feeding of the infant is the mother's."[35]

The Academy extolled the benefits of breastfeeding. It cited what it described as "strong evidence" that breastfeeding reduced the incidence of numerous infectious diseases in infants and children such as diarrhea, respiratory infections, meningitis, and otitis media (ear infections).

The Academy cited additional benefits, including "*possible* protective effect[s] . . . against sudden infant death syndrome, . . . diabetes[,] . . . Crohn's disease," and other chronic illnesses, as well as the "*possible* enhancement of cognitive development."[36] The Academy also touted "*possible* health benefits for mothers"[37] and noted that breastfeeding would save an average family $400 in the costs of food and formula during a child's first year.[38]

In 2005, the Academy ramped up its promotion of breastfeeding by issuing a new policy statement.[39] Notably, it eliminated its 1997 statement that breastfeeding was the mother's decision to make.[40] It declared that "postneonatal infant mortality rates in the United States are reduced by [an astonishing] 21% in breastfed infants." This bold statement was based on *one* study of *accidental* deaths, despite the obvious fact that the connection between breastfeeding and accidental deaths appears tenuous, to say the least, because there is no plausible biological mechanism to support a causal relationship between them.[41] The new policy statement identified "neurodevelopment" as a separate benefit of breastfeeding and also cited studies suggesting that breastfed infants were less likely to suffer from obesity and asthma as older children or adults.[42] For the first time the Academy recommended that premature and low birthweight infants receive either their mother's pumped milk or the milk of other mothers obtained from milk banks, to be fortified with nutritional supplements.[43] Additionally, the Academy asserted that increased breastfeeding would bring "community benefits," including "decreased annual health care costs of $3.6 billion in the United States," decreased costs for the federal WIC Program (the Special Supplemental Nutrition Program for Women, Infants, and Children), reduced parental absenteeism from work and thus less income lost, and smaller environmental and energy burdens due to decreased formula consumption.[44]

In 2012 the Academy issued yet another policy statement that made even more extravagant claims for breastfeeding's benefits. This statement explicitly framed the decision not to breastfeed as risky to children's health. It asserted that the "risk" of myriad infant and childhood illnesses, including the risk of suffering from child abuse and neglect, was reduced by exclusive breastfeeding for the first three to four months, with risk reductions ranging from 15 to 77 percent.[45] *Any* breastfeeding at all was said to reduce the risk of gastroenteritis, ear infections, Type

2 diabetes, and obesity. Further, the Academy cited a study claiming that more than 900 infant lives annually could be saved if 90 percent of American mothers breastfed exclusively for six months.[46] The Academy claimed that breastfed infants had higher IQ scores and teacher ratings.[47]

The Academy acknowledged that "the majority of published reports are observational cohort studies and systematic reviews/meta-analyses," but it failed to discuss the scientific implications of these research methods. The Academy did not rely on randomized controlled studies—the scientific gold standard—which are the only sure way to demonstrate that the claimed outcomes are the result of an intervention—here, breastfeeding—rather than confounding variables.[48] This is a serious omission, because association is not the equivalent of causation.[49] In the case of breastfeeding, the mother's educational background, economic status, IQ, smoking status, and prior commitment to breastfeeding are each important independent variables that can lead to the positive outcomes that the Academy claimed for breastfeeding. Notably, the studies the Academy cited did not show a clear dose–response relationship between breastfeeding and the desired heath outcome (i.e., whether the children were breastfed exclusively or only occasionally, and whether it was for a short time or many months), something that would be expected if breastfeeding were indeed the "magic bullet" that the Academy claimed. Further, these studies did not address whether it is the *act of breastfeeding* or the *consumption of human milk* that makes the difference. Most notably, the policy statement failed to discuss the difference between absolute and relative risk, which would have made it clear that relative differences in risk, even *if* they are supported by strong evidence, are unlikely to have an impact for most children because of the rarity of the events under discussion.

The policy statement ended with a triumphant and sweeping declaration of breastfeeding's benefits, without raising any caveats: "[B]reastfeeding and the use of human milk confer unique nutritional and nonnutritional benefits to the infant and mother and ... optimize infant, child and adult health. ... Recently, published evidence-based studies have confirmed and quantitated the risks of not breastfeeding. Thus, *infant feeding should not be considered as a lifestyle choice but rather as a basic health issue.*"[50]

B. How the Government Became a Key Player in Efforts to Increase Breastfeeding

The federal government has been involved in breastfeeding policy since the early 1980s. Prodded by infant formula manufacturers, the Reagan administration initially opposed international efforts to limit marketing of formula. However, after President Reagan appointed pediatric surgeon C. Everett Koop as Surgeon General, the Department of Health and Human Services (HHS) began to promote breastfeeding.[51] In 1990 the United States signed the Innocenti Declaration, committing the federal government to developing a comprehensive national strategy to increase breastfeeding.[52] During the Clinton administration, Surgeon General David Satcher framed breastfeeding promotion as part of a broader effort to improve the health of all Americans. HHS issued a Blueprint for Action on Breastfeeding, which declared that structural changes in the culture, economy, and legal and health care systems were necessary to make breastfeeding a realistic option for more women.[53]

After the George W. Bush administration took office in 2001, HHS shifted away from systemic reform efforts and ignored the legal impediments to breastfeeding and larger problems of health care access. Instead, HHS focused solely on the *marketing* of breastfeeding so that it would be "recognized as the normal and preferred method of feeding...."[54]

1. THE HHS CAMPAIGN FOR BREASTFEEDING: "BABIES WERE BORN TO BE BREASTFED"

In 2004, the Bush administration launched a national multimedia advertising campaign targeted at first-time parents "who would not normally breastfeed their baby"—that is, poor, less-educated women, and women of color.[55] The campaign hammered home the twin messages that the ideal standard for infant care was exclusive breastfeeding for six months and that all women have "what it takes" to breastfeed.[56] Basing their approach on research with African-American women, the campaign's creators determined that *"[b]reastfeeding benefits need to be recast to have greater perceived consequence"* because "[t]here was no perceived real disadvantage if you didn't breastfeed."[57]

In consequence, HHS released a media blitz about breastfeeding that was deliberately designed to elicit a fear of disaster on the part of non-nursing women. Mothers were transformed from competent adult decisionmakers and women with independent personal and professional lives into "vectors of risk" for their infants.[58] The campaign's centerpiece was a thirty-second television commercial showing a very pregnant African-American woman riding a mechanical bull in a bar, surrounded by a huge crowd. While the bull gyrated fiercely, the woman desperately tried to hold on. The screen turned black, followed by text declaring, "You wouldn't take risks before your baby is born." When the action resumed, the woman was thrown to the ground and the crowd gasped. After the woman stood up, the crowd cheered. The screen again turned black, and the text asked, "Why Start After?" An off screen voice declared, "Babies were born to be breastfed. Recent studies show [that] babies who are breastfed are less likely to develop ear infections, respiratory illnesses and diarrhea . . . ." At the same time, the screen stated, "Breastfeed Exclusively for 6 Months" and then displayed a website and an "800" number for more information about breastfeeding.[59] This sensational tone and a focus on risk pervaded the campaign. Another television commercial showed two pregnant white women engaging in log rolling in white water, with one woman falling off, and the same "risk" message that was presented in the bucking bull ad.[60] A print advertisement displayed a dish with two scoops of ice cream with cherries at their centers, apparently intended to represent female breasts. The photograph was captioned, "Breastfeed for 6 Months. You May Help Reduce Your Child's Risk for Childhood Obesity."[61]

The "Babies Were Born to Be Breastfed" campaign unleashed a storm of criticism. Infant formula manufacturers, as well as many women, objected to the campaign's emphasis on the "risks" of not breastfeeding.[62] Clayton Yeutter, a former Secretary of Agriculture, lobbied on behalf of formula manufacturers and succeeded in having the campaign changed before it began.[63] Arguing that mothers should not be made to feel guilty if they did not nurse, Yeutter also challenged the evidence to support some of the claimed "risks" of not breastfeeding, such as increased risks of leukemia and diabetes.[64] Critics of the critics objected to the formula manufacturers' lobbying, saying that the campaign's pro-breastfeeding message was being "watered down."⁶⁵ The Academy of Pediatrics tried to stake out a middle ground and recommended the elimination of some claims about risk. Ironically, the Academy was criticized as being biased because it received significant financial contributions from formula manufacturers.⁶⁶

Still others questioned the campaign's basic premise—that the reason women do not breastfeed is due to a lack of awareness about its benefits. The philosopher and medical ethicist Rebecca Kukla was blunt. She pointed out that "the information that 'breast is best' [is] . . . now disseminated in every form, from this bare slogan through detailed medical information, through health institutions, media campaigns, physicians, nurses, advice books, prenatal classes, websites, outreach programs for mothers at risk. . . ."⁶⁷ Kukla argued that it was the systemic barriers to breastfeeding—the lack of skilled assistance with breastfeeding mechanics, the failure of workplaces and public spaces to make breastfeeding a realistic possibility, and the economic pressures that made many mothers decide to return to work—that were the actual impediments to breastfeeding, rather than women's failure to appreciate breastfeeding's benefits.⁶⁸ Other commentators questioned whether such negative advertising was either appropriate or effective. Evidence is mixed on whether "fear appeals," advertisements that focus on risk, are persuasive.⁶⁹ Some research shows that optimal results occur at an "'intermediate' level of fear, where the amount of arousal is neither too weak nor too strong."⁷⁰ This approach is much more likely to change behavior than "attempts to frighten people . . . with images of death and injury."⁷¹

The "Babies Were Born to Be Breastfed" campaign was deeply disturbing, because it removed breastfeeding from the realm of normal childrearing choices, which are guided by the advice of health care professionals but remain decisions for individual parents to make. Like the rhetoric of the "bonding" movement thirty years earlier, the government's pro-breastfeeding government marketing campaign articulated a narrow range of acceptable maternal behaviors as being *medically* necessary for a healthy childhood. By implying that women who do not, or cannot, breastfeed are "bad mothers" who put their children at serious risk, the campaign inappropriately placed all the responsibility for childhood health on new mothers. It portrayed nonbreastfeeding mothers as morally deficient and made them feel guilty for making that choice,[72] instead of addressing the multiple obstacles to breastfeeding, which we will turn to shortly.

2. THE SURGEON GENERAL'S CALL TO ACTION

In 2011 President Obama's Surgeon General Dr. Regina Benjamin issued *The Surgeon General's Call to Action to Support Breastfeeding*. Like the "Babies Were Born to Be Breastfed" campaign that preceded it, the *Call to Action* was a highly charged polemic that slanted the scientific evidence in support of breastfeeding and downplayed the equivocal nature of the data on which it relied. For example, the *Call to Action* relied heavily on a 2007 meta-analysis of much of the research on breastfeeding's benefits, conducted by the Agency for Health Care Research and Quality (AHRQ), the research arm of HHS. Yet the AHRQ report made it clear that virtually all of the available studies were observational, not randomized clinical trials, and that much of the underlying data was of middling quality.[73] In contrast, the *Call to Action* soft-pedaled the data's limits, emphasizing the "health risks associated with formula feeding and early weaning from breastfeeding."[74]

C. The Overselling of Breastfeeding

1. HISTORY GIVES REASONS TO BE SKEPTICAL

One need not be a cynic to recognize that medical and scientific certainty is fleeting. One generation's professional wisdom quickly becomes the next era's discredited theory.[75] For example, over the past twenty years professional pediatrics organizations have drastically altered their views on the causes of sudden infant death syndrome (SIDS), completely reversing their recommendations for proper infant sleeping positions. While pediatricians now instruct parents that infants should be placed on their backs when they go to sleep, they had previously urged, with equal certainty and vigor, that infants be put to sleep on their stomachs.[76] Likewise, in the 1930s, '40s, and '50s, pediatricians were convinced that tonsillectomy was the best way to treat children's upper respiratory infections. As a result, the overwhelming majority of children had such surgery, until that too went out of fashion.[77] A similar wave of medical overenthusiasm occurred during the 1980s and '90s, when amoxicillin was routinely administered for sore throats and ear infections, even though less than one-quarter of the children had infections that would respond to antibiotics.[78] Public health experts now assert that this created a dangerous threat to public health, as an entire generation has developed resistance to first-line antibiotics.[79]

2. THE SCIENCE IN SUPPORT OF BREASTFEEDING'S BENEFITS IS WEAK

Many critics have challenged the science put forward to support the claim that breastfeeding improves children's health.[80] Almost all of the research cited by the Academy of Pediatrics consists of retrospective observational studies. These are not randomized clinical trials, in which potential subjects who are matched for demographic and clinical backgrounds are randomly assigned to a treatment or nontreatment group.[81] Many of the studies conflated association with causation. As the 2007 AHRQ report noted, while many studies showed an *association* between breastfeeding and a reduction in some childhood illnesses, *a causal relationship* between breastfeeding and the asserted health outcomes noted *should not be inferred*, because the studies were observational rather than randomized clinical trials.[82] Often the studies were unable to eliminate the influence of confounding variables. Even the authors of a study that claimed to show positive effects of breastfeeding conceded that "causality is difficult to demonstrate for any specific part of the interaction between the breastfeeding mother and her child. *It may be that breastfeeding represents a package of skills, abilities, and emotional attachments that mark families whose infants survive and that it is these factors that produce the benefits seen, rather than breastfeeding or breast milk per se.*"[83] The actual decision to breastfeed may reflect a constellation of confounding variables, encompassing a mother's overall approach to parenting, that are the *real* factors that lead to better health outcomes for breastfed infants, rather than either breastfeeding or human milk.[84]

Indeed, pediatricians who specialized in SIDS research reached precisely this conclusion. After reviewing epidemiologic studies on SIDS' relationship to breastfeeding, the 2005 Academy statement on SIDS declared that "[the studies' inconsistent] results suggest that *factors associated with breastfeeding, rather than breastfeeding itself, are protective.*"[85] These pediatricians hypothesized that maternal smoking might be the true cause of SIDS, because it is associated both with an increased incidence of SIDS and a decreased incidence of breastfeeding.

A basic flaw in many studies relied on by the Academy of Pediatrics, the "Breast Is Best" campaign, and the Surgeon General's *Call to Action* is the lack of a plausible biological mechanism to explain exactly *how* breastfeeding contributes to a claimed health or cognitive benefit. For example, one might anticipate that breastfeeding would confer some immunological protections on newborns and thus decrease the incidence of infectious diseases such as respiratory infections and diarrhea. However, studies do not always show that these immunological responses are at work or demonstrate a dose–response relationship: that is, that the longer a mother breastfeeds, the better outcome her child has. Further, when studies did find that breastfeeding had benefits, it was often for only one gender, or affected conditions that occurred rarely.[86] Many of the studies cited by the Academy examined the impact of breastfeeding for a short duration, while others found that breastfeeding's apparent positive effects diminished over time.[87]

Significantly, the studies relied on by the Academy of Pediatrics and the *Call to Action* fail to demonstrate whether it is human milk or the act of breastfeeding that provides the asserted benefits. Although some of the benefits claimed for human milk might be related to its immunological attributes, other benefits appear connected to a breastfeeding mother's physical proximity to her child, such as close bodily contact and attention focused on the infant.[88] Obviously, such physical closeness can be readily provided by a male or female caregiver feeding a baby with a bottle containing either formula or breast milk.[89]

But what is really missing from the Academy of Pediatrics' policy statements are broader relative risk analyses, which would assess the benefits of breastfeeding compared with other health-promoting behaviors, such as infant vaccination, parents' quitting smoking,[90] children's eating more nutritious food after infancy, and parents' earning enough money to pay for adequate food and housing. Relative risk assessments are critical to developing effective public health policy, because of the need to set priorities in deploying scarce government resources.[91] When physicians and government policymakers decide to make breastfeeding a core strategy to improve children's health, they ignore the impact of other medical interventions. For example, nearly one-third of American infants are born by caesarean section, which makes breastfeeding more difficult for many women.[92]

A recent sibling study supports the conclusion that many studies relied on by the government and the AAP are scientifically flawed. Professors Cynthia Colen and David Ramey suggested strongly that many of the benefits attributed to breastfeeding are in fact the result of racial, economic, and educational differences among mothers. The study analyzed long-term health outcomes for a group of more than 7,000 children from more than 3,000 families, gathered over a period of 24 years. This was a very large longitudinal study, which examined 11 cognitive, behavioral, and health outcomes. By comparing the outcomes of siblings who were born to and raised by the same mother (with at least one breastfed and one formula-fed infant per family), this study automatically controlled for the mother's intelligence, race, ethnicity, and social, economic, and educational status, as well as other intangible factors that might affect children's health outcomes. The study found that *for 10 of the 11 outcomes there was no statistically significant difference between the breastfed and nonbreastfed siblings*. For asthma, the eleventh outcome, the study found that breastfeeding duration was consistently associated with *poorer* health. The authors concluded that these results called into question the prevailing view that breastfeeding leads to major positive outcomes. Instead, the authors suggested, the results reflect pre-existing demographic differences between the *mothers* of breastfed and nonbreastfed children. Because of their finding that it was the mothers themselves, and not their breastfeeding decisions, that led to the observed outcomes, they questioned whether the claimed benefits of breastfeeding are sufficient to justify recommending it as a preferred method of child nourishment.[93]

3. THE RISKS OF BREASTFEEDING

Even assuming that breastfeeding has benefits, it also carries risks. Mothers may transmit diseases to their infants through breastfeeding, including HIV and active tuberculosis. In developed countries, women with these diseases are encouraged not to breastfeed.[94] The Academy of

Pediatrics advises women not to breastfeed if they are receiving chemotherapy or radiation treatment, if they are taking certain prescription drugs, such as antidepressants, or if they are using other illegal or legal drugs.[95]

In other instances there have been heightened medical surveillance and even criminal prosecutions of nursing mothers. The official recommendation of the American Academy of Pediatrics is that mothers who wish to have an occasional glass of beer or wine should imbibe right after nursing, in order to minimize the concentration of alcohol concentration in their milk.[96] Yet in 2014 a breastfeeding mother in Arkansas was arrested for "endangering the welfare of a child" after a waitress reported to the police that the mother had consumed two beers while eating dinner at a restaurant.[97] Also in 2014 an Oregon woman who used legal medical marijuana during her pregnancy was advised against breastfeeding while using marijuana. When the mother insisted that there was no data showing that marijuana was transmitted through human milk and that, in any case, she had the right to make the decision herself, doctors offered a compromise. They agreed to release the mother from the hospital only after she signed a "'waiver acknowledging her use of marijuana and the potential risks involved,'" evidence of the hospital's goal of protecting itself from legal liability.[98]

Mothers who ingest illicit drugs, which can be passed to their infants by nursing, are increasingly being subjected to criminal prosecution. In the past several years, at least three women have been charged with homicide based on allegations that their breastfeeding poisoned their infants; one was convicted of murder and another pled guilty to voluntary manslaughter. The third mother is, at this writing, still awaiting trial. Other mothers have been found guilty of lesser charges when the child tested positive for drugs but did not die.[99] In 2006 a California woman pled guilty to child endangerment pursuant to a plea bargain, after her child died and was found to have high levels of methamphetamine in its system, allegedly transmitted through breastfeeding.[100]

Human milk also contains environmental toxins to which women have been exposed,[101] although the Academy has concluded that these chemicals do not usually pose a risk to infants.[102] More recently, environmentalists and some pediatricians have been concerned about infants' exposure to lead through prolonged breastfeeding, as well as the effects of BPA and other endocrine disruptors on breastfed children.[103]

Additionally, women who have had surgery to enhance or reduce their breast size are often unable to provide sufficient breast milk to breastfeed.[104] Tragically, women are not always informed about this possibility. In 1997, Tabitha Walrond, a young African-American woman in New York City who had breast reduction surgery as a teenager, was charged with murder after her two-month-old child died, apparently from malnutrition and dehydration because Ms. Walrond was not producing sufficient milk. At trial, medical witnesses admitted that Ms. Walrond was never told that her breast reduction surgery could make it impossible for her to produce sufficient milk. Other witnesses testified that although Ms. Walrond brought her son to be seen by a pediatrician, she was turned away for lack of a Medicaid card. The card did not arrive until two months after her son died. After her son's death an autopsy disclosed a previously undiagnosed endocrine problem that had contributed to his death.[105]

Prosecutors initially proceeded on the theory that Ms. Walrond deliberately decided not to feed her child because she was angry at the child's father, who jilted her mid-pregnancy after finding another girlfriend with whom he also fathered a child. Prosecutors later abandoned that theory. Instead, they contended that Ms. Walrond's failure to recognize and respond to signs that her son was malnourished established her negligence, which was not excused by the breakdown of the medical and health insurance bureaucracies. Jurors deliberated for less than three hours before finding Ms. Walrond guilty of criminally negligent homicide, asserting that she had failed her duty as a mother to recognize the symptoms of malnutrition. After her conviction, the trial judge condemned Ms. Walrond for failing to recognize how malnourished her infant had become, saying that she should not be absolved of criminal responsibility because of the failings of the health care system and the Medicaid bureaucracy.[106]

Up to 10 percent of breastfed infants suffer from hypernatremia,[107] a serious condition in which the kidneys retain excess sodium, leading to dehydration. Hypernatremia has become more common in conjunction with the rise of breastfeeding and the typical practice of early discharge of infants from hospitals, often without adequate follow-up.[108] It can be difficult for new parents to recognize the symptoms of hypernatremia. As a result, some children are not diagnosed until they have suffered permanent injury, including neurological damage and death.[109]

III. How Social Pressures, Law, and Government Policy Support or Discourage Breastfeeding

A. Obstacles to Breastfeeding

Many American women find it difficult to nurse their children, a problem that is often exacerbated by a return to work. They cite a variety of medical, cultural, economic, and legal obstacles, which in turn are frequently linked to a lack of health care access. Women who have been sexually abused often find it difficult to breastfeed and can even suffer episodes of posttraumatic stress while nursing.[110] In general, women who choose to breastfeed are more likely than their non-breastfeeding peers to have good prenatal and postpartum care, which is correlated with, though not guaranteed by, having adequate health insurance and a good relationship with their physician.[111]

B. Cultural Constructions of the Breast and Breastfeeding

Deeply held cultural norms about the sexual aspects of the breast underlie the frequent objections to breastfeeding in public.[112] As feminist Iris Marion Young has observed, "Western . . . patriarchal logic defines an exclusive border between motherhood and sexuality." Breasts are scandalous because they disrupt that border.[113] While some state laws protect the right of women to breastfeed in public spaces, or in places of public accommodation, there are wide variations among states. Women have been harassed and arrested for breastfeeding on public transportation and in other public venues; a few cities, including New York, Philadelphia, and Pittsburgh, have responded by providing lactation rooms in public buildings.[114] In 2006, a mother was ejected from a Delta and Freedom Airlines flight when she was nursing her child and refused to cover up; in response, women staged "lactivism" events, nursing their infants en masse.[115]

Psychological support for breastfeeding, as well as community norms, is important. If a woman's husband, partner, or mother does not agree with her decision to nurse her child, she is less likely to begin or to continue breastfeeding.[116] For some African-American women, the legacy of slavery and the institution of "mammies," who were forced to nurse white women's children and to neglect their own, may make breastfeeding distasteful.[117] Further, in some ethnic and cultural communities, the entire family is expected to assist a new mother with feeding and caring for a baby,[118] which is easier if the infant is formula-fed.

C. Failures of the Health Care System

The health care system contributes significantly to the sharp drop-off in breastfeeding rates shortly after infants are discharged from the hospital.[119] Women are most likely to nurse if they receive extra support and encouragement by health care professionals soon after a child's birth, but hospitals differ in the extent of support they provide.[120] Lactation consultants, who often know more about nursing than physicians, can provide technical expertise and encouragement to new mothers, but they are both scarce and expensive.[121] Medicaid has only recently begun to require states to cover lactation consultants.[122] The Affordable Care Act requires insurers to cover women's consultations with health care providers about breastfeeding and to provide them with breast pumps; however, many of the women who are able to find lactation consultants end up paying for the services out of their own pockets.[123]

While breastfeeding usually begins in the hospital, many hospitals fail to fully support breastfeeding, either because the staff are not knowledgeable about lactation or give inconsistent messages about breastfeeding. There are also financial and structural obstacles to breastfeeding. The Baby-Friendly Hospital Initiative is part of an international effort to increase breastfeeding. To be certified as "Baby-Friendly," a hospital must meet ten criteria that maximize the opportunities for mothers to succeed at breastfeeding, including a requirement that the hospital not distribute formula samples or coupons when the infant is discharged.[124] Despite studies that demonstrate that giving away free samples discourages breastfeeding,[125] it is difficult for hospitals to end the lucrative financial arrangements they have with formula manufacturers, because ending these arrangements would have a negative impact on their bottom line.[126] Women who deliver at "Baby-Friendly" hospitals are more likely to initiate and continue breastfeeding.[127] However, fewer than 400 of the more than 3,000 hospitals in the United States have been certified as "Baby-Friendly." While this number has grown in recent years, these hospitals deliver less than 20 percent of American infants.[128] Other hospitals give conflicting messages when, despite encouraging new mothers to breastfeed, they send them home with free samples of infant formula, diaper bags labeled with a formula manufacturer's name, and coupons for free formula, which are a key part of manufacturers' marketing strategy.[129]

In contrast, New York City may have gone to the opposite extreme. Launched in 2012, Latch on NYC is a voluntary program in which participating New York City hospitals are to inform mothers of their right to breastfeed and encourage them to do so by educating them about its benefits before providing formula. While initially it was reported that hospitals would keep formula under lock and key, available to new mothers only if they have a physician's order permitting them to feed their infants with formula, the New York City Department of Health disputes that. What is clear is that while the program was designed to promote nursing by making it the normative, preferred behavior, many mothers fear that it will also fail to honor women's desire to choose what is best for them and their children.[130]

D. Workplace Obstacles

Even women who have successfully breastfed in the weeks following delivery may find it difficult to continue after returning to work.[131] Most American employers offer only brief maternity leaves, which are much shorter than those required in other developed nations.[132] Indeed, the United States is the only industrialized nation not to mandate paid childbirth leave.[133] While the Family and Medical Leave Act permits employees to take as much as twelve weeks of unpaid leave to address their family members' medical needs, including the birth or adoption of a child, for many women this is not financially feasible.[134] Accordingly, women who return to work during the first twelve weeks after giving birth are the least likely to continue to breastfeed.[135] While most women's initial decision about breastfeeding is not influenced by their employment status, six months after giving birth those women who work full time are much less likely to breastfeed than those who work part time or only in the home,[136] primarily because of the lack of support from their employers.[137]

There is a clear class divide in women's ability to pump their milk at work, which is necessary to maintain their milk supply. Unsurprisingly, women at higher-paying and professional jobs are more likely to have the flexibility and privacy necessary to pump, while women at lower-status jobs are often unable to take a break to pump their milk or to have a private space in which to do so.[138] More than 60 percent of American women work at hourly or minimum-wage jobs.[139] Even when employers encourage women to breastfeed, salaried women and women who work in offices are more likely to continue breastfeeding than women who work in factories or receive hourly wages.[140]

About one-fifth of all employers promote women's breastfeeding through "corporate lactation programs."[141] These programs reduce parental absenteeism due to an infant's illness and have been shown to save the employer the costs of health care and the expense of training new workers to replace mothers who leave.[142] Women working for such employers are more likely to continue to breastfeed.[143]

E. Legal Obstacles

Law, or the lack thereof, is a major impediment to breastfeeding. Until the enactment of the Affordable Care Act, no federal law required employers to support women who wish to breastfeed after returning to work. Courts were generally dismissive of women's desire to breastfeed, treating it as a matter of maternal choice, and rejected women's claims that their employers' refusal to support breastfeeding constituted gender discrimination.[144] Although of course only women can breastfeed, courts ruled repeatedly that neither lactating nor the act of breastfeeding was a part of pregnancy, which *is* protected against discrimination under Title VII of the Civil Rights Act.[145] At the same time, because breastfeeding is a normal human activity, it cannot constitute a disability under the Americans with Disabilities Act (ADA), which requires employers to make accommodations for employees with disabilities.[146]

In 2007 the case of Sophie Currier dramatized the lack of legal support for breastfeeding women who work outside the home. Dr. Currier, who had recently graduated from Harvard Medical School, could not begin her medical residency without taking a national licensing exam. The National Board of Medical Examiners refused her any accommodation to pump milk for her four-month-old infant. While the Board granted accommodations to test-takers who needed extra time because of physical or learning disabilities (including Dr. Currier), it declared that it could not provide her with a break to pump her milk because breastfeeding was not a disability under the ADA. Eventually a Massachusetts Appeals Court judge ordered the Board to grant Dr. Currier extra time on the exam and a private place to pump her milk. The Massachusetts Supreme Judicial Court affirmed the Appeals Court's ruling in 2012, relying on Massachusetts, not federal, law.[147]

Two developments since 2010 have begun to shift the legal landscape for working mothers who want to breastfeed. The first is the Affordable Care Act, which mandates that employers support these women at work by providing a private place to pump their milk while at work and an opportunity to do so. The ACA is more demanding than many state laws,[148] which often exempt employers if they can demonstrate that accommodating breastfeeding mothers would "seriously disrupt the operations of the employer"[149] or otherwise constitute a severe hardship.[150] Under the ACA, all employers of fifty or more people must provide "reasonable break time" (which may be unpaid) for nursing mothers who need to pump their milk at work. Employers must provide a private workplace location, other than a bathroom, in which nursing mothers can pump, as well as a refrigerator in which the pumped milk may be stored during the work day.[151] The ACA requires smaller employers to comply with the break time and pumping rules but excuses them from the break time requirement if complying would "impose a severe hardship." The United States Department of Labor has issued guidance to employers on how to implement the new law.[152] It appears that litigation is likely on questions of the type of private pumping space that employers must make available, as well as the timing and frequency of breaks that employers need to provide. The only remedy available to nursing mothers under the ACA is to ask the Department of Labor to intervene on their behalf. Alternatively, women can quit their jobs and claim that their employer's behavior constituted a "constructive discharge" from employment, but this is not a satisfactory option for most working mothers.

The second major change in the law, whose impact has not yet been fully realized, is the 2013 decision in *E.E.O.C. v. Houston Funding II,*

Ltd. In that case the United States Court of Appeals for the Fifth Circuit became the first federal court to hold that if an employee was fired because she was breastfeeding or lactating, that constituted gender discrimination under Title VII of the Civil Rights Act, because "lactation is a related medical condition of pregnancy for purposes of the PDA [Pregnancy Discrimination Act]." The case, which was eventually settled, is frequently cited by other courts and may end up establishing a new legal rule to protect women who claim that their employers have discriminated against them because they are breastfeeding.[153] In March 2016 a federal jury in Alabama found that the city of Tuscaloosa had discriminated against a lactating police officer when it demoted her after she attempted to exercise her right to pump her milk at work.[154] The ACA also authorized a change in the Internal Revenue Code to permit tax deductions for breast pumps and other equipment necessary to make breastfeeding more successful and thus more likely. Realistically, only wealthier women are likely to benefit from this change, because only their families earn enough to itemize deductions.[155] However, Congress has also failed to enact other laws or policies that would provide concrete support for women who decide to breastfeed. Congress has declined to promote the Baby-Friendly Hospital program, either by requiring hospitals to comply as a condition of Medicaid eligibility or other federal support, by offering financial incentives to make it easier for hospitals to end their reliance on financial support from formula manufacturers,[156] or by providing nursing bras and other breastfeeding support to indigent women.[157]

Conclusion

The evidence about the impact of breastfeeding and human milk on children's health is decidedly mixed, as well as hotly contested. But if the government actually wants to make breastfeeding a viable option for most women, it must remove the structural obstacles they currently face. The government must require employers to make meaningful adjustments in workplace policies for all mothers in the labor force, must legalize breastfeeding in all places of public accommodation, and must provide positive support, rather than disincentives, for poor women who choose to breastfeed.

7

The "Good Mother" and Crimes of Omission

Introduction

In 1978 Ginger McLaughlin, a twenty-year-old mother of three, was convicted of criminal child neglect after she went to the store and her husband brutally beat and killed their two-month-old infant in her absence. Ms. McLaughlin and her husband had argued shortly before she left about whether she needed to run this errand and the fact that he would have to care for their child in her absence. The prosecution's theory of the case was that because Ms. McLaughlin knew that her husband had a violent temper and had previously assaulted her and beaten her two older children eight months previously, her decision to leave their child with him was criminally negligent. The Oregon Court of Appeals reversed Ginger McLaughlin's conviction, holding that the trial judge should never have permitted the case to go to the jury because there was insufficient evidence that she was negligent. The court ruled that despite her husband's history of bad temper and violence, Ms. McLaughlin's act of leaving her child with him and "doing an ordinary family chore" did not reach the threshold of "a high degree of likelihood that he would cause an injury to the child" sufficient to meet "the reasonable person" standard of negligence.[1]

This case typifies the problem of the criminal prosecution of mothers for failing to prevent harm to their children at the hands of the mother's husband or boyfriend. Focusing on the repugnance of the killing and viewing the incident with the benefit of hindsight, it is tempting for prosecutors to charge, and juries to convict, mothers who fail to protect their children.

Child abuse is an emotionally charged subject. The words themselves summon horrific mental images and arouse strong feelings; it is difficult to understand how any adult could inflict hideous injuries on a defenseless child.[2] The child abuse cases that are the subject of this chapter have particular emotional force because they involve parents who were criminally prosecuted not for their own actions but for failing to protect their child from the violence of another. In American criminal law, an omission—a failure to act when one has a duty to act—is the equivalent of a physical action. In the case of non-abusive parents, their duty flows either from the parents' traditional, common law duty to protect their children, or from modern statutes that make it a crime to "cause" or "permit" a child to be abused or neglected.[3]

This chapter examines the striking gender asymmetry in the law's treatment of non-abusive parents and explores the economic, psychosocial, and legal factors that make such unequal treatment possible. Each year American mothers are charged with criminal child abuse, as well as murder and manslaughter, when the actual abuser is the mother's male partner—her husband or boyfriend.[4] While the abusers themselves are generally prosecuted, usually this does not prevent the non-abusive mother from being charged. The converse—criminal prosecution of a father based on child abuse committed by his wife or girlfriend—occurs much less frequently.[5] As one experienced child abuse professional observed, "'In the 16 years I've worked in the courts, I have never seen a father charged with a failure to protect when the mom is the abuser. Yet, in virtually every case where Dad is the abuser, we charge Mom with failure to protect.'"[6] Since 1960 there have been 108 published appellate cases in which parents were convicted of child abuse or homicide based on a *failure* to act. Eighty-seven of the defendants were mothers; eleven were fathers, and in ten additional cases the defendants were stepparents or the girlfriend or boyfriend of the abusive parent. While this is a relatively small number of cases, they illustrate the increasing tendency of prosecutors, judges, and juries to treat mothers as the absolute guarantors of their children's health, even when harm is inflicted by others, and even though the mothers themselves may be victims of the same abuser.

This chapter examines the factors that make it more likely that mothers, not fathers, will be prosecuted for *failing to prevent harm* to their children. It analyzes the subtle but powerful ways in which the unconscious processes of assessing risk and assigning responsibility intersect with theoretically neutral principles of criminal law to affect the decisions of investigators and prosecutors, jurors and judges, leading these legal decisionmakers to initiate a criminal investigation and decide to indict, convict, or impose a harsh sentence. The result is an uneven playing field, slanted decidedly against mothers. The power of unconscious mental processes—including unarticulated worldviews; racial, gender, and class biases; as well as the hindsight bias; the fundamental attribution error; and other mental shortcuts—is so strong that once a child has been abused or killed, the mother is the most likely culprit, based not on what she has done, but what she failed to do.

The argument is *not* that women who fail to protect their children from the violent acts of their partners should never be prosecuted. Each case involves a distinct set of facts, and there are cases in which a mother's failure to protect her child clearly demonstrates legal complicity in the abuse or death of her child. However, there are also many cases in which the mother's inaction is the product of physical abuse and psychological coercion by the same man who has harmed her child. Family violence encompasses both child abuse and intimate partner violence (also called domestic violence); the two are frequently connected because abusive men use violence—and the threat of future violence—against women and their children to control the women.[7] Frequently, prosecutors portray mothers who have not prevented harm to their children as having deliberately put their relationship with a lover—their husband or boyfriend—above their maternal obligations. As we shall see, the motif of "choice" looms large in many assertions made by prosecutors, judges, and jurors, consistent with American law's emphasis on individual action and responsibility. The factual, legal, and rhetorical question, "Why didn't she leave?" permeates criminal prosecutions of non-abusive mothers. Even in cases where there is no evidence that the mother was victimized by her child's abuser, it appears that unconscious racial, class, and gender biases, along with idealized visions of motherhood, affect the decisions of social workers, prosecutors, juries, and judges.

I. Child Abuse in Context

A. The History of Child-Abuse Investigation and Prosecution in America

Child abuse was not a recognized phenomenon in English common law or in the American colonies. Parents were not only permitted but were actually expected to physically discipline their children as a necessary means of achieving their educational, moral, and spiritual improvement. The biblical maxim "Spare the rod and spoil the child" reflects that era.[8] While parents' "correction" of their children was supposed to be undertaken "in a reasonable manner," the outer boundary of that reasonableness appears to be that a father could not kill or "permanently injure" his child.[9] Notably, the same rule applied to husbands' "chastisement" of their wives, as beating was permitted as a form of "correction."[10]

Even in the nineteenth century, parents and other adults were rarely prosecuted for what today we would describe as child abuse. In 1874 a highly publicized case captured the nation's attention. Ten-year-old Mary Ellen Wilson lived in New York City with foster parents who beat her almost every day. When the abuse was finally discovered, the resulting public outrage fueled the formation of "child protection" agencies across the nation. Reformers did not push for the criminal prosecution of child-abusing adults. Instead, they emphasized removing children from abusive homes or providing social support services to abusive parents to enable them to provide better care for their children.[11] Later, during the Progressive Era of the late nineteenth and early twentieth centuries, advocates sought to promote children's health and welfare by limiting child labor, establishing juvenile courts, and conducting research on children's health and poverty.[12] At mid-twentieth century, public attitudes toward corporal punishment of children were generally lenient. Professionals like social workers asserted that the best response to child abuse was to provide counseling and support to perpetrators.[13] Criminal prosecutions against parents for child abuse were extremely rare;[14] prosecutions of the non-abusive parent appear to have been even rarer.

The "rediscovery" of child abuse by a group of pediatric radiologists in the early 1960s changed everything. The 1962 publication of an article, "The Battered Child Syndrome," in the *Journal of the American Medical Association* was a watershed moment.[15] The article announced "the battered child syndrome" as a medical diagnosis, identifiable by X-rays and other clinical evidence. The immediate response was a rush of media attention, followed by a burst of legislative activity. Within five years of the publication of the article, every state had enacted a mandatory child abuse reporting law.[16] Since 1974 when Congress enacted legislation providing financial incentives for states to adopt uniform rules for child-abuse reporting, investigation, and intervention, forty-eight states and the District of Columbia have enacted child endangerment and/or failure-to-protect statutes.[17] In consequence, the number of potential child abuse cases that came to the attention of social services agencies and law enforcement skyrocketed, rising from 150,000 cases in 1963 to 1.3 million by 1982.[18] After some spectacular child abuse trials in the 1980s, reported rates of child abuse and child homicide began to decline in the 1990s.[19]

Criminal prosecutions of non-abusive parents take place against the background principle of American law that government should stay out of family life. This view of the sanctity of family privacy free from outside intervention stems from America's highly individualistic culture and an anti-government mindset. In this idealized vision, families are to be granted deference in raising their children in a manner consistent with parents' personal values, religious beliefs, and cultural traditions. This perspective is expressed in the legal aphorism that "the child is not the mere creature of the state"[20] and the more colloquial expression of a patriarchal society that "Father Knows Best."[21] The reluctance to interfere with actions and decisions within the family is historical, cultural, and legal, embodied in government's traditional hands-off approach to domestic violence, as well as private institutions' hesitancy to actively intervene to prevent, and condemn, child abuse.

This approach has been sanctioned by two decisions of the Supreme Court, *DeShaney v. Winnebago County Dep't. of Social Services*[22] and *Town of Castle Rock v. Gonzales*.[23] In these cases the Court declined to hold local government agencies accountable for failing to act to protect endangered children, even when the agencies had reliable evidence that the child had been abused or threatened in the past. In 1989 the Court ruled in *DeShaney* that government social workers had no constitutionally based obligation to protect a young boy from his father's severe beatings, despite the fact that the social workers had been warned repeatedly about the risk of serious harm. The Court held that as long as the boy was not physically in state custody (i.e., living in a juvenile facility) the state had no duty to act to reduce the risk of harm. [24] Sixteen years later, in *Town of Castle Rock v. Gonzales*,[25] the Supreme Court again held that the Constitution did not impose a legally enforceable duty on government authorities to protect potential child abuse victims. Here, the Court held that local Colorado police did not violate due process when they failed to respond to a mother's frantic phone calls asking them to enforce an existing judicial restraining order against a battering husband and father, who kidnapped and ultimately murdered his three daughters.[26]

Government attitudes and public opinion have only recently begun to shift. On rare occasions child abuse investigators have been charged with criminal homicide on the theory that their failure to adequately investigate abuse allegations led to a child's death. In other cases state agencies have been successfully sued in tort for failing to protect children from known abusers.[27] Extensive media coverage of domestic violence may also be changing public opinion. The National Football League's failure to impose sanctions on its players in notorious cases of domestic violence has recently brought heightened scrutiny of the problem of intimate partner violence and extreme corporal punishment.[28] The question of how private institutions and government should and will respond to all aspects of domestic violence is an open one.

B. The Demographics of Child Abuse

In recent years about 700,000 American children are estimated to suffer physical and emotional injuries at the hands of adults.[29] Men commit about 46 percent of all child abuse and neglect, compared with 54 percent committed by women. This apparent overrepresentation of women is not surprising given that a third of American children live with a single parent, usually the mother. Fathers constitute a little more than half of male perpetrators of child abuse; surrogate fathers—stepfathers, adoptive parents, and mothers' boyfriends—account for another quarter of male abusers. In contrast, 86 percent of female perpetrators are mothers; only 4 percent are surrogate mothers. Men are responsible for more severe physical abuse and more sexual abuse than women. Women are more likely than men to be guilty of child neglect,[30] a broad term that encompasses the failure to provide adequate food, clothing, and medical attention, as well as extreme indifference to a child's emotional and physical needs.[31]

Every child's death at the hands of an adult is tragic; nearly 1,600 children die from child abuse or neglect each year.[32] Most of these children are killed recklessly or inadvertently, sometimes as a result of excessive physical "discipline." While intentional killings make headlines, they are quite rare.[33] Seventy percent of children killed by a parent are six years old or younger; a third are less than a year old. Of the estimated 600 to 800 child homicide victims who are five years old or less, approximately 33 percent are killed by their fathers and 30 percent by their mothers. An additional 27 percent of these young children are killed by other men the children know, 8 percent are killed by other women they know, and 3 percent are killed by male strangers.[34]

These patterns of child abuse and neglect are the product of poverty and of profound changes in the American family. The number of children who live with two parents has plummeted in the past fifty years. Between 1910 and 1970, 85 percent of American children lived with two parents.[35] By 1990 that share had declined to 73 percent; today only 64 percent of children live with both parents.[36] Nearly 25 percent of all American children live in a one parent home headed by a single mother; only 4 percent live with single fathers. In contrast, 94 percent of fathers who live with their children also live with the children's mother.[37] The grim economic circumstances of many single parent families, especially those headed by women, set the stage for many cases of child abuse and neglect. *More than three-quarters* of children ages eight and younger who live with a single mother are poor or low-income; *two-thirds* of families headed by a single mother receive no financial support from the child's father.[38] Children are seven times more likely to be maltreated if they live in a poor family. While most single mothers live alone, about a fifth live with a partner.[39] Single women living with their children experience violence from their partners at a rate more than ten times that of married women with children.[40]

C. How Child Abuse Is Investigated and Prosecuted: Opportunities for Discretion

Child abuse and neglect cases usually are investigated and resolved by the civil child protection system;[41] criminal prosecutions are less common.[42] Discretionary decisionmaking permeates the legal apparatus directed at child abuse. Doctors and teachers decide whether to report suspected abuse or to just speak to the parents; social workers determine whether a family needs further monitoring and social support or should be reported to law enforcement. The police can refer a case to social services or the district attorney's office. Prosecutors, in turn, can seek an indictment, offer a plea bargain, or bring a case to trial. Once a case reaches trial, jurors and judges also make discretionary decisions. Each decisionmaker is inevitably influenced by the subliminal psychological processes of risk construction and the conscious and unconscious biases we have already noted. While much has been written about the impact of racial and gender bias, class bias also affects how prosecutors exercise their discretion. Professor Jennifer Collins has identified significant class disparities in the prosecution of parents who accidentally left their child in a hot car, leading to the child's death from hyperthermia. She found that parents with white collar jobs or who were married to a white collar spouse were prosecuted in just over 23 percent of these cases. In contrast, parents who were unemployed, had blue collar jobs, or otherwise presented evidence of lower socioeconomic status, were prosecuted in nearly 86 percent of potential cases.[43]

Many people have unconscious yet powerful views about motherhood, such as the belief that mothers should always be nurturing and put their children's needs above their own. Studies have shown that "sex-based stereotypes lead to the application of higher standards of parenting to mothers than to fathers." Professor Melissa Breger writes, "Motherhood bias is distinct from gender bias, yet interwoven and interrelated. . . . [I]mplicit societal expectations of mothers hold[ ] . . . mothers to the highest possible, almost unattainable, standards. Mothers instinctually are supposed to know how to raise children and raise them well. Mothers are envisioned as selfless and self-sacrificing, . . . ever nurturing and ever protective of their children."[44] Prosecutors often share these beliefs. Because they are the prime actors in initiating criminal proceedings, their unconscious biases can have far-reaching effects, particularly when these biases are shared by jurors and judges.[45] For example, in one case in which a mother was prosecuted for failure to protect her child from her husband's abuse, a juror declared, "She should have protected that baby with everything that she had."[46] Another prospective juror stated, "The biggest part of being a mother is protecting the child from the world."[47] In an unreported case, *State v. Lindley*, Dallas prosecutor Carmen White charged Arlena Lindley with failure to protect her child from the murderous rage of her boyfriend.

Ms. White declared, "[As a mother], I would sacrifice my life 10 times out of 10" and that a mother should "'lay her life, if she has to, on the line for her child.'" [48] These exalted views of motherhood are strong enough to trump mitigating evidence. For example, in *Johnson v. State*, a Florida prosecutor recommended a sentence of three to seven years in prison for Brenda Johnson, a mother who had not prevented the brutal killing of her daughter by her boyfriend. Ms. Johnson pled no contest to manslaughter. The prosecutor recommended leniency because Ms. Johnson had had a loving relationship with her daughter, had never physically harmed her, and had herself been victimized by her boyfriend's violence. The trial judge was not persuaded. He sentenced Ms. Johnson to the statutory maximum of fifteen years, declaring that the mother had so "abandoned or abdicated" her duty of care for her child that no lesser sentence was sufficient.[49]

There is much that we do not know about discretionary decision-making in child abuse cases. There is scant data on *how* decisions are reached to initiate criminal child abuse proceedings in addition to the civil proceedings, which are usually heard in family court. Prosecution rates *after* a referral from law enforcement or child protective agencies vary enormously across jurisdictions; one study found referral rates from 28 to 94 percent.[50] It is hard to know how often criminal child abuse cases go to trial rather than being resolved by plea bargaining, although prosecutors frequently bring indictments accompanied by the offer of a plea bargain, in order to exert leverage over reluctant witnesses.[51] In one national survey, nearly 80 percent of prosecutors indicated that they would consider prosecuting a non-abusive parent for child abuse, *even* if he or she was a victim of domestic violence or other coercion by the same perpetrator.[52] Sometimes this is a simple matter of needing to find adult eyewitnesses to the abuse. However, in other cases prosecutors will not charge a non-abusive parent if her testimony is necessary for the case against the principal perpetrator.[53] In a case that garnered national headlines in the 1980s, Lisa Steinberg was battered to death by her adoptive father, Joel Steinberg. New York prosecutors originally indicted Lisa's adoptive mother, Hedda Nussbaum, who was also brutally beaten by Steinberg, but ultimately concluded that they needed Nussbaum's testimony to convict Steinberg of murder, so the charges against her were dismissed.[54]

After criminal charges are brought, most child abuse cases are resolved by guilty plea.[55] Of the remaining handful of convictions that are the result of a full trial, only a small fraction will be addressed in published judicial opinions. These published decisions often do not reveal the full context of the cases, because judges are focused on the narrow legal issues presented on appeal, rather than all the facts surrounding the relationship between the child, the abuser, and the non-abusive parent. Appellate decisions rarely consider the connection between the two forms of domestic violence—intimate partner violence and child abuse—despite their substantial overlap. This may be because the non-abusing parent did not assert her own victimization as a defense or, if she did, was precluded from offering all relevant evidence. In addition to the published judicial decisions on which this chapter is based, a recent study by journalist Alex Campbell sheds some light on current prosecutorial practices. Campbell examined seventy-three cases between 2004 and 2014, in eleven states, in which a child was killed or seriously injured by a parent or the parent's partner. In each case the non-abusive parent was charged with homicide or child abuse by omission, convicted, and sentenced to at least ten years in state prison. In sixty-nine of the cases the child's mother was the non-abusive parent; in only four cases was the child's father charged based on his failure to act to prevent his partner's abuse.[56]

II. When Are Mothers Prosecuted?

The earliest reported decision, from 1960, is *Palmer v. State*.[57] *Palmer* is in many ways the prototypical child abuse by omission case. Barbara Ann Palmer became pregnant at fifteen. She married the baby's father but quickly separated from him and returned to live with her parents. After taking up with one McCue, a man five years older than her, she became estranged from her parents and, along with her young daughter, moved to another state with McCue. One month later her daughter was dead, a result of McCue's repeated brutal beatings. Palmer was charged with and convicted of involuntary manslaughter.

The Maryland Court of Appeals upheld Palmer's conviction, finding that there was sufficient evidence that Palmer was criminally negligent and that her failure to act was the actual and proximate cause of her child's death.[58] On the negligence issue, the court used the violence of McCue, whom the court referred to as Palmer's "paramour," as evidence that Palmer was negligent, because "any reasonable person [would be put on notice] that the child's life was in real and imminent peril."[59] Ruling on the question of whether Palmer's failure to act had caused her child's death, the court focused on "the foreseeability of the consequence of . . . [Palmer's omission to act, in] permitting McCue to 'discipline' the child by repeated and violent beatings."[60] Despite the court's determination that McCue's beatings were the "direct and immediate cause" of the child's death, it found that his violence *did not* constitute an "'intervening efficient cause'" sufficient to extinguish Palmer's responsibility for her child's death.[61]

Palmer is a classic case in two respects. First, its facts are typical, involving a young, emotionally immature woman, usually an adolescent who becomes pregnant at an early age and quickly separates from her baby's father. The teenager often finds it difficult to live with her parents and so moves in with another man with whom she has formed a romantic attachment, looking to him for emotional, if not financial, support. The case is classic legally as well. The prosecutor used a traditional crime—here, manslaughter—and charged that the mother was negligent in failing to foresee the possibility of harm and that it was her failure to act (when, as the mother, she had a legal duty to act) that was the legal cause of her child's death, because by failing to remove her child from her partner's violence she contributed to that death. Her omission to act was thus both the actual and proximate cause of the child's death.

Following *Palmer*, in the 1970s and '80s prosecutions for homicide and child abuse based on a parent's failure to act increased significantly. Some of these charges were predicated on the same type of "omission" analysis used in *Palmer*. Other prosecutions were made possible by legislatures' enactment of more expansive child abuse laws, including laws that explicitly made it a crime to "fail to protect" children from the abuse of others.[62] For example, New Mexico enacted a statute punishing a parent who either "causes" or "permits" child abuse to occur.[63] One goal of such a statute is to permit the criminal conviction of *all* adults who could have committed child abuse, when the abuse is clear but not who committed it.[64] However, these statutes also leave open the possibility that non-abusive parents can be convicted of the very serious crime of "intentionally" permitting child abuse. Only recently have some courts determined that there is a distinction in blameworthiness between an adult who intends to cause harm to a child and one who fails to prevent it, so that only the former group can face the most serious penalty of imprisonment for life.

In many child abuse cases children have been severely injured or killed when a parent, stepparent, or other partner used excessive discipline for minor acts of disobedience or normal childhood behaviors like bedwetting, sneaking candy and then lying about it, or refusing to eat. Often, in cases where the abuser is a man, his acts of violence appear to have stemmed from his resentment of his wife or girlfriend previously having had children with another man, particularly if the child resembles his biological father.[65]

As the number of mothers prosecuted when the actual abuser was the mother's husband or boyfriend began to rise, law professors and other commentators began to write critically about this trend, suggesting a pattern of gender, class, and race bias.[66] Two Wisconsin cases illustrate the possibility that fathers and mothers are receiving disparate treatment in the criminal justice system.[67] In 1986, in *State v. Williquette* the Wisconsin Supreme Court held that a mother, Terri Williquette, could be prosecuted for felony child abuse under a statute making it a crime to "subject[ ] a child to cruel maltreatment," because she did not prevent the children's father—her husband—from physically and sexually abusing their children.[68] Mrs. Williquette argued that because she was not present during the abuse she was not within the statute's reach. The Wisconsin Supreme Court disagreed. In reasoning similar to that of the court in *Palmer*, it ruled that the child abuse statute encompassed "situations in which a person *with a duty toward a child* exposes the child to a *foreseeable risk of abuse*," so that "a parent who fails to take any action to stop instances of child abuse can be prosecuted as a principal [the primary actor]."[69] The court found that there was sufficient evidence to justify prosecution, in light of testimony that Mrs. Williquette "regularly left the children in the father's exclusive care and custody despite allegedly knowing . . . [of his abuse,]" and that she had not reported her husband to the authorities.[70]

Seven years later, in *State v. Rundle*,[71] the Wisconsin Supreme Court reversed a father's conviction for child abuse that resulted in his daughter's death, based on his failure to intervene to protect the child from severe physical abuse by his wife. The court found that neither his failure to intervene to prevent the abuse despite knowing of his wife's violence for a long time nor his failure to seek appropriate medical care was sufficient to convict him as an accomplice of his wife.[72] Although the Wisconsin Supreme Court distinguished the two cases on the ground that the prosecutions were brought under different statutes, in reality the prosecution's theory was the same in both cases. In *Rundle* the prosecutor argued that the father "'stood back' and did nothing to protect his child's physical well-being against his wife's abuse."[73] Similarly, in *Williquette* the prosecutor argued that the mother's failure to act while knowing about her husband's abuse made her criminally responsible.[74]

III. The Impact of Intimate Partner Violence (IPV) on Child Abuse and the Mothers Who Are Prosecuted

A. How IPV and Child Abuse Overlap

There is an enormous overlap in the incidence of intimate partner violence (commonly referred to as domestic violence) and child abuse. Jeffrey Edleson, an author of the *Greenbook*, a resource for family court judges, reviewed multiple studies and found a 30 to 60 percent overlap in households in which a man commits intimate partner violence and abuses or injures a child. Some researchers have suggested that the extent of overlap is even greater if one looks only at the abuse inflicted by so-called intimate terrorists. For these men, for whom physical violence against their female partners serves as a means of exercising psychological coercion and control, physical and sexual abuse of children is simply an additional means of exercising control.[75] In the published cases analyzed for this chapter, 41 percent of the cases in which a mother was prosecuted for failing to protect her children include evidence that the mother had also been violently abused by the same man. Journalist Alex Campbell observed a similar pattern in his 2014 study, finding that in 40 percent of the cases in which the passive parent was the mother or girlfriend there was significant evidence of intimate partner violence as well as child abuse. In contrast, in the four cases where the father was the passive parent, there was no evidence that he had been abused by his female partner.[76]

Intimate partner violence is pervasive in American society, yet it is often downplayed or disbelieved by police, prosecutors, and judges.[77] An estimated 2 to 6 million American women suffer violence at the hands of their male partners annually; 25 to 35 percent of the women who seek emergency room treatment are there because of their partners' assaults.[78] Not only do police frequently not credit women's reports of abuse,[79] but judges also reject the testimony of abused women, finding them to be literally incredible.[80] One Maryland judge, ruling in the case of a woman who sought an order of protection from her partner's abuse, declared:

> I don't believe anything that you're saying. . . . The reason I don't believe it is because I don't believe that anything like that could happen to me. If I was you and someone had threatened me with a gun, there is no way that I would continue to stay with them. There is no way that I could take that level of abuse from them. Therefore, since I would not let that happen to me, I can't believe that it happened to you.[81]

These comments are not just an extreme example of judicial gender bias. Whether a judge is overtly hostile to women's claims of abuse or simply unfamiliar with the extent and effects of intimate partner violence on women and their children, despite the growing literature about such violence, it is extremely difficult for a woman to receive a fair hearing when she is charged with a crime based on her failure to act to protect her children.[82]

Further, even when judges or prosecutors are familiar with intimate partner violence, they often view it in a limited context, focusing on the paradigmatic case of a woman who, after suffering years of abuse at the hands of her partner, one day has had enough and kills him. These women often claim that they were acting in self-defense, a defense that is often sharply contested, particularly when, at first glance, the woman does not appear to have been in imminent fear for her life. But even prosecutors who are willing to accept the possibility that abused women may act in self-defense appear to have great difficulty in understanding why an abused woman would *not* act against an abusive partner who injured her child.

In some jurisdictions, institutional constraints appear to affect prosecutors' ability to connect intimate partner abuse and child abuse. One national survey found that more than a third of prosecutors' offices had separate domestic violence (intimate partner violence) and child abuse units, less than half had units addressing all family violence together, and about a sixth had units addressing either domestic violence or child abuse, but not both. Not one of the offices with separate domestic violence and child abuse units had protocols requiring prosecutors in one unit to communicate with their counterparts in the other abuse unit.[83]

Perhaps as a result of this bifurcated understanding of the impact of family violence on women and their children, prosecutors often assert that abused women who do not protect their children have chosen to put their relationship with a man above their duty to their children. The factual, legal, and rhetorical question, "*Why didn't she leave?*" permeates criminal proceedings against mothers who failed to protect their children against a violent abuser.

In other cases, prosecutors use evidence of victimization *against* mothers who have suffered intimate partner violence. Some assert that a mother's prior unsuccessful efforts to leave her abuser should be held against her, arguing that these efforts demonstrate that the mother was aware of the dangers her children faced and was either "reckless" or "negligent" in failing to protect the children.[84] In one recent case an Oklahoma prosecutor reframed the mother's status as a victim of physical and other abuse into a personal preference. He argued, "*She made the choice to stay* . . . . It's about putting your child at risk because of the *choices* you make, and the *choices* you make to stay in an abusive relationship."[85] As we will see later, judges have echoed this theory, asserting, for example, that a mother's "*lust*" for her batterer "completely overcame her sense of duty to her child."[86]

Professor Elizabeth Schneider argues that it is overly simplistic to treat abused women either as helpless victims or as active agents. They are both, acting in response to physical abuse, trauma, and coercion but also capable of making choices within the constraints of an abusive relationship to try to end the violence against them and their children.[87] However, acknowledging that battered women who try to make rational calculations in regard to their abuser have some agency in their lives is not the equivalent of saying that they have control over their situation.[88] Let us now examine the reality of intimate partner violence and child abuse in the daily lives of American women.

B. Why Don't Women Leave?

There are multiple reasons why women who are abused themselves or are mothers of abused children do not leave the abusers and take their children with them. Many mothers, both single and married, face daunting economic circumstances. Financial constraints can both contribute to and exacerbate violence against mothers and children. While intimate partner violence occurs at all income levels and across all cultures and races, it is experienced in distinct ways by women of color and low-income women. Poor women are more likely to be trapped in an abusive relationship because of their poverty.[89] Women who depend economically on their husbands or boyfriends are more likely to be abused because of that dependency; their abuse is also more likely to be severe. Men who are unemployed, as was Ginger McLaughlin's husband, are also more likely to engage in violence against the women and children in the household, perhaps as an effort to reassert their masculinity and power.[90] Mothers at all income levels must leave their children with their husbands or boyfriends on occasion, to go to work or to perform routine household tasks like grocery shopping.[91] More than three-quarters of children eight years old or younger who live with a single mother are poor or low-income. Three-quarters of single mothers work outside the home, but most are employed in low-wage jobs.[92] As a result of this economic vulnerability, it is hard for many women to leave abusive relationships, because they simply have no place to go. Today, more than a quarter of the families living in New York City shelters are there because of domestic violence. Shelters can provide temporary housing, but without access to long-term affordable housing many abused mothers end up returning to their batterers.[93]

Published cases illustrate the considerable economic pressures faced by many mothers with young children. Although few of the published decisions discuss the economic circumstances of abused children, those that do so point to families living in extreme poverty. For example, they indicate that the family lived in a trailer, motel, or public housing, was supported by food stamps, or was eligible for Medicaid.[94] In *State v. Maupin*, the court noted the mother's testimony that she was estranged from her parents, not receiving child support from the father of her children, and was on public assistance but still needed to sell her blood to make ends meet. She lived with her boyfriend in the hope that he would bring additional financial resources to her children, but this hope was not realized.[95]

In other cases the mother worked at low-wage jobs and relied on her husband or boyfriend to watch her children, either because he was not working or because of the high cost of child care.[96] For example, in *People v. Barrientos*, Nancy Barrientos, a mother of a three-year-old who worked at a fast-food restaurant, was charged with murder after her unemployed boyfriend, Rudy Marquez, brutally beat and abused her son, causing his death.[97] In *People v. Kuykendall*, Miranda Kuykendall worked the night shift at a health care facility and left her children, one nearly four and the other nearly two years old, with her boyfriend, Chris Elliott. Although Kuykendall was aware of Elliott's abuse, she continued to work because she needed "to save money so she could leave . . . [Elliott] and get her children away from him before [the youngest child]. . . . ended up dead." Unfortunately, her plan was unsuccessful, and Elliott killed her son.[98]

Even among women who are not living in extreme poverty, staying with an abusive partner can appear to be a rational choice, at least in the short run. The *Greenbook* for family court judges underscores the need to address intimate partner violence and child abuse together. It describes the complex calculus that an abused woman must undertake in endeavoring to protect her children. At any given moment she must decide whether placating her abuser or defying him will place her child in greater danger. She must also consider the larger questions of how and when to leave her abuser, asking who will care for her children while she is working; how she will provide them with food, housing in a safe neighborhood, and health insurance; and whether the act of leaving will provoke worse violence than she and her children currently experience.[99] Many of the published cases involve women who had lived with an abusive man for only a few weeks. While one could argue that even a day is too long to spend with a man who is violent to a woman or her children, for at least some of these women the man's violence might appear to be an isolated incident, rather than a demonstration of a pattern of dangerous abuse. In these circumstances a woman could make a rational decision to stay with her abuser until she could figure out an escape plan that was likely to be successful. In *People v. Barrientos*, for example, the abused single mother, who worried about her child's safety, made arrangements for her boyfriend's mother to take care of her child for several days until the boyfriend departed on a scheduled trip to Mexico. However, the boyfriend removed her child from his mother's house, took him to the couple's home, and beat him to death.[100]

Only recently have some courts begun to recognize how intimate partner violence can affect mothers' ability to protect their children from violent abusers. In the 2004 case of *Nicholson v. Scopetta*,[101] the New York Court of Appeals held that in civil failure to protect cases, a trial judge evaluating whether an abused mother had neglected her child must focus on whether she has met the standard of "the reasonable and prudent person in similar circumstances." The court ruled that this standard must be tailored to take into account the particular circumstance of a mother concerned about her children's safety as well as her own. These circumstances necessarily include:

> [the] risks attendant to leaving, if the batterer has threatened to kill her if she does; risks attendant to staying and suffering continued abuse; risks attendant to seeking assistance through government channels, potentially increasing the danger to herself and her children; risks attendant to criminal prosecution against the abuser; and risks attendant to relocation.[102]

Surely, if in a civil case "the reasonable parent" standard must be tailored to the actual circumstances the parent faces, the criminal law should do no less.

C. Why Don't Women Get Help?

In hindsight, it may seem clear that a woman whose child was at risk of harm from her husband or boyfriend should have contacted police, but in practice there are many reasons why women do not. Women often refrain from calling 911 because of mandatory arrest policies in many cities and towns, particularly those that require both parties to be arrested.[103] An arrest can also trigger the loss of public housing benefits, jeopardizing a family's stability and economic security.[104] Many women of color, who are disproportionately represented among mothers prosecuted for child abuse by omission,[105] are reluctant to contact the police. In part, this reflects a general distrust of law enforcement in communities of color, along with a desire to keep one's private life free from government surveillance and intrusion. Further, some women may hesitate to report their partners, given the reality that men of color, especially African-American men, are imprisoned at much higher rates and for longer periods of time than white men.[106] African-American, Latina, and Asian-American women are also more likely than white women to have difficulty acknowledging and responding to intimate partner violence because of reluctance to report their partners to friends, family, or law enforcement, especially if they are illegal immigrants and fear revealing that status to legal authorities.[107]

In addition, women are often afraid to seek help from law enforcement because of the growing number of public nuisance ordinances that penalize landlords who fail to effectively control crime on their premises. In practice these laws, which "count" every police visit to the landlord's property as an instance of public nuisance, encourage landlords to evict any woman who calls the police in response to violence in her home. As a result, many women remain silent, enduring violence from a spouse or partner because they fear the consequences of eviction more than physical injuries and psychological terror from the abuser. Recent studies have shown that these ordinances, which are increasingly popular around the country, have a disproportionate impact on victims of domestic violence.[108]

Other women are afraid to contact law enforcement because the abuser has threatened to retaliate if they do. In *Commonwealth v. Lazarovich*, a mother was charged with failing to prevent her husband's violent attacks on their daughter. Janice Lazarovich testified that her husband's violence began early in their marriage. He violently assaulted her throughout her second pregnancy, but when she tried to call the police, he ripped the phone from the wall and choked her with the phone cord. On another occasion, after her husband threw her on the floor she called the police when he was out of the room. The police came to the house but took no action. After they left, her husband picked up a knife with one hand and her young son with another; he threatened to cut their son's throat the next time she called the police.[109]

Similar fears can dissuade women from seeking medical attention for their children after a partner has abused them. In *Lazarovich*, Janice

Lazarovich testified that after her husband beat her daughter, she delayed seeking medical treatment because she didn't want to leave her other children alone with their father while she went to the hospital.[110] In addition, many women are reluctant to seek medical treatment out of fear that they will lose their children,[111] a fear that their batterers often exploit. In *State v. Fernane*, when a mother returned from a twenty-minute trip to the grocery store to find her two-year-old unconscious, her boyfriend dissuaded her from immediately seeking medical treatment, saying, "No, we'll all go down for this."[112]

IV. How Psychosocial Processes Affect Essential Legal Decisionmakers
A. *"The Reasonable Person" Standard and Parental Duty*

As we have noted throughout this book, unconscious mental processes have a powerful effect on how legal decisionmakers apply fundamental legal concepts, such as "the reasonable person." The construction of "the reasonable person," which operationalizes the standard of criminal negligence, is supposed to be simultaneously objective and subjective. Defendants are to be evaluated based on what a hypothetical reasonable person would do in the particular circumstances facing a defendant.[113] As the New York Court of Appeals emphasized in *Nicholson v. Scopetta*, the determination of whether a particular woman has met the standard of "the reasonable mother" accused of child abuse or neglect must take into account all of the circumstances she faces. Among these circumstances are the risks of leaving, including her abuser's threats to kill her if she tries to leave; the risks of staying and continuing to be abused; the risks of contacting social service or law enforcement, which could exacerbate the situation rather than solve it; and the risks created by trying to find safe housing for herself and her children.[114]

Yet in practice, as jurors and judges devise and apply the standard of "the reasonable person" to the defendant, they are likely to imbue "the reasonable parent" and "the reasonable mother" with heightened solicitude for her children's welfare, as well as "better-than-average" abilities to achieve it. This version of "the reasonable mother" is likely to have superhuman powers, including the ability to foresee and forestall all potential harmful acts of her partner; this leads in many cases to mothers' being held to a higher standard than fathers.[115] Prevailing cultural views of maternal nurturance, care, and prudence inevitably find their way into the law. As Professor Mayo Moran observed in her analysis of "the reasonable person," discussed in chapter 2, when judges and jurors construct "the reasonable person," they take gender into account in determining the appropriate standard of behavior. Attitudes toward women appear to have changed remarkably little since Judge Cooley's decision in the *Hasseneyer* case in the nineteenth century. Discussing the concept of negligence, he declared:

> [W]e should probably agree that a woman would be likely to be more prudent, careful and particular in many positions and in the performance of many duties than a man would. She would . . . be more vigilant and indefatigable in her care of a helpless child; . . . she would be more particular to keep within the limits of absolute safety.[116]

That mothers should display these attributes of extraordinary care and selflessness is a consistent theme in in the comments made by legal decisionmakers. Jurors who insist that a mother "should have protected that baby with everything she had," prosecutors who assert that a mother's obligation is to "lay her life . . . on the line for her child,"[117] and judges who impose heavy sentences to condemn a mother who "abandoned or abdicated" her duty are all employing a standard to evaluate accused mothers that is more rigorous than the law demands. One judge went so far as to assert that when one parent is the abuser and the other parent either knows or should have known of that abuse, the non-abusing parent has an even higher duty to act, because the child has no other advocate.[118]

How is it that mothers who fail to protect their children are subject to such elevated legal standards? Several unconscious psychological processes are at work. One is the fundamental attribution error, the subconscious coping mechanism that helps us make sense of disturbing and tragic events. In order to continue to believe in a world that is just, in which "good things happen to 'good' people and bad things happen to 'bad' people," we engage in "defensive attribution." The fundamental attribution error permits us to maintain a belief in a just world by retrospectively interpreting events in a way that attributes adversity to people's internal characteristics, which are often flawed, rather than to external circumstances that are beyond their control.[119] The fundamental attribution error permits our unconscious stereotypes to be activated, which "may distort judgments about blame and responsibility." When "an actor's behavior appears to confirm a stereotype about the actor's group, we tend to attribute that behavior to a dispositional factor within the control of the actor. If, however, the behavior is inconsistent with our ... [group stereotype], we are apt to seek out an external explanation and attribute the behavior to situational forces."[120] Thus, when mothers live with men who abuse their children, especially men to whom they are not married, jurors may draw upon unconscious stereotypes and biases about motherhood and determine that the abuse in this case happened because the women were "bad mothers," whose character and conduct were far below that of the ideal self-sacrificing, protective, and nurturing mother. There is significant evidence that jurors, judges, and prosecutors are animated, in red, blue, and purple states, to believe that single mothers are highly sexualized beings, whose actions must be closely scrutinized for evidence that lust overcame their maternal instincts.[121] Finally, the fundamental attribution error can also trigger unconscious stereotyping based on a defendant's race and ethnicity, which again can affect how jurors determine causation.

Jurors' assessments of whether a mother behaved "reasonably" can also be shaped by their unconscious reliance on "biased prototypes." As Martha Chamallas explains, the use of biased prototypes is an unconscious attempt to "assimilate" new situations. It permits people to fit new information into their existing mental categories by looking for "a family resemblance between the new case and the prototypical case."[122] But because the biased prototype is inaccurate—that is, the family resemblance is merely superficial—jurors often draw misleading conclusions when they rely upon it. For example, a mother prosecuted for failing to protect her children from a violent partner may offer evidence of her own victimization by the same man, seeking to explain why she failed to report his abuse to the authorities. Because many jurors are aware of intimate partner violence but not its connection to child abuse, they may carry in their heads a biased prototype of domestic violence, relying on the writings of Lenore Walker and others who focus on one type of battered woman, who tolerates abuse for a long time but ultimately asserts herself and strikes back to kill her abuser in self-defense. These jurors may not be able to fairly evaluate a battered mother who does not kill her abuser, who does not act aggressively to protect her children. Her risk calculus may be different because she must take into account the short- and long-term consequences, for her children and herself, of contacting law enforcement or seeking other avenues of escape from the abuse.

B. Causation

Most of the cases examined in this chapter are predicated on a *mother's* failure to act. As in *Palmer v. State*, a mother can be convicted of the abuse or death of a child if a jury or judge finds, beyond a reasonable doubt, that the mother's omission to act is both the "actual cause"—setting in motion a chain of events that resulted in the ultimate harm—and "proximate cause" of the harm. It is this framing of events that permits prosecutors to persuade jurors and judges that it is the *mother's* conduct that is the source of harm to her child, not the violence and abuse of the mother's partner. This framing is commonplace. When the question asked is "Why didn't the mother leave?" rather than "Why didn't the man stop abusing the children?" the expected answer is inevitable. Thus, in *People v. Abramson*, the Appellate Court of Illinois ruled that it was a *"fundamental fact* that [the mother's] . . . *failure to intercede* to protect her two very young children . . . directly *resulted in death just as sure as if she would have struck those blows herself."*[123]

How does this framing occur, and why is it so successful? While actual cause and proximate cause might appear to be objectively ascertainable, in reality both are psychologically and socially constructed at a very deep level. The identification of a defendant's action or inaction as an "actual cause" of harm hinges on the way in which a factual scenario of events is framed. As Martha Chamallas and Jennifer Wriggins have noted, this process—called "causal attribution"—does not flow inevitably from the laws of physics but rather relies on unconscious psychological mechanisms. Making decisions about causation implicates the "active process of social construction," which will vary according to the decisionmaker's "'time, place, culture and interest.'"[124]

Similarly, Professor Joshua Dressler recognizes that "courts and juries don't discover the proximate cause of harm—they select it."[125] Indeed, under the Model Penal Code juries are explicitly asked to make a value judgment, to decide whether the result that occurred was contemplated or foreseeable by the defendant or otherwise "too remote or accidental in its occurrence to have a [just] bearing on the actor's liability or on the gravity of his offense."[126]

The historic approach of American criminal law toward causation preferred a single, unitary source of harm. The naïveté of this view is now widely accepted, as most scholars today recognize that causation is multifactorial. Nonetheless, most lay people still believe that causation can be determined through a simple and straightforward reasoning process. "[P]eople tend to be 'content to rely on what first strikes them as a plausible sufficient cause for an event.'"[127]

These two strands of causation theory—a focus on foreseeability and a quest for a single simple cause—converge when parents are prosecuted for failing to protect their children. Even when prosecutors acknowledge that more than one individual contributed to the harm suffered by a child, they construct a narrative framework in which they identify an omission—the parent's failure to act—as the actual cause of harm, which sets in motion a cascading chain of events leading eventually to the child's injury or death. Prosecutors then argue that the consequences of the parent's failure to act were entirely foreseeable, so that the failure to act is also the proximate cause of the harm.

Prosecutors succeed in this reframing because jurors' causal attributions are influenced by a host of unconscious psychological mechanisms. First, prosecutors rely on the anchoring heuristic. Anchoring provides decisionmakers with a specific reference point that frames the choices available to them, subtly influencing their responses. For example, in a tort suit alleging that the defendant caused the plaintiff to suffer injuries, the anchor may be the specific number presented by the plaintiff's attorney as the amount of money necessary to compensate the plaintiff for his injuries. Both judges and jurors are strongly influenced by anchoring.[128] Prosecutors anchor their causation arguments when they assert that it is a parent's omission to act, not the physical abuse and violence of the parent's partner, that begins the causal chain. This provides jurors with a frame of reference, which increases the odds that they will find the omission to be the "actual cause" of harm to the child.[129]

Arguments about causation also implicate the fundamental attribution error. As noted in the discussion of "the reasonable person," jurors deciding cases of children's abuse or death want to believe in a just (and safe) world. As a result, they are likely to construct a narrative of the trial that focuses on the defendant's character ("a bad mother"), rather than view the horrific events in a broader, situational context, in which the terrible events are understood as the result of difficult circumstances that were external to the defendant.

In contrast to actual cause, proximate cause is defined by foreseeability. Here, the unconscious hindsight bias can powerfully shape our perceptions of whether events, particularly adverse outcomes, were actually foreseeable at the time that relevant decisions were made. Professor Baruch Fischhoff has shown that "[f]inding out that an outcome has occurred increases its perceived likelihood," a classic example of 20–20 hindsight. The hindsight bias leads people to "assess the quality of a decision not by whether the process was sound but by whether its outcome was good or bad."[130] In a criminal trial in which a mother is charged with child abuse or homicide based on her inaction, the hindsight bias can readily lead judges or juries to conclude that because a bad outcome occurred after the mother decided not to act, her decisionmaking process was itself flawed, and the bad outcome was foreseeable.[131] The hindsight bias was at work in *State v. McLaughlin*,[132] making it easy for the prosecutor to persuade the jury that *because* Ginger McLaughlin's husband killed their infant son while she ran an errand, it was foreseeable that he could have done so, since Ginger was aware of his bad temper and prior abusive acts. Because judges are also subject to the hindsight bias, they may not exercise their proper screening function to evaluate the sufficiency of the evidence before submitting a case to the jury. As the Texas Court of Criminal Appeals ruled in *State v. Williams*, "[It] is not enough to provide the jury with a set of legally correct definitions and then simply turn them [sic] loose and accept whatever they decide."[133]

Conclusion

The cases in which parents do not prevent their children from being harmed by the parent's abusive or violent partner are heartrending. Undoubtedly some of these parents should be prosecuted and punished severely. Nonetheless, before mothers—and fathers—are prosecuted, convicted, and sentenced, it is essential to try to minimize the impact of idealized norms of parenting, unconscious biases, and other psychological processes that can distort the legal standards that prosecutors, jurors, and judges are charged with applying and enforcing. Indeed, in these cases of triangulated violence, rather than focus on the after-the-fact condemnation of women as bad mothers, a far better way to protect children from abuse, injury, and death is to respond effectively to the man's violence against the mother—offering her social and economic support and stepping up law enforcement against abusive partners.

PART III

Environmental Hazards to Children

Toxic Substances and Contagious Diseases

8

Childhood Lead Poisoning and Other People's Children

Introduction

A. The Case of Steven Thomas

In 1991 Steven Thomas was living in Milwaukee. At the age of fourteen months he was found to have significant levels of lead in his system. His blood lead level (BLL) was 18μg/dL, well above the 10μg/dL level that was viewed as risky in 1978, when the United States banned the use of leaded paint in residential settings.[1] Eight months later, Steven's blood lead level had risen to 40 μg/dL; and it rose further, to 49 μg/dL by the time he was three years old. Despite receiving painful chelation therapy to remove the lead from his blood, Steven was permanently affected by his exposure to lead at a young age, when lead is most harmful because it moves easily from the bloodstream into the brain. Steven was diagnosed with significant cognitive impairments, language deficits, attention deficit hyperactivity disorder, and problems with fine motor skills. *After* Steven was found to have high blood lead levels, the two homes where he lived—one built in 1900 and the other in 1905—were found to have paint with high concentrations of lead. This was hardly surprising, given that paints containing up to 50 percent lead pigment were used extensively in interior house painting from the late 1800s through the 1940s. The three landlords who owned the two homes were found to have violated lead paint regulations.[2]

One of the landlords agreed to provide partial compensation for Steven's injuries, but the others resisted paying for the harm Steven suffered. Steven sued those landlords, as well as the manufacturers of lead paint and lead pigments who had done business in Wisconsin in the early twentieth century. Although the landlords settled with Steven, the lead paint and pigment manufacturers did not. They contended that because Steven could not identify the manufacturer of the specific lead paint or pigment found in the homes where he had lived, he could not meet the requirement of causation that is essential for tort liability.[3] In 2005, in a landmark decision, *Thomas ex rel. Gramling v. Mallett*, the Wisconsin Supreme Court declared that Steven had the right to sue the paint and pigment manufacturers. Under the "risk contribution" theory first articulated in *Collins v. Eli Lilly Co.*, people injured by lead poisoning could sue manufacturers of dangerous products even though they could not prove which manufacturer had produced the particular product that caused them injury.[4]

The response to the court's decision was swift. The business lobbying group Wisconsin Manufacturers & Commerce spent heavily to defeat Justice Louis Butler, the lead author of the *Thomas* decision, asserting that the decision was "'judicial activism of the worst kind.'" Justice Butler became the first Wisconsin justice to lose a bid for reelection in more than forty years.[5] After Scott Walker became governor of Wisconsin in 2011, the state legislature enacted a law that explicitly overturned the *Thomas v. Mallett* decision. Asserting that its goal was "to return tort law to its historical, common law roots," it declared that *Thomas* had improperly expanded the risk contribution theory first articulated in *Collins*. The law also established limits on future products liability cases, focusing particularly on product identification and time limitations.[6] This law effectively placed the full costs of injuries caused by lead contamination on individual families and, to a lesser extent, the state and local governments that provided lead remediation and medical treatment. Of course, overturning a state court decision is well within legislative prerogative under the separation of powers doctrine. However, in this case the new law was made retroactive. Plaintiffs representing other children injured by lead paint poisoning went to court to challenge the law's retroactive application to all cases pending at the time of enactment. In *Gibson v. American Cyanamid*, the United States Court of Appeals for the Seventh Circuit held that these other lead poisoning cases, which had relied on *Thomas*, could go forward.[7] In addition, a Wisconsin trial court has declared that the statute's retroactive effect violates the due process clause of the Wisconsin Constitution.[8]

When Steven Thomas' case went to trial, expert witnesses and lawyers for the manufacturers asserted that even though Steven had ingested significant amounts of lead as a young child, his having done so was not the cause of his low IQ, poor academic performance, or behavioral problems. Instead, the manufacturers' key expert witness testified, Steven's limited abilities were the product of "'the home, the environment, [and] the genetics that he came from.'" The witness emphasized that Steven's parents had IQs in the "borderline range"; other documents provided to the jury asserted that Steven was born into a "'[c]haotic household'" and was the ninth child of a mother with a "history of alcohol abuse" and a "poor diet." The witness also claimed that Steven's elevated blood lead levels were "too low" to explain his poor academic performance.[9] The jury was apparently persuaded by these arguments; it returned a verdict declaring that the lead contamination in the two apartments had *not* caused Steven's intellectual, neurological, or behavioral problems.[10]

The case of Steven Thomas exemplifies many of the problems with the American legal system's response to childhood lead poisoning. First, his injuries were entirely preventable, *if* the government had required housing contaminated with lead to be cleaned up—by their owners or lead products manufacturers—before young children were allowed to live there. Second, the case illuminates the connections between unconscious mental processes, including risk construction, and putatively neutral legal principles, demonstrating how easy it is to distance ourselves from the harm suffered by other people's children.[11] Despite the fact that a young child was exposed to high doses of a poison that is known to cause precisely the neurological, physical, and behavioral impairments from which he suffered, the manufacturers of that poison were not held legally accountable. Instead, the child's mother, a woman with a low IQ and a substance abuse problem, was deemed to be responsible for his deficiencies.

B. Lead Poisoning in Context

Lead is ubiquitous throughout the United States. It is found in the air we breathe, the water we drink, and our homes, yards, and playgrounds.[12] Lead is the most well studied of environmental toxins,[13] as well as the most harmful.[14] When the United States banned the use of leaded paint in residential settings in 1978, more than 64 million American homes (three-quarters of the nation's housing) contained lead paint.[15] Thirteen and a half million children one to five years old were deemed to be at risk of mental and physical impairment because their blood lead levels were greater than 10µg/dL.[16] Almost forty years after this ban, more than 500,000 American children under the age of six—one in thirty-eight—are *still* victims of lead poisoning every year.[17] In cities across the nation, lead found in tap water and deteriorating dwellings is destroying the health and intellectual capabilities of *hundreds of thousands* of American children, condemning them to a lifetime of physical and mental impairments, behavioral problems, and struggles with academic and economic achievement.[18] In 2012 this recognition prompted the Centers for Disease Control to declare that *there is no safe level* of lead exposure.[19]

This chapter focuses on lead, the most serious threat to the health of American children today. It examines the biology, history, and sociology of lead poisoning in this country and confronts the ways in which the American legal system has permitted lead poisoning to be a disease that primarily afflicts the poor and children of color, who often live in dilapidated housing and populate our inner cities. It explores the limitations of traditional tort actions in compensating children injured by lead, as well as the prevailing skepticism about the precautionary principle. It asks, once again, why we are more likely to find mothers, rather than others, responsible for risking harm to their children's health.

This chapter also highlights the important role given to "choice" in American law. The concept of choice appears to be applied unevenly in different health care contexts, often in ways that depend on gender, socioeconomic class, and race. In chapters 4 and 5 we saw how the law denies pregnant women the opportunity to make basic health care decisions for themselves and for their children. In situations ranging from making advance medical directives and determining whether or not to undergo a caesarean section, to deciding about the use of legal and illegal drugs, pregnant women are frequently denied the choice given to other adults. In chapter 6 we observed that new mothers are generally allowed to decide whether to breastfeed their infants, within the constraints of medical advice and family economics and values. However, a mother's choice can also lead to criminal prosecution if, in retrospect, it appears that she made the wrong decision, because breastfeeding did not provide adequate nourishment for, or inadvertently transmitted a drug to, her infant.

In chapter 7 we saw *choice* employed in a different sense. In cases in which a mother did not prevent her child from being harmed by a violent or abusive partner, prosecutors frequently allege that the mother "chose" to stay in an abusive relationship, or "chose" to put her sexual relationship with her partner above the needs of her child. Invoking the legal principles of causation, prosecutors hold the mother's ostensible "choice" not to intervene on behalf of her child against her. First, prosecutors frame the mother's failure to act as the actual cause of the harm inflicted by her husband or boyfriend. Then they assert that because her partner's violent or abusive conduct was foreseeable, the mother's inaction was also the proximate cause of the harm to her child.

In the context of childhood lead poisoning, *choice* is used in two distinct ways. First, choice is the remedy that Congress selected as a way to protect children from exposure to hazardous levels of lead. Under a 1992 statute, the Residential Lead-Based Paint Hazard Reduction Act,[20] renters and purchasers of homes where young children live must be informed of the possibility that lead paint is present and could be harmful to children. Renters and purchasers can choose whether to rent or buy the home, but the law imposes no obligation on landlords or sellers to remove any lead that is present.

Second, *choice* or its analogue, *control*, is invoked in discussing the principles of causation. Manufacturers of lead paints and pigments were aware in the late nineteenth and early twentieth centuries that lead was highly toxic to children. Yet, despite this awareness, they strenuously resisted government efforts to limit or ban the use of lead in paint. As a direct result of their resistance it was not until the late 1970s that the federal government banned lead paint, a half-century after most other industrialized nations had acted. Today when child plaintiffs suffering from lead poisoning seek to hold these manufacturers legally accountable, they resist liability by invoking theories of "choice" and "control." First, the manufacturers assert that they did not *choose* to create a risk of harm, because lead paint is dangerous to children only when it deteriorates, and by the time that occurs, in old and crumbling housing, the lead pigments and paint are no longer under the manufacturers' control. In essence, they argue that the decision to create conditions hazardous to children was not theirs, that it was instead landlords and property owners who *chose* not to protect children by failing to adequately maintain structures that were painted with lead paint at a time when it was legal. Second, they argue that any intellectual impairments or behavioral problems of a child with an admittedly high blood lead level were not caused by the child's ingestion of lead paint or lead dust but should instead be attributed to the mother's limited academic abilities and poor parenting skills.

Historically, the harms created by lead exposure have been addressed after the fact: once a child has been discovered to have high levels of lead in his body. Today, America's children—especially those who are poor and racial minorities—serve as canaries in the coal mine. Only *after* a child is tested and found to have high blood levels of lead will public health officials seek to identify the source of that lead—in deteriorating paint or drinking water—and reach out to other children living at the same address or in the same neighborhood who might be at risk.[21] Indeed, in some cities and states children's blood lead levels must be well above levels known to be harmful before public health authorities will order an inspection of the child's home to determine the extent of lead contamination.[22] In the vast majority of cases, children receive monetary relief only after individual litigation, an extraordinarily expensive and time-consuming way to reduce the risk of harm.[23] Despite widespread awareness of the significant health risk that lead poses to children living in older, deteriorating housing, the most obvious and effective way to decrease that risk—removing the lead before children live there—is attempted in far too few instances, a result of funding choices made by Congress and state and local governments.[24]

If half a million American children were the victims of an infectious disease—such as polio in the 1950s—there would be a public outcry. Undoubtedly that outrage would result in the deployment of massive public and private resources to investigate the source of harm and to develop a comprehensive strategy to treat affected children and prevent harm to future generations, as was indeed the case with polio. Yet a major public health initiative to prevent childhood lead poisoning has not materialized. Public lead abatement programs are woefully underfunded. This is so despite multiple studies showing that preventive action would more than pay for itself when compared with the continuing costs of treating afflicted children and cleaning up lead-contaminated sites, considering *only* the economic, and not human, benefits of preventing lead poisoning in the first place.[25] Indeed, in the past five years Congress has repeatedly cut federal funding for lead poisoning prevention and abatement.[26] Lawsuits seeking injunctive relief or money damages to compensate children injured by lead poisoning and to clean up hazardous lead paint in deteriorated housing, brought under products liability or public nuisance theories, continue to face an uphill battle in the courts.

I. How Lead Poisoning Occurs
A. How Children Are Exposed to Lead

Lead has been used in manufacturing for more than 5,000 years—to make tools and toy soldiers, to make wine sweeter, to avoid "knocking" in the internal combustion engine, and to make paint shinier and longer-lasting.[27] The ancient Greeks and Romans recognized that lead was dangerous to human health, observing the harmful impact of exposure to lead on workers and recommending against the use of lead pipes to convey water.[28]

In the United States, lead was first used in paint around 1800.[29] By the late nineteenth century it was well known that lead paint poisoned children and adults. Many medical and scientific articles published in the late 1800s and early 1900s revealed lead's toxicity at every level of exposure. The manufacturers of lead pigments and paints were well aware of these studies. For example, a 1900 internal Sherwin-Williams Company document noted, "It is also familiarly known that white lead is a deadly cumulative poison. . . ." During World War I, Sherwin-Williams recommended that the government revise its specifications for painting soldiers' helmets—which requested the use of 50 percent white lead carbonate paint—because of the dangers that lead paint posed. As an alternative, the company recommended that the government substitute another Sherwin-Williams paint that was lead-free.[30]

Lead products manufacturers also knew that lead poisoning had a disproportionate impact on poor inner-city children who were members of racial minorities. In the mid-1930s Manfred Bowditch, the Director of Health and Safety of the Lead Industries Association, a major trade group, acknowledged the risk that lead paint posed to children. He described childhood lead poisoning as "'a major 'headache,' this being in part due . . . to the fact that the only real remedy lies in educating a relatively ineducable category of parents." In a classic illustration of the fundamental attribution error he commented, "'The basic solution is—to get rid of our slums, but—even Uncle Sam can't seem to swing that one.

Next in importance is to educate the parents, but most of the cases are in Negro and Puerto Rican families, and how does one tackle that job?"[31]

Despite their recognition of the disastrous human consequences of exposure to lead from deteriorating paint, manufacturers continued to produce and promote lead paint for institutional and residential use. Many paints contained 50 percent lead,[32] even though companies also manufactured nonleaded alternatives. While many European nations banned lead-based paints at the beginning of the twentieth century, American paint manufacturers lobbied hard against similar action by American governments, claiming that efforts to ban lead paint were "a sinister plot by labor interests."[33] From the early 1900s until the beginning of World War II, manufacturers coordinated national advertising campaigns to encourage consumers to use lead-based paints.[34] As a result, today, almost four decades after the federal government's ban on lead in paint, more than a third of American housing stock still contains lead from old paint. Nearly a quarter of American homes pose significant hazards because lead-based paint has deteriorated and improper repairs have resulted in interior lead dust and lead in the soil around the house.[35]

Children encounter lead whenever housing is not well maintained, leading to peeling paint, paint chips, and lead dust. Lead-based paint accounts for 85 percent of children's lead exposure.[36] Even where lead paint is intact, lead dust is released every time a window or door is opened or shut.[37] Lead is released into the atmosphere when bridges and other public works previously painted with lead paint are "upgraded" through sandblasting without proper containment.[38] Children are also exposed to lead dust when their parents bring lead-contaminated clothing home from work.[39]

To a lesser extent, children are exposed to lead through drinking water or by licking or chewing toys that contain lead. In 2007 there was a flurry of media attention when it was discovered that many toys imported from China contained high levels of lead. In response, the Consumer Product Safety Commission (CPSC) issued multiple toy recalls, individual parents sued toy manufacturers on behalf of their children, and Congress enacted a statute aimed at reducing this hazard, expressly limiting the lead content of toys and authorizing the CPSC to promulgate regulations to reduce the risk that future children will be harmed by lead exposure from toys.

Lead is released into drinking water when chemicals used to disinfect the water supply leach lead from old pipes that contain lead or lead soldering.[40] In 1986 Congress revised the Safe Drinking Water Act, directing the EPA to establish drinking water regulations that set permissible contaminant levels so that "no known or anticipated effects on the health of persons occur and which allows an adequate margin of safety."[41] Five years later, the EPA promulgated the Lead and Copper Rule. The rule limits the concentration of lead in drinking water to 15 parts per billion (ppb) per one liter of water, measured at the tap. This takes into account the very real possibility that water which is safe to drink at a municipal processing plant becomes contaminated as lead leaches into the water system along the way to children's homes, or even from lead pipes or solder in the house's plumbing.[42] Between 2001 and 2004 about 42,000 young children and developing fetuses in Washington, D.C., were exposed to elevated levels of lead in drinking water in violation of the Lead and Copper Rule; more than 900 children were found to have elevated blood lead levels as a result.[43] The crisis in Flint, Michigan, a result of a decision to save money by using water from the Flint River as the city's water supply, has made it apparent how easy it is for public water systems to be contaminated with dangerous levels of lead.[44] In 2014 more than 7 percent of the Flint children tested had elevated blood lead levels.[45] Other cities, including Providence, Rhode Island, and Portland, Oregon, also have high levels of lead in their public drinking water.[46] Indeed, in June 2016 the National Resources Defense Council estimated that more than a thousand public water systems, serving nearly 4 million people, had water with lead levels higher than those permitted by the Lead and Cooper Rule.[47]

B. How Lead Harms Children and Leads to Lifelong Impairments

Lead is especially dangerous to young children because it enters their bodies when they are developing rapidly. Lead in the bloodstream readily enters the brain and literally shapes its development, because young children have an immature blood-brain barrier. Children absorb lead much more easily than adults and retain much more of the absorbed lead in their systems.[48] Studies have found that even small increases in BLL, from 1 to 4 µg/dL, are associated with a decrease in IQ between two to five points. In 2012 this led the CDC to stop referring to 10 μg/dL as the "blood lead level of concern," sufficient to trigger medical and public health investigations, because this would overlook many children at risk.[49] The CDC cited recent research showing that children with blood lead levels at or lower than 10 μg/dL still had physical, mental, and behavioral problems[50] and concluded that the 10 μg/dL cutoff did not provide an adequate margin of safety, because individual children vary in their susceptibility to lead's adverse effects.[51] Toddlers are particularly likely to ingest lead because they are active explorers, putting everything in their mouths, including paint chips and toys and blankets, which may be contaminated with lead dust. Lead paint chips taste sweet and are even sweeter at higher lead concentrations. A California court found recently that "[a] chip of lead paint that is approximately the size of a period at the end of a sentence is sufficient to cause a BLL of 20 micrograms per deciliter [20 μg/dL] if ingested by a young child."[52] Children whose diets lack basic nutrients like iron and calcium are more likely to be adversely affected by lead because lead is absorbed more readily when these nutrients are absent.[53]

Blood lead levels peak around age two, a time of great vulnerability for children because of their developing brains. Children who are exposed to lead as infants and toddlers are much more likely to suffer permanently from hyperactivity, impulsivity, distractibility, and restlessness, as well as cognitive impairments, than children who are either never exposed to lead or who are exposed to it when older. Lead is stored in bone and teeth, so the impact of lead poisoning is cumulative.[54] A major longitudinal study of low-income African-American children in Philadelphia examined their development from birth through age twenty-two. It found that for boys lead poisoning was "*the most significant predictor* of school disciplinary problems"; it was also a leading predictor of juvenile delinquency and adult criminal activity.[55]

II. Government Responses to the Risks of Lead

The federal government has responded in disparate ways to the dangers of lead poisoning depending on the source of the lead and, at least in part, the people who were most at risk of exposure.

A. Risks from Lead Paint

In response to the lobbying efforts of paint and pigment manufacturers, the federal government acted slowly to address the risks from lead-based paints, despite substantial evidence that lead was extraordinarily dangerous to children.[56] While some cities and states enacted bans on lead paint for residential and commercial buildings, including Baltimore in 1951, New York City in 1960, and Chicago in 1972, lead-based paint remained on the market even after these bans.[57]

Congress did not act until 1971, when it passed the Lead-Based Paint Poisoning Prevention Act. The law's major achievements were requiring federally funded public housing programs to sample the lead content of paint in apartments where young children lived and limiting the interstate transportation of paint containing lead in amounts greater than permitted by the Consumer Product Safety Commission (CPSC).[58] In 1972 the CPSC issued a partial ban on lead paint, limiting the sale of lead-based paint for interior and exterior residential use to paint containing less than 0.5 percent lead. Six years later the CPSC issued a more comprehensive ban, prohibiting the sale of paint for residential use that contained more than .006 percent lead.[59]

However, the decision to ban the use of lead in paint did nothing to abate existing lead paint hazards. Nearly forty years later, more than a third of American homes still contain lead-based paint, which will inevitably disintegrate if it is not well maintained.[60] Ninety-five percent of homes built before 1950 contain some lead. Homes built before 1950 are likely to have paint with higher concentrations of lead than houses built between 1950 and 1978.[61] In urban areas where most poor children live, the proportion of houses with lead-based paint is even higher. In Philadelphia, for example, more than 90 percent of the housing stock was built before 1978.[62]

In 1992, Congress recognized the need "to develop a national strategy to build the infrastructure . . . to eliminate lead-based paint hazards in all housing as expeditiously as possible,"[63] because more than three million American children under age six were then affected by low level lead poisoning.[64] As a result, Congress enacted the Residential Lead-Based Paint Hazard Reduction Act (RLBPHRA or Act).[65] The law's supporters acknowledged that lead poisoning was "the No. 1 environmental health problem facing American children today."[66]

However, Congress' choice of strategy was at once inadequate and typically American. While the law provided some funding for lead abatement in federally funded housing programs, it imposed no obligation on lead and lead paint manufacturers to clean up the poisons they had already marketed. Instead, the Act provided an "educational" remedy, a mandatory disclosure obligation. *In essence, Congress' primary weapon in the battle to decrease children's exposure to lead was a form letter.* The Act required sellers and landlords of all property built before 1978 to advise potential purchasers and renters of the possibility that lead paint was present at the property as well as any actual knowledge they had about lead paint there. The ostensible purpose of this notice requirement was to permit buyers and renters to make an informed choice about whether to buy or rent a particular property.[67] It took nearly four years for the EPA and the Department of Housing and Urban Development (HUD) to develop an appropriate disclosure form.[68] The sole remedy for buyers or renters who were not informed about the risks of lead paint was monetary, limited to three times the amount of property damages incurred as a result of the failure to disclose, including the costs of cleanup and the decrease in the value of the property due to the presence of lead, plus attorneys' fees. Buyers or renters who did not receive the required notice about the existence of a lead hazard were not permitted to rescind (undo) their agreement to purchase or rent the house.[69]

The Act's reliance on disclosure is consistent with American law generally, reflecting an underlying belief that knowledge is power and that individuals should be free to make their own decisions, no matter how ill advised.[70] While that belief is congenial with American culture, as well as a legal and political system that places its faith in freedom of contract and a theoretically competitive marketplace, it is an inadequate basis for public health policy. People who lack economic means, language skills, and consumer sophistication will not be protected by a disclosure obligation from agreeing to rent or buy housing that is dangerous to their children.

Further, the law ignores the reality that for many renters, as well as some buyers, the "choice" not to rent or buy a lead-contaminated home is illusory. In cities where affordable housing is scarce, most people have no option other than to sign a lease for a home in an old building with deteriorating paint. As a Baltimore attorney who represented thousands of Baltimore children in suits seeking compensation for lead poisoning explained, "'That's the sad fact to [sic] life in the ghetto that the only living conditions people can afford will likely poison their kids. . . . If you only have $250 per month, you're going to get a run down, dilapidated house where the landlord hasn't inspected it the entire time they've owned it.'"[71]

The Act did *not* obligate sellers and landlords to abate lead-based paint hazards and it failed to provide compensation for medical treatment or other harms suffered by children who were exposed to lead paint or lead dust at those premises. Courts faced with lawsuits brought on behalf of children poisoned by lead have repeatedly held that Congress did not intend to authorize a legal remedy for these children. In many cases the courts have also said that the children lacked standing to sue because they were not a party to the lease—that is, not the purchaser or tenant. Only one court has ruled to the contrary.[72]

A few states have gone further than the federal government and have mandated lead paint abatement in all residences where children under age six reside. A Massachusetts law that has been accompanied by aggressive lead screening efforts has been credited with dramatically reducing the incidence of serious lead poisoning in that state and, to a limited extent, with improving children's academic outcomes.[73] Some states require screening of all children under age six, while others have limited the screening requirement to children eligible for Medicaid or WIC, who, because their poverty or poor nutritional status, are statistically most at risk for lead poisoning.[74] Many states have failed to satisfy even this minimal screening obligation.[75] But even assuming that targeted screening is the best use of scarce health care dollars, it does not change the reality that most government agencies are relying on "secondary prevention"—using children with elevated blood lead levels to identify real estate that is likely to be contaminated with lead paint—rather than on "primary prevention"—getting the lead out of housing *before* children are injured.[76] Only rarely have cities or states focused on primary prevention of lead poisoning. Rochester, New York, has targeted its lead abatement efforts on neighborhoods that have the highest incidence of lead poisoning, mandating inspection and cleanup of all apartments with lead hazards, rather than waiting for young children to test with high levels of lead in their blood.[77]

B. Lead in Drinking Water

The disaster that occurred when Flint, Michigan, switched its municipal water supply from Detroit's public system to the Flint River is a reminder of how easy it is for lead to leach from old lead pipes into drinking water.[78] Washington, D.C., suffered a drinking water crisis in 2001–04. After the Army Corps of Engineers decided to use the chemical chloramine, instead of chlorine, to disinfect Washington's water supply, the chloramine caused lead to leach from pipes into drinking water. Even though the D.C. Water and Sewer Authority (DCW) detected elevated lead levels in tap water, it did not immediately respond to this risk and it did not promptly disclose the potential harm to Washington residents or educate them about taking precautionary measures.[79] As in Flint, a number of D.C. children were found to have blood lead levels that were well above the level where it is agreed that cognitive, neurological, and behavioral problems can occur. However, both individual lawsuits and a class action brought by parents of injured children have been dismissed.[80]

C. Atmospheric Lead: A Very Different Story

In striking contrast to the very slow and limited governmental response to lead in deteriorating homes and in public drinking water, the federal government has responded aggressively to concerns about high levels of airborne lead. The history of government action in this area demonstrates that precautionary regulation to protect the public's health can be effective, *if* it is accompanied by sufficient political will. The problem of atmospheric lead was created early in the twentieth century, when automobile makers were trying to make engines more efficient and avoid the problem of engine "knocking." Their solution was to add a potent poison—tetraethyl lead (TEL)—to gasoline. While TEL did indeed make cars run more smoothly and efficiently, it also killed the factory workers who produced it. When TEL was first produced in the United

States, employees at all three TEL factories died; many more became psychotic after being exposed to its fumes. Although the United States Surgeon General imposed a temporary moratorium on TEL production, the Public Health Service quickly lifted that moratorium after the Ethyl Corporation agreed to cap its concentration at 3 cc of TEL per gallon of gasoline.

For many years no further concerns were raised about atmospheric lead, but after World War II, when automobile use expanded rapidly, much more lead was released into the air. Simultaneously, the Ethyl Corporation's patent expired, opening it to competition from other suppliers. Improved gasoline fuels also meant that less TEL was necessary. In a bold effort to preserve its business, Ethyl Corporation sought approval from the Public Health Service to increase the amount of TEL in gasoline to 4 cc per gallon.

By the late 1960s the public began to be concerned about atmospheric lead. In 1966 Senator Edmund Muskie held hearings on a proposed Clean Air Act. At the hearings he directly challenged Ethyl Corporation's witnesses, who denied that increased automobile travel resulted in more atmospheric lead or that it posed any health risk. Muskie argued forcefully that harm could be measured in terms other than deaths, reinforced by the Surgeon General's concern about the risk of harm at low lead exposure levels to pregnant women, fetuses, and children.[81] In response, Congress enacted the Clean Air Act of 1970, which authorized the Administrator of the recently created Environmental Protection Agency to regulate any fuel additive whose emissions products "will endanger the public health or welfare."[82]

In 1973, responding to a petition brought by the Natural Resources Defense Council, the EPA promulgated regulations reducing the use of TEL in gasoline in a graduated, step-down fashion. The Ethyl Corporation challenged the EPA, contending that it had not met its burden under the Clean Air Act to show that atmospheric lead was hazardous to human health. However, writing for the United States Court of Appeals for the District of Columbia Circuit, Judge J. Skelly Wright interpreted the Act's "will endanger" language broadly, explicitly invoking the precautionary principle—that one may act based on evidence of risk, without waiting for harm to materialize.[83] "[E]ndanger," he said, "means something less than actual harm. When one is endangered, harm is *threatened*; no actual injury need ever occur."[84] Relying on this understanding of what Congress intended by its choice of language in the Clean Air Act, the majority opinion held that even though the EPA could not demonstrate specific *actual harm*—either that a significant portion of the population had high lead levels, or that lead from gasoline was the cause of those high levels—the agency had established a significant *risk of harm*. The court considered the facts demonstrating risk: the known toxicity of lead at high exposure levels, the fact that 90 percent of the lead in the ambient air came from leaded gas, and that people living in urban areas, especially children, were already likely to have greater lead exposure than other citizens.[85]

The *Ethyl Corp.* decision also provided a case study of the effectiveness of precautionary regulation. Even while the Ethyl Corporation was seeking to rescind the EPA regulations by political means, research showed that the regulations had dramatically reduced the level of lead in the ambient air, decreasing virtually in lockstep with the regulations' phased reduction of TEL in gasoline. Between 1975 and 1984 lead in gasoline decreased by 73 percent while lead in the atmosphere decreased by 71 percent.[86] Eventually, Congress mandated the elimination of all lead additives in gasoline.[87]

The *Ethyl Corp.* decision was important in another way. Judge Wright was prescient in identifying the dangers to urban children of lead from peeling paint, which he anticipated would be difficult and expensive to abate, even though "the ingestion of lead paint ... is generally regarded as 'the principal environmental source in cases of severe acute lead poisoning in young children.'" He also noted that "*there is no concerted national effort at removal*, and the danger to children living in dilapidated housing will remain for some time."

D. Lead in Toys

Most recently the government has acted to protect children from lead exposure in toys, again illustrating that government is most likely to respond to a risk that is perceived as affecting all of the nation's children. In 2007 the media gave prominent attention to toys that were contaminated with high levels of lead, almost all imported from China. They included a wide range of toys: Thomas the Tank Engine trains, Polly

Pockets dolls, Barbie doll accessories, building blocks, jewelry, paint sets, and action figures.[88] The public was outraged; in response, the Consumer Product Safety Commission (CPSC) and some manufacturers agreed that the toys would be recalled.[89] Congress held hearings and considered legislation to protect children from dangerous toys. The law Congress ultimately enacted, the Consumer Product Safety Improvement Act of 2008, was modest.[90] The Act imposed lower limits on certain toy contaminants, including lead, required more testing for toy safety as well as warning labels, and authorized the CPSC to impose increased penalties for knowing violations of the law.[91] However, critics contended that the law failed to address the two biggest problems in toy safety. First, the vast majority of toys bought by American consumers are manufactured in countries with lax safety standards. More important, the CPSC is so severely underfunded that it lacks the staff necessary to inspect imported toys and other household products or to verify their safety.[92]

Simultaneously, many American consumers pursued litigation against toy manufacturers. The cases were consolidated for trial and ultimately settled. In 2010 a federal judge in California approved a $50 million class action settlement in which Mattel and its subsidiary Fisher-Price agreed to pay partial refunds for all purchasers of lead-contaminated toys and to reimburse parents for the costs of having their children's blood lead levels tested, but only for the first $600,000 of requested reimbursements.[93] Mattel and Fisher-Price agreed to a $12 million settlement with thirty-eight states arising from the same toy recall. What is striking about the 2007 tainted toy crisis is the extensive media coverage it received, as well as the rapid response by government and private corporations to address a potential risk to children's health. Although a few children were seriously injured by the ingestion of lead from toys, for most children the risk was entirely hypothetical. As Dr. Helen Binns, a professor of pediatrics and preventative medicine, observed, while a child may play with a toy for a few moments a day, he is constantly being exposed to lead if his home is being remodeled or when paint is chipped or peeling. Dr. Binns declared that in "85% of lead-poisoning cases . . . the source is deteriorating paint where the child lives or spends time."[94] Yet there is scant media attention to the hundreds of thousands of children, largely poor, African-American, and urban, who have already suffered serious and irreversible harm after ingesting lead-based paint and inhaling lead dust.[95] It is this invisibility of risk when "other people's children" are involved that is at the heart of this chapter, and that has prompted some children's health advocates to pursue products liability and public nuisance litigation against lead pigment and paint manufacturers.

III. Efforts to Use the Tort System to Provide More Protection to Lead-Poisoned Children

A. Introduction

Almost four decades after the United States banned lead-based paint, children who are the victims of lead poisoning remain uncompensated for their injuries, and millions of children live in homes where the risk of lead poisoning is as great as ever. This section examines the reasons *why* the legal system has not protected children from injury. First, it analyzes the legal rules governing causation, products liability, and public nuisance. It then explores the ways in which unconscious psychological processes can affect the decisions of judges, jurors, and legislators as they apply these rules or create new ones. It also examines the role of the socially constructed tort standards of "the reasonable person" and "the reasonable mother" in cases of children's lead poisoning.

Since deteriorated lead paint is the major cause of children's lead poisoning, there are three categories of likely defendants in tort suits for negligence, products liability, and public nuisance: (1) manufacturers of lead pigments used in paint, (2) manufacturers of lead-based paint (who are often the same entities), and (3) owners of dilapidated buildings who have failed to maintain their premises in habitable condition. Most plaintiffs are the children injured by lead poisoning. Typically, these suits seek the abatement of lead in contaminated homes and compensatory damages, including the costs of providing medical treatment and special education and enrichment services, as well as the lifetime loss of earning power due to impaired intellectual and executive functioning abilities.[96] In public nuisance suits, plaintiffs are usually local governments, which seek the abatement of lead paint hazards. Sometimes they also seek reimbursement for the costs of treating children poisoned by lead and developing educational programs to increase public awareness about the risks of lead.[97] Each group of lawsuits has proved an uphill battle, primarily because of the difficulty that plaintiffs face in establishing causation.

B. The Problem of Causation: Actual Cause and Causal Attribution

Lead poisoned children suing to recover against lead pigment and paint manufacturers have relied on two tort theories: products liability and public nuisance. Since the 1960s most products liability lawsuits have been premised on the theory of strict liability in tort. Strict liability applies to products that were either defectively designed or manufactured, as well as to those that were "unavoidably unsafe" and marketed without an adequate consumer warning.[98] Public nuisance lawsuits assert that a defendant has created a condition injurious to the public health that must be eliminated in order to protect the public. In both products liability and public nuisance cases the plaintiffs' biggest challenge has been to establish causation.[99]

Causation, we know, is proven by establishing both "actual" and "proximate" cause. Actual cause is sometimes referred to as "cause-in-fact," encapsulated in the "but/for" test—but for the defendant's action, the harm would not have occurred.[100] Proximate cause is a restriction on liability, limiting legal responsibility to harmful results that were foreseeable at the time of the alleged tortious conduct.[101] For many years the legal rules of causation have effectively shielded manufacturers from liability,[102] with actual cause being the stumbling block to successful litigation. Plaintiffs have found it difficult to establish actual cause because they cannot show that a *specific* lead pigment or paint manufacturer either produced or sold the lead product that was the source of lead subsequently ingested or inhaled by a particular child. Of course, if plaintiffs *can* establish actual cause, it should be easy to establish proximate cause as well. It is quite clear, from the medical literature, internal company documents, and company officials' statements to outsiders, that by the early 1900s paint and pigment manufacturers were well aware of the risk posed by lead-based paints and pigments. The risks that they knew about are precisely the ones that materialized. Leaded paint was expected to deteriorate, and children who ingested lead paint chips or inhaled lead dust suffered significant cognitive, physical, and behavioral impairments.

Plaintiffs in lead paint poisoning cases find it hard to prove "actual cause." The typical plaintiff is like Steven Thomas: a young child living in a home built before 1978 that has peeling and chipped paint surfaces. The plaintiff is usually discovered to have elevated blood lead levels during a routine physical examination or, perhaps, a screening program. This test result will prompt a local health or housing authority to test the home for lead hazards; if they are present, the plaintiff will sue.[103] The plaintiff's initial hurdle is to establish who manufactured the product that is the source of the lead paint or lead dust in the home. Even though the connection between a plaintiff's elevated BLL and the lead paint chips and lead dust in the home appears obvious, it will be virtually impossible to identify the particular brands of lead paint that were used. With most homes built in the early 1900s it will be rare for there to be a century's worth of records indicating which paint was applied over that time, especially since many homes have had multiple owners. Absent a paper record, it is impossible to identify the manufacturer of the particular paint used in a home. Even paint sample analysis reveals only broad classes of leaded paint, such as lead carbonate, lead sulfate, or lead chromate.[104]

This evidentiary problem gives rise to three separate defenses, each based on actual cause. First, manufacturers of lead pigments or lead paint will assert that because the plaintiff cannot identify the specific defendant who produced or sold the product that is the "actual cause" of the plaintiff's injuries, he cannot establish causation and cannot win. Under the "but/for" test for actual causation the plaintiff cannot establish a causal link between any particular lead-products manufacturer and his subsequent injuries. Second, manufacturers will contend that, in any event, it is not the lead pigment or lead paint itself that caused the child's injuries but rather the negligence of the landlord who failed to maintain the child's home in a safe and habitable condition. Here the manufacturers will assert that even *assuming* they had manufactured the pigment or paint found in the dwelling, the negligence of the landlord is an intervening or superseding cause of the plaintiff's harm, which "cuts off" the causal chain from the manufacturer, precluding liability.[105] Third, the manufacturers will argue that even if it could be shown that "their lead" was present in the child's apartment and he had an elevated blood lead level, the lead in his apartment was not the actual cause of his cognitive, neurological, and behavioral difficulties; these are, they contend, the product of his genetics and upbringing.

This last argument can be devastatingly effective because it relies on unconscious psychological processes and prejudices. As a leading commentary on childhood lead poisoning litigation notes, "*the chief defense strategy in such cases is to 'trash' the family.*"[106] Defense counsel may assert that the fact that the child plaintiff with an elevated blood lead level has an IQ that is below average and exhibits learning and behavior problems is due entirely to the genetic contribution of parents who themselves have limited intellectual and cognitive abilities, as well as poor parenting skills.[107] As explained by Professor Jennifer Wriggins, this amounts to "genetic essentialism"—the assertion that "'personal traits are predictable and permanent, determined at conception, [and] "hard-wired" into the human constitution.'"[108] Further, the not so subtle import of such reasoning is that it does not matter that vulnerable young children ingested toxic amounts of lead from apartments contaminated with lead, because these children are already destined to be not so bright due to their parents' intellectual and academic deficits. This reasoning is remarkably similar to that of the Lead Industries Association's Manfred Bowditch, who described childhood lead poisoning as simply "a slum problem," which could not be solved easily because of "ineducable" "Negro and Puerto Rican" parents.[109]

Landlords defending against liability for the lead poisoning of their tenants' children are likely to make a similar argument. In many cases a landlord will concede that a plaintiff can establish "general causation"— the fact that lead in paint and dust can cause cognitive, neurological, behavioral, and physical harms in children who ingest or inhale lead. However, the landlord will contend that the plaintiff in this particular case cannot establish actual causation, asserting that the child's intellectual deficits and other problems are due not to lead poisoning but instead are attributable to the child's parents. The parents' contribution to their children's cognitive functioning and behavior is thus asserted to "supersede" any harm caused by the landlord.[110] This argument is especially likely to be directed at mothers, because in many cases the children are being raised by a single parent.[111] Here landlords use a two-pronged attack. First, they argue that the child's intellectual or learning deficits reflect the parent's/mother's genetic contribution, perhaps compounded by a failure to support children's learning (helping with homework, reading aloud, etc.). Second, landlords will argue that parents were negligent in failing to supervise their child and prevent him from eating lead paint chips or engaging in other dangerous activities.[112]

Landlords seeking to rebut causation or reduce damages will usually move for discovery, hoping to find evidence that could persuade a jury that a lead poisoned child's cognitive impairments and other learning problems are the result of heredity, not lead.[113] In addition to seeking a plaintiff child's full medical history, they may also ask the child's mother to take an IQ test and to produce her own academic records. Of course, defendants are entitled to make discovery requests to obtain information that might be relevant to causation and damages.[114] However, while evidence of the child's medical and developmental history, including pregnancy and birth, is certainly pertinent, other requests exceed the normal limits of relevancy and appear designed primarily to harass and intimidate the plaintiff and obfuscate the issues. As Jennifer Wriggins has noted, these expansive discovery requests have been directed *only* at mothers, not fathers; they have been granted *only* in cases in which the plaintiffs were African-American or Latino.[115]

In recent years, some courts have curtailed aggressive discovery requests in individual cases.[116] In *Andon v. 302–304 Mott Street Associates*, the landlord sought to compel a child plaintiff's mother to take an IQ test, relying on an affidavit from its expert, stating that "studies" showed that a mother's IQ is "'extremely relevant' in assessing a child's potential cognitive development." The trial judge ordered the mother to submit to an IQ test, but the appellate court reversed this decision, finding that the landlord's arguments were speculative and the discovery request was unduly intrusive, because one's IQ is a private matter.[117] In other, extreme, cases, landlords have insisted on a quid pro quo—arguing that if the court will not compel a mother to take an IQ test, the plaintiff should not be able to offer expert testimony on the crucial issues of causation and damages. One federal court absolutely rejected compelling a plaintiff's mother to submit to an IQ test,[118] as has one New York court. However, in a similar Maryland case the court upheld the landlord's position.[119]

The second line of defense for landlords is to argue that even if a child did absorb lead from chipped paint or lead dust due to the apartment's poor condition, it was the parent's fault for failing to prevent the child from eating paint chips, failing to keep the house clean, or failing to adequately supervise the children. Landlords will usually contend that it was the child's mother who was negligent, not only because of gender-based stereotypes about which parent provides child care and housecleaning but also because many children poisoned by lead live only with their mothers. These defendants will argue that a mother's negligence is either an absolute bar to landlords' liability, under the theory of contributory negligence, or should reduce their liability, based on the modern theory of comparative negligence.[120]

Landlords and manufacturers who make these arguments are appealing to the conscious and unconscious biases of legal decisionmakers. As explained by Professors Martha Chamallas and Jennifer Wriggins, these biases of race, gender, and class can powerfully influence the decisions of judges and juries. In the first instance, judges who order wide-ranging discovery of a mother's intellectual and academic abilities may rely on stereotypes about poor, minority, and less-well-educated parents that are implicitly predicated on notions of genetic determinism and poor parenting. In the second instance, jurors may be influenced by their own unconscious biases when they conclude that even if a landlord leased an apartment with peeling paint and doors and windows that unleash lead dust whenever they are opened or shut, the landlord should not be held liable, finding that the mother's failure to keep her house immaculate or to prevent her young child from playing with contaminated materials was the actual cause of the child's injuries. Only some courts have rejected such reasoning, acknowledging what most parents know firsthand: that young children are constantly exploring their environment, handling interesting objects and putting them in their mouths, activity that is virtually impossible to prevent.[121]

Professors Martha Chamallas and Jennifer Wriggins have explored the connections between the substantive law governing causation, the procedural rules for discovery, and the psychosocial construction of risk and responsibility. First, they assert that the "cultural context of lead paint cases is ... ripe for operation of the fundamental attribution error." As we know from chapter 2, in order for people to feel safe and believe in a just world, when bad things happen they tend to place responsibility for these bad outcomes on the victim, attributing the harm to the victim's internal, "dispositional" characteristics. In contrast, when bad things happen to *us* we are likely to view the harm as caused by external factors beyond our control. This unconscious, after the fact reconstruction of events is especially likely to occur when the victim is an outsider, someone who is not a member of "our" group.[122] Professors Chamallas and Wriggins contend, "In the racialized context of lead paint litigation, a 'dispositional' explanation for cognitive disorders, and in particular for low IQs of exposed children, is readily activated by stereotypes about poor minority families headed by women." They suggest that when judges are asked to make discretionary decisions about discovery their decisions to order overly broad discovery may be the result of the fundamental attribution error.

Chamallas and Wriggins also note the potent influence of another psychological mechanism, the "normality bias," which can "dispose a factfinder [a judge or jury] toward genetic and socioeconomic explanations for the plaintiffs' harms, despite strong scientific evidence linking cognitive injuries to lead exposure." Indeed, the trial of *Thomas v. Mallett* shows that this is exactly what defense lawyers hope that judges and juries will do. In *Thomas*, the defendants' key expert psychological witness testified, essentially, that Steven Thomas' limited intellectual capabilities and behavioral problems had nothing to do with lead poisoning but were entirely his parents' fault. The witness focused on the parents' low IQs, which were in "'the borderline range,'" and poor childrearing skills. The defendants also offered evidence that Steven was the ninth child of a mother with a "'history of alcohol abuse'" and that he lived in a "'chaotic household.'" This is an illuminating example of how successful a "trash the family" strategy can be. If defense lawyers are able to discover, and then introduce at trial, evidence about the plaintiff's mother (or siblings) to support the arguments that lower intelligence, poor academic achievement, and language deficits are typical of low income children and that conditions like ADHD are primarily the result of the parents' genetic contributions, they are very likely to defeat liability.[123] Under this approach, "a poor minority child from a 'bad' neighborhood ... [who] experience[s] problems in school and behavioral and learning disorders is regarded as a normal, if regrettable, state of affairs." Even though there is overwhelming scientific evidence that lead causes measurable harms even at very low doses, plaintiffs' lawyers may find it difficult to convince jurors that this specific child's difficulties were attributable to his exposure to toxic levels of lead.[124] The fundamental attribution error and the normality bias may distort the jurors' reasoning and lead them to reject compelling evidence that the defendants' actions were the actual cause of the plaintiff's harm.

C. Products Liability: The Evolution of the Common Law

The biggest hurdle faced by child plaintiffs suing the manufacturers of lead pigments and paints is to prove "actual cause"—that is, that the lead the child ingested or inhaled in rundown housing was manufactured by a particular corporation. Although the common law of products liability law has evolved over the past half century to make it much easier for people injured by defective products to be compensated for that harm, thus far children who have suffered lead poisoning have not been able to successfully sue the manufacturers of those products. Strikingly, over the past forty years there have been only two categories of toxic torts in which injured plaintiffs *have* successfully sued the manufacturers of dangerous and defective products when they cannot link their harm to the specific product manufactured by a particular defendant, and thus prove actual cause. The first successful plaintiffs are the so-called DES daughters, woman who developed a distinctive type of cancer many years after their mothers took DES (diethylstilbestrol), a drug prescribed to prevent miscarriages. The second group of plaintiffs are workers—primarily men—who were exposed to asbestos on the job and developed lung cancer, mesothelioma, and other lung diseases many years after exposure. The requirements of actual causation have also been relaxed for this group of plaintiffs, albeit under a different theory from that applied to the DES daughters. This section will examine these two groups of cases to understand how the courts crafted new theories of causation to permit their recovery. Then the situation of lead-poisoned children will be reexamined, to consider why they may have been treated differently.

1. DES AND THE THEORY OF MARKET SHARE LIABILITY

DES, a synthetic form of estrogen, was widely prescribed to pregnant women from 1947 to 1971. DES was believed to prevent miscarriages, and the FDA approved its marketing for this purpose on an experimental basis. While there was some evidence that DES was carcinogenic, the manufacturers did not investigate this possibility. And, although the FDA required the manufacturers to provide a warning label, they marketed DES without such a warning. More than 200 companies manufactured DES, primarily in a generic form. Many years later, the causal relationship between the DES mothers' ingestion of DES and their daughters developing adenocarcinoma, a rare cancer of the cervix and vagina, was discovered. By that time it was difficult for most of the plaintiffs to determine *who* had manufactured the DES that their mothers had taken, given the passage of time, the fact that much of the DES was generic, and that many pharmacies no longer had records of drugs dispensed years earlier. Nonetheless, the DES daughters were a sympathetic group of plaintiffs. They had developed cancer as a result of a toxic substance to which they had been exposed *in utero* and were often rendered infertile by the surgery necessary to treat the cancer.

In 1980, in *Sindell v. Abbott Laboratories*,[125] the California Supreme Court created an innovative legal theory to provide legal relief to a group of DES daughters. *Sindell* was a class action suit brought by a group of women whose mothers had been prescribed DES while pregnant; the daughters had all developed adenocarcinoma. Most of the plaintiffs were unable to identify the specific manufacturer of the DES their mothers had taken. Thus, they could not prove actual cause by establishing that but for their mothers' ingestion of a particular defendant's "brand" of DES they would not have developed adenocarcinoma.[126]

The California Supreme Court responded to the perceived unfairness of this situation by fashioning a new theory of liability that permitted the plaintiffs to recover against a group of companies known to have manufactured or sold DES in California. Under this "market share" theory, once the plaintiffs established that the defendants they were suing constituted a "substantial percentage" of the DES market, the entire group of defendants would be held liable for the harm to the plaintiff class, with liability apportioned based on each company's market share.[127] Thus, the court effectively shifted the burden of proof on the actual cause issue to the defendants. Only if a defendant could prove that it had *not* manufactured the DES ingested by the plaintiff's mother would it escape liability.

Although the court framed its decision in *Sindell* as a rather slight expansion of previous case law, in reality it was a major doctrinal shift. The court relied on *Summers v. Tice*,[128] a case in which the plaintiff had been injured while hunting with two friends but could not prove which one had shot him. Both had negligently shot in his direction, using identical shotguns and ammunition. The court held that because both defendants had negligently created a risk of harm by shooting in the plaintiff's direction, they would be found jointly and severally liable *unless* either could completely exonerate himself.

In *Sindell* the California Supreme Court offered several justifications for its ruling. First, it emphasized the unfairness of leaving the plaintiff DES daughters without a remedy, since the drug's manufacturers had been aware of the risk that DES might be a carcinogen and thus had arguably breached a duty of care, based on the foreseeability of harm.[129] *Sindell* also relied on utilitarian grounds, reasoning that as between the innocent plaintiffs and the defendants, the latter were in a superior position to insure against liability as a cost of doing business. First, the court asserted that the common law must evolve to meet the needs of a "complex industrialized society," in which scientific and technical advances could lead to the production of "fungible goods" that can harm consumers but "cannot be traced to any specific producer." The court concluded that because a product "manufacturer is in the best position to discover and guard against defects in its products and to warn of harmful effects," holding it liable for the defects and for failure to warn would provide an incentive to create and market safe products.[130] Minimizing the extent to which "market share" liability was a departure from traditional tort law principles, *Sindell* emphasized the difficult situation facing DES daughters. It noted that all DES had an identical chemical formula and that DES was biologically capable of causing the particular injuries alleged, meeting the requirements of general causation. Further, it observed that the difficulty of identifying the specific manufacturer of the DES taken by plaintiffs' mothers was attributable to the long latency period between the manufacture of the DES and the manifestation of harm. Finally, because the plaintiffs had sued a substantial portion of potential defendants, the court found it plausible to conclude that if a particular defendant had had a specific share of the market during the relevant period, that defendant had a comparable likelihood of having caused a particular plaintiff's injuries.[131]

A number of state courts have followed *Sindell* and fashioned a theory of liability similar to California's market share doctrine. However, most courts limited their rulings to the DES context.[132] For example, in *Collins v. Eli Lilly Co.*, the Wisconsin Supreme Court announced that DES daughters could sue under a "risk contribution theory."[133] *Collins* based its decision on a provision in the Wisconsin Constitution that declared, "Every person is entitled to a certain remedy in the laws for all injuries, or wrongs which he may receive in his person, property, or character." Following its prior decisions, the court held that this provision authorized the court to "fashion an adequate remedy."[134] In *Collins* the Wisconsin Supreme Court ruled that once a plaintiff could show that she suffered injury as a result of her mother's ingesting DES *and* that the defendants she sued represented a substantial share of the DES market, the burden shifted to defendants to show that they had *not* manufactured the DES taken by the plaintiff's mother. As in *Sindell*, the court explained why this approach was logical and just. First, "each defendant contributed to the *risk* of injury to the public and, consequently, the risk of injury to individual plaintiffs. . . ." Second, "between the injured plaintiff and the possibly responsible drug company, the drug company [was] in a better position to absorb the cost of the injury" through insurance, absorbing the damage award, or passing the costs along to the public. Third, "the cost of damages awards will act as an incentive for drug companies to test adequately the drugs they place on the market for general medical use."[135]

2. NOVEL THEORIES OF LIABILITY FOR WORKERS INJURED BY ASBESTOS EXPOSURE

Over the past forty years courts have also developed an innovative approach to liability to provide a remedy to plaintiffs injured by exposure to asbestos, who might otherwise not have been able to establish actual cause. People exposed to asbestos—nearly always men who encountered it while working in the mining, manufacturing, shipbuilding, and construction industries—have been highly successful in suing the manufacturers of asbestos for their injuries, despite being unable to identify the particular manufacturer(s) whose asbestos was the source of harm. This causation hurdle was especially difficult to surmount because the plaintiffs were often exposed to multiple sources of asbestos over many years. Plaintiffs usually brought these suits as a way to avoid the limits of workers' compensation law, which not only bars employees from suing their employers but also provides very limited remedies.[136] Plaintiffs have prevailed in asbestos litigation despite significant scientific disagreement over whether the diseases that stem from exposure to asbestos—lung cancer, asbestosis, and mesothelioma—can be initiated by a single toxic "insult" or require multiple exposures over time.[137] In addition, many plaintiffs were heavy smokers, and smoking is causally linked to lung cancer, heart disease, and other illnesses. While in other contexts this behavior might be regarded as contributory or comparative negligence, evidence of prior smoking has not barred plaintiffs in asbestos cases from recovering.

The courts that have found defendants liable in asbestos cases did not invoke a market share theory. Instead, as the California Supreme Court ruled in *Rutherford v. Owens-Illinois, Inc.*, for a plaintiff to prevail, he must first show that he was exposed to the defendant's products containing asbestos and then "establish in reasonable medical probability that a particular exposure or series of exposures was a 'legal cause' of his injury; i.e., a *substantial factor* in bringing about the injury. . . . The plaintiff need *not* prove that fibers from the defendant's product were the ones, or among the ones, that actually began the process of malignant cellular growth."[138]

There have been many critics of decisions that have adopted a "causation lite" approach to tort liability in the asbestos cases.[139] Professor Anita Bernstein has offered particularly trenchant criticism, focusing on the gender connections in asbestos litigation. Bernstein observes that both the plaintiffs and judges in these cases are overwhelming male; she suggests that the relaxation of traditional causation requirements may reflect judges' unconscious "fellow-feeling" toward plaintiffs who either already have or are worried about developing a disabling disease. She also notes that asbestos litigation is unique in permitting plaintiffs exposed to asbestos to sue without proof of physical harm, by creating an "inactive" or "deferred" docket, for causes of action that are based solely on having a "*risk*" of developing an asbestos-related disease.[140]

3. LEAD-EXPOSED CHILDREN HAVE BEEN TREATED DIFFERENTLY

In sharp contrast, nearly all the cases in which child plaintiffs injured by lead poisoning have sued lead pigment and paint manufacturers have been unsuccessful.[141] Only the Wisconsin Supreme Court has determined that the same market share or "risk contribution" theories used to permit suits by DES daughters are also appropriate for lead-poisoned children. Its decision in *Thomas ex rel. Gramling v. Mallett* made it possible for Steven Thomas to sue multiple manufacturers, even though he was unsuccessful at trial. In *Thomas*, the Wisconsin Supreme Court's analysis began and ended with the same rationale employed in the risk contribution theory in *Collins*: that without an alternative means of establishing causation, innocent plaintiffs who had been injured by the manufacturers of a defective product would be left without a remedy. The court rejected the manufacturers' argument that it was unnecessary to extend the risk contribution theory to children poisoned by lead poisoning because they could always sue their landlords, as Steven Thomas had. The court observed that although this might be true for Steven Thomas, it would not necessarily be true for future children, since landlords increasingly had insurance policies with a "pollution exclusion" that precluded coverage for harms caused by pollutants, including lead.[142]

The court also observed multiple similarities between the parties in *Collins* and *Thomas*. It noted that Steven Thomas and the DES daughters were all innocent plaintiffs, who suffered severe harm from the products marketed by the respective defendants. The court found that the risk contribution theory was a good match with the defendants' conduct. It observed that the defendant lead pigment and paint manufacturers were well aware of the risks posed by lead-based paint, yet continued to manufacture, market, and promote it despite that knowledge. Thus, they "contributed to the risk of injury to the public and, consequently, the risk of injury to individual [child] plaintiffs."[143] The court found that compared with Steven Thomas, these defendants were "in a better position to absorb the cost of the injury," similarly to the DES manufacturers in *Collins*.[144] The court also ruled that "fungibility" of products does not require chemical identity. It found that, like DES, the various formulations of lead paint and pigments made and sold by these manufacturers were inherently hazardous and that lead carbonate, the specific pigment used in the *Thomas* case, was chosen by the manufacturers because of its "hiding power" (the ability to cover the underlying surface), despite their knowledge of its hazardous nature. The court declared simply, "Harm is harm, whether it be 'signature' or otherwise."[145] The court rejected the manufacturers' "lack of control" argument, because the harm that was realized was indeed the one they foresaw.[146] The court was particularly dismissive of the defendants' effort to distinguish *Collins* on the ground that the nine-month gestation period for each injured DES plaintiff was much shorter than the many years in which lead-based paint was present in the homes where Steven Thomas lived. In essence, the court said, the manufacturers were "arguing that their negligent conduct should be excused because they got away with it for too long . . . [,]" and emphatically rejected that argument.[147] Finally, the court emphasized that the application of the risk contribution theory did not eliminate the issue of causation from trial but merely eased the plaintiff's burden of establishing the source of the lead carbonate he had ingested, similarly to the shifting of the burden of proof in the case of DES plaintiffs.[148]

D. Public Nuisance

Public nuisance is another tort that, in theory, appears to be a good candidate for addressing the problem of lead poisoning. Originating in early English common law, nuisance actions were historically brought on behalf of the Crown to address a problem of concern to the community at large. Today, the tort of public nuisance is aimed at protecting the public's interest, particularly interests in health. It requires proof that the nuisance constitutes "an unreasonable interference with a right common to the general public."[149] Classic examples of public nuisance include maintaining a pond that breeds malarial mosquitos, storing explosives in the center of the city, and widely disseminating foul odors, dust, and smoke.[150] The usual remedy for public nuisance is abatement: a court orders injunctive relief, commanding the creator of the nuisance to end it and clean up the harm already caused. In a few states, like California, the law of public nuisance is embodied in state statutes.[151]

One might anticipate that public nuisance cases brought against lead pigment and paint manufacturers would be successful. After all, lead causes harm to young children even at very low "doses," and approximately a third of the country's housing still contains lead-based paint, which is often in poor condition. There is overwhelming evidence that during the first three-quarters of the twentieth century, these manufacturers were well aware of lead's harmfulness and that poor, inner-city children of color were at the greatest risk of suffering that harm, because they were more likely to live in substandard housing, where lead paint would inevitably deteriorate. Despite this knowledge, the manufacturers lobbied successfully to prevent the United States and individual state governments from banning lead-based paint and continued to manufacture it, market it, and actively promote its sale, even in the face of an impending federal ban on lead paint.[152]

Thus, through their actions, the manufacturers created a public nuisance, a chronic public health problem affecting hundreds of thousands of vulnerable American children, just as surely as if they had dumped toxic chemicals in a public waterway.[153] The existence of deteriorated lead paint places an enormous burden on the community at large, impairing public health and public finances. While individual children bear the brunt of the harm from lead poisoning, the cities and states where they live struggle to bear the financial costs of lead poisoning, including the cost of abating lead hazards when landlords and private homeowners fail to do so[154] and the cost of providing medical treatment and special education services to children poisoned by lead.[155] These cities also suffer from the long-term economic burden of an undereducated and underemployed work force, as well as the crimes committed by some lead-poisoned victims.[156]

Yet, of the five public nuisance suits that have been litigated since 2000 only one has been successful. That case, *People v. Atlantic Richfield Co.*,[157] is still on appeal. All of the unsuccessful suits were brought by city or state governments in the Northeast and the Midwest. The plaintiffs in these lawsuits included Milwaukee,[158] where Steven Thomas lived, and the cities of St. Louis, Missouri;[159] Newark, New Jersey;[160] and Chicago.[161] In one case, Rhode Island's attorney general brought a public nuisance suit on behalf of the entire state.[162] In three of the cases the court rejected the very idea that the tort of public nuisance could or should be applied to provide a remedy to cities struggling with the task of remediating thousands of homes with deteriorating lead paint;

in the fourth, while the court recognized a potential cause of action, the jury found no liability. In *City of St. Louis v. Benjamin Moore & Co.*, the city of St. Louis sued the major lead paint and pigment manufacturers, seeking reimbursement for the expenses of abating the lead paint hazard in some privately owned housing in St. Louis.[163] The Missouri Supreme Court declared that all tort plaintiffs must establish both actual and proximate cause and found that St. Louis had not met that burden here. The court rejected the city's argument that "actual causation can be proven by showing that the defendants substantially contributed to the public health hazard created by lead paint" by demonstrating the defendants' "community wide marketing and sales of lead paint."[164] The court essentially treated the suit as a products liability action and declined to permit recovery under what it viewed as a "market share" approach to liability.[165]

The reasoning of the New Jersey Supreme Court in *In re Lead Paint Litigation* is striking, if not dumbfounding. The court rendered its decision three days after the *City of St. Louis v. Benjamin Moore & Co.* case was decided. The court ruled that prior actions of the New Jersey legislature, which were taken in recognition of the serious health risks posed by lead paint, including imposing a duty on landlords to clean up lead paint hazards, precluded the plaintiffs, twenty-six New Jersey cities, from bringing a public nuisance suit. The court completely accepted the "lack of control" arguments made by the lead paint and pigment manufacturers. It ruled that in order to constitute a public nuisance, a defendant must have exercised control over the alleged nuisance at the time it became a nuisance (here, when lead-based paint began to deteriorate), rather than, as alleged by the plaintiffs, having created a situation—the use of a dangerous poison in family residences—that it knew would result in harm to children in the future.[166]

In contrast to the three cases just discussed, in *City of Milwaukee v. NL Industries* the Wisconsin Court of Appeals recognized that a claim of public nuisance *was* viable even if the city was unable to identify the manufacturer of the paint used in any particular home.[167] Writing in 2004, the year before the Wisconsin Supreme Court's *Thomas* decision, the court relied on a 1998 study finding that one-fifth of Milwaukee children suffered from lead poisoning, as well as evidence showing that the defendants, two manufacturers of lead paint, had promoted the sale of lead paint, despite knowing of its hazards, and thus contributed to the creation of homes where lead poisoning was likely to occur. One of the defendants had, in fact, urged its sales representatives to encourage paint stores to sell their older, lead-based paint first, knowing that a ban on lead paint was imminent.[168] When the case went to trial, a jury found, by a vote of 10–2, that the presence of lead paint in Milwaukee housing was a public nuisance. However, it also found that the defendant lead pigment and paint manufacturers had not *unreasonably* engaged in activity that created this nuisance and thus were not liable.[169]

In March 2014 it appeared that plaintiffs' losing streak was coming to an end. In *People v. Atlantic Richfield* ten cities and counties in California brought suit against the major lead paint and pigment manufacturers who had done business in California, alleging that they had created a public nuisance by promoting the sale of their lead-based products when they knew that lead was a deadly and cumulative poison, causing serious harm to children. After a lengthy trial, Santa Clara County Superior Court Judge James Kleinberg found that the manufacturers had indeed created a public nuisance—"a clear and present danger" posed by the enormous number of homes with high levels of deteriorated lead paint where young children lived—through their marketing of lead paints and pigments. He further determined that because they were well aware of the dangers posed by their products, the manufacturers were responsible for abating the nuisance, by paying for the inspection and cleanup of interior lead paint in all homes where it was found.[170] The case is now on appeal.[171]

Several aspects of the court's decision are noteworthy. California defines public nuisance by statute, providing that "Anything which is injurious to health . . . so as to interfere with the comfortable enjoyment of life or property . . . is a nuisance." Further, a "public nuisance is one which affects at the same time an entire community or neighborhood, or any considerable number of persons, although the extent of the annoyance or damage inflicted upon individuals may be unequal."[172]

Most notably, the court took a different approach to causation from that of other courts. First, the court applied the California "substantial factor" test for causation, also used in asbestos litigation, instead of the "but/for" test used in many other states. Using this test, the plaintiffs did not need "to identify the specific location of a nuisance or a specific product sold by Defendants," as long as they could establish that lead paint exists in homes within the plaintiff localities. Second, the court rejected the defendants' argument that they lacked control of lead-based products at the time they posed an immediate threat to public health, finding, "There is no intervening or superseding cause." The court continued, "*Blaming the well-worn stereotypes of 'slum landlords,' 'bad parents,' 'the poor,' and 'the government' does not relieve Defendants of liability....*"[173]

Finally, after holding the defendants "jointly and severally liable," as in *Summers v. Tice*, the court ordered abatement of the lead hazard as the only remedy that would adequately protect the lives and health of California children. Rather than ordering injunctive relief, the court translated the costs of the necessary action into monetary terms, requiring the defendants to pay into a newly created fund administered by the local governments that had expertise in addressing lead contamination in housing. While acknowledging that this was a "massive" remedy, the court also concluded that it was the only way to address appropriately the concerns of thousands of children who are "presently and potentially" victims of lead poisoning, who are likely to "suffer from diminished intellectual capacity" and "may develop behavior problems including antisocial behavior." The court observed, "Ultimately society will pay for these problems over time."[174]

Conclusion

This chapter has disclosed a disturbing, if paradigmatic, case of risk assessment, risk management, and attribution of legal responsibility. Although the federal government banned the use of lead paint in 1978, in a belated recognition of the substantial risks that lead paint creates when it deteriorates, subsequent governmental efforts—at the federal, state, and local levels—have proved inadequate to protect children from the harms caused by lead exposure. Today it is widely acknowledged that lead causes serious and irreversible harm to approximately *a half million American children each year*. Yet the American legal system has proved inhospitable, if not downright hostile, to attempts to provide a remedy for children suffering from lead poisoning. These children are most likely to be poor African-American and Latino children living in the inner city. As a result of lead poisoning they are likely to have difficulty in school and in gaining employment. With the exception of the EPA's 1973 decision to phase out lead in gasoline, which improved the health of *all* of America's children, government has generally taken a reactive—not proactive—approach to protecting children from lead poisoning. Even the federal government's major proactive effort, the requirement that property owners disclose lead-based hazards before they sell or lease a home, precludes remedies for injured children. Individual lead poisoning plaintiffs rarely succeed in obtaining the abatement of lead hazards or compensation for their injuries. Corporate defendants have been held accountable in only one major case. Landlords who are sued for causing toxic exposures and their resultant injuries often push back against the mother of an injured child, asserting that it is her genetics and her bad parenting that are the real source of her child's mental and physical disabilities, rather than the toxic quantities of lead to which the child has been exposed by the landlord's negligence. This chapter illuminates the difficulty of using the law to promote children's health when the children most at risk can be seen as "other people's children."

9

The Vaccination Paradox

Introduction

A. The Problem

In the past decade there have been notable outbreaks of serious contagious diseases across the United States, including frequent outbreaks of pertussis (whooping cough) and multiple large measles outbreaks in 2014 and 2015. The incidence of pertussis among children less than one year old, when it is most likely to be fatal, has been on an upward trajectory since 1980.[1] In the spring of 2014 nearly 400 cases of measles were diagnosed in Amish communities in Ohio.[2] Later, a measles epidemic that began at Disneyland in December 2014 quickly spread, leaving more than 300 people infected in the United States and Canada. Nearly half of those who contracted measles were unvaccinated. The 2014 measles resurgence was the largest in the United States in two decades, with 667 cases reported in 27 states, a result of 23 separate outbreaks. By the summer of 2015 more than 178 measles cases had been documented.[3] In 2015 nearly 190 people became infected with the measles. They included a Washington State woman in her twenties who died after contracting the measles while being treated at a health care facility; this was the first measles fatality in the United States in twelve years.[4]

Although overall rates of childhood immunization remain relatively high, with about 7 percent of California children and approximately 6 percent nationwide not receiving all recommended vaccinations, in some communities *half* of all children are unvaccinated because their parents have refused to vaccinate their children in accordance with the vaccination schedule mandated by state law and recommended by the American Academy of Pediatrics and the Centers for Disease Control. In Colorado, for example, less than 82 percent of all kindergarten students had received the mandated vaccinations for measles, mumps, and rubella (MMR). Eleven states have rates of exemption from vaccination of 4 percent or more, with Oregon the highest at more than 7 percent.[5] Many people are put at risk for contracting measles, pertussis, and other contagious diseases, including unvaccinated children, children who cannot be vaccinated for medical reasons, and children who were vaccinated but whose vaccination did not "take." Pregnant women and the elderly are also at risk.[6]

It is widely accepted that the only way to protect an entire community from contagious diseases is through the process of "herd immunity."[7] Herd immunity is achieved when the vast majority of a population is vaccinated against a disease, making it much harder for the disease to spread because the means of disease transmission are interrupted. The extent of vaccination necessary to achieve herd immunity varies with each disease's infectiousness. For example, herd immunity against polio is achieved by community immunization rates of about 80 percent, while achieving herd immunity against measles requires that 95 percent of the population be vaccinated.[8] When immunization rates are low, the risk of a disease outbreak increases. For example, nine out of ten unvaccinated people exposed to measles will contract the disease.[9] Further, as Professor Saad Omer notes, "'[V]accine refusal clusters geographically.... Therefore, even if only ten of 100 people refuse vaccines but most of them live in the same neighborhood, the likelihood of outbreaks increases due to local breakdown of herd immunity.'"[10] The rapid spread of measles during the Disneyland epidemic was a result of the large number of unvaccinated children in particular communities. In Quebec, Canada, all but two of the measles cases were concentrated in just twenty-eight families who had religious or philosophical objections to vaccination. Since 2004 the number of measles cases has been on an upward trend, with a large spike in 2014.[11] The Disneyland epidemic also illustrates the way in which global travel can exacerbate the problem of inadequate herd immunity. Non-immunized children traveling abroad can readily contract a disease and bring it home, infecting many other children who in turn spread the disease.[12]

In the past decade, a growing chorus of physicians and public health advocates, parents of vaccinated children, and state officials has pushed to make it harder for parents to "opt out" of vaccination.[13] In June 2015 the American Medical Association adopted a policy resolution calling on state legislatures to end nonmedical exemptions, as well as to have medical societies and physicians work harder to educate the public about the benefits of vaccines and the risk to individual and public health of not vaccinating.[14] California followed suit, enacting legislation to eliminate religious and philosophical exemptions. California pediatrician and state senator Richard Pan declared, "When you have pockets of low vaccination . . . we need to do more to protect our communities. . . . This is a matter of public safety."[15] Vermont eliminated its philosophical exemption and other states tightened the process for obtaining an exemption, including Colorado, Connecticut, Michigan, South Dakota, and West Virginia.[16]

Yet anti-vaccination activists have a very different perspective. Believing that vaccines are dangerous to children, Barbara Loe Fisher, the president and co-founder of the National Vaccine Information Center (formerly known as Dissatisfied Parents Together [DPT]),[17] has framed the situation this way: "In America today, there is an unprecedented assault on the human right to exercise informed consent to medical risk-taking . . . led by one of the most powerful and wealthy corporate empires in the world: the global pharmaceutical industry. . . . What is at stake for the American people is our health and our liberty."[18] This small but vocal group contends that vaccines pose a greater risk to children's health than contagious diseases and that an overreaching government and greedy pharmaceutical companies are undermining parental decisionmaking for their children. They assert that parents should have the absolute right to exempt their children from vaccination. Campaigning against a proposed California law that would limit parents' ability to opt out, Robert Kennedy, Jr., "likened mandatory vaccines to the Holocaust." Kennedy alleged that children "get the shot, that night they have a fever of 103, they go to sleep, and three months later their brain is gone. This is a Holocaust, what this is doing to our community."[19]

Vaccine advocates and their foes offer sharply contested constructions of risk. Most American parents, government officials, public health experts, and physicians believe that contagious diseases pose a substantial risk to children's health. They see the complement of vaccines now available as the best way to minimize injury, death, and human suffering, to say nothing of saving billions of dollars in public and private resources.[20] The CDC recognized the development of vaccines against contagious diseases as one of the great public health success stories of the twentieth century, a major reason that Americans' life expectancy increased by thirty years between 1900 and 1999.[21] This majority further contends that parents who opt out of vaccination for their own children are essentially "free riders," whose children are protected from contagious diseases by the broader community's herd immunity, while avoiding any possible risk from vaccines.[22] In contrast, many parents who refuse vaccines for their children believe that some contagious diseases are not harmful, that naturally acquired immunity is preferable to immunity conferred by vaccination, or that their children are not at risk for particular diseases. They also believe that they can prevent them from contracting a contagious disease by embracing a "natural" lifestyle, including breastfeeding and providing nutritious foods, keeping children out of day care, and avoiding toxic chemicals in the home.[23] This chapter first explores these conflicting risk perspectives. Then it examines how American law views parental (and maternal) responsibility for children's well-being in the context of contagious diseases and the public's health.[24]

B. The Vaccination Controversy: Who Bears Responsibility for Protecting Children's Health?

Just as in the previous chapter, which addressed the risks to children from lead poisoning, the legal framework that governs childhood diseases and vaccination involves risk assessment and risk management. However, government has been much more active in promoting children's health in regard to contagious diseases and vaccination than it has in combatting the epidemic of childhood lead poisoning. In this chapter we shall see how the federal government and state governments work in tandem to develop public health policies that support the development of vaccines and encourage or mandate their use. In the case of contagious diseases and vaccination, the federal government has embraced the precautionary principle, through researching and paying for vaccines that have virtually eliminated many childhood diseases and providing extensive and ongoing evaluation of vaccine safety. State governments are also highly proactive, mandating that all children be vaccinated as a requirement for admission to school and day care with the goal of safeguarding all children from contagious diseases via herd immunity. At the same time, state governments authorize exemptions from vaccination to parents who seek to spare their children from vaccination mandates.

The controversy over childhood vaccination offers a potent counternarrative to the previous five chapters. This chapter explores the construction of risk in the context of the debate over immunization mandates and parental opt-outs, revealing the singular role that American law gives to parental choice in this one area of children's health. The legal system's response to childhood vaccination is the exception that proves my central thesis—that the unconscious processes of risk construction intersect with American law to make it more likely that mothers, instead of others, are held responsible for their children's health. Again, I make three main points. First, risk is psychologically and socially constructed on an individual level, reflecting individual worldviews, unconscious stereotypes and biases, and the unconscious resort to heuristics in perception and decisionmaking. Second, ostensibly neutral principles of the law simultaneously reflect and reinforce the psychosocially constructed nature of risk. Thus conscious and unconscious racial, class, and gender biases, as well as a variety of cognitive shortcuts, shape the views of legal decisionmakers who act with broad discretion—judges, jurors, legislators, regulators, and bureaucrats. In the case of childhood vaccination, purportedly neutral legal rules—primarily constitutional law doctrine—permit decisionmakers to have it both ways. Courts have upheld childhood immunization mandates as a necessary means of protecting the public's health, rejecting Fourteenth Amendment substantive due process challenges. At the same time, over the past several decades state legislatures have been increasingly generous in providing medical, religious, and philosophical exemptions to mandatory vaccination, thereby permitting parents, primarily well-educated mothers with sufficient time and money to pursue the exemption process, to opt out of those mandates for their own children. Only recently has there been a pushback against broad exemptions, a response to increases in disease outbreaks attributable, at least in part, to unvaccinated children. Third, in stark contrast with other situations in which children's health is at risk, in the case of mothers who *choose* not to have their children vaccinated against highly contagious diseases, threatening the health of those children and others in the community, the unconscious processes of risk construction intersect with fundamental principles of American law to make it more likely that *mothers will not be blamed* or held legally responsible for potential harm to children's health.[25] Indeed, anti-vaccination activists contend that it is *others*—pharmaceutical manufacturers, doctors, and government—who are risking harm to children by producing vaccines, promoting or mandating vaccination, and limiting parental opt-outs.

I. The Risks of Contagious Diseases and the Vaccines Designed to Protect against Them

A. Contagious Diseases

Today, most people acknowledge that vaccines can prevent the spread of infectious diseases, particularly those that are caused by airborne organisms and are transmitted by casual contact.[26] However, with the passage of time since the great polio, measles, and pertussis epidemics of the mid–twentieth century, fewer parents, physicians, and public health officials can remember what it was like when children routinely died of or suffered permanent injuries from diseases that have now been virtually eliminated from the United States. Many have never seen a case of measles.[27] In this context it is much easier for parents to focus on rare, but potentially serious, side effects of vaccines. Simply put, vaccines have become the victim of their own success.[28]

The development of vaccines has made possible a remarkable expansion of life expectancy in the United States since the beginning of the twentieth century. Contagious diseases are no longer the leading cause of death in the United States.[29] In 1900 one in ten infants born in the United States died before his first birthday.[30] More than 30 percent of all American deaths were those of children under age five.[31] At this time, smallpox was the only disease for which vaccination was widely available. Even then, despite the fact that smallpox was usually disfiguring and frequently fatal, there were pockets of resistance, as we shall see when we discuss the 1905 vaccination case of *Jacobson v. Massachusetts*.[32] From 1900 to 1904 there were an average of 48,000 smallpox cases each year and more than 1,500 deaths due to smallpox. Periodically there would be outbreaks of smallpox in particular localities, and public health officials would respond by mandating vaccination for those who had not been immunized previously. As a result of states' enactment of mandatory vaccination laws for children and adults, smallpox was eliminated in the United States in 1949. It was declared eliminated worldwide in 1977.[33]

In the first third of the twentieth century, children were particularly at risk for contracting pertussis (whooping cough), diphtheria, and tetanus, as well as polio, measles, rubella, and chicken pox.[34] Pertussis averaged about 200,000 cases and 4,000 deaths each year. In the peak year of 1934 there were 265,000 cases and 7,500 deaths from pertussis. After vaccinations for diphtheria, pertussis, and tetanus were developed in the 1910s and '20s these illnesses decreased, but it was not until 1948, when the combined vaccine against all three diseases was introduced, that the incidence of these diseases, particularly pertussis, really began to decline. Even in the 1930s and '40s there were an average of 21,000 cases of diphtheria and 1,800 deaths every year. For tetanus, in the 1940s there was an annual average of 580 cases and 472 deaths.[35]

Even by the 1950s and the advent of penicillin and other antibiotics, more than 2,000 Americans died *each year* from diseases that are now preventable by vaccines. Many diseases are caused by viruses, which do not respond to antibiotics.[36] In some years, the death toll for contagious diseases exceeded 3,500. Data on three of the most deadly diseases illustrate the extent of the risk. In the year 1950 alone there were 120,000 cases of pertussis and 1,118 deaths from that disease. There were also 33,000 cases of polio and 1,904 deaths.[37] The peak year for harm caused by polio was 1952, with more than 3,100 deaths.[38] After the polio vaccine was developed by Dr. Jonas Salk in 1955, both the disease incidence and number of deaths declined rapidly after 1963.[39] Polio was declared eliminated in North and South America in 1991. In the 1950s and '60s measles averaged more than 500,000 cases a year, with an average of more than 400 deaths annually. In 1958 there were more than 763,000 cases of measles, and more than 550 deaths caused by the disease. Since the development of vaccines against measles, mumps, and rubella in the 1960s, the incidence of these diseases has been substantially reduced; indeed, measles was declared to be "eliminated" in the United States in 2000. Nonetheless, measles and mumps continue to infect and injure children and adults, primarily because some parents are opting out of vaccination for their children, making them vulnerable to infection from those who "import" the diseases from abroad.[40]

Rubella is a disease that usually does not seriously harm children, but it has severe consequences when pregnant women become infected, particularly during the first trimester. Pregnant women are often unaware that they have rubella, but their children are born suffering from blindness, deafness, mental retardation, and other birth defects, collectively termed congenital rubella syndrome. A rubella epidemic in 1964 and 1965 afflicted more than 12 million Americans; about 11,000 fetuses were lost to miscarriage, stillbirth, or abortion. Twenty thousand babies were born with congenital rubella syndrome. Of these, 2,000 infants died shortly after birth, 12,000 were deaf, 3,500 were blind, and nearly 2,000 suffered from permanent mental disabilities. The incidence of rubella has declined dramatically since the measles, mumps, and rubella (MMR) vaccine was introduced, and in 2015 rubella was declared to have been eradicated in North and South America.[41]

Additional vaccines were developed against other common and serious diseases in the 1970s, '80s, and '90s, including meningitis, pneumococcal disease, Hepatitis A and B, Haemophilus influenzae type b (Hib), rotavirus, and varicella (chicken pox). All have been effective in dramatically reducing the numbers of cases, hospitalizations, and deaths due to these diseases. While some of these diseases are not household names, all have the capacity to harm thousands of American children. For example, before the Hib vaccine was licensed in 1985, each year there were about 20,000 cases, more than half in children less than a year old, with an average of 1,000 deaths. "Hib was the leading cause of childhood bacterial meningitis and postnatal mental retardation."[42] Rotavirus is the most common cause of severe gastroenteritis in young children; almost all children become infected with it before age five. Before the rotavirus vaccine was introduced in 1998, each year there were about 3 million cases of rotavirus-caused gastroenteritis in infants and children, leading to more than 400,000 physician visits, more than 200,000 visits to the emergency room, 62,000 children hospitalized, and between 20 and 60 deaths.[43]

Since the beginning of the twenty-first century, vaccines to prevent other diseases have been developed, including those caused by the human papillomavirus, or HPV. The HPV vaccine, like the vaccine against Hepatitis B before it, prevents cancers that kill thousands of Americans each year. HPV is the most common sexually transmitted disease in the United States, affecting about 20,000,000 men and women at any given time. HPV causes genital warts; without identification and treatment HPV leads to cervical cancer, anal and genital cancer, and throat cancer.[44] Each year about 4,000 American women die from cervical cancer and more than a thousand people die from other cancers causes by HPV.[45] Hepatitis B is also a serious illness, transmitted through blood transfusions, through sexual contact, and during birth. Before mandatory vaccination against Hepatitis B began in the 1990s, between 30 and 40 percent of all chronic Hepatitis B infections were transmitted from pregnant women to their newborns during labor and delivery. Children younger than ten are most likely to be afflicted by Hepatitis B, but they are frequently asymptomatic. As a result, the fact that they are infected becomes apparent only much later in life, when their long term chronic infection emerges as full blown Hepatitis B and liver cancer. This is why Hepatitis B vaccine is given to newborns at the hospital.[46]

Currently the Advisory Committee on Immunization Practices of the Centers for Disease Control recommends that children be vaccinated against fifteen diseases, including influenza.[47] In 2011 it was estimated that giving the standard schedule of childhood vaccines for American children prevents more than 42,000 deaths and 20,000,000 cases of disease for each birth cohort. At the same time, following the recommended schedule saves nearly $14 billion in direct heath care costs and $69 billion in broader costs to society, including the costs of surveillance in the event of a disease outbreak.[48] A 2013 study that crunched massive quantities of data found that since 1924, childhood vaccinations have prevented more than 103 million cases of serious contagious diseases, or more than a million cases a year. In the decade from 2003 to 2013 an estimated 26 million cases of serious illness were prevented.[49]

The benefits of vaccination are available to all immunized children, as well as adults and other children whom widespread immunization protects through herd immunity. Historically, poor children and children of color were less likely than middle- and upper-class white children to be fully immunized and thus more likely to contract vaccine-preventable diseases, because they lacked insurance and access to health care, even though it was theoretically available through Medicaid and SCHIP (the State Children's Health Insurance Program).[50] Many immigrant children lack access to good health care because their parents have language difficulties or are hesitant to seek health care out of fear that their illegal immigrant status will be disclosed or because the children themselves are illegal immigrants.[51] Congress and the Centers for Disease Control have endeavored for several decades to bridge the vaccination gap in poor communities through financial assistance to state and local governments to ensure that poorer children have access to vaccines when their parents cannot afford them.[52] Today the Affordable Care Act requires all public and private health insurers and managed care organizations to provide all necessary preventative care, including immunizations recommended by the CDC.[53] Of course, because more than a third of the states have chosen not to participate in the Medicaid expansion offered under the Affordable Care Act, many low-income children still have difficulty obtaining all necessary vaccinations.[54]

In addition to the enormous benefits measured by lives saved and illnesses avoided, vaccination saves massive amounts of public and private health care resources. For example, during a massive measles outbreak during 1989–91, there were 55,000 cases of measles, 11,000 hospitalizations, and 130 deaths. The direct costs of providing medical care to these patients were $150 million.[55] In 2008, a much smaller measles outbreak, involving only fourteen unvaccinated patients, cost nearly $800,000 to contain.[56]

Yet, in an era in which most parents, and many health care providers, have never seen a child afflicted with polio, pertussis, or measles,[57] a small but growing number of parents are focused not on the risk that their child might contract a disease preventable by vaccination but on the fear that vaccination could lead to autism or other childhood diseases whose causes are still not well understood.[58] While historically undervaccinated children have tended to be poor, African-American, or Latino, today they are much more likely to be the children of white, affluent, and well educated parents.[59]

B. The Risks of Vaccines: Science v. Fear, Data v. Anecdote

Vaccine proponents and opponents acknowledge that vaccines are not 100 percent safe. Many children (and adults) have minor adverse reactions to vaccination, including elevated temperature, tenderness and pain around the vaccination site, headache, upper respiratory tract infection, fever, fussiness, and vomiting. Adolescents and young adults sometimes faint when given vaccinations, a phenomenon known as syncope.[60] On rare occasions children have more severe reactions to vaccinations, including high fevers, encephalopathy (brain swelling), seizures, and even death.[61] In addition, children have sometimes been harmed when they were given a vaccine that contained live, rather than inactivated, viruses. In 1955, just as the successful creation of a vaccine against polio by Dr. Jonas Salk was being hailed as a medical miracle, some batches of the vaccine manufactured at Cutter Laboratories in California contained polio viruses that were not completely inactivated. As a result, thousands of children were infected with the live polio virus, resulting in 260 cases of paralytic polio and 11 deaths. In response, the federal government increased regulatory oversight of the vaccine production process.[62] In other instances vaccination actually increased the chances of a child's becoming ill. Most recently, after a rotavirus vaccine was approved in 1998 it was discovered that the vaccine increased the chances that a child would develop intussusception, a bowel blockage that is rarely, but sometimes, fatal. In response, the vaccine was withdrawn from the market less than a year later. After further research and development, two new vaccines against rotavirus were licensed, in 2006 and 2008. Both have been demonstrated to be safe and effective.[63]

The medical and scientific communities contend that in the aggregate, vaccines are incredibly safe, and they have the studies to back up this assertion. They assert that the overall risk-benefit calculus strongly supports vaccination against all childhood diseases as the best way to minimize the chances that any individual child will contract a contagious disease and suffer serious adverse consequences, as well as the chances that others in the community will be similarly affected. Most parents appear willing to accept this risk.[64] The American Academy of Pediatrics notes, for example, that the chances of one's developing encephalitis or other serious central nervous system disorders are more than a thousand times greater (1 out of every 800 cases) if a person contracts measles than if a child receives the measles vaccine (less than 1 in 1,000,000).[65] One recent study suggests that the vaccine may not cause encephalitis at all.[66]

However, opponents of vaccines are convinced, and claim publicly, that the adverse effects of vaccines are much more numerous and severe than medical and governmental authorities admit.[67] An important part of the reason that some parents believe that severe illnesses have been caused by their child's vaccination is the temporal overlap between vaccinations and the development of childhood illnesses, particularly developmental disorders. Children routinely receive many vaccinations during early childhood, particularly in the period from eighteen months to three years when autism, developmental delays, and other neurological problems become apparent. Therefore it is not surprising that parents would associate the onset of the child's illness with vaccination.[68]

The specific allegations of vaccine opponents have shifted over time, but they share some core concerns. Most notably, since the smallpox vaccine became widely available opponents of vaccines have expressed concern over the injection of "foreign" material into a person's body. Initially the "foreignness" of vaccines was attributable to their animal origin (early inoculations against smallpox were in fact injections of cowpox, which was observed by Edward Jenner to protect milkmaids against smallpox).[69] Later, opponents focused on vaccines as a source of "filth," because initially smallpox vaccination required the injection into one person of a small amount of diseased material from a person who had already contracted smallpox. Subsequently, the mere fact that a vaccine contained live but attenuated virus, cultivated in a lab, was enough to concern some vaccination critics. In addition, "foreignness" referred to immigrants and other outsiders. Historically, proponents of mandatory vaccination often focused on the poor and immigrant groups (which often overlapped) in their campaign for widespread vaccination. At the time of a major outbreak of smallpox in Boston in the early 1900s, doctors were accompanied into boardinghouses and crowded tenements by burly policemen, who would physically restrain reluctant adults in order for them to be vaccinated.[70] Today, metaphors of foreignness or filth are frequently invoked by vaccine opponents in two different ways. First, it is suggested that while some people (the lower classes, immigrants, and social deviants) might need vaccination, morally upright people, including mothers who protect their children through a "natural" and healthy lifestyle, do not.[71] Second, concerns that vaccines are "contaminated" with foreign materials (chemicals, animal parts, and cell lines derived from aborted fetuses) are frequently voiced.[72]

In the 1980s some parents believed that their children had suffered adverse effects from the DPT vaccine. The Institute of Medicine, the Centers for Disease Control, and the FDA convened two major panels to address these safety concerns. Around the same time, fearing massive tort liability, several vaccine manufacturers threatened to pull out of the vaccine market altogether, unless some way to protect them from financial ruin was found. In response, Congress enacted the National Childhood Vaccine Injury Act of 1986 (hereafter NCVIA or the Act).[73] The Act provides vaccine manufacturers with immunity from lawsuits in exchange for the establishment of a faster, alternative compensation system that relies on administrative law judges rather than on juries. Children (and adults) proven to have been injured as a result of a vaccine are compensated through a fund that is paid for by a 75-cent tax on every vaccination given in the United States. Under this system any person who believes he has been injured by a vaccine can bring a claim in the United States Court of Federal Claims. When the claimant's injury is acknowledged by the Department of Health and Human Services (HHS) to be a common adverse reaction, a so-called "table claim," it creates a presumption of causation, which HHS can rebut but rarely does. In cases where the asserted adverse reaction is not a table claim, the claimant must prove to an administrative law judge that his injuries were caused by a vaccination according to the usual "preponderance of the evidence" standard of proof used in tort suits.[74] While some parents have of course expressed disappointment when they have been unsuccessful, compensation has been awarded in about a quarter of the cases since the court began proceedings in 1988.[75]

More recent concerns about the foreignness of vaccines cluster around four major concerns. The first is that vaccines cause autism, based on the vaccine's contents. The measles, mumps, and rubella (MMR) vaccine is the primary culprit asserted here, based on a now-discredited publication by British physician Andrew Wakefield, who claimed that there was "an association" between the MMR vaccine and autism, basing his conclusion on a twelve child sample. Second, it is argued that vaccines cause autism[76] because they contain dangerous contaminants, especially thimerosal, which is a preservative that contains ethylmercury.[77] Third, other contaminants are alleged to be harmful, in unspecified ways, including aluminum and formaldehyde.[78] Fourth, some vaccine opponents assert that it is the number and frequency of vaccines that are harmful, noting that the current vaccine schedule includes many more vaccines than were available in the 1950s and '60s.

Each of these contentions has been rejected by numerous scientific panels, most recently in two reports from the Institute of Medicine, a part of the National Academies of Science, one issued in 2012 and the other in 2013.[79] The primary claim, that the MMR vaccine or any other vaccine causes autism, has been completely refuted. Andrew Wakefield's work could never be replicated and it was later retracted by the British medical journal *Lancet*. Wakefield was disciplined by British medical authorities and stripped of his license to practice medicine in the United Kingdom. It was later determined that several of the cases in the *Lancet* study were referred to Wakefield by a lawyer who hoped that Wakefield's study would support a lawsuit.[80]

In addition, the Institute of Medicine (IOM) has rejected any connection between the use of thimerosal in vaccines and autism or adverse reactions to vaccine. The IOM convened eight separate review panels between 2001 and 2004 to address the separate allegations that vaccines containing thimerosal caused autism and that the MMR vaccine caused autism.[81] Writing in the formal and careful language of science, for each allegation of harm the IOM found that the "evidence favors rejection of a causal relationship" between vaccination and autism.[82] Nonetheless, thimerosal free vaccines are now used in all immunizations mandated for children under six in the United States, although it is present in the optional influenza vaccine.[83] Ironically, it appears that efforts by government and vaccine manufacturers both to enhance vaccine safety and assuage safety concerns may have had the opposite result. When, out of an abundance of caution, the IOM recommended that thimerosal be removed from routine childhood vaccines, this action only fueled suspicions that thimerosal *was in fact* harmful.[84] Additional studies, published in 2010 and 2014, have affirmed that there is no causal relationship between the MMR vaccine or thimerosal in vaccines and autism,[85] yet celebrity anti-vaccine activists like Robert F. Kennedy, Jr., continue to raise baseless concerns about the dangers of vaccines.[86]

In regard to the third allegation, that vaccine additives such as formaldehyde and aluminum are harmful to children and cause adverse reactions, physicians and scientists point out that both compounds are already present in children's bodies, in much higher amounts than vaccines contribute. Both are necessary to make the vaccine more effective. Aluminum is an adjuvant, used to boost the body's immune response; without it people would need more doses of vaccines to be protected. The amount of aluminum in vaccines is about the same as the amount in a quart of infant formula. Formaldehyde is used to detoxify diphtheria and tetanus toxins or to inactivate viruses. Formaldehyde is normally found in the human bloodstream "at levels higher than in vaccines."[87]

In regard to the fourth concern, in 2013 the Institute of Medicine released a report addressing the scheduling of vaccines, considering the ages at which vaccines are administered and the multiple vaccines that are now available to combat childhood illnesses and mandated. The report noted that although children today receive more vaccinations than previously, "children now receive fewer antigens, which are the components of vaccines that stimulate the immune system," as a result of technological advances. The report recognized parental concerns about what some see as a rigid immunization schedule. However, it countered by noting that delaying or refusing immunization contributes to disease outbreaks across the country. The report found that the available data on the vaccine safety are reassuring, although it suggested that further research on the schedule itself would be useful.[88]

In addition to voicing concerns about vaccine side effects that are always shifting, some opponents of mandatory vaccination continue to press a broader claim that the government is hiding information about adverse vaccine effects.[89] The federal government asserts that, to the contrary, it is highly proactive in assessing vaccine safety, providing continuing oversight during the process of vaccine development and surveillance of clinical trials, as well as after a vaccine has been approved and is in general use. The FDA requires all vaccines to meet safety and efficacy requirements in order to be licensed. In addition, the FDA works closely with the CDC's Advisory Committee on Immunization Practices (ACIP) to determine, in conjunction with professional groups like the American Academy of Pediatrics, what diseases should be targeted for vaccine development, as well as the appropriate formulation and schedule of new vaccines.[90] Finally, once a vaccine is licensed, the CDC continues to oversee vaccine safety.[91] The Vaccine Adverse Event Reporting System (VAERS) was established by Congress in 1986 to encourage the reporting of all serious adverse health events that might be related to vaccination.[92] VAERS data are reviewed for possible patterns of injury, which are investigated further.[93]

C. The Impact of Unconscious Processes of Risk Construction

Yet despite the overwhelming evidence of vaccine safety, in general and for particular vaccines and vaccine ingredients, many parents remain skeptical about, if not adamantly opposed to, vaccinating their children. To understand why parents may be unpersuaded by an expert's straightforward factual explanations, we must return to our discussion in chapter 2 about the psychosocial construction of risk.

First, we learned that individuals' perceptions and decisions are highly affected by the availability heuristic—that is, if they have experienced something personally or heard about it (from a friend or the media), they are more likely to perceive something as risky.[94] Rare events capture our imagination, but they do not help us accurately predict future events.[95] Stories are frequently more powerful than statistics, especially when they arouse emotions, such as fear.[96] Risk communications that appeal to people's fears are successful; "the stronger the fear appeal, . . . the greater the severity of the threat perceived."[97] With the incredible availability of information on the Internet, it is easy for a parent who is concerned about the possibility of harm from vaccination to find information that fuels fears about potential risks.[98] And indeed, what parent would not be concerned about possible vaccine risks, when few current parents of young children have personally experienced the diseases that vaccines protect children from and every parent wants to keep her child as safe as possible?[99]

Second, people tend to assess risk based on their unconscious worldviews—that is, their visions of a just society. Those with "individualist" and "hierarchical" worldviews tend to minimize concerns about environmental risk. In contrast, those holding "egalitarian" and "communitarian" worldviews generally are more likely to rate environmental risks as dangerous. "Egalitarians" do so because they view technology as risky, while "communitarians" "find it congenial to believe that commerce and industry, activities they associate [with] inequity and selfishness, cause societal harm."[100]

Finally, trust—in medicine, science, and government—is also related to power and status. As noted in chapter 2, white women and nonwhites of both genders are more likely than white males to perceive risk in a given potential hazard. As Paul Slovic has observed, "risk perceptions seem to be related to individuals' power to influence decisions about the use of hazards."[101] Many parents, particularly mothers, feel powerless to influence government decisions about vaccine policy. However, they can try to protect their children from what they perceive to be risky immunizations by "opting out" of vaccination for their children, using the exemptions provided by state law that we shall discuss shortly.

Historically, many African-Americans had good reason not to trust doctors. Physicians have participated in major human rights abuses, including the infamous Tuskegee syphilis experiment, in which the United States Public Health Service recruited African-American men with syphilis to study its effects and then deliberately denied the men treatment and deceived them about what they were doing.[102] Other abuses include the involuntary sterilization of many African-American women, often without their knowledge and consent, and sometimes as an explicit condition of receiving welfare benefits.[103] More recently, investigative journalist Rebecca Skloot revealed significant bioethical lapses by Johns Hopkins University in its care of a poor African-American woman, Henrietta Lacks, whose cancerous cells were used to culture an experimental cell line, without disclosure or permission.[104] Today, some African-Americans continue to distrust their doctors, based on experiences of patronizing attitudes and substandard practice.[105] Historically the rates of immunization among African-American children were lower than those of white children, because of lack of access to preventative health services. Although the immunization rates of white children continue to be higher than those of African-American, Latino, or Native American (but not Asian-American) children, the disparities are growing smaller, as more affluent parents are opting out of vaccination.[106]

D. Why These Concerns about Risk Are So Prevalent Now

The concerns that some American parents have about vaccines reflect a confluence of factors. First, Americans now have fewer children, and give birth to them later, than in past decades. And, ironically, because Americans have a greater life expectancy than ever before, due largely to the vanquishing of many childhood illnesses, parents simply do not anticipate that their children will die or develop debilitating diseases. Parents naturally want to protect their children from all possible risks, including, for some parents, the remote risk of an adverse reaction to vaccination. As a result of living in an era in which the serious illness or death of a child is not the norm, especially for middle-class children, parents are much more likely to look for a villain, a remedy, or both, when death or illness does occur. According to Professor Lawrence Friedman, the twentieth century's medical and technological successes fueled Americans' rising expectations that all accidents or misfortunes that are not the victim's fault must have a remedy, especially a legal one.[107] In the case of vaccines it is therefore not surprising that the rising incidence of previously rare conditions like autism has spurred some parents to look for a simple and apparently straightforward explanation, even when the explanation is unsupported by reputable scientific research.[108]

Second, we are living at a time of great uncertainty and anxiety. This is fertile ground for the development of what Richard Hofstadter has called "the paranoid style in American politics," an apocalyptic belief that our nation is under siege from a vast and powerful conspiracy that threatens physical harm to our citizens as well as the even more insidious destruction of our way of life (a highly individualistic capitalist democracy).[109] Whether it is fear of terrorism, a vociferous debate about gun control, or a concern about a sluggish economy, many Americans evince a deep sense of unease.[110] Worry over the economy has become a central preoccupation in the United States since the global debt crisis began in 2008, contributing to a general state of anxiety.[111] Today, even as concerns about the strength of the economy are abating, there is increasing awareness of income inequality, which also triggers anxiety and leads many people to turn inward and focus on getting "what's mine."[112] Many have become more fearful and less trusting in all aspects of their lives,[113] rendering them susceptible to the sensational claims of anti-vaccination activists.[114] Many Americans distrust government, corporations, physicians, and scientists.[115] This distrust, in turn, is highly correlated with perception of greater hazards. Those who lack trust in expert authority are more likely to find activities to be risky than those who generally trust experts. In practice, then, we should not be surprised that many anti-vaccine websites assert that "Vaccine Policy Is Motivated by Profit," claiming not only that pharmaceutical companies develop vaccines in order to make huge profits but also that individual physicians have a financial interest in promoting vaccination and that government regulators are covering up adverse reactions to vaccines.[116]

Third, ours is the age of information overload, shaped by the Internet and the proliferation of partisan cable news programs, and the lack of effective means of screening and evaluating the truth of statements presented as scientific fact, even among those who are generally well educated.[117] Many people turn to the Internet in search of health information, as a supplement to, or substitute for, conversations with their physicians.[118] Official government websites are sometimes criticized for not providing direct access to the journal articles they cite, making it harder for web consumers to educate themselves about the relevant science. This lack of full access to "hard" scientific evidence has made it easier for parents to be persuaded by misinformation and emotional anecdotes that are often found on anti-vaccination websites.[119] This problem is compounded by the decline over the past two decades in scientifically trained journalists who can present complex scientific information accurately and in a way that most readers can understand.[120] Further, it appears that some journalists have so embraced the mantra of "even-handedness" that they present as possessing equal validity the peer-reviewed research by reputable scientists, anecdotes from individual parents, and opinions of anti-vaccine activists like Jim Carrey and Barbara Loe Fisher.[121] For example, when actress Jenny McCarthy was questioned on *Oprah* about the basis for her assertions that vaccines were dangerous and caused autism, she responded by touting her "Mommy instincts" and declared, "The University of Google is where I got my degree from."[122]

Today growing numbers of American parents, particularly middle- to high-income ones, try to protect their children through individual action, without trying to persuade government to enact protective regulation. This is a phenomenon that Professor Brenda Cossman calls "anxiety governance," in which increasing numbers of parents, especially mothers, seek to safeguard their children's health on their own, primarily by acting as conscientious consumers.[123] These "eco-moms" do not engage in political advocacy to try to change laws to ban dangerous substances. Instead, they try to keep their children safe by buying things, such as BPA-free baby bottles, organic foods, cribs made of wood without preservatives, and nontoxic cleansers.[124] These mothers often believe that they must take complete responsibility for their families' well-being. By electing to channel their "toxic vigilance" into searching the Internet for advice on safe products and buying accordingly, rather than lobbying government safety agencies, these mothers perpetuate the cycle of "anxiety governance," with mothers believing that they must act to protect their children because no one else will.[125] This phenomenon has significant implications, not just for the future of American democracy but also for the health of other people's children, whose parents may lack the education, time, and financial resources to try to purchase better health for their children.

II. American Law's Response to Competing Risk Perspectives

This section will address three major legal and policy concerns. First, it will examine the legal and regulatory regimens established to promote vaccine safety. Second, it will analyze the legal and constitutional requirements that laws mandating vaccination and providing exceptions to those mandates must satisfy. Here, the analysis will focus on the Fourteenth Amendment's substantive due process and equal protection clauses, the First Amendment's "free exercise" and "establishment" clauses, and the common law doctrine of informed consent. Third, this section will consider whether vaccine mandates, with and without exemptions, are sound public policy.

A. The Law's Response to Concerns about Vaccine Risks

Government has responded to parental concern about the actual and potential risks of vaccination on two fronts, a division of authority that reflects the American federal system. First, Congress has enacted laws to expand federal government oversight of vaccines and vaccine safety. Second, state governments—through the actions of their legislatures, courts, and administrative agencies—permit parents to exempt their children from vaccination for medical, religious, or philosophical reasons.

1. THE FEDERAL GOVERNMENT'S ROLE

The FDA, CDC, and other federal government agencies provide extensive oversight of vaccine development and safety, as discussed previously. In addition to convening multiple expert panels to address concerns raised by parents and others about vaccine safety and potential adverse events, the government also created a no-fault compensation scheme for children whose injuries were caused by vaccination. Under the framework established by the National Childhood Vaccine Injury Act, parents can seek compensation for their children's injuries if they can establish that the injuries were caused by a vaccination.[126] In the past two decades, many parents whose children suffer from autism or an autism spectrum disorder have filed claims with the United States Court of Federal Claims, asserting that the child's condition was caused by vaccination.[127] These claims were consolidated and in 2009–10 they were unanimously rejected in the Omnibus Autism Proceedings. In six separate cases, the special masters presiding over those cases found that there *was no causal relationship between vaccination and autism*, either in general, as a matter of biological plausibility, or in the specific cases litigated.[128] As a result of this unsuccessful litigation, many parents whose children suffer from autism or another developmental disorder are deeply dissatisfied,[129] a problem that was compounded by the Supreme Court's 2011 decision in *Bruesewitz v. Wyeth LLC*.[130] In *Bruesewitz*, the Supreme Court held that the National Childhood Vaccine Injury Act barred state tort law claims against vaccine manufacturers alleging that the vaccines were defectively designed. Thus, parents can raise causation arguments only in the administrative proceedings authorized by the Act; if they lose there, they have no further legal remedy. Many parents who have lost in these administrative proceedings continue to believe that vaccination was to blame and often share their beliefs on the Internet and prominent media outlets.

2. STATE OPTIONS FOR PARENTS WHO OBJECT TO VACCINATING THEIR CHILDREN

Each state establishes its own requirements for childhood immunization, but in practice most states follow the recommendations of ACIP, although some of the newer vaccines are not required in every state.[131] Every state exempts children from vaccination mandates for medical reasons. Forty-seven states authorize exemption for religious reasons. Only California, Mississippi, and West Virginia lack religious exemptions.[132] In addition, twenty states permit exemption based on parents' philosophical or personal beliefs.[133] Religious and philosophical exemptions are now under challenge across the United States, as the increased frequency of outbreaks of disease, particularly measles and pertussis, has driven concern among public health officials, doctors, and many parents that the health of the majority of children may be put at risk when some parents choose not to vaccinate their children.

Medical exemptions are granted for children whose parents present documentation that they have previously had a severe allergic reaction to a particular vaccine, presently have a moderate or severe illness that makes vaccination inadvisable, or have a compromised immune system, due, for example, to cancer or HIV/AIDS.[134] Medical exemptions account for about 20 percent of exemptions granted nationwide.[135]

a. Religious Exemptions and the First Amendment

Exemptions based on parents' religious and philosophical beliefs exemptions account for the remaining 80 percent of opt-outs from childhood vaccination mandates.[136] Most states began to authorize religious exemptions beginning in the 1970s, in response to the federal law, noted in chapter 7, that encouraged states to enact child abuse reporting laws, but provided exemptions for parents who did not seek medical treatment because of their religious beliefs. The federal law was repealed, but most states retained their religious exemption laws.[137] Religious exemptions to laws governing children's health, including vaccination, are not aimed at the risk of vaccines or other medical procedures. Rather, they are designed to safeguard parents' "free exercise" of their religion, which is protected by the First Amendment.[138] The First Amendment also safeguards religious freedom through the "establishment clause," which prohibits the government from placing a particular religion in a favored position, as was the case in Great Britain with the Church of England. The establishment clause also forbids the government from "excessive entanglement" with religion.[139]

Historically many states enacted narrow religious exemption laws, limiting exemption to "bona fide members of a recognized religious organization" or members of "a nationally recognized ... church ... opposed to medical immunization against disease."[140] Other states, like New York, added a requirement that the religious belief be "sincerely held."[141] New York courts have struggled for many years to apply this requirement, because it forces them to inquire into the sincerity of parents' religious beliefs, an act that itself might be seen as violating the establishment clause.[142] Nonetheless, New York still enforces its law, which exempts children "whose parent, parents, or guardian [holds] genuine and sincere religious beliefs which are contrary to" mandatory vaccination.[143] The Wyoming Supreme Court has taken a different approach, ruling that once the legislature enacts a religious exemption to vaccination, courts and administrative agencies are not permitted to scrutinize the sincerity of a parent's asserted religious beliefs.[144]

When parents have challenged a denial of a requested religious exemption, courts have frequently found that existing laws ran afoul of the First Amendment. *Boone v. Boozman* illustrates the problem. In *Boone* a federal district court invalidated Arkansas' religious exemption because it was available only to those parents who opposed vaccination "on the grounds that immunization conflicts with the religious tenets and practices of a *recognized church or religious denomination* of which the parent ... is an adherent or member."[145] While the goal of the statute may have been to protect religious liberty, the court found that the law as phrased infringed on religious liberty because of the narrowness of its exemption criteria. The law effectively limited religious exemptions to parents who were Christian Scientists or members of another group that espoused faith healing as part of its religious doctrine. The *Boone* court found that this exemption violated both the free exercise clause and the establishment clause of the First Amendment.[146] In response, the Arkansas legislature adopted a greatly expanded exemption, making it much easier for parents to opt out of vaccination for their children. The new Arkansas law provides: "This section shall not apply if the parents or legal guardian of that child [objects] thereto on the grounds that immunization conflicts with the *religious or philosophical beliefs* of the parent or guardian."[147]

b. Philosophical Exemptions

The Arkansas statute is typical of laws in the seventeen states that now permit parents to refuse vaccination for their child on the basis of philosophical or personal belief.[148] These statutes, as well as more broadly worded religious exemption laws, make it much easier for parents to obtain an exemption, increasing the rates of exemption overall. For example, a New York mother who sought a religious exemption to vaccination claimed "religious beliefs" that closely tracked the arguments that secular opponents of mandatory vaccination make. The mother asserted:

> I am requesting this religious exemption because it is my strong belief that all vaccines are made in violation of God's word. Vaccines are made with toxic chemicals that are injected into the bloodstream by vaccination. All vaccines are made with foreign proteins (viruses and bacteria). . . . I feel [that] vaccinat[ing] my child conflicts with my religious beliefs because I believe that man is made in God's image and the injection of toxic chemicals and foreign proteins into the bloodstream is a violation of God's directive to keep the body (which is to be treated as a temple) holy and free from impurities.[149]

While the court found the mother's declaration was not "religious" in nature and thus did not warrant exemption under New York law, the same statement would likely be sufficient for a philosophical exemption in a state that authorized such exemptions.

In practice, the ease of obtaining exemption depends not only on the statutory language used but also on the number and difficulty of procedural requirements to claim an exemption. A 2013 study of state religious and philosophical exemption laws grouped states into three roughly equal groups of "easy," "medium," and "difficult." "Easy" states required only that parents sign and submit a standardized form that was readily available from the child's school or the Internet; some forms had interactive "prompts" or required short answers. "Medium" states added other obligations, such as requiring parents to attend an educational session about vaccines with the school nurse or to submit an original statement of the grounds for their objection.[150] "Difficult" states imposed additional hurdles, such as requiring parents to have the exemption request notarized and/or to write a letter explaining why they were opposed to vaccination. This study made two key findings that confirmed previous research. First, states that made it relatively easy to claim an exemption had higher exemption rates. Second, states that granted philosophical and religious exemptions had higher exemption rates than states that authorized exemption on religious grounds only.[151]

c. Consequences of Exemptions
Notably, states with higher rates of exemption also have a greater incidence of outbreaks, particularly of measles and pertussis.[152] One study found that school age children whose parents had exempted them from vaccination were thirty-five times more likely to contract measles than their vaccinated peers; younger children were at even greater risk.[153] The correlation between high exemption rates and disease outbreaks is unsurprising, because parents seeking exemption are often clustered geographically, whether they are members of the same religious community, like the Amish, or are concentrated in culturally "progressive" and relatively affluent communities. For example, in the early twenty-first century, at a time when the exemption rate across Washington State averaged 6 percent, exceeding the then national average of 2.5 percent, the exemption rates in different Washington counties ranged from just over 1 percent to more than 26 percent.[154] Even within counties, different school districts may have different rates of parental opt-outs. A recent California news story found that vaccination rates for children in Beverly Hills and Santa Monica, on Los Angeles' affluent west side, had plummeted as "incidents of whooping cough surged."[155] Other studies have found that in some districts in California as many as half of all children are entering school without vaccinations.[156] The growing use of vaccination exemptions increases the risk of disease outbreaks that can spread rapidly. Individual parents appear unaware that the decisions they make for their own children, whom they believe they can protect through breastfeeding, healthy eating, and a healthy "lifestyle," will affect other, less well-off children. As noted by Daniel Rubin and Sophie

Kasimov, "While some groups of like-minded parents have formed tightly knit communities in solidarity with each other, they may not see themselves in solidarity with a family two zip codes away."[157]

In addition to the total rejection of vaccinations, growing numbers of parents have embraced "alternative vaccination schedules" that are contrary to those recommended by the Centers for Disease Control and the American Academy of Pediatrics.[158] As many as a fifth of all parents of young children now rely on alternative vaccination schedules. Some parents skip vaccinations for certain diseases altogether; others delay and "spread out" recommended immunizations.[159] More than half of the parents deviating from the recommended immunization schedule have devised the schedule themselves or with the help of a friend.[160] Many apparently believe that they have the expertise to determine what particular vaccines their child will need.[161] While these parents may believe these delays and omissions do not matter because their children will eventually need to be vaccinated—or exempted—in order to attend school or day care, the result of their choices is that the children who are now at greatest risk of contracting contagious diseases are younger children, who are more likely than older children to be severely affected by the diseases they contract, require hospitalization, and die.[162] Some physicians are now turning away parents who refuse to vaccinate their children, because they find it "untenable" to have unvaccinated children in their waiting rooms.[163]

d. The Role of Parens Patriae *and Informed Consent*

Parents who claim that they should be able to refuse to have their children vaccinated assert that they have an absolute "right" to make medical decisions for their children. They contend that making these decisions is inherent in the right of parents to raise their children as they see fit and in accordance with their religious and philosophical beliefs. Parents also argue that they know their children better than anyone and, therefore, their views should take precedence over those of the government and the child's physician. Frequently they invoke the doctrine of "informed consent," which, as Professor Wendy Parmet notes, has attained "a fundamental, if not 'sacramental' status, in contemporary thought." Indeed, "informed consent" is the mantra of the National Vaccine Information Center, a self-proclaimed informational organization that is active in the anti-vaccination movement. Its website declares, "Your Health. Your Family. Your Choice."[164] In contrast, those who assert that the government has, and should have, the right to insist that all children be vaccinated against contagious diseases rely on two other legal doctrines. They contend that the police power (the obligation to protect the health and safety of the entire community) and the doctrine of *parens patriae* (the obligation of the state to protect children and other incompetent individuals from harm) both support the mandatory vaccination of children.

In order to decide which view is "correct" or, preferably, to see if it is possible to accommodate the apparent conflicts between these competing doctrines, we must first examine the principles that underlie each. In essence, informed consent requires that before a medical intervention takes place, the patient must be told about the risks, as well as the benefits, of the proposed intervention and its alternatives, including the alternative of doing nothing.[165] Informed consent doctrine reflects several legal and cultural values. One that readily springs to mind is the promotion of individual self-determination and human dignity. John Stuart Mill articulated this view when he declared, "[T]he sole end for which mankind are warranted, individually or collectively, in interfering with the liberty of any of their number, is self-protection.... [T]he only purpose for which power can be rightfully exercised over any member of a civilized community, against his will, is to prevent harm to others. His own good, physical or moral, is not a sufficient warrant.... Over himself, over his own body and mind, the individual is sovereign."[166] In 1914 Judge Benjamin Cardozo ruled in accordance with this principle in a tort case in which a patient asserted that while she was under anesthesia her surgeon operated in violation of her express wishes. She claimed that this unauthorized intrusion into her body was a battery, an "unconsented touching." In *Schloendorff v. Society of New York Hospital* Judge Cardozo agreed, declaring, "Every human being of adult years and sound mind has a right to determine what shall be done with his own body."[167] *Schloendorff*, along with important later cases like *Canterbury v. Spence*[168] and *Truman v. Thomas*,[169] laid the groundwork for modern bioethics discourse.

The second core value of informed consent doctrine is the belief that shared decisionmaking between a doctor and her patient leads to better health outcomes. When physicians and patients discuss the risks and benefits of proposed medical interventions, as well as the risks and benefits of alternative approaches, each party gains valuable insights. Physicians can understand their patients' personal circumstances and values, while patients become better equipped to choose the treatment most likely to achieve their health goals while being consonant with their core values. Thus, informed consent is a process, not a form.[170] In the context of childhood vaccinations many physicians seek to educate the parents of their patients about vaccination's safety and efficacy, discussing its benefits for the individual child and children in the larger community and emphasizing the extremely low risks of a serious adverse reaction, particularly when compared with the risks if the child contracts the disease that could be prevented by vaccination. However, some physicians are finding it increasingly frustrating to have discussions with parents who seem not to be open to a realistic discussion of risks and benefits. Other doctors express concern that the presence of unvaccinated children in their waiting rooms poses an unacceptable risk to other children, including, in rare cases, the risk of death should they contract a vaccine-preventable disease.[171]

A third, closely related goal of informed consent is to compensate patients who are injured by a medical procedure to which they have agreed, if that agreement was achieved by inadequate disclosure of the procedure's risks and benefits.[172] The National Childhood Vaccine Injury Compensation Program (VICP) was designed to ensure that children and adults injured by vaccination are compensated for those injuries. As noted, some children suffer from chronic illnesses that their parents attribute to vaccination, but the parents have been unsuccessful in proving causation in court.

Informed consent is, of course, different when the patient is a child rather than an adult, because young children lack the experience, maturity, and reasoning ability necessary to make an informed decision. In practice, parents have traditionally given consent for their children's medical treatment; they usually know their child well and are presumed to act out of love. Having parents give consent on behalf of their children is easy when the parents agree with the physician's recommendation. However, there is longstanding friction between physicians and parents about whether parents should be presumed to act in their child's best interests. Some physicians contend that they, rather than the parents, are in the best position to identify and protect the interests of the child who is their patient.[173] While this might be attributed to medical paternalism, it is also possible that in choosing—or declining—treatment, the parent may not be acting in her child's best interests.

The doctrine of *parens patriae* reflects the principle that sometimes the state must intervene to protect a child from harm, whether it is the result of parental malice or intent, or the product of a parent's unreasonable or flawed judgment. Although American law usually defers to parental decisions about childrearing, reflecting the high value that American law and culture place on individual autonomy and family privacy,[174] nonetheless the child is not the parent's property, subject to treatment at the parent's whim. Indeed, that is the essential rationale for civil and criminal child abuse laws, discussed in chapter 7.

The question of what is best for the child has arisen frequently in cases when parents reject medical treatment for their children, either because they oppose the particular treatment recommended by physicians or because they eschew all medical treatment, for religious or philosophical reasons. The Supreme Court has expressed its view in several decisions, most notably *Prince v. Massachusetts*. There the Court declared, "Parents may be free to become martyrs themselves. But it does not follow [that] they are free, in identical circumstances, to make martyrs of their children before they have reached the age of full and legal discretion when they can make that choice for themselves."[175] Similarly, state courts have sometimes acted to compel medical treatment over parental objection, as noted earlier, when parents have objected to medical treatment for their children on religious grounds—for example, blood transfusions for the children of Jehovah's Witness parents,[176] or based on more general skepticism about the efficacy of mainstream medicine.[177]

Professor Wendy Parmet contends that even though states are fully justified in mandating childhood vaccination under their police power and *parens patriae* authority, the central purposes of informed consent—enhancing patient self-determination, preventing injuries that could be avoided by a full risk-benefit disclosure, and compensating patients for those injuries can still be achieved, even if they are not strictly required.[178] Parmet explains that given the purpose of informed consent—to acquire a patient's informed agreement to a given procedure—

parents contemplating vaccination of their children must be given sufficient information to make an informed choice about whether to accept vaccination or to seek a religious or philosophical exemption.[179] The goal is *not* to satisfy legal formalities but to prompt a discussion between parents and physicians about the risks and benefits of a particular vaccine, which should address not only the risks and benefits for the parent's child but also for the broader community.[180] Further, when public health officials and pediatricians educate parents about herd immunity and urge them to accept vaccination as an obligation of membership in a community, it only makes sense that their children should be compensated in the rare case of a serious adverse reaction.[181] Both vaccine skeptics and proponents agree that the national Vaccine Injury Compensation Program needs to be updated to provide prompt relief to children who have been injured as a result of vaccination.[182]

Meeting these goals of informed consent will also promote trust between physicians, parents, and patients, as well as between citizens and the public health system. As Dr. Louis Cooper, a noted proponent of childhood vaccination, explains, "Every time a mother holds her healthy infant to be immunized, she is demonstrating great faith in the potential benefit and safety of the vaccine and trust in the clinician who recommended it.... This trust is an expression of a special social contract that is one key to the success of immunization programs."[183]

III. How Current Vaccination Laws Reflect the Psychosocial Construction of Risk and Mothers' Responsibility for Children's Health

Current debates over vaccination policy, conducted in legislatures, on the Internet and television and radio talk shows, as well as in doctors' offices and family living rooms, illuminate the psychosocial nature of risk construction. We know that people's risk perceptions—and decisions about how to manage that risk—depend heavily on cognitive shortcuts like the availability heuristic; the "omission bias," which views actions as more significant than omissions; and individual worldviews, including trust or distrust in institutions. The way in which American law has implemented competing constructions of risk—by mandating vaccines against contagious diseases and granting parents either a narrow or expansive ability to refuse to vaccinate their own children—says a great deal about how the law views parents' obligations to protect their children's health, as well as the health of other children. Only three states have chosen to limit vaccination exemptions to medical grounds—for example, that for this child, on this particular day, vaccination is medically inadvisable. In all other states, opting out of vaccination is relatively easy, particularly if the state has enacted a "philosophical" exemption in addition to a religious one.

Among all the aspects of children's health addressed in this book, it is only in the case of vaccine refusals that mothers are not held legally accountable *either* for risking their own children's health *or* for inflicting harm on other people's children as a result of a failure to vaccinate. While in recent years there has been increasing discussion about holding nonvaccinating parents liable in tort for causing harm to other children, this has not yet happened.[184] In contrast, in chapters 4 through 7 we saw that many mothers and pregnant women have faced severe legal consequences for acts and omissions that potentially risk their children's health. When pregnant women refused blood transfusions or cesarean sections on the grounds of religious or personal belief, they were frequently overruled by courts. Readers will recall the pregnant Jehovah's Witness whom a New York court ordered to receive a blood transfusion over her objection, the Georgia woman who was ordered to undergo a cesarean section over her religious objections, and Florida mothers Samantha Burton and Laura Pemberton, who were forced by court order to undergo medical treatments recommended by their physician.[185] In each of these cases judges declared that the woman's religious or philosophical beliefs were insufficient to override the state's interest in ensuring the delivery of a healthy child. Similarly, when mothers who lived with violent and abusive men did not prevent their child from being abused or killed by those men, the mothers faced criminal charges ranging from child neglect to murder. Prosecutors and judges contended that these mothers *chose* to put their children's health at risk by having a sexual relationship with an abusive partner.[186] All of these cases portrayed pregnant women and mothers who failed to act to protect their children's health as "bad mothers," whose conduct fell below the standard of the "reasonable parent" or "reasonable mother."

The markedly different ways in which American law treats mothers who choose not to vaccinate their children and mothers who are asserted to have neglected their children (both born and "unborn") speaks volumes about the psychological and social underpinnings of risk perception, as well as the complex ways in which constructed risk intersects with American law. The major differences between these two groups of mothers are those of color and class. In previous chapters most of the women prosecuted have been poor, racial and ethnic minorities, or immigrants. Frequently they are single mothers; often they lack education and social supports. In contrast, most mothers (and fathers) who choose not to have their children vaccinated are white, well educated, middle- to upper-class, and married.[187] They typically assert that they are willing to run the risk that their child might contract a contagious disease because they believe that they can protect their child by breastfeeding, healthy eating, and avoiding day care.[188] These mothers claim the ability to make an individualized risk-benefit calculus, the very same right that is denied pregnant women who refuse blood transfusions or cesarean sections, as well as mothers who are victims of intimate partner violence who try to calculate the best way to extract their child from a violent or abusive situation.

Not only have nonvaccinating mothers not faced legal action, they have been rarely vilified in public discourse. Their actions have been frequently viewed with tolerance, if not outright sympathy. These mothers see themselves, and are often seen by others, as embodying the rugged individualism that is a core value in American society and American law, even though it is now often the neoliberalism of the twenty-first century, in which individuals act to protect their children and families through prudent economic and social choices.[189] These mothers often wrap themselves in the mantle of "family values."[190] *Only* in the realm of childhood vaccination have we found that mothers who choose not to act in conformity with majoritarian legal requirements are greeted with applause, rather than imprisonment.

This chapter's examination of the legal system's treatment of parents who opt out of mandatory immunization for their children also illuminates the elusive and ever-changing role of "choice" in American law. Nonvaccinating parents are treated very differently from other parents who do not provide their children with medical treatment. During the past fifty years many parents have been criminally prosecuted for forgoing lifesaving medical treatment for their children (for cancer, for diabetes, and for congenital birth defects). In several cases in the late twentieth century Christian Science parents were charged with manslaughter when they failed to seek medical treatment for an ill child who they thought was suffering from the flu or other minor illness. During the past decade at least one fundamentalist Christian couple was convicted of murder after they failed to summon medical help for their seven-month-old son, who later died.[191] In other cases physicians and hospital authorities have sought court orders to compel medical treatment over parental objections, whether the objections are grounded in religion or instead reflect parental beliefs that they know what is best for their children.[192] Similarly, courts have also upheld medical interventions to safeguard children's health such as mandatory screening of newborns for metabolic diseases, even when the parent challenged the screening as a matter of religious belief.[193] Whether they are Christian Scientists, fundamentalist Christians, or believers in holistic health and alternative healing, parents who fail to provide mainstream medical treatment for their children are frequently viewed by the larger community as religious zealots, modern-day Abrahams who have sacrificed their children on the altar of misguided or blind faith. Many have been convicted and sentenced to prison.[194]

In striking contrast, parents who refuse to accept mainstream medicine by having their children vaccinated do not simply risk the health of their own children, by making them highly vulnerable to contracting a contagious disease if an outbreak occurs. They also threaten the health of other people's children, who may be at risk of contracting a disease and suffering harm as a result, because they are too young to be vaccinated, are unable to be vaccinated because of a compromised immune system, or were vaccinated but the vaccine was less effective than usual. Yet to date no nonvaccinating parent has faced a tort suit or criminal prosecution for putting other children at risk.

If low-income children were not receiving mandatory vaccinations—assuming that their nonvaccinated status came to the attention of authorities—it is likely that their parents would be investigated for child abuse or neglect, or that doctors would seek a court order compelling the parents to permit their children to receive medical treatment. In these cases, the government would assert that the parent was acting unreasonably by refusing permission for her child to receive a treatment that was widely recognized by competent medical and public health authorities as safe and effective. Indeed, in Colorado and other states, parents of unvaccinated children have faced the loss of their welfare benefits if they fail to comply with state vaccination mandates.[195] Recently, the Conservative government in Australia adopted a similar policy.[196]

Finally, the construction of risk in the vaccination debates—and the law's reaction to it—illuminates a systemic issue in American law and society. American law typically focuses on the risk to specific, identified children. Frequently the focus is on harm after it has occurred. A risk that has been realized gives rise to tort suits, civil child abuse proceedings, or criminal prosecutions. But when attempts are made to use law in a precautionary, prophylactic way (as in the case of public nuisance lawsuits seeking remediation of lead contamination) or when legislative or regulatory action is proposed to protect all of a community's children (such as restricting parents' ability to refuse children's vaccination), these actions are frequently challenged as impermissible government overreaching or belittled as the intrusive arm of the "nanny state." Yet without legally imposed obligations to protect and improve the health of the community as a whole, many American children will continue to live shorter, less healthy, and less productive lives.

PART IV

A New Framework for Risk Assessment and Risk Reduction

10

Moving beyond Blame

Real Solutions for Children's Health

Introduction: So Where Are We Now?

This book has analyzed how the unconscious processes of risk perception, risk communication, and risk management affect the way that American society and the American legal system have responded to concerns about children's health. With the operation of cognitive shortcuts like the availability heuristic, the hindsight bias, and the fundamental attribution error, as well as unconscious biases of class, race, and gender, the emphasis on mothers as a source of harm is not surprising, because mothers *do* play a key role in their children's lives. The book has considered children's health in a broad range of contexts, from conception to birth and beyond—from infancy to school age to adolescence. In each context we have examined how American law, medicine, and the media, as well as the public, view mothers and pregnant women, and confronted the prevailing view that mothers are the virtual guarantors of their children's health and well-being. "Good mothers" are idealized as paragons of care and nurturance, while other mothers are held strictly accountable if they fail to live up to these heightened expectations. On many occasions mothers are held legally responsible for failing to do enough to protect their children from harm, facing civil and criminal sanctions, including civil commitment and imprisonment, based on their actions or inaction. At the same time, our society—and our legal system—has not acknowledged the substantial contributions to children's health made by other key players—fathers and other men, private individuals and corporations, and government policymakers. Actions by each of these players can also create risks and cause harm to children. In addition, poverty, racism, and social isolation have profound effects on children's health.

We have seen that "the law" encompasses both official pronouncements and informal, discretionary actions. American law is formally constructed by legislators who enact statutes, presidents and governors who sign those statutes into law, judges who interpret the law, and agency policymakers who promulgate regulations to make those laws enforceable. Yet our laws become real only through the discretionary decisions of many individual actors, including persons who may not be formally identified as part of the legal system. We readily acknowledge that county clerks, police officers, prosecutors, and judges are legal players, with clearly defined roles in implementing the law. But others, inside and outside the government, also play an important part in deciding whether legal proceedings should be initiated. These include health care professionals, who decide whether a pregnant patient or a newborn baby should be tested for drugs and "referred" to a prosecutor, social services investigators who recommend social and economic support or initiate child neglect proceedings when a mother is the victim of intimate partner violence, and jurors who decide whether a mother is guilty of homicide when she failed to perceive that the infant she was breastfeeding was not receiving adequate nourishment.

All of these actors—including legislators, prosecutors, health care professionals, and jurors—make legal decisions that are influenced by the unconscious processes of risk construction. When the governor of Tennessee signs into law a bill that makes the use of drugs while pregnant a crime, regardless of whether the baby has been harmed, he is exercising discretionary judgment about risk, shaped by psychosocial processes of which he is unaware. For each of us, subliminal mental shortcuts, unconscious biases and stereotypes, and personal worldviews intersect with prevailing cultural values to reach conclusions about legal responsibility for actual, or potential, harm.

The decisions of individuals and American law writ large are also influenced by a broad array of unconscious assumptions and background norms. Many of these are rooted in English common law, but American law has evolved over centuries to reflect the United States' unique history. That history includes a valuing of "rugged" individualism and family privacy, the subjugation of women and racial minorities, and hefty skepticism about the role of government. American values are also shaped by social and economic anxiety, initiated by the September

11 attacks, exacerbated by the severe economic downturn of the Great Recession of 2008, and continuing concern about income inequality and the place of the United States in the global economy. This anxiety is also fueled by the broad array of (mis)information available on the Internet and in other media. Living in an age in which we are "literally afraid of everything," it is easy to try to make sense of the world by zeroing in on those who are most often "proximate" to children—mothers—and make their behavior the focus of efforts to protect children.

This book is not a brief for bad mothers. It does not contend that mothers should never be held civilly or criminally responsible for causing harm to their children. Instead, it argues that action is needed on three fronts. First, we must acknowledge the reality of unconscious risk construction and its impact on American law and the American health care system. Second, laws and law enforcement must become more even-handed, taking account of, and endeavoring to avoid, unconscious biases and prejudices. "It's the mother's fault" should not be the automatic response whenever a child's health is seen to be at risk. Third, we should recognize the challenging and complex circumstances that confront many parents trying to raise healthy children. In response to this complexity, we must develop and implement comprehensive strategies that will improve the health of all of America's children. We need to identify what children need for good health and a successful life in a rapidly changing and often stressful world and then provide those necessities, supporting parents rather than engaging in retrospective blaming. The health of America's children demands that we embrace the precautionary principle, acting to prevent harm rather than reluctantly cleaning it up afterward.

Responses

I. Acknowledge Unconscious Risk Construction and Its Impact on the Law

At the outset, we must acknowledge that all people engage in unconscious risk construction. We cannot change how people are wired, nor would we want to, but we can act with awareness that making legal decisions—about broad legal principles and case-specific application of legal rules—is affected by subconscious mental processes. Armed with this knowledge, we can revise the law to channel and constrain the exercise of discretion in ways that will make legal rules and decisions fairer to individual parents, at the same time that we pursue better health care outcomes for children. In light of overwhelming evidence of racial, gender, and class bias throughout the legal system, we should carefully evaluate proposed legal rules for their potential disparate impact on particular groups of people and reformulate those rules to avoid such effects. If, for example, a goal of public health policy is to protect fetuses from exposure to alcohol, nicotine, and other drugs *in utero* out of concern that such exposure will lead to impaired physical or cognitive development, then the criteria for testing pregnant women for drugs must include *all* obstetrics patients, in private physician practices as well as public clinics, and drug screens must include both legal and illegal drugs.[1] If a public health goal is to increase the rates of vaccination against contagious diseases to protect the entire community via herd immunity, then legislatures should consider limiting vaccination exemptions on religious or philosophical grounds. If they choose to permit exemptions, legislatures should establish criteria and procedures for exemption that do not favor one racial or economic group over another.[2]

In addition, our legal system must build in rigorous safeguards to review and constrain the exercise of discretion. For example, we observed in chapters 5 and 7 that prosecutors' decisions to indict are rarely reviewed. In practice, once a decision has been made to bring a case to trial, juries are highly likely to convict, even if the prosecution's case is weak. This puts tremendous pressure on defendants to plead guilty even if they believe they are not. To reduce the potential for unfair convictions, the law could mandate a system of internal, pre-prosecution review or consultation.[3] Large district attorney's offices could require the prosecutors who bring child abuse or homicide cases to consult with prosecutors in the same office who handle intimate partner violence cases. This could help the first group of prosecutors to understand the perspective of mothers who are victims of intimate partner violence when their children are being abused by the same man and to consider whether the criminal prosecution of a non-abusive mother is the best response. Other systematic review processes could be implemented. For example, prosecutors could be required to determine whether the criteria for indicting pregnant women for putting the health of a developing fetus at risk through drug use are comparable to the criteria used in prosecuting the men who supply them with drugs or who terrorize them with violent attacks.[4]

More rigorous judicial review of the exercise of prosecutorial discretion is also necessary, particularly when prosecutors are interpreting a statute broadly or applying it in novel circumstances. The dangers of "judicial withdrawal" from the judiciary's obligation to oversee prosecutorial charging and plea bargaining decisions[5] are all too obvious in an age in which fetal personhood is a sharply contested moral and political question. This is necessary to avoid situations in which defendants are induced to accept a plea deal because the risk of going to trial is too great. Dissenting Judge Patricia Riley voiced her concern in *Bei Bei Shuai v. State*. When Ms. Shuai was prosecuted for murder and attempted feticide after she tried to commit suicide by ingesting rat poison, Judge Riley decried the prosecution as an unwarranted statutory expansion. She warned, "If the feticide statute is interpreted as advocated by the State and applied to women's prenatal conduct, it could have an unlimited scope and create an indefinite number of new 'crimes,'" including taking over-the-counter cold remedies or sleeping pills while pregnant, as well as smoking or drinking alcohol. Judge Riley asserted that the judiciary lacked the constitutional authority to condone such broad statutory interpretations by prosecutors. Rather, she contended, decisions about criminalizing the conduct of pregnant women are properly left to the legislature, a forum where they can be thoroughly investigated, studied, and debated.[6]

There is a similar need to constrain the exercise of discretion by health care professionals, who frequently take it upon themselves to interpret the law governing child abuse and neglect and report pregnant women to law enforcement after they have disclosed personal information in the course of treatment. Confidentiality is essential in caring for pregnant women, as it is in all health care relationships. If patients do not believe that they can speak candidly with the physician, nurse, or other health care provider who is treating them, without fear of legal repercussions, they will simply withhold information that would improve their health and the health of their developing fetus. Christine Taylor (the Iowa woman who fell down the stairs and, while seeking medical treatment, told a health care worker that she was ambivalent about her pregnancy because her husband had just abandoned her and their two young children) and Alicia Beltran (the woman who confided to a physician's assistant that although she had been dependent on an addictive prescription drug, she had weaned herself off it) are only two of many women who undoubtedly wish they had not been so forthcoming, after the health care providers called law enforcement because they concluded that the women were risking their fetuses' health. Not only did these disclosures violate the health care professionals' fiduciary duty to their patients,[7] but in arrogating to themselves the role of bedside lawyer these health care providers were impermissibly reaching conclusions about the law that they were not qualified to make.[8] While the major professional organizations for medicine and nursing have condemned the resort to legal and judicial intervention to restrict the conduct of pregnant women as unethical,[9] many of the members of these organizations appear unaware of the ethical commands of their profession. Further training of physicians and nurses on the front lines of providing care is essential, going beyond formal instruction on HIPAA and other confidentiality laws to the heart of the patient–provider relationship.

II. Accept and Embrace Complexity

Instead of throwing up our collective hands and declaring that it is too difficult to confront the core causes of children's poor health, especially poverty, we should embrace the connections between different sources of risk to children's health. Each potential source of harm should be viewed as an opportunity for intervention. Poverty is the biggest single threat to children's health and well-being. It is correlated with poorer health, poorer academic achievement, and shorter lifespans.[10] Addressing poverty in the United States would be the single most important way to improve the health of all American children.[11] It is not simply that being poor makes it harder to gain quality health care, because of lack of health insurance, transportation barriers, or other economic impediments. Being poor makes it hard to have a well-balanced diet, which is essential for healthy pregnancies and the development and growth of healthy children. A nutritious diet can also ameliorate some of the harms from lead exposure. Being poor makes it more likely that children will live in substandard, inner-city housing, where they are at high risk of being poisoned by lead. Children who are poor are much more likely to live in a dangerous neighborhood, to have either been a victim of violence themselves, or to have witnessed violence to others, which leads to stress and other contributors to poor health. Stress literally shortens lives, causing harm at the cellular level that leads to chronic illness and early death.[12] Children who live with single mothers, who are poorer than their married counterparts, are more than seven times as likely as children living with both parents to be the victims of child abuse; their mothers are more than ten times as likely to be the victims of intimate partner violence as married mothers.[13] Children who are poor are more likely to be homeless, to lack social and economic supports, and to lead less stable lives. They move more often, finding it harder to make friends and to succeed in school. Eradicating poverty requires government action on multiple fronts, including raising the minimum wage, increasing earned income tax credits, and enhancing educational opportunities so that parents, and their children, can be better informed citizens and have greater earning power.

This book has shown that all aspects of children's health are interconnected, from pre-conception to pregnancy to birth, from early childhood to adolescence and then adulthood, when the cycle begins anew. Impediments to good health, including contagious diseases, family violence (intimate partner violence *and* child abuse), poor nutrition, substandard housing, dangerous neighborhoods, and other environmental hazards, affect children of all ages. Accordingly, it makes sense to offer, but not mandate, interventions at all stages of children's lives, to improve their health and the health of future generations.

III. Develop Structural Solutions That Respond to Risk at Multiple Junctures

We might start, somewhat arbitrarily, with conception as the place to begin addressing the question of children's health. Certainly, as the use of assisted reproductive technology (A.R.T.) has grown rapidly over the past four decades, there is mounting evidence that children conceived through this technology face elevated health risks, whether it is the risk of premature delivery and low-birthweight infants, especially if they are twins or triplets, or a slightly increased risk of being diagnosed with autism or an autism spectrum disorder.[14]

A. PRIOR TO CONCEPTION

But for most children, whether or not they are born with the assistance of A.R.T., the best time to prevent health risks is before conception. Adolescence is a critical time to ensure that prospective parents are well prepared for their roles, both physically and emotionally. Teenagers should receive immunizations against Hepatitis B, HPV, and other contagious diseases that can be transmitted to future children as well as to others. Counseling and assistance with contraception should be made readily available, in order to reduce teen pregnancies. For prospective parents of all ages, their nutritional status, educational attainment, and income levels affect their overall health and access to health care. Planned pregnancies are more likely to result in the birth of healthy babies than those that are unplanned. Accordingly, all women and men should have access to contraception, fertility treatment, and other reproductive health services. When men resist the use of condoms (which protect against sexually transmitted diseases and pregnancy) their female partners may need economic *and* social support when they feel that they cannot insist on condom use because they are economically dependent on their partners or confront cultural views that "real men don't use condoms." Women who are the victims of intimate partner violence are also frequently reluctant or unable to insist that their partners use condoms.[15] Both men and women contemplating childbearing should be educated about potential safety risks in their work and home environments. This includes the risks of prenatal exposure to second-hand smoke from parents and others, which can contribute to the development of asthma and other respiratory conditions in children, as well as preterm birth, lower birthweights, and SIDS. In addition, prospective parents must be made aware of the possibility that they are being exposed to lead, mercury, or other dangerous chemicals that can affect fetal development and children's health, and be provided with assistance in reducing harmful exposures.

B. PREGNANCY: PROMISE AND PREVENTION

Once a woman is pregnant, prenatal care is obviously important, although prenatal care cannot erase the impact of years of inadequate health care. Prenatal care is most effective when it begins early in pregnancy. While Medicaid currently pays for nearly one-half of the births in the United States, African-American women and Latinas are less likely to have access to Medicaid coverage early in their pregnancies. The Affordable Care Act was designed to ensure that all women have access to reproductive health care, including high-quality obstetric care, although the refusal of many states to participate in the Medicaid expansion authorized by the ACA means that many low-income women still lack prenatal care. When preterm births and other pregnancy losses (miscarriages, stillbirths, or premature deliveries that end in an early death) occur, as they do in a very large portion of pregnancies, they should be viewed as the opportunity for a careful retrospective assessment of the health risks facing a particular woman, even though the cause of many adverse pregnancy events cannot be determined.[16] Rarely, if ever, should these events give rise to criminal prosecution.

Pregnancy also provides the occasion for screening women for adverse health conditions and other circumstances that can jeopardize a successful pregnancy. Health care professionals must screen for domestic violence, homelessness, mental illness, substance abuse, HIV and other sexually transmitted diseases, and make appropriate nonjudgmental referrals. If, as politicians avow, a major goal of American society is to promote the birth of healthy babies, the best way to achieve that goal is for health care providers to foster relationships of trust with their patients. This will ensure that they can provide appropriate care and honor patients' expectations that their treatment preferences will be respected *and* their statements will be kept confidential. Nurse-Family Partnership programs are an excellent example of the benefits of health care professionals establishing a close and trusting relationship with pregnant women and new mothers.

When pregnant women disclose that they are using drugs, whether legal or illegal, the most important thing a health care provider can do is to help the woman find a treatment program that will meet her needs and urge her to participate in that treatment. Pregnant women currently confront many obstacles in obtaining effective drug treatment. Federal law requires that pregnant women have priority access to drug treatment, receiving a referral within forty-eight hours of their request, but so far that mandate has not been met. In 2005 only 6 percent of pregnant drug users seeking treatment were able to access it.[17] Two federal laws, the Wellstone–Domenici Mental Health Parity and Addiction Equity Act of 2008 and the Affordable Care Act, hold out the promise of increasing access to drug and mental health treatment for all Americans, emphasizing the need to treat substance abuse and mental illness on a par with physical illness and giving priority to preventative health care services. It is too soon to assess the impact of these laws once they are fully implemented, given historic disparities among women and racial minorities in receiving health care, especially substance abuse treatment.[18] When, in 2014, the Tennessee legislature enacted the law making the use of a drug while pregnant a crime, with the sole defense being that the woman had entered and completed drug treatment, it was well known that there were not enough treatment programs in the state to meet the needs of all pregnant drug users, and that the shortage was particularly acute in rural areas. For pregnant women with children, the path to obtaining treatment is even more arduous. While these women would often benefit from inpatient treatment, because it provides more intensive care and offers a safe and protective environment, few programs offer inpatient treatment to pregnant women with children.[19]

It is also critical that substance abuse programs provide treatment that meets the mental health needs of affected women, whether or not they are pregnant. Pregnant women with substance abuse problems also frequently need economic and social support, including decent housing in a location that safeguards them from violent or abusive partners. Although substance abuse crosses all racial and class lines, for pregnant women who are poor and/or homeless, more extensive supports are necessary.

C. FAMILY VIOLENCE (INTIMATE PARTNER VIOLENCE AND CHILD ABUSE)

Family violence is a risk to health at all stages of children's and adults' lives. In a perverse sense, family violence can be seen as the "trifecta" of health risks. Not only does such violence harm women and children directly by the infliction of physical injuries, but it also makes it much more likely that they will suffer from mental illness and have serious substance abuse problems. Intimate partner violence affects more than a quarter of American women over their lifetimes.[20] Multiple studies have documented that a significant proportion of women who abuse drugs were also the victims of child abuse, particularly sexual abuse.[21] Family violence puts the health of pregnant women and the developing fetus at risk in multiple ways. Assault by an intimate partner is a major cause of miscarriage, stillbirth, and other fetal harms. Homicide is the second-leading cause of death of pregnant women, with most of the homicides being committed by the men who were the women's abusers.[22] Intimate partner violence (IPV) often increases pregnant women's drug use, either because they turn to drugs as a means of temporary escape or because their partners insist on it as a means of enforcing control. Many studies have documented the lack of adequate screening for IPV when women seek medical treatment, either at an emergency room or at their doctor's office. The United States Preventative Services Task Force and the Institute of Medicine both recommend that all women be screened for IPV as part of their regular, routine health care service.[23] The fact that such care is not now routinely provided contrasts sharply with the extensive training that health care professionals now receive about child abuse.

IPV overlaps with child abuse to an astonishing degree. The 1999 *Greenbook*, the guide for family court judges, observed that the overlap between families in which there is IPV and child abuse is between 30 and 60 percent.[24] Intimate partner violence is consistently underreported by its victims; only when social workers make inquiries about IPV do they discover its extraordinary prevalence.[25] Many women who suffer from IPV were the victims of physical and sexual abuse as girls, making them especially vulnerable as adults to the pressures of an abusive partner.

Reviews of the long-term impact of legal interventions against child abuse have often been discouraging. One study found that many children do not receive the mental health services that are recommended and that nearly half of the mothers who reported being the victim of IPV continue to be victimized eighteen months later. Other studies have concluded that the adversarial nature of intervention by child protective services may have two undesired consequences. First, social services investigators may focus on evidence collection and other aspects of building a case, neglecting to make referrals to address the long-term needs of children at risk. Second, even if supportive services are offered, parents may be put off by an intrusive investigation and decline to cooperate. In addition, even if short-term interventions are offered and accepted, they frequently do not have a long-term impact, because they do not address the fundamental challenges faced by parents in many families where there is child abuse—poverty and a lack of social support.[26]

Yet if a finding of IPV or child abuse is properly addressed, it can provide the occasion for successful intervention by legal, medical, or social work professionals. For example, a three year pilot project at four Philadelphia community health centers found that having a dedicated social worker specializing in intimate partner violence to whom health care professionals could refer their patients led to increased patient self-disclosure and follow-up. Unfortunately, once the pilot project ended, the identification and referrals of patients who were victims of IPV reverted to their previous levels.[27] Other studies have found that providing financial and social support, along with appropriate psychotherapy, can have lasting impacts on the well-being of children and their parents.[28] All children, adolescents, and adults should have access to comprehensive medical, mental health, and substance abuse treatment, providing both acute and preventative care, which are now mandated by federal law.

Over the past four decades prosecutors have devoted substantial resources to improving both prosecution rates and the way in which IPV prosecutions take place. In many cases they have succeeded in getting violent men off the street and away from their wives, girlfriends, and children.[29] Yet the rates of domestic assault and homicide are still high.[30] Enforcement at the street level is uneven; some police take IPV violence seriously and others do not. When IPV is not taken seriously, there is often no second chance for the women and children at risk.[31] The enactment of city ordinances that treat the act of calling the police as a "nuisance" discourages tenants, including women who are the victims of domestic violence, from seeking help from law enforcement.[32] Rather than treating a call for police assistance as an annoyance, cities should use these calls as the occasion for active intervention, putting victims of domestic violence in touch with social service and health care workers who can provide economic and social support and medical treatment that, in combination, can make it possible for women to leave partners who abuse them and their children.

D. NEWBORNS AND INFANTS

New parents need support in caring for their infants. They frequently do not have any idea what they are doing, and they suffer from sleep deprivation, stress, and, in the case of some new mothers, postpartum depression. Mothers who have just had C-sections may be in significant discomfort. Providing a child with appropriate nourishment, to support growth and healthy development, is a challenging task. Breastfeeding is touted by the American Academy of Pediatrics and the federal government as a way to reduce the risk that children will develop upper respiratory infections and other illnesses, and to enhance their cognitive development. However, the evidence that supports these claims is weak, because it relies heavily on observational studies that show an association, rather than a causal relationship, between mothers' breastfeeding and the claimed beneficial outcomes.

But even if the benefits of breastfeeding are real, current American law and government health policy provide little structural support for mothers who would like to nurse their infants. Although the Affordable Care Act requires employers with fifty or more employees to permit nursing mothers to pump their milk in a private place and to provide a refrigerator where they can safely store their milk, pumping at work is still difficult for many women. Many women work for smaller employers, who can seek a hardship exemption from the ACA's mandate. Others work for employers who can make pumping at work onerous and uncomfortable, arguably complying with the letter, but not the spirt, of the law. More significantly, the United States is the only wealthy nation that does not mandate paid maternity or paternity leaves, making it financially impossible in most families for new mothers to take the time off from work if their employer does not provide paid parenting leave.[33] Providing tax deductions for lactation consultants and breast pumps is not a meaningful way to encourage most women to breastfeed, because only the wealthiest women earn enough money to take itemized deductions. Women who receive their health care through Medicaid or who depend on the WIC program to nourish themselves and their children do not receive the same level of practical support for nursing that middle- and upper-class women can afford to purchase for themselves. On the state level, many states' laws do not adequately protect the ability of mothers to nurse their babies in stores, parks, or other places of public accommodation, which is necessary if children are to be well nourished, particularly when they are very young.

In contrast, what has been shown to work, particularly for low income women, who are the least likely to breastfeed, is to pair a new mother—during and after pregnancy—with a nurse who will be her cheerleader and support her if she chooses to breastfeed. There is a long tradition of providing nursing support to low income mothers, going as far back as the late nineteenth century and the settlement house movement led by Jane Addams and others, in Chicago, New York, and other large cities.[34] Today, programs like the Nurse-Family Partnership can make a huge difference in the lives of mothers and their children.

E. PROTECTING CHILDREN FROM ENVIRONMENTAL HARMS AT ALL AGES

In the twenty-first century, some of the biggest risks to children's health are environmental. As the risks of contracting a contagious disease have been reduced, though certainly not eliminated, more and more parents are, rightfully, concerned about harms from the environment, both known and unknown. As noted in chapters 3 and 8, today American children are most at risk from heavy metals (lead, mercury, and arsenic), air pollutants (including, in addition to heavy metals, sulfur dioxide, and PAHs [polycyclic aromatic hydrocarbons]), and pesticides and other toxic chemicals (PCBs and endocrine disruptors like BPA). While historically all American children were exposed to lead through atmospheric exposure to emissions from leaded gasoline, today the children most at risk are poor, primarily African-American and Latino children living in cities, who, as a result of their poverty, are much more likely to live in rundown housing, where they are exposed to lead on a daily basis, with devastating physiological, cognitive, and behavioral consequences. The single most important action to improve the health of America's children would be for the government to mandate, and fund where necessary, the total abatement of lead from all homes in the United States. This is an issue where prevention is both cost-effective and a moral imperative. We simply cannot continue to condemn generations of low income children, already at risk of poor health because of inadequate nutrition, lack of access to health care, the stress of living in poor neighborhoods, and a greater incidence of child abuse, to a lifetime of physical and intellectual impairments.

Children also confront other environmental hazards; here again, the poor are most at risk. This is because of three major factors. First, they often live close to sources of pollution—such as coal-burning power plants, municipal waste incinerators, and major urban highways. Second, their parents are more likely to work in industrial or agricultural settings where they are exposed to toxic chemicals, which they bring home on their skin and on their work clothes. If they live in rural areas, they may rely heavily on locally caught fish and wildlife, which are likely to have high levels of mercury and lead, respectively. Finally, their parents are least able to afford efforts to mitigate these harms, for example, by purchasing organic food to avoid pesticide residues or buying nontoxic cleaning products. Indeed, the parents of poor children generally have difficulty affording nutritious and healthful food, which can help mitigate the harms of toxic exposures.

Although Congress acted in the 1990s to amend the Clean Air Act to limit exposure to heavy metals like lead and mercury as well as other air pollutants, during the past three decades the politicization of environmental policy has become extreme. The EPA has frequently not acted to limit air pollution during Republican presidential administrations, and its actions under Democratic administrations have frequently been successfully challenged in the courts.[35] If we are truly to protect our children's health from environmental toxins, we must move beyond political rhetoric that decries all environmental or health regulations as "job killers."

F. PROTECT THE POPULATION AGAINST CONTAGIOUS DISEASES

The evidence is overwhelming that vaccines are an extraordinarily effective means of protecting everyone in society against the spread of contagious diseases with very minimal risk of harm to those who are vaccinated. Over the past ninety years, vaccines have prevented an estimated 103 million cases of diseases in the United States. During the past decade alone they prevented an estimated 26 million cases of serious illnesses.[36] Vaccines are highly cost-effective, saving billions of dollars in direct health care costs and many billions more in indirect costs, including parents' lost wages while caring for their children and the costs of public health surveillance in the event of an outbreak. Yet precisely because these diseases are much less prevalent today some parents view them as both unlikely and not very serious, believing that they can protect their children from disease by a good diet and healthy living. Recent outbreaks of pertussis and measles have made it clear that when it comes to infectious diseases, no man is an island. In order to protect all of America's children, as well as vulnerable adults, vaccine mandates are necessary and they should be strictly enforced, with only limited medical and religious exemptions. Parents' desire to make health care choices for their own children should not be privileged above the need to protect other people's children.

Conclusion: Choosing the Precautionary Principle to Protect Everyone's Children

Real accomplishments in improving the health of all of America's children can be achieved only by a coordinated and comprehensive health policy response, in which a public that is better educated about risk demands—and gets—laws that will minimize the risks to children's health at both immediate and distant levels. Direct government intervention is necessary to reduce the number of children living in poverty, by taking actions as diverse as raising the minimum wage, increasing the earned income tax credit, and enhancing opportunities for education and training so that parents can earn enough to support their children.

It is time to embrace the precautionary principle, on multiple levels. This means, first, that children (and their parents) must have access to quality health care that addresses acute and chronic health care needs, providing preventative health services and treatment for physical and mental illness as well as substance abuse. *Voluntary* opportunities for parents, especially young mothers, to interact with skilled and compassionate health care professionals can pay significant dividends in terms of children's health, cognitive development, academic achievement, and emotional well-being. Second, structural changes in government policy, including rules for the workplace, must be initiated to make it more possible for mothers who wish to breastfeed to do so. Third, to respond effectively to childhood sexual abuse and physical violence against children and their parents, there must be an integrated criminal justice and public health strategy that permanently removes the perpetrators of physical and sexual abuse from the home and provides social, economic, and psychological support to the children and parents who have endured this trauma. Fourth and finally, American law must be changed, particularly at the federal level, to curtail children's exposure to lead, mercury, and a wide array of toxic chemicals and hazardous substances. Dilapidated housing must be repaired, lead removed, and neighborhoods rebuilt.

Above all, collective action to improve the health of all of America's children is essential. We must embrace the social compact envisioned by the nation's founders, in which the government acts to protect the health of the entire population, not just that of individuals. At the same time we must eschew "anxiety governance," in which the wealthiest parents seek to protect their own children through individual action and ignore the needs of other people's children.

APPENDIX

Criminal Prosecutions of Parents Based on a Failure to Act

People v. Abraham, 629 N.E.2d 148 (Ill. App. Ct. 1993).
State v. Adams, 557 P.2d 586 (N.M. Ct. App. 1976).
State v. Alfred, 657 So.2d 116 (La. Ct. App. 1995).
State v. Austin, 172 N.W.2d 284 (S.D. 1969).
Austin v. Erickson, 477 F.2d 620 (8th Cir. 1973).
Bailey v. State, No. 03C01-9207-CR-00226, 1993 WL 480428 (Tenn. Crim. App. Nov. 22, 1993) (unpublished).
Barrett v. State, 675 N.E.2d 1112 (Ind. Ct. App. 1996).
People v. Barrientos, No. E057285, 2014 WL 1901173 (Cal. Ct. App. May 13, 2014), *rev. denied* (Aug. 13, 2014) (unpublished).
State v. Baughman, No. 1-09-38, 2010 Ohio App. LEXIS 1045, (Ohio Ct. App. Mar. 29, 2010) (unpublished).
People v. Bernard, 500 N.E.2d 1074 (Ill. App. Ct. 1986).
State v. Best, 232 N.W.2d 459 (S.D. 1975).
Boone v. State, 668 S.W.2d 17 (Ark. 1984).
Brewington v. State, 98 So.3d 628 (Fla. Dist. Ct. App. 2012).
Comm. v. Brown, 721 A.2d 1105 (Pa. Super. Ct. 1998).
Brown v. State, 770 N.E.2d 275 (Ind. 2002).
State v. Brown, 799 N.E.2d 1064 (Ind. 2003).
State v. Burciaga, 328 P.3d 782 (Or. Ct. App. 2014).
People v. Burden, 140 Cal. Rptr. 282 (Cal. Ct. App. 1977).
State v. Burrell, 160 S.W.3d 798 (Mo. 2005).
People v. Burton, 788 N.E.2d 220 (Ill. App. Ct. 2003).
State v. Cabezuela, 265 P.3d 705 (N.M. 2011).
State v. Cabral, 810 P.2d 672 (Haw. Ct. App. 1991).
State v. Cabral, 883 P.2d 638 (Haw. Ct. App. 1994).
State v. Cacchiotti, 568 A.2d 1026 (R.I. 1990).
C.G. v. State, 841 So.2d 281 (Ala. Ct. App. 2001).
Ex parte C.G., 841 So.2d 292 (Ala. 2002).
Campbell v. State, 999 P.2d 649 (Wyo. 2000).
Comm. v. Cardwell, 515 A.2d 311 (Pa. Super. Ct. 1986).
Cardwell v. State, 461 So.2d 754 (Miss. 1984).

People v. Carroll, 715 N.E.2d 500 (N.Y. 1999).
Conine v. State, 752 So.2d 4 (Fla. Ct. App. 2000).
State v. Crosky, No. 06AP-816, 2007 WL 4285153 (Ohio Ct. App. 2007) (unpublished).
Daumer v. State, 381 So.2d 1014 (Miss. 1980).
State v. Davis, 407 S.W.3d 721 (Mo. Ct. App. 2013).
Duncan v. State, 624 So.2d 1084 (Ala. Crim. App. 1993).
Elder v. State, 993 S.W.2d 229 (Tex. App. 1999).
State v. Engle, 660 N.E.2d 450 (Ohio 1996).
Fabritz v. State, 351 A.2d 477 (Md. 1975).
Fabritz v. Traurig, 583 F.2d 697 (4th Cir. 1978).
State v. Fernane, 914 P.2d 1314 (Ariz. Ct. App. 1995).
State v. Gaver, 944 S.W.2d 273 (Mo. Ct. App. 1997).
State v. Goetzinger, 326 P.3d (Or. Ct. App. 2014).
Graham v. State, 521 S.E.2d 249 (Ga. Ct. App. 1999).
Graves v. State, 612 S.E.2d 37 (Ga. Ct. App. 2005).
Hawkins v. State, 891 S.W.2d 257 (Tex. Crim. App. 1994).
Hawkins v. State, 855 S.W.2d 881 (Tex. App. 1993).
Hawkins v. State, 910 S.W.2d 176 (Tex. App. 1995).
State v. Hoffman, 639 P.2d 507 (Mont. 1982).
Hopper v. State, No. 02-11-00492-CR, 2013 WL 4679166 (Tex. App. Aug. 29, 2013) (unpublished).
Comm. v. Howard, 402 A.2d 674 (Pa. Super. Ct. 1979).
State v. Hunter, No. COA01-1126, 2002 N.C. App. LEXIS 2333 (N.C. Ct. App. Aug. 6, 2002) (unpublished).
Hutcheson v. State, 213 S.W.3d 25 (Ark. Ct. App. 2005).
Jakubczak v. State, 425 So.2d 187 (Fla. Dist. Ct. App. 1983).
Johnson v. State, 508 So.2d 443 (Fla. Dist. Ct. App. 1987).
Johnson v. State, 224 P.3d 105 (Alaska 2010).
State v. Jones, 778 So.2d 1131 (La. 2001).
Comm. v. Knox, 735 S.W.2d 711 (Ky. 1987).
State v. Kuykendall, No. 32,612, 2014 WL 5782937 (N.M. Ct. App. Sep. 23, 2014), *cert. granted*, 344 P.3d 988 (N.M. 2014), *cert. quashed* 370 P.3d 472 (N.M. 2015).
Lane v. Comm., 956 S.W.2d 874 (Ky. 1997).
Ellison v. Comm., 994 S.W.2d 939 (Ky. 1999).
Comm. v. Lazarovich, 547 N.E.2d 940 (Mass. App. Ct. 1989).
Comm. v. Lazarovich, 574 N.E.2d 340 (Mass. 1991).
State v. Leal, 723 P.2d 977 (N.M. Ct. App. 1986).
Leet v. State, 595 So.2d 959 (Fla. Dist. Ct. App. 1991).
State v. Legg, 623 N.E.2d 1263 (Ohio Ct. App. 1993).
State v. Lopez, 164 P.3d 19 (N.M. 2007).
Lott v. State, 686 S.W.2d 304 (Ct. App. Tex. 1985).
Lucas v. Comm., No. 2009-CA-000159-MR, 2012 WL 2360112 (Ky. Ct. App. 2012) (unpublished).

State v. Lucero, 647 P.2d 406 (N.M. 1982).
Mallory v. State, 563 N.E.2d 640 (Ind. Ct. App. 1990).
People v. Mathis, No. 279352, 2008 WL 4549001 (Mich. Ct. App. Oct. 21, 2008) (unpublished).
State v. Maupin, 859 S.W.2d 313 (Tenn. 1993).
State v. McLaughlin, 600 P.2d 474 (Or. Ct. App. 1979).
Michael v. State, 805 P.2d 371 (Alaska 1991).
Michael v. State, 767 P.2d 193 (Alaska Ct. App. 1988).
State v. Miranda, 878 A.2d 1118 (Conn. 2005).
State v. Morrison, 437 N.W.2d 422 (Minn. Ct. App. 1989).
State v. Mott, 931 P.2d 1046 (Ariz. 1997).
Mott v. Stewart, No. 98-CV-239, 2002 WL 31017646 (D. Ariz. Aug. 30, 2002) (unpublished).
Muehe v. State, 646 NE.2d 980 (Ind. Ct. App. 1995).
State v. Muro, 695 N.W.2d 425 (Neb. 2005).
People v. Novy, 597 N.E.2d 273 (Ill. App. Ct. 1992).
People v. Ogg, 161 Cal. Rptr 3d 584 (Cal. Ct. App. 2013).
People v. Super. Ct. (Selene Beatriz Olmos, Real Party in Interest), No. B250586, 2013 WL 6729916 (Cal. Ct. App. Dec. 20, 2013) (unpublished).
People v. Osuna, No. G041029, 2010 WL 4467302 (Cal. Ct. App. Nov. 9, 2010) (unpublished).
P.S. v. State, 565 So.2d 1209 (Ala. Crim. App. 1990).
Palmer v. State, 164 A.2d 467 (Md. Ct. App. 1960).
State v. Parker, 752 N.W.2d 452 (Iowa Ct. App. 2008).
State v. Peters, 780 P.2d 602 (Idaho Ct. App. 1989).
People v. Peters, 586 N.E.2d 469 (Ill. App. Ct. 1991).
Phelps v. State, 439 So.2d 727 (Ala. Crim. App. 1983).
Pickle v. State, 635 S.E.2d 197 (Ga. Ct. App. 2006).
State v. Pickles, 218 A.2d 609 (N.J. 1966).
People v. Pollock, 780 N.E.2d 669 (Ill. App. Ct. 2002).
Porter v. State, 532 S.E.2d 407 (Ga. Ct. App. 2000).
State v. Portigue, 481 A.2d 534 (N.H. 1984).
Qualley v. State, 206 S.W.3d 624 (Tex. Crim. App. 2006).
Comm. v. Raposo, 595 N.E.2d 773 (Mass. 1994).
State v. Rathbone, No. E2007-00602-CCA-R3-CD, 2008 WL 1744581 (Tenn. Crim. App. Apr. 16, 2008) (unpublished).
People v. Ray, 399 N.E.2d 977 (Ill. App. Ct. 1979).
Rice v. State, 949 P.2d 262 (Nev. 1997).
People v. Rolon, 73 Cal. Rptr.3d 358 (Cal. Ct. App. 2008) (partially unpublished).
State v. Rundle, 500 N.W.2d 916 (Wis. 1993).
State v. Sammons, 391 N.E.2d 713 (Ohio 1979).
State v. Smith, 408 N.E.2d 614 (Ind. Ct. App. 1980).
State v. Smith, 927 P.2d 14 (Nev. 1996).

People v. Stanciel, 606 N.E.2d 1201 (Ill. 1992).
People v. Swanson-Birabent, 7 Cal. Rptr. 3d 744 (Cal. Ct. App. 2003).
Tharp v. Comm., 40 S.W.3d 356 (Ky. 2000).
State v. Vasquez, 232 P.3d 438 (N.M. Ct. App. 2010).
United States v. Webb, 747 F.2d 278 (5th Cir. 1984).
State v. Widdison, 4 P.3d 100 (Utah Ct. App. 2000).
State v. Williams, 670 P.2d 122 (N.M. Ct. App. 1983).
State v. Williquette, 385 N.W.2d 145 (Wis. 1986).
Woodbury v. State, 440 S.E.2d 461 (Ga. 1994).
People v. Zamora, No. C067275, 2012 WL 6561195 (Cal. Ct. App. Dec. 17, 2012).
Zile v. State, 710 So.2d 729 (Fla. Dist. Ct. App. 1998).
State v. Zobel, 134 N.W.2d 101 (S.D. 1965).

NOTES

CHAPTER 1. ARE MOTHERS HAZARDOUS TO THEIR CHILDREN'S HEALTH?

1. David Pimentel, *Criminal Child Neglect and the "Free Range Kid"? Is Overprotective Parenting the New Standard of Care?*, 2012 Utah L. Rev. 947, 968–69 (2012) (hereafter *Criminal Child Neglect*); see also Bridget Kevane, *Guilty as Charged*, Brain Child Magazine (Summer 2009), available at http://www.brainchildmag.com/tag/bridget-kevane/ (last visited Sept. 6, 2016) (hereafter *Guilty as Charged*).
2. KJ Dell'Antonia, *Teenage Obesity Linked to Poor Mother–Child Bond*, N.Y. Times Motherlode Blog, Dec. 29, 2011.
3. Taryn W. Morrisey et al., *Maternal Employment, Work Schedules, and Children's Body Mass Index*, 82 Child Development 66, 76 (Jan./Feb. 2011).
4. See, e.g., April L. Cherry, *The Nonconsensual Medical Treatment of Pregnant Women and Implications for Female Citizenship*, 6. U. Pa. J. Const. L. 723, 741 (2004); and Jennifer M. Collins, *Lady Madonna, Children at Your Feet: The Criminal Justice System's Romanticization of the Parent–Child Relationship*, 93 Iowa L. Rev. 131, 179 (2007).
5. Linda Thomson, *Mother Is Charged in Stillbirth of a Twin*, Deseret Morning News, Mar. 12, 2004, at A1, available at 2004 WLNR 16942122; Katha Pollitt, *Pregnant and Dangerous*, Nation, Apr. 26, 2004, at 9, available at http://www.thenation.com/doc/20040426/pollitt; Pamela Manson, *Mother Is Charged in Stillborn Son's Death*, Salt Lake Trib., Mar. 12, 2004, at A1.
6. *People v. Jorgensen*, 41 N.E. 3d 778 (N.Y. 2015), *rev'g* 978 N.Y.S. 2d 361 (App. Div. 2d Dept. 2014); Andrew Smith, *Mom Gets 3 to 9 Years in Baby's Death*, Newsday.com (Jun. 22, 2012), http://www.newsday.com/long-island/suffolk/mom-gets-3-to-9-years-in-baby-s-death-1.3799074.
7. Lee Rood, *"I Never Said I Didn't Want My Baby": Mom Won't Be Prosecuted*, Des Moines Register, Feb. 10, 2010, at A1; and John Mangalonzo, *Feticide Charges Dropped; New Information About Pregnancy Emerges*, Hawkeye, (Feb. 11, 2010), www.thehawkeye.com/story/Fetus-death-021110.
8. *Burton v. Florida*, 49 So. 3d 263, 265 (Fl. Ct. App. 2010).
9. U.S. Dep't of Health & Human Servs., National Breastfeeding Campaign, video clip and transcript of "Ladies Night" commercial, available at http://www.4woman.gov/breastfeeding/ index.cfm?page=ladiesnight (last visited Mar. 20, 2009).

10 N.Y.C. Dep't of Health and Mental Hygiene, Latch on NYC, available at http://www.nyc.gov/html/doh/downloads/pdf/ms/initiative-description.Pdf (last visited Aug. 7, 2012).
11 Martha Chamallas, *Deepening the Legal Understanding of Bias: On Devaluation and Biased Prototypes*, 74 S. Cal. L. Rev. 747, 778 (2001) (hereafter *Deepening the Legal Understanding of Bias*).
12 *See, e.g.*, Jeffrey J. Rachlinski et al., *Does Unconscious Racial Bias Affect Trial Judges*, 84 Notre Dame L. Rev. 1195, 1195–97 (2009) (hereafter *Does Unconscious Racial Bias Affect Trial Judges*).
13 American children are, however, less healthy (on average) than their peers in other developed nations. See data discussed in chapter 3.
14 National Center for Health Statistics, Health, United States 2014: With Special Features on Adults Aged 55–64, at 85, Table 16, (2015); *see also* Elizabeth Arias, Changes in Life Expectancy by Race and Hispanic Origin in the United States, 2013–2014, NCHS Data Brief No. 244 (April 2016), available at http://www.cdc.gov/nchs/products/databriefs/db244.htm (last visited Aug. 11, 2016).
15 Centers for Disease Control, *Achievements in Public Health 1900–1999: Family Planning*, 48 Morbidity and Mortality Report (MMWR) 1073, 1073 (Dec. 3, 1999), available at https://www.cdc.gov/mmwr/preview/mmwrhtml/mm4847a1.htm (last visited Aug. 24, 2016); *cf.* Eula Biss, On Immunity: An Inoculation 62 (Graywolf Press, 2014) (hereafter On Immunity).
16 Donald G. McNeil, Jr., *Sharp Drop Seen in Deaths from Ills Fought by Vaccine*, N.Y. Times, Nov. 14, 2007, at A18). In the 1940s, before the vaccine against pertussis became available, there were more than 200,000 cases of pertussis each year. Centers for Disease Control, Epidemiology and Prevention of Vaccine-Preventable Diseases G-1, G-3, G-7, 215 (William Atkinson et al., eds., 12th ed. 2011) (hereafter Atkinson, *Epidemiology and Prevention of Vaccine-Preventable Diseases*); Kevin M. Malone and Alan R. Hinman, *Vaccination Mandates: The Public Health Imperative and Individual Rights,* in Law and Public Health Practice 262, 266 (Richard Goodman et al., eds., 2003) (hereafter *Vaccination Mandates*); Leticia Stein, *Measles Cases Rise as More Shun Shot*, St. Petersburg Times (Fla), July 8, 2011, at 1B (hereafter *Measles Cases Rise*).
17 These include milk pasteurization, sewage treatment, and a clean public water supply. CDC, *Achievements in Public Health, 1900–1999: Healthier Mothers and Babies*, 48 Morbidity and Mortality Weekly Report 849 (1999) (hereafter *Healthier Mothers and Babies*), available at http://www.cdc.gov/mmwr/preview/mmwrhtml/mm4838a2.htm; *see also* S. Jay Olshansky et al., *A Potential Decline in Life Expectancy in the United States*, 352 New Eng. J. Med. 1138, 1138 (2005).
18 Grant Miller, *Women's Suffrage, Political Responsiveness, and Child Survival in American History*, 123 Q. J. Econ. 1287, 1288–91 (2008).
19 Widespread use of sulfa drugs and penicillin contributed to significant declines in infant mortality from 1930 to 1949. *Healthier Mothers and Babies, supra* n. 17. The death rate from childhood cancer continues to decline, despite an increased

incidence in childhood cancer. CDC, *Many Cancer Rates Continue to Decline*, (Mar. 28, 2012), http://www.cdc.gov/Features/dsCancerAnnualReport/.

20 For smallpox, diphtheria, and polio the reduction in mortality was 100 percent. For four other diseases, for which vaccination was developed much more recently—Hepatitis A and B, invasive pneumococcal disease, and varicella—the decline was less than 90 percent. Kenneth D. Kochanek et al., *Deaths: Preliminary Data for 2009*, 59 Nat'l Vital Statistics Report 3, Mar. 16, 2011, available at www.cdc.gov/nchs/data/nvsr/nvsr59/nvsr59_04.pdf (last visited Oct. 17, 2011). Infants are still at the greatest risk for most vaccine-preventable illnesses, because they cannot yet be fully immunized, although the elderly are more likely to die than any other age group from complications of influenza. See Atkinson, *supra* n. 16, at 154–55, 217 (noting the mortality statistics from influenza and pertussis, respectively).

21 In 2011, the infant mortality rate in the United States was 6.2 deaths per 1,000 live births, nearly three times the rate in Iceland (2.2), the top performer, and higher than that of 28 other nations, including the Slovak Republic (5.7) and Estonia (3.3). OECD, *Health: Key Tables from OECD—Infant Mortality*, No. 9 (2012). doi: 10.1787/inf-mort-table-2012-1-en. In 2010, nearly 12 out of every 100 babies was born prematurely, a rate higher than that of nearly every European nation, Russia, China, Mexico, most of South America, and most of North Africa. C. P. Howson et al., World Health Organization, *Born Too Soon: The Global Action Report on Preterm Birth* 3, 12 (2012), available at http://whqlibdoc.who.int/publications/2012/9789241503433_eng.pdf (hereafter *Born Too Soon*).

22 See, e.g., Report of Surgeon General David Satcher, *Commentary: Our Commitment to Eliminate Racial and Ethnic Health Disparities*, 1 Yale J. Health Pol'y, L. & Ethics 1 (2001); and Rick Mayes and Thomas R. Oliver, *Chronic Disease and the Shifting Focus of Public Health: Is Prevention Still a Political Lightweight?*, 37 J. Health Politics, Pol'y, and L. 180, 182 (2012).

23 See, e.g., Joel Teitelbaum et al., *Translating Rights into Access: Language Access and the Affordable Care Act*, 38 Am. J.L. & Med. 348, 373 (2012); Perri Klass, *Poverty's Lasting Ills*, N.Y. Times, May 14, 2013, at D4.

24 Vincent J. Felitti, *Relationship of Childhood Abuse and Household Dysfunction to Many of the Leading Causes of Death in Adults: The Adverse Childhood Experiences (ACE) Study*, 14 Am. J. Preventative Med. 245, 251 (1998) (hereafter *Childhood Abuse and Household Dysfunction*); see also Jack P. Shonkhoff and Deborah A. Phillips, From Neurons to Neighborhoods: The Science of Early Childhood Development, Washington, D.C. (National Academies Press, 2000) (hereafter *From Neurons to Neighborhoods*).

25 Institute of Medicine, U.S. Health in International Perspective: *Shorter Lives, Poorer Health*, Washington, D.C. (Steven H. Woolf and Landon Aron, eds., National Academies Press, 2013) (hereafter *Shorter Lives*).

26 Sarah Gonzalez, *New Jersey River Polluters Fund Toxic Fish Swap—But There's a Snag*, NPR (Jan. 16, 2016), available at http://www.npr.org/sections/the-

salt/2016/01/26/462918329/new-jersey-river-polluters-fund-toxic-fish-swap-but-there-s-a-snag.

27 I am indebted to Joan Wolf for the term "vector of risk." Joan B. Wolf, *Is Breast Really Best? Risk and Total Motherhood in the National Breastfeeding Awareness Campaign*, 32 J. Health Pol., Pol'y & L. 595, 618 (2007) (hereafter *Is Breast Really Best?*).

28 *Burton v. Florida*, 149 So. 2d 263 (Fl. Ct. App. 2010), *cf. Jefferson v. Griffin Spaulding County Hospital Authority*, 274 S.E. 2d 457 (Ga. 1981) (per curiam); *but see* Nancy K. Rhoden, *The Judge in the Delivery Room: The Emergence of Court-Ordered Caesareans*, 74 Cal. L. Rev. 1951, 1959–60 (1986) (hereafter *The Judge in the Delivery Room*).

29 Anne D. Lyerly et al., *Risk and the Pregnant Body*, 39 Hastings Center Rpt. 34, 34–40 (2009) (hereafter *Risk and the Pregnant Body*); *cf.* American College of Obstetrics and Gynecology, *ACOG Committee Opinion: Patient Choice in the Maternal–Fetal Relationship*, 65 Int'l J. of Gynecology & Obstetrics 213, 213–15 (1999); *see also* Susan J. Westrick and Katherine Dempski, Essentials of Nursing Law and Ethics 273–77, Boston (Jones & Bartlett 2009).

30 Fear of malpractice is discussed in detail in chapter 4.

31 Joyce A. Martin et al., *Births: Final Data for 2013*, 64 National Vital Statistics Reports 2, 7 (Jan. 15, 2015).

32 This case is discussed in detail in chapter 4.

33 Current studies estimate that in certain areas of the country 0.2 to 1.5 children per thousand births present with the symptoms of FAS; studies of children at ages seven to nine indicate that 0.3 out of 1,000 appear to have symptoms of FAS. Children of low-income mothers are more likely to be diagnosed with FAS than their wealthier counterparts. Center for Disease Control and Prevention, *Fetal Alcohol Spectrum Disorders (FASDs)*, http://www.cdc.gov/ncbddd/fasd/data.html (last visited July 21, 2015); *see also* Ernest L. Abel, *An Update on Incidence of FAS: FAS Is Not an Equal Opportunity Birth Defect*, 17 Neurotoxicology and Teratology 437, 440–41 (1995). Estimates of the numbers of children who suffer from fetal alcohol spectrum disorders are higher. CDC, *More Than 3 Million US Women at Risk for Alcohol-exposed Pregnancy* (Feb. 2, 2016), http://www.cdc.gov/media/releases/2016/p0202-alcohol-exposed-pregnancy.html; *see also* National Institute on Alcohol Abuse and Alcoholism, *Fetal Alcohol Spectrum Disorders: Understanding the Effects of Prenatal Alcohol Exposure*, No. 82, http://pubs.niaaa.nih.gov/publications/AA82/AA82.pdf.

34 CDC, *Key Findings: Lifestyle During Pregnancy Study. Cf. CDC Advisory on Alcohol Use in Pregnancy* (2005) (http://www.cdc.gov/ncbddd/fasd/alcohol-use.html, updated Apr. 17, 2014) (last visited Aug. 30, 2015).

35 Civil commitment is a form of deprivation of liberty which is "civil" in nature because, in theory, it is designed not to punish but to prevent harm, either to the person who is being committed (self-harm), or to a third party. Historically, civil commitment has been authorized and used most often against the mentally ill

and persons with substance abuse, including alcoholism. Civil commitment laws do not have all the procedural safeguards (and constitutional guarantees) of a criminal trial (proof beyond a reasonable doubt, right to be represented by counsel, and the privilege against self-incrimination, among others) and civil commitment can be indefinite in nature, as opposed to imprisonment after a criminal conviction, which is frequently a definite, limited term. For a good introduction to civil commitment, see Christopher Slobogin et al., *Law and the Mental Health Systems: Civil and Criminal Aspects*, 804–8, 904–58 (West Publishing Corp. 6th ed. 2014)

36 Erik Eckholm, *Case Explores Rights of Fetus Versus Mother*, N.Y. Times, Oct. 24, 2013, at A1. Eventually the Wisconsin federal district court dismissed Ms. Beltran's petition for a writ of *habeas corpus* as moot, because she was no longer in custody and the case against her had been dismissed. *Beltran v. Strachota*, 2014 WL 4924668 (E.D. Wis. 2014).

37 Ali H. Mokad et al., *Actual Causes of Death in the United States, 2000*, 291 J. Am. Med. Ass'n. (JAMA) 1238 (2004).

38 Barbara L. Thompson et al., *Prenatal Exposure to Drugs: Effects on Brain Development and Implications for Policy and Education*, 10 Nature Reviews—Neuroscience 303, 304, 306 (2009), available at https://www.franklincollege.edu/science_courses/Amazing_brain/prenatal%20drug%20exposure.pdf; and Harriet Dinegar Milks, Annotation, *Smoking as Factor in Child Custody and Visitation Cases*, 36 A.L.R. 5th 377 (1996) at § 2[a].

39 *See, e.g., Scott v. Steelman*, 953 S.W.2d 147, 150 (Mo. Ct. App. S.D. 1997); and *Lizzio v. Lizzio*, 618 N.Y.S. 2d 934, 937 (N.Y. Fam. Ct. 1994); *see also* Milks, *supra* n. 38, at § 3.

40 Anne D. Lyerly et al., *The National Children's Study: A Golden Opportunity to Advance the Health of Pregnant Women*, 99 Am J. Pub. Health 1742 (2009).

41 *Id.; see also* Lyerly et al., *Risk and the Pregnant Body*, *supra* n. 29, at 34–40; and Andrew Solomon, *The Secret Sadness of Pregnancy with Depression*, N.Y. Times Magazine, May 31, 2015, at 35–39,52.

42 Linda C. Fentiman, *In the Name of Fetal Protection: Why American Prosecutors Pursue Pregnant Drug Users (and Other Countries Don't)*, 18 Colum. J. Gender & L. 647, 653–56 (2009) (hereafter *In the Name of Fetal Protection*).

43 Kirsten Scharnberg, *Prosecutors Target Pregnant Drug Users; Some Fear Women Will Shun Treatment*, Chicago Tribune, Nov. 23, 2003, at C1; *see also State v. McKnight*, 576 S.E. 2d 168, 171 (S.C. 2003), and 661 S.E.3d 354 (S.C. 2008); and National Advocates for Pregnant Women, S.C.: Leading the Nation in the Prosecution of Pregnant Women, http://www.advocatesforpregnantwomen.org/issues/punishment_of_pregnant_women/south_carolina_leading_the_nation_in_the_prosecution_punishment.php (last visited Feb. 18, 2009).

44 *See* Linda C. Fentiman, *Pursuing the Perfect Mother: Why America's Criminalization of Maternal Substance Abuse Is Not the Answer: A Comparative Legal Analysis*, 15 Mich J. Gender & L. 389, 400–6 (2009) (hereafter *Pursuing the Perfect Mother*).

45 *State v. McKnight*, 576 S.E.2d 168 (S.C. 2003), *Ex parte Ankrom*, 152 So.3d 397 (Ala. 2013); and *Health Experts Warn Alabama Court of Criminal Appeals That Prosecuting Pregnant Women as Drug Labs Is Bad for Babies*, National Advocates for Pregnant Women, July 12, 2010, available at http://advocatesforpregnantwomen.org/blog/2010/07/health_experts_wanr_alabama_co.php (last visited July 19, 2010).
46 Tenn. Code Ann.§ 39-13-107 (c) (2); *see also* 7/16/14 MSMBC All In With Chris Hayes, 2014 WLNR 19298913.
47 In March 2010 Utah enacted a law making it homicide for a woman to "recklessly or negligently cause the death of her unborn child." Utah Code Ann. § 76-5-201.
48 Fentiman, *Pursuing the Perfect Mother*, at 390-91, 466-69.
49 American College of Obstetricians and Gynecologists (ACOG), Committee on Ethics and American Academy of Pediatrics Committee on Bioethics, Committee Opinion Number 501, *Maternal-Fetal Intervention and Fetal Care Centers* 2 (Aug. 2011, Reaffirmed 2014), available at http://www.acog.org/Resources-And-Publications/Committee-Opinions/Committee-on-Ethics/Maternal-Fetal-Intervention-and-Fetal-Care-Centers (hereafter ACOG AAP Committee Opinion 501); *see also Ex Parte Ankrom*, 152 So. 3d 397, 433 (Ala. 2013) (Malone, C.J., dissenting).
50 Jacqueline H. Wolf, Don't Kill Your Baby: Public Health and the Decline of Breastfeeding in the Nineteenth and Twentieth Centuries 1, 42, 47-49, Columbus (Ohio State University Press, 2001).
51 Jane E. Brody, *Personal Health: The Ideal and the Real of Breast-Feeding*, N.Y. Times, Jul. 24, 2012, at D7; *see also* Cynthia G. Colen and David M. Ramey, *Is Breast Truly Best? Estimating the Effects of Breastfeeding on Long-term Child Health and Wellbeing in the United States Using Sibling Comparisons*, 109 Social Science and Medicine 55 (2014).
52 Centers for Disease Control and Prevention, Breastfeeding Report Card, United States/2014 at 2, 4 (2014); available at http://www.cdc.gov/breastfeeding/BreastfeedingReportCard2014.pdf.
53 Section 2713, Affordable Care Act, 111 Pub. L. 148, 124 Stat. 119, see also *Breastfeeding benefits*, https://www.healthcare.gov/coverage/breast-feeding-benefits/ (last visited Feb. 25, 2016).
54 Dell'Antonia, *supra* n. 2 (citing 2012 Save the Children State of the World's Mothers Report).
55 Department of Health and Human Services, Administration for Children and Families, Child Maltreatment 2014, 21, available at http://www.acf.hhs.gov/sites/default/files/cb/cm2014.pdf (last visited August 11, 2016) (hereafter Child Maltreatment 2014). These numbers are similar to earlier data. See Child Maltreatment 2011 ix, available at http://www.acf.hhs.gov/programs/cb/resource/child maltreatment 2011 (last visited June 1, 2013). *See also* Thomas L. Hafemeister, *Castles Made of Sand? Rediscovering Child Abuse and Society's Response*, 36 Ohio N.U. L. Rev. 819, 823 (2010) (hereafter *Castles Made of Sand*).

56 National data show that about 25 percent of girls and 10 percent of boys are the victims of childhood sexual abuse, although these numbers may underestimate the actual prevalence of sexual abuse. Annette Hernandez et al., *An Integrated Approach to Treating Non-Offending Parents Affected by Sexual Abuse*, 7 Soc. Work Ment. Health 533–55 (2009).

57 International Child Abuse Network, Child Abuse Statistics, available at http://www.yesican.org/stats.html (last visited June 20, 2011); *see also* Child Maltreatment 2014, *supra* n. 54, at 24.

58 See discussion in chapter 5.

59 Child Welfare Information Gateway, *Long Term Consequences of Child Abuse and Neglect* (2008), available at http://www.childwelfare.gov/pubs/factsheets/long_term_consequences.cfm#sitetop (last visited June 19, 2011).

60 One estimate is that "one-third of abused and neglected children will eventually victimize their own children." *Id.*; *see also Penn Study Finds Physically Abused Boys May Be More Likely to Commit Domestic Violence as Adults*, U. Penn. Medical School Release Oct. 17, 2005, available at http://www.uphs.upenn.edu/news/News_Releases/ oct05/chldabse.htm (last visited June 20, 2011).

61 Sheigla Murphy and Marsha Rosenbaum, Pregnant Women on Drugs: Combating Stereotypes and Stigma 50–52, New Brunswick, N.J. (Rutgers University Press, 1999); Wendy Chavkin, *Enemy of the Fetus? The Pregnant Drug User and the Pregnancy Police*, Health/PAC Bulletin, Winter 1992, at 5, 9.

62 Dorothy Roberts, *Motherhood and Crime*, 79 Iowa L. Rev. 95, 110–11 (1993); Saundra Chung, *Mama Mia! How Gender Stereotyping May Play a Role in the Prosecution of Child Fatality Cases*, 9 Whittier J. Child & Fam. Advoc. 205, at 205–6, 207–10 (2009–10) (hereafter *Mama Mia*); Jeanne A. Fugate, *Note, Who's Failing to Protect Whom? A Critical Look at Failure-to-Protect Laws*, 76 N.Y. U. L. Rev. 272, 273–74 (2001) (hereafter *Who's Failing to Protect Whom*); and Alex Campbell, *Battered, Bereaved, and Behind Bars*, Methodology Section, *These Women Were Sentenced to at Least 10 Years for Failing to Protect*, BuzzFeed (Oct. 2, 2014), available at https://www.buzzfeed.com/alexcampbell/how-the-law-turns-battered-women-into-criminals?utm_term=.je97AYvxod#.hkWvNe86J3 (last visited Aug. 24, 2016).

63 *Childhood Maltreatment, supra* n. 55, *see also* Alexia Cooper and Erica L. Smith, *Homicide Trends in the United States, 1980–2008*, 2, 4. Bureau of Justice Statistics, U.S. Dep't of Justice 6–7 (Nov. 2011) [NCJ236018].

64 Rose M. Kreider and Renee Ellis, Living Arrangements of Children 2009 (U.S. Census Bureau, Current Population Reports 3 (June 2011) [P70–126] (hereafter Living Arrangements of Children); and Jonathan Vespa et al., *America's Families and Living Arrangements: 2012*, U.S. Census Bureau 21 (Aug. 2013), http://www.census.gov/prod/2013pubs/p20-570.pdf (hereafter *America's Families and Living Arrangements*).

65 Vespa, *supra* at 13, *see also* Mark Mather, *U.S. Children in Single-Mother Families*, Population Reference Bureau (May 2010), http://www.prb.org/Publications/

PolicyBriefs/singlemotherfamilies.aspx (last visited June 18, 2013) (hereafter *U.S. Children in Single-Mother Families*). Two-thirds of these families function without any financial support from the child's father. *Id.* at 2.

66 *Id.*
67 Maltreatment of children is seven times more likely in poor families than in higher-income ones; unemployed parents are also more likely to commit child abuse than employed ones. Cynthia Godsoe, *Parsing Parenthood*, 17 Lewis & Clark L. Rev. 113, 125–26 (2013); *see also* Andrea J. Sedlak et al., Fourth National Incidence Study of Child Abuse and Neglect (NIS-4) 11 (2009–2010) (hereafter Fourth National Incidence Study).
68 Katie Roiphe, In Praise of Messy Lives: Essays 16, New York (The Dial Press, 2012); *see also* Jason De Parle and Sabrina Tavernise, *For Women Under 30, Most Births Occur Outside Marriage*, N.Y. Times, Feb. 17, 2012, at A1; and Claire Cain Miller, *Single Motherhood, in Decline Over All, Rises for Women 35 and Older*, N.Y. Times, May 9, 2015, at A/2.
69 Roberts, *supra* n. 62, at 111–13; and Elaine Chiu, *Confronting the Agency in Battered Mothers*, 74 S. Cal. L. Rev. 1223 (2001).
70 Centers for Disease Control, CDC's National Surveillance Data (1997–2007), available at http://www.cdc.gov/nceh/lead/data/national.htm; Advisory Committee on Childhood Lead Poisoning Prevention, Centers for Disease Control, *Low Level Lead Exposure Harms Children: A Renewed Call for Primary Prevention* 1–11 (Jan. 4, 2012) (hereafter *Low Level Lead Exposure Harms Children*), available at http://www.cdc.gov/nceh/lead/ACCLPP/Final_Document_030712.pdf.
71 *Ethyl Corp. v. EPA*, 541 F.2d 1, 12–13 (D.C. Cir. 1976); and *Small Refiner Lead Phase-Down Task Force v. EPA*, 705 F.2d 506, 527–28 (D.C. Cir. 1983).
72 Russell T. Gips, *From China with Lead: The Hasty Reform of the Consumer Product Safety Commission*, 46 Hous. L. Rev. 545 (2009) (hereafter *From China with Lead*).
73 *See, e.g., In re Mattel, Inc. Toy Lead Paint Product Liability Litigation*, 588 F. Supp. 2d 1111, 1117–20 (C.D. Cal. 2008).
74 Kim M. Cecil et al., *Decreased Brain Volume in Adults with Childhood Lead Exposure*, 5 PLoS Medicine 0741 (May 2008).
75 Deborah W. Denno, *Considering Lead Poisoning as a Criminal Defense*, 20 Fordham Urb. L. J. 377, 396 (1993) (hereafter *Lead Poisoning as a Criminal Defense*).
76 *Cf.* Virginia McGee Richards and Ben A. Hagood, Jr., *Hazardous House: Obligations and Remedies After Discovering Lead-Based Paint*, 17 S.C. Law. 28, 29–33 (2006) (hereafter *Hazardous House*).
77 *People v. Atlantic Richfield Co.*, 2014 WL 1385823 (Cal. Super Ct. [Santa Clara County] Mar. 26, 2014). That decision is now on appeal.
78 McGee Richards and Hagood, *supra* n. 76, at 30–33. *See also* Donald G. Gifford and Paolo Pasicolan, *Market Share Liability Beyond DES Cases: The Solution to*

the Causation Dilemma in Lead Paint Litigation?, 58 S.C. L. Rev. 115, 127 (2006) (hereafter *Market Share Liability Beyond DES Cases*).
79 Martha Chamallas and Jennifer B. Wriggins, The Measure of Injury: Race, Gender, and Tort Law 141–46, New York (NYU Press, 2010) (hereafter The Measure of Injury).
80 *Id.* at 139–53, *but see Andon v. 302–304 Mott Street Associates*, 731 N.E. 2d 589 (N.Y. 2000).
81 *See, e.g.*, Institute of Medicine, Financing Vaccines in the 21st Century: Assuring Access and Availability 42–44 (2004) (hereinafter Financing Vaccines); and Mark A. Hall, *The Scope and Limits of Public Health Law*, 46 (# 3 Supp.) Perspectives in Biology and Medicine S199, S204–05 (Summer 2003).
82 Wendy E. Parmet, *Informed Consent and Public Health: Are They Compatible When It Comes to Vaccines?*, 8 J. Health Care. L. & Pol'y 71, 89–90 (2005) (hereafter *Informed Consent and Public Health*).
83 Centers for Disease Control, *Ten Great Public Health Achievements—United States, 2001–2010*, 60 Morbidity and Mortality Weekly Report 619, 619 (2011) (hereafter *Ten Great Public Health Achievements, 2001–2010*).
84 *Bruesewitz v. Wyeth, LLC*, 131 S. Ct. 1068, 1072 (2011); *see also* Steve P. Calandrillo, *Vanishing Vaccinations: Why Are So Many Americans Opting Out of Vaccinating Their Children?*, 37 U. Mich. J. L. Reform 353, 359, 362 (2004) (hereafter *Vanishing Vaccinations*).
85 Atkinson, *supra* n. 16, at 32, Appendix G-8; Associated Press, *Fewer Kids Getting Vaccines; Parents Opting Out of School Shots Due to Fears, Paranoia, Laziness*, Nov. 29, 2011, available at http://www.nydailynews.com/life-style/health/kids-vaccines-parents-opting-school-shots-due-fears-paranoia-laziness-article-1.984004#ixzz2M3C7PKhk (last visited Feb. 26, 2013); Trine Tsouderos et al., *Vaccine Rates Raise Risk of Outbreaks; More Schools Fall Below State's Recommended Protection Level*, Chicago Tribune, June 19, 2011, at C1 (hereafter *Vaccine Rates Raise Risk of Outbreaks*).
86 Priya Shetty, *Experts Concerned about Vaccination Backlash*, 375 The Lancet 970, 970 (2010) (hereafter *Experts Concerned about Vaccination Backlash*).
87 Amanda F. Dempsey et al., *Alternative Vaccination Schedule Preferences Among Parents of Young Children*, 128 (#5) Pediatrics (Oct. 3, 2011), available at www.pediatrics.org/cgi/doi/10/1542/peds.2011–0400 (hereafter *Alternative Vaccination Schedule Preferences*).
88 Kathryn M. Edwards, *State Mandates and Childhood Immunization*, 284 JAMA 3171, 3171 (2000) (hereafter *State Mandates and Childhood Immunization*); *see also* Ken Haller, *Discard the Myths: Childhood Vaccines Save Lives, That's the Plain and Simple Truth*, St. Louis (MO) Post-Dispatch, Feb. 9, 2012, at A15, 2012 WLNR 2797654.
89 Tsouderos, *supra* n. 85; *see also* Elliot Njus, *High Opt-Out Rate for Vaccinations Challenges County*, The Oregonian (Portland, OR), June 18, 2011 (hereafter *High Opt-Out Rate*).

90 Heidi J. Larson et al., *Addressing the Vaccine Confidence Gap*, 378 Lancet 526, 529–30 (2011); *see also* Institute of Medicine (IOM), Immunization Safety Review: Vaccines and Autism 7 (2004) (hereafter IOM Immunization Safety Review).
91 Philip J. Smith et al., *Association Between Health Care Providers' Influence on Parents Who Have Concerns About Vaccine Safety and Vaccination Coverage*, 118 Pediatrics e1287, e1291 (2006) (hereafter *Health Care Providers' Influence on Parents and Vaccination Coverage*).
92 *See, e.g., Commonwealth v. Twitchell*, 617 N.E. 2d 609 (Mass. 1993); and *Walker v. Superior Court*, 763 P. 2d 852 (Cal. 1988).
93 *See, e.g., Mueller v. Auker*, 576 F.3d 979 (9th Cir. 2009); *In re Custody of a Minor*, 393 N.E. 2d 836 (Mass. 1979); and *In re McCauley*, 565 N.E. 2d 411 (Mass. 1991).
94 Stephen L. Isaacs and Steven A. Schroeder, *Class, The Ignored Determinant of the Nation's Health*, 351 N.E. J. Med. 1137 (2004).
95 Shonkhoff and Phillips, *supra* n. 24.
96 Hillary Rodham Clinton, *It Takes a Village and Other Lessons Children Teach Us*, 9–10, 15–18, 21–23 (Large Print ed. 1996).
97 Daniel B. Rubin and Sophie Kasimov, *The Problem of Vaccination Noncompliance: Public Health Goals and the Limits of Tort Law*, 107 Mich. L. Rev. First Impressions 114, 115 (2009) (hereafter *The Problem of Vaccination Noncompliance*).

CHAPTER 2. THE SOCIAL, PSYCHOLOGICAL, AND LEGAL CONSTRUCTION OF RISK

1 American Law Institute, Model Penal Code, Official Draft (1962) (hereafter Model Penal Code) §2.02 (2) (d) and Restatement (Third) of Torts: Physical and Emotional Harm § 3, Negligence.
2 Roger E. Kasperson et al., *The Social Amplification of Risk: A Conceptual Framework*, in Paul Slovic, The Perception of Risk 232, New London (EARTHSCAN Publications, 2000).
3 Alison C. Cullen and Mitchell J. Small, *Uncertain Risk: The Role and Limits of Quantitative Assessment*, in Risk Analysis and Society: An Interdisciplinary Characterization of the Field (hereafter Risk Analysis and Society) 163–67 (Timothy McDaniels and Mitchell J. Small, eds., Cambridge University Press, 2004) (hereafter *Uncertain Risk*). Uncertainty and variability are two distinct concepts. "'Uncertainty forces decision makers to judge how probable it is that risks will be overestimated or underestimated for every member of the exposed population, whereas variability forces them to cope with the certainty that different individuals will be subjected to risks both above and below any reference point one chooses.'" *Id.* at 165. In practice, "dose-response uncertainty is often the largest and most important source of error in an integrated health risk assessment." *Id.* at 167.
4 *Id.* at 165–67, 172–73; *see also* Mary R. English, *Environmental Risk and Justice*, in Risk Analysis and Society, *supra* n. 3, at 140.

5 Cullen and Small, *supra* n. 3, at 172–74. The use of such subjective values is often referred to as Bayesian analysis. *Id.* at 173.
6 Advisory Committee on Childhood Lead Poisoning Prevention, Centers for Disease Control, *Low Level Lead Exposure Harms Children: A Renewed Call for Primary Prevention* 1–11 (Jan. 4, 2012) (hereafter CDC, *Low Level Lead Exposure Harms Children*).
7 Paul Slovic, The Perception of Risk, *supra* n. 2, at xxxvi.
8 *Id.*
9 Paul Slovic, *Trust, Emotion, Sex, Politics, and Science: Surveying the Risk-Assessment Battlefield*, 19 Risk Analysis 689 (1999).
10 Mandana Vahabi, *The Impact of Health Communication on Health-related Decision Making, A Review of Evidence*, 107 Health Education 27, 33–34 (2007); Paul Slovic, Baruch Fischoff, and Sarah Lichtenstein, *Response Mode, Framing and Information-processing Effects in Risk Assessment*, in Slovic, *supra* n. 2, at 157–58.
11 Slovic, *supra* n. 2, at xxxvi.
12 Slovic, Fischoff, and Lichtenstein, *supra* n. 10, at 158.
13 Pew Research Center, U.S. Survey Research. *Questionnaire Design*, http://www.pewresearch.org/methodology/u-s-survey-research/questionnaire-des/ (last visited Aug. 19, 2015); Tarik Abdel-Monem et al., *Climate Change Survey Measures: Exploring Perceived Bias and Question Interpretation*, Publications of Affiliated Faculty: Nebraska Public Policy Center. Paper 35 (2014).
14 Dan M. Kahan et al., *Who Fears the HPV Vaccine, Who Doesn't, and Why? An Experimental Study of the Mechanisms of Cultural Cognition*, 34 Law Hum. Behav. 501, 502 (2010) (hereafter *Who Fears the HPV Vaccine*).
15 Thomas B. Newman, *The Power of Stories Over Statistics*, 327 Brit. Med. J. 1424, 1426 (2003); *see also* Vahabi, *supra* n. 10, at 35.
16 *See* Newman, *supra* n. 15, at 1426–27.
17 *See, e.g.*, Thomas M. Burton, *FDA Bans BPA in Baby-Food Packaging: Agency Doesn't Take Action on the Chemical's Use in Food Cans*, Wall Street J., July 11, 2013.
18 *See, e.g.*, English, *supra* n. 4, at 124; Abigail Goldman, *Lead-Paint Toys Aren't the Biggest Risk*, L. A. Times, Sept. 23, 2007 (hereafter *Lead-Paint Toys Aren't the Biggest Risk*).
19 As described by Cass Sunstein, "When people lack statistical knowledge, they consider risks to be significant if they can easily think of instances in which those risks came to fruition." Cass R. Sunstein, Laws of Fear 5 (Cambridge University Press, 2005); *see also* Peter Bennett and Kenneth Calman, Risk Communication and Public Health 8–9, 29, (Oxford University Press 1999). *See* Mike Stobbe, AP, *CDC: Young Adults Ignoring Skin-Cancer Warnings*, available at http://news.yahoo.com/cdc-young-adults-ignoring-sking-cancer-warnings-202758143.html (noting that about 9,200 Americans are expected to die from melanoma [skin cancer] in 2012); and CDC, *Unintentional Drowning: Get the Facts*, available at http://www.cdc.gov/HomeandReacreationalSafety/Water-Safety/waterinjuries-

factsheet.html (noting that about 4,000 Americans died from drowning or boating accidents each year from 2005–9).

20 Vicky M. Bier et al., *Risk of Extreme and Rare Events*, in McDaniels and Small, Uncertain Risk, *supra* n. 3, at 74, 78, 86.

21 This concern is at the heart of chapter 9 and will be discussed in detail there. See, e. g., Associated Press, *Fewer Kids Getting Vaccines; Parents Opting Out of School Shots Due to Fears, Paranoia, Laziness*, Nov. 29, 2011); Tsouderos, *Vaccine Rates Raise Risk of Outbreaks*, *supra* (chapter 1, n.85); Larson, *Addressing the Vaccine Confidence Gap*, *supra* (chapter 1, n.90) at 529–30; *see also* IOM, Immunization Safety Review, *supra* (chapter 1, n.90).

22 English, *supra* n. 4, at 124.

23 Vahabi, *supra* n. 10, at 35; and Carol B. Anderson, Inside Jurors' Minds: The Hierarchy of Juror Decision-Making 47–49, 67–68, 81 (National Institute for Trial Advocacy 2012) (hereafter Inside Jurors' Minds).

24 Jennifer A. Reich, *Neoliberal Mothering and Vaccine Refusal: Imagined Gated Communities and the Privilege of Choice*, 28 Gender & Soc. 679, 685, 688, 692–95 (2014) (hereafter *Neoliberal Mothering*).

25 Anderson, *supra* n. 23, at 47.

26 *Id*. at 47–49 (relying on Leon Festinger, *A Theory of Cognitive Dissonance* [1957] and 79–80); *see also* Baruch Fischhoff, *Hindsight ≠ Foresight: The Effect of Outcome Knowledge on Judgment Under Certainty*, 1 J. Experimental Psychology: Human Perception and Performance 288, 292, 295, 297–98 (1975) (hereafter *Hindsight ≠ Foresight*); Jon Hanson and Kathleen Hanson, *The Blame Frame: Justifying (Racial) Injustice in America*, 41 Harv. C.R.—C.L. L. Rev. 413, 419 (2006) (hereafter *The Blame Frame*); and Chamallas, *Deepening the Legal Understanding of Bias*, *supra* (chapter 1, n. 11), at 793–94.

27 Ann Bostrom, *Vaccine Risk Communication: Lessons from Risk Perception, Decision Making and Environmental Risk Communication Research*, 8 Risk: Health, Safety & Environment 173, 176 (Spring 1997) (hereafter *Vaccine Risk Communication*); Geoffrey Evans et al., U.S. Dep't of Health & Human Services, Accelerated Development of Vaccines 2002, The Evolution of Vaccine Risk Communication in the United States: 1982–2002, 60–61.

28 M. Granger Morgan, *Risk Communication: A Mental Models Approach* 12 (Cambridge University Press 2002); Anderson, *supra* n. 23, at 125.

29 Anderson, *supra* n. 23 at 125; *see also* Paul Slovic et al., *Response Mode, Framing and Information-processing Effects in Risk Assessment*, in Slovic, *supra* n. 2, at 163–64.

30 Anderson, *supra* n. 23, at 125.

31 Anderson, *supra* n. 23, at 129–30; Chamallas, *supra* n. 26, at 778–95.

32 Robert J. Smith and Justin D. Levinson, *The Impact of Implicit Racial Bias and the Exercise of Prosecutorial Discretion*, 35 Seattle Univ. L. Rev. 795, 798–99 (2012) (hereafter *The Impact of Implicit Racial Bias*).

33 Shima Baradaran, *Race, Prediction and Discretion*, 81 Geo. Wash. L. Rev. 157, 211 (2013) (hereafter *Race, Prediction and Discretion*); Smith and Levinson, *supra* n. 32.

34 Justin Murray, *Reimagining Criminal Prosecution: Toward a Color-Conscious Professional Ethic for Prosecutors*, 49 Am. Crim. L. Rev. 1541, 1573 (2012); Smith and Levinson, *supra* n. 32; Besiki Kutateladze et al., *Race and Prosecution in Manhattan, Research Summary* 3, 5–6 (Vera Institute of Justice July 2014); Mona Lynch and Craig Haney, *Looking Across the Empathic Divide: Racialized Decision Making on the Capital Jury*, 2011 Mich. St. L. Rev. 573, 577–79 (2011).
35 Kathryn Roe Eldrige, *Racial Disparities in the Capital System: Invidious or Accidental?*, 14 Cal. Def. J., 305, 320–22 (2002), and Lynch and Haney, *supra* n. 34, at 577–79.
36 Rachlinski, *Does Unconscious Racial Bias Affect Trial Judges?*, *supra*, at 1221–1226.
37 Matt Apuzzo, *Shoot First, and He Will Answer Questions*, N.Y. Times, Aug. 2, 2015, at A1; Kate Abbey-Lambertz, *These 15 Black Women Were Killed During Police Encounters. Their Lives Matter, Too*, Huffington Post (Feb. 2, 2015), http://www.huffingtonpost.com/2015/02/13/black-womens-lives-matter-police-shootings_n_6644276.html.
38 Ariel R. White et al., *What Do I Need to Vote? Bureaucratic Discretion and Discrimination by Local Election Officials*, 109 Am. Poli. Sci. Rev. 129, 140 (Feb. 2015) (hereafter *What Do I Need to Vote*).
39 Kahan et al., *supra* n. 14, at 502–3.
40 Slovic, *supra* n. 2 at xxxiv, 44; Melissa L. Finucane et al., *Gender, Race, and Perceived Risk: The 'White Male' Effect*, 2 Health, Risk & Soc'y 159, 163–64 (2000).
41 Finucane, *supra*.
42 *Id.*; *see also* Dan M. Kahan et al., *Culture and Identity-Protective Cognition: Explaining the White Male Effect in Risk Perception*, 4 J. Empirical Legal Studies 465, 480–83 (2007).
43 Jan L. Hitchcock, *Gender Differences in Risk Perception: Broadening the Contexts*, 12 Risk: Health Safety & Env't 179, 182, 188, 201–2 (2001).
44 Ruth Graham, *Don't Blame Parents for Vaccine Resistance: Blame Mothers*, Slate, available at http://www.slate.com/articles/double_x/doublex/2015/02/women_and_vaccine_resistance_mothers_make_health_care_decisions_for_their.html (last visited Feb. 15, 2016) (noting that mothers are more likely than fathers to make health care decisions for their children).
45 Kahan et al., *supra* n. 42, at 483 (reviewing the literature); *see also* Finucane, *supra* n. 40, at 160–61, 170.
46 Kahan et al, *supra* n. 14, at 503.
47 Dan Kahan et al., *Culture and Identity-Protective Cognition: Explaining the White Male Effect in Risk Perception* 5 (Yale Faculty Scholarship Series, Paper 101, 2007), http://digitalcommons.law.yale.edu/fss_papers/101.
48 Kahan et al., *supra* n. 14, at 503.
49 Kahan, *supra* n. 47, at 6, 9.
50 Michael D. Shear and Coral Davenport, *Obama Vetoes Effort by Republicans to Force Approval of Keystone Pipeline*, N.Y. Times, Feb. 25, 2015, at A16.

51 *See, e.g.*, Barbara Loe Fisher, *The Health Liberty Revolution & Forced Vaccination*, declaring: "In America today, there is an unprecedented assault on the human right to exercise informed consent to medical risk-taking . . . led by one of the most powerful and wealthy corporate empires in the world: the global pharmaceutical industry. . . . What is at stake for the American people is our health and our liberty." http://www.nvic.org/NVIC-Vaccine-News/August-2011.aspx (last visited Aug. 24, 2016).

52 Deborah Lupton, *Risk as Moral Danger: The Social and Political Functions of Risk Disclosure in Public Health*, 23 Int'l J. Health Services, 425, 425–26 (1993) (hereafter *Risk as Moral Danger*), citing Mary Douglas, *Risk as a Forensic Resource*, Daedalus 1, 3 (Fall 1990).

53 Lupton, *supra* n. 52, at 425–27.

54 *Id.* at 429.

55 *Id.* at 430.

56 Slovic, Fischoff, and Lichtenstein, *supra* n. 10, at 165–66.

57 Dan Kahan, *Fixing the Communications Failure*, 463 Nature 296–97 (Jan. 21, 2010); *see also* Kahan et al., *supra* n. 14.

58 Cullen and Small, *supra* n. 4, at 168.

59 *See* Paul A. Offit, Autism's False Prophets: Bad Science, Risky Medicine, and the Search for a Cure, 79–80 (Columbia University Press, 2010) (hereafter Autism's False Prophets); *cf.* Biss, on Immunity, *supra*, at 100–1.

60 Cullen and Small, *supra* n. 3, at 168.

61 Kahan, *supra* n. 47, at 36 (emphasis added).

62 *See, e.g.*, Hitchcock, *supra* n. 43, at 204; *see also* Association of State and Territorial Health Officials (ASTHO), *Communicating Effectively about Vaccines: New Communication Resources for Health Officials* 13 (Nov. 2010) (hereafter *Communicating Effectively about Vaccines*), http://www.vdh.state.va.us/clinicians/pdf/vaccinations (last visited Mar. 15, 2012).

63 Kahan, *supra* n. 14, at 513.

64 Kathryn M. Edwards, *State Mandates and Childhood Immunization*, *supra* (chapter 1, n. 88), at 3171.

65 Between 2000 and 2004 the national Institute of Medicine (IOM) convened eight separate task forces to evaluate the scientific evidence of an asserted causal connection between vaccination and autism. IOM, Immunization Safety Review: 2 *supra* n. 21. This review, which considered multiple studies of the effects of administering vaccines with and without thimerosal (including populations in Denmark, Sweden, the United States, and the United Kingdom), found no credible evidence of a causal relationship between thimerosal exposure via vaccines and the incidence of autism. *Id.* at 6.5. Recent studies have confirmed the lack of relationship between thimerosal and autism. *See* Luke A. Taylor et al., *Vaccines Are Not Associated with Autism: An Evidence-Based Meta-analysis of Case-Control and Cohort Studies*, 32 Vaccine 3623, 3623–25 (2014); and Cristofer S. Price et al.,

Prenatal and Infant Exposure to Thimerosal from Vaccines and Immunoglobulins and Risk of Autism, 126 Pediatrics 656. 656 (2010).
66 *See, e.g.*, ASTHO, *Communicating Effectively about Vaccines*, supra n. 62; and Bostrom, *supra* n. 27, at 177.
67 Gerd Gigerenzer et al., *Helping Doctors and Patients Make Sense of Health Statistics*, 8 Psychological Science in the Public Interest 53, 54 (2008).
68 *Id.*
69 Emily Oster, Expecting Better, 34–40, 81–84 (Penguin Books, 2013) (hereafter Expecting Better); and Heidi Murkoff and Sharon Mazel, What to Expect® When You're Expecting 69–79, 501–02 (Workman Publishing Co., Inc., 4th ed. 2008) (hereafter What to Expect®).
70 Prakesh S. Shah et. al., *Maternal Exposure to Domestic Violence and Pregnancy and Birth Outcomes: A Systematic Review and Meta-Analysis*, 19 J. Women's Health 2017, 2017 (2010).
71 Jeani Chang et al., *Homicide: A Leading Cause of Injury Deaths among Pregnant and Postpartum Women in the United States, 1991–1999*, 95 Am. J. Pub. Health 471, 471–72 (2005) (hereafter *Homicide: A Leading Cause of Injury Deaths among Pregnant and Postpartum Women*).
72 Sandra L. Martin et al., *Violence and Substance Use among North Carolina Pregnant Women*, 86 Am. J. Pub. Health 991, 991, 996–97 (1996) (hereafter *Violence and Substance Use among North Carolina Pregnant Women*).
73 Michelle Tulen et al., *Partner Violence Impacts the Psychosocial and Psychiatric Status of Pregnant, Drug-Dependent Women*, 29 Addictive Behaviors 1029, 1032–33 (2004).
74 Shah, *supra* n. 70, at 2019, 2024.
75 *See, e.g.*, Charles P. Larson, *Poverty During Pregnancy: Its Effects on Child Health Outcomes*, 12 Paediatric Child Health 673, 673–75 (2007) (hereafter *Poverty During Pregnancy*); Martin, *supra* n. 72, at 997; Jill Davies, Building Comprehensive Solutions to Domestic Violence: Policy Blueprint on Domestic Violence and Poverty, Policy and Practice Paper 15, available at http://www.vawnet.org/Assoc_Files_VAWnet/BCS15_BP.pdf; Futures Without Violence, *The Facts on Health Care and Domestic Violence* 2, futureswithoutviolence.org/userfiles/file/HealthCare/healthcare.pdf (last visited Feb. 3, 2014) (hereafter *Policy Blueprint on Domestic Violence and Poverty*).
76 Slovic, *supra* n. 2, at xxxv.
77 *See, e.g.*, *DOE Study: Fracking Chemicals Didn't Taint Water*, Associated Press, July 19, 2013; Suzy Khimm, *Study: GOP Votes Drive Public Opinion on Climate Change*, Washington Post (Reuters), Feb. 9, 2012.
78 Kahan, *supra* notes 14 and 42; *see also* Khimm, *supra*. n. 77.
79 Daniel T. Willingham, *Trust Me, I'm a Scientist: Why So Many People Choose Not to Believe What Scientists Say*, Scientific American May 5, 2011 (hereafter *Trust Me, I'm a Scientist*).

80 Lawrence O. Gostin, *Public Health Law in a New Century, Part III: Public Health Regulation: A Systematic Evaluation*, 283 J.A.M.A. 3118, 3120–22 (2000) (hereafter *Public Health Law in a New Century, Part III*); and Timothy F. Malloy, *Principled Prevention*, 46 Ariz State L. J. 105, 140 (2014).

81 Michigan Center for Public Health Preparedness, U. Mich. School of Pub. Health, *Confounding*, available at http://practice/sph.umich.edu/micphp/epicentral/confounding.php (last visited July 25, 2015).

82 This will be discussed at length in chapter 6.

83 Susan FitzGerald, *'Crack Baby' Study Ends with Unexpected But Clear Result*, Philadelphia Inquirer, July 22, 2013 (available at http://articles.philly.com/2013-07-22/news/40709969_1_hallam-hurt-so-called-crack-babies-funded-study).

84 *See, e.g.*, Shonkhoff and Phillips, *From Neurons to Neighborhoods*.

85 *Id.*; *see also* Carla Kemp, *Poverty Threatens Health of U.S. Children*, AAP News, May 4, 2013 (American Academy of Pediatrics), available at http://aapnews.aappublications.org/content/early/2013/05/04/aapnews.20130504-2.full (last visited Oct. 29, 2013).

86 Donald G. Gifford, *The Challenge to the Individual Causation Requirement in Mass Product Torts*, 62 Wash. & Lee L. Rev. 873, 882–88 (2005); *see also* Michael L. Rustad, *Torts as Public Wrongs*, 38 Pepp. L. Rev. 443, 525–27 (2011); and Joshua Dressler, Understanding Criminal Law 14–16 (4th ed. 2006) (hereafter Understanding Criminal Law).

87 Sanford H. Kadish, Stephen J. Schulhofer, and Carol S. Steiker, Criminal Law and Its Processes: Cases and Materials 80–83, 90–91 (Aspen Publishers, 8th ed. 2007).

88 *See, e.g.*, Steven Hetcher, *The Jury's Out: Social Norms' Misunderstood Role in Negligence Law*, 91 Geo. L. J. 633, 656 (2003) (hereafter *The Jury's Out*).

89 For an excellent brief discussion of the common law, see Karl N. Llewellyn, *The Bramble Bush* (Oceana Publications, 1930).

90 *See, e.g.*, Federal Administrative Procedure Act, 60 Stat. 237 (1945); Cal. Gov't Code §§ 11400–11529 (West Supp. 1996).

91 Anderson, *supra* n. 23.

92 *Id.* at 9, 24.

93 *Id.* at 119–20; Sunstein, *supra* n. 19 at 5.

94 Anderson, *supra* n. 23, at 22–25.

95 Chamallas, *supra* n. 26, at 778.

96 Dressler, *supra* n. 86 , at 617–18, 625–28.

97 *Id.* at 624.

98 Chamallas, *supra* n. 26, at 778–89.

99 Anderson, *supra* n. 23, at 47—49, 79-80; Fischhoff, *supra* n. 26, at 292–98; Hanson and Hanson, *supra* n. 26, at 419; and Chamallas, *supra* n. 26, at 793–94.

100 Anderson, *supra* n. 23, at 67–68.

101 *Id.* at 68.

102 *Id.* at 63, Fischhoff, *supra* n. 26, at 292–98.

103 Anderson, *supra* n. 23, at 63–64.

104 Anderson, *supra* n. 23, at 66.
105 *State v. Scruggs*, 905 A.2d 24, 26–28, 41 (Conn. 2006).
106 *Id.* at 29–30.
107 *Id.* at 36–38. The court declared:
 We find the application of hindsight to be particularly troubling in this context.... [T]he state cannot decline to prosecute persons who maintain such conditions because it believes the risk to children is either within an acceptable range or is speculative and then, only when catastrophic harm occurs, use that as evidence that the risk was unacceptable and foreseeable.
 Id. at 38, n. 10.
108 *See, e.g.*, Robert V. Percival, *Who's Afraid of the Precautionary Principle?*, 23 Pace Envtl. L. Rev. 21, 22 (2005–06) (hereafter *Who's Afraid of the Precautionary Principle?*).
109 A tort is a "civil wrong," a breach of duty to which the law responds by awarding monetary compensation for the injury suffered and, in rare cases, punitive damages, designed to punish as well as deter. William Prosser, Handbook on the Law of Torts § 2, at 9–10 (4th ed. 1971). Torts are distinct from violations of criminal law, as well as breaches of contract. *Ankiewicz v. Kinder*, 563 N.E. 2d 684, 686 (Mass. 1990). A contract is breached when one party does not fulfill her side of a promised bargain with another. *See, e.g.*, Restatement (Second) Contracts § 1.
110 *See* Restatement (Third) of Torts: Physical and Emotional Harm § 3, Negligence (hereafter Third Restatement of Torts).
111 *See* Restatement of Torts (Third) § 3, Negligence, Comment a. Implicit in the finding that a defendant is negligent is that s/he had a duty to act in a reasonable manner which was breached by the defendant's actions or failure to act. The reasonableness of a defendant's actions is measured in part by foreseeability: "In order to determine whether appropriate care was exercised, the factfinder must assess the foreseeable risk at the time of the defendant's alleged negligence." Third Restatement of Torts § 7, Duty, Comment j. Judge Learned Hand, in his famous formula for negligence, also incorporated notions of foreseeability when he declared: "[T]o provide against resulting injuries is a function of three variables: (1) The probability that she will break away; (2) the gravity of the resulting injury, if she does; (3) the burden of adequate precautions. *United States v. Carroll Towing Co.*, 159 F.2d 169, 173 (2d Cir. 1947).
112 484 P. 2d 1167, * (Wa. Ct. App. 1971).
113 At the time *Williams* was decided, the Washington manslaughter law embodied the civil law standard of simple negligence. This was subsequently changed to gross (criminal) negligence, which is the standard of criminal liability in almost every state. *State v. Norman*, 808 P.2d 1159, 1164 (Wash. App. Ct. 1991); *see also* Dressler, *supra* n. 86, at 140–41.
114 Hetcher, *supra* n. 88, at 634.
115 *Id.* at 647.
116 *Id.* at 636.

117 *Id.* at 640 (emphasis added).
118 *Id.* at 641.
119 *Id.* at 636.
120 As noted previously, negligence law generally presumes that all actors have a duty to avoid physical harm when their conduct creates a risk of harm to others, unless they fall into a category in which policy considerations militate against imposing a duty, as a matter of law. Third Restatement of Torts § 7, Duty, Comment a.
121 *Cf.* Michael D. Green, *Symposium, Flying Trampolines and Falling Bookcases: Understanding the Third Restatement of Torts*, 37 Wm. Mitchell L. Rev. 1011, 1015 (2010).
122 Diane P. Wood, *Sex Discrimination in Law and Life*, U. Chicago L. Forum 5 (1999); and Karen Czapanskiy, *Domestic Violence, the Family, and the Lawyering Process: Lessons from Studies on Gender Bias in the Courts*, 27 Fam. L. Q. 247, 252–53 (1993).
123 Mayo Moran, *The Reasonable Person: A Conceptual Biography in Comparative Perspective*, 14 Lewis & Clark L. Rev. 1233, 1243–49 (2010) (hereafter *The Reasonable Person*).
124 12 N.W. 155 (Mich. 1882).
125 *Id.* at 157 (emphasis added).
126 These cases are *Grodin v. Grodin*, 310 N.W.2d 869 (Mich. Ct. App. 1981); *Stallman v. Youngquist*, 531 N.E.2d 355 (Ill. 1988); *Bonte v. Bonte*, 616 A.2d 464 (N.H. 1992); *Chenault v. Huie*, 989 S.W.2d 474 (Tex. App. 1999); *Nat'l Cas. Co. v. N. Trust Bank of Fla., N.A.*, 807 So. 2d 86 (Fla. Dist. Ct. App. 2001); and *Remy v. MacDonald*, 801 N.E. 2d 260 (Mass. 2004).
127 *Stallman*, 531 N.E.2d 355; *National Casualty*, 807 So. 2d 86; and *Remy*, 801 N.E. 2d 260; are the cases in which the pregnant woman's driving was alleged to be negligent. In *Bonte*, 616 A.2d 464 (N.H. 1992), the pregnant woman was an allegedly negligent pedestrian.
128 *Grodin*, 301 N.W.2d 869, 869.
129 *Chenault*, 989 S.W.2d 474.
130 *Grodin*, 301 N.W. 2d 869.
131 *Bonte*, 616 A.2d at 466; *Nat'l Cas. Co.*, 807 So.2d at 87.
132 *Stallman v. Youngquist*, 531 N.E.2d 355.
133 *Id.* at 360.
134 *Id.* at 359–60.
135 Nancy S. Erickson, *Battered Mothers of Battered Children: Using Our Knowledge of Battered Women to Defend Them against Charges of Failure to Act*, 1A Current Perspectives in Psychological, Legal and Ethical Issues 197, 198 (1991) (hereafter *Battered Mothers of Battered Children*).
136 In cases in which women are prosecuted based on their asserted failure to act when they had a duty to act, this duty may be found in a specific statute or derived from the common law. *See, e.g., Lane v. Commonwealth*, 956 S.W.2d 874 (Ky. 1997), discussed in Lissa Griffin, *"Which One of You Did It?" Criminal Liability for*

"*Causing or Allowing*" *the Death of a Child*, 15 Ind. Int'l & Comp. L. Rev. 89 (2004) (hereafter "*Which One of You Did It?*"). *See also* Erickson, *supra* n. 135, at 198–203.

137 Third Restatement of Torts § 6, Negligence. Even then, foreseeability will not always be enough to impose liability, because of other policy considerations, *see, e.g.*, W. Jonathan Cardi, *Purging Foreseeability: The New Vision of Duty and Judicial Power in the Proposed Restatement (Third) of Torts*, 58 Vand. L. Rev. 739, 762–67 (2005). *See also*, Dressler, *supra* n. 86, at 204, noting that "foreseeability is a matter of considerable significance in proximate-causation analysis," though its application also depends on the circumstances of an asserted intervening cause.

138 *Cf.* Jo Goodie, *Toxic Tort and the Articulation of Environmental Risk*, 12 Law/Text/Culture 69, 73, 78 (2008); and Anderson, *supra* n. 23, at 90.

139 Model Penal Code, *supra* n. 2, § 2.03 (1); *see also* Dressler, *supra* n. 86, at 196, 201, 204.

140 This was the basic premise of Christopher Columbus Langdell, the originator of the "case method" of legal analysis and the founder of "modern" legal education. *See* Laura I. Appleman, *The Rise of the Modern American Law School: How Professionalization, German Scholarship, and Legal Reform Shaped Our System of Legal Education*, 39 New Eng. L. Rev. 251, 252 (2005).

141 Restatement (Third) of Torts: Liability for Physical and Emotional Harm §34, *Intervening Acts and Superseding Causes*, Comment a (emphasis in original).

142 In the criminal law context the Model Penal Code relies on foreseeability as a means of determining proximate cause. *See, e.g.*, MPC § 2.03 (3), which asks whether the defendant was aware, or should have been aware, of the risk that materialized, or that the foreseeable risk differed in that it was a different person or property injured or affected than foreseen, or that the harm foreseen was more severe than that which materialized. The authors of the Third Restatement of Torts acknowledge that the role of proximate cause in setting limits on tort liability has evolved since the advent of comparative negligence and other doctrines for apportioning liability, and that the concept of foreseeability is highly malleable. In some jurisdictions foreseeability is the touchstone for determining proximate cause. Third Restatement of Torts: § 34, Comments a, c, and d.

143 *See, e.g.*, *People v. Brady*, 29 Cal. Rptr. 3d 286 (Cal. Ct. App. 1st Dist., Div. 3 2005).

144 Dressler, *supra* n. 86, at 195–96.

145 See Hetcher, *supra* n. 88, at 642–46.

146 Chamallas and Wriggins, The Measure of Injury, *supra*, 122–23.

147 Dressler, *supra* n. 86, at 201 (emphasis in original).

148 Eric A. Johnson, *Knowledge, Risk and Wrongdoing: The Model Penal Code's Forgotten Answer to the Riddle of Objective Probability*, 59 Buffalo L. Rev. 507, 509–12 (2011) (hereafter *Knowledge, Risk and Wrongdoing*).

149 Chamallas and Wriggins, *supra* n. 146, at 124.

150 Erickson, *supra* n. 135, at 197–98 and 205.

151 Alternatively, the prosecution may assert that the mother failed to meet her duty of providing medical care when she returned and found her child injured. Erick-

son, *supra* n. 135, at 200–2, citing *State v. Atkins*, 125 Cal. Rptr. 855 (Cal. App. 1975), and *State v. Williquette*, 385 N.W.2d 145 (Wis. 1986).

152 This evidence can support a finding that the mother was criminally culpable when she failed to act to remove the child from harm. *See, e.g., Commonwealth v. Cardwell*, 515 A.2d 311 (Pa. Super. 1986); *see also* Michelle S. Jacobs, *Criminal Law: Requiring Battered Women Die: Murder Liability for Mothers Under Failure to Protect Statutes*, 88 J. Crim. L. & Criminology 579, 585 (1998) (hereafter *Requiring Battered Women Die*).

153 Chung, *Mama Mia, supra* (chapter 1, n. 62) at 213–14; Dorothy E. Roberts, *Is There Justice In Children's Rights? The Critique of Federal Family Preservation Policy*, 2 U. Pa. J. Const. L. 112, 117 (1999).

154 Private nuisance law evolved significantly during the nineteenth century, changing in response to the economic interests of industrialists. Morton J. Horowitz, *The Transformation of American Law, 1780–1860*, 74–76 (Harvard University Press, 1977 4th printing 1981).

155 *Id.* at 76–78; Restatement of Torts (Second) § 821C.

156 For the ruminations of this paragraph I am indebted to Robert V. Percival et al., Environmental Regulation: Law, Science, and Policy 178–96 (Aspen Publishers, 5th ed. 2006). *See also* Zygmunt J. B. Plater et al., "A Short Historical Sketch of the Evolution of U.S. Environmental Law," at 3, in *Environmental Law and Policy: Nature, Law and Society* (Aspen Publishers, 4th ed. 2010); and Gordon Morris Bakken, *Lawyers in the American West, 1820–1920: A Comment*, 1 Nev. L. J. 88, 96–97 (2001).

157 Plater, *supra* n. 156, at 3; and Matthew Warren, *Note, Active Judging: Judicial Philosophy and the Development of the Hard Look Doctrine in the D.C. Circuit*, 90 Geo. L. J. 2599, 2605 (2002).

158 The precise contours of the precautionary principle are not well defined. It first gained international environmental recognition in Principle 15 of the Rio Declaration of 1992, which stated, "Where there are threats of serous or irreversible damage, lack of full scientific certainty shall not be used as a reason for postponing cost-effective measures to prevent environmental degradation.'" Robert V. Percival, *Who's Afraid of the Precautionary Principle?, supra* n. 108, at 21–24. *See also* Cass R. Sunstein, *The Paralyzing Principle*, Regulation 32 (Winter 2002–8).

159 541 F.2d 1 (D.C. Cir. 1976) (*en banc*) (interpreting § 211 (c) (1) (A) of the Clean Air Act, focusing on the meaning of "will endanger").

160 *Id.* at 8.
161 *Id.* at 11–12.
162 *Id.* at 12–13.
163 *Id.* at 8–9.
164 *Id.* at 13–17.
165 Powell's memo is available at http://law2.wlu.edu/deptimages/Powell%20Archives/PowellMemorandumTypescript.pdf (last visited Aug. 24, 2016).
166 448 U.S. 607 (1980).

167 This observation is suggested by Percival, *supra* n. 156, at 183–96.
168 Pub. L. 91–596, Dec. 29, 1970, 84 Stat. 1590, embodied in 29 U.S.C. § 651 *et seq.*
169 448 U.S. at 639–43.
170 This observation is suggested by Percival, *supra* n. 156, at 183–96.
171 Adam Liptak, *The Polarized Court*, N.Y. Times, May 11, 2014 at SR1.
172 Mitch Smith, *As Flint Fought to Be Heard, Distant Lab Sounded Alarm*, N.Y. Times, Feb. 7, 2016, at A12.

CHAPTER 3. HOW HEALTHY ARE AMERICA'S CHILDREN?

1 *See, e.g.*, Woolf and Aron, *Shorter Lives* 2–6 (chapter 1, n. 25); Gopal K. Singh et al., *Persistent Socioeconomic Disparities in Infant, Neonatal, and Postneonatal Mortality Rates in the United States, 1969–2001*, 119 Pediatrics e928, 928–33, 937 (2007) (hereafter *Persistent Socioeconomic Disparities*); Foundation for Child Development, 2012 National Child and Youth Well-Being Index (CWI) 2 (2012).
2 Howson, *Born Too Soon* 1, 4, 81–86 (chapter 1, n. 21).
3 Michael Kelly, *The 1992 CAMPAIGN: The Democrats—Clinton and Bush Compete to Be Champion of Change; Democrat Fights Perception of Bush Gain*, N.Y. Times, Oct. 31, 1992, at A1. Anyone who is concerned about children's health must acknowledge, along with the American Academy of Pediatrics, that the biggest single determinant of children's health status and health outcome is whether they were born into, and continue to live, in poverty. *See, e.g.*, Charles P. Larson, *Poverty During Pregnancy*, 673 (chapter 2, n. 75); and Kemp, *Poverty Threatens Health of U.S. Children* (chapter 2, n. 85).
4 Julian Laubenthal et al., *Cigarette Smoke–induced Transgenerational Alterations in Genome Stability in Cord Blood of Human F1 Offspring*, 26 Fed'n Am. Societies for Experimental Biology (Faseb) J. 3946, 3953–54 (October 2012), available at http://www.fasebj.org/content/26/10/3946.full.pdf.(hereafter *Cigarette Smoke–induced Transgenerational Alterations in Genome Stability*).
5 "Most women are infected with HIV through heterosexual sex." Centers for Disease Control, *HIV Among Women*, http://www.cdc.gov/hiv/topics/women/ (last visited Aug. 23, 2012).
6 *See, e.g.*, Benedict Carey, *Study Finds Risk of Autism Linked to Older Fathers*, N.Y. Times, Aug. 23, 2012, at A1; Judith Shulevitz, *Why Fathers Really Matter*, N.Y. Times, Sept. 9, 2012, SR 1; Benjamin M. Neale et al., *Patterns and Rates of Exonic De Novo Mutations in Autism Spectrum Disorders*, Nature 2012, doi:10.1038/nature11011; Stephen J. Sanders et al., *De Novo Mutations Revealed by Whole-Exome Sequencing Are Strongly Associated with Autism*, Nature 2012, doi: 10.1038/nature10945.
7 Agency for Toxic Substances And Disease Registry, Case Studies in Environmental Medicine (CSEM), Principles of Pediatric Environmental Health. The Child as Susceptible Host: A Developmental Approach to Pediatric Environmental Medicine (Feb. 15, 2012) (hereafter Pediatric Environmental Health), http://www.atsdr.cdc.gov/csem/ped_env_health/docs/ped_env_health.pdf (last visited Aug. 30,

2013); *see also* Sharon Drozdowsky and Stephen G. Whittaker, Workplace Hazards to Reproduction and Development: A Resource for Workers, Employers, Health Care Providers, and Health & Safety Personnel, Washington State Dep't of Labor (Aug. 1999) (hereafter Workplace Hazards).
8   Woolf and Aron, *Shorter Lives*, at 170.
9   Inna Gaisler-Salomon, *Inheriting Stress*, N.Y. Times Sunday Review, March 7, 2014.
10 National Center for Health Statistics, Health, United States 2014: With Special Features on Adults Aged 55–64, Table 16, p. 85 (2015); *see also* Elizabeth Arias, *Changes in Life Expectancy by Race and Hispanic Origin in the United States, 2013–2014, supra* (chapter 1, n. 14).
11 Elizabeth Arias, *United States Life Tables, 2010*, cdc.gov, at 45–46 (Nov. 6, 2014), http://www.cdc.gov/nchs/data/nvsr/nvsr63/nvsr63_07.pdf (noting an average life expectancy of 59.0 for children born in 1925 and a life expectancy of 68.8 for children born in 1953).
12 Woolf and Aron, *Shorter Lives*, at 22.
13 Donald G. McNeil, Jr., *U.S. Fares Badly in Early Births In Global Study: Higher Premature Rate*, N.Y. Times, May 3, 2012, at A1.
14 Howson, *Born Too Soon*, at 1, 17.
15 McNeil, *supra* note 13, and Annie E. Casey Foundation, Kids Count Data Center, at http://datacenter.kidscount.org/data/tables/18-preterm-births?loc=1&loct=2 (last visited Jul. 29, 2013).
16 Woolf and Aron, *Shorter Lives*, at 73.
17 *Id.*; *see also* Sally C. Curtin et al., *Recent Declines in Nonmarital Births in the United States* (Aug. 2014); CDC, NCHS Data Brief No. 162, available at http://www.cdc.gov/nchs/data/databriefs/db162.pdf (last visited Aug. 26, 2016).
18 Joyce A. Martin et al., *Births: Final Data for 2010*, 61 (# 1) National Vital Statistics Reports 4–5, 8 (Aug. 28, 2012).
19 Denise Mann, *U.S. Teen Pregnancy Rate Continues to Fall*, HealthDay, June 20, 2012, available at http://consumer.healthdy.com/Article.asp?AID=665913 (last visited June 27, 2012); *see also* June Carbone and Naomi Cahn, *The Triple System for Regulating Women's Reproduction*, 43 J. Law, Med. & Ethics 275–82 (2015).
20 Centers for Disease Control, *Ten Great Public Health Achievements, United States, 1900–1999*, 48 Morbidity and Mortality Weekly Report 243–46 (Apr. 4, 1999) (hereafter CDC, *Ten Great Public Health Achievements 1900–1999*); and Ahmedin Jemal et al., *Annual Report to the Nation on the Status of Cancer,1975–2009, Featuring the Burden and Trends in Human Papillomavirus (HPV)–Associated Cancers and HPV Vaccination Coverage Levels* 4 (2013), http://jnci.oxfordjournals.org/content/early/2013/01/03/jnci.djs491.full.pdf+html (*hereafter HPV-Associated Cancers*).
21 Kochanek, Deaths: Preliminary Data for 2009 (chapter 1, n. 20).
22 Singh, *supra* n. 1, at e929.
23 Central Intelligence Agency, World Fact-Book, https://www.cia.gov/library/publications/the-world-factbook/rankorder/2091rank.html (last visited Aug. 26, 2013); *see also* Woolf and Aron, *Shorter Lives*.

24 In 1994 the American Academy of Pediatrics launched its Back to Sleep campaign. Singh, *supra* n. 1, at e938. *See also* Carrie K. Shapiro-Mendoza, *Recent National Trends in Sudden, Unexpected Infant Deaths: More Evidence Supporting a Change in Classification or Reporting*, 163 Am. J. Epidemiology 762, 762–66 (2006). *See also* M. T. Neary et al., *Hypoxia at the Heart of Sudden Infant Death Syndrome?*, Pediatric Research 2013 Jul. 17, 2013; and M. H. Malloy, *Prematurity and Sudden Infant Death Syndrome: United States 2005–2007*, 33 J. Perinatology 470, 470, 473–74 (2013).

25 Kochanek, *supra* n. 21, at 6.

26 Julie Steenhuysen, *U.S. Baby's Cure From HIV Raises Hope, New Questions*, Reuters Mar. 4, 2013; Centers for Disease Control, HIV Among Pregnant Women, Children, and Infants in the United States, Dec. 2012, http://www.cdc.gov/hiv/pdf/risk_WIC.pdf (last visited Aug. 19, 2015).

27 *See* Daniel B. Fishbein et al., *New, and Some Not-so-New, Vaccines for Adolescents and Diseases They Prevent*, 121 Pediatrics, Supp. 1, 55, 58 (Jan. 2008) (hereafter *New, and Some Not-so-New, Vaccines*).

28 Centers for Disease Control, *Ten Great Public Health Achievements—United States, 2001–2010*, 60 Morbidity and Mortality Weekly Report 619, 620 (May 20, 2011) (hereafter CDC, *Ten Great Public Health Achievements 2001–2010*).

29 Centers for Disease Control, 10 Leading Causes of Death by Age Group, United States 2010, http://www.cdc.gov/wisqars/pdf/10LCID_All_Deaths_By_Age_Group_2010-1.pdf (last visited Aug. 26, 2013).

30 Woolf and Aron, *Shorter Lives*, at 69, 75–78.

31 CDC, *supra* n. 20 at 243–46; and CDC, *supra* n. 28, at 619.

32 Jeanne Van Cleave et al., *Dynamics of Obesity and Chronic Health Conditions among Children and Youth*, 303 JAMA 623 (Feb. 17, 2010).

33 Glenn Hess, *High Court Weighs EPA Mercury Rule*, 93 (18) Chemical and Engineering News 22–24, May 4, 2015, http://.cen.acs.org/articles/93/i18/High-Court-Weighs-EPA-Mercury.html?h=10000686 (last visited May 7, 2015).

34 Philip J. Landrigan et al., *Environmental Pollutants and Disease in American Children: Estimates of Morbidity, Mortality, and Costs for Lead Poisoning, Asthma, Cancer, and Developmental Disabilities*, 110 Environ. Health Perspectives 721, 721–23 (2002) (hereafter *Environmental Pollutants and Disease in American Children*).

35 Alan J. Zametkin et al., *Suicide in Teenagers: Assessment, Management, and Prevention*, 286 JAMA 3120, 3121 (Dec. 26, 2001) (hereafter *Suicide in Teenagers*); Centers for Disease Control, 10 Things to Know About New Autism Data, available at http://www.cdc.gov/features/dautismdata/index.html (last visited Aug. 19, 2015).

36 In 2011, 21.4 percent of American children lived in families below the federal poverty level. The Foundation for Child Development, National Child and Well-Being Index (CWI) *supra* n. 1 1, 12.

37 *See, e.g.*, Landrigan, *supra* n. 34, at 721; and Office of Environmental Justice, EPA, Environmental Justice, Children's Environmental Health and Other Distribu-

tional Considerations, Chapter 10 of Guidelines for Preparing Economic Analyses 10–20 (May 2014), http://yosemite.epa/gov/ee/epa/eerm.nsf/vwAN/EE-0568-10.pdf/sfile/EE-0568-10.pdf (last visited Aug. 27, 2015).
38 Pediatric Environmental Health, *supra* n. 7, at 29.
39 Abigail English et al., *Clinical Preventative Services for Adolescents: Position Paper of the Society for Adolescent Medicine*, 35 Am. J. L. and Med. 351, 352–53 (2009).
40 *See* Minal R. Patel et al., *Perceived Parent Financial Burden and Asthma Outcomes in Low-Income, Urban Children*, 90 J. Urban Health 329 (2012).
41 Head-off Environmental Asthma in Louisiana (HEAL) Project, http://heal.niehs.nih.gov/ (last visited Sept. 4, 2013); *see also* Landrigan, *supra* n. 34, at 723.
42 President's Task Force on Environmental Health Risks and Safety Risks to Children, Coordinated Federal Action Plan to Reduce Racial and Ethnic Asthma Disparities, at x (May 2012).
43 Woolf and Aron, *Shorter Lives*, at 5, 28.
44 Margot Sanger-Katz, *America Starts to Push Away from the Plate*, N.Y. Times, July 26, 2015, at A1.
45 Dan Glickman et al., Accelerating Progress in Obesity Prevention: Solving the Weight of the Nation 1 (Institute of Medicine 2012).
46 Woolf and Aron, *Shorter Lives*, at 3, 61.
47 Jess Alderman et al., *Application of Law to the Childhood Obesity Epidemic*, 35 J. L., Med. & Ethics 90, 92–100 (Spring 2007); Woolf and Aron, *Shorter Lives*, at 61.
48 Melissa Mitgang, *Childhood Obesity and State Intervention: An Examination of the Health Risks of Pediatric Obesity and When They Justify State Involvement*, 44 Colum. J. L. & Soc. Probs. 553, 554 (2011); *see also* Woolf and Aron, *Shorter Lives*, at 71.
49 Glickman, *supra* n. 45, at 1; *see also* P. K. Newby, *Are Dietary Intakes and Eating Behaviors Related to Childhood Obesity? A Comprehensive Review of the Evidence*, 35 J. L., Med. & Ethics 35, 35 (Spring 2007).
50 Thomas L. Hafemeister, *Castles Made of Sand?* (chapter 1, n. 55) at 822–24; and Kathleen Noonan et al., *Legal Accountability in the Service-Based Welfare State: Lessons from Child Welfare Reform*, 34 Law & Soc. Inquiry 523, 526 (2009) (hereafter *Legal Accountability in the Service-Based Welfare State*); *see also* Child Maltreatment 2014, *supra*, at 21.
51 Hafemeister, *supra* n. 50, at 824–25, 830–45; and Noonan, *supra* n. 50, at 527–30.
52 Hafemesiter, *supra* n. 50, at 823–24. In one study, 84 percent of women seeking substance abuse treatment had a history of violent assault or PTSD. Susan R. B. Weiss et al., *Emerging Issues in Gender and Ethnic Differences in Substance Abuse and Treatment*, 3 Current Women's Health Reports 245, 247 (2003) (hereafter *Gender and Ethnic Differences in Substance Abuse and Treatment*). In a study of twins in the general population, women who had experienced sexual abuse as girls were three times more likely to become alcohol- or drug-dependent as adults. Patrick Zickler, *Childhood Sex Abuse Increases Risk for Drug Dependence in Adult Women*, 17 (No. 1) NIDA Notes (Apr. 2002), citing K. S. Kendler et al., *Childhood Sexual*

Abuse and Adult Psychiatric and Substance Abuse Disorders in Women: An Epidemiological and Co-Twin Control Analysis, 57 Archives of Gen. Psychiatry 953–59 (2000).
53 Firearm and Injury Center at Penn, Firearm Injury in the U.S. 32 (2011), available at ficap.uphs.upenn.edu.
54 CDC, *Ten Great Public Health Achievements 2001–2010*, supra n. 28, at 621; *see also* Karen Bouffard, *Lead Poisoning Declines*, Detroit News, Jan. 31, 2009, at A3.
55 William Wheeler and Mary Jean Brown, *Blood Lead Levels in Children Aged 1–5 Years: United States, 1999–2010*, 62 MMWR 245, 245 (2013) (hereafter *Blood Lead Levels in Children Aged 1–5 Years*); *see also* Associated Press, *Lead Poisoning Rates Rise in U.S. After CDC Lowers Blood Cutoff*, Apr. 5, 2013.
56 Low Level Lead Exposure Harms Children (chapter 1, n. 69); *see also* Denno, *Lead Poisoning as a Criminal Defense*, at 396 (chapter 1, n. 74).
57 Hess, *supra* n. 33.
58 Wendy Thomas, *Through the Looking Glass: A Reflection on Current Mercury Regulation*, 29 Colum. J. Envtl. L. 145, 147–55 (2004); *see also* Kathryn J. Kitzmiller, *The Not-So-Mad Hatter: Occupational Hazards of Mercury*, https://www.cas.org/news/insights/science-connections/mad-hatter (last visited Aug. 10, 2016).
59 The Supreme Court invalidated these regulations in *Michigan v. EPA*, 135 S.Ct. 2699 (2015). *See also* 76 FR 24976-01, 24977–80 (2011) (noting that "[c]hildren, and, in particular, developing fetuses, are especially susceptible to MeHg effects because their developing bodies are more highly sensitive to its effects").
60 Thomas, *supra* n. 58, at 159–67.
61 Hess, *supra* n. 33.
62 Donna S. Eng et al., *Bispheonol A and Chronic Disease Risk Factors in US Children*, 132 Pediatrics e637 (Sept. 2013); and Leonardo Trasande et al., *Association Between Urinary Bisphenol A Concentration and Obesity Prevalence in Children and Adolescents*, 308 JAMA 1113 (Sept. 19, 2012); Marija Kundakovic et al., *Sex-Specific Epigenetic Disruption and Behavioral Changes Following Low-Dose in Utero Bisphenol A Exposure*, PNAS Early Edition 1 (2013), available at pnas.org/cgi/doi/10.1037/pnas.1214056110; *see also* Jennifer T. Wolstenhome et al., *Gestational Exposure to Bisphenol A Produces Transgenerational Changes in Behaviors and Gene Expression*, 153 Endocrinology 3828 (Aug. 2012); *see* 77 FR 41899, http://www.gpo.gov/fdsys/pkg/FR-2012-07-17/pdf/2012-17366.pdf; *see also* Sabrina Tavernise, *F.D.A. Makes It Official: BPA Can't Be Used in Baby Bottles and Cups*, N.Y. Times, July 18, 2012, at A15.
63 Claire D. Brindis et al., *The Unique Health Care Needs of Adolescents*, 13 (1) The Future of Children 117, 117 (2002).
64 *Id.*
65 CDC, *Ten Great Public Health Achievements 2001–2010*, supra n. 28, at 621.
66 *See* Laura Bach, *How Parents Can Protect Their Kids from Becoming Addicted Smokers*, Campaign for Tobacco-Free Kids (May 28, 2015), https://www.tobaccofreekids.org/research/factsheets/pdf/0152.pdf; *See also* J. E. Milam et al., *Perceived*

Invulnerability and Cigarette Smoking among Adolescents, 25 Addictive Behaviors 71–80 (2000).
67 Sabrina Tavernise, *In All Flavors, Cigars Draw in Young Smokers*, N.Y. Times, Aug. 18, 2013, at A1.
68 *See* Priscilla Callahan-Lyon, *Electronic Cigarettes: Human Health Effects*, 23 Tobacco Control ii36, ii36–37 (2014), http://tobaccocontrol.bmj.com/content/23/suppl_2/ii36.full.pdf+html; *see also* cdc.gov, Press Release, *More Than a Quarter-million Youth Who Had Never Smoked a Cigarette Used E-cigarettes in 2013* (Aug. 25, 2014), http://www.cdc.gov/media/releases/2014/p0825-e-cigarettes.html (last visited Aug. 30, 2015); cdc.gov, Press Release, *E-cigarette Use Triples among Middle and High School Students in Just One Year* (Apr. 16, 2015), http://www.cdc.gov/media/releases/2015/p0416-e-cigarette-use.html.
69 Brindis, *supra* n. 63; Alan J. Zametkin et al., *Suicide in Teenagers*, *supra* n. 35, at 3121; CDC, 10 Leading Causes of Death by Age Group, United States 2010, *supra* n. 25.
70 Amy T. Schalet, *Beyond Abstinence and Risk: A New Paradigm for Adolescent Sexual Health*, 21–3S, S5, S5 (2011); Joyce C. Abma et al., Centers for Disease Control, National Center for Health Statistics, *Teenagers in the United States: Sexual Activity, Contraceptive Use, and Childbearing, National Survey of Family Growth 2006-08* 1–3 (June 2010); and Gilda Siegh et al., *Adolescent Pregnancy, Birth, and Abortion Rates Across Countries: Levels and Recent Trends*, 56 J. Adolesc. Health 223, 226 (2015), available at http://www.sciencedirect.com/science/article/pii/S1054139X14003875(last visited Aug. 26, 2016).
71 *See, e.g.*, Shanta R. Dube et al., *Childhood Abuse, Household Dysfunction, and the Risk of Attempted Suicide Throughout the Life Span*, 286 JAMA 3089 (2001); and Weiss, *Gender and Ethnic Differences in Substance Abuse and Treatment*, *supra* n. 52, at 247.
72 *See* Betsy McAlister Groves, *Mental Health Services for Children Who Witness Domestic Violence*, 9 Domestic Violence & Children 122, 122–23 (1999).
73 Brindis, *supra* note 63, at 117–24; English, *supra* note 39; and Butler Center for Research, Research Update: Substance Abuse, Dependence, and Mental Health Severity among Lesbian, Gay, Bisexual, Transgender, and Questioning (LGBTQ) individuals (Nov. 2013), available at https://archive.org/details/LGBTQresearch-Nov13 (last visited Aug. 26, 2016).
74 Paul W. Newacheck et al., *Trends in Private and Public Health Insurance for Adolescents*, 291 JAMA 1231, 1235 (2004).
75 Brindis, *supra* n. 63, at 117–24; *see also* Barry R. Furrow et al., Health Law: Cases, Materials and Problems 838–40 (West Publishing Corp., 7th ed. 2013); and Sara Rosenbaum et al., *Public Health Insurance Design for Children: The Evolution from Medicaid to SCHIP*, 1 J. Health & Biomed. L. 1 (2004).
76 See Ruqaiijah Yearby, *Breaking the Cycle of "Unequal Treatment" with Health Care Reform: Acknowledging and Addressing the Continuation of Racial Bias*, 44 Conn. L. Rev. 1281, 1315 (2012).

77 Newacheck, *supra* n. 74, at 1236; Kaiser Commission on Medicaid and the Uninsured, Health Coverage of Children: The Role of Medicaid and CHIP (July 2012), www.kff.org.
78 132 S. Ct. 2566 (2012).
79 Gardiner Harris and Abby Goodnough, *Obama Takes Health Care Momentum into G.O.P. Territory*, N.Y. Times, July 1, 2015, at A17. *See also* John Holahan et al., The Cost of Not Expanding Medicaid, Kaiser Commission on Medicaid and the Uninsured (July 2013), www.kff.org (last visited Aug. 8, 2013).

CHAPTER 4. CONCEPTIONS OF RISK

1 Joan B. Wolf, *Is Breast Really Best?*, *supra* (chapter 1, n. 27), at 611 and 620.
2 410 U.S. 113 (1973).
3 Lynn M. Paltrow and Jeanne Flavin, *Arrests of and Forced Interventions on Pregnant Women in the United States, 1973–2005: Implications for Women's Legal Status and Public Health*, 38 J. Health Politics, Pol'y and L. 299, 316–18 (2013) (hereafter *Arrests of and Forced Interventions on Pregnant Women*).
4 Today, A Child Is Born is in its fourth edition and is a bestseller worldwide. For a fuller discussion of the impact of this visual separation of the fetus from the pregnant woman, see E. Ann Kaplan, *Look Who's Talking, Indeed: Fetal Images in Recent North American Visual Culture*, 121, 125–28, in Mothering, Ideology, Experience, and Agency (Evelyn Nakano Glenn, Grace Chang, and Linda Rennie Forcey, eds. 1994).
5 In 1999, *USA Today* showed a photograph of a twenty-two-week-old fetus' hand reaching outside the uterus during fetal surgery. Robert Davis, *Spinal Surgery in Womb Tests Faith, Technology*, USA Today, Dec. 13, 1999, at D7; *see also* Murkoff and Mazel, What to Expect®, *supra*, at 66 (chapter 2, n. 69).
6 Rita Kempley, *They Grin Before They Bear It: Peek-A-Boo: Prenatal Portraits for the Ultrasound Set*, Washington Post, Aug. 9, 2003, at C01.
7 Linda L. Layne, Motherhood Lost: A Feminist Account of Pregnancy Loss in America, 81, 85, 88 New York (Routlege, 2003).
8 Jeremy W. Peters, *G.O.P. Rethinks the Way It Talks about Abortion*, N.Y. Times, July 27, 2015, at A1.
9 *Stuart v. Camnitz*, 774 F.3d 238 (4th Cir. 2014), *cert. denied Walker-McGill v. Stuart*, 135 S. Ct. 1838 (2015) (striking down North Carolina's ultrasound requirement as unconstitutional).
10 *Cf.* Kaplan, *supra* n. 4, at 132; *see also Commonwealth v. Morris*, 142 S.W. 3d 654, 655–57 (Ky. 2004).
11 Ken L. Bassett et al., *Defensive Medicine During Hospital Obstetrical Care: A By-Product of the Technological Age*, 51 Soc. Sci. & Med. 523, 530 (2000).
12 138 Mass. 14, 15, 17; 52 Am. Rep. 242 (Ma. 1884).
13 65 F. Supp. 138, 142 (D.D.C. 1946).
14 Jill D. Washburn Helbling, *Note, to Recover or Not to Recover: A State by State Survey of Fetal Wrongful Death Law*, 99 W. Va. L. Rev. 363, 364–65 (1996); *see, e.g., Smith v. Brennan*, 157 A.2d 497 (N.J. 1960).

15 Bassett, *supra* n. 11. This view is beginning to regain currency. Howson, *Born Too Soon*, *supra*, at 33.
16 Bassett, *supra* n. 11.
17 *Id.* at 530 (citing research showing that electronic fetal monitoring has not proven better than nurses' using stethoscopes in identifying fetuses at risk of oxygen deprivation ["fetal distress"]).
18 Roni Caryn Rabin, *Weighted Toward C-Sections*, N.Y. Times, Jan. 12, 2016, at D4.
19 Rhoden, *The Judge in the Delivery Room*, at 1955 (chapter 1, n. 28); Helen I. Marieskind, *Cesarean Section in the United States: Has It Changed Since 1979?*, 16 Birth 196, 196 (1989); Joyce A. Martin et al., *Births: Final Data for 2013*, 64 National Vital Statistics Reports 2, 7 (Jan. 15, 2015); Luz Gibbons et al., *The Global Numbers and Costs of Additionally Needed and Unnecessary Caesarean Sections Performed per Year: Overuse as a Barrier to Universal Coverage*, World Health Report, Background Paper No. 30, 7 (2010), available at http://www.who.int/healthsystems/topics/financing/healthreport/30C-sectioncosts.pdf.
20 Ernest L. Abel and Michael Kruger, *Physician Attitudes Concerning Legal Coercion of Pregnant Alcohol and Drug Abusers*, 186 Am. J. Obstetrics & Gynecology 768, 769–71 (2002); Stephen D. Brown et al., *Do Differences in the American Academy of Pediatrics and the American College of Obstetricians and Gynecologists Position on the Ethics of Maternal–Fetal Interventions Reflect Subtly Divergent Professional Sensitivities to Pregnant Women and Fetuses?*, 117 Pediatrics 1382, 1382–87 (2006); *cf.* ACOG AAP Committee Opinion 501, *supra* (chapter 1, n. 49).
21 Oster, Expecting Better, *supra*, at xii, xvi, xvii–xviii, 35–39 (chapter 2, n. 69); Linda Geddes, *Telling Pregnant Women to Drink No Alcohol Is Counterproductive*, The Guardian, Feb. 19, 2013, http://www.theguardian.com/science/2013/feb/19/advising-pregnant-women-drink-no-alcohol; Meghan Holohan, *New Study Shows No Harm from Moderate Drinking in Pregnancy, but Experts Urge Caution*, Today.com, Jan. 3, 2014, http://www.today.com/parents/new-study-shows-no-harm-moderate-drinking-pregnancy-experts-urge-2D11849699; Elizabeth M. Armstrong, Conceiving Risk, Bearing Responsibility: Fetal Alcohol Syndrome & the Diagnosis of Moral Disorder 205–7 (Johns Hopkins Univ. Press, 2003) (hereafter Conceiving Risk).
22 Center for Drug Evaluation and Research, FDA, *General Considerations for the Clinical Evaluation of Drugs* 7 (1997), available at http://www.fda.gov/downloads/ScienceResearch/SpecialTopics/WomensHealthResearch/UCM131186.pdf.
23 Janine A. Clayton and Francis S. Collins, *NIH to Balance Sex in Cell and Animal Studies*, 509 Nature 282, 282–83 (May 2014).
24 Michael B. Brimacombe et al., *Comparison of Fetal Demise Case Series Drawn from Socioeconomically Distinct Counties in New Jersey*, 26 Fetal and Pediatric Pathology 213, 214, 219–21 (2007); N. Tanya Nagahawatte and Robert L. Goldenberg, *Poverty, Maternal Health, and Adverse Pregnancy Outcomes*, 1136 Ann. N.Y. Acad. Sci. 80, 82–83 (2008); Katherine Harmon, *U.S. Stillbirths Still Prevalent, Often Unexplained*, Scientific American, Dec. 13, 2011; and *ACOG Issues New Guidelines on Managing Stillbirths*, Feb. 20, 2009, available at http://www.acog.org/About-

ACOG/News-Room/News-Releases/2009/ACOG-Issues-New-Guidelines-on-Managing-Stillbirths (last visited Sept. 5, 2016); *see also* 113 Obstet. & Gynecology 748–61 (2009); Melinda Wenner Moyer, *How Much Alcohol Is Safe for Expectant Mothers*, Scientific American Jan. 4, 2013.
25 Layne, *supra* n. 7, at 93–95.
26 Harmon, *supra* n. 24.
27 Nicholas Bakalar, *Pregnancy Rates Sank Over Last 20 Years*, N.Y. Times, July 3, 2012, at D7.
28 *Miscarriage*, Planned Parenthood (Jan. 25, 2014), http://www.plannedparenthood.org/health-topics/pregnancy/miscarriage-19894.htm.
29 Institute of Medicine, Preterm Birth: Causes, Consequences, and Prevention 1 (2007).
30 *Pregnancy Loss*, March of Dimes (Jan. 25, 2014), http://www.marchofdimes.com/loss/stillbirth.aspx.
31 Layne, *supra* n. 7, at 93–95; *see, e.g.*, Michelle Reese, *After Mom's Heart Procedure, Mesa Family Welcomes Miracle Baby*, East Valley Tribune (Mesa, Arizona), Sept. 16, 2012.
32 Anahad O'Connor, *Risks: Caffeine's Link to Birth Weight*, N.Y. Times, Feb. 26, 2013, at D4; Linda Searing, *Caffeine During Pregnancy Shows No Effect on Child Behavior in Study*, Washington Post, July 16, 2012; Oster, Expecting Better, *supra* n. 17, at 77–87, 135–46 (2013) (chapter 2, n. 69); *see also* sources cited in Christopher M. Burkle et al., *Punishing Maternal Behavior: Potential Legal Consequences for Obesity-Associated Poor Fetal Outcome in the United States*, 34 J. Legal Med. 251, 254, 269–70 (2013); Anahad O'Connor, *Health Officials Call for More Fish in Children and Pregnant Women*, N.Y. Times, June 11, 2014, at A14.
33 Oster, Expecting Better, *supra*, at xvii–xviii and 35–39.
34 Janice Humphreys et al., *Increasing Discussions of Intimate Partner Violence in Prenatal Care Using Video Doctor Plus Provider Cueing: A Randomized, Controlled Trial*, 21 Women's Health Issues 136, 136–37 (2011).
35 Chang, *Homicide: A Leading Cause of Injury Deaths among Pregnant and Postpartum Women*, *supra*, at 471–72 (chapter 2, n. 71).
36 Humphreys, *supra* n. 34, at 137; *see also* Nagahawatte and Goldenberg, *supra* n. 24.
37 The American College of Obstetricians and Gynecologists, Intimate Partner Violence, 518 Committee Opinion 3 (Feb. 2012), http://www.acog.org/-/media/Committee-Opinions/Committee-on-Health-Care-for-Underserved-Women/co518.pdf?dmc=1&ts=20150826T1416360065; *see also* Futures Without Violence, *The Facts on Health Care and Domestic Violence 2*, available at futureswithoutviolence.org/userfiles/file/HealthCAre/health-care.pdf (last visited Feb. 3, 2014), and Antonia Zerbisias, *Killings Reopen Debate on Rights of Fetuses*, Toronto Star, Oct. 10, 2007, at L1.
38 Perry Klass, *Poverty's Lasting Ills*, N.Y. Times, May 14, 2013, at D4; and Annie Lowrey, *50 Years Later, War on Poverty Is a Mixed Bag*, N.Y. Times, Jan. 5, 2014, at A1 and A4.

39 *See* Nagahawatte and Goldenberg, *supra* n. 24, at 81, 83–84; *cf.* Cara V. James, et al., *Putting Women's Health Care Disparities on the Map: Examining Racial and Ethnic Disparities at the State Level*, The Henry J. Kaiser Family Foundation, June 2009, at 62, available at http://kaiserfamilyfoundation.files.wordpress.com/2013/01/7886.pdf.

40 *Id.*; *see also* Singh et al., *Persistent Socioeconomic Disparities, supra*, at e937 (chapter 3, n. 1); and Paula Braverman et al., *Poverty, Near-Poverty, and Hardship around the Time of Pregnancy*, 14 Matern. Child Health J., 20, 20–21 (2010).

41 Jane Perkins, *Medicaid: Past Successes and Future Challenges*, 12 Health Matrix 7, 12 (2002).

42 Between 2008 and 2010, Medicaid paid for an average of 45 percent of American births. Anne Rossier Markus et al., *Medicaid Covered Births, 2008 Through 2010 in the Context of the Implementation of Health Reform*, 23 Women's Health Issues e273 (2013).

43 Eduardo Porter, *New Front in the Fight with Infant Mortality*, N.Y. Times, Oct. 23, 2013, B1, B2. Barely 70 percent of American women receive prenatal care in their first trimester of pregnancy. Nearly 12 percent of African-American women and 9 percent of Hispanic women lack prenatal care in their last trimester, compared with 5 percent of white women. National Bureau of Vital Statistics, *Expanded Data for the New Birth Certificate, 2008*, 59 National Vital Statistics Report 6–7 (July 27, 2011); *see also* David E. Hayes-Bautista et al., UCLA, Timely Access to Prenatal Care: Prime Necessity for Latina Mothers (2003).

44 132 S. Ct. 2566 (2012).

45 Hani K. Atrash et al., *Preconception Health Care for Improving Perinatal Outcomes: The Time to Act*, 10 Matern. Child Health J. S3, S4-S8 (2006); and Elizabeth Harrison et al., *Environmental Toxicants and Maternal and Child Health: An Emerging Public Health Challenge*, 1–4, 2009 (published by Women's and Children's Health Policy Center, Johns Hopkins Bloomberg School of Public Health).

46 Lawrence B. Finer and Stanley K. Henshaw, *Disparities in Rates of Unintended Pregnancy in the United States, 1994 and 2001*, 38 Persp. On Sexual and Reproductive Health 90, 90 (2006) (finding that 49 percent of pregnancies in American women aged fifteen to forty-four were unplanned, with unplanned pregnancy rates higher among those who are poorer, younger, less well educated, and African-American or Hispanic).

47 Sabrina Tavernise, *Fertility Rate Stabilizes as the Economy Grows*, N.Y. Times, Sept. 6, 2013, at A15 (citing study from National Center for Health Statistics).

48 Jason DeParle and Sabrina Tavernise, *Unwed Mothers Now a Majority Before Age 30*, N.Y. Times, Feb. 18, 2012, at A1.

49 Jill Davies, *Building Comprehensive Solutions to Domestic Violence: Policy Blueprint on Domestic Violence and Poverty*, Policy and Practice Paper 15, available at http://www.vawnet.org/Assoc_Files_VAWnet/BCS15_BP.pdf.

50 Singh et al., *Persistent Socioeconomic Disparities*, *supra*, at e937 (chapter 3, n. 1); *see also* Larson, *Poverty During Pregnancy*, at 673–74; Nagahawatte and Goldenberg, *supra* n. 24, at 80, 81–84.
51 Singh et al., *supra*, at e928, e929.
52 Howson, *Born Too Soon*, *supra*, at 12; and Press Release, Inst. of Med. of the Nat'l Acads., Preterm Births Cost U.S. $26 Billion a Year; Multidisciplinary Research Effort Needed to Prevent Early Births (July 13, 2006), available at http://www.nationalacademies.org/onpinews/newstem.aspx?RecordID=11622 (hereafter IOM Preterm Birth Report Press Release).
53 *Id.* at vii, 1, 9, 17; Christopher V. Almario et al., *Risk Factors for Preterm Birth Among Opiate-Addicted Gravid Women in a Methadone Treatment Program*, 201 Am. J. Obstetrics & Gynecology 326.e1, 326.e1 (2009).
54 IOM Preterm Birth Report Press Release, *supra* n. 52.
55 Nevada Maternal and Child Health Advisory Board, Maternal and Child Health Issue Brief: Access to Prenatal Care (Feb. 2009); *see also* Marian MacDorman et al., *Recent Trends in Out-of-Hospital Births*, 58 J. Midwifery and Women's Health 494, 495 (Sept.–Oct. 2013) (noting that low birth weight is defined as 2.5 kg or less).
56 Howson, *Born Too Soon*, *supra*, at 17 (chapter 1, n. 21), and IOM Preterm Birth Report Press Release, *supra* n. 52.
57 Gerd Gigerenzer et al., *Helping Doctors and Patients Make Sense of Health Statistics*, *supra* at 53 (chapter 2, n. 67); *see* Peter H. Schwartz and Eric M. Meslin, *The Ethics of Information: Absolute Risk Reduction and Patient Understanding of Screening*, J. Gen. Intern. Med. 867, 867–69 (2008).
58 Cass R. Sunstein, *The Laws of Fear* 5 (2005) (chapter 2, n. 19); *see also* Peter Bennett and Kenneth Calman, Risk Communication and Public Health 8–9, 29 (1999).
59 Neal Feigenson, *Legal Blame: How Jurors Think and Talk About Accidents* 51–57 (2000) (quoting John Stuart Mill, *A System of Logic* 469 [1864]).
60 Melissa L. Finucane et al., *The Affect Heuristic in Judgment of Risks and Benefits*, in Paul Slovic, *The Perception of Risk* 413, 414–416, 425–26 (2000).
61 Gerd Gigerenzer et al., *supra* n. 57, at 53, 54–56.
62 *See, e.g.*, Bassett, *supra* n. 11, at 530; Emily R. Carrier et al., *Physicians' Fears of Malpractice Lawsuits Are Not Assuaged by Tort Reforms*, 29 Health Affairs 1585, 1588–91 (2010); and Dorthe Fuglenes et al., *Obstetricians' Choice of Cesarean Delivery in Ambiguous Cases: Is It Influenced by Risk Attitude or Fear of Complaints and Litigation?*, 200 Am. J. Obstetrics & Gynecology 48.e1, e4–e6 (2009).
63 *See, e.g.*, Elliott M. Perlman, *Well-Managed Case Gets Caught in Malpractice Fervor*, Am. Med. News, Feb. 21, 1994; and Fuglenes et al., *supra* n. 62, at 48.e4; *see also* Bassett, *supra* n. 11, at 528–33.
64 Overall, American women are delaying having children and are having fewer of them. Judith Shulevitz, *The Grayest Generation*, The New Republic, Dec. 20,

2012, at 9, 9, 12; *see also* Sabrina Tavernise, *Fertility Rate Stabilizes as the Economy Grows*, N.Y. Times, Sept. 6, 2013, at A15.
65 Carrier, *supra* n. 62, at 1585, 1587; Helen I. Marieskind, *supra* n. 19, at 199; Dawn Durain, *Politics in the Nursing Room*, 37 Nursing Clinics of North America 795, 800 (2002); *see also* Armstrong, *supra* n. 21, at 135.
66 Abigail Zuger, *Good Care and Bad, All at Once*, N.Y. Times, Jan. 12, 2016 at D5.
67 American College of Obstetricians and Gynecologists, Committee on Ethics, Committee Opinion No. 321, *Maternal Decision Making, Ethics, and the Law*, 106 Obstetrics and Gynecology 1127, 1131 (2005) (hereafter ACOG Committee Opinion No. 321); *see also* Janice Blanchard and Nicole Lurie, *R-E-S-P-E-C-T: Patient Reports of Disrespect in the Health Care Setting and Its Impact on Care*, 53 J. Fam. Practice 721, 721, 727 (2004).
68 ACOG Committee Opinion No. 321, *supra* n. 67, and Ernest L. Abel and Michael Krugerer, *Physician Attitudes Concerning Legal Coercion of Pregnant Alcohol and Drug Abusers*, 186 Am. J. Obstetrics & Gynecology 768, 770–71 (2002).
69 Marian MacDorman et al., *Recent Trends in Out-of Hospital Births*, *supra* n. 54, at 495; *see also* Edmund G. Howe, *When a Mother Wants to Deliver with a Midwife at Home*, 24 J. Clinical Ethics 172 (2013); and Frank A. Chervenak et al., *Planned Home Birth in the United States and Professionalism: A Critical Assessment*, 24 J. Clinical Ethics 184 (2013).
70 MacDorman, *supra* n. 54; *see also* American College of Nurse Midwives, News Release, *New Analysis Reveals Women Choosing Midwife-Led, Out of Hospital Births at an Increasing Rate*, Sept. 24, 2013; and Marian MacDorman et al., *Trends and Characteristics of Home and Other Out-of-Hospital Births in the United States, 1990–2006*, 58 (#11) Nat'l Vital Statistics Reports 2, 6 (Mar. 3, 2010).
71 *See* Monica Campo, *Trust Power and Agency in Childbirth: Women's Relationships with Obstetricians*, 22 Outskirts Online J. (May 2010), http://www.outskirts.arts.uwa.edu.au/volumes/volume-22/campo.
72 *Ferguson v. City of Charleston, S.C.*, 532 U.S. 67 2001; *see also* April L. Cherry, *The Rise of the Reproductive Brothel in the Global Economy: Some Thoughts on Reproductive Tourism, Autonomy, and Justice*, 17 U. Pa. J.L. & Soc. Change 257, 266 (2014).
73 Lyerly, *Risk and the Pregnant Body*, *supra*, at 34–40 (chapter 1, n. 29).
74 Oster, *supra*, at 201–2.
75 Bassett, *supra* n. 11, at 525–33. In the United States, the caesarean section rates have increased from about 5 percent in 1965 to nearly 33 percent today. The rate increased every year from 1996 to 2009, peaking at 32.9 percent of all births. It is currently at 32.7 percent. *See, e.g.*, Rhoden, *The Judge in the Delivery Room*, at 1955; Marieskind, *supra* n. 19, at 196; Joyce A. Martin et al., *Births: Final Data for 2013*, 64 National Vital Statistics Reports 2, 7 (Jan. 15, 2015). In contrast, the World Health Organization recommends a C-section rate between 5 and 15 percent; most developed countries exceed that. T. A. Wiegers, *General Practitioners and Their Role in Maternity Care*, 66 Health Policy 51, 52 (2003).

76 Dan Frosch, *Refusals Cut Options after C-Sections*, N. Y. Times, Apr. 15, 2014, at D3.
77 Oster, *supra*, at 201–4. Sometimes physicians request that their patients agree to a definite time for labor induction. *Cf.* Heidi Murkhoff and Sharon Mazel, What to Expect®, *supra*, at 368, and Utah Dep't of Health, *Should I Schedule My Baby's Day of Birth*, accessed at http://health.utah.gov/mihp/pregnancy/preged/duringpreg/Birth_scheduling.html (Mar. 14, 2014).
78 Yvonne W. Cheng et al., *Second Stage of Labor and Epidural Use: A Larger Effect Than Previously Suggested*, Obstetrics & Gynecology 1, 7–8 (2014)
79 Rabin, *supra* n. 18.
80 *See, e.g.*, Erick Eckholm, *Case Explores Rights of Fetus Versus Mother*, N.Y. Times, Oct. 24, 2013, at A1; *see also* Michele Goodwin, *Fetal Protection Laws: Moral Panic and the New Constitutional Battlefront*, 102 Cal. L. Rev. 781, 806–8 (2014); and Michelle Oberman, *Mothers and Doctors' Orders: Unmasking the Doctor's Fiduciary Role in Maternal-Fetal Conflicts*, 94 Nw. U. L. Rev. 451, 474–82 (2000).
81 Eckholm, *supra*; *see also* Ira J. Chasnoff et al., *The Prevalence of Illicit-Drug or Alcohol Use During Pregnancy and Discrepancies in Mandatory Reporting in Pinellas County, Florida*, 322 New Eng. J. Med. 1201, 1202 (1990) (hereafter *Discrepancies in Mandatory Reporting in Pinellas County, Florida*).
82 ACOG AAP Committee Opinion 501, *supra*; Pam Belluck, *Risk and Reward in Utero*, N.Y. Times, Feb. 12, 2011 (describing successful fetal surgeries as well as the risks to mothers and the fetus); *see also* Anna Smajdor, *Ethical Challenges in Fetal Surgery*, 37 J. Med Ethics 88, 88–90 (2011); and Jan A. Deprest et al., *Fetal Surgery Is a Clinical Reality*, 15 Seminars in Fetal and Neonatal Med. 58, 58–59 (2010).
83 *Schloendorff v. Society of New York Hospital*, 105 N.E. 92, 93 (N.Y. 1914).
84 Barry R. Furrow et al., Health Law 310–11 (2d ed. 2000); Patient Self-Determination Act, 42 U.S.C. §1395cc (2012).
85 *Canterbury v. Spence*, 464 F. 2d 772, 780–88 (D.C. Cir. 1972); and *Truman v. Thomas*, 611 P.2d 902, 905–8 (Cal. 1980); *also see, e.g.*, N.Y. Pub. Health L. § 2805-d.
86 *Cruzan v. Director, Missouri Dep't. of Health*, 497 U.S. 261 (1990); *Washington v. Harper*, 494 U.S. 210 (1990); and *In re Dubreil*, 629 So. 2d 819 (Fla. 1993).
87 April Cherry, *The Detention, Confinement, and Incarceration of Pregnant Women for the Benefit of Fetal Health*, 16 Columbia Journal of Gender & Law 147 (2007).
88 201 A.2d 537, 538 (N.J. 1964).
89 *In re Jamaica Hospital*, 491 N.Y.S. 2d 898 (Sup. Ct. Special Term, Queens County 1985).
90 *See, e.g., In re Baby Boy Doe*, 632 N.E. 2d 326 (Ill. App. Ct. 1994).
91 *See Fosmire v. Nicoleau*, 551 N.E. 2d 77, 79 (N.Y. 1990) and *In re Fetus Brown*, 689 N.E. 2d 397, 399 (Ill. App. Ct. 1997).
92 *See, e.g., Stamford Hospital v. Vega*, 674 A.2d 821, 831–32 (Conn. 1996); *In re Fosmire v. Nicoleau*, 551 N.E. 2d at 83–84; and *In re Fetus Brown*, 689 N.E. 2d at 405.
93 *Jefferson v. Griffin Spalding County Hospital Authority*, 274 S.E. 2d 457, 458–59 (Ga. 1981).

94 *Id.* at 458–60; and Hill, P. J., concurring, 274 S.E. 2d at 461. *See also* Rhoden, *The Judge in the Delivery Room*, *supra*, at 1960, n. 60.
95 *Jefferson v. Griffin Spalding County Hospital Authority*, (Smith J., concurring), 274 S.E. 2d at 461.
96 *See, e.g.*, Oberman, *supra* n. 80, at 474–82; Lisa C. Ikemoto, *Furthering the Inquiry: Race, Class, and Culture in the Forced Medical Treatment of Pregnant Women*, 59 Tenn. L. Rev. 487, 511–12 (1992).
97 10 Pa. D. & C. 3d 90 (Allegheny County Ct. 1978).
98 566 N.E. 2d 1319 (Ill. 1990).
99 *In re A.C.*, 573 A.2d 1235, 1238–41 (D.C. Ct. App. 1990). One of the doctors testified that Ms. C. could understand the discussion of the C-section and, while on a respirator, mouthed the words, "I don't want it done." *Id.* at 1241.
100 Angela Carder's family reached a settlement with the George Washington University Medical Center that included not only money damages but also an agreement to change protocols in dealing with future patients like Ms. Carder. *Stoners v. George Washington University Hospital et al.*, No. 88–05433 (Sup. Ct. D.C. 1990).
101 *In re A.C.*, 573 A.2d 1235, at 1249.
102 ACOG Committee Opinion Number 501, *supra*, at 1, 3, and 5; ACOG Committee Opinion No. 321, *supra*, at 5, 9; American Medical Association, H-420.969, *Legal Interventions During Pregnancy* (reaffirmed 1999).
103 ACOG Committee Opinion Number 501, *supra*, at 2.
104 Abel and Kruger, *supra* n. 20; and Brown et al., *supra* n. 20.
105 *Husband to Challenge Court Order in Lawsuit Over Wife's Refusal of Caesarean Section*, Penn. L. Weekly, Jan. 26, 2004; Keyetv.com, *New Questions about Childbirth Rights*, Keyetv.comalth_story_140110423.html/resources_storyPrintableView (last visited Oct. 12, 2004).
106 Paltrow & Flavin, *supra* n. 3, at 307.
107 *Pemberton v. Tallahassee Memorial Regional Med. Center, Inc.*, 66 F. Supp. 2d. 1247, 1251 (N.D. Fla. Tallahassee Div. 1999).
108 Paltrow & Flavin, *supra* n. 3, at 307.
109 *Pemberton*, 66 F. Supp. 2d at 1251.
110 *Id.* at 1252.
111 *See, e.g.*, Oberman, *supra* n. 80.
112 550 U.S. 124, 132, 168 (2007). The medical name for the banned procedure, which is performed during the second trimester, is an "intact dilation and evacuation." *Id.* at 173.
113 *Id.* at 159–60.
114 *See, e.g.*, Margo Kaplan, *"A Special Class of Persons": Pregnant Women's Right to Refuse Medical Treatment after Gonzales v. Carhart*, 13 U. Pa. J. Const. L. 145, 176–79 (2010) (hereafter *"A Special Class of Persons"*).
115 *Burton v. State*, 49 So. 3d 263 (Fla. Dist. Ct. App. 2010).
116 *Id.* at 266.

117 *N.J. Div. of Youth & Family Servs. v. V.M. (In re J.M.G.)*, 974 A.2d 448, 450 (N.J. Super. Ct. App. Div. 2009) (per curium) (Carchman, J., concurring).
118 Jessica L. Waters, *In Whose Best Interest? New Jersey Division of Youth and Family Services v. V.M. and B.G. and the Next Wave of Court-Controlled Pregnancies*, 34 Harv. J. L & Gender 81, 106 (2011).
119 *Id.* at 86–87.
120 Hedy R. Bower, *How Far Can a State Go to Protect a Fetus? The Rebecca Corneau Story and The Case for Requiring Massachusetts to Follow the U.S. Constitution*, 31 Golden Gate L. Rev. 25 (Sept. 24, 2010); *Barbara F. v. Bristol Div. of Juvenile Court*, 735 N.E. 2d 357, 358 (Mass. 2000); Marilyn L. Miller, *Note: Fetal Neglect and State Intervention: Preventing Another Attleboro Cult Baby Death*, 8 Cardozo Women's L. J. 71, 71 (2001).
121 Paltrow and Flavin, *supra* n. 3, at 317.
122 *Id.*
123 Centers for Disease Control, HIV Among Pregnant Women, Children, and Infants in the United States, Dec. 2012, available at http://www.cdc.gov/hiv/pdf/risk_WIC.pdf (last visited Aug. 19, 2015).
124 Michael Ulrich, *With Child, Without Rights? Restoring a Pregnant Woman's Right to Refuse Medical Treatment Through the HIV Lens*, 24 Yale J. L. & Feminism 303, 321 (2012).
125 148 F. Supp. 2d 462 (D. N.J. 2001).
126 *See* New York Comp. Codes R. & Regs. tit. 10, § 69 (1997); *see also* Michael A. Stoto et al., Reducing the Odds: Preventing Perinatal Transmission of HIV In The United States (National Academy Press, 1999).
127 U.S. Dep't of Health & Human Services, Aidsinfo, *Recommendations for Use of Antiretroviral Drugs in Pregnant HIV-1-Infected Women for Maternal Health and Interventions to Reduce Perinatal HIV Transmission in the United States* (last updated Aug. 6, 2015), available at https://aidsinfo.nih.gov/guidelines/html/3/perinatal-guidelines/0.
128 Centers for Disease Control, *HIV among Pregnant Women, Children, and Infants in the United States*, Dec. 2012, *supra* n. 132.
129 Centers for Disease Control, *HIV among Women*, http://www.chdc.gov/hiv/topics/women (last visited Aug. 23, 2012).
130 Press Release, N.Y. Academy of Medicine, *Study in Academy's Journal of Urban Health Finds Condom Use Lagging in HIV Positive Injection Drug Users* (Oct. 9, 2007), http://www.nyam.org/news/press-releases/2007/2977.html.
131 In chronological order, the cases are *Grodin v. Grodin*, 310 N.W.2d 869 (Mich. Ct. App. 1981); *Stallman v. Youngquist*, 531 N.E.2d 355 (Ill. 1988); *Bonte v. Bonte*, 616 A.2d 464 (N.H. 1992); *Chenault v. Huie*, 989 S.W.2d 474 (Tex. App. 1999); *Nat'l Cas. Co. v. N. Trust Bank of Fla., N.A.*, 807 So. 2d 86 (Fla. Dist. Ct. App. 2001); and *Remy v. MacDonald*, 801 N.E. 2d 260 (Mass. 2004). A recent Wisconsin decision, *Tesar v. Anderson*, 789 N.W.2d 351 (Wis. App. 2010), raised a similar issue. The case involved a child who was stillborn after his pregnant mother was involved in

a car accident; both she and the driver of another car were alleged to have driven negligently. *Tesar* was a wrongful death lawsuit, a suit brought by survivors to recover compensatory damages for the loss of the deceased person, such as loss of consortium or support. *Black's Law Dictionary* (9th ed. 2009). In *Tesar*, the Court of Appeals of Wisconsin declined to draw a distinction in the wrongful death context between a fetus and a living child. *Id.* at 361–64.

132 *Stallman*, 531 N.E. 2d 355 (Ill. 1988), *National Casualty*, 807 So. 2d 86 (Fla. Dist. Ct. App. 2001), and *Remy*, 801 N.E. 2d 260 (Mass. 2004) are the cases in which the pregnant woman's driving was alleged to be negligent; in *Bonte*, 616 A.2d 464 (N.H. 1992), the pregnant woman was an allegedly negligent pedestrian.

133 *Grodin v. Grodin*, 301 N.W.2d 869, 869 (Mich. Ct. App. 1980).

134 *Chenault v. Huie*, 989 S.W. 2d 474 (Tex. App. 1999).

135 The three cases which found that lawsuits based on prenatal conduct by pregnant women could be brought were *Grodin v. Grodin*, 310 N.W.2d 869 (Mich. Ct. App. 1981); *Bonte v. Bonte*, 616 A.2d 464 (N.H. 1992); and *Nat'l Cas. Co. v. N. Trust Bank of Fla., N.A.*, 807 So. 2d 86 (Fla. Dist. Ct. App. 2001).

136 *Nat'l Cas. Co. v. N. Trust Bank of Fla., N.A.*, 807 So. 2d 86 (Fla. Dist. Ct. App. 2001) and *Grodin v. Grodin*, 310 N.W. 2d 869 (Mich. Ct. App. 1981), explicitly stated the goal of providing compensation for injuries as a rationale for their decisions. In *Bonte v. Bonte*, 616 A. 2d 464, 466 (N.H. 1992), this reasoning was implicit.

137 In *Grodin*, the Michigan Court of Appeal framed the question as a simple factual question for the jury: did the woman's Tetracycline use constitute a "reasonable exercise of parental discretion"? *Grodin*'s reasoning has been criticized by subsequent Michigan decisions. *See, e.g., Mayberry v. Pryor*, 134 Mich. App. 826 (1984), and *Thelin v. Thelin*, 174 Mich. App. 380 (1989).

138 The three cases that rejected the imposition of a tort duty on pregnant women based on alleged negligence while pregnant were *Stallman v. Youngquist*, 531 N.E.2d 355 (Ill. 1988); *Chenault v. Huie*, 989 S.W.2d 474 (Tex. App. 1999); and *Remy v. MacDonald*, 801 N.E. 2d 260 (Mass. 2004).

139 *Stallman v. Youngquist*, 531 N.E.2d 355, 359 (Ill. 1988).

140 *Id.*

141 *Remy v. MacDonald*, 801 N.E. 2d 260, 263 (Mass. 2004).

142 *United States v. Carroll Towing Co.*, 159 F. 2d 169, 173 (2d Cir. 1947). Judge Hand articulated the rule for determining negligence as follows: "[T]he owner's duty, as in other similar situations, to provide against resulting injuries is a function of three variables: (1) The probability that she will break away; (2) the gravity of the resulting injury, if she does; (3) the burden of adequate precautions. Possibly it serves to bring this notion into relief to state it in algebraic terms: if the probability be called P; the injury, L; and the burden, B; liability depends upon whether B is less than L multiplied by P: i.e., whether B less than PL."

143 Mayo Moran, *The Reasonable Person, A Conceptual Biography in Comparative Perspective*, 14 Lewis & Clark L. Rev. 1233, 1238–49, 1283 (2010); and Lu-in Wang,

Negotiating the Situation: The Reasonable Person in Context, 14 Lewis & Clark L. Rev. 1285, 1288 (2010).
144 *Remy* at 263, *Stallman* at 359–60, *Chenault* at 477.
145 *Stallman* at 359.
146 Fischhoff, *Hindsight ≠ Foresight, supra*, at 292–97 (1975) (citing Wohlstetter).
147 Daniel Kahneman, *Thinking, Fast and Slow* 13–14 (Farrar, Straus and Giroux, 2011).
148 *Chenault* at 478.
149 *Stallman*, 531 N.E. 2d at 360.
150 *Chenault* at 478, *Stallman* at 360.
151 *Stallman* at 359.
152 *Chenault v. Huie*, 989 S.W. 2d 474, at 478.
153 *Stallman*, 531 N.E. 2d at 361. See also Nancy K. Young et al., *Substance-Exposed Infants: State Responses to the Problem*, HHS Pub. No. (SMA) 09-4369 (2009) (hereafter *State Responses to Substance-Exposed Infants*); *cf.* Dorothy E. Roberts, *Punishing Drug Addicts Who Have Babies: Women of Color, Equality, and the Right of Privacy*, 104 Harv. L. Rev. 1419, 1445 (1991).
154 [1999] 2 S.C.R. 753 (Can.).
155 *Id.* at PP's 37–70, 77–80.
156 Pamela Manson, *Mother Is Charged in Stillborn Son's Death, supra* (chapter 1, n. 5); Linda Thomson and Pat Reavy, *Rowland's Out of Jail, Heading to Indiana*, Deseret Morning News, Apr. 30, 2004; Doug Smith and Linda Thomson, *Rowland in New Trouble*, Deseret Morning News, May 27, 2004.
157 *Commonwealth v. Pugh*, 960 N.E. 2d 672, 676–79 (MA. 2012).
158 *Id.* at 685–88.
159 *Id.* at 686.
160 *Id.* at 692, citing *Remy v. MacDonald*, 801 N.E. 2d 260 (2004).
161 *Id.* at 693.
162 See Amie Newman, *Help for Christine Taylor: Victim of Iowa's Feticide Law*, RH Reality Check (Feb. 25, 2010), http://rhrealitycheck.org/article/2010/02/25/help-christine-taylor-victim-iowas-feticide/.
163 Rood, *"I Never Said I Didn't Want My Baby," supra* (chapter 1, n. 7); and Mangalonzo, *Feticide Charges Dropped, supra* (chapter 1, n. 7).
164 Michele Goodwin, *Fetal Protection Laws: Moral Panic and the New Constitutional Battlefront*, 102 Cal. L. Rev. 781 (2014).
165 Charles Wilson (Associated Press), *Ind. Woman Rejects Plea Deal in Death of Newborn*, July 13, 2012, available at http://cnsnews.com/news/article/ind-woman-rejects-plea-deal-death-newborn.
166 *Id.*
167 *People v. Jorgensen*, 41 N.E. 3d 778 (N.Y. 2015), *rev'g* 978 N.Y. S. 2d 361 (App. Div., Dep't. 2014); *see also* pre-trial ruling in *People v. Jorgensen*, unpublished opinion at 907 N.Y.S. 2d 439, at *5 (2010).
168 410 U.S. 113, 163–65 (1973).

169 *Id.* at 158.
170 *See, e.g.*, Burwell v. Hobby Lobby Stores, Inc., 134 S. Ct. 2751 (2014), and *Whole Woman's Health v. Hellerstedt*, 136 S. Ct. 2292 (2016).
171 505 U.S. 833 (1992).
172 *Id.* at 852.
173 550 U.S. 124, 159 (2007).
174 *See* Kaplan, *supra* n. 122, at 176–80.
175 Although a Mississippi "personhood" initiative was defeated at the polls in 2011, other states and Congress are considering personhood initiatives. Other state laws seek to limit access to abortion on the ground that fetuses can experience pain, have heartbeats, and are otherwise "alive." *See* Dina Schoental Butcher, *The Personhood Debate*, N.Y. Times, July 5, 2014, at A18; Jeremy W. Peters and Michael D. Shear, *A Ruling That Both Sides Can Run With*, N.Y. Times, June 30, 2014, at A1; *see also* Anna Stolley Persky, *Reproductive Technology and the Law*, Washington Lawyer, July/Aug. 2012, at 27.
176 Fetal Homicide Laws, National Conference of State Legislatures, available at http://www.ncsl.org/research/health/fetal-homicide-state-laws.aspx#States%20 Laws (Mar. 2015) (last accessed Aug. 27, 2015); *see also* Unborn Victims of Violence Act, Pub. L. No. 108–212, 118 Stat. 568 (2004).
177 *Id.*; *see, e.g.*, Ala. Code 13A-6-1 (defining a "person" under the criminal law to include "an unborn child in utero at any stage of development, regardless of viability"), and Kansas Stat. Ann. § 21–5419 (West 2016). This fetal homicide law prohibits killing "an unborn child," defined as "a living individual organism of the species *Homo Sapiens* in utero, in any state of gestation from fertilization to birth."
178 *See, e.g.*, Deborah Tuerkheimer, *Conceptualizing Violence against Pregnant Women*, 81 Ind. L. J. 667, 694–97 (2006).
179 Justin Waddell, *Dead Letters: Protecting the Intentions of a Living Will Declarant with a Dedicated Advocate*, 25 Geo. J. Legal Ethics 801, 806 (2012).
180 *See, e.g.*, Brophy v. New England Sinai Hospital, 497 N.E. 2d 626 (Mass. 1986), and *Cruzan v. Director, Missouri Dep't of Health*, 497 U.S. 261 (1990).
181 Tex. Health & Safety Code § 166.049 (West 2016).
182 Megan Greene and Leslie R. Wolfe, *Pregnancy Exclusions in State Living Will and Medical Proxy Statutes* 1–5, Center for Women Policy Studies, Washington, D.C. (Aug. 2012).
183 Manny Fernandez and Erik Eckholm, *Pregnant and Forced to Stay on Life Support*, N.Y. Times, Jan. 8, 2014, at A1; Manny Fernandez, *Texas Woman Is Taken Off Life Support after Order*, N.Y. Times, Jan. 27, 2014, at A9; Jeffrey L. Ecker, *Death in Pregnancy—An American Tragedy*, 370 New Eng. J. Med. 889 (Feb. 5, 2014); and *Muñoz v. John Peter Smith Hospital*, Cause No. 096-270080-14 (District Ct., Tarrant County, Tex., 96th Judicial District, Jan. 24, 2014, Judge R. H. Wallace, Jr.).
184 Wade Goodwyn, "In Tight Texas Lt. Gov. Race, Little Space Left on the Right," All Things Considered, npr.org., Mar. 3, 2014.

185 See, e.g., Rachel Warren, *Pro [Whose?] Choice: How the Growing Recognition of a Fetus' Right to Life Takes the Constitutionality out of Roe*, 13 Chapman L. Rev. 221–22, 245–47 (2010).
186 *University Health Services v. Piazzi*, No. CV86-RCCV-464 (Superior Court of Richmond County, Ga., Aug. 4, 1986) discussed in Daniel Sperling, *Maternal Brain Death*, 30 Am. J. L. and Med. 453, 494–95 (2004); and James M. Jordan III, *Incubating for the State: The Precarious Autonomy of Persistently Vegetative and Brain-Dead Women*, 22 Ga. L. Rev. 1103, 1109–10 (1988).
187 Jordan, *supra* n. 186, at 1110, n. 25; *Baby Born to Brain-Dead Woman Dies*, Atl. J., Aug. 17, 1986, at 1-B.
188 United Press International, *Coma Mom Dies, then Baby—Dispute Over*, Orlando Sentinel (Aug. 17, 1986). http://articles.orlandosentinel.com/1986-08-17/news/0240370243_1_piazzi-drug-overdose-hadden.
189 *DiNino v. Washington*, 684 P. 2d 1297 (Wash. 1984); and *Gabrynowicz v. Heitkamp*, 904 F. Supp. 1061 (N.D. N. D. 1995).
190 See Stephen H. Miles and Allison August, *Courts, Gender, and the Right to Die*, 18 L. Med & Health Care 85 (1990) (finding that courts have historically treated men and women differently in regard to exercising self-determination about medical treatment).
191 573 A. 2d 1235.

CHAPTER 5. DRUG USE BY PREGNANT WOMEN
1 See, e.g., Young et al., *State Responses to Substance-Exposed Infants*, *supra* (chapter 4, n. 153), at 7.
2 The National Center on Addiction and Substance Abuse at Columbia University, Women Under the Influence (hereafter Women Under the Influence) 48–49 (2006).
3 U.S. Dep't Health & Hum. Serv., *The Health Consequences of Smoking: 50 Years of Progress: A Report of the Surgeon General* 17 (Jan. 2014), available at http://www.surgeongeneral.gov/library/reports/50-years-of-progress/full-report.pdf (hereafter HHS, *The Health Consequences of Smoking*).
4 John Rolfe, available at http://www.nps.gov/jame/historyculture/john-rolfe.htm (last visited June 9, 2014).
5 Mark Pendergrast, *Uncommon Grounds: The History of Coffee and How It Transformed Our World* (Basic Books, 2nd ed. 2010).
6 Ira J. Chasnoff et al., *The 4P's Plus© Screen for Substance Use in Pregnancy: Clinical Application and Outcomes*, 25 J. Perinatology 368, 373 (2005) (hereafter *The 4P's Plus© Screen*); Robert H. Nishimoto and Amelia C. Roberts, *Coercion and Drug Treatment for Postpartum Women*, 27 Am. J. Drug Alcohol Abuse 161, 175 (2001); and Linda M. Whiteford and Judi Vitucci, *Pregnancy and Addiction: Translating Research into Practice*, 44 Social Science & Medicine 1371, 1371 (1997); Chasnoff et al., *Discrepancies in Mandatory Reporting in Pinellas County, Florida*, *supra* (chapter 4, n. 81), at 1202, 1206; Gene M. Heyman, Addiction: A Disorder of Choice 35–39 (Harvard University Press, 2009).

7 *Reyes v. Super. Ct.*, 141 Cal. Rptr. 912, 912 (Ct. App. 1977).
8 Michael Tonry, *Rethinking Unthinkable Punishment Policies in America*, 46 UCLA L. Rev. 1751, 1767–81 (1999); *see also* Meda Chesney-Lind and Lisa Pasko, The Female Offender: Girls, Women, and Crime (Sage Publications, 2d ed. 2003).
9 *State v. McKnight*, 576 S.E.2d 168, 171 (S.C. 2003). The actual charge against McKnight was "homicide by child abuse," which is committed if one "causes the death of a child . . . while committing child abuse or neglect, and the death occurs under circumstances manifesting an extreme indifference to human life."
10 American Psychological Association standards for intellectual disability, or mental retardation, declare 70 to be the cutoff point for "normal" intellectual functioning; approximately 1 to 3 percent of the population has an IQ of 70 to 75 or lower. *Atkins v. Virginia*, 536 U.S. 304, 308–9 (2002). More recently, in *Hall v. Florida*, 134 S. Ct. 1986 (2014), the Supreme Court expanded the prohibition against executing defendants with an intellectually disability, ruling that an IQ test is not the sole indicator of intellectual disability.
11 Robyn E. Blumner, *Moralists' New Target: Pregnant Women*, St. Petersburg (Florida) Times, Aug. 10, 2003, at 7D.
12 *State v. McKnight*, 576 S.E. 2d 168, 171, 173 (S.C. 2003).
13 *McKnight*, 661 S.E. 2d at 359.
14 *McKnight*, 576 S.E. 2d at 171.
15 Sarah Fowler, *Judge Dismisses Rennie Gibbs' Depraved Heart Murder Case*, The Dispatch, Apr. 3, 2014; *see also State v. Rennie Gibbs*, Case No. 2007-0031-CR1, Order of Cir. Ct. Lowndes County, Miss., Apr. 2, 2014 (Judge Kitchen).
16 *See, e.g.*, Robert M. Silver et. al, *Work-Up of Stillbirth: A Review of the Evidence*, 196 Am. J. Obstet. & Gynecol. 433–44 (May 2007).
17 Dana Stone, *Is Meth Murder Charge Useful?*, Oklahoman, Dec. 19, 2007; and Jay F. Marks, *For Meth Mom, a Tough Road Ahead*, Daily Oklahoman, Dec. 22, 2007. Ms. Hernandez was released from prison after serving nearly a year, when the judge modified her sentence to ten years' probation, conditioned on her spending three months in inpatient drug rehabilitation. Sean Murphy, *Woman in Stillborn Case Leaves Prison*, AP, Nov. 8, 2008.
18 Ada Calhoun, *Mommy Had to Go Away for Awhile*, N.Y. Times Sunday Magazine, Apr. 29, 2012, at MM 30.
19 *Ex parte Ankrom*, 152 So. 3d 297 (Ala. 2013), upholding the applicability of Ala. Code § 26–15–3.2 to prenatal harms.
20 Calhoun, *supra* n. 18.
21 Jessica Vanegeren, The Capital Times (Madison, WI), Mar. 19, 2014, 2014 WLNR 7504737 (citing National Advocates for Pregnant Women); *see also* Lynn Paltrow and Jeanne Flavin, Are Pregnant Women Persons After 20 Weeks? (updated January 2015), http://advocatesforpregnantwomen.org/main/publications/articles_and_reports/are_pregnant_women_persons_after_20_weeks_updated_january_2015_1.php (visited Aug. 15, 2016).

22 *See* Paltrow and Flavin, *Arrests and Forced Interventions on Pregnant Women* (chapter 4, n. 3), at 312, Figure 1 and the cases discussed in this chapter.
23 Erik Eckholm, *Case Explores Rights of Fetus Versus Mother*; Vanegeren, *supra* n. 21.
24 Calhoun, *supra* n. 18.
25 *See* Nina Martin, *Take a Valium, Lose Your Kid, Go to Jail* (Sept. 23, 2015) (finding that between 2006 and mid-2015, 479 pregnant women were prosecuted under the Alabama child endangerment statute, https://www.propublica.org/article/when-the-womb-is-a-crime-scene (last visited 8/15/16); Alicia Gallegos, *Fetal Endangerment Ruling Could Criminalize Prescribing*, Am. Med. Ass'n (Jan. 28, 2013), http://www.amednews.com/article/20130128/government/130129951/6/; and *The Alabama Supreme Court Further Solidifies Protection to the Unborn*, SLI Educational Update (Southeast Law Institute, Birmingham, AL), Feb. 1, 2013, http://www.southeastlawinstitute.org/news.asp?record_no=25068.
26 Substance Abuse and Mental Health Services Administration (SAMHSA), 2012 National Survey on Drug Use and Health 31.
27 *Id.* at 33.
28 *The Health Consequences of Smoking*, *supra* n. 3, at 17.
29 *Id.*; *see also* SAMHSA, 2013 National Survey on Drug Use and Health 50 (Sept. 2014) (hereafter SAMHSA 2013 Survey on Drug Use).
30 *Id.* at 51.
31 U.S. Food & Drug Admin., *Caffeine Intake by the U.S. Population* 53, 63 (Sept. 2009, last updated Dec. 2012), available at http://www.fda.gov/downloads/AboutFDA/CentersOffices/OfficeofFoods/CFSAN/CFSANFOIAElectronicReadingRoom/UCM333191.pdf.
32 SAMHSA 2013 Survey on Drug Use, *supra* n. 29, at 15–17. Results from the SAMHSA Behavioral Health Trends in the United States, 2014 National Survey on Drug Use and Health (Sept. 2015), were very similar. See http://www.samhsa.gov/data/sites/default/files/NSDUH-FRR1-2014/NSDUH-FRR1-2014.pdf.
33 *Id.* at 18; *see also* Press Release, *New Research Reveals the Trends and Risk Factors behind America's Growing Heroin Epidemic*, Centers for Disease Control and Prevention (July 7, 2015), http://www.cdc.gov/media/releases/2015/p0707-heroin-epidemic.html; Katharine Q. Seelye, *In Heroin Crisis, White Families Seek Gentler War on Drugs*, N.Y. Times, Oct. 31, 2015, at A1, http://www.nytimes.com/2015/10/31/us/heroin-war-on-drugs-parents.html; Michael McAuliff and Ryan Grim, *Congress Finally Gives a Damn about Heroin Addiction*, Huffington Post (Feb. 15, 2016), http://www.huffingtonpost.com/entry/heroin-capitol-hill_us_56be63bde4b0c3c5505184c5; Governor Peter Shumlin's 2014 State of the State Address, available at http://governor.vermont.gov/newsroom-stateo-of-state-speech-2013 [*sic*] (last visited Feb. 25, 2014).
34 SAMHSA 2013 Survey on Drug Use, *supra* n. 29, at 26.
35 Gail Winger et al., *Behavioral Perspectives on the Neuroscience of Drug Addiction*, 84 J. Experimental Analysis of Behavior 667, 671–79 (2005); Nora D. Volkow

and Ting-Kai Li, *Drug Addiction: The Neurobiology of Behavior Gone Awry*, in Principles of Addiction Medicine 3 (Lippinncott, Williams & Wilkins [Richard K. Ries et al., eds.], 4th ed. 2009); Heyman, *supra* n. 6, at 40–41; and Sana Loue and Beatrice Ioan, *Legal and Ethical Issues in Heroin Diagnosis, Treatment, and Research*, 28 J. Leg. Med. 193, 197–98 (2007). Helge Waal and Jorg Mørland, *Addiction as Impeded Rationality*, in Addiction: Entries and Exits 121, 123 (Russell Sage Foundation [Jon Elster, ed.], 1999); *see also* George F. Koob and Michel Le Moal, *Neurobiology of Addiction* 432 (Academic Press, 2006).

36 Eliot L. Gardner, *The Neurobiology and Genetics of Addiction: Implications of the Reward Deficiency Syndrome for Therapeutic Strategies in Chemical Dependencies*, *in* Addiction, Entries and Exits, *supra* n. 35, at 68–72. Because of its ubiquity some view dopamine as the key to understanding addiction, while others, like Koob and Le Moal, suggest that it as mere "oil in the machine.'" Koob and Le Moal, *supra* note 35, at 447.

37 Volkow and Li, *supra* n. 35, explain that the dopamine increases occasioned by drug use may be five to ten times greater than those caused by normal stimuli and last longer as well. *See also* Marianne J. Legato, *Why Men Never Remember and Women Never Forget* 35 (Rodale Books, 2005).

38 *See, e.g.*, Koob and Le Moal, *supra* n. 35, at 5, 7, 19; Waal and Morland, *supra* n. 39, at 126–127; Heyman, *supra* n. 6, at 46–48 and 53–54; and Winger, *supra* n. 35, at 668, 673.

39 Gardner, *supra* n. 36, at 69–71, 73–74; *see also* Wendy J. Lynch et al., *Biological Basis of Sex Differences in Drug Abuse: Preclinical and Clinical Studies*, 164 Psychopharmacology 121, 127 (2002).

40 Volkow and Li, *supra* n. 35, at 5. *See also* George R. Uhl and Robert W. Grow, *The Burden of Complex Genetics in Brain Disorders*, 61 Archives of General Psychiatry 223, 224 (2004). Almost all genetic contributions to brain disorders involve multiple genes and complex interactions between genes and environmental factors, making reductionist assumptions or genetic "quick fixes" both unwise and unlikely. *See* Uhl and Grow, *supra*, at 224–28.

41 There is a significant overlap between those who abuse illegal drugs and those who abuse alcohol. One survey found that alcoholics were ten times more likely to abuse illegal drugs than those in the general population. George R. Uhl et al., *Genetic Influences in Drug Abuse*, in Floyd E. Bloom and David J. Kupfer, eds., Psychopharmacology: The Fourth Generation of Progress 1793, 1795 (1995).

42 Heyman, *supra* n. 6, at 91; Ming T. Tsuang et al., *The Harvard Twin Study of Substance Abuse: What We Have Learned*, Harvard Rev. Psychiatry 267, 269 (Nov./Dec. 2001); Legato, *supra* n. 37, at 36; Gardner, *supra* n. 36, at 74.

43 Uhl, *supra* n. 41, at 1793.

44 Tsuang, *supra* n. 42, at 271; Gardner, *supra* n. 36, at 81–84.

45 Volkow and Li, *supra* n. 35, at 6–7; and Rosa M. Crum, *The Epidemiology of Substance Abuse Disorders* 17, in Principles of Addiction Medicine, *supra* n. 35. *See also* Comm. on Addictions of the Group for the Advancement of Psychiatry, *Re-*

sponsibility and Choice in Addiction, 53 Psychiatric Serv. 707, 707 (2002) (hereafter Comm. on Addictions); and Felitti, *Childhood Abuse and Household Dysfunction*, at 251 (chapter 1, n. 24).

46 See, e.g., Bradley T. Conner et al., *Genetic, Personality, and Environmental Predictors of Drug Use in Adolescents*, 38 J. Substance Abuse Treatment 178, 186–87 (2010).

47 Larry Cahill, *His Brain, Her Brain*, 292 Scientific American 40, 40 (2005). *See also* Larry Cahill, *Why Sex Matters for Neuroscience*, Nature Rev. Neuroscience, May 10, 2006, at 1–7; and Cora Lee Wetherington, *Sex-Gender Differences in Drug Abuse: A Shift in the Burden of Proof?*, 15 Experimental and Clinical Psychopharmacology, 411, 411 (2007).

48 Sheila B. Blume, *Women: Clinical Aspects*, in *Substance Abuse: A Comprehensive Textbook* 645 (Williams & Wilkins [Joyce Lowinson et al., eds.], 3rd. ed., 1997).

49 *Id.* at 649. T. Flensborg-Madsen et al., *Amount of Alcohol Consumption and Risk of Developing Alcoholism in Men and Women*, 42 Alcohol and Alcoholism 442, 444–45 (2007).

50 Stephanie S. Covington, *Women and Addiction, A Gender-Responsive Approach*, Clinician's Manual 14 (2007); *see also* Daniel W. Hommer et al., *Evidence for a Gender-Related Effect of Alcoholism on Brain Volumes*, 158 Am. J. Psychiatry 198, 199–203 (2001).

51 Blume, *supra* n. 48.

52 Wetherington, *supra* n. 47, at 411, 414 (citing a study showing a study showing that "women were three to four times more likely to become addicted to cocaine within 24 months of the first time they used it"); *see also* Cahill, *Why Sex Matters for Neuroscience*, *supra* n. 47, and Lynch, *supra* n. 39, at 127–29.

53 *Id.*; *see also* Wetherington, *supra* n. 47, at 414.

54 Beginning with the ancient Greeks, drinking by women has periodically been proscribed, and public drinking has been particularly stigmatizing. Elizabeth R. Morrissey, *Power and Control through Discourse: The Case of Drinking and Drinking Problems among Women*, 10 Contemp. Crises 157, 165 (1986). *See also* Women Under the Influence at 48–49, and Glen R. Hanson, *In Drug Abuse, Gender Matters*, 17 (No. 2) NIDA Notes, May 2002.

55 Lynch, *supra* n. 39, at 123; Kathleen T. Brady and Carrie L. Randall, *Gender Differences in Substance Use Disorders*, 22 Psychiatric Clinics of North America 241, 243 (1999).

56 Thomas M. Brady and Olivia Silber Ashley, eds., Department of Health and Human Services, Substance Abuse and Mental Health Services Administration, Office of Applied Studies, Women in Substance Abuse Treatment: Results from the Alcohol and Drug Services Study (ADSS) 7 (2005); available at http://www.oas.samsha.gov/WomenTX/WomenTX.htm (last visited July 15, 2009). *See also* Stephen R. Kandall, Substance and Shadow: Women and Addiction in the United States 270 (1996) and Shelly F. Greenfield, *Women and Substance Abuse Disorders*, in Jensvold et al., Psychopharmacology and Women: Sex, Gender, and Hormones 299, 300, 306 (1996).

57 *See also* HHS, Substance Abuse and Mental Health Serv. Admin, Office of Applied Studies, Results from the 2008 National Survey on Drug Use, http://www.dpft.org/resources/NSDUHresults2008.pdf at 15, 24 (hereafter 2008 National Survey on Drug Use) (visited Aug. 16, 2016).
58 Blume, *supra* n. 48, at 647; *see also* Suniya S. Luthar et al., *Gender Differences among Opioid Abusers: Pathways to Disorder and Profiles of Psychopathology*, 43 Drug and Alcohol Dependence 179, 179 (1996); and Sharon C. Wilsnack and Richard W. Wilsnack, *Drinking and Problem Drinking in US Women: Patterns and Recent Trends*, in *12 Recent Developments in Alcoholism: Women and Alcoholism* 29, 46 (Marc Galanter, ed. 1995).
59 Lisa Najavits et al., *The Link Between Substance Abuse and Posttraumatic Stress Disorder in Women: A Research Review*, 6 Am. J. on Addictions 273, 274–78 (1997).
60 Sheigla Murphy and Marsha Rosenbaum, *Pregnant Women on Drugs*, *supra*, 8–9, 49–50 (chapter 1, n. 60); Susan R. B. Weiss et al., *Emerging Issues in Gender and Ethnic Differences in Substance Abuse and Treatment*, 3 Current Women's Health Reports 245, 247 (2003) (finding that 84 percent of women seeking substance abuse treatment had a history of violent assault or PTSD). In a study of twins in the general population, women who had experienced sexual abuse as girls were three times more likely to become alcohol- or drug-dependent as adults. Patrick Zickler, *Childhood Sex Abuse Increases Risk for Drug Dependence in Adult Women*, 17 (No. 1), NIDA Notes (Apr. 2002), citing K. S. Kendler et al., *Childhood Sexual Abuse and Adult Psychiatric and Substance Abuse Disorders in Women: An Epidemiological and Co-Twin Control Analysis*, 57 Archives of Gen. Psychiatry 953–59 (2000). Many other researchers have found that childhood sexual abuse is a significant predictor of both depression and posttraumatic stress disorder, which in turn make substance abuse much more likely. *See, e.g.*, Blume, *supra* n. 48, at 62, Weiss, *supra*, at 247.
61 Rochelle Hanson et al., *Relations among Gender, Violence Exposure, and Mental Health: The National Survey of Adolescents*, 78 Am. J. Orthopsychiatry 313, 314 (2008).
62 Najavits, *supra* n. 59, at 274.
63 Louann Brizendine, The Female Brain 132–33 (Broadway Books, 2006).
64 *Id.*; *see also* Weiss, *supra* n. 60, at 246–47; *see also* Wilsnack and Wilsnack, *supra* n. 58, at 49. *Cf.* Najavits, *supra* n. 59, at 280; and Morrissey, *supra* n. 54, at 159, 165.
65 Binta Lambert et al., *Ethical Issues and Addiction*, 29 J. Addictive Diseases 164, 164 (2010); *see also* Weiss, *supra* n. 60, at 247; and Murphy and Rosenbaum, *supra*, at 89–96. *See also* T. J. Mathews and Brady E. Hamilton for the Centers for Disease Control, *Delayed Childbearing: More Women Are Having Their First Child Later in Life*, Data Brief No. 21 (Aug. 2009), available at http://www.cdc.gov/nchs/data/databriefs/db21.htm (last visited May 25, 2010).
66 Murphy and Rosenbaum, *supra*.

67 *Id.* at 50; Maureen O. Marcenko and Michael Spence, *Social and Psychological Correlates of Substance Abuse Among Pregnant Women*, 19 Social Work Research 103, 103 (1995).
68 Guttmacher Inst., *Unintended Pregnancy in the United States* 1 (Dec. 2013), available at http://www.guttmacher.org/pubs/FB-Unintended-Pregnancy-US.pdf; *see also* Lawrence B. Finer and Stanley K. Henshaw, *Disparities in Rates of Unintended Pregnancy in the United States, 1994 and 2001*, 38 (2) Perspectives on Sexual & Reprod. Health 90, 94 (2006).
69 Murphy and Rosenbaum, *supra*, at 4, 52–54.
70 Thirty-two states and the District of Columbia prohibit the use of Medicaid funding for abortion. Guttmacher Inst., *State Policies in Brief: An Overview of Abortion Laws* (July 1, 2014), available at http://www.guttmacher.org/statecenter/spibs/spib_OAL.pdf (last visited Feb. 20, 2016). In 2011, 89 percent of American counties lacked any physician who could provide an abortion. Guttmacher Inst., *State Facts About Abortion: Texas* 2 (2014), http://www.guttmacher.org/pubs/sfaa/pdf/texas.pdf. *See also Whole Woman's Health v. Hellerstedt*, 126 S. Ct. 2292, 2313 (2016).
71 Murphy and Rosenbaum, *supra*, at 8–9, 49–50; *see also* Peter D. Jacobson et al., *Reciprocal Obligations: Managing Policy Responses to Prenatal Substance Exposure*, 81 Milbank Q. 475, 481–82 (2003).
72 Murphy and Rosenbaum, *supra*.
73 *Id.* at 17–28.
74 *Id.* at 8; Wendy B. Kissin et al., *Characterizing Pregnant Drug-Dependent Women in Treatment and Their Children*, 21 J. Substance Abuse Treatment 27, 29 (2001).
75 Murphy and Rosenbaum, *supra*, at 41–45; Covington, *supra* n. 50, at 15; and Kissin, *supra* n. 74.
76 Murphy and Rosenbaum, *supra*, at 33, 41–45. "Neighborhood disorganization," a sociological construct encompassing multiple aspects of neighborhood poverty, crime, social isolation, and marginalization, is associated with higher rates of premature births and babies born with lower birth weight, at least some of which may be attributed to the physiological effects of stress. *See* Margaret L. Holland et al., *The Effects of Stress on Birth Weight in Low-Income Unmarried Black Women*, 19 Women's Health Issues 390, 391, 394–95 (2009). *See also* Debra Niehoff, *Invisible Scars: The Neurobiological Consequences of Child Abuse*, 56 DePaul L. Rev. 847, 854–57 (2007) (describing the debilitating mental and physical health effects of chronic stress).
77 *See, e.g.*, Weiss, *supra* n. 60, and Brady and Ashley, *supra* n. 56.
78 Murphy and Rosenbaum, *supra*, at 35–41.
79 Kissin, *supra* n. 74, at 30.
80 Murphy and Rosenbaum, *supra*, at 50–52.
81 *See* Covington, *supra* n. 50, at 15–16; Deborah A. Frank et al., *Forgotten Fathers: An Exploratory Study of Mothers' Report of Drug and Alcohol Problems among Fathers of Urban Newborns*, 24 Neurotoxicology & Teratology 339, 345 (2002);

Wendy Chavkin, *Enemy of the Fetus: The Pregnant Drug User and the Pregnancy Police*, Health/Pac Bull., Winter 1992 at 5, 9 (noting in a study of 146 female drug users, "over half had been sexually abused.... There was a clear-cut statistical association among a history of sexual abuse, the severity of drug use, and the likelihood that the woman would be involved as an adult with a man who coercively urged continued drug use"); and Sandra L. Martin et al., *Violence and Substance Abuse among North Carolina Pregnant Women*, 86 Am. J. Pub. Health 991–92, 997 (1996).

82 Murphy and Rosenbaum, *supra*, at 58–61.
83 *Id.* at 4; Suzanne Pursley-Crotteau, *Perinatal Crack Users Becoming Temperant: The Social Psychological Process*, 22 Health Care for Women Int'l 49, 62 (2001).
84 Calhoun, *supra* n. 18; *see also* Marvin Wang, *Perinatal Drug Abuse and Neonatal Drug Withdrawal*, Apr. 12, 2010, available at http://emedicine.medscape.com/article/978492 (last visited June 1, 2010).
85 Murphy and Rosenbaum, *supra*, at 4; *see also* Bjørg Hjerkinn et al., *Substance Abuse in Pregnant Women, Experiences from a Special Child Welfare Clinic in Norway*, 7 BMC Pub. Health 322, p. 5 (2007) and Part VI, *infra*.
86 Murphy and Rosenbaum, *supra*, at 74; *see also* Kissin, *supra* n. 74, at 32.
87 Sarah C. M. Roberts and Amani Nuru-Jeter, *Women's Perspectives on Screening for Alcohol and Drug Use in Prenatal Care*, 20 Women's Health Issues 193, 194–98 (2010); *see also* Diane Phillips et al., *Factors That Influence Women's Disclosure of Substance Use During Pregnancy: A Qualitative Study of Ten Midwives and Ten Pregnant Women*, 37 J. Drug Issues 357, 359, 367–68 (2007).
88 *See, e.g.*, Lambert, *supra* n. 65, at 171, and Howell, *infra* n. 214, at 209.
89 Murphy and Rosenbaum, *supra*, at 88–93; Roberts and Nuru-Jeter, *supra* n. 87.
90 Roberts & Nuru-Jeter, *supra* n. 87. In most states, physicians and other health care professionals are mandated to report suspected child abuse or neglect to child protective services. In fourteen states and the District of Columbia, prenatal drug exposure is explicitly defined as evidence of child abuse. Child Welfare Information Gateway, U.S. Dep't of Health & Human Services, Definitions of Child Abuse and Neglect: Summary of State Laws (July 2009), available at www.childwelfare.gov (last visited June 23, 2010). *See, e.g.*, Ariz. Rev. Stat. § 8-201 (22). A referral to child protective services triggers an investigation, which in turn will start the clock ticking on mandatory decisionmaking about termination of parental rights under the Adoption and Safe Families Act of 1997 (ASFA), which authorizes the termination of parental rights if children have been in foster care for fifteen of the previous twenty-two months. For details of this process see Annette R. Appell, *Protecting Children or Punishing Mothers: Gender, Race, and Class in the Child Protection System*, 48 S. C. L. Rev. 577, 581–89 (1997) and Catherine J. Ross, *The Tyranny of Time: Vulnerable Children, "Bad" Mothers, and Statutory Deadlines in Parental Termination Proceedings*, 11 Va. J. Soc. Pol'y & L. 176, 196–217 (2004).
91 Mokdad et al., *Actual Causes of Death in the United States*, *supra*, at 1240–41.

92   Id. From 2006 to 2010, an average of 87,798 Americans died annually from alcohol-related causes. Centers for Disease Control, Alcohol and Public Health: Alcohol-Related Disease Impact (ARDI), available at http://apps.nccd.cdc.gov/ DACH_ARDI/Default/Report.aspx?T=AAM&P=f6d7eda7-036e-4553-9968-9b17ffad620e&R=d7a9b303-48e9-4440-bf47-070a4827e1fd&M=AD96A9C1-285A-44D2-B76D-BA2AE037FC56&F=&D=.
93   Armstrong, *Conceiving Risk, supra,* at 208–9 .
94   Mokdad, *supra,* at 1240, 1242.
95   Centers for Disease Control and Prevention, *Fetal Alcohol Spectrum Disorders (FASDs),* http://www.cdc.gov/ncbddd/fasd/data.html; *see also* Ernest L. Abel, *An Update on Incidence of FAS: FAS Is Not an Equal Opportunity Birth Defect,* 17 Neurotoxicology and Teratology 437, 440–41 (1995). In 2016 new clinical guidelines for the diagnosis of fetal alcohol spectrum disorders were proposed by the National Institutes of Health. https://www.niaaa.nih.gov/news-events/news-releases/nih-releases-improved-guidelines-diagnosing-fetal-alcohol-spectrum.
96   Estimates of drinking among pregnant women in Europe cover a wide range, varying from 23 to 66 percent across countries. Ingrid de Chazeron et al., *Is Pregnancy the Time to Change Alcohol Consumption Habits in France?,* 32 Alcohol Clin. Exp. Res. 868, 870–71 (2008); and Ludmila N. Bakhireva et al., *Paternal Drinking, Intimate Relationship Quality, and Alcohol Consumption in Pregnant Ukrainian Women,* 72 J. of Studies on Alcohol and Drugs 536, 536 (July 2011).
97   Elizabeth M. Armstrong and Ernest L. Abel, *Fetal Alcohol Syndrome: The Origins of a Moral Panic,* 35 Alcohol & Alcoholism 276, 279–80; and Abel, *supra* n. 95.
98   Philip A. May and J. Phillip Gossage, *Maternal Risk Factors for Fetal Alcohol Spectrum Disorders,* 34 Alcohol Research & Health 15, 17 (2011).
99   Chasnoff et al., *The 4P's Plus ©, supra* n. 6 , at 372–73.
100 Armstrong, *supra,* at 3–5, 7.
101 Abel, *supra* n. 95, at 440.
102 Armstrong, *supra* n. 93, at 82, n. 51; May and Gossage, *supra* n. 98, at 21.
103 *See, e.g.,* Centers for Disease Control, *Alcohol Use in Pregnancy,* available at http://www.cdc.gov/ncbddd/fasd/alcohol-use.html (last updated Apr. 17, 2014); and *More Than 3 Million US Women at Risk for Alcohol-Exposed Pregnancy,* CDC (Feb. 2, 2016), http://www.cdc.gov/media/releases/2016/p0202-alcohol-exposed-pregnancy.html.
104 Armstrong, *supra* n. 93, at 205–7.
105 BJOG: Int. J. Obstetrics & Gynaecology, *Danish Studies Suggest Low and Moderate Drinking in Early Pregnancy Has no Adverse Effects on Children Aged Five* (June 20, 2012), http://www.bjog.org/details/news/2085661/Danish_studies_suggest_low_and_moderate_drinking_in_early_pregnancy_has_no_adver.html.
106 Laubenthal et al., *Cigarette Smoke-induced Transgenerational Alterations in Genome Stability,* at 3953–54.
107 N. Kistin et al., *Cocaine and Cigarettes: A Comparison of Risks,* 10 Paediatr. Perinat. Epidemiol. 269 (1996); *see also* Lane Anderson, *Study: Poverty, Not Cocaine,*

Causes Children More Harm, Deseret Morning News, May 5, 2014, 2014 WLNR 12005617.

108 M. H. Malloy, *Prematurity and Sudden Infant Death Syndrome: United States 2005-2007*, 33 J. Perinatol. 470, 473 (2013); and Colleen M. O'Leary et al., *Maternal Alcohol Use and Sudden Infant Death Syndrome and Infant Mortality Excluding SIDS*, 131 Pediatrics e770, e771 (2013).

109 Catherine Saint Louis, *Quick Gains after a Smoking Ban*, N.Y. Times, Apr. 1, 2014, at D4.

110 See, e.g., Denise Grady, *Pregnancy Problems Tied to Caffeine: Long-Held Concerns about Miscarriages Are Focus of New Study*, N.Y. Times, Jan. 21, 2008, at A10.

111 Emily Oster, Expecting Better, *supra*, at xii, xvi, xvii-xviii, 37-39, 53-62 (2013); and Murkoff and Mazel, What to Expect When You're Expecting, *supra*, at 66, 69-70.

112 Young, *supra*, at 7.

113 National Conference of State Legislatures, *States' Responses to Maternal Drug and Alcohol Use: An Update* (2000).

114 Wendy Chavkin, *Commentary, Cocaine and Pregnancy—Time to Look at the Evidence*, 285 JAMA 1626, 1626 (2001) (citing Deborah A. Frank et al., *Growth, Development, and Behavior in Early Childhood Following Prenatal Cocaine Exposure: A Systematic Review*, 285 JAMA 1631 [2001]).

115 Susan Okie, *The Epidemic That Wasn't*, N.Y. Times, Jan. 27, 2009, at D1; and Laura M. Betancourt et al., *Adolescents with and without Gestational Cocaine Exposure: Longitudinal Analysis of Inhibitory Control, Memory and Receptive Language*, 33 Neurotoxicol. & Teratol. 36-46, 9, 12 (2011); see also Anderson, *supra* n. 107.

116 Katherine Harmon, *U.S. Stillbirths Still Prevalent, Often Unexplained*, Scientific American, Dec. 13, 2011; and Am. C. Obstetricians & Gynecologists (ACOG) Practice Bulletin, *Management of Stillbirth*, 113 Obstet. & Gynecol. 748, 748-51 (2009).

117 Nagahawatte and Goldenberg, *Poverty, Maternal Health, and Adverse Pregnancy Outcomes*, *supra*, at 80-83 (chapter 4, n. 24).

118 *In re Winship*, 397 U.S. 358, 364 (1970).

119 *Reyes v. Super. Ct.*, 141 Cal. Rptr. 912, 912 (Ct. App. 1977).

120 *McBoyle v. United States*, 283 U.S. 25, 27 (1931).

121 AP, *Pregnant Woman Is Charged with Child Abuse for Drinking*, N.Y. Times, Jan. 22, 1990, at B8; Tamar Lewin, *Drug Use in Pregnancy: New Issue for the Courts*, N.Y. Times, Feb. 5, 1990, at A1; and AP, *Woman in Fetal Alcohol Case Gives Birth to Healthy Infant*, N.Y. Time, June 17, 1990.

122 *Ferguson v. City of Charleston*, 532 U.S. 67, 70-73 (2001); see also Kary L. Moss, *Forced Drug or Alcohol Treatment for Pregnant and Postpartum Women: Part of the Solution or Part of the Problem?*, 17 New Eng. J. Crim. & Civ. Confinement 1, 2 (1991).

123 Dorothy E. Roberts, *Unshackling Black Motherhood*, 95 Mich. L. Rev. 938, 941-44 and sources cited therein (1997).

124 *Ferguson*, 532 U.S. 67, at 84-85.

125 *Johnson v. State*, 602 So. 2d 1288, 1290 (Fla. 1992); see also *State v. Luster*, 419 S.E. 2d 32, 34-35 (Ga. Ct. App. 1992); and *Sheriff, Washoe County, Nev. v. Encoe*, 885 P. 2d 596, 598-99 (Nev. 1994).

126 At the time, Wis. Stat. § 940.01, first-degree intentional homicide, provided that: "(a) . . . whoever causes the death of another human being with intent to kill that person or another is guilty of a Class A felony."
127 Armstrong, *supra*, at 2.
128 *State v. Deborah J.Z.*, 596 N.W. 2d 490, 491 (Wis. Ct. App. 1999). The child was born with a blood alcohol level of .199 and physical features showing the effects of fetal alcohol exposure. *Id. See also* Armstrong, *supra*, at 1–2.
129 *Id.* at 492–96.
130 *Id.* at 495.
131 *Id.*, citing *Hillman v. Georgia*, 503 S.E. 2d 610, 613 (Ga. Ct. App. 1998).
132 *Whitner v. South Carolina*, 492 S.E.2d 777 (S.C. 1997).
133 *State v. McKnight*, 576 S.E.2d 168, at 171.
134 *Atkins v. Virginia*, 536 U.S. 304, 308–9 (2002). Traditionally 70 has been the cut-off point for "normal" intellectual functioning; approximately 1 to 3 percent of the population has an IQ of 70 to 75 or lower. *See* discussion of *Atkins* in n. 10, *supra*.
135 *State v. McKnight*, 576 S.E. 2d 168, 171, 173 (S.C. 2003).
136 The trial judge declared a mistrial after several jurors conducted Internet "research" on pertinent medical issues. *State v. McKnight*, 661 S.E. 2d 354. 356, 358 (S.C. 2008).
137 *Id.* at 358–59.
138 The court suspended the sentence upon service of twelve years in prison. *McKnight*, 576 S.E. 2d at 171.
139 *Id.* at 172–73, citing *State v. Jarrell*, 564 S.E.2d 362, 366 (S.C.Ct. App. 2002).
140 *McKnight*, 661 S.E. 2d at 358–59; *see also* Sharon Greene, *Regina McKnight Released from Prison*, abc15News, June 19, 2008, http://wpde.com/news/videos/regina-mcknight-released-from-prison (last visited Sept. 5, 2016).
141 The cases are discussed in more detail in Fentiman, *Pursuing the Perfect Mother*, *supra*, at 405–6.
142 According to the prosecutor, the indictment was a necessary "'wake-up call,'" so that "'we will never see a case like this again.'" Ken Kobayashi, *Mother Gets Probation in Ice Death*, Honolulu Advertiser, Aug. 26, 2004, at 1B. The trial judge concurred. *State v. Aiwohi*, FC, CR. NO. 03-1-0036 (Haw. Cir. Ct. Aug. 25, 2004), at http://www.courts.state.hi.us/docs/stat_v_aiwohi/state_v_aiwohi2.pdf.
143 *Id.*
144 The court held, in a technically worded opinion, that the attendant circumstance that the victim be a person at the time of the defendant's conduct was an essential element of manslaughter, and thus her conviction could not stand. *State v. Aiwohi*, 123 P. 3d 1210, 1223 (Haw. 2005).
145 *See, e.g.*, Stone and Marks, both *supra* n. 17; and Adam Nossiter, *Rural Alabama County Cracks Down on Pregnant Drug Users*, N.Y. Times, Mar. 15, 2008, at A10; *see also* Calhoun, *supra* n. 18.
146 Armstrong, *supra*, at 11–12.
147 *Morissette v. United States*, 342 U.S. 246, 250 (1952).

148 Barry C. Feld, *Race, Politics, and Juvenile Justice: The Warren Court and the Conservative "Backlash,"* 87 Minn. L. Rev. 1447, 1526–39 (2003).
149 Joan E. Jacoby, The American Prosecutor: A Search for Identity, 11–17, 20, 22–25 (1980); and John L. Worrall, *Prosecution in America: An Historical and Comparative Account*, in The Changing Role of the American Prosecutor, 4–5, 8–9 (John L. Worrall and M. Elaine Nugent-Borakove, eds., 2008).
150 See Fentiman, *In the Name of Fetal Protection, supra*, at 659 (chapter 1, n. 41).
151 Daniel S. Medwed, *The Zeal Deal: Prosecutorial Resistance to Post-Conviction Claims of Innocence*, 84 B.U. L. Rev. 125, 153–54 (2004).
152 *See, e.g.*, Sue Anne Pressley, *S.C. Verdict Fuels Debate Over Rights of the Unborn: Jury Finds Mother Guilty of Homicide*, Wash. Post, May 27, 2001, at A03.
153 Calhoun, *supra* note 18.
154 Nat. Dist. Atty's Assoc., *Resolution Regulation of Precursor Chemicals* (Apr. 30, 2005), available at http://www.ndaa.org/pdf/res_regulation_precursor_chemicals_april_30_05.pdf.
155 AP, *Judge Drops 'Meth Baby' Charge*, Casper Star-Tribune, Sept. 29, 2005.
156 Michael Tonry, *Determinants of Penal Policies*, 36 Crime & Just. 1, 24 (2007); *cf. Bordenkircher v. Hayes*, 434 U.S. 357 (1978).
157 Besiki Kutateladze et al., *Race and Prosecution in Manhattan*, Research Summary 1, 5–7 (Vera Institute of Just. July 2014); *see also* Michele Goodwin, *The Invisible Classes in High Stakes Reproduction*, 43 J. L., Med. & Ethics 289–91 (2015).
158 Brian Forst, *Prosecution Policy and Errors of Justice*, in The Changing Role of the American Prosecutor, *supra* n. 149, at 51–52.
159 Kent Roach, *Canada*, in *Criminal Prosecution: A Worldwide Study* 85 (Craig M. Bradley, ed., 2d ed. 2007).
160 Abraham Goldstein, *The Passive Judiciary* 5 (LA State Univ. Press 1981).
161 *Id.* at 5, 57.
162 See *Bei Bei Shuai v. State*, 966 N.E. 2d 619 (Ind. Ct. App. 2012) (Riley, J., concurring and dissenting).
163 *See* Nat'l Conference of State Legislatures, *Fetal Homicide Laws*, (Mar. 2015), http://www.ncsl.org/research/health/fetal-homicide-state-laws.aspx#State%20 Laws (last visited Feb. 20, 2016).
164 *See, e.g., Whitner v. State*, 492 S.E. 2d 777 (S.C. 1997); *Ex parte Ankrom*, 152 So. 3d 297 (Ala. 2013); and *Ex parte Hicks*, 153 So. 3d 53 (Ala. 2014) (opinions of Parker J., and Moore, C.J., concurring).
165 Calhoun, *supra* n. 18.
166 *See, e.g.*, Pressley, *supra* n. 152, at A07 (quoting Condon); *see also* David Firestone, *Woman Is Convicted of Killing Her Fetus by Smoking Cocaine*, N.Y. Times, May 17, 2001, at A12.
167 Calhoun, *supra* n. 18.
168 *Ex parte Hicks*, 153 So. 3d 53 (Ala. 2014).
169 *Ex parte Ankrom*, 152 So. 3d 297 (Ala. 2013).

170 *Ex parte Hicks*, 153 So. 3d 53, at 72–73, citing *Roe,* 410 U.S. 113 (1973) and *Casey,* 505 U.S. 833 (1992), respectively.
171 Cynthia Lee, Murder and the Reasonable Man: Passion and Fear in the Criminal Courtroom 217–20 (New York University Press, 2003).
172 Peter Gorman, *D.A. Rewrites the Law,* Fort Worth Weekly (July 28, 2004), http://archive.fwweekly.com/content.asp?article=504. The district attorney's interpretation of the law was subsequently determined to be invalid by the Texas attorney general, who stated that the Texas Controlled Substance Act neither authorized prosecution of drug-using pregnant women nor required physicians to report their drug usage to law-enforcement officials. Tex. Atty' Gen. Op. GA-0291 (Jan. 5, 2005).
173 Martha S. Chamallas, *Gaining Some Perspective in Tort Law: A New Take on Third-Party Criminal Attack Cases,* 14 Lewis & Clark L. Rev. 1251, 1252 (2010); and Mayo Moran, *The Reasonable Person, supra,* at 1233–49 (chapter 2, n. 123).
174 Lee, *supra* n. 171, at 203–12, 235–45.
175 531 N.E. 2d 355, 360 (Ill. 1988).
176 Similarly, a defendant is reckless in the eyes of the criminal law if he or she disregarded the risk of an unjustifiable result that a law-abiding (i.e., reasonable) person in that situation would have recognized. *See, e.g.,* Model Penal Code § 2.02 (1) (c) (defining "recklessly") (American Law Institute, Model Penal Code Official Draft 1962). Some jurisdictions, such as Massachusetts, require only "objective" recklessness. *See, e.g., Commonwealth v. Welansky,* 55 N.E. 2d 902, 910 (Mass. 1944).
177 *Youngquist,* 531 N.E. 2d at 360.
178 Roberts, *supra* n. 123, at 943, n. 28.
179 Chasnoff et al., *Discrepancies in Mandatory Reporting in Pinellas County, Florida, supra* note 6, at 1202.
180 Chasnoff, *The 4P's Plus© Screen, supra* n. 6, at 370, 372–73; *see also* Moss, *supra* n. 122, and Roberts, *supra* n. 123.
181 Kahneman, *Thinking, Fast and Slow* 4, 25, 28 (2011).
182 Martha Chamallas, *Deepening the Legal Understanding of Bias, supra,* at 778.
183 *See* Marlee Kline, *Complicating the Ideology of Motherhood: Child Welfare Law and First Nation Women,* 18 Queen's L.J. 306, 306–9 (1993); *cf.* Elizabeth Rapaport, *Mad Women and Desperate Girls: Infanticide and Child Murder in Law and Myth,* 33 Fordham Urb. L.J. 527, 530–31, 556–59 (2006); and Carol Sanger, *1989 Survey of Books Relating to the Law, III. Law and Society: Seasoned to the Use,* 87 Mich. L. Rev. 1338, 1339–40, 1364 (1989) (analyzing The Good Mother and Presumed Innocent).
184 Emily Oster, *Witchcraft, Weather and Economic Growth in Renaissance Europe,* 18 J. Econ. Perspectives 215–28 (14) (2004); and Samuel K. Cohn, *The Black Death and the Burning of Jews,* 196 Past and Present 3–4 (Oxford University Press, 2007).
185 *Cf.* Goodie, *Toxic Tort and the Articulation of Environmental Risk, supra,* at 69, 73, 78 (chapter 2, n. 138). *See also* Armstrong, *Conceiving Risk, supra,* at 11–12; and

William P. Marshall, *National Healthcare and the American Constitutional Culture*, 35 Harv. J. L. & Pub. Pol'y 131, 139–44 (2012).

186 *See, e.g., June v. Union Carbide Corp.*, 577 F. 3d 1234, 1239–44 (10th Cir. 2009); and Restatement (Third) of Torts: Liability for Physical and Emotional Harm §§28 (Burden of Proof) and 29 (Limitations on Liability for Tortious Conduct); compare Chamallas and Wriggins, *supra*, at 121–28.

187 The concept of foreseeability is highly malleable; it is also important in many jurisdictions since foreseeability is the touchstone for determining proximate cause. Restatement (Third) of Torts: Liability for Physical and Emotional Harm §§ 29 and 34, Comments a, c, and d.

188 As Daniel Kahneman has observed, "We are prone to overestimate how much we understand about the world and to underestimate the role of chance in events. Overconfidence is fed by the illusory certainty of hindsight." Kahneman, *supra* n. 180, at 14.

189 Chamallas and Wriggins, *supra*, at 124.

190 *See, e.g.*, Marks and Stone, both *supra* n. 17.

191 Chorioamnionitis is an infection of the placental tissues and amniotic fluid that can precede rupture of the membranes leading to labor. It has been associated with preterm labor and early gestational age fetal demise. *McKnight*, 576 S.E. 2d at 172; and Michael B. Brimacombe et al., *Comparison of Fetal Demise Case Series*, *supra* at 220 (chapter 4, n.24).

192 Nina Martin, *A Stillborn Child, A Charge of Murder, and the Disputed Case Law on 'Fetal Harm,'* Propublica (Mar. 18, 2014, 12:00 PM), http://www.propublica.org/article/stillborn-child-charge-of-murder-and-disputed-case-law-on-fetal-harm.

193 414 N.E. 2d 660 (N.Y. 1980). The New York Court of Appeals reversed the decision of a mid-level appeals court, which had reversed the decision of the trial judge. 417 N.Y.S. 2d 997 (N.Y. App. Div. 2d Dep't 1979).

194 414 N.E. 2d at 662–66.

195 Under Utah Code Ann. § 76-5-202, punishing aggravated murder, a defendant may receive the death penalty.

196 Staci Visser, *Prosecuting Women for Participating in Illegal Abortions: Undermining Gender Equality and the Effectiveness of State Police Power*, 13 J. L. & Fam. Stud. 171, 171 (2011).

197 Utah Code Ann. § 76-5-201.

198 Tenn. Code Ann. § 39-13-107. In 2016 the Tennessee legislature voted to end the law, because of its unintended consequences, including driving some pregnant women away from health care professionals and incentivizing others to seek abortion. Meghan Tompson, *Tennessee Discontinues Controversial Fetal Assault Law*, Mar. 27, 2016, http://www.pbs.org/newshour/bb/tennessee-discontinues-controversial-fetal-assault-law/ (visited Aug. 16, 2016).

199 Ala. Code § 22-52-1.2; Alaska Stat. § 47.37.190; Ark. Code Ann. § 20-64-815; Cal. Welf. & Inst. Code § 3050; Colo. Rev. Stat. § 27-82-108; Conn. Gen. Stat. Ann. § 17a-685; Del. Code Ann. tit. 16, § 2212; D.C. Code Ann. §7-1303.04; Fla. Stat. Ann.

§ 397.675; Ga. Code Ann. § 37-7-41; Haw. Rev. Stat. Ann. § 334-60.2; Idaho Code Ann. § 66-329; Ind. Code Ann. § 12-23-11-1; Iowa Code § 125.75; Kan. Stat. Ann. § 59-29b54; Ky. Rev. Stat. Ann § 222.430; La. Rev. Stat. Ann. § 28:54; Mass. Ann. Laws ch. 123, § 35; Minn. Stat. § 626.5561; Miss. Code Ann. § 41-30-27; Neb. Rev. Stat. Ann §§ 71-908, 71-919; N.H. Rev. Stat. Ann. § 135-C:27; N.M. Stat. Ann. § 43-2-8; N.C. Gen. Stat. § 122C-201; N.D. Cent. Code § 12.1-04.1-22; Ohio Rev. Code Ann. § 5119.90; Okla. Stat. tit. 63 § 1-546.5; R.I. Gen. Laws § 21-28.2-3; S.C. Code Ann. § 44-52-50; S.D. Codified Laws § 34-20A-70; Tenn. Code Ann. §§ 33-1-101, 33-6-501 to -502; Tex. Health & Safety Code Ann. § 574.034; Va. Code Ann. §§ 37.2-800, -809; Wash. Rev. Code Ann. § 70.96A. 140; W. Va. Code Ann. § 27-5-2; Wis. Stat. Ann. § 51.15; Wyo. Stat. Ann. § 25-10-110. See Fentiman, *Pursuing the Perfect Mother*, at 422.

200 Minn. Stat. § 626.5561, Okla. Stat. tit. 63 § 1-546.5, N.D. Cent. Code § 12.1-04.1-22, S.D. Codified Laws § 34-20A-70, Wis. Stat. Ann. § 51.15.
201 Judith M. Nyhus Johnson, *Minnesota's "Crack Baby" Law: Weapon of War or Link in a Chain?*, 8 Law & Ineq. 485, 486-87 (1990); *see also* Doug Grow, *Judge Turns from Anger, Hoping to Help Addicted Mother*, Minneapolis Star-Tribune, Nov. 10, 1989, at 1B.
202 532 U.S. 67 (2001).
203 Minn. Stat. § 626.5561; *see also* Johnson, *supra* note 201.
204 *State ex rel. Angela M.W. v. Kruzicki*, 561 N.W. 2d 729 (1997).
205 Okla. Stat. tit. 63 § 1-546.5, N.D. Cent. Code § 12.1-04.1-22, S.D. Codified Laws § 34-20A-70.
206 Eckholm, *supra* n. 23; and *Beltran v. Strachota*, 2014 WL 4924668 (E.D. Wid. 2014).
207 Marilyn L. Poland et al., *Punishing Pregnant Drug Users: Enhancing the Flight from Care*, 31 Drug & Alcohol Dependence 199, 201-2 (1993).
208 Winnipeg Child & Family Servs. (Nw. Area) v. G. (D.F.), [1997] 3 S.C.R. 925 (Can.).
209 *Id.* at 950-51, para. 41.
210 White men account for 42 percent of all substance-abuse treatment admissions in the United States compared with white women, who constitute 18 percent of those admissions. In every racial group women receive much less treatment than men. Black men are 16 percent of treatment admissions, black women 7.5 percent; Hispanic men constitute nearly 7 percent but Hispanic women are 2 percent. Native American and Asian men are admitted at even lower rates, although still they occupy more treatment spots than their female counterparts. Weiss, *supra* n. 60, at 249. Brady & Ashley, *supra* n. 56, at 6, 17.
211 Martin, *supra* n. 192, at 997. See Covington, *supra* n. 50, at 16; *see also* author's interview with Peter Bernstein, M.D., Ariela Frieder, M.D., and Evelyn Diaz, L.C.S.W., at Montefiore Hospital, Bronx, N.Y. (on file with the author); and V. A. Gyarmathy et al., *Drug Use and Pregnancy—Challenges for Public Health*, 14 (#9) Eurosurveillance 1, 3 (Mar. 2009), available at www.eurosurveillance.org.

212 Marilyn Daley et al., *The Impact of Substance Abuse Treatment Modality on Birth Weight and Health Care Expenditures*, 33 J. Psychoactive Drugs 57, 59 (Jan.–Mar. 2001); Weiss, *supra* n. 60; and Brady and Ashley, *supra* n. 56, at 6.

213 Bernstein et al. Interview, *supra* n. 211; *see also* Claire D. Brindis et al., *California's Approach to Perinatal Substance Abuse: Toward a Model of Comprehensive Care*, 29 J. of Psychoactive Drugs 113, 119 (1997). Historically, many drug-treatment programs excluded pregnant women. See Marcenko and Spence, *supra* n. 67; Vicki Breibart, Wendy Chavkin, and Paul H. Wise, *The Accessibility of Drug Treatment for Pregnant Women: A Survey of Programs in Five Cities*, 84 Am J. Pub. Health 1658, 1658–61 (1994). Often, as was the case with Ms. G.D.F., women face such lengthy delays that they simply give up and return to drug use. Whiteford & Vitucci, *supra* n. 6, at 1371.

214 Karol Kaltenbach and Loretta Finnegan, *Prevention and Treatment Issues for Pregnant Cocaine-Dependent Women and Their Infants*, Annals N.Y. Acad. of Sciences 329, 332 (1998); Lauren M. Jansson et al., *Pregnancy and Addiction: A Comprehensive Care Model*, 12 J. Substance Abuse Treatment 321, 322 (1996).

215 The data are mixed as to whether inpatient or outpatient treatment for alcoholism and other substance abuse is more effective, although one study found that women who were given the opportunity to have their children live with them during treatment remained in treatment much longer. *See, e.g.*, Embry M. Howell et al., *A Review of Recent Findings on Substance Abuse Treatment for Pregnant Women*, 16 J. Substance Abuse Treatment 195, 210, 215–16 (1999). Some studies have shown that what most contributes to long-term abstinence from drug and alcohol use is treatment completion, which usually correlates with a longer (six months) and more intense period of treatment. Perhaps significantly, the women in these studies were older, with an average age of thirty, which is consistent with the theory that many addicts eventually age out of heavy drug use. Lawrence Greenfield et al., *Effectiveness of Long-Term Residential Substance Abuse Treatment for Women: Findings from Three National Studies*, 30 Am. J. Drug & Alcohol Abuse 537, 538, 542, 547–49 (2004). Studies also suggest that treatment which addresses both substance abuse and mental illness leads to women's staying in treatment longer than women who participate only in substance abuse treatment. Brady and Ashley, *supra* n. 56, at 31–35, 37.

216 Weiss, *supra* n. 60, at 250; *see also* Blume, *supra* n. 48, at 650–51; and Mary-Lynn Brecht et al., *Coerced Treatment for Methamphetamine Abuse: Differential Patient Characteristics and Outcomes*, 31 Am. J. Drug and Alcohol Abuse 337, 350 (2005).

217 Murphy and Rosenbaum, *supra* ; Peter D. Jacobson et al., *supra* note 71, at 477; Kissin, *supra* n. 74, at 32; Whiteford and Vitucci, *supra* n. 6, at 1373–74.

218 Marcenko and Spence, *supra* n. 67, at 106; Jane E. Corrarino et al., *Linking Substance-Abusing Pregnant Women to Drug Treatment Services: A Pilot Program*, 29 J. of Obstetric, Gynecologic, & Neonatal Nursing 369, 370 (2000); *see also* Walter B. Connolly, Jr., and Alison B. Marshall, *Drug Addiction, Pregnancy, and*

Childbirth: Legal Issues for the Medical and Social Services Communities, 18 Clinics in Perinatology 147, 180–81 (1991).
219 Chavkin, *Enemy of the Fetus?*, *supra* n. 81, at 9; Vicki Breitbart et. al, *supra* n. 213 at 1660; Bernstein et al. interview, *supra* n. 211.
220 Pursley-Crotteau, *supra* n. 83, at 57–59, 61.
221 Young, *supra* n. 1, at 28–29, citing Federal Substance Abuse Prevention and Treatment Block Grant, as well as treatment program data. For more recent data see http://www.samsha.gov/data/sites/files/spot110-trends-pregnant-women-2013.pdf and http://wwwdasis/samsha.gov/webt/state_data/US11.pdf.
222 Sarah H. Heil et al., *Effects of Voucher-Based Incentives on Abstinence from Cigarette Smoking and Fetal Growth among Pregnant Women*, 103 Addiction 1009, 1009–18 (2008); and Rebecca J. Donatelle et al., *Incentives in Smoking Cessation: Status of the Field and Implications for Research and Practice with Pregnant Smokers*, 6 Nicotine & Tobacco Res. S163, S173–75 (2004).
223 Donatelle, *supra*, at S173; and Diane M. Morrison et al., *Beliefs about Substance Use among Pregnant and Parenting Adolescents*, 8 J. Research on Adolescence 69, 92 (1998); *cf.* Brindis et al., *supra* n. 213, at 116.
224 *See, e.g.*, Stephen T. Higgins et al., *Contingent Reinforcement Increases Cocaine Abstinence During Outpatient Treatment and 1 Year of Follow-Up*, 68 J. Consulting & Clinical Psychol. 64, 65–69 (2000).
225 Higgins, *supra*; Heil *supra* n. 222; Donatelle, *supra* n. 222, and Michael Prendergast et al., *Contingency Management for Treatment of Substance Abuse Disorders: A Meta-Analysis,* 101 Addiction 1546, 1547 (2006). One study examined the impact of adding case management services to behavioral interventions (including incentive payments for "clean" urine samples) to try to reduce the use of illegal drugs among pregnant women but did not have a control group of drug-using women who were not provided with behavioral interventions or case management. Hendree Jones et al., *The Effectiveness of Incentives in Enhancing Treatment Attendance and Drug Abstinence in Methadone-Maintained Pregnant Women*, 61 Drug & Alcohol Dependence 297, 302–5 (2001).
226 *See* Covington, *supra* n. 50, at 34.
227 *See, e.g.*, Higgins, Heil, & Prendergast, *supra* notes 222, 224.
228 *See, e.g.*, Covington, *supra* n. 50, and Marcenko and Spence, *supra* n. 67, at 107.

CHAPTER 6. CAUGHT IN THE CROSSFIRE
1 Jean-Jacques Rousseau, *Emile (or On Education)*, trans. A. Bloom (1979).
2 U.S. Dep't of Health & Human Servs., "Ladies Night" Spot Transcript, Ad Council Materials, National Breastfeeding Campaign; *see also* http://www.womenshealth.gov/breastfeeding/programs/nbc/adcouncil/transcript_ladiesnight.cfm (last visited Oct. 1, 2009); *see also* Judith Warner, *Why Vilify Mothers Who Bottle Feed*, N.Y. Times, June 22, 2006, available at http://opinionator.blogs.nytimes.com/2006/06/22/why-vilify-mothers-who-bottle-feed/comment-page-3/?login=email&_r=0.

3 Nina Bernstein, *Bronx Woman Convicted in Starving of her Breast-Fed Son*, N.Y. Times, May 20, 1999; Nina Bernstein, *Trial Begins for Mother in Breast-Fed Infant's Starvation Death*, N.Y. Times, Apr. 28, 1999; Nina Bernstein, *Mother Charged with Starving Baby Tells of Frantic Efforts to Save Him*, May 19, 1999.

4 *See, e.g.*, American Academy of Pediatrics, Section on Breastfeeding, *Policy Statement: Breastfeeding and the Use of Human Milk*, 129 Pediatrics e827, e827 (2012) (dismissing a woman's decision not to breastfeed as an unimportant "lifestyle choice") (hereafter 2012 AAP Policy Statement on Breastfeeding).

5 Gretchen Livingston, *Among 38 Nations, U.S. Is the Outlier When It Comes to Paid Parental Leave*, Pew Research Center, Dec. 12, 2013, http://www.pewresearch.org/fact-tank/2013/12/12/among-38-nations-u-s-is-the-holdout-when-it-comes-to-offering-paid-parental-leave/ (last visited Aug. 28, 2016).

6 Armstrong, *Conceiving Risk*, at 11–12.

7 Naomi Baumslag and Dia L. Michels, *Milk, Money, and Madness: The Culture and Politics of Breastfeeding* 39–45 (1995).

8 Jill Lepore, Book of Ages: The Life and Opinions of Jane Franklin 17 (2013) (quoting Cotton Mather, Elizabeth in Her Holy Retirement 35 (Boston: B. Green, 1710) (italics and full quote in original).

9 Nestlé used wheat, cow's milk, malt, and sugar to create a substitute for human milk. Alice Lesch Kelly, *Keeping Up with Mother's Milk*, L.A. Times, Feb. 20, 2006, at F1.

10 Ann Hulbert, Raising America: Experts, Parents, and a Century of Advice about Children 67–69 (2003), quoting L. Emmett Holt, M.D., author of The Care and Feeding of Children, one of the leading childrearing advice books in the late nineteenth and early twentieth centuries. *See also* Jacqueline H. Wolf, Don't Kill Your Baby, *supra at* 15) (chapter 1, n. 49).

11 As many new mothers will attest, breastfeeding is exhausting and time-consuming, particularly at the beginning. *See, e.g.*, Pamela Kruger, *Calling It Quits*, in Unbuttoned 133–38 (Dana Sullivan and Maureen Connolly, eds. 2009).

12 Wolf, *supra* n. 10, at 1, 42, 47–49.

13 *Id.* at 42–44, 74–82.

14 *Id.* at 15, 19–20 (2001); U.S. Dep't of Agric., Victor Oliviera et al., WIC and the Retail Price of Infant Formula, Food Assistance and Nutrition Research Report No. 39, at 16 (2004); Baumslag and Michels, *supra* n. 7, at xxi.

15 Hulbert, *supra* n. 10, at 102–3; Rebecca Kukla, Mass Hysteria: Medicine, Culture, and Mothers' Bodies 174–75 (2005).

16 Oliviera et al., *supra* n. 14, at 16.

17 Sergio Stagno and Gretchen A. Cloud, *Working Parents: The Impact of Day Care and Breast-Feeding on Cytomegalovirus Infections in Offspring*, 91 Proc. Nat'l Acad. Sci. U.S. 2384, 2385 (1994).

18 Am. Acad. of Pediatrics, *Breastfeeding and the Use of Human Milk*, 100 Pediatrics 1035 (1997) (hereafter 1997 AAP Policy Statement on Breastfeeding).

19 Wolf, *supra* n. 10, at 192.

20 Bob D. Cutler and Robert F. Wright, *The U.S. Infant Formula Industry: Is Direct-to-Consumer Advertising Unethical or Inevitable?*, Health Marketing Q., 2002, at 39, 41–42 (2002). *See also* Laura Epstein, *Women and Children Last: Anti-Competitive Practices in the Infant Formula Industry*, 5 Am. U. J. Gender & L. 21, 24 (1996).
21 Kukla, *supra* n. 15, at 175.
22 *Id.* at 174–75.
23 Donna V. Porter, Cong. Research Serv., *Breast-feeding: Impact on Health, Employment and Society* (July 18, 2003) (citing Jon Weimer, U.S. Dep't of Agric., The Economic Benefits of Breast Feeding: A Review and Analysis, Food Assistance and Nutrition Research Rep. No. 13 [2001]).
24 Oliviera et al., *supra* n. 14, at 16; Alan S. Ryan et al., *Breastfeeding Continues to Increase into the New Millennium*, 110 Pediatrics 1103, 1104 fig.1 (2002).
25 Diane E. Eyer, *Mother Infant Bonding: A Scientific Fiction*, 5 Hum. Nature 69, 85, 89 (1994).
26 Kukla, *supra* n. 15, at 150; *see also* Jules Law, *The Politics of Breastfeeding: Assessing Risk, Dividing Labor*, 25 Signs: J. Women Culture & Soc'y 407–8 (2000).
27 Eyer, *supra* n. 25, at 8, 10–11.
28 Anne L. Wright and Richard J. Schanler, *The Resurgence of Breastfeeding at the End of the Second Millennium*, 131 J. Nutrition 421S, 421S (2001); *see also* Stagno and Cloud, *supra* n. 17, at 2385.
29 Ryan et al., *supra* n. 24; *see also* Ctrs. for Disease Control & Prevention, Breastfeeding Among U.S. Children Born 1999–2006, CDC National Immunization Survey, http://www.cdc.gov/BREASTFEEDING/DATA/NIS_data/index.htm (last visited Sept. 15, 2009).
30 Centers for Disease Control and Prevention (CDC), *Breastfeeding Report Card*, United States/2014 at 2, 4 (2014); https://www.cdc.gov/breastfeeding/pdf/2014breastfeedingreportcard.pdf; *see also* Porter, *supra* n. 23, at 5.
31 Porter, *supra* n. 23, at 2; *see also* 2012 AAP Policy Statement on Breastfeeding, *supra* n. 4, at e828; Melanie Besculides, Katina Grigoryan, and Fabienne Laraque, *Infant Feeding Survey* 5–7 (2000) (examining trends in New York City hospitals) (on file with the author); Ryan, *supra* n. 24, at 1105–6; Ctrs. for Disease Control & Prevention, *supra* n. 30.
32 Christina M. Gibson-Davis and Jeanne Brooks-Gunn, *Couples' Immigration Status and Ethnicity as Determinants of Breastfeeding*, 96 Am. J. Pub. Health 641, 643 (2006).
33 Am. Acad. of Pediatrics, *supra* n. 18, at 1035.
34 *Id.* at 1037.
35 *Id.* at 1036.
36 *Id.* at 1035 (emphasis added).
37 These included the suppression of menstruation (and a concomitant reduced risk of becoming pregnant), a decrease in post-partum bleeding, a speedier return to pre-pregnancy shape and weight, a lowered risk of breast and ovarian cancer, and

a reduction in hip fractures post-menopause. Am. Acad. of Pediatrics, *supra* n. 18, at 1035.
38   *Id.* at 1035–36.
39   *See* Am. Acad. of Pediatrics, *Breastfeeding and the Use of Human Milk,* 115 Pediatrics 496 (2005) (hereafter 2005 AAP Policy Statement on Breastfeeding).
40   Am. Acad. of Pediatrics, *supra* n. 18, at 1036.
41   Am. Acad. of Pediatrics, *supra* n. 39, at 496. *See* Aimin Chen and Walter J. Rogan, *Breastfeeding and the Risk of Postneonatal Death in the United States,* 113 Pediatrics e435, e435 (2004).
42   *Id.* at 497.
43   *Id.* at 500.
44   *Id.* at 497.
45   *2012 AAP Policy Statement on Breastfeeding, supra* n. 4, at e828–31.
46   *Id.* at e829.
47   *Id.* at e830–31.
48   *See, e.g.,* Jane Brody, *The Ideal and the Real of Breast-Feeding,* nytimes.com (July 23, 2012), http://well.blogs.nytimes.com/2012/07/23/the-ideal-and-the-real-of-breast-feeding/.
49   Michael B. Brakken, Risk, Chance, and Causation: Investigating the Origins and Treatment of Disease (Yale University Press, 2013).
50   2012 *AAP Policy Statement on Breastfeeding, supra* n. 4, at e837 (emphasis added).
51   Sami Shubber, The International Code of Marketing of Breast-Milk Substitutes: An International Measure to Protect and Promote Breast-feeding 2, 43 (1998); U.S. Dep't of Health & Human Servs., Report of the Surgeon General's Workshop on Breastfeeding & Human Lactation iii (1984), available at http://profiles.nlm.nih.gov/NN/B/C/G/G/_/nnbcgg.pdf; C. Edward Koop (1982–1989), http://www.surgeongeneral.gov/about/previous/biokoop.html (last visited Aug. 26, 2014).
52   UNICEF Innocenti Declaration on the Protection, Promotion and Support of Breastfeeding, July 30, 1990. *See also* U.S. Dep't of Health & Human Servs., HHS Blueprint for Action on Breastfeeding 3, 18 (2000) (hereafter Breastfeeding Blueprint).
53   U.S. Breastfeeding Comm., *Breastfeeding in the United States: A National Agenda* 7, 11, 13, 14 (2001), http://www.usbreastfeeding.org/Portals/0/Publications/National-Agenda-2001-USBC.pdf.
54   *Id.* at 11.
55   The campaign used radio, television, print media, and outdoor advertising. Press Release, U.S. Dep't of Health & Human Servs., *Public Service Campaign to Promote Breastfeeding Awareness Launched* (June 4, 2004), http://www.hhs.gov/news/press/2004pres/20040604.html. The campaign relied on public service announcements. The television advertisements ended in 2005, the radio commercials ended in April 2006, and print media were available until the end of 2006. U.S. Dep't of Health & Human Servs., National Breastfeeding Awareness Campaign, http://www.womenshealth.gov/breastfeeding/programs/nbc/index.cfm (last visited

Oct. 17, 2009) (hereafter Breastfeeding Awareness Campaign). Ctrs. for Disease Control & Prevention, *Infant Feeding Practices Study II*, http://www.cdc.gov/ifps/index.htm.

56 Suzanne G. Haynes, National Breastfeeding Awareness Campaign Results: Babies Were Born to Be Breastfed! 4, http://www.womenshealth.gov/breastfeeding/programs/nbc/results/campaign_results.ppt.
57 *Id. See also* Joan B. Wolf, *Is Breast Really Best?*, at 611, 620 (emphasis added).
58 Wolf, *supra*, at 618.
59 HHS, "Ladies Night" Spot, *supra* n. 2; see also https://www.youtube.com/watch?v=wC1RAr52xFo.
60 HHS, http://www.womenshealth.gov/breastfeeding/programs/nbc/adcouncil/CNBA4130-E01NY.mpg (last visited Oct. 17, 2009).
61 Kukla, *supra* n. 15, 190 fig. 6.1; *see also* http://www.womenshealth.gov/breastfeeding/government-in-action/national-breastfeeding-campaign/adcouncil/Ice_Cream.pdf (last visited Aug. 28, 2016)..
62 Brian Ross and Jill Rackmill, *Breast-Feeding Ads Stalled, 'Watered Down,'* June 4, 2004, http://abcnews.go.com/2020/story?id=124271&page=1.
63 *Id.*
64 Marc Kaufman and Christopher Lee, *HHS Toned Down Breast-Feeding Ads, Formula Industry Urged Softer Campaign*, Washington Post, Aug. 31, 2007, at A1, A4.
65 John Toscano, *Ion Politics*, Queens Gazette, July 14, 2004, http://www.qgazette.com/news/2004-07-14/Political_Page/Ion_politics.html.
66 Ross and Rackmill, *supra* n. 62; *see also* Melody Petersen, *Breastfeeding Ads Delayed by a Dispute Over Content*, N.Y. Times, Dec. 4, 2003, at C1.
67 Kukla, *supra* n. 15, at 192.
68 *Id.* at 193.
69 Robert A.C. Ruiter et al., *Scary Warnings and Rational Precautions: A Review of the Psychology of Fear Appeals*, 16 Psychol. & Health 613, 614 (2001).
70 Robin L. Snipes et al., *A Model of the Effects of Self-efficacy on the Perceived Ethicality and Performance of Fear Appeals in Advertising*, 19 J. Bus. Ethics 273, 274 (1999).
71 Ruiter et al., *supra* n. 69, at 626.
72 *See, e.g.*, Elizabeth Vargas et al., *Is the Breast Best? Ad Campaign Rattles Mothers on Breast-Feeding Controversy*, July 13, 2006, http://abcnews.go.com/2020/print?id=2188066; and Wolf, *Is Breast Really Best?*, at 600–1, 615–17, 620–22.
73 Stanley Ip, et al., Evidence-Based Practice Ctr., Breastfeeding and Maternal and Infant Health Outcomes in Developed Countries 160–62 (2007) (hereafter AHRQ Report on Breastfeeding), available at http://archive.ahrq.gov/downloads/pub/evidence/pdf/brfout/brfout.pdf (last visited Sept. 2, 2016).
74 HHS, Office of the Surgeon General, *The Surgeon General's Call to Action to Support Breastfeeding* 1–2 (2011) (hereafter *The Surgeon General's Call to Action*), http://www.surgeongeneral.gov.
75 *See generally* Hulbert, *supra* n. 10, at 7–9.

76 See, e.g., Am. Acad. of Pediatrics, *The Changing Concept of Sudden Infant Death Syndrome: Diagnostic Coding Shifts, Controversies Regarding the Sleeping Environment, and New Variables to Consider in Reducing Risk*, 116 Pediatrics 1245, 1246 (2005); *see also* Dawne Gurbutt and Russell Gurbutt, *Risk Reduction and Sudden Infant Death Syndrome*, 80 Community Practitioner 24, 25 (2007).

77 Rand E. Rosenblatt, Sylvia A. Law, and Sara Rosenbaum, *Law and the American Health Care System* 6 (1997); and Charles D. Bluestone, *Current Indications for Tonsillectomy and Adenoidectomy*, 101 Annals Otology, Rhinology & Laryngology 58 (1992).

78 Sherry Boschert, *Otitis Behind Most Antibiotics Used Before Age 6*, Fam. Prac. News, Sept. 1, 2000, http://findarticles.com/p/articles/mi_7342/is_17_30/ai_66168850; Eugene Leibovitz, *Acute Otitis Media in Pediatric Medicine: Current Issues in Epidemiology, Diagnosis, and Management*, 5 Pediatric Drugs (Supplement) 1, 1–12 (2003); Jeffrey A. Linder et al., *Antibiotic Treatment of Children with Sore Throat*, 294 JAMA 2315 (2005).

79 See, e.g., Nicholas Bakalar, *Antibiotic Use in First Year May Increase Asthma Risk*, N.Y. Times, June 19, 2007, at F7.

80 For an excellent review of the literature supporting and arguing against the benefits of breastfeeding see Wolf, *Is Breast Really Best?*, at 601–10; and Rebecca Goldin et al., *What Science Really Says about the Benefits of Breast-Feeding (and What the New York Times Didn't Tell You)*, June 20, 2006, http://www.stats.org/stories/breast_feed_nyt_jun_20_06.htm.

81 Brakken, *supra* n. 49.

82 AHRQ Report on Breastfeeding, *supra* n. 73, at v, 3–7.

83 Chen and Rogan, *supra* n. 41, at e438 (emphasis added).

84 Wolf, *Is Breast Really Best?*, at 602.

85 Am. Acad. of Pediatrics, *supra* n. 76, at 1250 (emphasis added). In October 2016 the AAP issued new guidance on infant sleep, recommending exclusive breastfeeding for six months to reduce the risk of SIDS. However, the AAP still noted only an association, rather than a causal relationship, between not breastfeeding and SIDS. AAP, *SIDS and Other Sleep-Related Infant Deaths: Updated 2016 Recommendations for a Safe Infant Sleeping Environment*, 138 (5) Pediatrics e20162938 at 4 (2016).

86 Posting of Dr. Steven Parker to WebMD Blog, *Breast-Feed or Else*, http://blogs.webmd.com/healthy-children/2006/07/breast-feed-or-else.html (May 17, 2008) (citing Anushua Sinha et al., *Reduced Risk of Neonatal Respiratory Infections among Breastfed Girls but Not Boys*, 112 Pediatrics e303 (2003); and Wendy H. Oddy et al., *Breastfeeding Duration and Academic Achievement at 10 Years*, 127 Pediatrics e137 (2011).

87 Mary Ann Hylander et al., *Human Milk Feedings and Infection among Very Low Birth Weight Infants*, 102 Pediatrics e38, 1, 4 (1998); and Goldin et al., *supra* n. 80.

88 Kukla, *supra* n. 15, at 148.

89 *Id.* at 148–50, 160–63.

90 Dale Tavris et al., *Evaluation of a Pregnancy Outcome Risk Reduction Program in a Local Health Department*, 99(2) Wisc. Med J. 47, 50 (2000); Donatelle, *Incentives in Smoking Cessation*, *supra*, at S163, S164 (chapter 5, n. 222); and M.M.T.

Vennemann et al., *Do Immunisations Reduce the Risk for SIDS? A Meta-Analysis*, 25 Vaccine 4875, 4878 (2007).

91 *See* Lawrence O. Gostin, *Public Health Law in a New Century, Part III: Public Health Regulation: A Systemic Evaluation*, 283 JAMA 3118, 3120–22 (2000).

92 Vincenso Zanardo et al., *Elective Cesarean Delivery: Does It Have a Negative Effect on Breastfeeding?*, 37 Birth 275, 276–77 (2010).

93 Cynthia G. Colen and David M. Ramey, *Is Breast Truly Best? Estimating the Effects of Breastfeeding on Long-term Child Health and Wellbeing in the United States Using Sibling Comparisons*, 109 Social Science and Medicine 55 (2014) [at 3–4, 10–23 in manuscript form].

94 In the United States, the Centers for Disease Control and the AAP counsel HIV-positive women against breastfeeding because formula feeding is "safe, affordable, and culturally acceptable." Am. Acad. of Pediatrics, *supra* n. 42, at 497; Jennifer S. Read and the Comm. on Pediatric AIDS, *Human Milk, Breastfeeding, and Transmission of Human Immunodeficiency Virus Type 1 in the United States*, 112 Pediatrics 1196, 1196 (2003). However, in the developing world, experts conclude that breastfeeding, even with HIV, is safer than using formula. Lawrence K. Altman, *Scientists Urge New Look at Feeding in AIDS Fight*, N.Y. Times, Feb. 27, 2007, at A15.

95 2005 AAP Policy Statement on Breastfeeding, *supra* n. 39, at 497. See also AAP 2012 Statement, *supra* n. 4, at e833–34.

96 *2012 AAP Policy Statement on Breastfeeding*, *supra* n. 4, at e833; *see also* 2005 AAP Statement, *supra* n. 39, at 497.

97 Tara Culp-Ressler, *Arkansas Mother Thrown in Jail for Breastfeeding While Drinking a Beer*, ABC News 20/20, Mar. 27, 2014.

98 Caroline Bologna, *Mom Who Smokes Pot Fights for Her Right to Breastfeed Her Preemie*, Huffington Post, Aug. 12, 2014, 2014 WLNR 22085428.

99 *See, e.g.*, Thaddeus Greenson, *Mom Gets Six Years in Prison for Son's Death; Wortman Leaves Plea in Place in Methamphetamine Breast Milk Case*, Times Standard, Mar. 20, 2012; Harriet McLeod, *Mom in Drugged Breast-Milk Murder of Baby Gets 20 Years in Prison*, Reuters Apr. 4, 2014; Doyle Murphy, *California Baby Dies after Drinking Mother's Drug-Laced Milk*, N.Y. Daily News, Sept. 2, 2013; Darrell Smith, *Citrus Heights Mom Gets 12 Years After Infant Son's Fatal Overdose*, Sacramento Bee, March 27, 2015, at http://www.sacbee.com/news/local/crime/article16488236.html (visited Sept. 2, 2016); KGW Staff, *Hillsboro Mother Accused of Breastfeeding Meth to Child*, Sept. 16, 2009, http://www.kgw.com/story/news/nation/ (last visited Sept. 12, 2014); *see also* Warner Todd Huston, *Idaho Woman Arrested for Breastfeeding her Baby While on Meth*, http://www.breitbart.com/big-government/2016/06/10/idaho-woman-arrested-breastfeeding-baby-meth/ (June 10, 2016); and Keith Kinnaird, *Mother Imprisoned for Exposing Baby to Meth*, Bonner County Daily Bee, May 20, 2016; http://www.bonnercountydailybee.com/local_news/20160520/mother_is_imprisoned_for_exposing_baby_to_meth (last visited Sept. 2, 2016).

100 Maeve Reston, *Plea Deal in Perris Mom Meth Case*, L.A. Times, Sept. 19, 2006, http://articles.latimes.com/print/2006/sep/19/local/me-meth19 (last visited Oct. 3, 2014).
101 Florence Williams, *Toxic Breast Milk?*, N.Y. Times Magazine, Jan. 9, 2005, at 21–24; Wolf, *Is Breast Best?*, at 614; *see also* Karen Fassuliotis, *The Science of Endocrine Disruption—Will It Change the Scope of Products Liability Claims?*, 17 Pace Envt'l. L. Rev. 351, 358 (1999).
102 2005 AAP Policy Statement on Breastfeeding, *supra* n. 39, at 497.
103 Betsy Lozoff et al., *Higher Infant Blood Lead Levels with Longer Duration of Breastfeeding*, 155 J. Pediatr. 663, [p. 5 of unnumbered article] (2009).
104 U.S. Food & Drug Admin. Ctr. for Devices & Radiological Health, Medical Devices Advisory Committee, General and Plastic Surgery Devices Panel, 66th Meeting (2005).
105 *Report on Baby's Death Prompts Delay in Trial*, N.Y. Times, Mar. 18, 1999, at B8.
106 *Id.*; Nina Bernstein, *Mother Convicted in Infant's Starvation Death Gets 5 Years' Probation*, N.Y. Times, Sept. 9, 1999, at B3; Cynthia McFadden, Hugh Downs, and Barbara Walters, ABC 20/20, Feb. 26, 1999, Transcript #99022603. The judge sentenced Ms. Walrond to five years' probation.
107 Rosa Manganaro et al., *Incidence of Dehydration and Hypernatremia in Exclusively Breast-Fed Infants*, 139 J. Pediatrics 673, 673 (2001); Michael L. Moritz et al., *Breastfeeding-Associated Hypernatremia: Are We Missing the Diagnosis?*, 116 Pediatrics e343, e345 (2005), http://www.pediatrics.org/cgi/doi/10.1542/peds.2004-2647; Arlan L. Rosenbloom, *Permanent Brain Damage from Hypernatremic Dehydration in Breastfed Infants: Patient Reports*, 43 Clinical Pediatrics 855–56 (2004).
108 I. A. Laing and C. M. Wong, *Hypernatraemia in the First Few Days: Is the Incidence Rising?*, 87 Archives Disease Childhood (Fetal Neonatal Edition) F158, F160 (2002), available at http://fn.bmj.com; Verity H. Livingstone et al., *Neonatal Hypernatremic Dehydration Associated with Breast-Feeding Malnutrition: A Retrospective Survey*, 162 Canadian Med. J. 647, 651 (2000); *see also* Jeanne M. Madden et al., *Effects of a Law Against Early Postpartum Discharge on Newborn Follow-up, Adverse Events, and HMO Expenditures*, 347 New Eng. J. Med. 2031, 2035 (2002).
109 Moritz et al., *supra* n. 107, at e343; Rosenbloom, *supra* n. 107, at 856.
110 Kukla, *supra* n. 15, at 194.
111 *See* Elsie M. Taveras et al., *Clinician Support and Psychosocial Risk Factors Associated with Breastfeeding Discontinuation*, 112 Pediatrics 108, 113 (2003).
112 Karen Springen, *Indecent Exposure?*, Newsweek, June 11, 2007, at 49.
113 Iris Marion Young, *Breasted Experience: The Look and the Feeling*, in On Female Body Experience: "Throwing Like a Girl" and other Essays 85, 88 (2005).
114 *See, e.g.*, Samantha Schmidt, *De Blasio Signs Bill Mandating Lactation Rooms in City*, N.Y. Times, Aug. 12, 2016, at A20; Kathleen Longcore, *Call for Cover-Up Stuns Nursing Mom, Complaints at County Building Prompt Solidarity 'Nurse-In,'* Grand Rapids Press, June 9, 2005, at A1; Bianca Prieto, *Breast-Feeding Mom*

Ticketed Citation Dismissed Law Passed Last Year Guarantees Her Right, Rocky Mountain News, July 29, 2005; Letter from Elisabeth Benjamin, N.Y. Civil Liberties Union Reproductive Rights Project, to Gerald L. Storch, Toys 'R' Us (Sept. 14, 2006) (challenging harassment of mother who breastfed her infant while shopping at a Toys 'R' Us store in New York City).

115 Geoff Elliott, *Mums Begin 'Lactivism' after Airline Bans Breastfeeding*, The Australian, Nov. 23, 2006, at 8.

116 *See* Karen Bonuck et al., *Country of Origin and Race/Ethnicity: Impact on Breastfeeding Intentions*, 21 J. Hum. Lactation 320 (2005); *see also* Samir Arora et al., *Major Factors Influencing Breastfeeding Rates*, at 2.

117 Wolf, *supra* n. 57, at 621.

118 *Id*. In African-American communities, this practice is sometimes referred to as "other-mothering." Laura T. Kessler, *The Politics of Care*, 23 Wis. J. L. Gender & Soc'y 169, 174–75 (2008).

119 Jose Labarere et al., *Efficacy of Breastfeeding Support Provided by Trained Clinicians During an Early, Routine, Preventative Visit: A Prospective, Randomized, Open Trial of 226 Mother-Infant Pairs*, 115 Pediatrics e139, e140 (2005), http://www.pediatrics.org/cgi/doi/10.1542/peds.2004-1362. See also Taveras, *supra* n. 11, at 113.

120 Arora, *supra* n. 116, at 1; Taveras et al., *supra*, at 113.

121 Interview with Miriam Labbok, M.D., Dir. Ctr. For Infant & Young Child Feeding & Care, Dep't of Maternal & Child Health, Univ. of N.C., and Mary Rose Tully, Dir. Of Lactation Servs., N.C. Women's and Children's Hosps., in Chapel Hill, N.C. (Aug. 29, 2009) (on file with the author). *See also* Breastfeeding Report Card, United States/2014, *supra* n. 30, at 2; and Indu B. Ahluwalia et al., *Why Do Women Stop Breastfeeding? Findings from the Pregnancy Risk Assessment and Monitoring System*, 116 Pediatrics 1408, 1410–11 (2005); *see also* Christine M. Furber and Ann M. Thomson, *Midwives in the UK: An Exploratory Study of Newborn Feeding Support for Postpartum Mothers in the Hospital*, 52 J. Nurse-Midwifery 142, 143–46 (2007). New York City has recently initiated a program to connect visiting nurses with newly pregnant women who live in neighborhoods with high infant mortality rates. N.Y. City Dep't of Health & Mental Hygiene, Nurse-Family Partnership, http://home2.nyc.gov/html/doh/html/ms/ms-nfp.shtml. Such programs, organized nationally under the rubric of Nurse-Family Partnerships, have been found to be highly cost-effective in enhancing children's health status, improving family planning, increasing rates of maternal employment, and decreasing families' reliance on welfare programs. Julia B. Isaacs, Brookings Inst., *Cost-Effective Investments in Children 13–16* (2007); David L. Olds et al., *Effects of Nurse Home-Visiting on Maternal Life Course and Child Development: Age 6 Follow-Up Results of a Randomized Trial*, 114 Pediatrics 1550, 1550 (2004); *see also* Lynn A. Karoly et al., *Early Childhood Interventions: Proven Results, Future Promise* xxxviii (2005).

122 *See, e.g.*, New York State Medicaid Coverage of Lactation Counselling Services (March 2013), https://www.health.ny.gov/community/pregnancy/breastfeeding/medicaid_coverage/lactation_counseling_services.htm.

123 Catherine Saint Louis, *Breast-Feeding Services Lag the Law*, N.Y. Times, Oct. 1, 2013, at D6.
124 *See* Barbara L. Philipp et al., *Baby-Friendly Hospital Initiative Improves Breastfeeding Initiation Rates in a US Hospital Setting*, 108 Pediatrics 677–78 (2001); *see also* Shubber, *supra* n. 51, at 2, 43.
125 U.S. Gov't Accountability Office, *Breastfeeding: Some Strategies Used to Market Infant Formula May Discourage Breastfeeding; State Contracts Should Better Protect Against Misuse of WIC Name* app. I at 9 (2006); Katherine R. Shealy et al., U.S. Dep't Health & Human Servs., The CDC Guide to Breastfeeding Interventions i (2005), https://www.cdc.gov/breastfeeding/pdf/breastfeeding_interventions.pdf (last visited Aug. 15, 2016).
126 For example, in 1999 Boston Medical Center, a major teaching hospital serving an inner-city population, estimated that it lost $20,000 in annual revenue by giving up free formula. Philipp et al., *supra* n. 124, at 680.
127 *See, e.g.*, Sonja Merten et al., *Do Baby-Friendly Hospitals Influence Breastfeeding Duration on a National Level?* 116 Pediatrics e702, e708 (2005), http://www.pediatrics.org/cgi/doi/10.1542/peds.2005-0537.
128 Baby Friendly Hospital Initiative U.S.A, at www.babyfriendlyusa.org/find-facilities (last visited Feb. 29, 2016) (citing number of hospitals and birthing centers that meet Baby Friendly standards); *see also* Anne Merewood et al., *Breastfeeding Rates in US Baby-Friendly Hospitals: Results of a National Survey*, 116 Pediatrics 628 (2005).
129 Cutler and Wright, *supra* n. 20, at 46; *see also* Alison Steube, *The Risks of Not Breastfeeding for Mothers and Infants*, 2 Reviews in Obstetrics and Gynecology 222, 227 (2009).
130 Lorraine Boyd et al., *Latch on NYC: A Program to Support Mothers Who Choose to Breastfeed*, Presentation at the American Pub. Health Ass'n, Nov. 2–6, 2013; *see also* Latch on NYC Initiative-Myths http://www.nyc.gov/html/om/pdf/2012/latch_myth_fact.pdf (last visited Aug. 15, 2016); KJ Dell'Antonia, *Why the Backlash on Bloomberg's Breastfeeding Initiative*, N.Y. Times, Aug. 2, 2012, http://parenting.blogs.nytimes.com/2012/08/02/why-the-backlash-on-bloombergs-breastfeeding-initiative/; and Sumathi Reddy, *One Sure Formula for Controversy*, Wall St. J., Aug. 2, 2012, http://www.wsj.com/articles/SB10000872396390444320704577565443888428780.
131 Taveras et al., *supra* n. 111, at 111–12.
132 Nancy E. Dowd, *Race, Gender, and Work/Family Policy*, 15 Was. U. J. L. & Pol'y, 219, 220, n. 6, 232–35 (2004).
133 Rada K. Dagher et al., *Maternity Leave Duration and Postpartum Mental and Physical Health: Implications for Leave Policies*, 39 J. Health Politics, Pol'y & L. 369, 370 (2014).
134 Pub. L. No. 103-3, 107 Stat. 6 (1993); *see also* 29 U.S.C. § 2612 (b) (1).
135 Brian Roe et al., *Is There Competition Between Breast-Feeding and Maternal Employment?*, 36 Demography 157, 167 (1999).

136 Alan S. Ryan et al., *The Effect of Employment Status on Breastfeeding in the United States*, 16 Women's Health Issues 243, 247 (2006) (citing data showing a consistent pattern from 1984 to 2003). See also Alan S. Ryan and Wenjun Zhou, *Lower Breastfeeding Rates Persist among the Special Supplemental Nutrition Program for Woman, Infants, and Children Participants, 1978–2003*, 117 Pediatrics 1136, 1142 (2006).

137 Joan Ortiz et al., *Duration of Breast Milk Expression among Working Mothers Enrolled in an Employer-Sponsored Lactation Program*, 30 Pediatric Nursing 111, 116 (2004).

138 Jodi Kantor, *On the Job, Nursing Mothers Are Finding a 2-Class System*, N.Y. Times, Sept. 1, 2006, at A1.

139 Ryan et al., *supra* n. 136, at 249.

140 *Id.* See also Chen and Rogan, *supra* n. 41.

141 See, e.g., Am. Acad. of Pediatrics, National Worksite Breastfeeding Support Initiative, http://www.aapca3.org/resources/nbsi.pdf (last visited Sept. 19, 2009).

142 Carmella Bocchino, et al., U.S. Dep't of Health & Human Servs., *Advancing Women's Health: Health Plans' Innovative Programs in Breastfeeding Promotion* 78–81, http://www.womenshealth.gov/owh/pub/breastfeeding.cfm (last visited Oct. 4, 2009); Ortiz et al., *supra* n. 137, at 116; *see also* Sue Shellenbarger, *Employer, State Support Stalls for Mothers Who Nurse at Work*, Wall St. J., Nov. 22, 2005, at D4.

143 Shellenbarger, *supra* n. 142.

144 See, e.g., *Bd. of Sch. Dirs. of Fox Chapel Area Sch. Dist. v. Rosetti*, 411 A.2d 486, 488 (Pa. 1980), and *Barrash v. Bowen*, 846 F.2d 927, 930–32 (4th Cir. 1988).

145 Under the Pregnancy Discrimination Act of 1978, Title VII encompasses discrimination against women on account of pregnancy. See, e.g., *Fejes v. Gilpin Ventures, Inc.*, 960 F. Supp.1487, 1491 (D. Colo. 1997).

146 See, e.g., *Martinez v. N.B.C., Inc.*, 49 F. Supp. 2d 305, 308–09 (S.D.N.Y. 1999).

147 Carey Goldberg, *Board Won't Relent for Breast-Feeding Mother*, Boston Globe, June 23, 2007, 2007 WLNR 11944689; *Sophie C. Currier v. Nat'l Bd. of Med. Exam'rs*, No. 2007-J-0434 (Mass. App. Ct. 2007); *see also* Felicia Mello, *Ruling Gives Breast-Feeding Student Extra Break in Exam*, Boston Globe, Sept. 27, 2007, 2007 WLNR 18952115; and *Currier v. National Bd. of Medical Examiners*, 965 N.E. 2d 829 (Mass. 2012).

148 National Conference of State Legislatures, *Breastfeeding State Laws*, Mar. 31, 2015, available at http://www.ncsl.org/research.health/breastfeeding-state-laws.aspx (last visited Aug. 29, 2015).

149 Cal. Lab. Code § 1032.

150 Minn. Stat. Ann. § 181.939; Tenn. Code Ann. § 50-1-305.

151 This was accomplished by amending the Fair Labor Standards Act and adding a new section, 29 U.S.C.§ 207 (r).

152 U.S. Dep't of Labor, Wage and Hour Division, Fact Sheet #73: Break Time for Nursing Mothers Under the FLSA, available at https://www.dol.gov/whd/regs/compliance/whdfs73.htm (last visited Aug. 28, 2016).

153 717 F.3d 425, 428 (5th Cir. 2013); *see also* Alissa Wickham, *EEOC Settles Breastfeeding Bias Suit* (May 12, 2014), available at http://www.law360.com/articles/536737/eeoc-settles-breastfeeding-bias-suit (last visited Sept. 2, 2016).

154 *Alabama City Must Pay Cop Who Quit Over Breastfeeding Dispute*, 30 No. 17 Westlaw Journal Employment 15, March 15, 2016, at https://1.next.westlaw.com/Document/I92fb028dec3a11e598dc8b09b4f043e0/View/FullText.html?navigationPath=Search%2Fv3%2Fsearch%2Fresults%2Fnavigation%2Fi0ad6ad3a0000015699a3e8438527ae56%3FNav%3DANALYTICAL%26fragmentIdentifier%3DI92fb028dec3a11e598dc8b09b4f043e0%26startIndex%3D1%26contextData%3D%2528sc.Search%2529%26transitionType%3DSearchItem&listSource=Search&listPageSource=ec7ee386e3b8a41d6311d48b08d6d7af&list=ANALYTICAL&rank=13&grading=na&sessionScopeId=10f60c8e8ed83881799b8cde6122ad9a43154addcb730bbf22ea4b1c98eb46c0&originationContext=Search%20Result&transitionType=SearchItem&contextData=%28sc.Search%29 (visited Sept.2, 2016).

155 Anne E. Kornblut, *Michelle Obama's Remarks on Breast-feeding Draw Criticism from Palin, Bachmann*, Washington Post, Feb. 19, 2011, at A02 (stating that the mother must itemize deductions to get the tax benefit and only one-third of taxpayers itemize their taxes).

156 Two bills have been proposed during two recent sessions of Congress, Breastfeeding Promotion Act of 2011, H.R. 2758 (112th Cong., at § 101), and the Breastfeeding Promotion Act of 2011, H.R. Rep. 1463, 12th Cong., but neither was enacted.

157 *See, e.g.*, H.R. 2790, proposed by Representative Maloney in the 108th Congress, and its predecessor and successor legislation.

CHAPTER 7. THE "GOOD MOTHER" AND CRIMES OF OMISSION

1 *State v. McLaughlin*, 600 P.2d 474, 475–77 (Or. Ct. App. 1979).
2 Hafemeister, *Castles Made of Sand, supra* at 821 (chapter 1, n. 54).
3 New Mexico's child abuse statute is typical. It provides that child abuse "consists of a person knowingly, intentionally or negligently, and without justifiable cause, *causing or permitting* a child to be placed in a dangerous situation, tortured, or exposed to the weather." N.M. Stat. § 30-6-1 (D) (West. 2014) (emphasis added).
4 The chapter's analysis is based on 108 appellate court decisions, which are included in the appendix. Additional cases have been identified through media accounts. *See, e.g.*, Alex Campbell, *Battered, Bereaved, and Behind Bars, Methodology Section*, https://www.buzzfeed.com/alexcampbell/these-mothers-were-sentenced-to-at-least-10-years-for-failin?utm_term=.ksaO64oQNM#.xtqe3AD9yo (last visited Sept. 5, 2016).
5 Legal scholars have been writing about this problem, in both the criminal and civil contexts, for several decades. This chapter seeks to acknowledge their work and build upon it. These scholars include Nancy Erickson, *Battered Mothers of Battered Children*, at 198; Michelle S. Jacobs, *Requiring Battered Women Die*;

Melissa L. Breger, *The (In)Visibility of Motherhood in Family Court Proceedings*, 36 N.Y.U. Rev. L. & Soc. Change 555 (2012); Myrna S. Raeder, *Preserving Family Ties for Domestic Violence Survivors and Their Children by Invoking a Human Rights Approach to Avoid the Criminalization of Mothers Based on the Acts and Accusations of Their Batterers*, 17 J. Gender, Race & Just. 105 (2014); Saundra Chung, *Mama Mia!*, at 205–6, 207–10; and Fugate, Note, *Who's Failing to Protect Whom?*, supra, at 273–74 (chapter 1, n. 62).

6   Fugate, *supra*, at 274.
7   Matthew J. Breiding et al., *Prevalence and Characteristics of Sexual Violence, Stalking, and Intimate Partner Violence Victimization: National Intimate Partner and Sexual Violence Survey, United States, 2011*, Ctrs. for Disease Control & Prevention, U.S. Dep't of Health & Human Servs. (Sept. 5, 2014). *See also* Michael P. Johnson, *A Typology of Domestic Violence: Intimate Terrorism, Violent Resistance, and Situational Couple Violence* 1–4, 5–6, 10–12, and 16–17 (2008).
8   Proverbs 13:24.
9   Stephen J. Pfohl, *The "Discovery" of Child Abuse*, 24 Soc. Probs. 310, 310–11 (1976–77); *see also* Jill Elaine Hasday, *Parenthood Divided: A Legal History of the Bifurcated Law of Parental Relations*, 90 Geo. L.J. 299, 310–11, citing 1 William Blackstone, Commentaries *440–41, and 2 James Kent, *Commentaries on American Law* 253–54.
10 *See, e.g.*, Reva B. Siegel, *"The Rule of Love": Wife Beating as Prerogative and Privacy*, 105 Yale L.J. 2117 (1996).
11 Hafemeister *supra*, at 821; Noonan, *Legal Accountability in the Service-Based Welfare State*, *supra*, at 526.
12 Hafemeister, *supra*, at 834–35; Pfohl, *supra* n. 9, at 312–14.
13 Hafemeister, *supra*, at 835–36, Pfohl, *supra* n. 9, at 314–15.
14 Kathleen Kelley Reardon and Christopher T. Noblet, *Childhood Denied: Ending the Nightmare of Child Abuse and Neglect* 97–102 (2008).
15 C. Henry Kempe et al., *The Battered Child Syndrome*, 181 J.A.M.A. 17 (1962).
16 Hafemeister, *supra*, at 838–40.
17 Hafemeister, *supra*, at 842–43; *see also* Kathleen G. Noonan et al., *Legal Accountability in the Service-Based Welfare State*, *supra* (chapter 3, n. 50), at 526.

These states, and the relevant statutes are: Ala. Code § 13A-13-6; Ala. Code § 26-15-3.2; Alaska Stat. § 11.51.100; Alaska Stat. § 11.51.110; Ariz. Rev. Stat. § 13-3619; Ariz. Rev. Stat. § 13-3623; Ark. Code Ann. § 5-27-205; Ark. Code Ann. § 5-27-206; Ark. Code Ann. § 5-27-207; Ark. Code Ann. § 5-27-221; Cal. Penal Code § 273a; Colo. Rev. Stat. § 18-6-401; Conn. Gen. stat. § 53–21; Del. Code Ann. tit. 11, § 1102; D.C. Code § 22-1101; Fla. Stat. Ann. § 827.03; Ga. Code Ann. § 19-7-2; Haw. Rev. Stat. § 709-903.5; Haw. Rev. Stat. § 709-904; Idaho Code Ann. § 18-1501; 720 Ill. Comp. Stat. 5/12C-5; 720 Ill. Comp. Stat. 5/12C-15; 720 Ill. Comp. Stat. 646/50; Ind. Code § 31-34-1-2; Iowa code § 726.6; Iowa code § 726.6A; Iowa code § 124.401C; Kan. stat. ann. § 21–5601; Ky. Rev. Stat. Ann. § 508.100; Ky. Rev. Stat. Ann. § 530.060; Ky. Rev. Stat. Ann. § 218A.1441; Ky.

Rev. Stat. Ann. § 218A.1442; Ky. Rev. Stat. Ann. § 218A.1443; Ky. Rev. Stat. Ann. § 218A.1444; La. Rev. Stat. Ann. § 14:91.4; Me. Rev. Stat. tit. 17-A, § 554; Mass. gen. Laws ch. 265, § 13J; Minn. Stat. § 609.378; Miss. Code Ann. § 97-5-39; Miss. Code Ann. § 97-5-40; Mo. Rev. Stat § 568.045; Mo. Rev. Stat. § 568.050; Mont. Code Ann. § 45-5-622; Mont. Code Ann. § 45-5-628; Neb. Rev. Stat. § 28-707; Nev. Rev. Stat. § 200.508; N.H. Rev. Stat. Ann. § 639:3; N.J. Stat. Ann. § 2C:24-4; N.M. Stat. Ann. § 30-6-1; N.Y. Penal Law § 260.10; N.C. Gen. Stat. § 14-318.2; N.C. Gen. Stat. § 14-318.4; N.D. Cent. Code § 14-09-22; Ohio Rev. Code Ann. § 2903.15; Ohio Rev. Code Ann. § 2919.22; Okla. Stat. tit. 21 § 701.7; Okla. Stat. tit. 21 § 843.5; Okla. Stat. tit. 21 § 852.1; Or. Rev. Stat § 163.575; 18 PA. Cons. Stat. Ann. § 4304; R.I. Gen Laws § 11-9-5; S.C. Code Ann. § 16-3-85; S.C. Code Ann. § 16-3-95; S.C. Code Ann. § 63-5-70; S.D. Codified Laws § 26-10-30; Tenn. Code Ann. § 39-13-102; Tenn. Code Ann. § 39-15-401; Tenn. Code Ann. § 39-15-402; Tex. Penal Code § 22.04; Utah Code Ann. § 76-5-109; Vt. Stat. Ann. tit. 13, § 1304; Vt. Stat. Ann. tit. 13, § 1305; Va. Code Ann. § 18.2-371.1; Va. Code Ann. § 40.1-103; Wash rev. Code Ann. § 9A.42.035; W. Va. Code § 61-8D-1; W. Va. Code § 61-8D-4; W. Va. Code § 61-8D-4A; Wis. Stat. § 948.03; Wyo. Stat. Ann § 6-4-403.

18 Reardon and Noblet, *supra* n. 14, at 102.
19 Robert Reinhold, *2 Acquitted of Child Molestation in Nation's Longest Criminal Trial*, N.Y. Times, Jan. 19, 1990, at A1; *see also* Jennifer L. Truman and Erica L. Smith, Bureau of Justice Statistics, U.S. Dep't of Justice, NCJ 238799, *Prevalence of Violent Crime among Households with Children, 1993–2010* (Sept. 2012).
20 *Pierce v. Soc'y of Sisters*, 268 U.S. 510, 535 (1925).
21 "Father Knows Best" was the title of a hugely popular American television series that ran from 1954 to 1960. "Father Knows Best," http://fatherknowsbest.US/history (last visited Mar. 18, 2015).
22 *DeShaney v. Winnebago Cnty Dep't of Soc. Servs.*, 489 U.S. 189 (1989).
23 *Town of Castle Rock v. Gonzales*, 545 U.S. 748 (2005).
24 *DeShaney*, 489 U.S. 189 at 201–03.
25 *Gonzales*, 545 U.S. 765–67.
26 The Supreme Court's decision was condemned by the Inter-American Commission on Human Rights. In 2011 the Commission found that the Castle Rock police department had denied the girls and their mother important rights guaranteed by international human rights law, including the right to equal protection before the law, the right to judicial protection, and, for the three girls, the right to life. *Jessica Lenahan (Gonzales) v. United States*, Report No. 80/11, Case 12.626, Inter-Am. Comm'n H.R. 2, 5 (Jul. 2011), http://www.oas.org/en/iachr/decisions/2011/US-PU12626EN.doc.
27 *See, e.g.*, Oren Yaniv, *New York Child Welfare Workers Charged in Starvation Death of 4-Year-Old Marchella Brett-Pierce*, N.Y. Daily News (Mar. 23, 2011), http://www.nydailynews.com/news/crime/new-york-child-welfare-workers-charged-starvation-death-4-year-old-marchella-brett-pierce-article-1.123475; Mosi

Secret, *Ex–Child Welfare Caseworkers Plead Guilty in Death of a 4-Year-Old*, N.Y. Times, Dec. 18, 2013, at A24; *see also Anderson v. Nebraska Dep't of Social Servs.*, 538 N.W.2d 732, 738–39 (Neb. 1995).

28 Ken Belson, *Goodell Admits He Was Wrong in Rice Case*, N.Y. Times, Aug. 29, 2014, at B8; Rachelle Cohen, *Violence Roughs Up the NFL's Image*, Boston Herald, Sept. 18, 2014, http://www.bostonherald.com/news_opinion/opinion/op_ed/2014/09/rachelle_cohen_violence_roughs_up_nfl_s_image.

29 In 2014 an estimated 702,000 American children were estimated to have been abused or neglected. *Child Maltreatment 2014*, supra (chapter 1, n. 55), at 21. These numbers are similar to earlier data. In 2012, an estimated 686,000 children nationwide were the victims of abuse and neglect. U.S. Dep't Health & Human Serv., Admin. Child., Youth & Fam., Child. Bureau, *Child Maltreatment 2012* xi, http://www.acf.hhs.gov/sites/default/files/cb/cm2012.pdf.

30 Office of the Assistant Secretary for Planning & Evaluation, U.S. Dep't of Health & Human Servs., *Male Perpetrators of Child Maltreatment: Findings from NCANDS*, v, 1, 7, 9, 13 (Jan. 2005), available at http://www.aspe.hhs.gov/hsp/05/child-maltreat/report.pdf.

31 *See* The Child Abuse Prevention and Treatment Act as Amended by P.L. 111–320, the CAPTA Reauthorization Act of 2010, at 6, 42 U.S.C. §§ 5101 and 5116. *See also* Child Welfare Information Gateway, Children's Bureau, *Act of Omission: An Overview of Child Neglect* 2 (Aug. 2012), available at https://www.childwelfare.gov/pubPDFs/acts.pdf.

32 For federal fiscal year 2012, an estimated 1,593 American children died from abuse and neglect. *Child Maltreatment 2012*, supra n. 29, at xii.

33 *See, e.g.*, Benjamin Mueller and John Surico, *Queens Father Killed 3 and Himself, Police Say*, N.Y. Times, Jan. 25, 2015, at A19. *Cf.* Rick Bragg, *Carolina Jury Rejects Execution for Woman Who Drowned Sons*, N.Y. Times, July 29, 1995, at 1 (Susan Smith), and *Yates v. State*, 171 S.W.3d 215 (Tex. 2005) (Andrea Yates).

34 Alexia Cooper and Erica L. Smith, Bureau of Justice Statistics, U.S. Dep't of Justice, NCJ 236018, *Homicide Trends in the United States, 1980–2008*, at 5–7 (2011); *Child Maltreatment 2012*, supra n. 29, at 19; and Timothy Y. Mariano et al., *Toward a More Holistic Understanding of Filicide: A Multidisciplinary Analysis of 32 Years of U.S. Arrest Data*, 236 Forensic Sci. Int'l 46, 48 (2014).

35 Kreider and Ellis, *Living Arrangements of Children* at 3 (chapter 1, n. 64).

36 *Id*. *See also* Vespa, *America's Families and Living Arrangements* at 21 (chapter 1, n. 64).

37 Vespa et al., *supra*, at 13. *See also* Mather, *U.S. Children in Single-Mother Families* at 2 (chapter 1, n. 65).

38 Mather, *supra* n. 37, at 2.

39 Jane Waldfogel et al., *Fragile Families and Child Wellbeing*, 20 The Future of Children 87, 88 (2010), http://www.futureofchildren.org/futureofchildren/publications/docs/20_02_05.pdf; *see also* Kreider and Ellis, *supra* n. 35, at 13; and Vespa, *supra* n. 36, at 16, Table 6.

40 Shannan Catalano, *Intimate Partner Violence, 1993–2010*, Bureau Just. Stat., U.S. Dep't Just 1 (Nov. 2012).
41 Theodore P. Cross et al., *Prosecution of Child Abuse: A Meta-Analysis of Rates of Criminal Justice Decisions*, 4 Trauma, Violence, & Abuse 323, 324 (2003).
42 *Id.* at 323, 337; Andrea J. Sedlak et al., *Child Protection and Justice Systems Processing of Serious Child Abuse and Neglect Cases*, 30 Child Abuse & Neglect 657, 660 (2006).
43 Jennifer M. Collins, *Crime and Parenthood: The Uneasy Case for Prosecuting Negligent Parents*, 100 NW. U. L. Rev. 807, 831–32 (2006).
44 Breger, *supra* n. 5, at 564, 566–67.
45 Breger, *supra* n. 5, at 560–77.
46 Nolan Clay, *Kelsey's Mother Gets 27 Years in Prison*, Oklahoman (Sept. 10, 2007), http://newsok.com/kelseys-mother-gets-27-years-in-prison/article/3122794.
47 Chung, *supra* n. 5, at 213–14.
48 Campbell, *supra* n. 4, at 3 and 18 of 21. The facts of the case are discussed briefly in an unpublished decision, *Lindley v. State*, 2010 WL1076138 (Tex. Ct. App. 2010).
49 *Johnson v. State*, 508 So. 2d 443, 444–47 (Fl. Dist. Ct. App. 1987) (Zehmer, J., dissenting).
50 Cross, *supra* n. 41, at 330.
51 *See* Harmon M. Hosch et al., *A Comparison of Anglo-American and Mexican-American Jurors' Judgments of Mothers Who Fail to Protect Their Children from Abuse*, 21 J. Applied Soc. Psychol. 1681, 1685 (1991).
52 *Id.* at III-6-6.
53 Interview with A.S., York City area prosecutor (June 3, 2013).
54 Evan Stark, *A Failure to Protect: Unravelling "The Battered Mother's Dilemma*," 27 W. St. U. L. Rev. 29, 32 (1999–2000); *see also* Patricia Volk, *The Steinberg Trial: Scenes from a Tragedy*, N.Y. Times Magazine, Jan. 15, 1989, available at http://www.nytimes.com/1989/01/15/magazine/the-steinberg-trial-scenes-from-a-tragedy.html?pagewanted=all.
55 Cross, *supra* n. 41, at 330, 332
56 Campbell, *supra* n. 4, Methodology, 2 of 37. While the study can be criticized as selective, because it did not examine prosecution practices in all fifty states, it provides a glimpse into the way that child abuse by omission is treated by prosecutors today.
57 *Palmer v. State*, 164 A.2d 467 (Md. 1960); *see also Commonwealth v. Lane*, 956 S.W.2d 874 (Ky. 1997) (Cooper, J., concurring, at 879) (noting that *Palmer* was the first case "to directly impose a duty upon a parent" to prevent the physical abuse of a child by the parent's "domestic companion").
58 *Palmer*, 164 A.2d at 473.
59 *Id.* at 468, 473.
60 *Id.* at 474.
61 *Id.* The negative view of single mothers, particularly those who are sexually active, has long been noted. *See, e.g.*, Roiphe, *In Praise of Messy Lives, supra* (chapter 1, n.

68), at 15–27; and Carol Sanger, *1989 Survey of Books Relating to the Law; III. Law and Society: Seasoned to the Use* (reviewing *Presumed Innocent* by Scott Turow and *The Good Mother* by Sue Miller), 87 Mich. L. Rev. 1338, 1350–58 (1989); and Dorothy Roberts, *Unshackling Black Motherhood*, 95 Mich. L. Rev. 938 (1997), who notes the special negative emphasis on the fertility of African-American women.

62 Alaska Stat. § 11.51.100; Ariz. Rev. Stat. § 13-3623; Ark. Code Ann. § 5-27-221; Cal. Penal Code § 273a; Del. Code Ann. tit. 11, § 1102; Fla. Stat. § 827.03; Haw. Rev. Stat. § 709-903.5; Idaho Code Ann. § 18-1501; 720 Ill. Comp. Stat. 5/12C-5; Iowa Code § 726.6; Ky. Rev. Stat. Ann. § 508.100; Me. Rev. Stat. tit. 17-A, § 554; Mass. Gen. Laws ch. 265, § 13J; Minn. Stat. § 609. 378; Miss. Code Ann. § 97-5-39; Nev. Rev. Stat. § 200.508; N.M. Stat. Ann. § 30-6-1; N.C. Gen. Stat. § 14-318.4; N.D. Cent. Code § 14-09-22; Ohio Rev. Code Ann. § 2903.15; Okla. Stat. tit. 21 § 843.5; Okla. Stat. tit. 21 § 701.7; Okla. Stat. tit. 21 § 852.1; S.C. Code Ann. § 16-3-85; S.C. Code Ann. § 16-3-95; S.C. Code Ann. § 63-5-70; S.D. Codified Laws § 26-10-30; Tenn. Code Ann. § 39-15-401; Tenn. Code Ann. § 39-15-402; Tenn. Code Ann. § 39-13-102; Tex. Penal Code § 22.04; Utah Code § 76-5-109; Va. Code Ann. § 18.2-371.1; W. Va. Code § 61-8D; Wis. Stat. § 948.03.

63 *State v. Cabezuela*, 265 P.3d 705 (N.M. 2011).
64 *See* Lissa Griffin, *Which One of You Did It?*, *supra* (chapter 2, n. 136).
65 *See, e.g., Phelps v. State*, 439 So. 2d 727 (Ala. 1983); *Boone v. State*, 668 S.W.2d 17, 19 (Ark. 1984); *People v. Super. Court*, Olmos, 2013 WL 6729916, at *2 (Ca. Ct. App. Dec. 20, 2013); *Daumer v. State*, 381 So. 2d 1014, 1015 (Miss. 1980); *State v. Lucero*, 647 P.2d 406, 407 (N.M. 1982); *Maupin v. State*, 1991 Tenn. Crim App. LEXIS 818, at *7 (Tenn. Crim. App. Oct. 7, 1991), *aff'd* 859 S.W.2d 313 (Tenn. 1993); and *Campbell v. State*, 999 P.2d 649 (Wyo. 2000).
66 *See, e.g.*, Annette R. Appell, *Protecting Children or Punishing Mothers: Gender, Race, and Class in the Child Protection System*, 48 S.C. L. Rev. 577 (1997); Erickson, *Battered Mothers of Battered Children*, at 198; Jacobs, *supra* n. 5; and Fugate, *supra*.
67 I am indebted to Linda J. Panko for identifying these contrasting cases in her article *Legal Backlash: The Expanding Liability of Women Who Fail to Protect Their Children from Their Male Partner's Abuse*, 6 Hastings Women's L.J. 67, 78–80 (1995).
68 *State v. Williquette*, 385 N.W.2d 145, 149 (Wis. 1986).
69 *Id.* at 149.
70 *Id.* at 152, 155.
71 500 N.W.2d 916 (Wis. 1993).
72 *Id.* at 919–24.
73 *Id.* at 919.
74 *Williquette*, 385 N.W. 2d. 149.
75 Jeffrey L. Edleson, *The Overlap Between Child Maltreatment and Woman Abuse*, Nat'l Online Resource Ctr on Violence Against Women 2–3 (Apr. 1999), available at http://www.vawnet.org/Assoc_Files_VAWnet/AR_overlap.pdf; *see also* J Susan Schechter and Jeffrey L. Edleson, *Effective Intervention in Domestic Violence and*

Child Maltreatment Cases: Guidelines for Policy and Practice, Recommendations from the National Council of Juvenile and Family Court Judges Family Violence Department 9 (hereafter *The Greenbook*) (1999); and Johnson, *supra* n. 7, at 5–12, 61–67, 81.

76 See this book's appendix for the published cases. See Campbell, *supra* n. 5, for the Methodology section, *supra*, at 2.

77 Somini Sengupta, *U.N. Reveals 'Alarmingly High' Levels of Violence against Women*, N.Y. Times, March 10, 2015, at A4.

78 Breiding et al., *supra* n. 7, at 2; Johnson, *supra* n. 7, at 1.

79 *See, e.g.*, *United States v. Webb*, 747 F.2d 978 (5th Cir. 1984).

80 Leigh Goodmark, *Telling Stories, Saving Lives: The Battered Mothers' Testimony Project, Women's Narratives, and Court Reform*, 37 Ariz. St. L. J. 709, 745–51 (2005).

81 Karen Czapanskiy, *Domestic Violence, the Family, and the Lawyering Process*, *supra*, at 252, citing *Gender Bias in the Courts: Report of the Maryland Special Joint Committee on Gender Bias in the Courts* 2–3 (1989) (emphasis added) (chapter 2, n. 122).

82 *Cf.* Schechter and Edleson, *The Greenbook*, *supra* n. 75.

83 Debra Whitcomb, *Children and Domestic Violence: The Prosecutor's Response*, Nat'l Inst. Just., U.S. Dep't Just. III-6-4, III-6-5 (2004).

84 *Cf.* Campbell, *supra* n. 4, at 8 of 21.

85 *Id.*

86 *State v. Cacchiotti*, 568 A.2d 1026, 1031 (R. I. 1990).

87 Elizabeth M. Schneider, *Feminism and the False Dichotomy of Victimization and Agency*, 38 N.Y.L. Sch. L. Rev. 387, 388–91 (1993).

88 Elaine Chiu, *Confronting the Agency in Battered Mothers*, *supra*, at 1257–59.

89 Breiding et al., *supra* n. 7, at 2; Johnson, *supra* n. 7, at 1.

90 Cynthia K. Sanders, *Economic Abuse in the Lives of Women Abused by an Intimate Partner: A Qualitative Study*, 21 (1) Violence Against Women 3, 5–6 (2015).

91 In 2012 nearly three-fifths of married women with children under eighteen worked outside the home. Vespa, *supra* n. 36, at 22, Table 8.

92 Mather, *supra* n. 37, at 3.

93 Sanders, *supra* n. 90, at 4–5; *see also* Mireya Navarro, *Homeless, Because They Are Abused at Home*, N.Y. Times, Nov. 11, 2014, at A1.

94 *See Phelps v. State*, 439 So. 2d 727, 730 (Ala. 1983); *State v. Bernard*, 500 N.E. 2d 1074 (Ill. 1986); *Cardwell v. State*, 461 So. 2d 754, 757, 761 (Miss. 1984); *Commonwealth v. Brown*, 721 A.2d 1105 (Pa. Super. Ct. 1998); and *Hawkins v. State*, 891 S.W.2d 257, 259 (Tex. Crim. App. 1994).

95 *State v. Maupin*, 1991 Tenn. Crim App. LEXIS 818, at *7 (Tenn. Crim. App. Oct. 7, 1991); *aff'd* 859 S.W.2d 313 (Tenn. 1993).

96 *People v. Barrientos*, 2014 WL 1901173 (Cal. Ct. App. May 13, 2014) (unpublished); *People v. Superior Court, Olmos*, 2013 WL 6729916 (Cal. Ct. App. Dec. 20, 2013); and *State v. Kuykendall*, 2014 WL 5782937 (Ct. App. N.M. Sept. 23, 2014), *cert. granted* 344 P.3d 988 (N.M. 2014), *cert. quashed* 370 P. 3d 472 (N.M. 2015).

97 In the case of *People v. Barrientos*, Nancy Barrientos was convicted of involuntary manslaughter and assault on a child causing great bodily injury, resulting in death.
98 *State v. Kuykendall*, 2014 WL 5782937 (Ct. App. N.M. Sept. 23, 2014), *cert. granted* 344 P.3d 988 (N.M. 2014), *cert. quashed* 370 P. 3d 472 (N.M. 2015). Kuykendall was convicted of negligently permitting child abuse resulting in death in regard to her younger son and negligently permitting child abuse not resulting in death in regard to her older son.
99 *The Greenbook*, *supra* n. 75, at 11. In many cases women are at greatest risk of harm from their abuser when they try to flee, a phenomenon known as separation assault. *See, e.g., State v. Ketchner*, 339 P.3d 645, 647 (Ariz. 2014) (discussing expert testimony on separation assault) and Michael D. Rosenbaum, *To Break the Shell Without Scrambling the Egg: An Empirical Analysis of the Impact of Intervention into Violent Families*, 9 Stan. L. & Pol'y Rev. 409, 414–15 (1998), citing Martha Mahoney, *Legal Images of Battered Women: Redefining the Issue of Separation*, 90 Mich. L. Rev 1, 71–72 (1991).
100 *People v. Barrientos*, 2014 WL 1901173 (Cal. Ct. App. May 13, 2014) at *1–3.
101 *Nicholson v. Scoppetta*, 820 N.E. 2d 840 (N.Y. 2004).
102 *Id.* at 846.
103 Meghan A. Novisky and Robert L. Peralta, *When Women Tell: Intimate Partner Violence and the Factors Related to Police Notification*, 21 (1) Violence Against Women 65, 67 (2015).
104 *Id.* at 79.
105 *See* Campbell, *supra* n. 4.
106 Elaine Chiu, *supra*, at 1250 (chapter 2, n. 33); *see also* Shima Baradaran, *Race, Prediction, and Discretion*, *supra*, at 160.
107 Chiu, *supra* n. 88, at 1249–51; *see also* Johnson, *supra* n. 7, at 35–36; Karin Wang, *Battered Asian American Women: Community Responses from the Battered Women's Movement and the Asian American Community*, 3 Asian L. J. 151, 156–67 (1996); and Jenny Rivera, *Domestic Violence Against Latinas by Latino Males: An Analysis of Race, National Origin, and Gender Differentials*, 14 B.C. Third World L. J. 231, 234, 241–52 (1994).
108 ACLU Women's Rights Project, *Silenced: How Nuisance Ordinances Punish Crime Victims in New York* 1–8. 10 (June 2015), available at https://www.aclu.org/sites/default/files/field_document/equ15-report-nuisanceord-rel3.pdf (last visited Aug. 29, 2016).
109 *Commonwealth v. Lazarovich*, 574 N.E. 2d 340, 342 (Mass. 1991).
110 *Id.*
111 Novisky and Peralta, *supra* n. 103, at 68; *see also People v. Burton*, 788 N.E.2d 220, 226 (Ill. App. Ct. 2003); *People v. Abraham*, 629 N.E.2d 148, 152 (Ill. App. Ct. 1993); and *Daumer v. State*, 381 So.2d 1014, 1017 (Miss. 1980).
112 914 P.2d 1314, 1316 (Ariz. Ct. App. 1995).
113 Model Penal Code § 2.02 (2) (d).

114 820 N.E. 2d at 846 (paraphrasing Judge Kaye's opinion).
115 Breger, *supra* n. 5, at 564–67.
116 12 N.W. 155, 157 (Mich. 1882).
117 Campbell, *supra* n. 4, at 3, 18.
118 *Muehe v. State*, 646 N.E.2d 980, 984 (Ind. Ct. App. 1995).
119 Anderson, Inside Jurors' Minds, *supra*, at 47–49 and 79–80 (chapter 2, n. 23); Chamallas and Wriggins, The Measure of Injury, *supra*, at 125–26; *see also* Hanson and Hanson, *The Blame Frame*, at 419 (chapter 2, n. 26).
120 Chamallas and Wriggins, *supra*, at 125–26.
121 Roiphe, *supra* n. 61; Sanger, *supra* n. 61; Roberts, *supra* n. 61.
122 Chamallas, *Deepening the Understanding of Bias*, *supra*, at 778.
123 629 N.E. 2d 148, 155 (Ill. App Ct. 1993) (emphasis added).
124 Chamallas and Wriggins, The Measure of Injury, *supra*, at 124 (chapter 1, n. 78).
125 Dressler, Understanding Criminal Law, *supra*, at 201.
126 Model Penal Code § 2.03 (2) (b) and (3) (b) (emphasis added).
127 Chamallas and Wriggins, The Measure of Injury, *supra*, at 125.
128 Anderson, Inside Jurors' Minds, *supra*; Chris Guthrie et al., *Inside the Judicial Mind*, 86 Cornell L. Rev. 777, 787–94 (2001).
129 This framing is of course permitted by the applicable rules of causation.
130 Fischhoff, *The Hindsight Bias*, *supra*, at 288, 292, 295, 297–98 (chapter 2, n. 26). See also Daniel Kahneman, *Thinking, Fast and Slow*, *supra*, at 202–3 (chapter 4, n. 147).
131 *See, e.g.*, *State v. Williams*, 235 S.W. 3d 742, 749, 753 (Tex. Crim. App. 2007).
132 600 P.2d 474.
133 *State v. Williams*, 235 S.W.3d 742,753.

CHAPTER 8. CHILDHOOD LEAD POISONING AND OTHER PEOPLE'S CHILDREN

1 Mary Jean Brown and Stephen Margolis, Lead in Drinking Water and Human Blood Lead Levels in the United States, 61 MMWR Supp. 4 (Aug. 10, 2012). One µg is a microgram, one-millionth of a gram; a dL is a deciliter, or a tenth of a liter. Lawrie Mott et al., Lead, in Our Children at Risk: The Five Worst Environmental Threats to Their Health 8, n.*, New York (National Resources Defense Council 1997). The lead ban is currently codified at 16 C.F.R. § 1303.1—1303.5 (West 2015).
2 *Thomas ex rel. Gramling v. Mallett*, 701 N.W. 2d 523, 528–30 (Wis. 2005). Steven Thomas' lawsuit was brought by a guardian *ad litem*, Susan Gramling.
3 *Id.* at 530. The paint and pigment manufacturers also claimed that because Steven had received some compensation from his landlords, he was not entitled to seek further relief from them.
4 *Id.* at 557–64. The court first developed the risk contribution theory in *Collins v. Eli Lilly Co.*, 342 N.W. 2d 37 (Wis. 1984). *Collins* is discussed in more detail in part III.C. of this chapter.
5 Bruce Vielmetti, *U.S. Appeals Court Reinstates Wisconsin Lead Paint Suit*, Milwaukee Journal Sentinel Proof and Hearsay Blog (July 24, 2014), http://www.jsonline.

com/news/statepolitics/appeals-court-reinstates-wisconsin-lead-paint-suit-b99317605z1-268494482.html (last visited Mar. 5, 2015).
6. Wis. Stat. Ann. § 895.046.
7. 760 F. 3d 600, 604 (7th Cir. 2014), *cert. denied*, 135 S.Ct. 2311 (May 19, 2015).
8. *Clark v. American Cyanamid Co.*, 2014 WL 1257118 (Wis. Cir. Mar. 25, 2014) (Trial Order); *cert. granted* 2015 WL 5684280 (Wis. 2015), *cert. vacated* 877 N.W.2d 117 (Wis. 2016).
9. *Thomas ex rel. Gramling v. Mallett*, 795 N.W. 2d 62, PP's 41–51 (Wis. Ct. App. 2010) (unpublished disposition).
10. *Id.* at PP's 2–5.
11. This phrase is taken from Samuel Kaplan, The Dream Deferred: People, Politics, and Planning in Suburbia 177 (Vintage Books 1977). Kaplan notes a comment made by a parent from Englewood Cliffs, New Jersey, a suburb of New York City: "You can't expect people who worked very hard to make a little money to pay for other people's children."
12. Brown and Margolis, *supra* n. 1; *see also* Rachel Hawkins, *EPA Shoots Down Lead Shot Regulation: Lead Ammo's Unreasonable Risk to Human Health and the Environment, and the Special Situation of the California Condor*, 5 Golden Gate U. Envt'l. L. J. 533, 537 (2012).
13. Chamallas and Wriggins, The Measure of Injury, *supra*, at 140, n. 75 (chapter 1, n. 78).
14. *See, e.g.*, Lead, Requirements for Disclosure of Known Lead-Based Paint and/or Lead-Based Paint Hazards in Housing, Final Rule, 61 Fed. Reg. 9064, 9065 (Mar. 6, 1996).
15. CCCH, Inc., *EPA Solicits Public Input on Lead-Based Paint Rules for Public and Commercial Buildings*, 31 No. 2 Hazardous Waste Consultant 2.1 (2013).
16. Brown and Margolis, *supra* n. 1.
17. William Wheeler and Mary Jean Brown, *Blood Lead Levels in Children Aged 1–5 Years: United States, 1999–2010*, 62 MMWR 245, 245 (2013) (hereafter *Blood Lead Levels in Children Aged 1–5 Years*); *see also* Associated Press, *Lead Poisoning Rates Rise in U.S. after CDC Lowers Blood Cutoff*, April 5, 2013.
18. Gerald Markowitz and David Rosner, Lead Wars: The Politics of Science and the Fate of America's Children 11–19 (University of California Press, 2013) (hereafter Lead Wars). *See also* Update: Blood Lead Levels 1991–1994, 46 MMWR 141, 141–42 (Feb. 21, 1997) (hereafter *Update: Blood Lead Levels 1991–1994*); *see also* CDC, *Low Level Lead Exposure Harms Children*, *supra* (chapter 1, n. 70), 7, 10.
19. *Low Level Lead Exposure Harms Children*, *supra*, at 16.
20. 42 U.S.C. §§ 4801–6.
21. *Low Level Lead Exposure Harms Children*, *supra*, at 15–17; and Carla Campbell et al., *Philadelphia's Lead Court Is Making a Difference*, 38 J. Health Pol., Pol'y & L. 709, 711–13 (2013). *See also* Montrece McNeill Ransom et al., *Toward Eradication: How Law and Public Health Practices Can Be Used to Prevent Childhood Lead Poisoning*, 22 Tulane Envtl. L. J. 1, 11–18 (2008).

22 Ransom, *supra*, at 27; and N.Y.C. Dep't of Health & Mental Hygiene, *Report to the New York City Council on Progress in Preventing Lead Poisoning in New York City* 1 (submitted Sept. 30, 2010) (hereafter *NYC Report to the City Council on Lead*).
23 Only rarely are attorneys' fees available for suits seeking compensation for injuries due to lead poisoning. *Cf. G.M.M. v. Kimpson*, No. 13-CV-5059, 2015 WL 1285704, at *17 (E.D.N.Y. Mar. 19, 2015) (Weinstein, J.). State law remedies vary. New York law, for example, does not provide for attorneys' fees because of failure to disclose the presence of lead-based paint. N.Y RPL § 234.
24 *Lead Wars*, *supra* n. 18, at 19–20; *see also* Campbell, *supra* n. 21, at 722–23; and Michael Wines, *Beyond Flint, Lead Poisoning Persists Despite Decades-Old Fight*, N.Y. Times, Mar. 4, 2016, at A1.
25 Studies have found that abating lead paint hazards is extremely cost-effective. For example, in 2014 the judge in *Atlantic Richfield* relied on testimony that "every dollar spent on reducing lead paint exposure results in societal savings between $12 and $155." *People v. Atlantic Richfield Co.*, 2014 WL 1385823, at *52 (Cal. Super Ct. [Santa Clara County] Mar. 26, 2014). *See also* Campbell, *supra* n. 21, at 715; and April Burbank, *Burlington Makes Slow [Progress] Toward Lead-Abatement Goals*, Burlington Free Press, Oct. 24, 2013.
26 Ransom, *supra* n. 21, and Wines, *supra* n. 24.
27 Howard Markel, *How a Doctor Discovered U.S. Walls Were Poisonous*, PBS NewsHour, Mar. 29, 2013, available at http://www.pbs.org/newshour/rundown/how-a-doctor-discovered-us-walls-were-poisonous/; Hawkins, *supra* n. 12, at 541; Brown and Margolis, *supra* n. 1, at 1.
28 Vincent T. Corvello and Jeryl Mumpower, *Risk Analysis and Risk Management: An Historical Perspective*, 5 Risk Analysis 103, 107 (1985).
29 Mott et al., *supra* n. 1, at 1.
30 Gerald Markowitz and David Rosner, *"Cater to the Children": The Role of the Lead Industry in a Public Health Tragedy, 1900–1955*, 90 Am. J. Pub. Health 36, at 36–39 (2000); *see also People v. Atlantic Richfield Co.*, 2014 WL 1385823, at *13–18 (Cal. Super Ct. [Santa Clara County] Mar. 26, 2014). Quote at *13).
31 *People v. Atlantic Richfield Co.*, 2014 WL 1385823, at *14 (Cal. Super Ct. [Santa Clara County] Mar. 26, 2014).
32 *Thomas*, 701 N.W.2d at 529.
33 *Id.* at 537.
34 *Atlantic Richfield*, 2014 WL 1385823, at *18–28.
35 *Low Level Lead Exposure Harms Children*, *supra* n. 18, at 33–34; *see also* Lindsey Konkel, *Stress+Pollution = Health Risks for Low-Income Kids*, Environmental Health News, June 6, 2012, http://www.environmentalhealthnews.org/ehs/news/2012/pollution-poverty-and-people-of-color-stress-day-3 (last visited April 14, 2015).
36 *Update, Blood Lead Levels 1991–1994*, *supra* n. 18, at 145; *cf.* Elise Gould, *Childhood Lead Poisoning: Conservative Estimates of the Social and Economic Benefits of Lead Hazard Control*, 117 Envtl. Health Perspectives, 1162, 1166 (2009).

37 Mott, *supra* n. 1, at 4.
38 *Williamsburg Around the Bridge Block Ass'n v. Giuliani*, 644 N.Y.S.2d 252, 254 (N.Y. App. Div. 1996).
39 Abigail Goldman, *Lead-Paint Toys Aren't the Biggest Risk*, *supra* (chapter 2, n. 18).
40 Brown and Margolis, *supra* n. 1, at 1, 4.
41 42 U.S.C. § 300g-1(b) (4) (A). While the EPA has not set maximum contamination levels for lead, it has achieved roughly the same purpose by setting "action levels" that trigger an obligation for a municipal water system to investigate and decontaminate its water supply. See 40 C.F.R. § 141.80(c)(1), (2), and (3), and U.S. EPA, *Lead and Copper Rule Monitoring and Reporting Guidance for Public Water Systems* 48–51 (Rev'd 2010), available at http://water.epa.gov/lawsregs/rulesregs/sdwa/lcr/upload/Revised-Lead-and-Copper-Rule-Monitoring-and-Reporting-Guidance-for-Public-Water-Systems.pdf.
42 Mark R. Powell, *The 1991 Lead/Copper Drinking Water Rule and the 1995 Decision Not to Revise the Arsenic Drinking Water Rule: Two Case Studies in EPA's Use of Science*, at 7 ([Resources for the Future Discussion Paper 97–05] 1997).
43 Robert McCartney, *CDC's Botched Handling of D.C. Lead Scare Reveals a Poisonous Bureaucracy*, Washington Post, May 27, 2010; *see also* David Brown, *Study Can't Pinpoint Extent of Lead Exposure; Several Factors Determine Any Harm to Children's IQ; Experts View Public Health Impact as Slight*, Washington Post, Jan. 31, 2009.
44 John Eligon, *A Question of Environmental Racism in Flint*, N.Y. Times, Jan. 22, 2016, at A1.
45 Wines, *supra* n. 24.
46 Rebecca Renner, *Exposure on Tap: Drinking Water as an Overlooked Source of Lead*, 118 Envtl. Health Perspectives A68, A69–73 (2010).
47 Erik Olson and Kristi Pullen Fedinick, *What's in Your Water? Flint and Beyond* 5 (National Resources Defense Council (June 2016), available at https://www.nrdc.org/sites/default/files/whats-in-your-water-flint-beyond-report.pdf (last visited Sept. 4, 2016).
48 World Health Organization, *Lead: Children's Health and the Environment: WHO Training Package for the Health Sector*, Slide 7 (July 2008) (hereafter WHO Training Package); *EPA Solicits Public Input on Lead-Based Paint Rule for Public and Commercial Buildings*, 31 No. 2 Hazardous Waste Consultant 2.1 (CCH) (2013).
49 *Low Level Lead Exposure Harms Children*, *supra* n. 18, at 7.
50 *Id.* at 4–13, 16, 29; *People v. Atlantic Richfield Co.*, 2014 WL 1385823, at *10 (Cal. Super Ct. [Santa Clara County] Mar. 26, 2014); CDC, *Update: Blood Lead Levels 1991–1994*, 46 MMWR 141, 141–144–45 (1997); *see also* Gould, *supra* n. 36, at 1163 (2009) (discussing chelation).
51 *Low Level Lead Exposure Harms Children*, *supra* n. 18, at ix, 4, 9.
52 *People v. Atlantic Richfield Co.*, 2014 WL 1385823, at *12 (Cal. Super Ct. [Santa Clara County] Mar. 26, 2014).
53 *Low Level Lead Exposure Harms Children*, *supra* n. 18, at 21.

54 Brown and Margolis, *supra* n. 1, at 1–2.
55 Herbert L. Needleman et al., *Bone Lead Levels and Delinquent Behavior*, 275 JAMA 363–68 (1996); and Deborah W. Denno, *Lead*, in Violence in America (Ronald Gottesman and Richard Maxwell Brown, eds., Scribner 1999).
56 *People v. Atlantic Richfield Co.*, 2014 WL 1385823, at *14–18 (Cal. Super Ct. [Santa Clara County] Mar. 26, 2014); *see also* Herbert L. Needleman, *Review: The Removal of Lead from Gasoline: Historical and Personal Reflections*, in Environmental Research Section A84, 20, 20–28 (2000), http://www.unc.edu/courses/2006fall/envr/230/001/Needleman_2000.pdf (last visited Aug. 19, 2015) (hereafter Needleman, *The Removal of Lead from Gasoline*).
57 Baltimore's Health Commissioner banned lead-based paint in 1951. *People v. Atlantic Richfield*, 2014 WL 1385823, at *37 (Cal. Super Ct. [Santa Clara County] Mar. 26, 2014). New York City restricted the use of paint containing more than 1 percent lead in 1960. New York City Health Code § 173.13 (c), Chicago Municipal Code Ch. 78, § 78-17.2. *See also* Matthew L. Wald, *Lead Paint: New Rules, Old Questions*, N.Y. Times, Feb. 12, 1995, and New Jersey Interagency Task Force on the Prevention of Lead Poisoning, Strategic Plan 2003–2008, at 4 (2003).
58 42 U.S.C. §§ 4821–41.
59 The ban was issued on February 27, 1978. 16 C.F.R. §§ 1303.1. and 1303.4–1303.5. In 2009, as part of the Consumer Product Safety Improvement Act of 2008, that limit was reduced to .0009 percent. 16 C.F.R. §§ 1303.1.
60 *Low Level Lead Exposure Harms Children*, *supra* n. 18, at 33–34; *see also* U.S. Dep't of Housing and Urban Development, *American Healthy Homes Survey: Lead and Arsenic* at 4, 33–34 (2011).
61 Campbell, *supra* n. 21, at 711.
62 *Id.*
63 42 U.S.C. § 4851a (1).
64 Statement of Senator Joseph Lieberman, Cong. Rec. S17904-2, 1992 WL 279561.
65 This law, also referred to as Title X of the Housing and Community Development Act of 1992, is codified at 42 U.S.C. §§ 4801–4806.
66 Statement of Mr. Wendell H. Ford, Cong. Rec. S17904-2, 1992 WL 279561.
67 42 U.S.C. § 4851a (7).
68 The joint EPA/HUD regulations were issued on March 6, 1996, 61 Fed. Reg. 9064-01. They are codified at 24 C.F.R. Part 35.
69 Federal Residential Lead-Based Paint Hazard Reduction Act of 1992, 42 U.S.C. § 4852d (b) and (c).
70 Indeed, Maryland had earlier tried a similar approach. In 1949 the Maryland legislature enacted a "toxic finishes" law that required children's furniture and toys painted with lead to be labeled as such. The Lead Industries Association vigorously lobbied Maryland officials; the law was repealed the next year. Steven Sarno, Comment, *In Search of a Cause: Addressing the Confusion in Proving Causation of a Public Nuisance*, 26 Pace Envtl. L. Rev. 225, 230, n. 25 (2009).

71 Terrence McCoy, *Freddie Gray's Life: A Study in the Sad Effects of Lead Paint on Poor Blacks*, Washington Post, Apr. 30, 2015.
72 *See, e.g., Mason ex rel. Heiser v. Morrisette*, 403 F.3d 28, 28–30 (1st Cir. 2005); *Brown v. Maple3, LLC*, 928 N.Y.S. 2d 740 (N.Y. App. Div. 2011); *Roberts v. Hamer*, 655 F.3d 578, 584 (6th Cir. 2011); *but see McCormick v. Kissel*, 458 F. Supp. 2d 944, 947–49 (S.D. Ind. 2006). *See also Skerritt v. Bach*, 805 N.Y.S. 2d 213, 214–15 (4th Dep't 2005).
73 *See, e.g.,* Mass. Gen. Laws Ch. 111, §§ 190–199; and Jessica Wolpaw Reyes, Working Paper, *Childhood Lead and Academic Performance in Massachusetts* 2, New England Public Policy Center at the Federal Reserve Bank of Boston (Aug. 2011), https://www.bostonfed.org/economic/neppc/wp/2011/neppcwp113.pdf; *see also* Darshak Sanghavi, *Pediatric Perspective: Lead May Be Even More Dangerous than We Thought*, Boston Globe, May 25, 2004.
74 Ransom, *supra* n. 21, at 11–18.
75 General Accounting Office, *Lead Poisoning: Federal Health Care Programs Are Not Effectively Reaching At-Risk Children* 5, 14, GAO/HEHS 99-18 (1999) (hereafter GAO Report on Lead Poisoning); *see also Memisovski v. Maram*, 2004 U.S. Dist. LEXIS 16772 (N.D. Ill. Aug. 23, 2004); and Cindy Mann, *CMCS Informational Bulletin, Targeted Lead Screening Plans*, Center for Medicaid and CHIP Services (June 22, 2012), http://www.medicaid.gov/federal-policy-guidance/downloads/cib-06-22-12.pdf.
76 *See* Diane Cabo Freniere, *Private Causes of Action against Manufacturers of Lead-Based Paint: A Response to the Lead Paint Manufacturers' Attempt to Limit Their Liability by Seeking Abrogation of Parental Immunity*, 18 B.C. Envtl. Aff. L. Rev. 381, 385 (1991) (hereafter *Private Causes of Action against Manufacturers of Lead-Based Paint*).
77 *Local Laws Key to Reducing Dangers of Lead Poisoning*, New Room, University of Rochester, May 6, 2013, http://www.urmc.rochester.edu/news/story/index.cfm?id=3823 (last visited Aug. 19, 2015); Katrina S. Korfmacher and Michael L. Hanley, *Are Local Laws the Key to Ending Childhood Lead Poisoning?*, 38 J. Health Pol., Pol'y & L. 757 (2013).
78 Wines, *supra* n. 24.
79 Carol D. Leonning and Bill Turque, *Lead Probe Sought in D.C.; Residents Fear Water Danger Was Downplayed*, Washington Post, Jan. 28, 2009.
80 *See, e.g., Parkhurst v. D.C. Water and Sewer Authority*, D.C. Superior Court, Civ. Action 13-0003814, and decision at 2013 WL 1438094 (Apr. 8, 2013 D.C. Super.) (Trial Order denying class certification). More recent decisions have ruled against the parents, at least in part. *See Beveridge & Diamond Defeats Negligence Claims Against DC Water*, Jan. 15, 2016, available at http://www.bdlaw.com/news-1829.html (last visited Aug. 29, 2016), and *Barkley v. D.C. Water & Sewer Auth.*, 2016 D.C. Super. LEXIS 1 (D.C. Super. Ct. 2016).
81 This brief history of tetraethyl lead is drawn from Hawkins, *supra* n. 12; at 540–42; and Needleman, *The Removal of Lead from Gasoline*, *supra* n. 55, at 20, 24–26.

82 Section 211 (c) (1) (A) of the Clean Air Act, 42 U.S.C. 1857f-6c (c) (1) (A) (added by the Clean Air Amendments of 1970, Pub. L. 91–604, Dec. 31, 1970.)
83 *Ethyl Corp. v. EPA*, 541 F.2d 1, 13 (D.C. Cir. 1976). The discussion of the EPA's rule making and other aspects of its regulatory response are drawn from *Ethyl Corp.* and Needleman, *supra* n. 57, at 28–30.
84 541 F.2d 1, at 12–13.
85 *Id*. at 8–9, 13–17.
86 Needleman, *supra* n. 57, at 30–32; *see also Small Refiner Lead Phase-Down Task Force v. EPA*, 705 F.2d 506, 527–29 (D.C. Cir. 1983).
87 U.S. Dep't of Health & Human Services, *Toxicological Profile for Lead* 3, 16 (Aug. 2007) (hereafter *HHS Toxicological Profile for Lead*).
88 Adam Edelman and Adam Nichols, *Big Recall Rerun by Mattel. 9.3 Million More Toys from China Have Lead Paint or Deadly Magnets*, N.Y. Daily News, Aug. 15, 2007, 2007 WLNR 15810278; Sarah Borchersen-Keto, Consumer Product Safety Guide Letter No. 900 Issue No. 1570, 2012 WL 5498114 (C.C.H.); *Mattel to Pay $2.3 Million for Violating Lead Paint Ban*, 27 (No. 9) Andrews Toxic Torts Litig. Rep. 11, June 17, 2009.
89 *Millions of Toys Recalled; Contain 'Date Rape' Drug*, CNNMoney.com, Nov. 8, 2007; Goldman, *supra* n. 39; *Mattel to Pay $2.3 Million for Violating Lead-Paint Ban*, 27 No. 9 Andrews Toxic Torts Litig. Rep. 11, June 17, 2009; *Mom Files $5 Million Class Suit Over Lead Paint on Toy Trains, Hesse v. Learning Curve Brands*, 14 Andrews Class Action Litig. Rep. 12 at *1, Aug. 21, 2007; *see also In re RC2 Corp. Toy Lead Paint Products Liab. Litig.*, 2008 WL 548772 (2008).
90 Pub. L. 110-314, codified as 15 U.S.C. § 1278a, implemented by CPSC regulations, *Children's Products Containing Lead; Interpretative Rule of Inaccessible Component Parts*, 74 Fed. Reg. 2439 (Jan. 15, 2009), codified at 16 C.F.R. § 1500.87.
91 Michael J. Keating and Thomas H. Case, *Corporate Compliance Series: Designing an Effective Products Liability Compliance Program, IV. Corporation's Statutory Liability for Defective Products, §1.19, Consumer Products Safety Improvement Act of 2008* (Westlaw 2010–11).
92 Gips, *From China with Lead*, at 560–72 (2009) (chapter 1, n. 71). In contrast, manufacturers expressed concern that the law made it too easy for plaintiffs to sue. *See, e.g.*, Frank Leone et al., *The Consumer Product Safety Improvement Act, Its Implementation and Its Liability Implications*, 76 Def. Couns. J. 300, 302–6 (July 2009).
93 *Judge OKs $50 Million Settlement in Toxic-Toys Case, In re Mattel Inc. Toy Lead Paint Prods. Liab. Litig.*, 17 No. 4 Westlaw J. Class Action 11, May 19, 2010.
94 Goldman, *supra*.
95 *Cf*. Wines, *supra* n. 24.
96 *See, e.g., Thomas ex rel. Gramling v. Mallett*, 701 N.W. 2d 523, 528–29 (Wis. 2005); *In re Lead Paint Litig.*, 924 A.2d 484, 486 (N.J. 2007) *Blanks v. Fluor Corp.*, 450 S.W.3d 308, (Mo. Ct. App. 2014); *Ford ex rel. Pringle v. Philadelphia Housing Auth.*,

848 A.2d 1038; and *German v. Fed. Home Loan Mortgage Corp.*, No. 93 CIV. 6941 (MBM), 1998 WL 812478, at *6 (S.D.N.Y. Nov. 16, 1998).

97 See, e.g., *In re Lead Paint Litigation*, at 486.
98 See, e.g., *Greenman v. Yuba Power Products*, 27 Cal. Rptr. 697, 700–01 (1963); and Restatement (Second) of Torts § 402A, *see especially* Comment K. Recently, the Restatement (Third) of Torts: Products Liability § 2 (1998) has returned to a negligence standard for two kinds of products liability suits, those alleging a defective design or a failure to warn of a product's dangers, although not all state courts have adopted the Third Restatement's reasoning. Kyle Graham, *Strict Products Liability at 50: Four Histories*, 98 Marquette L. Rev. 555, 556–57, 563–79 (2014).
99 Sarno, *supra* n. 70, at 226–27, 246–55.
100 Third Restatement of Torts: Phys. & Emot. Harm §§ 26 and 27. Some jurisdictions use the "substantial factor" test in cases in which two or more defendants each committed an act "but for" which the injury would not have occurred. These cases are often referred to as ones of "overdetermined harm." § 27. In addition, some paint and pigment manufacturers may argue that even if the child was exposed to lead from paint, the plaintiff has not ruled out other causes of lead poisoning, such as drinking water with high levels of lead. *Cf. Thomas ex rel. Gramling v. Mallett*, 701 N.W. 2d 523, 564–65.
101 Proximate cause is referred to as "scope of liability" in the Restatement (Third) of Torts: Physical & Emotional Harm Chap. 6, §29. *See also* the previous discussion in chapter 4 regarding tort suits against pregnant women.
102 Molly McDonough, *Risky Business: Wisconsin Court's Risk Analysis May Be Last Hope for Lead Paint Plaintiffs*, ABA J. 18, 19 (Feb. 2005) (quoting Peter Earle, attorney for plaintiff Steven Thomas).
103 Daniel J. Penofsky, *Childhood Lead-Based Paint Poisoning Litigation*, 66 Am. Jur. Trials 47, § 149 (2015); *see also Norwood v. Lazarus*, 634 S.W.2d 584, 586 (Mo. Ct. App. E.D. 1982).
104 This could eliminate some potential defendants, but it could not conclusively identify the defendant whose paint is in a particular dwelling. *See Thomas ex rel. Gramling v. Mallett*, 701 N.W. 2d 523, 529.
105 *Cf. Thomas*, 701 N.W. 2d at 552–57. In *Thomas*, the lead pigment and paint manufacturers contended that Steven Thomas should not have a remedy against them because he already had successfully sued two of his landlords. Most courts consider evidence of a statutory violation as evidence of negligence. *See, e.g., Brooks v. Lewin Realty III, Inc.*, 835 A.2d 616, 621 (Md. 2003); and *Juarez by Juarez v. Wavecrest Management Team Ltd.*, 694 N.Y.S.2d 115, 120–22 (N.Y. 1996). A current New York City law is typical: "Owners must prevent the reasonably foreseeable occurrence of lead hazards and remediate them, and the underlying defects that may cause lead hazards, using safe work practices." New York City Local Law No. 1 (2004).
106 Penofsky, *supra* n. 103, at § 131.

107 *Cf. Campbell v. Bonner*, No. 92-7771 (D.C. Super. Ct. Jan. 7, 1994), and other cases cited in Jennifer Wriggins, *Genetics, IQ, Determinism, and Torts: The Example of Discovery in Lead Exposure Litigation*, 77 B.U. L. Rev. 1025, 1042–43 and 1073–79 (1997).
108 Wriggins, *supra* n. 107, at 1036, quoting Professors Rochelle Cooper Dreyfuss and Dorothy Nelkin, *The Jurisprudence of Genetics*, 45 Vand. L. Rev. 313, 315–16 (1992).
109 *People v. Atlantic Richfield Co.*, 2014 WL 1385823, at *14 (Cal. Super Ct. [Santa Clara County] Mar. 26, 2014); and Lead Wars, *supra* n. 18, at 30–35.
110 *See, e.g., Canada By and Through Landy v. McCarthy*, 567 N.W.2d 496, 506-07 (Minn. 1997).
111 Chamallas and Wriggins, The Measure of Injury, *supra*, at 143.
112 *See, e.g., Norwood v. Lazarus*, 634 S.W. 2d 584, 587–88 (Mo. Ct. App. E.D. 1982).
113 "Discovery" is the pre-trial process in which the parties exchange information in their possession. It is designed to level the litigation playing field, ensuring that all parties have equal access to information and avoiding unfair surprise at trial. To some extent it may encourage settlement prior to trial. *See, e.g.*, Jack Friedenthal et al., Civil Procedure: Cases and Materials 831 (West Academic, 11th ed. 2013). Discovery obligations are much broader in civil cases than in criminal ones. *See, e.g.*, Mary Prosser, *Reforming Criminal Discovery: Why Old Objections Must Yield to New Realities*, 2006 Wis. L. Rev. 541, 582 (2006).
114 *See, e.g., Perez v. Fleischer*, 997 N.Y.S.2d 773, 774–75 (App. Div., Third Dep't 2014), and *Bunch v. Artz*, 71 Va. Cir. 358, at *7–10 (Cir. Ct. Va., Portsmouth Aug. 15, 2006).
115 Wriggins, *supra* n. 108, at 1028, and cases discussed in this section.
116 *See, e.g., Little by Little v. McIntyre*, 672 A.2d 1271, 1272–73 (N.J. App. Div. 1996).
117 731 N.E. 2d 589, 591–93 (N.Y. 2000). *Andon* has been followed widely in New York, including a recent decision, *Perez v. Fleischer*, 997 N.Y.S. 2d 773, 776 (App. Div., 3d Dep't 2014).
118 *Caban ex rel. Crespo v. 600 E. 21st Street Co.*, 200 F.R.D. 176 (E.D. N.Y. 2001).
119 *Baez v. Sugrue*, 752 N.Y.S. 2d 38, 386–87 (N.Y. App. Div. 2002); *Parker v. Housing Authority of Baltimore City*, 742 A.2d 522, 523–25 (Md. Ct. Spec. App. 1999).
120 *See, e.g.*, Freniere, *Private Causes of Action Against Manufacturers of Lead-Based Paint*, *supra* n. 76, at 396.
121 *Cf. Norwood v. Lazarus*, 634 S.W.2d 584, 587–88 (Mo. Ct. App. E.D. 1982). While some states, like New York, do not recognize a tort of negligent parental supervision, others do. *See, e.g., M.F. ex rel. Flowers v. Delaney*, 830 N.Y.S. 2d 412, 414 (App. Div., 4th Dep't 2007); *cf. Ankiewicz v. Kinder*, 563 N.E.2d 684, 685–87 (Mass. 1990).
122 Chamallas and Wriggins, *supra*, at 152 (chapter 1, n. 78); *see also* Anderson, Inside Jurors' Minds, *supra*, at 47–49 (chapter 2, n. 23).
123 Robert J. McCaffrey et al., *Essential Assessment, Lead Paint Injuries: Causation and Discovery*, 52 No. 1 DRI for Def. 36, at 6–9 (Jan. 2010).
124 Chamallas and Wriggins, *supra*, at 152.

125 607 P. 2d 924 (Cal. 1980).
126 *Id.* at 925–31.
127 *Id.* at 925–31, 937.
128 199 P.2d.1, 2–5 (Cal. 1948).
129 This emphasis on foreseeability of harm was an important part of California's products liability jurisprudence. See *Escola v. Coca Cola*, 150 P.2d 436, 441 (Cal. 1944) (Traynor, J., concurring).
130 607 P.2d 924, at 936.
131 *Id.* at 929–31, 936–37. *See also* M. Stuart Madden and Jamie Holian, *Defendant Indeterminacy: New Wine into Old Skins*, 67 Louisiana L. Rev. 785, 798 (2007).
132 Donald G. Gifford and Paolo Pasicolan, *Market Share Liability Beyond DES Cases: The Solution to the Causation Dilemma in Lead Paint Litigation?* 58 S.C. L. Rev. 115, 125 (2006); *see also* Madden and Holian, *supra*, at 799, n. 80, noting the split among state courts about whether to adopt some form of market share liability and whether it should be limited to the DES context.
133 342 N.W.2d 37 (Wis. 1984); see also *id.* at 53–55 (Abrahamson, J., concurring).
134 342 N.W.2d 37, 45 (Wis. 1984), citing Article I, Sec. 9 of the Wisconsin Constitution.
135 *Id.* at 49.
136 *Borel v. Fibreboard Paper Products Corp.*, 493 F.2d 1076 (5th Cir. 1973), was the first successful asbestos products liability case. See Jane Stapleton, *The Two Explosive Proof-of-Causation Doctrines Central to Asbestos Cases*, 74 Brook. L. Rev. 1011, 1017 (2009).
137 Stapleton, *supra*, at 1019–26; and *Rutherford v. Owens-Illinois, Inc.*, 67 Cal. Rptr. 2d 16, 30–32 (Cal. 1997).
138 See, e.g., *Rutherford*, 67 Cal. Rptr. at 32. *Id.* at 36. The "substantial factor" test, which was at issue in *Summers v. Tice*, applies in cases where there is more than one act that contributed to the plaintiff's injuries, but any one of them standing alone cannot necessarily meet the "but for" test. *See, e.g.*, Jane Stapleton, *Choosing What We Mean by "Causation" in the Law*, 73 Mo. L. Rev. 433, 442 (2008).
139 *See generally* Stapleton, *The Two Explosive Proof-of-Causation Doctrines Central to Asbestos Claims*, supra n. 136.
140 Anita Bernstein, *Fellow-Feeling and Gender in the Law of Personal Injury*, 18 J. L. & Pol'y 295, 302–4, 313–15, 330–47 (2009).
141 See, e.g., *Skipworth v. Lead Industries Ass'n*, 690 A.2d 169, 173 (Pa. 1996); *Brenner v. Am. Cyanamid Co.*, 699 N.Y.S. 2d 848 (N.Y. App. Div. 1999); and *Santiago v. Sherwin Williams Co.*, 3 F.3d 546, 550–51 (1st Cir. 1993).
142 *Mallett*, 701 N.W.2d at 554.
143 *Id.* at 558.
144 *Id.*
145 *Id.* at 563; *see also id.* at 569–70 (discussing "hiding power").
146 *Id.*

147 *Id.* at 562.
148 *Mallett*, 701 N.W.2d at 563.
149 Restatement (Second) of Torts § 821B provides:
(1) A public nuisance is an unreasonable interference with a right common to the general public.
(2) Circumstances that may sustain a holding that an interference with a public right is unreasonable include the following:
   (a) Whether the conduct involves a significant interference with the public health, the public safety, the public peace, the public comfort or the public convenience, or
   (b) whether the conduct is proscribed by a statute, ordinance or administrative regulation, or
   (c) whether the conduct is of a continuing nature or has produced a permanent or long-lasting effect, and, as the actor knows or has reason to know, has a significant effect upon the public right.
150 Restatement (Second) of Torts § 821B, Comment b.
151 Cal. Civ. Code §§ 3479 and 3480.
152 *City of Milwaukee v. N.L. Industries*, 691 N.W. 2d 888, 894 (Wis. Ct. App. 2004); see also Sarno, *supra* n. 70, at 246, n. 105 (discussing the case).
153 *Cf. City of St. Louis v. Benjamin Moore & Co.*, 226 S.W. 3d 110, 118 (Mo. 2007) (Wolff, J., dissenting).
154 *See* New Jersey law, discussed in *In re Lead Paint Litigation*, 924 A.2d 484, 493–94 (N.J. 2007).
155 *In re Lead Paint Litigation*, 924 A.2d 484, 492–502 (N.J. 2007).
156 *See, e.g.*, Denno, *Lead Poisoning as a Defense, supra*; and *People v. Atlantic Richfield Co.*, 2014 WL 1385823 (Cal. Super Ct. [Santa Clara County] Mar. 26, 2014).
157 *People v. Atlantic Richfield Co.*, 2014 WL 1385823, at *10.
158 691 N.W. 2d 888, 893–94 (Wis. Ct. App. 2004).
159 *City of St. Louis v. Benjamin Moore & Co.*, 226 S.W. 3d 110 (Mo. 2007).
160 *In re Lead Paint Litigation*, 924 A.2d 484 (N.J. 2007).
161 *City of Chicago v. Am. Cyanamid Co.*, 823 N.E. 2d 126 (Ill. Ct. App. 2005).
162 *Rhode Island v. Lead Industries Ass'n, Inc.*, 951 A.2d 428, 436–37 (R.I. 2008).
163 226 S.W.3d 110, 112–13 (Mo. 2007).
164 *Id.* at 114–16. Similar reasoning was used, and a similar result reached, in the public nuisance case brought by Chicago against lead pigment and paint manufacturers. *City of Chicago v. Am. Cyanamid Co.*, 823 N.E. 2d 126, at 137–40.
165 226 S.W. 3d 110, 116.
166 *Id.* at 495–502. In *Rhode Island v. Lead Industries Ass'n*, 951 A.2d 428 (R.I. 2008), the Rhode Island Supreme Court reversed a jury verdict that lead paint and pigment manufacturers had created a public nuisance. Using reasoning similar to the Missouri and New Jersey Supreme Court decisions discussed above, the Rhode Island Supreme Court accepted the "lack of control" argument advanced by the defendant paint and pigment manufacturers. The court also held that because the

Rhode Island legislature had provided some relief to lead-poisoned children, the tort of public nuisance was not available. 951 A.2d 428, 435.
167 691 N.W.2d 888, 893–94 (Wis. Ct. App. 2004).
168 *Id.* at 894.
169 *Id.* at 891–92; *see also* Sarno, *supra* n. 70, at 258, n. 105 (2009) (emphasis added).
170 *People v. Atlantic Richfield Co.*, 2014 WL 1385823, at *1–2, 51–62 (Cal. Super Ct. [Santa Clara County] Mar. 26, 2014). The plaintiffs estimated that 4.7 million homes were built in the ten cities and counties before lead paint was banned. More than half are estimated to contain lead-based paint hazards. *Id.* at *13. The court found that the defendants had actual or constructive knowledge of the hazards of lead. *Id.* at *25, 52–53.
171 *Atlantic Richfield Co. et al. v. Superior Court (The People)*, No. 100-CV-788657, has been consolidated, and is now named *People v. ConAgra Grocery Products Company et al.* Judicial Branch of California, Appellate Courts Case Information, 6th Appellate Dist., H040880, *The People v. ConAgra Grocery Products Company et al.*, http://appellatecases.courtinfo.ca.gov/search/case/mainCaseScreen.cfm?dist=6&doc_id=2073589&doc_no=H040880&search=party&start=1&query_partyLastNameOrOrg=ConAgra%20Grocery%20Products%20Company (last visited Sept. 4, 2016).
172 Cal. Civ. Code §§ 3479, 3480.
173 *People v. Atlantic Richfield Co.*, 2014 WL 1385823, at *44–45 (Cal. Super Ct. [Santa Clara County] Mar. 26, 2014).
174 *People v. Atlantic Richfield Co.*, 2014 WL 1385823, at **52–54, 56, 61–62 (Cal. Super Ct. [Santa Clara County] Mar. 26, 2014).

CHAPTER 9. THE VACCINATION PARADOX

1 *The Pink Book: Course Textbook*—13th Ed. 266 (2015), available at http://www.cdc.gov/vaccines/pubs/pinkbook/downloads/pert.pdf (hereafter *Pink Book*); *see also* Tami Skoff, *Update on Pertussis Epidemiology and Vaccination in the United States*, at 7–11, 15–22 (June 2013), http://www.cdc.gov/vaccines/ed/ciinc/downloads/2014-07-30/Skoff-pertussis.pdf; Centers for Disease Control (CDC), Pertussis Cases by Year (1922–2014), http://www.cdc.gov/pertussis/surv-reporting/cases-by-year.html; CDC, Provisional Pertussis Surveillance Report, Feb. 2015, http://www.cdc.gov/mmwr/preview/mmwrhtml/mmm6353md.htm?s_cid=mm6353md_w.
2 Sarah Jane Tribble, *Measles Outbreak in Ohio Leads Amish to Reconsider Vaccines*, Morning Edition, National Public Radio, June 24, 2014, http://www.npr.org/sections/health-shots/2014/06/24/323702892/measles-outbreak-in-ohio-leads-amish-to-reconsider-vaccines.
3 CDC, *Measles Cases and Outbreaks: 2015 Measles Cases in the U.S.*, http://www.cdc.gov/measles/cases-outbreaks.html; Karen Kaplan, *Vaccine Refusal Helped Fuel Disneyland Measles Outbreak, Study Says*, L.A. Times, Mar. 16, 2015; and Robbie Gonzalez, *The Disneyland Measles Outbreak Is Over in the U.S., But Not in Canada*, io9.com, Apr. 28, 2015, http://io9.com/thedisneylandmeaslesoutbreak-

isoverintheusbu1698536756; Adrienne LaFrance, *The New Measles*, The Atlantic, Jan. 23, 2015, http://www.theathlantic.com/health/archive/2015/01/the-new-measles/384738.

4   Kelly McEvers, *First Measles Death in 12 Years Raises Vaccination Concerns*, NPR News, July 6, 2015, npr.org/2015/07/06/420594973/first-measles-death-in-12-years-raises-vaccination-concerns; and Elahe Izadi, *The U.S. Just Recorded Its First Confirmed Measles Death in 12 Years*, Wash. Post, July 2, 2015.

5   Scott Hensley, *Vaccination Gap Helps Fuel Disneyland Measles Spread*, NPR, Mar. 16, 2015, available at http://www.npr.org/sections/health-shots/2015/03/16/393336901/vaccination-gap-helps-fuel-disneyland-measles-spread; *see also* Ranee Steither et al., *Vaccination Coverage among Children in Kindergarten, United States, 2013–1014 School Year*, 63 MMWR 913, 913–19 (Oct. 17, 2014).

6   Institute of Medicine, Financing Vaccines, *supra*, at 3, 27 (chapter 1, n. 81); Malone and Hinman, *Vaccination Mandates*, *supra*, at 262, 264 (chapter 1, n. 16); *see also* Oklahoma's Nursing Times, *Employee Vaccinations Help Protect Nursing Home Residents*, Sept. 9, 2011, http://www.ouhsc.edu/news/templates/?a=484.

7   Walter A. Orenstein et al., *Public Health Considerations—United States*, in Stanley A. Plotkin and Walter A. Orenstein, *Vaccines* 1006 (3d. ed. 1999); and Geoffrey P. Garnett, *Role of Herd Immunity in Determining the Effect of Vaccines against Sexually Transmitted Disease*, 191 (Suppl. 1) J. Infectious Diseases S97–106 (2005).

8   Pauline W. Chen, *Reopening a Door to Measles*, N.Y. Times, July 1, 2014, at D6; *see also* Malone and Hinman, *supra*, at 264. Throughout this chapter I will use the terms *immunization* and *vaccination* interchangeably.

9   CDC, *Measles, Health Care Professionals*, available at http://www.cdc.gov/measles/hcp (last visited July 16, 2015).

10 Shetty, *Experts Concerned about Vaccination Backlash*, *supra*, at 970 (chapter 1, n. 85).

11 CDC, *Measles Cases and Outbreaks: 2015 Measles Cases in the U.S.*, *supra* n. 3; Gonzalez, *supra* n. 3; and Kaplan, *supra* n. 3.

12 David E. Sugarman et al., *Measles Outbreak in a Highly Vaccinated Population, San Diego, 2008: Role of the Intentionally Undervaccinated*, 125 Pediatrics 747 (2010); Yvonne A. Maldonado, *Current Controversies in Vaccination Safety*, 288 JAMA 3155, 3156 (2002); and Leticia Stein, *Measles Cases Rise as More Shun Shot* (chapter 1, n. 16).

13 *See* Denise F. Lillvis et al., *Power and Persuasion in the Vaccine Debates: An Analysis of Political Efforts and Outcomes in the United States, 1998–2012*, 92 Millbank Quarterly 475, 478, 483 (2014); *see also AMA Supports Tighter Limitations on Immunization Opt Outs*, Press Release, June 8, 2015.

14 *AMA Supports Tighter Limitations on Immunization Opt Outs*, *supra*; *see also* American Medical Association Policy No. H-440.970, https://www.ama-assn.org/ssl3/ecomm/PolicyFinderForm.pl?site=www.ama-assn.org&uri=/resources/html/PolicyFinder/policyfiles/HnE/H-440.970.HTM.

15 Scott Neuman, *Calif. Moves Closer to Banning Vaccine 'Personal Belief' Exemptions*, NPR, May 14, 2015, available at http://www.npr.org/sections/thetwo-way/2015/05/14/406829769/calif-moves-closer-to-banning-vaccine-personal-belief-exemptions (last visited July 12, 2015); *see also* Jennifer Medina, *California Is Set to Toughen Rules on Vaccinations*, N.Y. Times, June 26, 2015, at A12.

16 Cal. Health & Safety Code §§ 12035, 120335, 120338, 120370, 120375 and Vt. Stat. Ann. tit. 18, §§ 1121–1125, 1129 (effective Jan. 1, 2016); *see also* National Conference of State Legislatures, *States with Religious and Philosophical Exemptions from School Immunization Requirements (Jan. 21, 2016)*, available at: http://www.ncsl.org/issues-research/health/school-immunization-exemption-state-laws.aspx (last visited Aug. 22, 2016).

17 Rebecca Coombes, *Vaccine Disputes*, 338 British Med. J. 1528, 1529 (2009); and Jordynn Jack, *Autism and Gender: From Refrigerator Mothers to Computer Geeks* 73 (University of Illinois Press, 2014).

18 Barbara Loe Fisher, National Vaccine Information Center, *The Health Liberty Revolution & Forced Vaccination*.

19 Medina, *supra* n. 15; and Joanna Waters, *Robert Kennedy Jr. Apologises for Holocaust Reference in Autism Speech*, The Guardian (U.K.), Apr. 13, 2015.

20 Allison Kennedy et al., *Vaccine Attitudes, Concerns, and Information Sources Reported by Parents of Young Children: Results from the 2009 HealthStyles Survey*, 127 Pediatrics Supp. 1, at S92, S93–94 (May 2011).

21 CDC, *Ten Great Public Health Achievements 1900–1999*, at 241.

22 Wendy E. Parmet, *Informed Consent and Public Health*, 89–90.

23 Doreen D. Fredrickson et al., *Childhood Immunization Refusal, Provider and Parent Perceptions*, 36 Family Medicine 431, 432–36 (2004); Jennifer A. Reich, *Neoliberal Mothering*, *supra* 685, 688, 692–95 (chapter 2, n.24).

24 Although parents of both genders oppose vaccination, a significant majority of these parents are mothers. In a recent nationwide survey, mothers were more likely than fathers to be concerned about "serious adverse effects from vaccines . . . and more likely to believe that some vaccines cause autism in healthy children and to have ever refused a vaccine for their child." Gary L. Freed et al., *Parental Vaccine Safety Concerns in 2009*, 125 Pediatrics 654, 658 (2010). This may also reflect the patterns of decisionmaking in many families, in which the mother is the primary decisionmaker about children's health. Reich, *supra* n. 23, at 685; *see also* Ruth Graham, *Don't Blame Parents for Vaccine Resistance*, *supra* (chapter 2, n. 44).

25 While the tide of public opinion may be shifting against parents who do not vaccinate their children, to date no parents have been prosecuted or been the subject of a civil suit for causing harm to their own or other people's children based on failure to vaccinate.

26 Strictly speaking, a distinction may be drawn between infectious diseases, which are caused when microorganisms enter the body and grow within it; contagious

diseases, which are transmitted either by direct or indirect contact with infected individuals or their bodily discharges; and communicable diseases, which are communicated from person to person, animal to animal, animal to person, or person to animal, either directly or indirectly. *Webster's Third New International Dictionary* (1993). In practice, most laypeople, as well as the *Oxford English Dictionary* (6th ed. 2007), use the terms interchangeably.

27 *See, e.g.*, Chen, *supra* n. 8.
28 *See* Steve P. Calandrillo, *Vanishing Vaccinations*, at 359, 362 (chapter 1, n. 83).
29 Landrigan, *Environmental Pollutants and Disease in American Children* 721 (chapter 8, n. 34).
30 *Cf.* Institute of Medicine, *Adverse Effects of Vaccines: Evidence and Causality* 27 (Kathleen R. Stratton et al., eds., National Academies Press, 2012) (hereafter *IOM Adverse Effects*).
31 CDC, *Achievements in Public Health 2001–2010*, at 621.
32 197 U.S. 11 (1905).
33 CDC, *Ten Great Public Health Achievements 1900–1999*, *supra*, at 243–44 (chapter 3, n. 20).
34 Sandra W. Roush et al., *Historical Comparisons of Morbidity and Mortality for Vaccine-Preventable Diseases in the United States*, 298 JAMA 2155, 2156 (2007).
35 *Id. See also* Willem G. van Panhuis et al., *Contagious Diseases in the United States from 1888 to the Present*, 369 New Eng. J. Med. 2152, 2154, 2156 (2013). Tetanus is a bacterium that enters the body through a wound. Tetanus is an infectious, but not contagious, disease. Children usually receive tetanus toxoid as part of the DTaP or Tdap immunizations, which also protect against diphtheria and pertussis. William Atkinson et al., *Epidemiology and Prevention of Vaccine-Preventable Diseases* 292–98 *supra* (chapter 1, n. 16).
36 *Cf.* IOM Adverse Effects, *supra* n. 30, at 27.
37 Atkinson, *Epidemiology and Prevention of Vaccine-Preventable Diseases*, *supra* n. 35, at G-1, G-3, G-7, and 252–53; and *Concise Oxford English Dictionary* (12th ed. 2011).
38 Roush, *supra* n. 34.
39 CDC, *Ten Great Public Health Achievements 1900–1999*, *supra*. The Salk vaccine was supplemented, and then superseded, by the Sabin oral vaccine, introduced in 1961. In 2000 the United States returned to the use of the inactivated virus (Salk) vaccine, in order to eliminate the very minimal risk (about eight cases a year) of contracting the disease through vaccination. Atkinson, *supra* n. 35, at 252–53.
40 CDC, *Ten Great Public Health Achievements*, *supra*, at 244–46; Roush, *supra* n. 34, at 2156; Centers for Disease Control, *Frequently Asked Questions about Measles in the U.S.*, http://www.cdc.gov/measles/about/faqs.html (last visited Aug. 10, 2015); and Mark Berman, *How the U.S. Went from Eliminating Measles to a Measles Outbreak at Disneyland*, Washington Post, Jan. 23, 2015.
41 *Id.* at 276; and Donald G. McNeil, Jr., *Rubella Has Been Eliminated from the Americas, Health Officials Say*, N.Y. Times, Apr. 30, 2015, at A7.

42 CDC, *Ten Great Public Health Achievements 1900–1999*, *supra* (chapter 3, n. 20), and Roush, *supra* n. 34.
43 Atkinson, *supra* n. 35, at G-7; CDC, *Pink Book*, *supra* n. 1; *see also* The American Academy of Pediatrics, available at https://www.healthychildren.org/English/safety-prevention/immunizations/Pages/Rotavirus-Vaccine-What-You-Need-to-Know.aspx (last visited Aug. 6, 2015).
44 David Bruce, *HPV Vaccination Being Given to Boys More Frequently*, Pittsburgh Post-Gazette, Jan. 1, 2012, at A-13; Jemal et al., *Annual Report to the Nation on the Status of Cancer Inst., 1975–2009, Featuring the Burden and Trends in Human Papillomavirus (HPV)—Associated Cancers and HPV Vaccination Coverage Levels*, 105 J. Nat'l Cancer Inst. 175, 175–76 (2013) (hereafter *Annual Report on the Status of Cancer*); and Immunise Australia, HPV School Vaccination Program for Parents, http://hpv.health.gov.au/for-parents/ (last visited Feb. 26, 2013). There are three FDA-approved vaccines against HPV. Gardasil® and Gardasil 9®, developed by Merck Pharmaceuticals, target four and nine strains of HPV, respectively. Cervarix®, developed by GlaxoSmithKline, targets two strains of HPV. Gardasil 9® provides more comprehensive coverage against the wide variety of cancers that HPV causes. National Cancer Institute, *Fact Sheet, Human Papillomavirus (HPV) Vaccines* (Apr. 29, 2015), http://www.cancer.gov/cancertopics/factsheet/prevention/HPV-vaccine (last visited June 30, 2015); *see also Recommendations on the Use of Quadrivalent Human Papillomavirus Vaccine in Males—Advisory Committee on Immunization Practices (ACIP), 2011*, 60 Morbidity and Mortality Weekly 1705 (Dec. 23, 2011).
45 CDC, HPV Vaccination Information Statement, http://www.cdc.gov/vaccines/hcp/vis/vis-statements/hpv-gardasil.pdf; Susan Hariri et al., *Human Papillomavirus, VPD Surveillance Manual*, chapter 5 (5th ed. 2011), http://www.cdc.gov; *see also* Jemal, *supra* n. 44; and Deborah Kotz, *HPV Vaccine Coverage Debated*, Boston Globe, July 23, 2011, at Metro p. 1; and *Throat Cancer on the Increase . . .*, Toronto Star, Mar. 31, 2011, at R3.
46 Infection with the Hepatitis B virus leads to acute, and then chronic, hepatitis. The Hepatitis B virus causes up to 80 percent of liver cancers, Atkinson, *supra* n. 35, at 115–17. It leads to an estimated 5,000 deaths per year because of cirrhosis and cancer. Fishbein, *New, and Some Not-so-New, Vaccines for Adolescents*, *supra*, at S10 (chapter 3, n. 27).
47 Centers for Disease Control, *Recommended Immunization Schedule for Persons Aged 0 Through 18 Years: United States, 2015*, available at http://www.cdc.gov/vaccines/schedules (last visited June 30, 2015).
48 CDC, *Ten Great Public Health Achievements 2001–2010* at 619.
49 van Panhuis et al., *supra* n. 35, at 2156; *see also* Steve Lohr, *Combing Years of Data, Doctors Show Big Benefit of Childhood Vaccines*, N.Y. Times, Nov. 28, 2013, at B3.
50 Kaiser Commission on Medicaid and the Uninsured, *State Children's Health Insurance Program (CHIP): Reauthorization History* 1 (Feb. 2009), http:/www.kff.org (Pub. No. 7743-02).

51 McNeil, *supra* n. 41; Tsouderos, *Vaccine Rates Raise Risk of Outbreaks*; see also Roxana Torrico, *Children, Youth & Families Practice Update: Meeting the Needs of Immigrant Children and Youth in Child Welfare* (Nat'l. Assn. of Social Workers 2010), http://www.naswdc.org/assets/secured/documents/practice/clinical/WKF-MISC-45510.ChildrenPU.pdf; and Kaiser Commission on Medicaid and the Uninsured, *Connecting Eligible Immigrant Families to Health Coverage and Care: Key Findings from Outreach and Enrollment Workers* 1–2 (Oct. 2011), at http://www.kff.org.

52 These include the Vaccines for Children Program and the "317" grant program. The Vaccines for Children Program provides free vaccines for eligible children, including those who are eligible for Medicaid, uninsured, underinsured, or Native American. Financing Vaccines, *supra* n. 6, at 7–9, 16, 34, 39, 46–47. The "317" program, which is administered by the Centers for Disease Control, is authorized by § 317 of the Public Health Services Act, 42 U.S.C. § 247(b). Malone and Hinman, *supra* n. 6, at 268. Research has found that in some medically underserved communities children who receive care from public health clinics have higher immunization rates than children who are cared for by private physicians. Jorge Rosenthal et al., *Immunization Coverage Levels among 19- to 35-Month-Old Children in 4 Diverse, Medically Underserved Areas of the United States*, 113 Pediatrics e296, e296 (2004).

53 42 U.S.C. 300gg-13 (a) (2) (Coverage of Preventative Health Services).

54 As of July 2016, nineteen states have rejected the opportunity to expand Medicaid under the Affordable Care Act. Kaiser Family Foundation, *Status of State Action on the Medicaid Expansion Decision* (as of July 7, 2016), http://kff.org/health-reform/state-indicator/state-activity-around-expanding-medicaid-under-the-affordable-care-act/ (last visited Aug. 22, 2016).

55 Financing Vaccines, *supra* n. 6, at 46.

56 Sanny Y. Chen et al, *Health Care-Associated Measles Outbreak in the United States after an Importation: Challenges and Economic Impact*, 203 J. Infectious Diseases 1517, 1523–24 (2011).

57 Edwards, *State Mandates and Childhood Immunization*, *supra*, at 3171 (chapter 1, n. 87), and Chen, *supra* n. 8.

58 Tsouderos, *supra* n. 51; *see also* Elliot Njus, *High Opt-Out Rate for Vaccinations Challenges County*, *supra* (chapter 1, n. 88).

59 Reich, *supra* n. 27, at 687; Whet Moser, *Why Do Affluent, Well-Educated People Refuse Vaccines?* Chicago Magazine (Mar. 26, 2014), http://www.chicagomag.com/city-life/March-2014/Why-Is-Vaccine-Refusal-More-Prevalent-Among-the-Affluent/; and Paloma Esquivel and Sandra Poindexter, *Plunge in Kindergartners' Vaccination Rate Worries Health Officials*, L.A. Times (Sept. 2, 2014).

60 *See Possible Side-effects from Vaccines*, CDC.gov, http://www.cdc.gov/vaccines/vac-gen/side-effects.htm; IOM Adverse Events, *supra* n. 30, at 18–24; and Andrea Kitta, Vaccinations and Public Concern in History: Legend, Rumor, and Risk Perception 20 (Routledge 2012).

61 *See, e.g.*, World Health Organization, *Information Sheet: Observed Rate of Vaccine Reactions—Measles, Mumps and Rubella Vaccines* 2–6 (May 2014), http://www.who.

int/vaccine_safety/initiative/tools/MMR_vaccine_rates_information_sheet.pdf.; World Health Organization, *What Are Some of the Myths—and Facts—about Vaccinations?*, Apr. 2013, www.who.int/features/qa/84/ent# (last visited July 19, 2015).

62 Parmet, *supra* n. 22, at 92, n. 141; *see also* Kitta, *supra* n. 60, at 21–22.

63 CDC, *Rotavirus Vaccine (RotaShield® and Intussusception)*, http://www.cdc.gov/vaccines/vpd-vac/rotavirus-rotashield-historical.htm (last visited Jul. 1, 2015); *see also Pink Book, supra* n. 1, at 311–17 (Apr. 2015).

64 Kennedy, *supra* n. 20.

65 American Academy of Pediatrics, *Immunization, Autism Facts, What Parents Should Know about Measles-Mumps-Rubella (MMR) Vaccine and Autism* (hereafter AAP, *Immunization, Autism Facts*), available at http://www2.aap.org/immunization/families/autismfacts.html (last visited July 1, 2015). See also Atkinson, *supra* n. 35, at 174, 189.

66 *12-Year Study Confirms Overall Safety of Measles Vaccines*, Sci. Daily, Jan. 6, 2015, available at http://www.sciencedaily.com/releases/2015/01/150106095242.htm, citing Nicola P. Klein et al., *Safety of Measles-Containing Vaccines in 1-Year-Old Children*, 135 Pediatrics e321 (2015).

67 *See, e.g.*, Barbara Loe Fisher, *In the Wake of Vaccines*, Mothering 38, 43 (Sept.–Oct. 2004). Fisher's complex claim began by asserting that "each year about 12,000 reports are made to the Vaccine Adverse Event Reporting System; parents as well as doctors can make those reports." She continued, "However, if that number represents only 10 percent of what is actually occurring, then the actual number may be 120,000 vaccine-adverse events. If doctors report vaccine reactions as infrequently as [former FDA Commissioner] Dr. [David] Kessler said they report prescription-drug reactions, and the number 12,000 is only 1 percent of the actual total, then the real number may be 1.2 million vaccine-adverse events annually."

68 AAP, *Immunization, Autism Facts, supra* n. 65; and Edward W. Campion, *Suspicions about the Safety of Vaccines*, 347 New Eng. J. Med. 1474 (2002).

69 Biss, On Immunity, at 51–52 (chapter 1, n. 15).

70 Kitta, *supra* n. 60, at 19–20.

71 Biss, *supra* n. 69, at 23–26.

72 Kitta, *supra* n. 60, at 81–82; *see also* Biss, *supra* n. 69, at 73–74.

73 42 U.S.C. §§ 300aa-2—300aa-33; *see also Bruesewitz v. Wyeth LLC*, 131 S. Ct. 1068, 1072 (2011).

74 Elizabeth C. Scott, *The National Childhood Vaccine Injury Act Turns Fifteen*, 56 Food Drug L. J. 351, 355–56 (2001); *see also Bruesewitz v. Wyeth LLC*, 131 S. Ct. 1068, 1073–74 (2011).

75 *See, e.g.*, Lauren L. Haertlein, *Immunizing against Bad Science: The Vaccine Court and the Autism Test Cases*, 75 Law & Contemp. Probs. 211, 223 (2012); Miranda Hitti, *Vaccine Court Rejects Autism Claims*, WebMD (Feb. 12, 2009); and U.S. Dep't of Health and Human Services, *National Vaccine Injury Compensation Program: Monthly Statistics Report*, hrsa.gov 2–3 (July 1, 2015), http://www.hrsa.gov/vaccinecompensation/statisticsreport.pdf.

76 "Autism is a complex and severe set of developmental disorders characterized by sustained impairments in social interaction, impairments in verbal and non-verbal communication, and stereotypically restricted or repetitive patterns of behavior and interests." IOM *Immunization Safety Review supra*, at 32 (chapter 1, n. 90). Autism's etiology (causation) is uncertain and multifaceted, although there appears to be a strong genetic component. Autism has been diagnosed with greater frequency over the past several decades, but the apparent increased incidence may be due, at least in part, to greater public awareness, broader diagnostic criteria, and increased numbers of health and psychological professionals prepared to assist children with autism and autism spectrum disorders. Neal A. Halsey et al., *Measles-Mumps-Rubella Vaccine and Autistic Spectrum Disorder: Report from the New Challenges in Childhood Immunizations Conference Convened in Oak Brook, Illinois, June 12–13, 2000*, 107 Pediatrics e84 2001, 1, 3–8. Recent research also points to fathers' genetic contribution to their children's autism. *See, e.g.*, Carey, *Study Finds Risk of Autism Linked to Older Fathers, supra*; and Shulevitz, *Why Fathers Really Matter, supra* (chapter 3, n. 6).

77 Methylmercury, the form of mercury released into the atmosphere by power plants and which bioaccumulates in fish, is a neurotoxin. The two forms of mercury are different. Not only is there no evidence showing that ethylmercury is toxic in the dose previously contained in vaccines, but it is excreted from the body from five to seven times faster than methylmercury, so there is no chance of its accumulating within a child's body as a result of vaccination. The World Health Organization has found that it is safe to continue to use vaccines with thimerosal. Thomas W. Clarkson et al., *The Toxicology of Mercury—Current Exposures and Clinical Manifestations*, 349 New Eng. J. Med. 1731, 1733–36 (2003).

78 Sandra J. Bean, *Emerging and Continuing Trends in Vaccine Opposition Website Content*, 29 Vaccine 1874, 1877 (2011); and Centers for Disease Control and Prevention (CDC), *Parents' Guide to Childhood Immunization* 34–35 Atlanta (U.S. Department of Health and Human Services, Centers for Disease Control and Prevention, 2015), available at https://www.cdc.gov/vaccines/parents/tools/parents-guide/downloads/parents-guide-508.pdf (last visited Aug. 22, 2016).

79 Larson, *Addressing the Vaccine Confidence Gap, supra*, at 529–30 (chapter 1, n. 89); IOM, Adverse Effects, *supra* n. 30; Institute of Medicine, *The Childhood Immunization Schedule and Safety: Stakeholder Concerns, Scientific Evidence, and Future Studies* 1–6 (2013) (hereafter The Childhood Immunization Schedule and Safety); *see also* IOM Immunization Safety Review, *supra* n. 76, at 7; and Maldonado, *supra* n. 12, at 3156.

80 IOM, Adverse Effects, *supra* n. 30, on MMR. On the controversy involving Wakefield's research, see Seth Mnookin, The Panic Virus: A True Story of Medicine, Science and Fear 299–302 (Simon and Schuster, 1st ed., 2011) (hereafter The Panic Virus); *see also* Editors, *Retraction-ileal-lymphid-nodular hyperplasia, non-specific colitis, and pervasive developmental disorder in children*, The Lancet (published

online Feb. 2, 2010) (retracting the 1998 Wakefield study finding a link between vaccination and autism because of its flawed science, which was addressed in the negative findings of the United Kingdom's General Medical Council's Fitness to Practice Panel on Jan. 28, 2010); and Nick Triggle, *MMR Scare Doctor 'Acted Unethically,' Panel Finds,* http://news.bbc.co.uk/2/hi/health/8483865.stm (last visited Nov. 11, 2011); Brian Deer, *How the Case against the MMR Vaccine Was Fixed,* British Medical Journal, Jan. 6, 2011, http://www.bmj.com/content/342/bmj.c5347.full.print?.

81 IOM Immunization Safety Review, *supra* n. 76, at 2.
82 *Id.* at 1. Other researchers have reached conclusions similar to those of the IOM. See additional sources cited in n. 84, *infra*.
83 IOM Immunization Safety Review, *supra* n. 76, at 185; Atkinson, *supra* n. 35, at 159 and B-19.
84 Offit, Autism's False Prophets, *supra,* at 79–80; *cf.* Biss, *supra* n. 69, at 100–1.
85 Taylor et al., *Vaccines Are Not Associated with Autism, supra,* at 3623–25. A 2010 study examining maternal and infant exposure to thimerosal also found no evidence of a causal relationship between prenatal and infant thimerosal exposure and the development of an autism spectrum disorder. Price et al., *Prenatal and Infant Exposure to Thimerosal, supra,* at 656.
86 See Medina, *supra* n. 15; and Waters, *supra* n. 19.
87 *Questions and Answers about Vaccine Ingredients,* American Academy of Pediatrics (Jan. 2013), https://www.healthychildren.org/English/safety-prevention/immunizations/Pages/Vaccine-Ingredients-Frequently-Asked-Questions.aspx; *see also* Biss, *supra* n. 69, at 73–74.
88 The Childhood Immunization Schedule and Safety, *supra* n. 47, at 1–6; *see also* American Academy of Pediatrics, *AAP Agrees With IOM Report on Safety of Vaccine Schedule,* Press Release, Chicago (Jan. 16, 2013), available at https://www.aap.org/en-us/about-the-aap/aap-press-room/pages/AAP-Agrees-With-IOM-Report-on-Safety-of-Vaccine-Schedule.aspx?nfstatus=401&nftoken=00000000-0000-0000-0000-000000000000&nfstatusdescription=ERROR:+No+local+token. (last visited Aug. 22, 2016).
89 *See, e.g.,* Fisher, *supra* n. 67.
90 Financing Vaccines, *supra* n. 6, at 57–59 and A71–72. *See also* Jean Clare Smith, *The Structure, Role, and Procedures of the U.S. Advisory Committee on Immunization Practices (ACIP),* 28S Vaccine A68, A68, A71 (2010); HHS, A Comprehensive Review of Federal Vaccine Safety Programs and Public Health Activities 53 (Dec. 2008), available at http://www.hhs.gov/nvop/nvac/documents/vaccine-safety-reviw.pdf (hereafter Comprehensive Review Federal Vaccine Safety Programs); and Orenstein, *supra* n. 7, at 1007.
91 Maldonado, *supra* n. 12, at 3157.
92 Orenstein, *supra* n. 7, at 1012; Comprehensive Review Federal Vaccine Safety Programs, *supra* n. 90, at 18.
93 Comprehensive Review Federal Vaccine Safety Programs, *supra* n. 90, at 18–23. *See also* Atkinson, *supra* n. 35, at 50–51; and Maldonado, *supra* n. 12, at 3155–57.

94 Thomas B. Neuman, *The Power of Stories Over Statistics*, 327 Brit. Med. J. 1424, 1426 (2003); and Paul Slovic, *Informing and Educating the Public about Risk*, at 184 in Paul Slovic, The Perception of Risk, *supra* (chapter 2, n. 2).
95 Bier, *Risk of Extreme and Rare Events*, *supra*, at 74, 78, 86 (chapter 2, n. 20).
96 Neuman, *supra* n. 94, at 1426; and Campion, *supra* n. 68, at 1475.
97 Kim Witte and Mike Allen, *A Meta-Analysis of Fear Appeals: Implications for Effective Public Health Campaigns*, 27 Health Education and Behavior, 591, 597 (2000).
98 Andrea Kata, *Anti-vaccine Activists, Web 2.0. and the Postmodern Paradigm—An Overview of Tactics and Tropes Used Online by the Anti-Vaccination Movement*, 30 Vaccine 3778, 3780 (2012).
99 Edwards, *State Mandates and Childhood Immunization*, *supra*, at 3171; *see also* Biss, *supra*.
100 Dan M. Kahan et al., *Who Fears the HPV Vaccine*, at 501, 503.
101 Slovic, The Perception of Risk, at xxxiv–xxxv.
102 James H. Jones, Bad Blood: The Tuskegee Syphilis Experiment 1–5, 188 (1993); *see also* Benjamin Roy, *The Tuskegee Syphilis Experiment: Biotechnology and the Administrative State*, 87 JAMA 56; Kimani Paul-Emile, *The Regulation of Race in Science*, 80 Geo. Wash. L. Rev. 1115, 1126–27 (2012).
103 Vernelia R. Randall, *Segregation and Racism: Trusting the Health Care System Ain't Always Easy! An African-American Perspective on Bioethics*, 15 St. Louis U. Pub. L. Rev. 191, 203–4 (1996); and Laura T. Kessler, *"A Sordid Case": Stump v. Sparkman, Judicial Immunity, and the Other Side of Reproductive Rights*, 74 Md. L. Rev. 833, 875–87 (2015).
104 Rebecca Skloot, The Immortal Life of Henrietta Lacks (Crown Publishers, 2010).
105 Randall, *supra* n. 103, at 191–92.
106 *See* National Center for Health Statistics, Health, United States 2014: With Special Features on Adults Aged 55–64, Table 72, pp. 237–39 (2015), http://www.cdc.gov/nchs/data/hus/hus14.pdf#072. National Committee for Quality Assurance (NCQA), *The State of Health Care Quality Report* 12–13 (2010) (noting that the "vaccination rate declined by almost four percentage points among commercial enrollees [who are wealthier] while it actually improved by nearly three percentage points among Medicaid plan members").
107 Lawrence M. Friedman, Total Justice (Russell Sage Foundation, 1994).
108 Larson, *supra* n. 82, at 529.
109 Richard A. Hofstadter, The Paranoid Style in American Politics and Other Essays 1, 7–9, 29 (Harvard University Press, 1965).
110 *See, e.g.*, Stephen Heuser, *Risk and The City*, Boston Globe, Apr. 21, 2013, at K1; Jonathan Weisman, *Gun Control Drive Blocked in Senate; Obama, in Defeat, Sees 'Shameful Day,'* N.Y. Times, Apr. 18, 2013, at A1.
111 Pew Research Center, *Five Years After Market Crash U.S. Economy Seen as 'No More Secure,'* Sept. 12, 2013, available at http://www.people-press.org/2013/09/12/five-years-after-market-crash-u-s-economy-seen-as-no-more-secure/ (last visited Aug. 22, 2016); *cf.* Noreen Malone, *Occupying Wall Street with Yoga, Pillow Fights,*

and Small Group Discussions, N.Y. Mag., Sept. 16, 2011, available at, http://nymag.com/daily/intelligencer/2011/09/will_occupy_wall_street_accomp.html (last visited Aug. 22, 2016).

112 Noam Scheiber and Dalia Sussman, *Inequality Troubles Americans across Party Lines, a Poll Finds*, N.Y. Times, July 4, 2015, at A1.

113 *See, e.g.*, Jeff Zeleny and Megan Thee-Brenan, *New Poll Finds a Deep Distrust of Government*, N.Y. Times, Oct. 26, 2011, at A1.

114 The claim by Barbara Loe Fisher, *supra* n. 67, is typical. *See also* Robert M. Wolfe et al., *Content and Design Attributes of Antivaccination Web Sites*, 287 JAMA 3245, 3247 (2002).

115 Daniel T. Willingham, *Trust Me, I'm a Scientist* (chapter 2, n. 79). One study of parental attitudes toward vaccination found that "[o]nly parents who fully vaccinated their children trusted their physicians, pharmaceutical companies, or the government." Andrea Kata, *supra* n. 98, at 3780.

116 *Id.* Bean, *supra* n. 78, at 1876; and Wolfe, *supra* n. 114, at 3247.

117 *See* Matthew A. Baum, *Red State, Blue State, Flu State: Media Self-Selection and Partisan Gaps in Swine Flu Vaccinations*, 36 J. Health Pol., Pol'y and L. 1021, 1023–24 (2011).

118 Kata, *supra* n. 98, at 3779 (2012). *See also* Kitta, *supra* n. 60, at 36–37.

119 Kitta, *supra* n. 60, at 41.

120 Mnookin, *supra* n. 80, at 84–86.

121 Larson, *supra* n. 79, at 529; and Gregory A. Poland and Robert M. Jacobson, *The Age-Old Struggle against the Antivaccinationists*, 364 New Eng. J. Med. 97 (2011). *See, e.g.*, Christopher Cadelago, *Tim Donnelly Soliciting Referendum Help from Jim Carrey*, Sacramento Bee, July 2, 2015.

122 Mnookin, *supra* n. 80, at 306; and Katrina van den Heuvel, *Jenny McCarthy's Vaccination Fear-Mongering and the Cult of False Equivalence*, The Nation, July 22, 2013, http://www.thenation.com/article/jenny-mccarthys-vaccination-fear-mongering-and-cult-false-equivalence/.

123 Brenda Cossman, *Anxiety Governance*, 38 Law & Soc. Inquiry 892, 898–905 (2013).

124 Cossman, *supra*; *see also* Michael Tortorello, *Is It Safe to Play Yet?*, N.Y. Times, Mar. 15, 2012, at D1.

125 Cossman, *supra* note 123, at 905–15.

126 *Bruesewitz v. Wyeth LLC*, 131 S. Ct. 1068, 1079–80 (2011); Mary J. Davis, *The Case against Preemption: Vaccines and Uncertainty*, 8 Ind. Health L. Rev. 291, 294 (2010/11); Betsey J. Grey, *The Plague of Causation in the National Childhood Vaccine Injury Act*, 48 Harv. J. on Legis. 343, 344 (2011); and Scott, *supra* n. 74.

127 Mnookin, *supra* n. 80, at 283–97; *see also Cedillo v. Secretary, Dep't of Health and Human Services*, 617 F.3d 1328 (Fed. Cir. 2010); and *Hazlehurst v. Secretary, Dep't of Health and Human Services*, 604 F.3d 1343 (Fed. Cir. 2010).

128 Haertlein, *supra* n. 75, at 211, 217–23. These proceedings are accessible through the website of the United States Court of Appeal for the Federal Circuit, http://www.uscfc.uscourts.gov/node/5026 (last visited Nov. 8, 2011).

129 *See, e.g.*, Haertlein, *supra* n. 75; and Hitti, *supra* n. 75. Parents may feel particular dissatisfaction because the VICP has not provided the speedy remedy that Congress promised. *See, e.g.*, Nora Freeman Engstrom, *A Dose of Reality for Specialized Courts: Lessons from the VICP*, 163 U. Penn. L. Rev. 1631, 1655–76 (2015).

130 562 U.S. 223 (2011). The Court held that the federal law had preempted state law remedies. It ruled that Congress' intent was to offer a "*quid pro quo*"—in exchange for continuing to manufacture necessary vaccines, manufacturers received immunity from state tort suits, but injured children would still be able to seek a legal remedy under the administrative procedures established by the Act. *Id.* at 228–40.

131 Malone and Hinman, *supra* n. 6, at 268. For each state's current vaccination requirements see Immunization Action Coalition, *State Information*, http://www.immunize.org/laws/ (last visited Aug. 22, 2016).

132 Cal. Health & Safety Code §§ 120325, 120335, 120338, 120370, and 120375. *See* James G. Hodge and Lawrence O. Gostin, *School Vaccination Requirements: Historical, Social, and Legal Perspectives*, 90 Ky. L. Rev. 831, 859 (2001–02).

133 Lillvis et al., *supra* n. 13, at 478–81, 496; National Conference of State Legislatures, States with Religious and Philosophical Exemptions from School Immunization Requirements, *supra* n. 16.

134 Chen, *supra* n. 8; Nina R. Blank et al., *Exempting Schoolchildren from Immunizations: States with Few Barriers Had Highest Rates of Nonmedical Exemptions*, 32 Health Affairs 1282–83 (2013); and Daniel A. Salmon et al., *Health Consequences of Religious and Philosophical Exemptions from Immunization Laws: Individual and Societal Risks of Measles,*, 281 JAMA 47, 47–48 (1999).

135 Blank, *supra* n. 134, at 1283.

136 *Id.*

137 The Child Abuse Prevention and Treatment Act of 1974 (CAPTA), 42 U.S.C. §5101, provided federal funding to states that adopted policies consistent with its requirements, including an exemption for religious beliefs. Ross D. Silverman, *No More Kidding Around: Restructuring Non-Medical Childhood Immunization Exemptions to Ensure Public Health Protection*, 12 Annals Health L. 277, 282 (2003); *see also* Henry J. Abraham, *Abraham, Isaac and the State: Faith-Healing and Legal Intervention*, 27 U. Rich. L. Rev. 951, 975 (1993).

138 The First Amendment protects religious freedom by providing that "Congress shall make no law respecting an establishment of religion, or prohibiting the free exercise thereof...." U.S. Const. amend. I. In *Cantwell v. Connecticut*, 310 U.S. 296, 303 (1940), the Supreme Court declared that the protections of the First Amendment were applicable to the states. The Religious Freedom Restoration Act of 1993 (RFRA), 42 U.S.C. §2000bb *et seq.*, limits the extent to which the federal government may interfere with the exercise of religious freedom. The scope and impact of that law is sharply contested. *See, e.g.*, *Burwell v. Hobby Lobby Stores, Inc.*, 134 S. Ct. 2751 (2014) (majority and dis-

senting opinions). RFRA does not apply to the states, *City of Boerne v. Flores*, 117 S. Ct. 2157 (1997), but twenty-one states have enacted mini-RFRAs. See National Conference on State Legislatures, *State Religious Freedom Restoration Acts* (Jun. 5, 2015), http://www.ncsl.org/research/civil-and-criminal-justice/state-rfra-statutes.aspx; Campbell Robertson and Richard Perez-Pena, *Bills on 'Religious Freedom' Upset Capitols in Two States*, N.Y. Times, Apr. 1, 2015, at A1.

139 *Boone v. Boozman*, 217 F. Supp. 2d 938 at 949–50 (E.D. Ark. 2002).
140 *See, e.g., Sherr v. Northport-East Northport Union Free Sch. Dist.*, 672 F. Supp. 81, 89–90 (E.D. N.Y. 1987); and *McCarthy v. Boozman*, 212 F. Supp. 2d 945, 949 (W.D. Ark. 2002) (similar exemption); *but see Kleid v. Bd. of Educ.*, 406 F. Supp. 902, 904, 906–7 (W.D. Ky. 1976).
141 N.Y. Pub. Health L. § 2164.
142 *Cf. Phillips v. City of New York*, 27 F. Supp. 3d 310, 312 (2014) (discussing plaintiffs' allegations), *aff'd by Phillips v. City of N.Y.*, 775 F. 3d 538, 540–43 (2d Cir. 2015), *cert. denied* 136 S. Ct. 104 (2015).
143 N.Y. Pub. Health L. § 2164 (9), applied and upheld in *Caviezel v. Great Neck Publ. Sch.*, 701 F. Supp. 414 (E.D. N.Y. 2010; *aff'd, Phillips v. City of N.Y.*, 775 F. 3d 538, 540–43 (2d Cir. 2015). *Cf. Farina v. Bd. of Educ.*, 116 F. Supp. 2d 503, 513 (E.D. N.Y. 2000).
144 In re *Le Page v. State of Wyoming Dep't of Health*, 18 P.3d 1177, 1179–81 (Wyo. 2001).
145 Ark. Code Ann. § 6-18-702(d) (2) (repealed and replaced by § 6–18–702(d)(4)), discussed in *McCarthy v. Ozark School Dist.*, 359 F.3d 1029 (8th Cir. 2004).
146 *Boone*, 217 F. Supp. 2d 938, 942–951.
147 Ark. Code. Ann. § 6-18-702 (4) (A) (emphasis added).
148 See National Conference of State Legislatures, *States with Religious and Philosophical Exemptions from School Immunization Requirements*, supra n.16; *see also* Lillvis, *supra* n. 13.
149 *Check v. N.Y. City Dep't of Ed.*, 2013 WL 2181045 (E.D. N.Y. 2013).
150 Blank, *supra* n. 134, at 1283.
151 Blank, *supra* n. 134, at 1282, 1284–87; *see also* Silverman, *supra* n. 137, at 278; Malone and Hinman, *supra* n. 11, at 274; Salmon et al., *Parental Vaccine Refusal in Wisconsin: A Case-Control Study*, 108 (#1) Wisc. Med. J. 17, 17 (2009).
152 Saad B. Omer et al., *Nonmedical Exemptions to School Immunization Requirements: Secular Trends and Association of State Policies with Pertussis Incidence*, 296 JAMA 1757, 1761 (2006).
153 Salmon et al., *supra* n. 134, at 47, 49. Similar patterns have been shown for pertussis. Daniel R. Feikin et al., *Individual and Community Risks of Measles and Pertussis Associated with Personal Exemptions to Immunization*, 284 JAMA 3145, 3147 (2000).
154 Omer et al., *supra* n. 152, at 1759.
155 Gina Bellafante, *Vaccine Fear Goes Viral*, N.Y. Times, Oct. 12, 2014, at MB1.

156 Valerie Richardson, *California to Tighten Vaccine Law*, The Washington Times, June 11, 2015, 2015 WLNR 17195378.
157 Rubin and Kasimov, *The Problem of Vaccination Noncompliance*, at 115 (chapter 1, n. 96).
158 Dempsey, *Alternative Vaccination Schedule Preferences among Parents of Young Children*, *supra* (chapter 1, n. 86).
159 K. J. Dell'Antonia, *The A.A.P. Has a New Vaccine Schedule. Will You Follow It?* The New York Times Blogs (Motherlode) Jan. 29, 2013; Dempsey, *supra*, n. 158; *see also* ASTHO, *Communicating Effectively about Vaccines*, at 12.
160 Dempsey, *supra*.
161 Reich, *supra* n. 23, at 10–14.
162 *See* Saad B. Omer et al., *Vaccine Refusal, Mandatory Immunization, and the Risks of Vaccine-Preventable Diseases*, 19 New Eng. J. Med. 1981, 1984 (2009).
163 Bellafante, *supra* n. 155.
164 Parmet, *supra* n. 22, at 81. *See* NVIC, at http://www.nvic.org (last visited July 15, 2015).
165 Simon N. Whitney et al., *A Typology of Shared Decision Making, Informed Consent, and Simple Consent*, 140 Ann. Intern. Med. 54, 54 (2003).
166 John Stuart Mill, *On Liberty*, in Mill, *Text Commentaries*, 48 (Alan Ryan ed., Norton 1997 ed.).
167 105 N.E. 92, 93 (N.Y. 1914).
168 464 F. 2d 772, 782–83 (D.C. Cir. 1972).
169 611 P. 2d 902, 906 (Cal. 1980).
170 Whitney et al., *supra* n. 165.
171 Bellafante, *supra* n. 155; *see also* Dorit Rubinstein Reiss, *Thou Shalt Not Take the Name of the Lord God in Vain: Use and Abuse of Religious Exemptions from School Immunization Requirements*, 65 Hastings L. J. 1551, 1565–66 (2014) (discussing two children who contracted measles in a doctor's waiting room and succumbed to subacute sclerosing panencephalitis [SSPE], a rare but fatal reaction to measles).
172 Parmet, *supra* n. 22, at 88–92; *see also Canterbury v. Spence*, 464 F.2d 772, 781–83 (D.C. Cir. 1972).
173 American Academy of Pediatrics, Committee on Bioethics, *Informed Consent, Parental Permission, and Assent in Pediatric Practice*, 95 Pediatrics 314, 315 (1995).
174 Lawrence O. Gostin, *When Terrorism Threatens Health: How Far Are Limitations on Personal and Economic Liberties Justified*, 55 Fla. L. Rev., 1105, 1141–58 (2003); Wendy E. Parmet, *Liberalism, Communitarianism, and Public Health: Comments on Lawrence O. Gostin's Lecture*, 55 Fla. L. Rev. 1221 (2003); *see also Pierce v. Society of Sisters*, 268 U.S. 510 (1925), and *Meyer v. Nebraska*, 262 U.S. 390 (1923).
175 321 U.S. 158, 170 (1944).
176 *See, e.g., Matter of McCauley*, 565 N.E. 2d 411 (Mass. 1991).
177 *See, e.g., In re Custody of a Minor*, 393 N.E. 2d 836 (Mass. 1979) or *Mueller v. Auker*, 576 F. 3d 979 (9th Cir. 2009).

178 Parmet, *supra* n. 22, at 81–107.
179 *Id.* at 95–97.
180 The National Childhood Vaccine Injury Compensation Act mandates that the CDC prepare Vaccine Information Sheets, which must be given to patients or their parents. 42 U.S.C. § 300aa-26 (a).
181 Parmet, *supra* n. 22, at 89–90.
182 *See* Nora Freeman Engstrom, *supra* n. 129, at 1698–706.
183 Louis Z. Cooper et al., *Promoting Public Trust in Immunization*, 122 Pediatrics 149, 149 (2008).
184 *See, e.g.*, Dorit Rubinstein Reiss, *Compensating the Victims of Failure to Vaccinate: What Are the Options?*, 23 Cornell J. L. & Pub. Pol'y 595, 597–98, 605–26 (2014); and Stephen P. Teret and Jon S. Vernick, *Gambling with the Health of Others*, 107 Mich. L. Rev First Impressions 110, 111–13 (2009).
185 The cases are *In re Jamaica Hospital*, 491 N.Y.S. 2d 898 (N.Y. Sup. Ct., Special Term, Queens County 1985); *Jefferson v. Griffin County Hospital Authority*, 274 S.E.2d 457, 458–59 (Ga. 1981); *Burton v. State*, 49 So.3d 263 (Fla. App. Ct. 2010); and *Pemberton v. Tallahassee Memorial Regional Medical Center, Inc.*, 66 F. Supp. 2d 1247, 1251 (N.D. Fla. 1999).
186 *State v. Cacchiotti*, 568 A. 2d 1026, 1031 (R.I. 1990).
187 Aamer Imdad et al., *Religious Exemptions for Immunization and Risk of Pertussis in New York State, 2000–2011*, 132 Pediatrics 37, 40–41 (Jul. 2013), citing P. J. Smith et al., *Children Who Have Received No Vaccines: Who Are They and Where Do They Live?*, 114 (1) Pediatrics 187–95 (2004); *see also* Reich, *supra* n. 23, at 2.
188 Reich, *supra* n. 23, at 14–17.
189 Reich, *supra* n. 23, 4–6; *see also* Cossman, *supra* n. 123.
190 *See, e.g.*, Jack, *supra* n. 17, at 73–81; and Reich, *supra* n. 23.
191 Examples of prosecution of Christian Science parents include *Commonwealth v. Twitchell*, 617 N.E. 2d 609 (Mass. 1993); and *Walker v. Superior Court*, 763 P. 2d 852 (Cal. 1988). *Commonwealth v. Schaible*, 2015 Pa. Super. Unpub. LEXIS 3377, 133 A.3d 69 (2015), was a murder prosecution of faith-healing parents.
192 *See, e.g.*, *Mueller v. Auker*, 576 F.3d 979 (9th Cir. 2009); *In re Custody of a Minor*, 393 N.E. 2d 836 (Mass. 1979); and *Matter of McCauley*, 565 N.E. 2d 411 (Mass. 1991).
193 *Spiering v. Heineman*, 448 F. Supp. 2d 1129 (D. Neb. 2006).
194 *See, e.g*, *Walker v. Superior Court*, 763 P. 2d 852 (Ca. 1988); *Commonwealth v. Twitchell*, 617 N.E. 2d 609 (Ma. 1993); and *State v. Hermanson*, 604 So. 2d 775 (Fl. 1992).
195 U.S. General Accounting Office (GAO), Report to Congressional Requesters, Welfare Reform: State Sanction Policies and Number of Families Affected 3, 5, 29–30 (Mar. 2000) (GAO/HEHS-00-44).
196 Wendy Parmet blog, available at http://blogs.law.harvard.edu/billof-health/2015/04/25/no-jab-no-pay-australias-misguided-approach-to-vaccine-refusal/; *see also* Jonathan Pearlman, *Aussie 'no jab, no pay' policy boosts vaccina-*

tion rates, It withholds benefits from parents who do not have their kids immunised from diseases, Straits Times (Singapore), Aug. 4, 2016, 2016 WLNR 23617037.

CHAPTER 10. MOVING BEYOND BLAME

1 See, e.g., Chasnoff, *The 4P's Plus© Screen for Substance Use in Pregnancy, supra,* at 373 (chapter 4, n. 81); Nishimoto and Roberts, *Coercion and Drug Treatment for Postpartum Women, supra,* at 175 (chapter 5, n. 6); Whiteford and Vitucci, *Pregnancy and Addiction, supra,* at 1371 (chapter 5, n. 6); and Chasnoff, *Discrepancies in Mandatory Reporting in Pinellas County, Florida, supra,* at 1206 (chapter 4, n. 81). Further, to ensure that such testing will actually result in improved health for developing fetuses, the statute must also authorize the spending of sufficient funds to ensure that there is a treatment slot available for every pregnant woman who wants one.
2 Lillvis, *Power and Persuasion in the Vaccine Debates, supra* (chapter 9, n. 13).
3 Gerald E. Lynch, *Our Administrative System of Criminal Justice,* 66 Fordham L. Rev. 2117 (1988).
4 *See United States v. Kimbrough,* 128 S. Ct. 558 (2007), and the recent decision of the Department of Justice and the United States Sentencing Commission to treat the amounts of cocaine possessed by a defendant as equivalent, regardless of whether the cocaine is in "crack" or powder form, ending more than three decades of sentencing practices that discriminated against those who possessed crack cocaine.
5 Goldstein, *The Passive Judiciary, supra,* at 5 (chapter 5, n. 159).
6 *Bei Bei Shuai v. State,* 966 N.E.2d 619, 635–36 (Ind. Ct. App. 2012, Riley J., concurring and dissenting).
7 Michelle Oberman, *Mothers and Doctors' Orders: Unmasking the Doctor's Fiduciary Role in Maternal–Fetal Conflicts,* 94 Nw. U. L. Rev. 451, 474–82 (2000).
8 Michele Goodwin, *Fetal Protection Laws: Moral Panic and the New Constitutional Battlefront,* 102 Cal. L. Rev. 781, 806–8 (2014).
9 Linda C. Fentiman, *The New "Fetal Protection": The Wrong Answer to the Crisis of Health Care for Women and Children,* 84 Denver U. L. Rev. 537, 569–70 (2006).
10 Institute of Medicine, *Shorter Lives, supra* (chapter 1, n. 25).
11 Anyone who is concerned about children's health must acknowledge, as has the American Academy of Pediatrics, that the biggest single determinant of children's health status and health outcome is whether they were born into, and continue to live in, poverty. Michael Kelly, N.Y. Times Oct. 31, 1992, at A1; Isaacs and Schroeder, *Class, the Ignored Determinants of the Nation's Health, supra* (chapter 1, n. 93); Larson, *Poverty During Pregnancy, supra* (chapter 2, n. 75); and Kemp, *Poverty Threatens Health of U.S. Children, supra* (chapter 2, n. 85).
12 Shonkoff and Phillips, *From Neurons to Neighborhoods, supra* (chapter 1, n. 24).
13 Catalano, *Intimate Partner Violence, 1993–2010, supra,* at 1 (chapter 7, n. 40).
14 Institute of Medicine, Preterm Birth: Causes, Consequences, and Prevention 162–64, 265, 371 (Richard E. Behrman and Adrienne Stith Butler, eds., National

Academies Press, 2007) (chapter 4, n. 29); and Centers for Disease Control, Key Findings: The association between assisted reproductive technology and autism spectrum disorder, available at http://www.cdc.gov/ncbddd/autism/features/artandasd.html (last visited Aug. 23, 2016).

15 Jane K. Stoever, *Stories Absent from the Courtroom: Responding to Domestic Violence in the Context of HIV and AIDS*, 87 N.C. L. Rev. 1157, 1175–77 (2009).

16 Brimacombe, *Comparison of Fetal Demise Case Series Drawn from Socioeconomically Distinct Counties in New Jersey, supra*, at 214, 219–21 (chapter 4, n. 24); Nagahawatte and Goldenberg, *Poverty, Maternal Health, and Adverse Pregnancy Outcomes, supra*, at 82–83 (chapter 4, n. 21); Harmon, *U.S. Stillbirths Still Prevalent, Often Unexplained, supra* (chapter 4, n. 21); and Wenner Moyer, *How Much Alcohol Is Safe for Expectant Mothers, supra* (chapter 4, n. 21).

17 Young, *Substance-Exposed Infants, State Responses to the Problem, supra*, at 28–29 (chapter 5, n. 1).

18 Susan R.B. Weiss, *Emerging Issues in Gender and Ethnic Differences in Substance Abuse and Treatment, supra*, at 249 (chapter 5, n. 60).

19 Nishimoto and Roberts, *Coercion and Drug Treatment for Postpartum Women, supra*, at 176–77 (chapter 5, n. 6); Roberts and Nuru-Jeter, *supra*, at 193–94 (chapter 5, n. 87).

20 CDC, *The National Intimate Partner and Sexual Violence Survey* (NISVS) 2010 Survey Report (2011).

21 Weiss, *supra* n. 18, at 247; Zickler, *Childhood Sex Abuse Increases Risk for Drug Dependence in Adult Women, supra* (chapter 5, n. 60); *see also* Najavits, *The Link between Substance Abuse and Posttraumatic Stress Disorder in Women, supra*, at 274 (chapter 5, n. 59).

22 Chang, *Homicide: A Leading Cause of Injury Deaths among Pregnant and Postpartum Women, supra*, at 471–72 (chapter 2, n. 71).

23 Jennifer Brown-Cranstoun, *Kringen v. Boslough and Saint Vincent Hospital: A New Trend for Healthcare Professionals Who Treat Victims of Domestic Violence*, 33 J. of Health L. 629 (2000); Task Force, *Screening for Intimate Partner Violence and Abuse of Elderly and Vulnerable Adults* (2012); and Institute of Medicine, Clinical Preventative Services for Women: Closing the Gaps (2011).

24 Schechter and Edleson, *The Greenbook, supra*, at 9.

25 Evan Stark, *The Battered Mother in the Child Protective Service Caseload: Developing an Appropriate Response*, 23 Women's Rts. L. Rep. 107, 110 (2002).

26 Kristine A. Campbell et al., *Household, Family, and Child Risk Factors after an Investigation for Suspected Child Maltreatment: A Missed Opportunity for Prevention*, 164 Arch. Pediatric Adolescent Med. 943 (2010).

27 Karin V. Rhodes et al., *The Anatomy of A Community Health Center System-Level Intervention for Intimate Partner Violence*, 91 J. Urban Health 107, 112–17 (2013).

28 Campbell, *supra* n. 26, at 6–7, 12.

29 Chiu, *Confronting the Agency in Battered Mothers, supra*, at 1223–35 (chapter 1, n. 69).

30 Catalano, *supra* n. 13.
31 *Town of Castle Rock v. Gonzales*, 545 U.S. 748 (2005).
32 ACLU Women's Rights Project, *Silenced: How Nuisance Ordinances Punish Crime Victims in New York, supra,* at 1–8, 10 (chapter 7, n. 108).
33 Tara Siegel Bernard, *In Paid Family Leave, U.S. Trails Most of the Globe*, N.Y. Times Feb. 23, 2013, at B1.
34 Jacqueline H. Wolf, Don't Kill Your Baby, *supra*, at 1, 42, 47–49 (chapter 1, n. 49).
35 *See, e.g., Michigan v. E.P.A.*, 135 S. Ct. 2699 (2015).
36 van Panhuis et al., *Contagious Diseases in the United States from 1888 to the Present, supra,* at 2154, 2156 (chapter 9, n. 35); and Lohr, *Combing Years of Data, Doctors Show Big Benefit of Childhood Vaccines, supra* (chapter 9, n. 49).

INDEX

AAP. *See* American Academy of Pediatrics
abatement, public nuisance and, 237
abortion: anti-abortion movement, 138; coercion and domestic violence, 120; criminal prosecution of pregnant women, 103–5; *Gonzales v. Carhart*, 89, 104–5; "intact dilation and evacuation" and, 89, 334n112; Medicaid and, 345n70; *Planned Parenthood of Southeastern Pennsylvania v. Casey*, 104, 138; *Roe v. Wade*, 71, 86, 88–89, 103–5, 138; teens and, 66
absolute risk, 34–35, 162. *See also* relative risk
abuse. *See* child abuse; drugs; physical abuse; sexual abuse
ACA. *See* Affordable Care Act
ACOG. *See* American College of Obstetricians and Gynecologists
actions. *See* duty to act; failure to act; individual action; legal actions, against pregnant women
"actual cause," 49, 143; lead poisoning and, 225–31
actual harm, 222
ADA. *See* Americans with Disabilities Act
addiction. *See* alcohol; drugs; drug treatment, for pregnant women; illegal drugs; smoking; tobacco; treatment
addiction legislation, 11, 112, 147–48, 288
adolescents: child abuse and, 188; death in, 60, 66; health of, 65–67; smoking and, 65
adoption, 98–99, 346n90

Adoption and Safe Families Act of 1997, 346n90
advance medical directives: living wills and, 10, 105; pregnant women and overriding, 105–8
affect heuristic, 80
Affordable Care Act (ACA), 7, 67, 78; breastfeeding and, 15, 156, 173; Medicaid, expansion of, 67, 287, 390n54; prenatal care and, 287; vaccinations and, 252; workplace and, 15, 176
African-Americans: asthma and, 62; breastfeeding and, 164; drugs and, 142; drug treatment and, 353n210; HIV/AIDS and, 93; homicide and, 77; men in prison, 196; "other-mothering" and, 363n118; physicians and trust in, 259; poverty and, 35, 37–38, 78; prenatal care and, 78, 330n43; risk and, 29; slavery and, 173; stillbirths in, 77, 125; Tuskegee syphilis experiment and, 259
Agency for Health Care Research and Quality (AHRQ), 166, 167
AIDS/HIV. *See* HIV/AIDS
Aiwohi, Tayshea, 131, 349n142, 349n144
alcohol: binge drinking, 115, 122; deaths, 11, 122, 347n92; fetal alcohol syndrome (FAS), 11, 122, 123, 304n33, 347n95, 349n128; gender and consumption of, 117–18; historical use, 109, 343n54; illegal drug use and, 342n41; pregnant women and, 11, 122, 123, 129, 304n33, 347n95, 347n96, 349n128; sexual abuse with drugs and, 16, 120, 289, 324n52, 344n60; "telescoping," 118

403

alternative vaccination schedules, 21, 268
aluminum, vaccinations and, 257
amendments. *See* Constitution, U.S.
American Academy of Pediatrics (AAP), 87, 321n3, 323n24; breastfeeding and, 158, 160–62, 168, 169–70, 291; vaccinations and, 253
American College of Obstetricians and Gynecologists (ACOG), 81–82, 87
American Medical Association, 87, 181, 244–45
American Psychological Association, 340n10
Americans with Disabilities Act (ADA), 15, 175–76
Amish, 267
amoxicillin, 167
"anchoring and adjustment" heuristic, 27–28, 40
Anderson, Carol, 40, 42, 142, 312n23
Andon v. 302–304 Mott Street Associates, 228
Angela M. W., 149
Ankiewicz v. Kinder, 317n109
Ankrom, 113
Ankrom, Hope, 111–12, 113
anti-abortion movement, 138
antidepressants, 12, 170
anxiety, mental health and, 31, 61, 66, 102, 118, 260, 281
anxiety governance, 262, 295
Armstrong, Elizabeth, 128, 132, 328n21, 332n65, 347n93
A.R.T. *See* assisted reproductive technology
asbestos exposure, in workplace, 234–35
assimilation, biased prototypes and, 41
assisted reproductive technology (A.R.T.), 285–86
association, versus causation, in breastfeeding, 167
asthma, 62, 169
Atkins v. Virginia, 349n134

atmospheric lead, 220–22
Australia, 59, 276
authority, 85, 88, 220; expert, 33, 36–37, 261; multiple sources of, 33–34
autism, 58, 61; defined, 392n76; vaccinations and, 34, 261, 263, 314n65
availability heuristic, 26, 40
AZT, 91, 92

"Babies Were Born to Be Breastfed" campaign, 164, 165
Baby Boomers, 58, 159
Baby-Friendly Hospital program, 173–74, 177
Back to Sleep campaign, 323n24
Barrientos, Nancy, 194, 373n97
battered child syndrome, 63, 181
Bei Bei Shuai v. State, 136, 283, 350n162, 400n6
Beltran, Alicia, 4, 11–12, 112, 149, 284, 305n36
Beltran v. Strachota, 305n36
Benjamin, Regina, 166
"the Benzene case," 54
Bernstein, Anita, 235
better than average bias, 42, 96, 130, 197
bias: better than average, 42, 96, 130, 197; cultural, 28; hindsight, 42, 43, 96, 202, 317n107; motherhood, 185; omission, 27, 35; of prosecutors, 185; racial, 28, 81; against single mothers, 370n61. *See also* gender bias; judges
biased prototypes, juries and, 41–42, 43, 80, 142
binge drinking, 115, 122
Binns, Helen, 223
birth: "born-alive rule," 74, 126, 137; children and life expectancy, 7, 58, 59–60, 246, 248; labor induction, 82, 333n77; Medicaid and, 330n42; premature, 35, 76, 113, 345n76; preterm, 59, 60, 76, 79, 125, 303n21; rates, 331n64; stillbirths, 76, 77, 79, 111, 125–26, 335n131;

VBACs, 82, 88. *See also* caesarean sections
bisphenol A. *See* BPA
Blackmun, Harry, 103
blood transfusions, as compulsory medical treatment, 10, 83–91
Bonbrest v. Kotz, 74–75
"bonding" hypothesis, 159, 165
Bonte v. Bonte, 336n135, 336n136
Boone v. Boozman, 265
"born-alive rule," 74, 126, 137
Bowditch, Manfred, 213, 227. *See also* lead poisoning
boys: physical abuse of, 15; sexual abuse rates, 307n56
BPA (bisphenol A), 26, 65, 171, 262
brain: dead, 106; development, 58, 61, 215; dopamine, 342n136, 342n137; drugs and, 116–17; genetics and, 342n140; mercury and, 64. *See also* IQ
breastfeeding: ACA and, 15, 156, 173; benefits, 161, 291, 357n37; campaigns, 14, 155, 163–66, 168; controversy, 5, 37, 156–57, 158; cultural constructions of, 172–73; government involvement in, 14–15, 163–66; health care system failure and, 173–74; history and, 166–67; HIV/AIDS and, 169, 361n94; homicide and, 155, 171; infant formula and, 5, 157, 158–59, 356n9, 364n126; legal obstacles, 175–77; in media, 164, 165, 358n55; Medicaid and, 173, 291–92; obstacles to, 15, 172, 356n11; overselling of, 166–72; on public transportation, 172; rates, 159–60; from "recommendation" to mandate, 160–62; risks, 169–72; science in support of, 158–62, 166–69; slavery and, 173; toxins in human milk, 170–71; workplace obstacles and, 15, 174–75, 177
"Breast Is Best" campaign, 168
breasts: cultural constructions of, 172–73; reduction, 171

Breger, Melissa, 185
Bruesewitz v. Wyeth LLC., 263, 391n73
Burton, Samantha, 5, 89–90, 273
Bush, George H. W., 54, 110
Bush, George W., 14, 54, 163
Butler, Louis, 208

caesarean sections (C-sections): criminal prosecution of pregnant women for choosing, 3–4, 10, 99; emergency and planned, 82; as medical treatment, court-ordered, 10, 83–91; rates, 75, 82, 332n75; VBACs, 82, 88
caffeine. *See* coffee consumption
Campbell, Alex, 187, 190
Canada, 59, 98, 114, 150–51; measles in, 243, 244; prosecutors in, 134, 135
Canterbury v. Spence, 269
Carder, Angela, 108, 334n100. See also *In re A.C.*
Cardozo, Benjamin, 83, 269
care. *See* duty of care; prenatal care
Carrey, Jim, 261
Carville, James, 57
"causal attribution": in context, 200; lead poisoning and, 225–31
causation: "actual cause," 49, 143, 225–31; breastfeeding and, compared to association, 167; child endangerment and, 144; choice and control with, 211; foreseeability and individual action with, 44, 48–51; harm and, 53–54, 201; pregnant women and, 50, 143–47; proximate cause, 49, 143, 144, 200, 202; psychosocial processes and legal decisionmakers with, 200–202; rules and criminal convictions, 143–47, 201
Centers for Disease Control (CDC), 123; on breastfeeding and HIV/AIDS, 361n94; on lead poisoning, 216; with "safe" exposure levels, 25; vaccinations and, 34, 245–46, 251, 257–58

Chamallas, Martha, 41, 49, 199, 200, 229, 230
Chenault v. Huie, 336n138
Chicago. See *City of Chicago v. Am. Cyanamid Co.*; lead poisoning
child abuse: *battered child syndrome* and, 63, 181; causation and, 51; cycle of, 307n60; deaths, 178, 183–88, 194–95, 340n9, 369n32; with definition expanded, 134; demographics, 183–84; economic status and, 16, 308n67; gender bias with, 16–17, 179; history of, 180–83; homicide by, 111, 144, 178, 340n9; investigated and prosecuted with discretion, 184–87; IPV affecting, 190–97; legislation, 188–89, 366n3, 396n137; men and, 178–79, 183–89, 194–95, 211; mothers and crimes of omission with, 180–87, 211; neglect and, 63, 178, 346n90; by omission and prosecutors, 370n56; physical abuse and, 8, 15, 61, 66, 180, 183, 190, 192, 201; poverty and, 16, 184, 308n67; rates, 15, 182, 369n29, 369n32; risks, 16; risk solutions, 288–91; single mothers and, 48, 184; women and, 48, 180–87, 190, 211. *See also* domestic violence; intimate partner violence
Child Abuse Prevention and Treatment Act of 1974, 396n137
A Child Is Born (Nilsson), 73, 327n4
child endangerment, 13, 43, 170; causation and, 144; charges of, 99, 110, 114, 126, 128, 129, 131; fetus and, 138; legislation, 129, 182
children: of abuse and link to prison, 16; boys, 15, 307n56; fetus conflated with, 136–38, 338n175; girls, 15, 46–47, 59, 307n56; HIV transmitted to, 8, 58; life expectancy, 7, 58, 59–60, 246, 248; mothers sued for prenatal harm by, 93–94, 336n137; as murder witnesses, 63; poverty and, 37–38, 57, 61, 78, 321n3, 400n11; "the reasonable pregnant woman" and, 47–48; sexual abuse rates, 15, 307n56; stress influencing, 7, 63; teen pregnancy, 59, 66; vaccination legislation for, 255, 263; Vaccines for Children Program, 390n52. *See also* adolescents; children's health; infants
children's health: adolescents, 65–67; birth, 7, 58–59, 60; chronic conditions, 61, 62–63; complexity of, 284–85; in context, 6–9, 56, 302n13; deaths, 7, 43, 59–60, 66, 79, 248–50, 302n19, 303n20, 303n21; DNA with, 58; environmental hazards, 64–65, 293; fathers and, 8; in future, 67; illness and injury, 61–62; with law and unconscious risk construction, 281–84; with lead poisoning exposure, 207–9, 213–16, 224–41, 384n149; neglect, 3, 63; obesity, 3, 62–63; poverty and, 37–38, 57, 61, 63, 321n3; precautionary principle and, 294–95; race and, 56, 59–60; risk solutions and, 285–94; SCHIP, 66–67; smoking and, 12, 57–58, 113; social class with, 57, 60; today, 279–81; vaccination legislation and mothers, 272–76; vaccine risks and options for parents, 264–72. *See also* breastfeeding
CHIP. *See* State Child Health Insurance Program
choice, causation and, 211
chorioamnionitis, 352n191
Christian Scientists, 22, 265, 275
Christie, Chris, 134
chronic conditions, childhood, 61, 62–63
Church of England, 265
City of Chicago v. Am. Cyanamid Co., 384n165
City of Milwaukee v. NL Industries, 239
City of St. Louis v. Benjamin Moore & Co., 239

civil commitment: defined, 304n35; drug use by pregnant women and, 148–51. *See also* Beltran, Alicia
Civil Rights Act, Title VII, 175, 177
Clean Air Act, 53, 64, 221–22, 293
climate change, 31, 36
Clinton, Bill, 57, 163
cocaine, 37, 124–25, 128, 146, 400n4
coffee consumption, 109, 115; as pregnancy risk, 76, 124; smoking and, 37
cognitive processes, unconsciousness and, 9, 17, 197. *See also* bias; heuristics; worldviews
Colen, Cynthia, 169
Collins, Jennifer, 185
Collins v. Eli Lilly Co., 208, 234
common law, 39; "born-alive rule," 74, 126, 137; duty to act, 318n136; English, 49, 74, 180, 237, 280; products liability and lead poisoning, 231–37. *See also* public nuisance law
Commonwealth v. Lazarovich, 196–97
Commonwealth v. Pugh, 99–100, 327n157
communication. *See* risk communication
communitarian worldviews, 29–30, 33
compulsory medical treatment. *See* treatment
conception: risk solutions prior to, 286; smoking prior to, 57–58, 113
condoms, 93, 286
Condon, Charles, 134, 137–38
confidentiality, 149–50, 283–84
Constitution, U.S.: First Amendment, 83, 84, 264–66, 396n138; Fourteenth Amendment, 83, 104, 247, 262; Fourth Amendment, 81
Consumer Product Safety Commission (CPSC), 214, 217, 223, 378n59
Consumer Products Safety Improvement Act of 2008, 223
contagious diseases, 387n26; in context, 248–52; outbreaks, 243–44, 267; problem, 243–48; vaccinations and, 243–62, 293–94

control: causation and, 211; gun, 20, 26. *See also* Centers for Disease Control; power
Cooley, Thomas, 46–47, 198
Cooper, Louis, 272
coping strategies, juries and, 42
Corneau, Rebecca, 90–91
corporations, 53, 222; with lactation programs, 175; lead poisoning by, 221, 223, 239–40, 374n3, 376n25. *See also* pharmaceutical industry
corruption, prosecutors and, 133
Cossman, Brenda, 262
costs: infant formula, 364n126; lead paint, reducing exposure to, 376n25; vaccinations and saved, 251
counterfactual thinking, 42–43
court-ordered treatment, 71, 92
CPSC. *See* Consumer Product Safety Commission
"crack babies," myth of, 37–38
crimes of omission. *See* mothers, crimes of omission and
criminal convictions: causation rules and, 143–47, 201; poverty and, 111; reversal of, 4, 13, 130–31, 146
criminalizing, of pregnancy, 147–48
criminal justice system: with discretion, 28, 40, 185; racism in, 28
criminal law: deterrence and, 38–39; principle of legality and, 126, 128, 129, 130; "the reasonable mother" in, 48, 50–51; "the reasonable parent" in, 48; "the reasonable person" in, 44
criminal liability, social construction and, 138–42
criminal prosecutions, 5; "fetal protection," first wave, 126–28; "fetal protection," second wave, 128–32; of pregnant women, 3–4, 98–105; of pregnant women for drug use, 109–15, 126–32; race and, 185
Cruz, Ted, 134

C-sections. *See* caesarean sections
cultural bias, 28
cultural constructions, of breastfeeding, 172–73
cultural scripts, 6, 40
cultural stereotypes, 9
cultural understanding, unconscious, 31
Curran v. Bosze, 86
Currier, Sophie, 175–76

deaths: adolescents, 60, 66; alcohol, 11, 122, 347n92; brain dead, 106; child abuse, 178, 183–88, 194–95, 340n9, 369n32; in childhood, 7, 43, 59–60, 66, 79, 248–50, 302n19, 303n20, 303n21; feticide, 4, 100–102, 105, 338n177; genocide, 58, 245; homicide, 35, 77, 155, 171, 178, 340n9, 349n126; infants, 7, 59–60, 79, 124, 166, 167–68, 250, 286, 302n19, 303n21; IPV, 194–95; from lead poisoning, 221; motor vehicles, 60; neglect, 183; preterm, 60, 125; smoking, 12; suicide, 66, 101, 107, 283; tobacco, 122. *See also* manslaughter; murder
decisionmaking: discretionary, 44–51; fundamental attribution error and, 27; issues with, 36; juries with cases and, 40–44; psychosocial processes and legal, 197–202
"defensive attribution," 27, 198
Denmark, 123
Denno, Deborah, 19, 308n75, 325n56, 378n55, 384n156
Department of Health and Human Services, 5, 163–66, 255
Department of Housing and Urban Development, 218
Department of Justice, 134
depression: mental health and, 16, 66, 118, 119, 154, 344n60; postpartum, 291
DES, market share liability theory and, 231–34

DeShaney v. Winnebago County Dep't. of Social Services, 182
deterrence, law and, 38–39
Dietrich v. Inhabitants of Northampton, 74
disabilities. *See* Americans with Disabilities Act
discretion: with child abuse, 184–87; criminal justice system with, 28, 40, 185; prosecutors and, 40, 133–36; racial bias and, 28
discretionary decisionmaking, substantive law and, 44–51
diseases: asthma, 62, 169; HPV, 32, 33, 250–51; illness in childhood, 61–62; measles, 243–44, 249, 252; obesity, 3, 62–63, 78, 161, 164; pertussis, 7, 244, 249, 267, 302n16; polio, 7, 249, 253, 303n20; rubella, 243, 249–50, 255; smallpox, 248–49, 254, 303n20; syphilis, 259. *See also* Centers for Disease Control; contagious diseases; HIV/AIDS; infectious diseases
Disneyland, 243, 244
DNA: with children, health of, 58; drug use and, 116–17
Dobson v. Dobson, 98
doctors. *See* physicians
Doe v. Div. of Youth and Family Services, 92
domestic violence: in media, 183; pregnancy and, 77; tolerance of, 8. *See also* intimate partner violence
dopamine, 342n136, 342n137
dose-response uncertainty, 310n3
Dressler, Joshua, 49, 200–201
drugs: brain and, 116–17; epidemiology, 115–16; gender and use and abuse of, 117–19; harm from use of, 121–26; history of, 110, 115–16; infant formula treated as, 5; legislation, 351n172; marijuana, 148, 170; poverty and, 50, 120, 150; pregnancy and use of, 119–21; race and, 141, 142; reasons for using, 109, 116–17; sexual abuse with alcohol and,

16, 120, 289, 324n52, 344n60; testing, covert, 127, 141; use and effects, 115–26; War on Drugs, 110, 126. *See also* alcohol; illegal drugs; pregnant women, drug use by; prescription medicine
drug treatment, for pregnant women: completion, role of, 354n215; effective, 153, 354n213; gender and, 151–52; special concerns, 152–53; studies, 355n225
drug treatment, race and, 353n210
duress, 39
duty of care, 3, 94, 97, 186, 233
duty to act, 48, 51, 99, 179, 182, 198, 318n136

economic status: child abuse and, 16, 308n67; IPV and, 193–94, 195; social class and, 57, 60. *See also* poverty
Edleson, Jeffrey, 190
E.E.O.C. v. Houston Funding II, Ltd., 176–77
EFM. *See* electronic fetal monitoring
egalitarian worldviews, 29–30, 33
electronic fetal monitoring (EFM), 75
Elliott, Chris, 194
Emile (Rousseau), 155
English common law, 49, 74, 180, 237, 280
Enlightenment, 143
environmental hazards: in childhood, 64–65, 293; risk solutions, 292–93. *See also* lead
environmental law, 52
environmental lawyers, 52–53
environmental movement: climate change and, 31, 36; precautionary principle and, 320n158
Environmental Protection Agency (EPA): criticism of, 293; *Ethyl Corp. v. Environmental Protection Agency*, 53, 222; on lead, 19, 215, 221, 222, 377n41; mercury and, 64
Erickson, Nancy, 366n5
Estonia, 303n21
Ethyl Corporation, 221

Ethyl Corp. v. Environmental Protection Agency, 53, 222
exemptions, vaccinations: consequences of, 267–68; First Amendment and religious, 264–66; with informed consent and *parens patriae*, 268–72; philosophical, 266–67
Ex parte Ankrom, 138
Ex parte Hicks, 138
expert authority, trust in, 33, 36–37, 261. *See also* scientists
exposure levels: asbestos in workplace, 234–35; CDC and "safe," 25; lead paint and reducing, 376n25; of toxic substances prior to conception, 58. *See also* lead poisoning
"external" risk, 31. *See also* "internal" risk
Eyer, Diane, 159

Facebook, 73
fact-finding, juries by, 97
failure to act: manslaughter and, 5, 44, 99; murder and, 5, 275
families: *Doe v. Div. of Youth and Family Services*, 92; domestic violence and, 8, 77, 183; legislation for adoption and safe, 346n90; Nurse-Family Partnerships, 287, 292, 363n121; with structures changing, 16; violence, 66, 180, 192, 285, 288–91; *Winnipeg Child & Family Services v. G.D.F.*, 150–51. *See also* children; fathers; infants; intimate partner violence; mothers; parents
Family and Medical Leave Act, 15, 174
FAS. *See* fetal alcohol syndrome
fathers: as child abusers, 183, 187–88, 189; with children, health of, 8; gender bias and, 9; as perpetrators of IPV, 5; with smoking prior to conception, 57–58, 113. *See also* parents
feminists, 86, 140, 159, 172
Ferguson v. City of Charleston, S.C., 81, 137, 141, 148

fetal alcohol syndrome (FAS), 11, 122, 123, 304n33, 347n95, 349n128
fetal assault legislation, 352n198
"fetal protection" prosecutions: first wave, 126–28; second wave, 128–32
feticide: criminal prosecution of pregnant women for, 100–103; legislation, 105, 338n177; murder and, 101, 147, 283; reasons for, 4
fetus, 327n5; child conflated with, 136–38, 338n175; child endangerment and, 138; chorioamnionitis and, 352n191; "fetal protection" prosecutions, first wave, 126–28; "fetal protection" prosecutions, second wave, 128–32; with lead in drinking water, 215; miscarriages, 76, 124, 125, 231, 289; as passenger in pregnant woman, 74, 103, 129, 131; religion and, 84; rights of, 74–75; as separate human entity, 73–74, 75, 86–91, 97, 105, 112, 136–38, 338n175. *See also* abortion; caesarean sections; pregnancy; pregnant women; prenatal care
First Amendment, 83, 84, 264–66, 396n138
Fischhoff, Baruch, 96, 202
Floyd, Mitch, 112–13, 134, 137, 139
foreseeability, 96; causation with individual action and, 44, 48–51; harm and, 383n129; in Model Penal Code, 319n142; negligence and, 44, 317n111, 319n137; role of, 352n187. *See also* hindsight bias
formaldehyde, vaccinations and, 257
Fourteenth Amendment, 83, 104, 247, 262
Fourth Amendment, 81
France, 114, 134, 135
Friedman, Lawrence, 260
fundamental attribution error, 27, 31, 42, 50, 80

gasoline, lead in, 19, 53
gender, 49; drug treatment and, 151–52; with drug use and abuse, 117–19; manslaughter and, 48; stereotypes, 18, 20, 96, 229–30; switching approach, 139; with vaccinations, opposition to, 387n24
gender bias: with child abuse, 16–17, 179; fathers and, 9; with harm, failure to prevent, 178–80; IPV and, 191; judges and, 46–47, 84, 191; negligence and, 46–47, 90
genetics: brain and, 342n140; DNA, 58, 116–17
genocide, 58, 245
Gibbs, Rennie, 111, 125, 145
Gibson v. American Cyanamid, 208
girls: gender bias and, 46–47; sexual abuse rates, 15, 307n56; teen pregnancy, 59
Goldstein, Abraham, 136
Gonzales v. Carhart, 89, 104–5
government: "anxiety governance," 262, 295; breastfeeding and involvement of, 14–15, 163–66; lead risks and response of, 19, 216–24; science and, 261; skepticism with precautionary principle and, 44, 51–54; vaccine risks and role of, 263
Gramling, Susan, 374n2
Greece, ancient, 157, 213, 343n54
Greenbook, 190, 194, 289, 373n99
Grodin v. Grodin, 336n135, 336n136, 336n137
gross negligence, 45, 317n113
"group-grid" worldview typology, 30
guilty pleas, to avoid prison, 135
guns, 20, 26, 60

Hand, Learned, 95, 317n111, 336n142
harm: actual, 222; causation and, 53–54, 201; civil commitment and, 304n35; from drug use, 121–26; foreseeability and, 383n129; gender bias with failure to prevent, 178–80; from lead poisoning, 215–16; negligence and, 318n120; overdetermined, 381n100; prenatal, 93–94, 336n137; reduction strategy with treatment, 153; from tobacco, 124. *See also* causation
healers, women, 143
health: AHRQ, 166, 167; National Institutes of Health, 76; OSHA, 53, 54; pub-

lic, 31–34; WHO, 332n75, 392n77. *See also* children's health; Department of Health and Human Services; Institute of Medicine; mental health
health care professionals. *See* nurses; physicians
health care system, breastfeeding and, 173–74
health insurance. *See* Affordable Care Act; Medicaid; State Child Health Insurance Program
The Health Liberty Revolution & Forced Vaccination (Loe Fisher), 314n51
Hepatitis B virus, 250, 251, 389n46
herd immunity, 21, 244, 246, 251, 272, 282
Hernandez, Theresa, 111, 125, 145, 340n17
heroin, 116, 121
Hetcher, Steven, 45
heuristics: affect, 80; "anchoring and adjustment," 27–28, 40; availability, 26, 40; risk perception, 26–28; unconsciousness and, 26, 27–28
Heyman, Gene, 153
hierarchical worldviews, 29, 30, 32
hindsight bias, 42, 43, 96, 202, 317n107
Hispanics: drugs and, 142; drug treatment and, 353n210; HIV/AIDS and, 93; prenatal care and, 78, 330n43
HIV/AIDS: breastfeeding and, 169, 361n94; in infants, 60; mandatory testing and treatment, 91–93; risk and, 31; transmission, 8, 10, 58, 85, 321n5
Hofstadter, Richard, 260
Holmes, Oliver Wendell, Jr., 74
Holocaust, 58, 245
home buyers, lead paint and, 218–19
homicide, 349n126; breastfeeding and, 155, 171; by child abuse, 111, 144, 178, 340n9; pregnant women and, 35, 77
Honduras, 59
hospitals: Baby-Friendly Hospital program, 173–74, 177; *Jefferson v. Griffin County Hospital Authority*, 85, 88; prison, 90; *Raleigh Fitkin-Paul Morgan Hospital v. Anderson*, 84; *Schloendorff v. Society of New York Hospital*, 269; *Stoners v. George Washington University Hospital et al*, 334n100
HPV: risk attitudes and, 33; vaccine, 32, 250–51
human milk, toxins in, 170–71. *See also* breastfeeding
human rights, 368n26
hypernatremia, 171–72

Iceland, 303n21
illegal drugs: alcohol and, 342n41; breastfeeding and, 170; cocaine, 37, 124–25, 128, 146, 400n4; deaths, 122; heroin, 116, 121; methamphetamine, 50, 111–12, 116, 131, 145, 170
illness, in childhood, 61–62
immunity. *See* herd immunity
immunization. *See* vaccines and vaccinations
individual action, 44, 48–51
individualist worldviews, 29, 32
Industrial Union Dept., AFL-CIO v. American Petroleum Institute, 54
infant formula: costs, 364n126; criticism of, 164–65; as drug, 5; invention of, 157, 356n9; popularity of, 158–59
infants: "crack babies," myth of, 37–38; deaths, 7, 59–60, 79, 124, 166, 167–68, 250, 286, 302n19, 303n21; HIV/AIDS in, 60; risk solutions for, 291–92; SIDS, 60, 124, 166, 167–68, 286; vaccinations and, 303n20
infectious diseases, 387n26, 388n35
informed consent: with medical treatment, compulsory, 83–86; pharmaceutical industry with, 314n51; with vaccination exemptions and *parens patriae*, 268–72; violations of, 83
injury, 49; in childhood, 61–62; vaccine, 255, 263, 270

Innocenti Declaration, 163
In re A.C., 86–87, 89, 108, 334n99
In re Lead Paint Litigation, 239
Inside Jurors' Minds: The Hierarchy of Juror Decision-Making (Anderson), 40
Institute of Medicine (IOM), 34, 256, 289, 314n65
"intact dilation and evacuation," 89, 334n112
Inter-American Commission on Human Rights, 368n26
"internal" risk, 31. *See also* "external" risk
Internet, vaccinations and, 261, 263
intimate partner violence (IPV): with child abuse and mothers prosecuted, 190–97; condoms and, 286; in context, 5; deaths, 194–95; judges and, 191, 198; juries and, 198–99; pregnant women and, 35; public nuisance ordinances and, 196; race and, 196; risk solutions, 288–91; women not getting help with, 195–97; women not leaving with, 193–95
investigations, child abuse, 184–87
involuntary manslaughter, 99, 187, 373n97
IOM. *See* Institute of Medicine
IPV. *See* domestic violence; intimate partner violence
IQ, 340n10, 349n134; breastfeeding and, 162; lead poisoning and, 20, 209, 215–16, 227, 228, 230

Jacobson v. Massachusetts, 248
Jefferson, Jessie Mae, 85
Jefferson v. Griffin County Hospital Authority, 85, 88
Jehovah's Witness, 271, 273
Jenner, Edward, 254
Jews, 58, 143, 245
Johnson, Brenda, 186
Johnson, Lyndon, 78
Johnson v. State, 128, 186
Jorgensen, Jennifer, 4, 13, 102–3

journalists, 34, 187, 190, 259, 261. *See also* media
Journal of the American Medical Association, 181
judges: with discretion, 28, 40; gender bias and, 46–47, 84, 191; IPV and, 191, 198; "judicial restraint" and criticism of, 136; with juries, construction of, 44–48
"judicial restraint," 136
juries: "anchoring and adjustment" heuristic and, 27–28, 40; biased prototypes and, 41–42, 43, 80, 142; counterfactual thinking and, 42–43; decisionmaking in cases, 40–44; with discretion, 28; with fact-finding, 97; IPV and, 198–99; judges and construction of, 44–48; media influencing, 40–41; "the reasonable person" and, 39–40, 44–48, 45

Kahan, Dan, 29
Kahneman, Daniel, 96, 142, 352n188
Kaplan, Samuel, 375n11
Kasimov, Sophie, 267–68
Kennedy, Anthony, 105
Kennedy, Robert, Jr., 245, 256
Kenya, 59
Kessler, David, 391n67
Kevane, Bridget, 3
Keystone XL pipeline, 31
Kimbrough, Amanda, 111–12, 400n4
King, Rebecca, 139
Kleinberg, James, 240
Koob, George F., 342n136
Koop, C. Everett, 163
Kukla, Rebecca, 165
Kuykendall, Miranda, 194

labor induction, pregnancy and, 82, 333n77
Lacks, Henrietta, 259
lactation programs, corporations with, 175
laissez-faire capitalism, skepticism and, 52

landlords: lead paint and, 228–29, 242, 374n3, 381n105; stereotypes of slum, 241
law: breast feeding and legal obstacles, 175–77; in context, 40, 55; deterrence and, 38–39; discretionary decision-making and substantive, 44–51; environmental, 52; government action and precautionary principle, 44, 51–54; juries and decisionmaking in cases, 40–44; procedural, 39; psychosocial processes and legal decisionmakers, 197–202; response to vaccine risks, 262–72; slippery slope, 95, 102, 150; unconscious risk construction influencing, 281–84. *See also* common law; criminal law; legislation; private nuisance law; public nuisance law; substantive law; tort law
lawsuits, against pregnant women, 93–98, 335n131
lawyers, 134; environmental, 52–53; lead poisoning and fees for, 376n23. *See also* prosecutors
Lazarovich, Janice, 196–97
lead: atmospheric, 220–22; brain development and, 61, 215; in drinking water, 8–9, 19, 54, 212, 215, 220; EPA on, 19, 215, 221, 222, 377n41; in gasoline, 19, 53; TEL, 220–21, 222; in toys, 19, 214, 222–24
Lead and Copper Rule, 215
Lead-Based Paint Poisoning Prevention Act, 217
Lead Industries Association, 378n70
lead paint: cost of reducing exposure to, 376n25; home buyers and, 218–19; landlords and, 228–29, 242, 374n3, 381n105; legislation, 211, 217–19, 378n65, 378n70; prevalence of, 385n170; renters and, 218–19, 227–28; risks from, 207, 211, 213–14, 217–20
lead pigment, 205, 211, 236, 237, 381n105; products liability and, 231; public nuisance law and, 224, 225, 240, 384n164; studies, 213
lead poisoning, 26; "actual cause," and, 225–31; children and exposure to, 207–9, 213–16, 224–41, 384n149; in context, 209–13, 241–42; by corporations, 221, 223, 239–40, 374n3, 376n25; deaths, 221; expert authority and, 37; government response to risks of, 19, 216–24; harm from, 215–16; increase in, 64; IQ and, 20, 209, 215–16, 227, 228, 230; lawyers, fees for, 376n23; poverty and, 19, 213, 217, 223–24; products liability and common law, 231–37; public nuisance law and, 20–21, 237–41; race and, 213–14, 216, 227; rates, 18; *Thomas* case, 207–9, 226, 230, 236, 238, 374n2, 374n3
Leahy, Patrick, 134
Lee, Cynthia, 139
legal actions, against pregnant women: blood transfusions and caesarean sections, 10, 83–91; HIV, mandatory testing and treatment, 91–93; informed consent violations and deprivation of liberty, 83
legislation: adoption and families, 346n90; advance medical directive, 106–7, 108; child abuse, 188–89, 366n3, 396n137; child endangerment, 129, 182; Civil Rights Act, Title VII, 175, 177; Clean Air Act, 53, 64, 221–22, 293; disabilities, 15, 175–76; drugs, 351n172; Family and Medical Leave Act, 15, 174; fetal assault, 352n198; feticide, 105, 338n177; lead paint, 211, 217–19, 378n65, 378n70; manslaughter, 317n113; mental health and addiction, 288; Occupational Safety and Health Act, 54; with pregnancy criminalized, 147–48; Safe Drinking Water Act, 215; toy safety, 223; vaccination, 255, 263, 266, 272–76. *See also* Affordable Care Act
Le Moal, Michel, 342n136

liberty, 314n51; deprivation of constitutionally protected, 83; pregnant women with deprivation of, 4–5. *See also* prison
Life (magazine), 73
life expectancy: Baby Boomers, 58; children, 7, 58, 59–60, 246, 248
Lindley, Arlena, 185–86
living wills, 10, 105
Loe Fisher, Barbara, 245, 261, 314n51
Lupton, Deborah, 31

malpractice. *See* medical malpractice
manslaughter, 128, 131, 170, 179, 349n144; Christian Scientists and, 22, 275; failure to act and, 5, 44, 99; gender and, 48; involuntary, 99, 187, 373n97; legislation, 317n113; motor vehicles and, 4, 13, 102
marijuana, 116, 148, 170
market share liability theory, DES and, 231–34
Marlowe, Amber, 87–88
maternal selfishness, 98–99, 112
Mather, Cotton, 157
McCarthy, Jenny, 261
McCaskill, Claire, 134
McFall v. Shimp, 86
McKnight, Regina, 111, 137, 145–46, 340n9; "fetal protection" prosecutions and, 129–31; with mistrial, 349n136; sentence and, 349n138. See also *State v. McKnight*
McLaughlin, Ginger, 193, 198, 202
measles, 243–44, 249, 252, 267
Measure of Injury: Race, Gender, and Tort Law (Chamallas and Wriggins), 49
media: breastfeeding in, 164, 165, 358n55; domestic violence in, 183; journalists, 34, 187, 190, 259, 261; juries influenced by, 40–41; with medical and political landscapes, 73–75, 327n5; with race and drugs, 142; risk portrayed by, 8, 34–35, 37–38

Medicaid, 66, 67, 78, 120, 171; abortion and, 345n70; ACA and expansion of, 390n54; birth and, 330n42; breastfeeding and, 173, 291–92; lead poisoning and, 219; prenatal care and, 287; WIC program, 161, 291
medical directive. *See* advance medical directives
medical interventions. *See* pregnant women, medical interventions against
medical malpractice, 80–81, 88, 93
medical marijuana, 170
medical parentalism, 81
medical risk-taking, informed consent and, 314n51
medicine. *See* prescription medicine
men: alcohol and, 117–18; as child abusers, 178–79, 183–89, 194–95, 211; condoms and, 286; drug treatment and, 353n210; HIV transmitted by, 8, 58; murder and, 179, 183, 185, 186, 194; in prison, 196; "the reasonable man," 140; white, 29, 196. *See also* fathers; intimate partner violence
mens rea, 99, 109
mental health: anxiety and, 31, 61, 66, 102, 118, 260, 281; civil commitment and, 304n35; depression and, 16, 66, 118, 119, 154, 344n60; legislation, 288; postpartum depression and, 291; poverty and, 63, 103; treatment for, 354n215. *See also* posttraumatic stress disorder
mercury: levels, 64–65, 293; methylmercury, 392n77; pregnancy risks and, 76–77
methamphetamine, 50, 111–12, 116, 131, 145, 170
methylmercury, 392n77
Michigan Central Railroad Co. v. Hasseneyer, 46–47, 198
Middle Ages, 74, 143
midwives, 88

milk: pasteurization, 14, 158, 302n17; toxins in human, 170–71. *See also* breastfeeding
Mill, John Stuart, 80, 269
Milwaukee. See *City of Milwaukee v. NL Industries*
miscarriages, 76, 124, 125, 231, 289
Model Penal Code, 201, 319n142
Moran, Mayo, 46–47, 198
mortality. *See* deaths
motherhood bias, 185
mothers: with boyfriends as child abusers, 183, 185–86, 187–88, 189, 194–95, 211; as child abusers, 183, 187, 190; IPV and prosecution of, 190–97; maternal selfishness and, 98–99, 112; "othermothering," 363n118; prenatal harm and, 93–94, 336n137; "the reasonable mother," 48, 50–51, 138–42, 197; single, 48, 184, 370n61; stereotypes of "good" and "bad," 142; with vaccination legislation and health of children, 272–76; as victims of IPV, 5. *See also* parents
mothers, crimes of omission and: child abuse in context, 180–87, 211; in context, 178–80, 202–3; IPV impacting child abuse and, 190–97; prosecution of, 187–90; psychosocial processes and legal decisionmaking with, 197–202
motor vehicles: deaths, 60; with lawsuits against pregnant women, 102–3, 335n131; manslaughter and, 4, 13, 102; negligence and, 318n127
Muñoz, Erick, 106, 107
Muñoz, Marlise, 4, 106–7
murder, 3–4, 48, 114, 128, 129, 145, 170; children as witnesses to, 63; failure to act and, 5, 275; feticide and, 101, 147, 283; homicide by child abuse, 111, 144; maternal selfishness and, 98–99; men and, 179, 183, 185, 186, 194; sentencing, 112, 130, 131
Muskie, Edmund, 221

National Advocates for Pregnant Women, 146
National Breastfeeding Awareness Campaign, 14, 155
National Casualty Co. v. Northern Trust Bank of Florida, N.A., 335n131, 336n135, 336n136
National Childhood Vaccine Injury Act of 1986, 255, 263
National Childhood Vaccine Injury Compensation Program, 270
National District Attorney's Association, 134
National Federation of Independent Businesses v. Sebelius, 67, 78
National Football League, 8, 183
National Institutes of Health, 76
National Resources Defense Council, 215
National Vaccine Information Center, 245
Native Americans, with mercury levels, 65
neglect: child abuse and, 63, 178, 346n90; childhood, 3, 63; cycle of, 307n60; deaths, 183; physical abuse and, 61
negligence: defined, 24, 95, 140; foreseeability and, 44, 317n111, 319n137; gender bias and, 46–47, 90; gross, 45, 317n113; Hand on, 317n111; harm and, 318n120; pregnant women and, 318n127. *See also* "the reasonable person"
"neighborhood disorganization," 345n76
Nestlé, Henri, 157, 356n9
Newman, Troy, 138
Nicholson v. Scopetta, 195, 197
Nilsson, Lennart, 73, 327n4
Nixon, Richard, 52–53
nuisance law. *See* private nuisance law; public nuisance law
Nurse-Family Partnerships, 287, 292, 363n121
nurses, 71, 267; with breastfeeding, 158; confidentiality and, 283, 284; with covert drug testing, 127; midwives, 88; power of, 6; with racial bias, 81; wet, 157

nursing. *See* breastfeeding
Nussbaum, Hedda, 186

Obama, Barack, 14
"Obamacare." *See* Affordable Care Act
obesity: breastfeeding and, 161, 164; childhood, 3, 62–63; poverty and, 78
Occupational Safety and Health Act, 54
Occupational Safety and Health Administration (OSHA), 53, 54
O'Connor, Sandra Day, 104
Omer, Saad, 244
omission: bias, 27, 35; prosecutors with child abuse by, 370n56. *See also* mothers, crimes of omission and
Omnibus Autism Proceedings, 263
Operation Rescue, 138
OSHA. *See* Occupational Safety and Health Administration
"other-mothering," 363n118
"overdetermined harm," 381n100

painkillers, 112, 116, 149
paint. *See* lead paint
Palmer, Barbara Ann, 187–88
Palmer v. State, 187–88, 189, 200
Paltrow, Lynn, 146
Pan, Richard, 245
parens patriae, informed consent and, 268–72
parents: medical parentalism, 81; physicians trusted by, 259, 395n115; "the reasonable parent," 17, 48; "the reasonable person" standard and duty of, 197–200; vaccine risks for children and options for, 264–72
Parker, Thomas, 138
Parmet, Wendy, 268, 271–72
pasteurization, milk, 14, 158, 302n17
Patrick, Dan, 107
Pediatrics (journal), 3
Pemberton, Laura, 88, 273

Pemberton v. Tallahassee Memorial Regional Medical Center, Inc., 86, 334n107
penicillin, 249, 302n19
People v. Abramson, 200
People v. Atlantic Richfield Co., 237, 240, 376n25
People v. Barrientos, 194–95, 373n97
People v. Kuykendall, 194
People v. Warner-Lambert Co., 146–47
People v. Williams, 44–45, 317n113
Percival, Robert, 54
Percocet, 11, 149
person. *See* "the reasonable person"
personhood initiative, 338n175
pertussis (whooping cough), 7, 244, 249, 267, 302n16
Pfannenstiel, Diane, 126–27
pharmaceutical industry, with informed consent, 314n51
philosophical exemptions, vaccinations and, 266–67
physical abuse, 8, 66, 180, 192, 201; of boys, 15; by men, 183; neglect and, 61; by women, 190. *See also* child abuse
physicians: civil commitment and, 148; medical malpractice and, 80–81, 88, 93; parents trusting, 259, 395n115; power of, 6; pregnancy and risk perception of, 10, 79–81; vaccinations and, 270. *See also* American Academy of Pediatrics
Piazzi, Donna, 107–8
Planned Parenthood of Southeastern Pennsylvania v. Casey, 104, 138
police officers: with discretion, 28, 40, 185; IPV and, 191, 196
polio, 7, 249, 253, 303n20
politics: media with medical landscape and, 73–75, 327n5; paranoid style of, 260; prosecutors with ambitions in, 134
postpartum depression, 291
posttraumatic stress disorder (PTSD): sexual abuse and, 344n60; in women, 118–19, 154, 324n52

poverty: breastfeeding and, 157–58; child abuse and, 16, 184, 308n67; children and, 37–38, 57, 61, 78, 321n3, 400n11; criminal convictions and, 111; drugs and, 50, 120, 150; lead poisoning and, 19, 213, 217, 223–24; mental health and, 63, 103; "neighborhood disorganization" and, 345n76; pregnancy and, 78–79; prenatal care and, 78, 127, 141; race and, 78; rates, 323n36; risks of, 9, 35, 125, 133, 284–85; vaccinations and, 251–52, 275; War on Poverty, 78

Powell, Lewis, 54

power: with defining risk, 26; of physicians and nurses, 6; of prosecutors, 133

precautionary principle: with children, health of, 294–95; environmental movement and, 320n158; skepticism with government action and, 44, 51–54

pregnancy: caesarean sections, 82; domestic violence and, 77; drug use and, 119–21; labor induction and, 82, 333n77; physicians and lay persons, risk perception of, 10, 79–81; poverty and, 78–79; risks, 35, 75–82, 124; risk solutions with promise and prevention, 287–88; statues and criminalizing of, 147–48; stillbirths, preterm deliveries, and adverse birth outcomes, 79; teen, 59, 66; unplanned, 78, 119, 122, 286

pregnant women, 9; alcohol and, 11, 122, 123, 129, 304n33, 347n95, 347n96, 349n128; causation and, 50, 143–47; criminal prosecution of, 3–4, 98–105; DES and, 231–34; homicide and, 35, 77; IPV and, 35; with liberty, deprivation of, 4–5; negligence and, 318n127; "the reasonable pregnant woman," 47–48, 95, 96, 138–42; smoking and, 141

pregnant women, drug use by, 50, 57, 82; civil commitment and, 148–51; in context, 11–14, 153–54; criminal prosecutions, history, 109–15, 126–32; criminal prosecutions, winning, 132–47; effects, 115–26; pregnancy criminalized, statutes, 147–48; treatment for, 151–53, 354n213, 354n215, 355n225

pregnant women, medical interventions against, 98–105; advance medical directives, overriding, 105–8; in context, 9–10; historical overview, 71–75; lawsuits against, 93–98, 335n131; legal actions against, 10, 83–93; pregnancy, risks during, 75–82

premature birth, 35, 76, 113, 345n76

prenatal care, 11, 13, 97, 129; confidentiality and, 149–50; lack of, 59, 91, 121; Medicaid and, 287; poverty and, 78, 127, 141; race and, 78, 330n43

prenatal harm, 93–94, 336n137

prescription medicine: amoxicillin, 167; antidepressants, 12, 170; AZT, 91, 92; DES, 231–34; marijuana, 170; painkillers, 112, 116, 149; Percocet, 11, 149; Suboxone, 149; Tetracycline, 47, 94, 336n137; withholding of, 81

preterm birth: deaths, 60, 125; poverty and, 79; rate, 59, 76, 303n21. *See also* premature birth

"priming," stereotypes and, 28

Prince v. Massachusetts, 271

"the principle of legality," 126, 128, 129, 130

prison, 114, 136; children of abuse and link to, 16; guilty pleas to avoid, 135; hospital, 90; race and, 196; sentencing, 103, 111, 112, 130, 147, 186, 187, 189, 275, 279, 340n17, 349n138

private nuisance law, 52, 320n154

procedural law, 39

products liability, with lead poisoned: children treated differently, 236–37; common law and, 231–37; DES and market share liability theory, 231–34; workers with asbestos exposure and, 234–35

Progressive Era, child abuse in, 181

prosecutors: bias of, 185; with causation rules and criminal convictions, 143–47, 201; child abuse by omission and, 370n56; with child abuse investigations, 184–87; corruption and, 133; discretion and, 40, 133–36; with fetus and child, conflation of, 136–38; with mothers and crimes of omission, 187–90; political ambitions in, 134; power of, 133; pregnant drug users and winning, 132–47; with risk construction, unconscious, 282–83; with social construction influencing criminal liability, 138–42
prototypes. *See* biased prototypes
proximate cause, 49, 143, 144, 200, 202
psychosocial processes: causation and, 200–202; legal decisionmakers and, 197–202; of risk and vaccination legislation, 272–76; of risk construction, 9, 40–44
PTSD. *See* posttraumatic stress disorder
"public good," vaccinations as, 21
public health: with authority, multiple sources of, 33–34; risk and, 31–32, 33
public nuisance law, 52; children with lead poisoning and, 237–41; lead pigment and, 224, 225, 240, 384n164; lead poisoning and, 20–21; as a tort, 237–41, 384n149
Puerto Rico, 134
Pugh, Alissa, 99–100

race, 49; with children, health of, 56, 59–60; criminal prosecutions and, 185; drugs and, 141, 142; drug treatment and, 353n210; HIV/AIDS and, 93; IPV and, 196; lead poisoning and, 213–14, 216, 227; mercury levels and, 65; poverty and, 78; prenatal care and, 78, 330n43; prison and, 196; risk and, 29; stereotypes, 18, 20, 96, 229–30; stillbirths and, 77, 125; vaccinations and, 252. *See also* African-Americans; Hispanics
racial bias, 28, 81
racism, in criminal justice system, 28
Raleigh Fitkin-Paul Morgan Hospital v. Anderson, 84
Ramey, David, 169
rape, prototype and, 41–42
rap music, 28
Reagan, Ronald, 54, 110, 163
realized harm, 54
"the reasonable man," 140
"the reasonable mother": child abuse and, 197; in criminal law, 48, 50–51; criminal liability with social construction of, 138–42
"the reasonable parent," 17, 48
"the reasonable person," 6, 17, 24, 44–46; with construction by jurors and judges, 44–48; juries and, 39–40, 45; parental duty and standard for, 197–200; "the reasonable man" and, 140
"the reasonable pregnant woman," 47–48, 95, 96; criminal liability with social construction of, 138–42
relative risk, media and, 34–35, 37. *See also* absolute risk
religion, 22, 267, 271, 273, 275; breastfeeding and, 157; fetus and, 84; with vaccination exemptions and First Amendment, 264–66
Remy v. MacDonald, 100, 336n138
renters, lead paint and, 218–19, 227–28
Residential Lead-Based Paint Hazard Reduction Act, 211, 217–19, 378n65
retribution, 39, 113
Reyes, Margaret, 110, 126
Reyes v. Superior Court, 110, 126
rights: Civil Rights Act, Title VII, 175, 177; of fetus, 74–75; human, 368n26
Riley, Patricia, 101–2, 136, 283
risk, 4–10, 12, 14–15, 18–19, 21–23. *See also* absolute risk; relative risk

risk analysis, 37
risk assessment, 25, 36, 72, 79, 110, 168, 246
risk communication, 6, 32–36
risk construction: law influencing unconscious, 281–84; psychosocial processes of, 9, 40–44; unconsciousness and, 36, 38, 40, 48, 52, 55, 247, 258–59, 281–84
risk contribution theory, 208, 234, 236–37, 374n4
risk management: in context, 6, 31; poverty and, 37–38; trust and, 36
risk perception: in context, 6, 24–26; heuristics, 26–28; of physicians with pregnancy, 10, 79–81; racial bias and, 28; worldviews, impact of, 29–32
risks: breastfeeding, 169–72; child abuse, 16; with connotations changing, 31; of harm, 53; law and response to vaccine, 262–72; from lead paint, 207, 211, 213–14, 217–20; media and portrayal of, 8, 34–35, 37–38; medical risk-taking, 314n51; poverty, 9, 35, 57, 125, 133, 284–85; power with defining, 26; pregnancy, 35, 75–82, 124; public health and, 31–32, 33; race and, 29; types of, 34–35; vaccination legislation psychosocial processes of, 272–76; vaccinations, 26–27, 32–33, 252–58, 262–76; of vaccines with contagious diseases, 252–58; "vector of risk," 9, 71, 304n27
Roe v. Wade, 71, 86, 88–89, 103–4; criticism of, 138; opponents of, 105
Romans, ancient, 213
Rousseau, Jean-Jacques, 155
Rowland, Melissa, 4, 10, 98–99
rubella, 243, 249–50, 255
Rubin, Daniel, 267–68
Rutherford v. Owens-Illinois, Inc., 235

Sabin oral vaccine, 388n39
Safe Drinking Water Act, 215
"safe" exposure levels, CDC and, 25

St. Louis. See *City of St. Louis v. Benjamin Moore & Co.*
Salk, Jonas, 249, 253, 388n39
Salk vaccine, 388n39
Satcher, David, 163
SCHIP. See State Child Health Insurance Program
schizophrenia, 58
Schloendorff v. Society of New York Hospital, 269
Schneider, Elizabeth, 192
science: breastfeeding supported by, 158–59, 167–69; government and, 261; with risks of vaccines, 252–58. See also journalists; media
scientists: Christian Scientists, 22, 265, 275; trust and disagreements among, 36
Scruggs, Daniel, 43
Scruggs, Judith, 43, 49
sentencing: criminal convictions reversed with, 4, 13, 130–31, 146; guilty pleas to avoid prison with, 135; murder, 112, 130, 131; prison terms, 103, 111, 112, 130, 147, 186, 187, 189, 275, 279, 340n17, 349n138. See also criminal prosecutions; prison
sex-based stereotypes, 185. See also gender; gender bias
sexual abuse, 63; children and rates of, 15, 307n56; drugs and alcohol with, 16, 120, 289, 324n52, 344n60; PTSD and, 344n60; rape, 41–42
Sherwin-Williams Company, 213
Shuai, Bei Bei, 101–2, 283
SIDS. See sudden infant death syndrome
Sindell v. Abbott Laboratories, 232–34
single mothers: bias against, 370n61; child abuse and, 48, 184
skepticism: about breastfeeding, 166–67; *laissez-faire* capitalism and, 52; with precautionary principle and government action, 44, 51–54
Skloot, Rebecca, 259

slavery, breastfeeding and, 173
slippery slope, 95, 102, 150
Slovak Republic, 303n21
Slovic, Paul, 25–26, 29, 36, 259
slum landlords, stereotypes of, 241
smallpox, 248–49, 254, 303n20
smoking: adolescents and, 65; with children, health of, 12, 57–58, 113; coffee consumption and, 37; deaths, 12; decline in, 115; pregnant women and, 141; prior to conception, 57–58, 113; SIDS and, 168, 286
social class: with health of children, 57, 60; stereotypes, 18, 20, 96, 229–30
social construction, criminal liability and, 138–42
South Carolina. See *Ferguson v. City of Charleston, S.C.*; *State v. McKnight*
Stallman v. Youngquist, 47–48, 97, 98, 140, 141, 336n138
State Child Health Insurance Program (SCHIP or CHIP), 66–67
State v. Aiwohi, 349n142, 349n144
State v. Deborah J.Z., 349n128
State v. Fernane, 197
State v. Gibbs, 145
State v. Hernandez, 145
State v. Lindley, 185–86
State v. Maupin, 193–94
State v. McKnight, 131, 145, 340n9, 349n136, 349n138
State v. McLaughlin, 202
State v. Norman, 317n113
State v. Rundle, 189–90
State v. Scruggs, 43, 49
State v. Williams, 202
State v. Williquette, 189, 190
Steinberg, Joel, 186
Steinberg, Lisa, 186
stereotypes: "crack babies," 38; cultural, 9; of gender, race, and social class, 18, 20, 96, 229–30; of "good" and "bad" mothering, 142; "priming" and, 28; role of, 17; sex-based, 185; of slum landlords, 241; unconscious bias and, 6, 24, 28, 46, 110, 130, 199, 247, 280
Stevens, John Paul, 54
stillbirths, 76, 77, 79, 111, 125–26, 335n131
Stoners v. George Washington University Hospital et al, 334n100
stress: children and influence of, 7, 63; "neighborhood disorganization" and, 345n76; PTSD, 118–19, 154, 324n52, 344n60
studies, lead pigment, 213
Suboxone, 149
"substantial factor," 235, 240, 381n100, 383n138
substantive law, 39; causation and, 44, 48–51; principles and discretionary decisionmaking, 44–51; "the reasonable person," 44–48
sudden infant death syndrome (SIDS), 60, 124, 166; breastfeeding and, 167–68; smoking and, 168, 286
suicide, 66, 101, 107, 283
Summers v. Tice, 233, 241, 383n138
Sunstein, Cass, 311n19
Supreme Court, United States, 8, 103–5, 134
Supreme Court of Canada, 98, 150–51
Surgeon General: on breastfeeding, 163, 166, 168; on lead poisoning, 221
syphilis, 259

Taylor, Christine, 4, 100–101, 283–84
teen pregnancy, 59, 66
TEL. *See* tetraethyl lead
"telescoping," alcohol and, 118
Tesar v. Anderson, 335n131
testing: covert drug, 127, 141; HIV/AIDS with mandatory treatment and, 91–93
Tetracycline, 47, 94, 336n137
tetraethyl lead (TEL), 220–21, 222
Texas Controlled Substance Act, 351n172
Thailand, 59

thimerosal: IOM on autism and, 314n65; in vaccinations, 33, 256, 393n85
Thomas, Steven: landlords and, 381n105; lead poisoning and, 207–9, 226, 230, 236, 238, 374n2, 374n3
Thomas ex rel. Gramling v. Mallett, 208, 230, 236
Title VII. *See* Civil Rights Act, Title VII
tobacco, 12, 109; deaths, 122; harm from, 124. *See also* smoking
tonsillectomy, 166
tort law, 49; deterrence and, 38–39; "the reasonable person" and, 44
torts, 319n142; defined, 317n109; and informed consent, 83. *See also* negligence; private nuisance; products liability; public nuisance
torts, with lead poisoning in children: causation, problem of, 225–31; in context, 224–25; products liability and common law, 231–37; public nuisance and, 237–41, 384n149
Town of Castle Rock v. Gonzales, 182
toxic substances: exposure prior to conception, 58; in human milk, 170–71; prevalence of, 61–62. *See also* environmental hazards; lead; mercury
toys, lead in, 19, 214, 222–24
treatment, 396n137; compulsory medical, 10, 83–93; court-ordered, 71, 92; HIV/AIDS testing with mandatory, 91–93; for mental health, 354n215. *See also* drug treatment, for pregnant women; informed consent
Truman v. Thomas, 269
trust: in expert authority, 33, 36–37, 261; between parents and physicians, 259, 395n115
Turkey, 59
Tuskegee syphilis experiment, 259

uncertainty, dose-response, 310n3
unconscious psychological processes: with bias and stereotypes, 6, 24, 28, 46, 110, 130, 199, 247, 280; biased prototypes and, 80, 142; cognitive processes and, 9, 17, 197; with cultural understanding, 31; heuristics and, 26, 27–28; hindsight bias and, 202; with juries and decisionmaking, 40–44; racism and, 28; risk construction and, 36, 38, 40, 48, 52, 55, 247, 258–59, 281–84
unemployment, 151, 185, 193, 194, 308n67
United Kingdom, 256
United States Preventative Services Task Force, 289
United States v. Carroll Towing Co., 317n111, 336n142
United States v. Kimbrough, 400n4
unplanned pregnancy, 78, 119, 122, 286

Vaccine Adverse Event Reporting System, 257–58, 391n67
vaccines and vaccinations, 390n52, 391n67; alternative vaccination schedules, 21, 268; aluminum in, 257; autism and, 34, 261, 263, 314n65; CDC and, 34, 245–46, 251, 257–58; contagious diseases and, 243–62, 293–94; controversy, 246–48; with costs saved, 251; exemptions, 264–72; gender and opposition to, 387n24; with government, role of, 263; herd immunity and, 21, 244, 246, 251, 272, 282; history of, 388n39; HPV, 32, 250–51; infants and, 303n20; law and response to risks of, 262–72; legislation, 255, 263, 266, 272–76; poverty and, 251–52, 275; problem, 243–46; as "public good," 21; race and, 252; risks, 26–27, 32–33, 252–58, 262–76; thimerosal in, 33, 256, 393n85
Vaccines for Children Program, 390n52
vaginal births after caesareans. *See* VBACs
variability, uncertainty and, 310n3

VBACs (vaginal births after caesareans), 82, 88
"vector of risk," 9, 71, 304n27
violence. *See* child abuse; domestic violence; families; intimate partner violence; physical abuse; sexual abuse
V.M. (Mrs.), 90, 91
voter registration process, racial bias in, 28

Wakefield, Andrew, 255
Walker, Lenore, 199–200
Walker, Scott, 208
Walrond, Tabitha, 155, 171
Warner-Lambert, 146–47
War on Drugs, 110, 126
War on Poverty, 78
Warren, Earl, 134
water, 302n17; lead in drinking, 8–9, 19, 54, 212, 215, 220; Safe Drinking Water Act, 215
Wellstone-Domenici Mental Health Parity and Addiction Equity Act of 2008, 288
wet nurse, 157
White, Carmen, 185–86
white men: in prison, 196; "white male effect," 29
white women: criminal prosecution and, 185; drug treatment and, 353n210; drug use and, 141; prenatal care and, 330n43; risk and, 29
Whitner v. State, 129, 130
WHO. *See* World Health Organization

whooping cough. *See* pertussis
WIC Program, 161, 291
Williquette, Terri, 189, 190
Wilson, Mary Ellen, 181
Winnipeg Child & Family Services v. G.D.F., 150–51
witches, 143
women: alcohol and, 117–18; child abuse and, 48, 180–87, 190, 211; feminists, 86, 140, 159, 172; as healers and witches, 143; HIV/AIDS and, 321n5; PTSD in, 118–19, 154, 324n52; white, 29, 141, 185, 330n43, 353n210. *See also* intimate partner violence; mothers; pregnant women
workplace: ACA and, 15, 176; asbestos exposure in, 234–35; breastfeeding and obstacles in, 15, 174–75, 177; unemployment, 151, 184, 193, 194, 308n67
World Health Organization (WHO), 332n75, 392n77
worldviews: on breastfeeding, 15; egalitarian and communitarian, 29–30, 33; "group-grid" typology of, 30; hierarchical, 29, 30, 32; individualist, 29, 32; risk perception and impact of, 29–32
Wriggins, Jennifer, 49, 200, 227, 228, 229, 230
Wright, J. Skelly, 53, 221–22

Yeutter, Clayton, 164

Zimmerman, Deborah, 128–29, 349n128

ABOUT THE AUTHOR

Linda C. Fentiman is Professor at the Elisabeth Haub Law School at Pace University. She is a distinguished legal scholar whose teaching and research reflect her broad experience in criminal law, health law, and environmental law. She was a Fulbright Scholar at the University of Warsaw in Poland and has taught at several American law schools. She lives in New York and is a Fellow of the New York Academy of Medicine.

www.ingramcontent.com/pod-product-compliance
Lightning Source LLC
Chambersburg PA
CBHW020348080526
44584CB00014B/940